THE
CRISIS

T0153669

THE
CRISIS.

NUMBER I. *To be continued Weekly.*

FRIDAY, January 20, 1775. [*Price Two-pence Halfpenny.*

Potior visa est Periculosa libertas quieto servitio.

SALUST.

To the People of ENGLAND and AMERICA.

Friends and Fellow Subjects,

 T is with the greatest Propriety I address this Paper to you: It is in your Defence, at this GREAT, this IMPORTANT CRISIS, I take the Pen in hand: A CRISIS big with the Fate of the most glorious Empire known in the Records of Time; and by *your* FIRMNESS and RESOLUTION ONLY, it can be saved from DESTRUCTION: By *your* FIRMNESS and RESOLUTION, you may preserve to yourselves, your immediate Offspring, and latest Posterity, all the glorious Blessings of FREEDOM, given by *Heaven* to undeserving Mortals: By *your* SUPINENESS and PUSSILANIMITY, you will entail on yourselves, your Children, and *Millions* yet unborn, MISERY and SLAVERY.

It is in your Defence I now stand forth to oppose, the most *sanguinary*, and *despotic* Court that ever disgraced a *free* Country.

It is in your Defence I now unsheath the Sword of Justice, to oppose the most profligate and abandoned Administration, that ever shewed the *Weakness*, or abused the *Confidence* of a Prince.

It

THE
CRISIS

A British Defense
of American Rights

1775–1776

Edited and with an Introduction by

Neil L. York

Liberty Fund
Indianapolis

This book is published by Liberty Fund, Inc., a foundation established
to encourage study of the ideal of a society of free and responsible individuals.

The cuneiform inscription that serves as our logo and as the design motif for our endpapers is the
earliest-known written appearance of the word "freedom" (amagi), or "liberty." It is taken from a
clay document written about 2300 B.C. in the Sumerian city-state of Lagash.

16 17 18 19 20 21 C   05   04   03   02   01
16 17 18 19 20 21 P   05   04   03   02   01

Library of Congress Cataloging-in-Publication Data

Names: York, Neil Longley, editor.
Title: The crisis : a British defense of American rights, 1775–1776 / edited
   and with an introduction by Neil L. York.
Description: Indianapolis : Liberty Fund, 2016. | Originally published:
   London : T.K. Shaw, 1775–1776. | Includes index.
Identifiers: LCCN 2016029374| ISBN 9780865978959 (pbk. : alk. paper) | ISBN
   9781614876519 (kindle) | ISBN 9781614879213 (pdf)
Subjects: LCSH: United States—History—Revolution,
   1775-1783—Causes—Sources. | United States—History—Revolution,
   1775-1783—Periodicals. | United States—Politics and
   government—1775-1783—Periodicals. | Great Britain—Politics and
   government—1760-1789—Periodicals.
Classification: LCC E211 .C96 2016 | DDC 973.3/11—dc23
LC record available at https://lccn.loc.gov/2016029374

Liberty Fund, Inc.
8335 Allison Pointe Trail, Suite 300
Indianapolis, Indiana 46250-1684

Contents

Acknowledgments

Once again, serendipity has helped set the course of my academic life. I happened to be at a Liberty Fund gathering in June of 2012 on the British debate over Colonial American resistance, 1764–1776, when *The Crisis* came up in conversation. Hans Eicholz, of Liberty Fund, and Jack Greene, professor emeritus at Johns Hopkins, were discussing the possibility of bringing out a scholarly edition of *The Crisis*—all ninety-two issues of it under one cover. I had written an article about this London weekly a few years before. They agreed that I was a logical choice for editor of a Liberty Fund compilation, and, four years later, here we are. Jack and Hans are fine scholars; I am flattered by their trust in me. Jeremy Black, at the University of Exeter, and Timothy Breen, now emeritus at Northwestern, were kind enough to read over my introductory essay. Pat Gallagher and Laura Goetz championed my cause at Liberty Fund. Laura skillfully copyedited and guided the manuscript through to Dan Kirklin, who expertly took the manuscript into production and handed it off to Otto Barz at Publishing Synthesis for typesetting. Kate Mertes then did the index. Bill Pidduck, publisher and chairman of Adam Matthew Digital, generously shared what his team had done with *The Crisis* in its online Eighteenth Century Journals Portal (www.amdigital.co.uk) so that this edition could be produced.

What Liberty Fund does to make historical texts available to modern readers reflects a rare commitment to the life of the mind. It is an honor to be associated with such an effort. I am quite certain that the men behind *The Crisis* would marvel at what Pierre Goodrich, founder of Liberty Fund, made possible through his vision and by his generosity.

Neil L. York

Introduction

EPITAPH on the Cruel Death of CRISIS,
  HERE to the flames poor CRISIS was configu'd,
  His body is consum'd, but not his mind,
  For, from his ashes, many forms shall rise,
  TRUTH may be burnt alive, but never dies.[1]

So observed the *Morning Post* about *The Crisis*, one member of the London press lamenting the passing of another, even as it sought to reassure readers that the quest for truth would not be deterred. As it turned out, *The Crisis* did not die a "cruel death," despite the efforts of government authorities to suppress it.[2] The third issue, which appeared on 4 February 1775, had been burned publicly at the order of Parliament. And yet, *The Crisis* continued to be printed for more than another year and a half, ninety-two issues in all, much to the irritation, no doubt, of those who hoped the public burning, followed by the prosecution of one of the publication's presumed printers, would crush it.

1. *The Morning Post and Daily Advertiser*, 8 March 1775.

2. What follows adds to what I have already written in "George III, Tyrant: *The Crisis* as Critic of Empire, 1775–1776" *History* 94 (2009):434–60. Edward Solly wrote briefly about "'The Crisis,' 1775–6" in *Notes and Queries*, 5th series 8 (1877): 14–15, but the first true scholarly interest was shown by Paul Leicester Ford, "The Crisis" *The Bibliographer* 1 (1902):139–52. *The Crisis* has thereafter been at least mentioned in various studies: in John A. Sainsbury, *Disaffected Patriots* (Kingston, Ont.: McGill-Queen's University Press, 1987), pp. 85–86; James E. Bradley, *Religion, Revolution, and English Radicalism* (Cambridge: Cambridge University Press, 1990), pp. 424–25; Kathleen Wilson, *The Sense of the People* (New York: Cambridge University Press, 1995), pp. 242–43; and, with more detail and greater gusto, in T. H. Breen, *American Insurgents, American Patriots* (New York: Hill and Wang, 2011), pp. 162–74.

But the men behind this weekly, men every bit as shadowy now as they were then, had made it clear that they would not be easily intimidated. "The CRISIS will be carried on with spirit, in defiance of Lawless Power, upon the true principles of the Constitution," they informed London readers as they prepared the first issue for publication. They pledged "even at the risk of every thing that is dear to man, to rescue the Liberty of the Press, the Natural Rights of mankind, and the Constitution of the British Empire in England and America, from that Ruin with which they are now threatened."[3] That they continued to print *The Crisis* each Saturday for so many months to come, was a testament to the growing power of the press and to the rise of a public whose political voice could not be silenced by legislative fiat or judicial decree.

The Crisis pursued its political objectives with a vituperative intensity that set it apart from its contemporaries in the London press. *The Crisis* oozed sarcasm from its pages; its sardonic tone most likely added to the anger of policy makers even as it fed the appetite of readers who relished the irreverence. It cleared the literary ground that others, perhaps most famously Thomas Paine in his *Common Sense*, would later seed. Nonetheless, different plants grew from this rhetorically similar soil. Paine criticized one king as a first step toward condemning monarchy altogether; the men behind *The Crisis* never went that far. For all of their complaints against crown and parliament, for all of their warnings that the wrongs committed against Americans might next be visited upon Britons, they did not advocate overthrowing George III. When rebellious Americans decided on an independent republic as the solution to their imperial problem, they and the authors of *The Crisis* parted ways. However hard *The Crisis* had worked to create a transatlantic community of protest, however much it drew on a philosophical tradition equally appealing to dissident colonists, their social circumstances and the political ideology that grew out of them were fundamentally different. Thus *The Crisis* provides a study of contrasts between what became revolution in America but remained protest in Britain.

---

3. *Morning Chronicle and London Advertiser*, 20 January 1775.

Just as Paine was not the first to put the call for "common sense" to good polemical use, there were others who had already titled their efforts at political consciousness-raising *The Crisis*. More than sixty years earlier, Richard Steele's pamphlet of that title urged readers to rely on their "common sense" and support the Hanoverian succession, thereby upholding the principles of the Glorious Revolution and preventing any return of Stuart absolutism. Parliament, Steele instructed readers, embodied the notion that all legitimate government was based on consent; the authority of the crown, he admonished, had to be limited because "absolute Power in one person" was but "clandestine tyranny;" and the people, he stressed, could justifiably resist any attack on their constitutional rights because those rights came from nature, not government.[4]

Where Steele focused on the British Isles, the anonymous author of *The Crisis* published in 1766 looked beyond them, to the larger empire, when protesting against the Stamp Act and the flawed thinking that led to its passage. He condemned any attempt to tax the colonists directly as unconstitutional, but he, like Steele before him, appealed to reason rather than emotion and avoided ad hominem attacks; stylistically, neither anticipated what would be done in *The Crisis* reprinted here.[5]

That far more strident *Crisis* debuted in London on 21 January 1775 and appeared weekly, without interruption, through 12 October 1776. More like a brief pamphlet than a true newspaper, a typical issue ran six pages with perhaps three thousand words in total, each issue composed of a single essay with nothing else to accompany it: no general news and

---

4. Richard Steele, Esq., *The Crisis* (London: Samuel Buckley, 1714), p. v, for "common sense" and "clandestine tyranny"; also see *Extracts from Sir Richard Steele's Crisis* (London: M. Cooper, 1746), which were reprinted as a guide to the next generation. For background see Calhoun Winton's *Captain Steele* (Baltimore: Johns Hopkins University Press, 1964), but there is still good reason to go back to Winton's "Richard Steele: The Political Writer" (Ph.D. dissertation, Princeton University, 1955), pp. 238–97.

5. *The Crisis. Or, A Full Defense of the Colonies* (London: W. Griffin, 1766). Eight pamphlets printed in London between 1722–1770 had "Crisis" in their title. Most dealt with some aspect of imperial affairs; all can be found in the text-searchable online compilation, Eighteenth Century Collections Online (ECCO).

no advertisements placed by others. It had to compete for readers in a city bustling with printers and publishers. Imperial affairs, and their implications for Britons, had become increasingly prominent in the press, with some writers—anonymously, as was the fashion—defending government as vigorously as others condemned it. As an anti-government weekly *The Crisis* followed in the wake of John Wilkes' *The North Briton* and, later, *The Whisperer.*[6] Failed attempts to silence them probably only added to their readership and emboldened those who eventually brought out *The Crisis*.

Important, too, were the bi- and thrice-weekly newspapers that carried essays critical of government policy. These essays were necessarily briefer than what appeared in a free-standing weekly like *The Crisis* because they had to be squeezed into the columns of four-page sheets, where usually half of the overall space was given over to advertisements. Still, those newspaper essays could deploy their fewer words to equal effect. Most notable among these stood the "Junius" series that

6. The first issue of *The North Briton* appeared on 5 June 1762 and the last in the regular run, the controversial No. 45, on 23 April 1763. The earliest compilations, which began to appear before the end of 1763, did not include No. 45. They can be found in ECCO (see n. 5 supra). See the discussion in George Nobbe, *The North Briton* (New York: Columbia University Press, 1939); and more broadly in George Rude, *Wilkes and Liberty* (Oxford: Clarendon Press, 1962), pp. 17–36; P. D. G. Thomas, *John Wilkes: A Friend to Liberty* (Oxford: Clarendon Press, 1996), pp. 27–56; and Arthur H. Cash, *John Wilkes* (New Haven: Yale University Press, 2006), pp. 65–120.The *Whisperer* ran from 17 February 1770 through 11 January 1772. "Printed for the Authors by W. Moore" appeared at the end of each issue. The original Fleet Street address eventually shifted to Chancery Lane. *The Whisperer* is now available online, as digitized by Adam Matthew in its Eighteenth Century Journals Portal. For the revolutionary American press in general see Philip Davidson, *Propaganda and the American Revolution, 1763–1783* (Chapel Hill: University of North Carolina Press, 1941); Arthur M. Schlesinger, *Prelude to Independence: The Newspaper War on Britain,1764–1776* (New York: Alfred A. Knopf, 1957); John B. Hench and Bernard Bailyn, eds., *The Press and the American Revolution* (Worcester: American Antiquarian Society, 1980); Jeffery A. Smith, *Printers and Press Freedom* (New York: Oxford University Press, 1988); Michael Warner, *The Letters of the Republic* (Cambridge: Harvard University Press, 1990; and Russ Castronovo, *Propaganda 1776: Secrets, Leaks, and Revolutionary Communications in Early America* (New York: Oxford University Press, 2014).

ran in the *Public Advertiser*.[7] Earlier essayists like Richard Steele had been no less didactic, but much more deferential. Nonetheless, caustic as "Junius" or John Wilkes or *The Whisperer* could be, none were as unrelentingly strident or as witheringly personal as what would be printed in the pages of *The Crisis*.

London, on the eve of the American rebellion, with its population of nearly a million, had just under twenty papers. Boston, by comparison, with a population of fewer than twenty thousand, had five weekly newspapers—an indication of higher literacy rates and a higher standard of living in the provincial town's laboring classes than in the imperial capital. The divisions that marked pro- and anti-government newspapers were not quite as pronounced in London as in Boston,[8] and yet there were tendencies in the London press that would distinguish a *Public Advertiser* (which had run "Junius") or *St. James Chronicle* from the more staid *London Gazette*.[9] None printed more than thirty-five hundred copies per issue; most printed far fewer than

7. Junius's first "letter" appeared on 21 January 1769, the last, the sixty-ninth, on 21 January 1772. See the compilation and analysis (including the difficulty of establishing authorship) in John Cannon, ed., *The Letters of Junius* (Oxford: Clarendon Press, 1978).

8. For Boston see *The History of Printing in America*, 2nd ed., 2 vols. (Albany: J. Munsell, 1874; orig. ed., 1810); Arthur M. Schlesinger, *Prelude to Independence: The Newspaper War on Britain, 1764–1776* (Boston: Alfred A. Knopf, 1958); Mary Ann Yodelis, "Boston's Second Paper War: Economics, Politics, and the Theory and Practice of Political Expression in the Press, 1763–1775" (Ph. D. dissertation, University of Wisconsin, 1971); and my case study in "Tag-Team Polemics: The 'Centinel' and His Allies in the *Massachusetts Spy*" *Proceedings of the Massachusetts Historical Society* 107 (1995):85–114.

9. Solomon Lutnick broke down print-run size and sympathies in *The American Revolution and the British Press, 1775–1783* (Columbia: University of Missouri Press, 1967), pp. 224–25. He listed seventeen titles that fit the newspaper category being printed in London in 1775, but also cautioned that the list excluded papers with too few surviving copies to effectively evaluate. Lutnick did not include *The Crisis*, though R. S. Crane and F. B. Kaye, *A Census of British Newspapers and Periodicals, 1620–1800* (Chapel Hill: University of North Carolina Press, 1927), from which he drew, did. See too Fred Junkin Hinkhouse, *The Preliminaries of the American Revolution as seen in the English Press, 1763–1775* (New York: Columbia University Press, 1926); and Troy Bickham, *Making Headlines: The American Revolution as Seen through the British Press* (DeKalb: Northern Illinois University Press, 2009). Neither of them allude to *The Crisis*.

that. *The Crisis*, with its weekly output of around two thousand, stood somewhere near the middle.[10]

All, regardless of size, were involved in a conscious effort to shape public opinion; even more, they were part of a reshaping of the public sphere itself.[11] By the time that *The Crisis* became part of London's political scene the expectation that opinion out-of-doors should play a role in shaping the policy made indoors at Whitehall and Westminster had grown increasingly insistent. The London coffeehouses, where so many newspapers were left for distribution and sale, grew in political importance as proceedings in the House of Commons were now being summarized regularly, whereas less than a decade before Parliament had banned such reporting.[12] Still barred from reporting debates in the House of Lords, the press nonetheless leaked news of the proceedings there, as peers passed along notes, even speeches, as their colleagues in the Commons had been doing for years. Consequently, what has been said about the American press and the rise of colonial protest could also be said of the press in London: just as colonists developed a greater sense of danger through what essayists in the press claimed imperial policies portended for their future, Britons, too, came to worry about tyranny anticipated as much as tyranny experienced. It was that agitated state of mind that *The Crisis* sought to heighten.[13]

10. At least, that was the size of the print run early on, as noted in the *London Evening-Post*, 2 February 1775.

11. Jürgen Habermas, *The Structural Transformation of the Public Sphere* (Cambridge: MIT Press, 1989; orig German ed., 1962). J. A. Downie questioned Habermas' basic argument in "Public and Private: The Myth of the Bourgeois Public Sphere" in Cynthia Wall, ed., *A Concise Companion to the Restoration and Eighteenth Century* (Malden, Mass.: Blackwell, 2005), pp. 58–79. Also see Jeremy Black's overview, *The English Press in the Eighteenth Century* (London: Croom Helm, 1987).

12. For parliamentary reluctance to have debates made public see P. D. G. Thomas, "The Beginnings of Parliamentary Reporting in Newspapers, 1768–1774" *English Historical Review* 74 (1959):632–36; Thomas' more general discussion in *The House of Commons* (Oxford: Clarendon Press, 1971); and J. R. Pole, *The Gift of Government* (Athens: University of Georgia Press, 1983).

13. See David Ramsay's comment that American colonists "were not so much moved by oppression actually felt, as by a conviction that a foundation was laid, and a precedent

The Crisis caught the attention of Parliament at the same moment as a just-published pamphlet with a similar title, *The Present Crisis*. Superficially they appear to be an odd pairing in parliamentary minds: *The Crisis* condemned the king and his men for doing too much, for oppressing the colonists with unconstitutional policies; *The Present Crisis*, by contrast, called on the king to do even more, to exercise his prerogative powers more aggressively and drive disobedient colonists back into line.[14] The pamphlet offended one group in Parliament, the weekly another, but they concurred that these attacks on the crown could not be tolerated. The House of Lords led, and the Commons followed, in a joint condemnation of both publications. With the third issue of *The Crisis* as their evidence, they censured the weekly "as a false, daring, infamous, seditious, and treasonable Libel on His Majesty, designed to alienate the Affections of His Majesty's Subjects from his Royal person and Government, and to disturb the Peace of the Kingdom." They chastised *The Present Crisis* with equally harsh language, adding that it was "an audacious insult on His Majesty, tending to subvert the fundamental Laws and Liberties of these Kingdoms, and to introduce an illegal and arbitrary Power."[15]

---

about to be established for future oppressions" in his *A History of the American Revolution*, 2 vols. (Indianapolis: The Liberty Fund, 1990; orig. ed., 1789), 1:105–106, as edited by Lester Cohen. Bernard Bailyn made a more elaborate argument along these lines in *The Ideological Origins of the American Revolution* (Cambridge: Belknap Press of Harvard University Press, 1967).

14. *The Present Crisis, With Respect to America, Considered* (London: T. Becket, 1775), criticized repeal of the Stamp Act, claiming that from that point on the colonists had become implacable; it also condemned members of the opposition in Parliament who had encouraged them. Britain was sovereign, Parliament supreme, and colonies necessarily subordinate—all of which, it emphasized, had to be insisted upon before those dissident colonists began seeking independence altogether.

15. For the House of Lords' resolutions of 24 February 1775, concurred in by the Commons three days later, see the *House of Lords Journals*, 30:324 and the *House of Commons Journals*, 35:159, resp. Also see R. C. Simmons and P. D. G. Thomas, eds., *Proceedings and Debates of the British Parliament Respecting North America, 1754–1783*, 6 vols. (Millwood, N.Y.: Kraus International Publications, 1982–1987), 5:456, 462 (Lords resolutions), and 5:464, 465 (Commons concurrence); *The Annual Register . . . For the Year*

To underscore their disgust, the Lords and the Commons had also agreed that the pamphlet and the offending issue of the weekly should be destroyed by the "common hangman." Handbills circulated around London, announcing "The Last DYING SPEECH of the CRISIS," which would be burned at the gate to the entrance of Westminster palace yard on the afternoon of March 6th, and the next afternoon in front of the Royal Exchange. *The Present Crisis* would join it in the blaze.

Authorities may have come away from the first staged display of governmental prowess feeling that they had made their point; not so the second. At Westminster, the sheriffs of the city of London and Middlesex County carried off their duties with no difficulties. The crowd of hundreds that gathered did nothing to disrupt the proceedings, beyond uttering some "Hissings and Shoutings." The hangman stacked wood, started a fire, and tossed copies of the offending pamphlet and disreputable weekly on the little pyre, with a ring of constables forming a circle around it.[16]

The orderly affair of that day was followed by chaos the next. The Royal Exchange, site of the second burning, was located on Threadneedle Street in the heart of London, across from the Bank of England and close by the lord mayor's mansion house. That was an area where crowds could more easily turn into mobs. Sure enough, events there were "abundantly more diverting," as one newspaper put it wryly afterward. The crowd that gathered was larger than at Westminster, the number of constables, smaller. The hangman had difficulty getting a fire started because people interfered with him; insults were hurled, dead cats and dogs and other

---

1775, 2nd ed. (London: J. Dodsley, 1777), Part I, Chronicle, pp. 94–95; and the typically acidic comments of Horace Walpole in A. Francis Steuart, ed., *The Last Journals of Horace Walpole during the Reign of George III from 1771–1783*, 2 vols. (New York: J. Lane, 1910), 1:439–41; and Walpole's letter of 28 February 1775 in W. S. Lewis, *Horace Walpole's Correspondence*, 48 vols. (New Haven: Yale University Press, 1937–1983), 28:180.

16. As recounted by the *Public Advertiser*, 7 March 1775, and the *London Evening-Post*, of that same day, which also noted, "A person unknown took an opportunity, while the Crisis was burning, to throw the Address of the Archbishop and Clergy of the Diocese of Canterbury to the King into the said flames."

Front of the Royal Exchange.

The Royal Exchange, as viewed from Cornhill Street in London. From a copper line engraving by John Green of the scene produced by painter and illustrator Samuel Wale. Originally printed in *London and its Environs Described,* 6 vols. (London: R. & J. Dodsley, 1761), where it appeared between pp. 280–81 in the fifth volume. Later removed and colored by hand. The attempt to burn a copy of the third issue of *The Crisis* here the day after another had been burned in the yard at Wesminster Palace produced a riot.

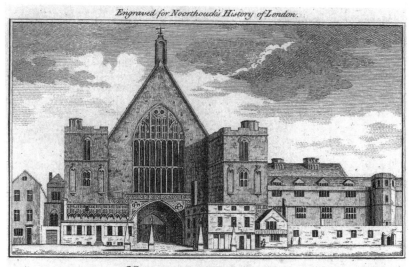

Engraved for Noorthouck's History of London.

WESTMINSTER HALL.

John Collyer's engraving of Westminster Hall, as reproduced on copper plate for and printed in John Noorthouck's *A New History of London* (London: R. Baldwin, 1773), p. 692. The third issue of The Crisis was publicly burned in the yard here without incident on 6 March 1775.

debris were flung at anyone representing authority; one of the sheriffs was pulled from his horse and beaten; the stack of wood and tinder was broken apart before the offending pieces were fully burned, smoldering bits being scattered along the street; three men seized by the sheriffs or constables were freed by the crowd so that no one could be charged with creating a public disturbance. What was intended to be a demonstration of governmental resolve instead turned into embarrassing street theatre.[17]

With that, parliamentary action against *The Present Crisis* ceased. No legal case against it was pursued. The real test for *The Crisis* still lay ahead. Parliament exercised its authority to direct Attorney General Edward Thurlow to prosecute those responsible for it. That freed Thurlow from the need to seek a grand jury indictment, which he knew he was not likely to get in London anyway because any attempt to stifle the press would be unpopular with the public.

When the men behind *The Crisis* had claimed, in their very first issue, that freedom of the press was a bulwark of English liberty, they repeated a widely shared sentiment. "The liberty of the press is indeed essential to the nature of a free state," wrote William Blackstone in his influential *Commentaries* on English law. Nonetheless, Blackstone's notion of a free press differed from that of most printers and high court judges sided with him, not the printers. Printers believed that truth should be a mitigating factor in any defense; Blackstone limited press protection to freedom from prior restraint. As Blackstone explained it, "provocation, and not falsity" was the key issue. Any printer who published "what is improper, mischievous, or illegal" must accept "the consequence of his own temerity." Any writing that demonstrated "a pernicious

---

17. "Diverting" comment in the *Public Advertiser*, 8 March 1775; also see the *Morning Post*, 8 March 1775, and *The General Evening Post* for the next day. The *St. James Chronicle*, 9 March 1775, reported that thousands of copies had been dispersed through the kingdom. Two centuries and three hundred books later, Parliament was coming to see that the exercise too often backfired. See Charles Ripley Gillett, *Burned Books*, 2 vols. (New York: Columbia University Press, 1932), 2:656–660 for *The Crisis* and *Present Crisis*.

tendency" and threatened "good peace and order" ought to be held legally liable for any resulting public unrest, its instigators punished for any harm done; such could be "the only foundation of civil liberty," Blackstone concluded.[18]

The use of prior restraint had ended by 1695, after Parliament allowed a licensing act that it first passed thirty-three years before to lapse. That 1662 act had expressed a concern that "heretical, schismatical, blasphemous, and treasonable books, pamphlets and papers" threatened the peace of the kingdom. Parliament therefore directed that no book be published without a proper royal license. It provided a second line of defense as well: no book concerning religion could be published without approval by the Archbishop of Canterbury; no book on the common law could be printed without first being reviewed by a lord chief justice.[19] Those printers who published without a license from the crown faced the possibility of being tried for and convicted of seditious libel, which meant that in an extreme case they could receive the same sentence as those convicted of high treason: death.

In the years since the end of licensing, seditious libel had been gradually reduced from a capital crime to a relatively minor offense. Guilty verdicts would usually result in a judge's sentence that involved jail time and possibly a fine rather than a long prison term or execution. Threat of prosecution for seditious libel nevertheless became the favored tool of government to combat its opponents in the press; after all, the stamp duties and advertising taxes imposed on printers increased costs but did

18. William Blackstone, *Commentaries on the Laws of England*, 4 vols. (Chicago: University of Chicago Press, 1979; orig. ed., 1765–1769), 4:150–153 (Book IV, Chapter 11); echoed in various legal compendia, such as *A Digest of the Law Concerning Libels* (London: J. Dodsley, 1770; orig. ed, 1765), by "A Gentleman of the Inner-Temple" [John Rayner?].

19. For the 1662 Act and its last renewal (for two years) in 1692 see Danby Pickering, ed., *The Statutes at Large*, 46 vols. (Cambridge: Joseph Bentham, 1762–1807) at 8:137–38 (14 Charles II c. 33) and 9:223 (4 & 5 William and Mary c. 24), resp.

not necessarily curtail criticism.[20] Attorney General Thurlow and Solicitor General Alexander Wedderburn understood that an allegation of
seditious libel against *The Crisis* or any other publication had to involve
more than simple defamation of a public official. Prosecutors needed to
prove malicious intent, with a further intention to incite public unrest.
Convincing jurors that they had made their case would be their most
difficult task, particularly since they were responding to a parliamentary
directive rather than proceeding on the basis of a grand jury indictment.
Moreover, there was increasing pressure for judges to allow jurors in libel
trials to determine questions of law (whether a libel actually occurred)
as well as matters of fact (whether the accused wrote or printed the text
in question).[21]

Deciding not to risk overshooting the mark, Thurlow and Wedderburn
made no mention of treason in their formal charge against *The Crisis*,
despite the complaint by the Lords and the Commons that it had com-

20. The basic study remains Frederick Seaton Siebert, *Freedom of the Press in England,
1476–1776* (Urbana: University of Illinois Press, 1952); but also see the important revisions offered by Philip Hamburger, "The Development of the Law of Seditious Libel
and the Control of the Press" *Stanford Law Review* 37 (1985):661–765. The Zenger case
decided in New York in 1735 had no effect on English law at this time. And even if it
eventually helped establish the idea of truth as a defense in Anglo-American courts, the
burden of proof still lay with the defendant in a libel case. See Stanley Nider Katz, ed.,
A Brief Narrative of the Case and Trial of John Peter Zenger (Cambridge: Belknap Press of
Harvard University Press, 1963). For the larger context see Richard Buel, Jr., "Freedom
of the Press in Revolutionary America: The Evolution of Libertarianism, 1760–1820"
in Bernard Bailyn and John B. Hench, eds., *The Press and the American Revolution*
(Worcester: American Antiquarian Society, 1978), pp. 59–97; Jeffery A. Smith, *Printers
and Press Freedom* (New York: Oxford University Press, 1988); and Leonard W. Levy,
Emergence of a Free Press (New York: Oxford University Press, 1985), where Levy recon-
sidered some of the arguments he made in *Legacy of Suppression: Freedom of Speech and
Press in Early America* (Cambridge: Belknap Press of Harvard University Press, 1960).

21. The right of jurors to pronounce "upon the whole matter"—on questions of law
as well as fact—in libel suits would be formalized by an act of Parliament in 1792. See
Pickering, ed., *Statutes at Large*, 37:627–28 (32 George III c. 60). For context see Thom-
as A. Green, "The Jury, Seditious Libel and the Criminal Law" in R. H. Helmholz and
Thomas A. Green, eds., *Juries, Libel, & Justice* (Los Angeles: William Andrews Clark
Memorial Library, 1984), pp. 39–91; and James Oldham, *English Common Law in the*

mitted a "treasonable Libel." And even though "Printed and published for the Authors, by T. W. Shaw" appeared on every issue of *The Crisis*, from the first through the last, Shaw was not prosecuted. Instead, another London printer, Samuel Axtell, was taken to court. It is indeed possible that more than one printer was involved and that the only witness the prosecution could muster agreed to testify against Axtell, with no mention of Shaw.[22] The real reasons remain elusive. London printers had become adept at keeping their presses from prying eyes. Listing the place of publication could be a ruse or even an act of hiding in plain sight, with journeymen doing the actual work and master printers not in the shop. Experience taught prosecutors that going after any of them legally could prove to be more trouble than it was worth. Axtell, for his part, was tried in absentia in June 1775, Axtell apparently choosing not to attend his own trial. Found guilty of being a "wicked[,] seditious[,] malicious and ill-disposed person" who "unlawfully[,] wickedly[,]" and "maliciously"maligned both crown and Parliament, the Court of King's Bench sentenced him to ninety days in jail.[23]

The Crisis continued to be published each week, trial regardless—as indeed had happened with other writers or printers charged with seditious libel over the past decade. Like them, the men funding *The Crisis* reaffirmed their commitment to a defense of English liberties. They repeated their warnings about how those liberties were in jeopardy, but they made no mention of Axtell's trial in their weekly. Per-

---

Age of Mansfield (Chapel Hill: University of North Carolina Press, 2004). American juries were already acting in this fashion. See Matthew P. Harrington, "The Law-Finding Function of the American Jury" *Wisconsin Law Review* (1999):377–439.

22. Although this witness also thought that William Moore, of *The Whisperer* fame, was somehow involved as well, Thurlow and Wedderburn decided not to charge Moore. The "Resolution and Order to Prosecute" is in PRO/[Public Record Office] TS [Treasury] 11/209/844, TNA [The National Archives], Kew. For the possibility of two printers being involved see note 1 to No. 1, at p. 1 infra.

23. For the formal charges, with Thurlow acting by order of the House of Lords, see PRO/KB [King's Bench] 33/5/8 TNA. Also see the large parchment roll in PRO/KB 10/39 part 2, TNA.

haps they foresaw that the days of book-burnings and prosecutions were ending, though English law did not formally abandon the charge of seditious libel until 2009. Interestingly enough, when Parliament that year finally discontinued seditious libel as the basis for a criminal prosecution, it tied itself to notions of press liberty and to deeper notions of freedom that *The Crisis* had relied on in its defense to the public over two centuries before.[24]

We now know slightly more than Attorney General Thurlow did about authorship of *The Crisis*, but only because three names appeared on essays published after Axtell's prosecution: William Stewardson, Philip Thicknesse and, most intriguingly, Thomas Shaw, the printer who was identified at the end of every issue. Stewardson, apparently a Southwark sailmaker by trade, had his name attached to issue No. 67. The tone of this piece was not as harsh as many of the others that bracketed it. Stewardson, if he was indeed the author, condemned bad policies and foolish ministers, but he was not so caustic in his criticism of the king. This was most likely the same Stewardson who also took an excursion into pamphlet writing on his own.[25]

Philip Thicknesse, identified as the author of No. 30, was one of the more colorful characters of his age. Thicknesse comes down to us as

24. In Section 73 of the Coroners and Justice Act passed that year. The law applies to Scotland, Wales and Northern Ireland as well. It does not preclude an individual from bringing a civil suit for an alleged libel, however, with the "intended malice" standard still being applied, as it had been under criminal law.

25. No. 67 is dated 27 April 1776 and reprinted infra at pp. 425–433. Two pamphlets appeared under Stewardson's name: *A Letter to the Hon. The Commissioners of His Majesty's Customs* (London, 1763) and *A Serious Warning to Great Britain* (London, [1778]), both printed at his expense, with no actual printer listed. The former protested what Stewardson alleged was fraud in the awarding of naval contracts; the latter condemned alleged fraud in the customs and excise services that helped precipitate the American war. In that second pamphlet, Stewardson claimed (on p. 16) to have written an account of a vision that he sent to the king that was subsequently printed in *The Whisperer* on 9 June 1770.

a quarrelsome, eccentric gadfly who made friends and enemies with equal ease. As a youth he sought adventure abroad, first in Georgia, then in Jamaica. He bought a commission in the Royal Marines after returning to England, retired to Bath after a middling military career, and then moved to a cottage outside of town, still a contentious contrarian.[26] An inheritance case that he lost on appeal to the House of Lords was the focus of issue No. 30, which stands as the great exception to an otherwise single-minded obsession with Britain, America, the empire, and a king failing to do his duty. Why, exactly, *The Crisis* took up Thicknesse's cause remains a mystery, like so much else about the weekly and the people who started it and kept it going.[27]

Shaw signed his name as the author of one piece, and to part of a second, phrased as if he were responding to another author who had written for the weekly. Unlike Thicknesse, Shaw kept the focus on larger concerns—on the issues that *The Crisis* had made its raison d'être.[28] That Shaw could affix his own name to the essay, roughly a month after Axtell's conviction, suggests that he did not fear prosecution, even if his tone was as harsh and his condemnations as sweeping as anything printed in earlier numbers. In the second essay he reaffirmed his determination "to support FREEDOM of the Press" and defend the "CHARTERED

---

26. Philip Gosse confessed in his biography of Thicknesse, *Dr. Viper* (London: Cassell and Company, 1952), p. 214, that he could "but marvel that nobody ever shot or bludgeoned him to death." Katherine Turner's sketch of Thicknesse for the *Oxford Dictionary of National Biography*, 60 vols. (Oxford: Oxford University Press, 2004), 54:202–6, essentially follows Gosse's account.

27. No. 30 appeared on 12 August 1775; printed infra at pp. 273–280. Several earlier issues had alluded to Thicknesse's case, though it is most unlikely that Thicknesse himself wrote them or that he had had anything to do with launching *The Crisis*. Thicknesse's failed appeal before the House of Lords was in February 1775; see the *House of Lords Journals*, 34:309, 316, 319, 329. I discuss more about Thicknesse, including why he was an unlikely author of anything other than issue No. 30, in "George III, Tyrant," pp. 452–53.

28. *The Crisis*, No. 28, dated 29 July 1775, and reprinted infra at pp. 243–250.

RIGHTS and CONSTITUTIONAL LIBERTIES of the BRAVE *Americans"* as well as the rights of Englishmen at home.[29]

Shaw's first essay used the same literary tactics as others in the series, ranging through the past to find examples that could be used for the present. Having already printed numerous pieces that decried the corruption and fall of republican Rome, Shaw railed against *"Neronian Cruelty,"* knowing that previous issues had set the stage for his historical allusion. Likewise, he could warn that conspiracies were afoot to destroy English and American liberties, and simply mention the king and his ministers without having to explain which particular ministerial or parliamentary actions he had in mind; those points too had already been raised. He placed God and Magna Carta on the side of good, arrayed against pensioners and placemen who personified the bad; he juxtaposed liberty and progress against slavery and ruin. These were all familiar tropes, words evoking symbols, symbols incarnated in the political reality he constructed for his readers. Although Shaw reminded those readers of their duty to defend their rights, when he called for Englishmen to rise up and fight oppression he did not mean literally, as the colonists were doing. Rather, he expected them to be able to make subtle distinctions, to know what separated Britons from Americans as well as what joined them in common cause.

ॐ　　ॐ　　ॐ

The Crisis is notable for the assumptions that Thomas Shaw and the other men behind it had about the intellectual world of their readers.[30] They played off Britons' deepest fears, capitalizing on a state of mind that they did not create but sought to reinforce. Conspiracy theory was as popular then as ever; not surprisingly, conspiracies loomed large in the Anglo-American political world described by *The Crisis*. Conspiracy against American rights marked imperial policy; con-

---

29. Ibid., No. 35, 16 September 1775, reprinted at pp. 319–325 infra.

30. That *The Crisis* was a group effort was emphasized repeatedly. See, for example, No. 1, 21 January 1775, pp. 1–11; No. 15, 29 April 1775; and No. 22, 17 June 1775, at pp. 129–134, and pp. 191–196, resp.

spiracy against the rights of Englishmen, in England itself, would come next, readers were warned. The weekly reserved its sharpest, harshest comments for those most responsible for these dark designs: Lord North, "engendered in the womb of hell,"[31] who headed a depraved ministry; the Earl of Bute, long out of power but still active behind the scenes, corrupting others with his baneful influence;[32] Lord Chancellor Apsley and Chief Justice Mansfield, who twisted the law to serve unjust ends; secretary of state for American affairs Lord George Germain and his predecessor, the Earl of Dartmouth, who endorsed and passed along the nefarious policies that brutalized Americans; General Thomas Gage, who in his dual role as army commander in North America and governor of Massachusetts, set loose the troops to murder and plunder; Samuel Johnson and John Wesley, mercenaries whose pens were for hire, defending the indefensible actions of "A Bloody Court, A Bloody Ministry, And A Bloody Parliament."[33]

Unlike other newspaper essays and pamphlets that attacked George III obliquely through his ministers, *The Crisis* targeted the King directly and repeatedly, utterly undeterred by Axtell's conviction in court. The authors did not mince words, even likening George III to Charles I and suggesting that he deserved the same fate. One issue addressed him derisively as his "TYRANNIC MAJESTY—the DEVIL" and ticked off a litany of his wrongs before concluding that in his case there could be only one proper judgment: the "Wages of these Sins is Death."[34] Nevertheless, *The Crisis* still held out hope that the empire could be restored and the nation saved if George III found his bet-

---

31. See issue No. 2, 28 January 1775, reprinted infra, at pp. 13–21.

32. In attacking both Bute and Mansfield, *The Crisis* played to an anti-Scots bias common in England at the time, where memories of "the '45" and "The Pretender" lingered. See, for example, No. 18, 20 May 1775, and No. 53, 20 January 1776, pp. 157–167 and pp. 477–484 infra, resp.

33. Issue No. 28, 29 July 1775, at infra pp. 243–250.

34. Issue No. 23, 24 June 1775, at pp. 197–207 infra.

ter self—that is, *if* he embraced Viscount Bolingbroke's notion of the
patriot king.[35] Remembering what George III himself had stated over
the years about his commitment to serving his subjects, Shaw and his
compatriots dismissed their flesh and blood monarch as a perversion
of Bolingbroke's ideal of the people's king who would selflessly protect
them and uphold the principles of the Glorious Revolution.[36] Asking,
rhetorically, "are we not Descendants" of those patriots who overthrew
James II and restored balanced government, *The Crisis* urged its readers to denounce Tyranny "in the Name of those Ancestors."[37]

Although the authors associated with *The Crisis* stood by the idea of
mixed and balanced government within a monarchical system, they
reflected the republican tendencies of what historian Caroline Robbins
called the "commonwealth" tradition.[38] There lay an inherent tension
between their own brand of libertarianism and their desire to preserve,
even strengthen, constitutional government. Like so many of their generation, including those whose politics may have differed from theirs,
the authors who wrote for *The Crisis* took it as a given that fundamental

35. Bolingbroke is alluded to twice in *The Crisis:* No. 36, 23 September 1775, and No.
40, 21 October 1775, reprinted at pp. 327–332 and pp. 363–368, resp. Also see No. 15, 29
April 1775, at pp. 129–134 infra.

36. See David Armitage, ed., *Bolingbroke: Political Writings* (Cambridge: Cambridge
University Press, 1997) for the *Patriot King* (1738) and related essays; Isaac Kramnick,
Bolingbroke and His Circle (Cambridge: Harvard University Press, 1968); and H. T.
Dickinson, *Bolingbroke* (London: Constable, 1970), with Dickinson's suggestion that
Bolingbroke may well have influenced the new king (p. 307). A new edition of Boling-
broke's writings that included *The Patriot King* had been printed in London by Thomas
Davis just days before the first issue of *The Crisis* went to press. See the advertisements
for it in *The Gazetteer and New Daily Advertiser*, 17 January 1775, and the *St. James
Chronicle*, 21 January 1775.

37. *The Crisis*, No. 37, 30 September 1775, at pp. 333–343 infra. For the complexities
of the Glorious Revolution as looking forward and backward simultaneously see Lois
G. Schwoerer, *The Declaration of Rights, 1689* (Baltimore: Johns Hopkins University
Press, 1989); and Lee Ward, *The Politics of Liberty in England and Revolutionary America*
(Cambridge: Cambridge University Press, 2004).

38. Caroline Robbins, *The Eighteenth-Century Commonwealthman* (Cambridge: Harvard University Press, 1959).

rights came from God and through nature, that all legitimate government depended on the consent of the governed, and that even though the king-in-parliament reigned supreme, no one stood above the law and no power short of God's could be unlimited. The Glorious Revolution had restored principles going back to the ancient constitution of Britain, historically difficult to reconstruct but no less real because of it, disappearing into a foggy Saxon past for some and back to even earlier Gothic antecedents for others.[39]

Where modern scholars have attempted to separate intellectual threads, *The Crisis* was typical of the age in weaving them all into its own ideological fabric. For example, one issue alluded approvingly to the great medieval jurists Henry de Bracton and Sir John Fortescue. "The king must not be under man but under God and under law, because law makes the king,"de Bracton had written, adding that there "is no *rex* where will rules rather than *lex*"—a position on limited government not so different from what *The Crisis* would champion five hundred years later.[40] That so many of the pen names of the authors in its pages—Junius, Brutus, Casca—were drawn from the history of republican Rome was indicative of the tendency to run ancient and modern together, to

---

39. John Phillip Reid, *The Ancient Constitution and the Origins of Anglo-American Liberty* (DeKalb: Norther Illinois University Press, 1984), p. 84, singled out an argument in *The Crisis* as typifying what he called "evolving permanency"—the notion of an ancient constitution that allowed for change in circumstance rather than principle, with fundamental law remaining immutable on that higher level. For context see J. G. A. Pocock, *The Ancient Constitution and the Feudal Law* (Cambridge: Cambridge University Press, 1957; revised ed., 1987); Glenn Burgess, *The Politics of the Ancient Constitution* (Basingstoke: Macmillan, 1992); and Colin Kidd, *British Identities Before Nationalism* (Cambridge: Cambridge University Press, 1999). An excellent example of a tract on the ancient constitution still circulating at the time of *The Crisis* is George St. Amand's *An Historical Essay on the Legislative Power of England*, first published in London in 1725, reprinted in 1767, and then appended to a 1770 reissue and update of the two-volume *A Complete Collection of the Lords' Protests*.

40. The allusion to Bracton and Fortescue is in *The Crisis*, No. 14, 22 April 1775; see infra pp. 123–128. The quoted passages can be found in Samuel E. Thorne, trans. and ed., *Bracton on the Laws and Customs of England*, 4 vols. (Cambridge: Belknap Press of the Harvard University Press, 1968–1977), 2:33.

deal in archetypes when advising those living in the present on how to avoid repeating the mistakes of the past.

Americans had been right, insisted *The Crisis*, to resist the foolish policies pursued by Lord North and, before him, the unconstitutional connivings of George Grenville. Virtual representation arguments had been a canard; Americans should have been allowed to tax themselves, which better and worthier men like Lord Camden and the Earl of Chatham—when Chatham was true to his principles, that is—understood.[41] Oppressed by crown and parliament, Americans had the right, even the duty, to resist, as indeed did all people who suffered from tyranny.[42] *The Crisis* hinted broadly that any conflict between mother country and colonies would eventually draw in France and Spain, a geopolitical awareness shared by dissident colonists across the Atlantic.[43]

When *The Crisis* first went to press it had not been difficult to draw analogies between British and American conditions, to speak of the common cause, a transatlantic association of the aggrieved. To those who defended government and contended that protesting Americans would not be satisfied with anything less than full independence, *The Crisis* countered that discontented colonists only wanted those rights guaranteed them as Englishmen: they would not leave the empire unless driven from it. Early on, Shaw and his associates seemed to believe that reconciliation was still possible, that the empire could serve the needs and meet the aspirations of Americans as well as Britons.

After the shooting started, *The Crisis* joined a chorus of those calling for commissioners to be sent out from London to negotiate a

41. See, notably, No. 65 of *The Crisis*, 13 April 1776, for Pitt, and No. 82, 10 August 1776, for Camden's speech against the Declaratory Act; infra at pp. 569–576 and 687–692, resp.

42. Ibid., at No. 5, 21 February 1775, No. 34, 9 September 1775 (at pp. 39–47 and 307–316, resp.) and several other issues in between.

43. See Issues No. 9, 18 March 1775, and No. 12, 8 April 1775, at pp. 75–82 and 97–112, resp., infra, as cases in point.

peaceful settlement.[44] When, after more than a year of bloodshed, it became evident that no accommodation could be reached, that Americans who had once argued they only wanted their rights within the empire now insisted they could only secure them outside it, *The Crisis* did not denounce them as disingenuous or as traitors to the common cause. It printed the Declaration of Independence, though basically without comment. Only seven more issues appeared thereafter, essentially to reaffirm traditional Whig principles as exemplified by the texts from which its authors drew.[45] It accepted, however reluctantly, a different future, where America could become a haven for the oppressed, separated from Britain, not united with it.[46] Indeed, the final issue closed with the men behind *The Crisis* stating that they themselves had decided to sail for more hospitable American shores.[47]

❧ ❧ ❧

Some of the earlier issues of *The Crisis* garnered American notice and were reprinted in New York, Newport, Philadelphia, and a few other places.[48] For modern readers unaware of the transatlantic nature of imperial protest, that by itself may well seem impressive; for those seeking

---

44. Ibid., No. 50, 30 December 1775, at pp. 451–460 infra. For Britain's halting steps toward a negotiated peace from that point on see my *Turning the World Upside Down* (Westport: Praeger, 2003), pp. 131–43

45. Issues No. 86, 87 and 88 (8, 14, and 21 September 1776, rep.) were drawn largely from Robert Molesworth's *The Principles of a Free Whig*; Issue No. 90, 6 October 1776, drew from *An Extract from the* Freeholder's *Catechism*, now usually attributed to Bolingbroke. See pp. 713–730 and 737–742, resp.

46. Ibid., No. 81, 3 August 1776, at pp. 681–686 infra.

47. Ibid., No. 91, 12 October 1776), at pp. 743–747 infra. This was the last of the 92 issues; *A Crisis Extraordinary* of 9 August 1775 (reprinted at pp. 261–272 infra) had not been numbered. The pledge to leave Britain for America may have been made for literary effect; we know too little about Shaw and his associates to say for certain.

48. American reprints are listed in Charles Evans, *American Bibliography*, 14 vols., reprint ed. (New York: Peter Smith, 1941–59), 5:112–25, 228. No. 3, the issue burned publicly in London, was reprinted in Hartford and Norwich, Connecticut, as well as Newport, Rhode Island, New York, and Philadelphia. They were all issued without any commentary added by the American printers. The list (though not the actual texts) can

a more coordinated, systematic sharing of ideas, its circulation around the empire probably appears fairly hit-or-miss. To be sure, *The Crisis* did not enjoy the reprint success of Paine's *Common Sense* or, earlier, of John Dickinson's Pennsylvania Farmer *Letters*. But then the actual influence of writers on readers, appealing as it is among historians to try and prove, is inherently elusive.

Even though *The Crisis* stood as a publication apart in its acerbic language and combative tone, it should also be considered alongside others that made their rights arguments less intemperately. They were all products of the same philosophical and political traditions. In the world that *The Crisis* shared with other defenders of English freedoms, fundamental law was real and basic human rights were antecedent to those bestowed by any government. Moreover, all legitimate government was a compact between ruler and ruled, the duties of the ruler being as great as the responsibilities of the ruled. In the British empire the rights of Englishmen extended fully to the colonies, with nothing lost through transatlantic migration. Charters, for colonists, were constitutions, just as they claimed, not mere contracts, revocable by crown decree.[49] If British-Americans were obliged, because of British tyranny, to rise in rebellion and eventually turn to revolution, *The Crisis* accepted that they did what men of conscience had always had the right to do. Ultimately the former colonists would point to their successful revolution as evidence of their exceptionalism, even as proof of their peculiar destiny in the larger world. It is curious if not ironic that a weekly British paper dedicated to saving the empire from itself promoted that very-American state of mind.

---

be found in the online version of the Evans Collection cited above, in Early American Imprints: Series One, Evans, 1639–1800.

49. The best introduction to the problems of defining constitutional rights in the British empire remains Jack P. Greene, *Peripheries and Center* (Athens, Ga.: University of Georgia Press, 1986). For the best examination of contentious constitutional issues dividing those who sought to define the empire—disputes over rights and responsibilities, over taxation and representation, and over the limits to imperial authority and extent of colonial autonomy—see John Philip Reid's magnum opus, *Constitutional History of the American Revolution*, 4 vols. (Madison: University of Wisconsin Press, 1986–1993).

Editorial Note

The printed source for this edition of *The Crisis* comes from the copy that is found in the Bodleian Library. We were able to access an electronic version of the source from the online Eighteenth Century Journals Portal of Adam Matthew Digital, a London-based company that makes many primary-source collections available digitally for the first time. The texts were then converted into a digital manuscript that was used as the basis for typesetting.

Following Liberty Fund practice, we have not altered the texts: we have retained original spelling and punctuation with a few exceptions (we have modernized long esses to *s* and removed repeated quotation marks at the beginning of each line of the quoted material). We have silently corrected typographical errors that appeared in the original source. The editor has created footnotes to provide the reader with information about people and events that will help put the writings in their historical context and also serve as a complement to the texts themselves. We have kept the footnotes that appeared in *The Crisis* in their original format (symbols, such as asterisks or daggers); new editorial notes appear beneath *The Crisis* notes and are indicated by arabic numerals.

For works cited frequently in the footnotes, the following shortened citations have been used:

Blackstone, *Commentaries:* William Blackstone, *Commentaries on the Laws of England*, 4 vols. (Oxford: Clarendon Press, 1765–1769; orig. ed.) (Chicago: University of Chicago Press, 1979).

Cobbett, *Parliamentary History:* William Cobbett et al., eds., *The Parliamentary History of England*, 36 vols. (London: T. C. Hansard, 1806–1820).

Labaree, *Papers of Franklin:* Leonard Labaree et al., eds., *The Papers of Benjamin Franklin*, 39 vols. (New Haven: Yale University Press, 1959—).

Namier and Brooke, *House of Commons*: Sir Lewis Namier and John Brooke, *The House of Commons, 1754–1790*, 3 vols. (London: Her Majesty's Stationery Office, 1964).

Oxford DNB: *The Oxford Dictionary of National Biography*, 60 vols. (Oxford: Oxford University Press, 2004).

Pickering, *Statutes*: Danby Pickering, ed., *The Statutes at Large*, 46 vols. (Cambridge: Joseph Bentham, 1762–1807).

Simmons and Thomas, *Proceedings and Debates:* R. C. Simmons and P. D. G. Thomas, eds., *Proceedings and Debates of the British Parliament Respecting North America, 1754–1783*, 6 vols. (White Plains, N.Y.: Kraus International Publications, 1982).6

THE
CRISIS

THE

CRISIS

NUMBER I   *To be continued Weekly.*

FRIDAY, JANUARY 20, 1775[1]   [*Price Two-pence Halfpenny.*

Potior visa est Periculosa libertas quieto servitio

SALLUST[2].

To the People of ENGLAND and AMERICA.

Friends and Fellow Subjects,

IT is with the greatest Propriety I address this Paper to you: It is in your Defence, at this GREAT, this IMPORTANT CRISIS, I take the Pen in hand: A CRISIS big with the Fate of the most glorious Empire known in the Records of Time; and by *your* FIRMNESS and RESOLUTION ONLY,

---

1. The date here, from the copy in the Bodleian Library used in this collection, is different from that on the British Library [BL] copy. There it is January 21, 1775. It seems likely that the January 20 date was a mistake, even though the actual date of publication, with public distribution the next day; that is, printed on a Friday, to be issued on Saturday. Given other typesetting differences, it also seems likely that two presses were involved in the actual printing, one getting the date "right," the other "wrong." For other misdatings, present on both the Bodleian and BL copies, see the Saturday, 31 [not 30, as printed] August 1776 issue; also nos. LXXXVI and XC, which should be dated 7 [not 8] September and 5 [not 6] October 1776, resp.

2. A phrase advising that it is better to have freedom with danger than peace with slavery, from Sallust's historical fragment that appeared in various London editions of

1

it can be saved from DESTRUCTION: By *your* FIRMNESS and RESOLU-
TION, you may preserve to yourselves, your immediate Offspring, and
latest Posterity, all the glorious Blessings of FREEDOM, given by *Heaven*
to undeserving Mortals: By *your* SUPINENESS and PUSSILANIMITY, you
will entail on yourselves, your Children, and *Millions* yet unborn, MIS-
ERY and SLAVERY.

It is in your Defence I now stand forth to oppose, the most *sanguinary*,
and *despotic* Court that ever disgraced a *free* Country.

It is in your Defence I now unsheath the Sword of Justice, to oppose the
most profligate and abandoned Administration, that ever shewed the
Weakness, or abused the *Confidence* of a Prince.

It is in your Defence I now stand forth, with a Firmness and Resolution
becoming an *Englishman* determined to be *free*, to oppose every ARBI-
TRARY. and every UNCONSTITUTIONAL Act, of a venal and corrupt *Majority*, smuggled into the present new fangled Court Parliament, through
the Villainy of Lord North,[3] and purchased with the PUBLIC MONEY, to

---

C. Crispus Sallustii Opera (see the translation offered later in the essay). It comes near
the end of a speech that Sallust (Gaius Sallustius Crispus), a first century BCE Roman
historian, attributed to Marcus Aemilius Lepidus. Thomas Gordon (of *Cato's Letters*
fame) in his 1744 translation of Sallust's *Works*, rendered it as: "The Liberty of my
Country, though attended with perils, is to me far more inviting, than a State of Subjection with all its Allurements of Tranquillity." (p. 280) Liberty Fund has made this edition available through the Interent as part of its Online Library of Liberty. The phrase
is repeated in a later issue (see infra XXII.1).

3. Frederick, Lord North, headed the ministry from 1770–1782. He did not actually
become a peer until 1790, when his father died and he entered the House of Lords as
the second Earl of Guilford. An effective leader in the House of Commons, George
III had had high hopes for him and his cabinet. North did not push hardline policies
until 1774, as a consequence of the Boston Tea Party, and even then they were tougher
measures only in comparison with those that had been pursued in the previous decade.
North vacillated throughout his ministry—in the crisis leading to war, during the war
itself, and when seeking peace. North's parliamentary critics (echoed by disenchanted
colonists) belittled him and his king in almost equal measure, though never on the
floor of the Lords and the Commons with the vituperative language that marked *The
Crisis*. North left few personal papers to posterity; his private life eludes us and his
public life has to be reconstructed on the basis of papers left in other collections. The

betray their TRUST, *enslave* the People, *subvert* the Protestant Religion, and destroy the *Glory, Honor, Interest,* and *Commerce,* both foreign and domestic, of *England* and *America*; and all this villainous Sacrifice of a *great Empire,* a *brave People,* and the glorious Truths of *Heaven*; to comply with the ambitious Views, and gratify the mean vindictive Spirit of ONE, assisted by a numerous Train of deputy TYRANTS, whose sole aim has been, to trample under Foot the *sacred* Rights of Mankind, and the English CONSTITUTION.

It is in your Defence, and in Defence of the Liberties of my Country, that I now stand forth, with a fixed Resolution to oppose, and shew to the World, unawed by Fear the dangerous Tendency of every Act of *lawless Power,* whether it shall proceed from the King, the Lords, or the Commons.

I will endeavour in Conjunction with my fellow Labourer in this great Work, to rescue the Liberty of the Press, (that Bulwark of Freedom)[4] from the RUIN with which it is now threatened, by *Special Juries* of *Middlesex,* and the arbitrary Decisions of a Scotch Chief Justice,[5] the glorious

---

best introduction to him is P. D. G. Thomas, *Lord North* (London: Allen Lane, 1976); Peter Whiteley, *Lord North* (London: Hambledon Press, 1996); and Andrew Jackson O'Shaughnessy's chapter on him in *The Men Who Lost America* (New Haven: Yale University Press, 2013), pp. 47–80.

4. The more common phrase was "bulwark of liberties:" thus William Blackstone, *Commentaries on the Laws of England,* 4 vols. (Oxford: Clarendon Press, 1765,–1769) referred to magna carta and trial by jury as bulwarks of English liberty (in, respectively, Book III, Chap. 23, at 3:350; and Book IV, Chap. 27, at 4:342) and even the Royal Navy as a "floating bulwark" (Book I, Chap. 13, at 1:405). "The liberty of the press," Blackstone wrote, "is indeed essential to the nature of a free state." (Ibid., Book IV, Chap. 11, at 4:151).

5. The anti-Scots sentiments revealed in this caustic allusion to William Murray, first Earl of Mansfield and chief justice of the court of king's bench, was typical of the London press at that time. Reflecting the uneasy joining of English and Scots as Britons, those underlying sentiments had risen to the surface during the early days of George III's reign, when the new king was criticized for still being under the sway of his old tutor, the Earl of Bute. Bute (see infra II.6) would serve as the great bogeyman and political scapegoat of his age. For the anti-Jacobitism that could spill over into a general anti-Scots sentiment, with Wilkeite agitation serving as a notable example, see Linda Colley, *Britons* (New Haven: Yale University Press, 1992).

Advocate for *despotic Sway*. The heavy Fines, and cruel Imprisonment of
the *two Woodfall's*,[6] without even the *Appearance* of Guilt, and contrary
to the Intention of the Jury, will be faithfully recorded by the Pen of
Truth, and fill many Pages in the black Catalogue of *Murray's* Crimes.

It shall be my Endeavour in this degenerate Age, to revive the *dying*
Embers of *Freedom*, and rouse my Countrymen in *England*, from that
lethargic State of *Supineness* and *Inattention*, in which they seem to sleep,
at this Time of *national Danger*, when a mighty Kingdom, and all the
dearest Rights of Men are hastening to their RUIN; that they may yet
stand high on the Roll of FAME, equal with their brave and virtuous
Brethren in *America*, who are now struggling in the glorious Cause of
Liberty, against the cruel Oppressions, and destructive Designs of *exalted*
Villains, whose Actions will be transmitted to Posterity in Characters of
Blood, and their Names forever branded with eternal Marks of Infamy;
while *America* will remain the Glory and Admiration of the World, and
be held in the highest Veneration to the end of Time. Let not the long
envied Glory of *Britain*, O! my Countrymen, be eclipsed by the virtuous
Actions of the *Americans* in the new World; our *Danger* is the *same, their*
Cause, is *our* Cause, with the constitutional Rights of *America*, must
fall, the Liberties of *England*; let us then, shew ourselves equal to them

---

6. Six London publishers were prosecuted in 1770 at the court of king's bench, Mansfield presiding, for printing the "Junius" letters (see infra VII.9), which had been critical
of George III, though not as caustic as *The Crisis* would prove to be five years later.
Prosecutions proceeded on the basis of an "information" (filed *ex officio* by the attorney
general on behalf of the king) because grand juries refused to indict the printers—an indication of the press's growing power among the public. Three printers were convicted,
but for minor offenses, not seditious libel; two were acquitted; and Henry Sampson
Woodfall, of the *Public Ledger*, convicted in a first trial, had the charges dropped when
a second trial was ordered. His brother William, his partner at the paper, was not prosecuted. See the discussion in Fred S. Siebert, *Freedom of the Press in England, 1476–1776*
(Urbana: University of Illinois Press, 1952), pp. 385–391, and the trial records for Woodfall, John Almon (the *London Museum*) and John Miller (the *London Evening-Post*) in
T. B. Howell, *A Complete Collection of State Trials*, 34 vols. (London: Longman, Hurst,
Rees and Orme, 1809–1826), 20:803–922; and James Burrows, ed., *Reports of Cases Ar-
gued and Adjudged in the Court of King's Bench*, 5 vols. (London; A. Strahan and W.
Woodfall, 1790), which has only Woodfall (5:2661–2670) and Almon (5:2686–2690).

in *Virtue*, *Courage*, Firmness, and Resolution, and as they have done, prove to the World, we are alike Enemies to *Tyranny*, and *lawless Power*, and that we never will be Slaves to One, nor to a *Majority* of FIVE HUNDRED AND FIFTY-EIGHT TYRANTS.[7]

We will strain every Nerve, and brave every Danger, to stimulate our Countrymen this Side the *Atlantic*, to a noble Exertion of their Rights as *Freemen*; to shew them the *Danger*; as well as the *Infamy* of remaining *quiet* Spectators of their OWN DESTRUCTION; and to remove that dark Cloud of Slavery, which now obscures the glorious Light of *Freedom*; and, but for the *Virtue* of our *Forefathers*, would Ages ago, have overwhelmed *this* Kingdom, like the States around us, in a long, a lasting Night of MISERY and RUIN.

Upon this Plan, and with these Principles we set out, and intend to proceed, that the present, (if not too far *degenerated*) and future Generations, may enjoy undiminished ALL the BLESSINGS of LIBERTY; To accomplish this End, we will risk every Thing that is dear to Man, and brave both *Royal* and *Ministerial* Vengeance, to preserve from RUIN (if *possible*) the NATURAL RIGHTS of MANKIND, THE *Sacred Constitution of the British Empire*, and the *Freedom of* our *Country*.

---

7. There were 558 members of the House of Commons in 1775, representing 314 constituencies. Those in England sent two representatives to Westminster for each parliamentary district, with seven exceptions; those in Scotland and Wales sent one each. The breakdown was: 245 English electoral districts, with 489 individuals representing 40 counties, 203 boroughs (5 with just one representative), and one representative each for Oxford and Cambridge; 45 Scottish districts, for 30 counties and 15 boroughs; and 24 Welsh districts, for 12 counties and 12 boroughs. For details on those constituencies and each of the House members during the American Revolutionary Era see Sir Lewis Namier and John Brooke, *The House of Commons, 1754–1790*, 3 vols. (London: Her Majesty's Stationery Office, 1964); P. D. G. Thomas, *The House of Commons in the Eighteenth Century* (Oxford: Clarendon Press, 1971) for parliamentary procedures; and the massive History of Parliament Online, sponsored by the Institute for Historical Research. Many Commons members are included in Alan Valentine, *The British Establishment, 1760–1784*, 2 vols. (Norman: University of Oklahoma Press, 1970); and, in an unparalleled resource, *The Oxford Dictionary of National Biography*, 60 vols. (Oxford: Oxford University Press, 2004), with its online access and addenda.

Agreeable to our Motto we shall ever think, *"Liberty* with *Danger, preferable* to *Servitude* with *Security."*[8]

We should glory in the Smiles of our Sovereign, but will never purchase them at the Expence of our *Liberty*; nor will we ever give up, but with our Lives, the Right to expose and publickly display in all its hideous Forms the cruel Despotism of *Tyrants*. We can conceive no Reason, why the *Laws* and *Religion* of *England* should be sported with, and trampled under Foot, by a Prince of the House of *Brunswick*, rather than by one of the House of *Stuart*,[9] surely upon every Principle of *Justice, Reason*, and *Common Sense*,[10] whatever is *Tyranny* and *Murder* in one Man, is equally so in another; and if it is *just* to *oppose* and *resist* one, it is as *just* to *oppose* and *resist* the other. It is not a *Name*, nor an *Office* however important, that can, or ought to bring Respect and Reverence to the Possessor, while he acts below, and is unworthy of them. Folly and Villainy ought to have no Asylum, nor can Titles sanctify *Crimes*, tho' in *our Days* they *protect Criminals*. A

8. The author(s)' translation for the passage from Sallust (see supra I.2).

9. When contemporaries referred to the House of Stuart, they had in mind monarchs on the Scottish throne since it had been joined with that of England when James VI of Scotland succeeded Elizabeth I as James I of England and Scotland. The House of Brunswick and the House of Hanover were joined by marriage to the House of Stuart through the mother of King George I, Sophia, who was a granddaughter of James I, daughter of the elector of Hanover, and ultimately electress in her own right. She was married to George I's father, Ernest Augustus, Duke of Brunswick-Lüneburg, whom she survived by well over a decade. When Anne I died in 1713, the last in the Stuart line to rule in Britain, leaders in Parliament turned to Hanover and the future George I, carrying through on an arrangement over a decade in the works. Had Sophia outlived Anne she would have succeeded her as queen of Great Britain.

10. This is the first of nine times that the author(s) would call on readers to use their "common sense," a common enough phrase on both sides of the Atlantic. See nos. 14, 16, 33, 47, 51, 56, 62, and 66 for the other eight. There would never be a reference to Thomas Paine's *Common Sense*, even though John Almon had begun reprinting copies in his Piccadilly shop by June 1776. The men behind *The Crisis* remained more traditionally Whig, supportive of monarchy even if hostile to the reigning monarch. The publishing history of *Common Sense* once it made it into Britain can be found in Thomas R. Adams, *The American Controversy*, 2 vols. (Providence: Brown University Press, 1980), 1:422–28.

Royal, Right Honourable, or a Right Reverend Robber, is the most dangerous Robber, and consequently the most to be *detested.*

Our modern Advocates for Villainy and Slavery, have found out a new Way of arguing and convincing the Judgements of Men; they make nice *Distinctions* without a *Difference,* and tell the World. what was Tyranny in the Time of *Charles* the *first,*[11] is not Tyranny in the Days of *George* the *Third,* and to this they add a long Catalogue of Virtues which he never possessed, they say he is *pious;* that his chief Aim is to render his Subjects, a *happy, great,* and *free* People; (and indeed he has more than once said so himself) these and many other *Falshoods* equally wicked and absurd, they endeavour to instill into the Minds of the too easily deluded *English.* These, and such like Artifices, have ever been made Use of in the Reigns of arbitrary Kings, to *deceive* the People, and make them with more ease and to Chains well *polished* submit their Necks, and even *Reverence* and *adore* the Hand that rivets them. Thus do Tyrants succeed, and the galling Yoke of Slavery, so much complained of by almost every Nation in the World, becomes a *Crime* of the first MAGNITUDE, in the PEOPLE through their own Credulity and vile SUBMISSION. Truth, in Spite of all the false colouring of venal Writers speaks a different Language, and declares in Opposition to the Pen of Falsehood, that *Bloodshed* and *Slaughter, Violence* and *Oppression, Popery* and *Lawless Power* characterise the present Reign; and we will defy even the pensioned *Johnson,* after the closest Examination of the two Reigns, to tell which is the best. *Charles* broke his *Coronation Oath, butchered* his SUBJECTS, made Ten Thousand *Solemn Promises* he never intended to *perform,* and often committed *Perjury:* (but these are no *Crimes* in a *King,* for ALL Kings have a DIVINE RIGHT, to be DEVILS) *He,* tried to overturn the Constitution by *Force,* but found his Mistake when it was too *late,* and that even *Royal Villainy* does not always succeed, and when the

---

11. Charles I succeeded his father James I to the throne in 1625 and lost it when he was beheaded in 1649, long after he had been beaten militarily and politically by Parliament. To eighteenth-century critics of the royal prerogative, he served as the symbolic embodiment of the monarch as tyrant.

just Vengeance of *Heaven* overtook him, he saw, (though he would not believe it before, and imagined, he had a *Divine Right* to shed HUMAN BLOOD) that the SAME POWER, which RAISED him UP, could PULL him DOWN: The present Sovereign, not wishing to make a Figure in History *without* a *Head*; and being more *mild* and *gentle, just* and *good*, has IMPROVED upon the Plan, and is now tearing up the CONSTITUTION by the Roots, under the FORM of LAW; this Method of Proceeding is certainly much *safer*, and more *judicious,* as well as *just*; for what Right can an ENGLISHMAN have to complain, when he is LEGALLY made a SLAVE by ACT OF PARLIAMENT. How wicked! How rebellious! must the *Americans* be, and what *leveling Principles* must they possess, to *resist* the *Divine Right* of the King, and the *divine Right* of the Lords and Commons, under the Sanction of a *divine* Act of Parliament, sent from *Heaven*, to PLUNDER, BUTCHER, STARVE, or ENSLAVE them, just as it shall come into their *divine* Heads, or the Heads of their *divine* Instruments; and when once they have carried this *divine* Law into Execution, according to their *righteous* Intention, WE shall soon see on this Side the *Atlantic*, that they have the same *divine Right*, to use US, in the SAME *merciful and divine* Manner. This is but the first *divine* Step, of a DIABOLICAL Plan for shedding HUMAN BLOOD, reducing an INDUSTRIOUS, BRAVE, FLOURISHING, and FREE People, from a State of AFFLUENCE, to that of MISERY, BEGGARY, and SLAVERY; and Nothing, but a Resolution in the People HERE, will be able to prevent the next *divine* Step of the same Plan, from laying in RUINS, ALL the RIGHTS of the *British*, with those of the *American* World.[12]

---

12. Stuart absolutism, which critics linked to divine right notions—easy enough to do, given what James I said from the throne in 1604—continued to play a symbolic role in British politics. In real terms, the idea that monarchs were answerable only to God, their authority otherwise irresistible, did not ever prevail in the Stuart Era. The views expressed by Robert Filmer in *Patriarcha*, first developed in the 1630s although not published posthumously until 1680, went beyond those of most enthusiasts for monarchy, even in Filmer's generation. By the reign of George III there were hardly any true Tories left in public life, much less divine-right monarchists; all were essentially Whigs of one stamp or another, with at least some commitment to the idea of limited government and natural rights. Filmer is most accessible in Johann P. Sommerville, ed., *Patriarcha and Other Writings* (Cambridge: Cambridge University Press, 1991). For the unfolding context see Gordon J. Schochet, *Patriarchalism in Political Thought* (Oxford

The Altar of Despotism is erected in *America*, and WE shall be the next Victims to LAWLESS POWER; all the Horrors of SLAVERY, now stare US in the Face; our Religion *Subverted,* Freedom, Law, and Right *artfully undermined,* the *Roman Catholic Religion,* not *tolerated,* but ESTAB-LISHED, a Majority of the House of Commons, and House of Lords mere *Creatures* of the King; in short, every Engine of OPPRESSION and ARBITRARY Power is at work to accomplish our RUIN.

O my Countrymen, that we could but inspire you with noble Senti-ments of LIBERTY, rouse you to a just sense of your immediate Dan-ger, and make you *feel,* sensibly *feel,* all the Blessings derived from FREEDOM, the natural Right of every Man, but more peculiarly of *Englishmen,* it is our *Birthright,* our *Inheritance,* it was handed down to us by our Ancestors, and *Sealed* often with their BLOOD; let us then, in Justice to them, to ourselves, and to Posterity, make a noble *constitutional* Stand, in *Conjunction* with our noble and spirited, but suffering fellow Subjects in *America,* against the present Plan, long fixed by the Minions of Power to destroy it, and overturn the Con-stitution, a Constitution ten Thousand Times superior to any System ever devised by the *Greeks* or *Romans.*[13]

At such a time as THIS, when the merciless, the relentless Hand of Tyran-ny is tearing out the Vitals of *Freedom,* sapping the Foundations of *public*

Basil Blackwell, 1975) and Lee Ward, *The Politics of Liberty in England and Revolutionary America* (Cambridge: Cambridge University Press, 2004).

13. Blackstone's *Commentaries,* 1:142–82 (Book I, Chap. 2) celebrated what is commonly called "mixed and balanced government," the forms (crown, Lords, Commons) restored with the accession of Charles II that have been preserved to the present, and in that sense a perpetuation of the understanding of Aristotle, who was still thought of as "the philosopher" in the American Revolutionary Era. Aristotle had talked in his *Politics* (Book III, Chap. 7) about the ineluctable tendency for power to concentrate in the hands of the one, the few or the many, as reflected in the governmental forms of mon-archy, aristocracy, and democracy; their perversions were a devolution into tyranny, oligarchy or anarchy. Aristotle's understanding of the distinction between form and function, as well as between government and politics, also survives to the present. Rich-ard McKeon's edition of *the Basic Works of Aristotle* (New York: Random House, 1941) is a good starting point (see pp. 1185–86 for the section noted above).

Security, making a *Mockery* of *Justice*, and destroying all the envied *Rights* of *Britain*, and the *Truths* of *Heaven*; I say, at such a Time, to be *inattentive* or *inactive*, is *Infamy*, and he who can *tamely* see his Country upon the Brink of RUIN, without putting out his Arm, and lending a helping Hand to rescue her from DESTRUCTION, must be an abandoned Wretch, a Disgrace to the Name of *Englishman* and to his Country.

N.B.[14] No.2, will contain the *secret* Reasons urged in the Cabinet for dissolving the last Parliament, and *smuggling* another of the same Complexion. &c. &c.

To the People of ENGLAND and AMERICA.

Some Time in the middle of *March* will be published, Price IS. 6d. in Quarto, on a fine Paper and new Type,

The Prophecy of R u i n, a Poem.

Ense velut stricto, quoties Lucilius ardens
Infremuit, rubet Auditor cui frigida Mens est,
Criminibus, tacita sudant Praecordia Culpa.

JUVENAL.[15]

Sharp as a Sword Lucilius *drew his Pen,*
And struck with panic Terror guilty Men,
At his just Strokes the harden'd Wretch would start,
Feel the cold Sweat, and tremble *at the Heart.*[16]

14. Nota Bene: Latin, to "note well."

15. Juvenal (Decimus Junius Juvenelis) was a Roman poet whose life spanned the late first century and early second century CE. He wrote the *Satires*, from which this passage is taken (see infra I.16), which were often cited by British writers in the eighteenth century.

16. The translation for the passage from the thirteenth chapter of Juvenal's *Satires* that appears above was taken from Peter Bayle's *The Dictionary Historical and Critical*, 5 vols

Printed and published for the Authors, by T. W. SHAW, in Fleet-Street, opposite Anderton's Coffee House, and by his appointment the Corner of Little Turnstile, Holborn, where Letters to the Publisher will be thankfully received.

(London, 1734) 3:905, or perhaps another edition of that same work. Bayle in turn most likely went to Thomas Creech's translation produced for John Dryden's *The Satires of Decimus Junius Juvenalis* (1693).

THE

CRISIS

NUMBER II   *To be continued Weekly.*

SATURDAY, JANUARY 28, 1775   [*Price Two-pence Halfpenny.*

A Bloody Court,

A Bloody Ministry,

And

A Bloody Parliament.

T HE sudden and unexpected Dissolution of the last ruinous Parliament,[1] gave a just and general Alarm to the whole Nation; and
we may search in vain the voluminous Pages of *Grecian, Roman,*
or *English* History, to find such another plan of PREMEDITATED

---

1. The seventh and final session of the Thirteenth Parliament convened on 13 January
1774 and adjourned the following June 22nd, then was dissolved to allow for an early
election–essentially as a hoped-for vote of confidence in the king and his ministers. After elections held at the end of September, the first session of the Fourteenth Parliament
convened on 29 November 1774 and was still in session at that moment. Legislation
designed to both punish and reform the American colonies, to be known eventually as
the Coercive Acts, had been passed in the previous session and became the focal point
of public debate over imperial policy. Those four acts, plus the Quebec Act, which,

Villainy, for destroying at one grand stroke of ROYAL and Ministerial Policy, all the Rights of a FREE PEOPLE. Lord North, engendered in the Womb of Hell, raised by the fostering Hand of *infernal Spirits*, and possessing Principles that have eclipsed ALL the GLORIES of his SATANIC Parents, had the Effrontery to declare in the Face of the House of Commons and the World, but a few Days before the Recess of the late Parliament, that they should meet AGAIN early in *October*, for the Dispatch of Business. When he uttered this Falshood, it was suspected by many, and he well knew it had been determined, that they should be dissolved, altho' the precise Time was not fixed. On the 16th Day of *September* 1774, a Notice was published in the *Gazette* for the last Parliament to MEET on the 15th of *November*; eleven Days had not elapsed before a Proclamation appeared for its DISSOLUTION, and the calling a *new* Parliament. Who can guard against *Deception, Artifice, and Villainy*, when stamped with ROYAL AUTHORITY? The very Thought of an HONEST House of Commons struck *Terror* into the guilty Soul of Lord North, the diabolical Minion of ROYAL Favour, and Instrument of ROYAL Vengeance; nay, even the King (*virtuous* as he is) had his FEARS; and in order to secure their own *Creatures* and *Dependents,* or, in other Words, to have the *old* Parliament new revived, and *smuggle* a Majority of *venal abandoned* Miscreants (who would deny their GOD, or sell their SOULS for *Money*) into the present House of Commons, Lord North sent Letters to ALL his Friends that THEY might be PREPARED, and it was known in the most distant Parts of *England,* and even the Time of Election fixed in several Boroughs in *Cornwall*, some Days BEFORE the Parliament was DISSOLVED. This is a TRUTH which *Lord North* with all his consummate Impudence cannot DENY.[2]

---

unfortunately for peace in the empire, was linked in many minds to that new policy, can be found in Danby Pickering, ed., *The Statutes at Large*, 46 vols. (Cambridge: Joseph Bentham, 1762–1807): the Boston Port Act (24 George III c.19) at 30:336–41; the Administration of Justice Act (24 George III c. 39) at 30:367–71; the Massachusetts Government Act (24 George III c. 45) at 30:381–90; a new quartering act (24 George III c. 54) at 30:410; and the Quebec Act (24 George III c. 83) at 30:549–54.

2. Lord North read the outcome of the September 1774 election for seats in the Commons, where he solidified a relatively narrow majority, as a vindication of his approach

The ministerial *Hacks* were immediately set to work to fabricate Lies (and publish them in the News-paper) to delude and deceive the Electors; that little or no Opposition might be made to the Tools of Government. One Report said, the Dissolution of Parliament was owing to some *disagreeable* Advices received from *America,* and that our *virtuous* King, with his still *more virtuous* Ministers, intended to adopt some *conciliating* Measures with Respect to the Colonies, and that it would betray a *Weakness* in the King to let the SAME Parliament meet AGAIN, to *repeal* those Acts, which they had but a *few* Months before *passed.* Another Report, equally TRUE, asserted it was on Account of Intelligence received from the North, of a very ALARMING Nature; and a Third, that it was occasioned by a Difference between the *French* and *English* Ministry, which rendered such a Step necessary, as there was great Reason to believe we should *soon* be involved in a War, and that it would be exceedingly improper to have the Nation put in a Ferment, by a general Election, at so critical a Time as that, and when the Assistance of Parliament, would be particularly wanted. A fourth Report was, that Lord Chatham and his Friends would be *immediately* taken into FAVOUR, and that there was to be an ENTIRE CHANGE in the Ministry. By these low Artifices and ministerial Lies, the People of *England* were lulled into a State of Supineness, and even made to lend a helping Hand to complete their OWN RUIN.[3]

---

to colonial policy, boosting his confidence (at least temporarily) in what was widely perceived as a hardline policy–but which he would follow with what he considered a conciliatory gesture in February 1775, itself the source of much contention. For the September 1774 election see Bernard Donoughue, *British Politics and the American Revolution* (London: Macmillan, 1964), pp. 177–200; and more generally Peter D. G. Thomas, *Tea Party to Independence* (Oxford: Clarendon Press, 1991).

3. William Pitt, now in the House of Lords as the Earl of Chatham, still held popular appeal as a leader of the parliamentary opposition, the onetime "Great Commoner" the conscience if not the voice of opposition to foolish policies. There were colonists who looked to him as their protector, the preferred alternative to Lord North and George Grenville before him. That the hated Townshend revenue program became law during his ministry (1766–1768) was either explained away or forgiven by those resting their hopes, however unrealistically, on him. While he did argue against Parliament taxing

The subsequent Part of this Paper shall unravel the diabolical Scheme. Lord North saw a powerful Opposition forming in every Part of *England*; he was fearful of ASSOCATIONS; he dreaded a SOLEMN LEAGUE and COVENANT, which he was certain the People would have entered into for the Preservation of their RIGHTS and LIBERTIES before next *May*, the Time when the Parliament would have been DISSOLVED of course; he trembled for the Event; conscious of his own Villainy, and that his HEAD had been long forfeited to the Justice of his Country, he determined to take the Electors by SURPRIZE, to put them off their GUARD, and rob them of TIME, that no Opposition might be made to his Creatures, and the People be prevented from fixing upon Men of honest independent Principles, to whom they might with safety delegate the important, the sacred Trust of Representation.

Lord North communicated his Fears to the King, painted the daring rebellious Spirit of the AMERICANS, and told him, that the People HERE were as *disloyal* and *disaffected*, and that Hints had been thrown out in the public Prints, of Plans forming in different Parts of ENGLAND, for keeping out of the new Parliament most of HIS Friends, and unless prevented by some well concerted Scheme, there was but too much Reason to believe, from the Spirit of the People, that they would succeed; an Event, says this TRAITOR, much FEARED, and greatly DREADED by every Well-wisher to your Person and Government: Should it ever take Place, and there is a Country Party, or a Majority of mock Patriots in the House of Commons, who are Enemies to all Order and Government, you must be reduced to a most degrading Situation indeed; your

---

the colonists directly and he was willing to deal with the Continental Congress as a de facto government, he believed that, ultimately, Britain had to be sovereign and Parliament supreme. And while he objected to the use of force as applied by the King and North, he did not rule out the possibility of applying it under different circumstances. For Pitt in an imperial context the best place to begin is Marie Peters' "The Myth of William Pitt, Earl of Chatham, Great Imperialist, Part II: Chatham and Imperial Reorganization, 1763–78" *Journal of Imperial and Commonwealth History* 22 (1994):393–431. See too my "When Words Fail: William Pitt, Benjamin Franklin and the Imperial Crisis of 1766" *Parliamentary History* 28 (2009):341–74.

present FRIENDS will then be unable to give you any Assistance; and instead of the Power being in YOUR Hands, it will then be in the Hands of the PEOPLE and you will be under the disgraceful Necessity of giving your Assent to the REPEAL of every Act which has been passed for the Purpose of raising a REVENUE, and ENFORCING a due Obedience to YOUR Authority: In short, you will be a King WITHOUT POWER, and subject to the Controul of a few Demagogues for Liberty, the Dregs of Mankind, and a common Rabble, who will always support them, nay, it may even endanger the Security of your Throne; for what will not a hot-headed Parliament do, with whom the VOICE of the People can have any Weight? the Plan for reducing the *Americans,* and making them dependent on your WILL, must be crushed; they will triumph in the Victory obtained over the just Power of Parliament and your Preroga-tive; your faithful Servants will be *compelled* to leave you, and you will be without A REAL FRIEND to advise with. If your Majesty can get a majority of *your Friends* re-chosen in the new Parliament, you will be able to raise what Money you please with THEIR Assistance; you will then be able to keep your present Ministers, and preserve them from the Resentment (which has been incurred by serving of YOU) of an enraged Rabble, who are made to believe through the Licentiousness of the Press, that they labour under a Load of accumulated Grievances. You will then be able to trample under foot, FACTION, SEDITION, and REBELLION throughout your Dominions, and to carry every Thing before you, agreeable to your royal Pleasure; with the Power of Par-liament, and your Majesty's *Firmness* and *Perseverance* you may bring *England* and *America* into a proper State of Subjection to your WILL. To accomplish this it will be necessary to prorogue the Parliament to some future Day, then to meet, and immediately after call a Council and *dissolve* them; in the mean Time YOUR Friends may be made acquainted with this Determination, and be PREPARED for the Elec-tion before any Opposition can possibly be made, or the People know any Thing of the Matter.

The King, firmly resolved on the People's RUIN, caressed his villainous Minion, admired the Plan formed for our Destruction, and, drunk with Prerogative, sucked in the baneful Advice and pursued it.

Thus the present Parliament was smuggled, and thus in a most shameful, unprecedented, artful and sudden Manner, was the last House of
Commons dissolved by the King, to answer his own and his Ministers
wicked, tyrannical, and bloody Designs against the People and Constitution of this Kingdom. Such an Instance, of an infamous Exertion of the royal Prerogative, and under the like Circumstances, is
not to be found in the History of *England*; such an INJURY and
INSULT was never before offered to a FREE PEOPLE, and never
ought to be FORGIVEN: It was a Piece of *Hanoverian* TREACH-
ERY, BASENESS, and INGRATITUDE, which has far exceeded all
the artful Villainy and low Cunning of the discarded *Stuarts*. His
Majesty (Heaven protest so much Goodness), out of a *Tenderness* to
the Constitution, could not make so BAD a USE of his Prerogative
(five Years back) as to DISSOLVE the same Parliament, when their
iniquitous Proceedings, and their Violations of Justice, had roused the
Indignation of the People, and he was requested to do it by upwards
of EIGHTY THOUSAND Freeholders (*signed*) and the general Voice
of the whole Nation: But in 1774 he got the better of that *Tenderness,*
and, to answer his own Purposes, could exert the Royal Prerogative,
(which he had absolutely *refused* to his Subjects, in the haughty Terms
of a Despot) with no other View, but to OVERTURN the Constitution of the *British* Empire in *England* and *America*, and DESTROY
or enslave the People.[4]

4. The author(s) condemned the calling of an election in September, well over six
months before one was required under the Septennial Act—the King and North, with
their "minions," seeking to coalesce control and pass their hated policies, or so the
author(s) charged. The implicit contrast is to the previous parliament (1768–1774),
where foolish policies may have been implemented but then had been rescinded once
it became clear that those policies hurt Britons as well as Americans. The author(s)
preferred to remember the North who came to power in 1770 and provided for partial
repeal of the Townshend Revenue Act; but that was also the North who continued the
duty on tea, for both political and financial reasons, and it was that North—not some
sort of completely new, utterly corrupted version—who came to predominate in 1774.
Ironically, North's flexibility early on only added fuel to the protest fires once they were
lit against him; thus the charges that he had been corrupted by ministerial authority
and his growing sense of power.

His Majesty, his Minions, and Instruments of Slaughter, are now *safe*, in robbing the People of their Property, by shameful and iniquitous Taxes in Time of Peace; *safe* in their Subversion of the Protestant Religion; *safe* and successful in their cruel Plan for *starving* the honest and industrious Inhabitants, and destroying the Trade of the Town of *Boston* in *America*, and the Commerce of *England*; *safe* so far, in their Attempt to destroy the *Lives, Rights, Liberties*, and *Privileges,* of Millions; I say they are *safe*, in all these Violations of, and Depredations on, our national Security, and natural Rights, because we are TAME.

> These MIGHTY CRIMES will sure ere long PROVOKE,
> The Arm of *Britain* to some noble Stroke.
> No wonder if such Deeds, should SOON compel
> *America* and *England* to REBEL:
> Then *George* may boast, that he, by ART and HIRE,
> Great *Nero*[5] like, has set the World on Fire;
> Might boast that *Thousands* by his Power fell,
> And that he could e'en *Nero* far *excell*:
> *Bute*[6] shall rejoice, and instantly restore,

---

5. Nero (more pompously Nero Claudius Caesar Augustus Germanicus, once he became emperor) ruled in Rome from 54–68 CE, succeeding his great-uncle Claudius. He was the last of the Julio-Claudian line; to many, then and since, only Caligula was worse. Nero was most infamous for the burning of Rome, which he was believed to have been behind, and the persecution of Christians. Most of what readers of *The Crisis* knew of him came from Tacitus's *Annals* (and that most likely in the *Works* translated by Thomas Gordon) or Suetonius's far more salacious *Lives of the Twelve Caesars* which, like Tacitus's writings, could be found in either Latin or English editions.

6. The best starting point for John Stuart, third Earl of Bute, is Karl Schweizer's sketch in the *Oxford DNB*, 53:173–179. Schweizer also edited *Lord Bute* (Leicester: Leicester University Press, 1988), a collection of essays by ten different authors (Schweizer included) exploring various aspects of Bute's career. Though Bute headed only one ministry under George III, and that but briefly (1762–1763), he worked for many more years behind the scenes, so much so that his supposed secret influence continues as a theme for British politics in that era. There is, after all, a certain timeless irresistibility to conspiracy theory explanations—including among Bute's contemporaneous political adversaries. For Bute and the American crisis see Peter Shaw's attempt at psycho-historical analysis in *American Patriots and the Rituals of Revolution* (Cambridge: Harvard University Press, 1981).

The *Stuart* Race, in all their cursed Power;
Shall seize upon the Throne he should defend,
And *Traitor* prove when *George* most wants a Friend.
This may not be; but should he still oppress
His injured Subjects, sure they'll seek redress,
When by Oppression, driven to despair,
If he don't LOVE them, they may *make* him FEAR;
And tho' by shameful Taxes, he has seiz'd
Their Treasure, and their Vitals squeez'd,
Yet he should know, that SWORDS and ARMS remain,
When call'd by WRONGS, are seldom us'd in VAIN;
And Freedom's Sons, with Liberty inspir'd,
With mighty Rage and Indignation fir'd
'Gainst *England's* mortal Foes, no longer'll yield,
To LAWLESS Power, arm'd with Virtue's Shield;
Their Case most Just, nay, HEAVEN's sacred Cause,
The Cause of TRUTH and VIOLATED LAWS,
Will draw th' avenging Sword, (O glorious Deed!)
Their LAWS to SAVE, and make those Traitors bleed;
Aided by Heav'n, all Danger will defy,
And nobly Conquer, or like Britons die,
Then, blessing FREEDOM with their parting Breath
Will BRAVELY fall into the Arms of Death:
A glorious Death much better in the Grave,
A FREEMAN buried, than a living SLAVE.
'Twas first decreed, by that great Pow'r above,
All should be FREE, and Heaven gave in Love
That Blessing to Mankind, a sacred TRUST,
He who'd resign it, is to *God* UNJUST.

N.B. As we shall always have a particular Pleasure, in giving Satisfaction to our Readers, and complying with their Requests; we do in this Number, agreeable to the Desire of an anonymous Writer of the 21st, give a Translation of the Motto at the Head of the first Number, although was explained in the third Page of that Paper.

Liberty with Danger is preferable to Servitude with Security.

The Motto to the Prophecy of Ruin is likewise translated in the under-written Advertisement.

No. III. will be addressed to the KING.

To the People of England and America.

On the 1st Day of *March* will be published, (Price 1s. 6d.) in Quarto, on a fine Paper and new Type,

The Prophecy of R u i n, a Poem.

Ense velut Stricto, quoties Lucilius ardens
Infremuit, rubet Auditor cui frigida Mens est,
Criminibus, tacita sudant Praecordia Culpa.

JUVENAL.

Sharp as a Sword Lucilius *drew his Pen,*
And struck with panic Terror guilty Men,
At his just Strokes the harden'd Wretch would start,
Feel the cold Sweat, and tremble *at the Heart.*

Printed and published for the Authors, by T. W. Shaw, Fleet Street, opposite Anderton's Coffee House, and by his appointment the Corner of Little Turnstile, Holborn, where Letters to the Publisher will be thankfully received.

THE

CRISIS

NUMBER III   *To be continued Weekly.*

SATURDAY, FEBRUARY 4, 1775   [*Price Two-pence HalfPenny.*

Thy Name, O! Chatham, (with some few more) is made, rare Instance, IMMORTAL by Defeat; and to thee—NEW HONOURS rise—from the RUINS of thy COUNTRY. While you live, never-fading Laurels, the just Reward of thy Virtue, Conduct, and Fidelity, shall crown thy hoary Head, and shade thy venerable Brow—And may thine and BRITAIN'S *ravished Eyes, behold thy FOES and Hers, for their TREACHERY and VILLAINY, dragged to EXECUTION, dressed and dishonoured in funeral ROSE-MARY and the baleful YEW.*

To the K I N G,

SIR,

TO follow you regularly through every Step of a fourteen Years SHAMEFUL and INGLORIOUS Reign, would be a Task as Painful, as Disagreeable, and far exceed the Bounds of this Paper: But we are called upon by the Necessity of the Times, the Measures you are pursuing, by every Principle of Justice and Self-preservation, and by the Duty we owe to GOD and our COUNTRY, to declare our Sentiments (with a Freedom becoming of Englishmen), on some of those dreadful Transactions and Oppressions which this Kingdom has laboured under, since the Glory and Lustre of the Crown of *England*, was doomed to fade upon your Brow; and, to point out to you, Sir, your own critical and DANGEROUS Situation.

Sir, it is not your rotten Troop in the present House of Commons; it is not your venal, beggarly, pensioned Lords; it is not your polluted, canting, prostituted Bench of Bishops; it is not your whole set of abandoned Ministers; nor all your Army of *Scotch* Cut-throats, that can protect you from the Peoples Rage, when drove by your Oppressions, and till now unheard of Cruelties, to a State of Desperation.

The Day, we Fear, is not far Distant, when you will have Reason, too much Reason, to wish you had acted like a Father, and not like a Tyrant, when you will be Bound to curse those TRAITORS, those exalted Villains, whom now in the Face of Day, without a Blush, you can be Base enough to call your Friends: be assured, Sir, your Danger is great amidst all this *fancied* Security; and it will be impossible for them to preserve YOU from the just Resentment of an enraged, long abused, and much injured Nation: Should that Day ever come, but Heaven avert the Stroke, where can you hide yourself from the tenfold Vengeance, of a brave and mighty People, with Law, Justice, Heaven, and all its sacred Truths on their Side.

Then like Wounds that bleed afresh, will be brought to their Minds, your barbarous, and unprovoked MASSACRE, in *St. George's Fields*, when Men and Women were indiscriminately and inhumanly Slaughtered, to gratify, what would have disgraced even your Footman; a PITIFUL REVENGE.[1] Then Sir, they will remember with Horror and Indignation, the Letter of THANKS, sent from the Secretary at

---

1. The St. George's Fields "massacre" occurred on 10 May 1768, when a crowd gathered to protest the incarceration of John Wilkes in King's Bench Prison. Waiting until the Riot Act had been read, regular soldiers then fired upon the crowd. William Allen, one of the half-dozen slain, came to symbolize the slaughter of innocents by marauding troops, though the soldier tried for murder was subsequently acquitted (see infra XXIII.7). The classic account remains George Rudé, *Wilkes & Liberty* (Oxford: Clarendon Press, 1962), pp. 37–56. The initial reports in the London press were relatively terse; it would take time for events to work their way into popular memory. The attempt to read

War by YOUR ORDER, to the Officer on Duty the 10th of *May*, 1768, (the Day of Carnage); and likewise your PENSIONING, and screening the Murderers from the Punishment of the Law. Then Sir, they will remember the horrid Plan laid at *Brentford*, for destroying the Right of Election; or in the most savage Manner, to take away the Lives of the Freeholders of *Middlesex*; which was (to make use of a word from your merciful royal Dictionary) EFFECTUALLY carried into Execution, and several People killed; to this Plan Sir, formed by *Procter* and your Minions, YOU must have been PRIVY, as the event afterwards sufficiently proved; Then Sir, they will remember, the mean, low, and criminal Subterfuge, you had Recourse to, to DISPENSE with the Laws, (and set aside the just Verdict of an HONEST JURY) to pardon those HIRED RUFFIANS, *Balf* and *Mack Quirk*,[2] convicted upon the clearest Evidence of PREMEDITATED MURDER. Then, Sir, they will remember the insults they received, and the ignoble Answers you gave, to the Remonstrances and Petitions, delivered by them to the Throne, praying a Dissolution of Parliament; Nor will they forget, Sir, the infernal Plan for smuggling the present House of Commons, and destroying all the Rights of this free Country. In a Word, Sir, these and every other despotic and bloody Transaction of your Reign, will rise fresh in their Minds; if they should be drove by your Encouragement of Popery, your Persecutions, your Oppressions,

---

symbolic importance into the conflict between soldiers and civilians even carried across the Atlantic to Boston, once troops there were involved in confrontations leading up to the "massacre" on 5 May 1770. See Hiller B. Zobel, *The Boston Massacre* (New York: W. W. Norton, 1970).

2. Lawrence Balf and Edward MacQuirk had been convicted of murder in January 1769 and then were pardoned by George III the following March. Their case had arisen out of a by-election riot at Brentford the previous December. John Glynn, prominent barrister, serjeant-at-law, and leading supporter of John Wilkes, had won a seat in the Commons in that election (see infra XII.5). One of his supporters had reputedly been beaten to death. Balf and MacQuirk were convicted on slight evidence, but their pardon raised a howl of indignation among Wilkes' supporters; the Duke of Grafton, head of the ministry, would be impugned by "Junius" in an essay for the *Public Advertiser* of 18 March 1769. For "Junius" see infra VII.9.

your Violations of Justice, your Treachery, and your Weakness, into a fatal and unnatural CIVIL WAR in *America*; I say they will rise fresh in their Minds, and stimulate them to Deeds of Glory; nay, they may pursue with implacable Revenge the Author of all their Miseries.

The People, Sir, with a Candour and Indulgence peculiar to English-men, passed over the Injuries and Insults in the first Part of your Reign, or, kindly laid the blame at the Door of your Ministers; but it is now evident to the whole World, that there was a Plan formed by Lord *Bute* and yourself, either before, or, immediately after you came to the Crown, for subverting the British Constitution in Church and State; which to our Grief, with indefatigable pains and too much Success, Lord *Bute's* Tools, and your infernal Minions, have carried into Execution; therefore, it no longer remains to determine who is now the greatest CRIMINAL in *England.*

Consider, Sir, if through the late and present iniquitous Measures, and an obstinate Resolution in your Majesty to pursue them, the SWORD is forced to be drawn in *America,* it cannot remain long unsheathed in *England*: we hope there is some Virtue HERE; and we entertain a better Opinion of our Countrymen, then to believe they are so far *degenerated*, as to TAMELY see a mercinary Army of Soldiers (who are at all Times a Terror to the peaceable Inhabitants of every free State) BUTCHER their BRETHREN and FELLOW SUBJECTS in *America,* because they are determined to defend their own Rights and the British Constitution; I say they never will TAMELY see that, without putting out a helping Hand, and sharing with them the GLORY of a decisive Victory over TYRANNY, and all the AGENTS of the infernal Monarch of the dark Regions of HELL, who would enslave the WORLD.

Should you, Sir, still pursue the same tyrannical Measures only to gratify a mean vindictive Spirit, and be the Author of such dreadful Mischiefs; O! we shudder at the Thought: the People will then perhaps, treat you, Sir, with as little Ceremony, as little Respect, and as little Mercy, as you and your Minions have treated them; for Sir, whenever the State is convulsed by civil Commotions, and the Constitution totters to its Centre, the Throne of *England* must shake with it; a Crown will then be no SECURITY, and at one Stroke all the gaudy Trappings of Royalty may be laid in the Dust; in such a Time of dreadful Confusion and Slaughter; when the Son's Weapon drinks the Father's Blood, and we see a Ruffian's Blade reeking from a Brother's Heart: When Rage is burning in the Breasts of Englishmen, provoked by Wrongs not to be borne by Men; all Distinctions must cease, the common Safety and the Rights of Mankind, will be the only Objects in View; while the King and the Peasant, must share one and the same Fate, and perhaps fall undistinguished together.

Let these Things, Sir, be well weighed; tremble for the Event; drive those Traitors from your Breast who now surround you; let the Just and Honest have your Confidence, and once more make your People HAPPY, GREAT, and FREE; be not the Instrument of their Destruction; consider the solemn and sacred Oath you made at your Coronation, to PROTECT your Subjects in ALL their Rights and Liberties, and the PROTESTANT Religion, as by Law established: Consider, Sir, what a Perversion of all Right and Justice that must be (besides the heinous Crime of PERJURY), when instead of being their PROTECTOR, you become their DESTROYER.

Your Plan, Sir, for bringing the Colonies by FORCE of ARMS into a State of Subjection to your WILL, is Cruel, Bloody, and (I hope) Impracticable; it is repugnant to every Principle of Humanity, Justice, sound Policy, and the natural Rights of Mankind; it is the foulest Disgrace to you, and will reflect eternal Infamy on your Reign and Memory, as the Sovereign and Father of a FREE PEOPLE; it is such a Plan of encroaching Violence and lawless Power, as the *Americans,* never can, never ought, nor never will Submit to; it is such a Scheme for enslaving, or destroying the human Race, as EVERY Man ought to execrate and condemn, and to oppose even till he Perish.

Men, Sir, at three thousand Miles Distance, must think it extremely hard to work, toil, and run Hazards; only to support the infamous Luxury of high pampered Lords, a rotten Court, and your Tribe of venal Senators, Minions, Pimps, and Parasites the Pests of Society; and to be taxed and mulct by them at their Pleasure: All Nature, Sir, revolts even at the Idea of such a State of human Misery.

Force, Sir, can never be used effectually to answer the End, without destroying the Colonies themselves. Liberty and Encouragement are necessary to keep them together; and Violence will hinder both. Any Body of Troops considerable enough to awe them, keep them in Subjection, and under the Direction of a needy *Scotch* Governor, sent only to be an Instrument of Slaughter, and to make his Fortune; would soon put an End to planting, and leave the Country to you, Sir, and your merciless Plunderers only; and if it did not, they would starve the Inhabitants and eat up all the Profit of the Colonies.[3] On the Contrary, a few prudent Laws, Sir, (but you seem to be a Stranger to Prudence, as well as to Justice and Humanity); and a little prudent Conduct, (that too, has been long despaired of by the Kingdom) would soon give us far the greatest Share of the Riches of ALL *America*; perhaps drive other Nations out of it, or, into our Colonies for Shelter.

If violent Methods be not used (at this Time) to prevent it, your Northern Colonies, Sir, must constantly increase in People, Wealth, and Power; their Inhabitants are considerably more than doubled since the Revolution; and in less than a Century, must become powerful States; and the more Powerful, the more People will flock thither: And, there are so many Exigencies in all States, so many foreign Wars, and domestic Disturbances, that these Colonies can seldom want Opportunities, if they watch for them, to do, what you, Sir, might be extremely Sorry for; throw off their Dependance on the Mother-Country: Therefore, Sir, it

3. The "needy Scotch governor" referred to derisively here was presumably John Murray, the fourth earl of Dunmore. Formerly governor of New York, Dunmore had presided as governor of Virginia since 1771. He became embroiled in competition with the House of Burgesses over imperial policy in the aftermath of the Coercive Acts and fought for control of the colony against patriot forces from the spring of 1775 until finally abandoning his post the following summer in the political and military aftermath of the Declaration of Independence. He was particularly reviled in Revolutionary American circles for forming his so-called Ethiopian Regiment in the Fall of 1775, which was composed of slaves who escaped from their masters with the promise of freedom if they fought for the king. John E. Selby wrote the sketch of Dunmore for the *Oxford DNB*, 39:955–56, which drew from his brief biography, *Dunmore* (Williamsburg, Va.: Virginia Independence Bicentennial Commission, 1977).

should be your first and greatest Care, that it shall never be their Interest to act AGAINST an Evil that can no otherwise be averted, than by keeping them fully employed in such Trades as will increase their own, as well as our Wealth; for, Sir, there is too much Reason to fear, if you don't find Employment for them, they may find some for YOU: Withdraw then, Sir, from *America*, your armed Ruffians, and make a full RESTORATION of the People's Rights; let them Tax themselves, and enjoy their Property unviolated by the Hand of Tyranny; thus, Sir, The subsequent part of your Reign, may yet be Happy and Glorious. May the Compact between you and the People be no more VIOLATED; may you be SPEEDILY reconciled to the just Demands of the Colonies: May Lord Bute, Lord Mansfield, Lord North, and all your Majesty's infamous Minions, who would precipitate you and the Kingdom into Ruin, answer with their HEADS (and soon) for their horrid CRIMES; and may the SUCCESSION IN YOUR MAJESTY's ROYAL HOUSE, AND THE RELIGION, LAWS, RIGHTS, AND LIBERTIES OF THE SUBJECT, go Hand in Hand down to all Posterity, until this Globe shall be reduced to its original Chaos, and Time be swallowed up in Eternity.

The Author of the PROPHECY of RUIN is extremely sorry, he is again under the necessity of putting off the Publication of his POEM to a future Day; but the Public may rest assured, it will be Published some time in the Middle of *March*.

To the People of ENGLAND and AMERICA.

Some Time in the middle of *March* will be published, Price 1s 6d. in Quarto, on a fine Paper and new Type,

The Prophecy of R u i n, a Poem.

Ense velut Stricto, quoties Lucilius ardens
Infremuit, rubet Auditor cui frigida Mens est,
Criminibus, tacita sudant Praecordia Culpa.

JUVENAL.

Sharp as a Sword Lucilius *drew his Pen,*
And struck with panic Terror guilty Men,
At his just Strokes the harden'd Wretch would start,
Feel the cold Sweat, and tremble *at the Heart.*

Printed and published for the Authors, by T. W. SHAW, Fleet Street, opposite Anderton's Coffee House, and by his appointment the Corner of
Little Turnstile, High Holborn, where Letters to the Publisher will be
thankfully received.

THE

CRISIS

NUMBER IV   *To be continued Weekly.*

SATURDAY, FEBRUARY 11, 1775   [*Price Two-pence Half penny.*

Ye CONSPIRATORS against the LIBERTIES of Mankind at St. JAMES's, in St. STEPHEN's CHAPEL, the HOUSE of LORDS, or amongst the BENCH of SATANICAL BISHOPS; you must surely think there is no GOD to JUDGE, nor HELL to RECEIVE you; or, you could never be so far ABANDONED as to stain your HANDS, and consent to DYE the PLAINS of AMERICA with the INNOCENT BLOOD of her INHABITANTS.

Nero had such Instruments of Slaughter.

THE steady and uniform Perseverance in a regular Plan of DESPOTISM, since the Commencement of this Reign, makes it evident to the meanest Capacity, that a Design was formed, (and it has with too much Success been carried into Execution) for subverting the Religion, Laws, and Constitution of this Kingdom, and establish upon the Ruins of PUBLIC LIBERTY, an arbitrary System of Government: in a Word, the Destruction of this Kingdom will soon be effected by a Prince of the House of *Brunswick.*

The BLOODY RESOLUTION has passed the House of Commons and the House of Lords to address our present HUMANE, GENTLE Sovereign, to give Directions for ENFORCING the cruel and unjust Edicts of the last Parliament against the *Americans*.[1] His Majesty possessing Principles which nothing can equal but the GOODNESS of his Heart, will no doubt, give immediate Orders for carrying EFFECTUALLY into Execution the MASSACRE in *America*; especially as he is to be SUPPORTED in polluting the Earth with BLOOD, with the LIVES and FORTUNES of his *faithful* Butchers, the Lords and Commons; would to God they ONLY were to fall a Sacrifice in this UNNATURAL CIVIL WAR.

The Day of Trial is at Hand; it is Time to prove the Virtue and rouse the Spirit of the People of *England*; the Prospect is too dreadful, it is too melancholy to admit of farther Delay.

The Lord Mayor of London ought immediately to call a Common Hall for the Purpose of taking the Sense of his Fellow Citizens, at this ALARMING CRISIS, upon presenting a Remonstrance to the Throne; couched in Terms, that might do Honour to the City, as the First and most Powerful in the World, and to them as Men determined to be FREE; in Terms that might strike CONVICTION into his Majesty's Breast; and TERROR into the Souls of his Minions: this is not a Time for *Compliments*, nor should Tyrants, or, the Instruments of Tyranny, ever be complimented.

The Merchants of London, it is to be hoped, and the whole commercial Interest of England, will exert themselves upon this great Occasion; by sending to the Throne spirited and pointed Remonstrances, worthy of Englishmen; by noble and generous SUBSCRIPTIONS, and in every

---

1. George III opened the new parliamentary session begun on 29 November 1774 with a speech from the throne that condemned the "daring spirit of resistance and disobedience to the law" in Massachusetts. The Lords endorsed the message by a vote of 46–9 (with those opposed issuing a "dissentient") and the Commons, 264–73 (technically a vote against amending the response to be less supportive). See William Cobbett, et al., eds., *The Parliamentary History of England*, 36 vols. (London: T. C. Hansard, 1806–1820), 18:33–47.

other Manner, give all the RELIEF, and all the Assistance in their Power, to their oppressed and injured Fellow Subjects in America.[2]

Let them heartily join the Americans, and see whether TYRANNY and LAWLESS POWER, or, REASON, JUSTICE, HEAVEN, TRUTH, and LIBERTY, will prevail.

Let them, together with the Gentlemen of landed Property, who must greatly Suffer by this unnatural CIVIL WAR, make a glorious stand against the Enemies of PUBLIC FREEDOM, and the constitutional Rights of the Colonies; for, with the ruin of America, must be involved that of England.

Let them in plain Terms, declare their own Strength, and the POWER of the People, a Power, that has hitherto withstood the united Efforts of Fraud and Tyranny; a Power, to which all Kings have ever owed their Crowns; a Power, which raises them to a Throne; and when unworthy of their DELEGATED TRUST, can pull them down.

Let them declare to the World, they will never be so base and cowardly, as QUIETLY to see any *Part* of their Fellow Subjects, BUTCHERED,

---

2. The Corporation of the City of London had actually thanked Chatham just the day before for his attempt to resolve the imperial dispute (see infra VI.1). In January, London and Bristol merchants had submitted a petition to the House of Commons, as did merchants elsewhere, most notably in Glasgow, Birmingham and Norwich, to be followed by a second petition from London merchants. All sought to support the Americans by calling for repeal of legislation going back to the Tea Act of 1773. See Cobbett, et al., eds., *Parliamentary History*, 18:168–98; and R. C. Simmons and P. D. G. Thomas, eds., *Proceedings and Debates of the British Parliament Respecting North America, 1754–1783*, 6 vols. (White Plains, N.Y.: Kraus International Publications, 1982), 5:287–323. Failing to move the Commons, London merchants (and others) shifted their attention to the king but did no better there. Even so, the petitions are an indication that a significant portion of the British public sympathized with dissident Americans and that the men behind *The Crisis* did indeed have an audience for their arguments. James E. Bradley reviews the attempts to influence policy through petitions in "The British Public and the American Revolution: Ideology, Interest and Opinion," in H. T. Dickinson, ed., *Britain and the American Revolution* (London: Longman, 1998), pp. 124–54, which builds on his earlier book, *Popular Politics and the American Revolution in England* (Macon, Ga.: Mercer University Press, 1986).

or ENSLAVED, either in England or America, to answer the Purpose of EXALTED Villainy; and by that Means, become the *detested* Instruments of their OWN DESTRUCTION.

Let them declare to the World, they are not yet ripe for SLAVERY, that their Forefathers made a noble Resistance, and obtained a decisive Victory over TYRANNY and LAWLESS POWER, when the *Stuarts* reigned; that they are determined to do THEMSELVES JUSTICE, and not to suffer any farther Attacks upon their FREEDOM, from the present Sovereign, who is exceedingly desirous, as well as ambitious, to destroy the Liberties of Mankind; but that they do INSIST upon a RESTORATION of their OWN violated Rights, and the Rights of British America.

Let them enter into an ASSOCIATION for the Preservation of their Lives, Rights, Liberties, and Privileges; and resolve at once to bring the whole Legion of *public Traitors*, who have wickedly entered into a Conspiracy to destroy the dear-bought Rights of this FREE NATION to condign Punishment, for their past and present diabolical Proceedings, which have already stained the Land with Blood, and threaten Destruction to the human Race.

A few spirited Resolutions from the City of *London*, and the whole Body of Merchants of *England*, would strike Terror into the Souls of those Miscreants, the Authors of these dreadful public Mischiefs.

The grand Principle of Self-preservation, which is the first and fundamental Law of Nature, calls aloud for such Exertions of public Spirit; the Security of the Nation depends upon it; Justice and the Preservation of our own, and the Lives of our fellow-Subjects in *America* demand it; the very being of the Constitution makes it necessary, and whatever is necessary to the public Safety, must be just.

The present Conspirators against the Peace and Happiness of Mankind, ought to know, that no Subterfuges, no knavish Subtilties, no Evasions, no Combinations, nor pretended Commissions, shall be able to screen or protect them from public Justice. They ought to know that the PEOPLE, can follow them thro' all their Labyrinths, and doubling Meanders; a Power, confined by no Limitations but of public Justice, and the public Good; a Power that does not always FOLLOW Precedents, but MAKES them; a Power which has this for its Principle, that extraordinary and unprecedented Villainies; ought to have extraordinary and unprecedented Punishments.

TO THE

Officers, Soldiers, and Seamen,

Who may be employed to butcher their Relations, Friends, and Fellow-Subjects in America.

You can neither be ignorant of, nor unacquainted with the arbitrary Steps, that the present King, supported by an abandoned Ministry, and a venal Set of prostituted Lords and Commons, is now persuing to overturn the sacred Constitution of the British Empire, which he had SWORN TO PRESERVE.

You are not, or will not long be ignorant that the King, the Lords and Commons, have, (to satiate their Revenge against a few Individuals) declared the whole People of America to be in a State of *Rebellion*, only because they have openly avowed their Resolution to support their Charters, Rights and Liberties, against the secret Machinations of designing Men who would destroy them: and you are fixed upon as the Instruments of their Destruction. However, I entertain too good an Opinion of you, to believe there is one TRUE ENGLISHMAN, who will undertake the BLOODY Work. Men without Fortunes, Principles or Connections, may indeed, handle their Arms in a desperate Cause, to oblige a Tyrant, or Monster in human Shape: But Men of Family and Fortune, or, of honest Principles, I hope could never be prevailed upon to sheath their Swords in the Bowels of their Countrymen. Englishmen, surely cannot be found to execute so diabolical a Deed, to imbrue their Hands in innocent Blood, and fight against their Friends and Country; Actions which must brand them with perpetual Marks of Reproach and Infamy.

O! my Countrymen, let neither private Interest, nor Friendship; neither Relations, nor Connections; prevail with, or induce you to obey (as you must answer at the last Day, before the aweful Judge of the World, for the Blood that will be wantonly and cruelly Spilt) the murderous Orders of an inhuman Tyrant; who, to gratify his lust of Power, would lay waste the World. No, rather enter into a solemn League, and join with the rest of your Countrymen, to oppose the present Measures of Government planned for our RUIN.

When your Country calls, then stand forth and defend the Cause of Liberty, despise the Degeneracy of the Age, the Venality of the Times, and hand Freedom down to Posterity; that your Children may smiling bless, not curse your war-like Resolution. To die gloriously fighting for the Laws and Liberties of your Country, is honourable, and would deserve a Crown of Martyrdom; to die fighting against it, is Infamy; and you would for ever deserve the heaviest Curses and Execration.

I hope neither you nor the Irish have forgot the shameful Insults you have received from the King, ever since the Conclusion, of the last war; you have been despised, neglected, and treated with Contempt; while a Parcel of beggarly Scotchmen only, have been put into every Place of Profit and Trust, in the East and West Indies, in England and America, and the Preference has, of Honours and Promotions, been constantly given to those People, nay even to Rebels; and some who have served in the French Service.

Be assured, if you can be prevailed upon to butcher, or enslave your fellow-Subjects, and to set up an arbitrary Power on the Ruins of public Liberty, that your Subsistance would soon be reduced to the miserable Pittance of foreign Troops; and you with the surviving Subjects of England and America, be reduced to the miserable Condition of being ruled by an Army of Scotch Janizaries, assisted by *Roman Catholics.*

Let every English and Irish Officer, Soldier, and Seaman, seriously Weigh these things; and then if they are Valiant, Courageous, Magnanimous and Free, like their Forefathers; if they are True to their King and their

Country; if they Value their Religion, Laws, Lives, Liberties, Families, and Posterity; no Consideration can prevail with them to engage against the Americans, in an Inhuman Bloody CIVIL WAR.

Let every Man then who is really and truly a Protestant, who wishes well to his Country, and the Rights of Mankind; lay aside his Prejudices, and consider the Cause of *America*, and her Success in this Struggle for Freedom, as a Thing of the last Consequence to England, upon which OUR Salvation depends, for the present plan of Royal Despotism is a Plan of *GENERAL RUIN*. I say let us all *SPEEDILY* unite and endeavour to defend them from their OPEN, and ourselves from our own secret and domestic Enemies, and if any are luke-warm in this great public Cause, at this Time of emminent Danger; let them be made an Example of *TREACHERY* and *COWARDICE*: that the present Generation may detest and abhor them, and Posterity declaim against and curse them, as unnatural Monsters, who would destroy the Human Race.

To the People of ENGLAND and AMERICA.

Sometime in the middle of *March* will be published, Price 1s 6d. in Quarto, on a fine Paper and new Type,

The Prophecy of R U I N, a Poem.

Ense velut Stricto, quoties Lucilius ardens
Infremuit, rubet Auditor cui frigida Mens est,
Criminibus, tacita sudant Praecordia Culpa.

JUVENAL.

Sharp as a Sword Lucilius *drew his Pen,*
And struck with panic Terror guilty Men,
At his just Strokes the harden'd Wretch would start,
Feel the cold Sweat, and tremble *at the Heart.*

Printed and published for the Authors, by T. W. SHAW, Fleet Street, opposite Anderton's Coffee House, and by his Appointment the Corner of Little Turnstile, High Holborn, where Letters to the Publisher will be thankfully received.

THE
CRISIS

NUMBER V *To be continued Weekly.*

SATURDAY, FEBRUARY 18, 1775 *[Price Two-pence Half-penny.*

Resistance to Tyrants and the Instruments of Tyranny is Justifiable, and Warranted, by all the Laws of GOD and MAN.

To the P E O P L E.

AT a juncture like the Present, when the National reputation of BRITAIN, as well as her absolute Safety, stands tottering on the brink of Destruction; when LIBERTY and FREEDOM, the great Pillars of the Constitution, are, by Force and Fraud, undermined, and tumbling into Ruins; when the BLOODY Sword of Tyranny is drawn against *America*, and soon to be plunged into the Bowels of her innocent Inhabitants; when the present Sovereign, aided by a despisable Junto, the REBEL, out-cast, and refuse of Scotland, and a Parliament not returned by the free Suffrages of the People, are rioting with IMPU-NITY in the Spoils of an insulted powerful Kingdom; when they, by cruel Oppression, have spread Terror and CIVIL WAR, in every Part of the British Empire; when they have destroyed or suspended her

Trade, and sapped the Credit of Public Security; when the most iniquitous and unjust Laws are Daily passed to curb the Spirit, and bind in Chains, the Hands of a BRAVE and FREE PEOPLE; when St. *James*'s is made the Slaughter House of *America*; when the Sovereign is become a national Executioner, and for a Scepter, carries a BLOODY KNIFE; when by a most Scandalous and Shameful profusion of the Public Money, we are hourly Robbed and Plundered, to answer all the Purposes of King-Craft and Villainy; When new Taxes are Daily imposed upon the People in time of Peace, to the almost intire Ruin of the State; when the Minions of Despotism are increasing the Land Forces, for the open and avowed Purpose of wading knee deep in Blood, through the Liberties of Britain; when the Protestant Religion is openly Subverted, and the British Subjects in *Canada*, deprived of those great Securities of their personal Liberty and Property, the HABEAUS CORPUS ACT, and Trial by JURIES; when a suspending, and dispensing Power is assumed by the Crown; when Opposition, to the most cruel and wanton Acts of LAWLESS POWER, is deemed REBELLION; when the Senators, designed the Protectors of the People, are become their Destroyers; when the appointed Guardians of Public Freedom, are become Base Apostates, and Conspirators against the Liberties of Mankind; when neither OATHS, nor CONSCIENCE, can bind the Sovereign or his Ministers; when both PUBLIC and PRIVATE JUSTICE is denied to a Subject, nay, to the whole Body of the People at Large; when our Lives are exposed to false Accusations, and our Persons to arbitrary Imprisonment, and heavy Fines; when the Judges before whom we are to stand upon Life and Death, and before whom all Cases concerning Liberty and Property, must be brought; too much devoted to the Will and Pleasure of the Crown, and Enemies to the natural Rights of Mankind; when Juries who are to decide our Fate, packed, bribed, or modeled to the pernicious Designs of a wicked and detestable Ministry; when every Post, Civil, Naval, and Military; is filled by Northern Flatterers and their Adherents, by Men of no Principles; by Parisites, Pimps, Catamites, and the Advocates for Arbitrary Power; when the People can see nothing but Misery and Slavery before their Eyes; when this vast and mighty Empire, the Admiration and envy of the World, is, through Corruption and Villainy, falling into RUINS.[1]

At such a Juncture as this, and under these dreadful and alarming Circumstances of experienced, and impending Danger, it becomes the Duty of every Englishman, to stand Forth to defend his Life, his Liberty, and his Property from Lawless Violence, and to save his Country from Perdition.

So highly did our Brave and Virtuous Ancestors, value and Esteem their Rights, Liberties, and Privileges, that they spared neither BLOOD nor Treasure in their Defence, when invaded, as they too often were, by some of our Kings, who, in the pursuit of Lawless Power, pulled down all the Fences of Liberty, and broke in, like the present Sovereign, upon the Constitution, so far, that the Lives, Liberties, and Properties, of the Subjects of this Realm, were Hourly in Danger, and many fell Sacrifices to Royal or ministerial Vengeance.

Then it was, that our generous Forefathers, nobly ASSOCIATED THEMSELVES in DEFENCE of their Inherent, and legal Rights, and made an offering of the best and choicest BLOOD in the Kingdom, to the Shrine of LIBERTY, that we, their Posterity, might be FREE and HAPPY. To them and the glorious Struggles they made, with Power, we owe all the Blessings we enjoy, and the English Constitution, our greatest Boast, and their greatest Glory.[2]

---

1. This sort of catch-all list would be typical of attempts by *The Crisis* to build a transatlantic community of protest. Thus, the public was warned, what began in Canada under the auspices of the Quebec Act could be extended to other American colonies and eventually to Britain itself—a domino effect for the American Revolutionary Era. But defenders of imperial policy at Whitehall and Westminster could counter that the Quebec Act showed sensitivity to the needs of colonists in one part of the empire, not a diabolical plot to undermine rights everywhere. See George M. Wrong, *Canada and the American Revolution* (New York: The Macmillan Company, 1935); and Philip Lawson, *The Imperial Challenge* (Montreal and Kingston: McGill-Queen's University Press, 1989).

2. The men behind *The Crisis* were making a veiled allusion to Magna Carta here, and as J. C. Holt, *Magna Carta*, 2nd ed. (Cambridge: Cambridge University Press, 1992; orig.

It was in such Times as these, when our brave Progenitors behaved like Britons, with a true Patriot zeal, with which almost every Breast was fired, they spurned the Yoke, and broke the Chains that were prepared for them, letting their King and his Minions know, they would not Suffer him, nor them, to destroy their Birthrights, and dispense with the known Laws of the Land, by which they were resolved to be Governed, and not by his WILL, or any other LAWLESS POWER upon Earth.

Let us at this Time, in this Hour of eminent Danger, follow so bright and glorious an Example, by a well timed, noble Resistance, to the present Royal, and ministerial Plan, for SUBVERTING the Laws and Religion, and overturning the Constitution of the British Empire, in England and America; a Resistance that will secure Freedom to posterity, and immortal Honour to ourselves; the Field of GLORY is open before us; let us rouse from a State of Apathy, and Exert ourselves in a Manner becoming of Englishmen, worthy of Men who love LIBERTY, and deserve to be FREE. Let us shew to the World, we are not to be enslaved by One, nor by Five Thousand Tyrants: for the Sons of CRUELTY, CORRUPTION, and DESPOTISM, will persue their Bloody designs, with greater Vigour, and with all the unrelenting Malice of Barbarians, against our fellow Subjects in America, in proportion as we are TAME and ACQUIESCING; and if once they can succeed, through our BASENESS and COWARDICE, the Sword will be immediately turned against us, the sacred Constitution of our Empire dissolved, and we shall fall DESPISED, UNLAMENTED, and DETESTED, into the same horrible Gulph of ARBITRARY POWER.

Let us take Advantage of the present Opportunity, while our Resentments boil high, while every English Breast is fired with Indignation against those who are the Authors of all our Past and present Calami-

---

ed., 1965) explained, the "Great Charter" was dear to English hearts. But they had more in mind, a frame of reference that made Magna Carta part of something far more inclusive. For that broader context see J. G. A. Pocock's *The Ancient Constitution and the Feudal Law* (Cambridge: Cambridge University Press, 1957; revised ed., 1987), and tracts like [John Sadler] *Rights of the Kingdom* (London: J. Kidgell, 1682); or Edward King's *An Essay on the English Constitution and Government* (London: Benjamin White, 1767).

ties, which now convulse the State to its CENTRE;—Let us by all proper, just, and legal Means, exemplary Punish the Parricides, and avowed Enemies of Mankind;—Let neither private Acquaintance, nor personal Alliance, stand between us and our DUTY to our COUN-TRY;—Let all who have a common Interest in the Public Safety—join in common Measures to DEFEND the Public Safety;—Let us persue to disgrace, destruction, and even Death, all those who have brought this Ruin upon us, let them be ever so GREAT, or ever so MANY;—Let us Stamp, and deep engrave in Characters legible to all Europe at Present, and to all Posterity hereafter, what vengeance is due to CRIMES, which have no less Objects in View, than the RUIN OF NATIONS, and the DESTRUCTION OF MILLIONS;—Let us frustrate their Present desperate, and wicked Attempt to destroy America, by joining with our injured fellow Subjects, and bravely striking, one HONEST and BOLD Stroke to destroy them—Nay, although the Designs of the Conspirators, should be laid deep as the Centre, although they should raise HELL itself, and should fetch le-gions of Votaries from thence to avow their Proceedings, yet let us not leave the Pursuit till we have their HEADS and their ESTATES.

Hear Part of the Address of your injured, and oppressed fellow Subjects in America, to you, upon this Melancholy occasion, upon the dreadful Prospect of impending Ruin; then let every Englishman lay his Hand upon his Heart, and declare, whether he does not think they have been most CRUELLY TREATED, and whether he can in Justice, Conscience, and Humanity, draw the Sword against them; or whether he would not rather join with them, and endeavour to obtain a DECESSIVE VIC-TORY over TYRANNY, or fall Gloriously with the LIBERTIES of his Country. These are their Words.[3]

---

3. The Continental Congress's address to the people of Great Britain, approved on 21 October 1774, can be found in Worthington Chauncey Ford, ed., *The Journals of the Continental Congress*, 34 vols. (Washington, D.C.: Government Printing Office, 1904–1937), 1:82–101. Congress ordered that one hundred twenty copies be printed (by Will-liam and Thomas Bradford of Philadelphia). It was also reprinted in London, early in 1775. John Almon had reprinted, as pamphlets, extracts from Congress's proceedings,

"WHEN a Nation, led to greatness by the Hand of Liberty, and possessed of all the Glory that Heroism, Munificence, and Humanity can bestow, descends to the ungrateful task of forging Chains for her Friends and Children, and instead of giving Support to Freedom, turns Advocate for Slavery and Oppression, there is Reason to suspect she has either ceased to be Virtuous, or been extremely Negligent in the appointment of her Rulers.

"In almost every Age, in repeated Conflicts, in long and Bloody Wars, as well Civil as Foreign, against the many powerful Nations, against the open assaults of Enemies, and the more dangerous Treachery of Friends, have the Inhabitants of your Island, your Great and glorious Ancestors, maintained their Independance, and transmitted the Rights of Men and the blessings of Liberty to you their Posterity.

"Be not surprised, therefore, that we, who are Descendents from the same common Ancestors; that we, whose Forefathers participated in all the Rights, the Liberties, and the Constitution, you so justly Boast, and who have carefully conveyed the same fair Inheritance to us, guaranted by the plighted Faith of Government, and the most Solemn compacts with British Sovereigns, should refuse to surrender them to Men, who found their Claims on no principles of Reason, and who Prosecute them with a design, that by having our Lives and Property in their Power, they may with the grater Facility ENSLAVE YOU.

"The Cause of America is now the Object of universal Attention: it has at length become very Serious. This unhappy Country has not only been Oppressed, but Abused and Misrepresented; and the Duty we owe ourselves and Posterity, to your Interest, and the general Welfare of the British Empire, leads us to address you on this very important Subject.

"We call upon you yourselves, to witness our Loyalty and Attachment to the common Interest of the whole Empire: did we not, in the last War,

---

which included the address, before the end of 1774. For context see Edmund Cody Burnett, *The Continental Congress* (New York: Macmillan, 1941); and Jerrilyn Marston Greene, *King and Congress* (Princeton, N.J.: Princeton University Press, 1987).

add all the Strength of this vast Continent to the Force which repelled our common enemy? Did we not leave our native Shores, and meet Disease and Death, to promote the Success of the British Arms in Foreign Climates? Did you not thank us for our Zeal, and even Reimburse us large Sums of Money, which, you confessed, we had advanced beyond our Proportion, and far beyond our Abilities? You did.

"To what Causes, then, are we to attribute the sudden Change of Treatment, and that system of Slavery which was prepared for us at the restoration of Peace.

"Let Justice and Humanity cease to be the Boast of your Nation! consult your History, examine your History, examine your Records of former Transactions, nay turn to the Annals of the many arbitrary States and Kingdoms that surround you, and shew us a single Instance of Men being condemned to suffer for imputed Crimes, unheard, unquestioned, and without even the specious Formality of a Trial; and that too by Laws made expressly for the Purpose, and which had no Existence at the Time of the Fact committed. If it be difficult to reconcile these Proceedings to the Genius and Temper of your Laws and Constitution, the Task will become more arduous when we call upon our ministerial Enemies to justify, not only condemning men untried, and by hearsay, but involving the innocent in one common punishment with the Guilty, and for the Act of thirty or forty, to bring Poverty, Distress and Calamity on thirty thousand souls, and those not your Enemies, but your Friends, Brethren, and Fellow-Subjects.

"Admit that the Ministry, by the Powers of Britain, and the aid of our Roman Catholic neighbours, should be able to carry the point of taxation, and reduce us to a state of perfect humiliation and slavery. Such an enterprize would doubtless make some addition to your national debt, which already presses down your Liberties, and fills you with Pensioners and Placemen.—We presume, also, that your Commerce will somewhat be diminished. However, suppose you should prove victorious—in what Condition will you then be? What Advantages or what Laurels will you reap from such a Conquest?

"May not a Ministry with the same Armies enslave you—it may be said, you will cease to pay them—but remember the taxes from America, the

Wealth, and we may add, the men, and particularly the Roman Catholics of this vast Continent, will then be in the Power of your Enemies—nor will you have any Reason to expect, that after making Slaves of us, many among us should refuse to assist in reducing you to the same abject State.

"Do not treat this as chimerical—Know that in less than half a century, the quit Rents reserved to the Crown, from the numberless Grants of this vast Continent, will pour large Streams of Wealth into the Royal Coffers, and if to this be added the Power of taxing America at Pleasure, the Crown will be rendered independant on you for Supplies, and will possess more Treasure than may be necessary to purchase the *Remains* of Liberty in your Island.—In a Word, take Care that you do not fall into the Pit that is preparing for us.

"We believe there is yet much VIRTUE, much JUSTICE and much public Spirit in the English Nation—To that Justice we now appeal. You have been told that we are seditious, impatient of Government, and desirous of Independency. Be assured that these are not Facts, but Calumnies—Permit us to be as free as yourselves, and we shall ever esteem a Union with you to be our greatest Glory and our greatest Happiness; we shall ever be ready to contribute all in our Power to the Welfare of the Empire—we shall consider your Enemies as our Enemies, and your Interest as our own.

"But if you are determined that your Ministers shall wantonly sport with the Rights of Mankind—If neither the Voice of Justice, the Dictates of the Law, the Principles of the Constitution, or the Suggestions of Humanity can restrain your Hands from shedding HUMAN BLOOD in such an impious Cause, we must then tell you, that we never will submit to be Hewers of Wood or Drawers of Water for any Ministry or Nation in the World.

"The People of England will soon have an Opportunity of declaring their Sentiments concerning our Cause. In their Piety, Generosity, and good Sense, we repose high Confidence; and cannot, upon a Review of past Events, be persuaded that *they*, the Defenders of true Religion, and the Assertors of the Rights of Mankind, will take Part against their affectionate Protestant Brethren in the Colonies, in Favour of *our open* and *their own secret* Enemies, whose Intrigues, for several Years past, have been wholly exercised in sapping the Foundations of civil and religious Liberty."

Printed and published for the Authors, by T. W. SHAW, in Fleet-Street, opposite Anderton's Coffee House, where Letters to the Publisher will be thankfully received.

THE

CRISIS

NUMBER VI   *To be continued Weekly.*

SATURDAY, FEBRUARY 25, 1775   [*Price Two-pence Halfpenny*

Is there not some hidden CURSE in the Stores of HEAVEN, Red with uncommon Wrath, to BLAST the Man who Owes his GREATNESS to his COUNTRY'S RUIN.

To the Right Honourable LORD NORTH, First Lord of the Treasury, Chancellor of the Exchequer, and Ranger of Bushy Park, &c. &c.

My LORD,

WE know not which is most to be detested your Lordship's PUSILLANIMITY, or your VILLAINY, such a Miscreant never before disgraced the Administration of any Country, nor the confidence of any King; one Day you are all Fire and Sword, *Boston* is to be laid in *Ashes*, and the Rivers of *America* are to run with the BLOOD of her Inhabitants; Ships are prepared, Troops embarked, and Officers appointed for the threatened Carnage; you no sooner find, the brave Americans are determined to resist your Instruments of Slaughter and to oppose the cruel Designs of a despotic Tyrant, to rob them of their Rights; than all the bravadoing, and all the blustering of your Lordship, is immediately softened into a Calm, and you Relax; FEAR seizes your dastardly Soul, and you sink beneath the Weight of accumulated Guilt.

One Day we hear of nothing but accusations, Proscriptions, Impeachments, and Bills of Attainder against the Patriots in *America*, and they are speedily to be apprehended, and to receive a Punishment due to their *Crimes*, due to *Rebels*; three Days do not elapse before this JUST and NOBLE resolution of your Lordship to bring those Traitors to a Trial is dropped, and lenient, or, no Steps are to be taken against them.

Another Day ALL the Colonies are in a state of REBELLION, and the last Advices received from America, you tell the House of Commons, were of a very alarming Nature, and such a daring Spirit of Resistance had manifested itself throughout the Continent, that it was now high time Parliament should adopt Measures for ENFORCING obedience to the late Acts, a Plan is no sooner proposed by you, but carried by a ROTTEN MAJORITY, for reducing them to a state of Subjection to your, and your Royal Master's WILL; and Bloodshed and Slaughter stare them in the Face; they laugh at your impotent Malice, and with a spirited firmness becoming of Freemen, DARE you to the Stroke; when behold, your Threats, and the resolutions of your venal Troop, (I will not call it a British Senate) become like the Threats and Resolutions of a Society of Coal Porters, who declare Vengeance against another Body of Men, who will not comply with their UNLAWFUL IMPOSITIONS, but, FEAR the next Day without even the shadow of Justice on their side to carry their desperate Designs into execution.

The Motion you made, my Lord, in the House of Commons on Monday last, for a SUSPENSION of the several American Acts, till it is known WHICH of the Provinces will raise a REVENUE, and contribute to the Luxuries of the parent State, subject to the Controul of the British Parliament, is a Subterfuge too low, and too thinly disguised to deceive the *Americans*, or to impose upon the understanding of the meanest Capacity; it is evident to the World this is only a villainous Plan to divide them, who, while united together, may bid defiance to all your Lord-ship's cunning fraud, force, and villainy.[1] The Americans, my Lord, are too Sensible and too Brave to be drawn into any Trap, either of your, or, your Royal Master's making, you may weave the Webb as artfully as you please, for their Destruction, and they will be sure to break it; their Cause is Just, 'tis the Cause of Heaven, and Built upon the solid founda-tion of TRUTH and LIBERTY, they will carefully watch over the sacred gifts of God, and never surrender them to you, nor any Power upon Earth, but with their Lives. You have found, my Lord, that your hostile Invasion, and all your Force and Violence would not Terrify them into a Compliance with your Measures, nor answer the infamous Design of making the King ABSOLUTE in *America*; and now you are determined to try whether by Fraud and Artifice you can effect your Purpose.

You have, my Lord, by the most cruel Oppressions, drove the Ameri-cans to a State of Desperation, you have destroyed their Charters, in-vaded their Rights, imposed Taxes contrary to every principle of Jus-tice, and to every idea of Representation, and by blockading the Port of BOSTON, reduced near Thirty Thousand People in easy Circum-stances, to a State of dependence upon the Charity and Benevolence of their Fellow-Subjects; and now, rare CONDESCENSION, a SUS-PENSION, of the several American Acts, or in other Words, Minis-terial Oppression and Villainy is to be granted them, provided they will raise a REVENUE in America, still subject to the CONTROUL of the King and Parliament in England: This *Suspension* Scheme, my Lord, will not do, the Americans will have a REPEAL of ALL the

---

1. North successfully proposed his conciliatory motion in the committee of the whole on 20 February 1775, which was formally approved by the House on the 27th. It came on the heels of Chatham's failed "provisional act" introduced in the Lords on February 1st. See Cobbett, et al., eds., *Parliamentary History*, 18:198–203 (for Chatham) and 18:319–58 (for North). North timed his proposal to follow debates beginning on February 2nd in the Commons over how to respond to the king on papers that he had presented to both houses when Parliament reconvened on January 19th after its Christmas break. Also see Simmons and Thomas, eds., *Proceedings and Debates*, 5:329–37 (Chatham) and 5:432–51 (North), and the *House of Commons Journal*, 35:161, for the resolution as it was reported on February 27th. Thomas, *Tea Party to Independence*, pp. 176–219, provides context.

Acts they complain of, and a full restoration of all their CHARTERS, RIGHTS, LIBERTIES, and PREVILIGES, before they grant you a single Farthing, and then not subject to the controul of a Banditti of Rotten Members in St. *Stephen's Chapel*, of your appointing, for where would be the difference, between their Taxing themselves, Subject to the CONTROUL, and at the DISPOSAL of the King and Parliament, HERE; or of the House of Commons in England Taxing them in the first Instance, there would be none, my Lord, and they would still be in the same situation they are now; still subjects to the WILL of the King, and the Corrupt influence of the Crown, this Scheme, my Lord, appears to me as ridiculous and absurd, as the NEGATIVE still vested in the Court of Aldermen, in the City of London, which gives a Power to a Majority of TWENTY-SIX, to set aside the Choice of SEVEN THOUSAND Liverymen, in the Election of their Mayors. Be assured, my Lord, this new Plan must fall to the Ground, with all your former ones in this Business; the Day of Trial is at Hand, the Americans will be firm, they will have a confirmation of all their Rights; they will have a redress of all their Grievances; they will levy their own Taxes, NOT SUBJECT, to any controuling Power; and they will fix the Constitutional Liberty of America, upon a Foundation not be again shaken by YOU, nor any PUSILANIMOUS, WEAK, WICKED, or CRUEL TYRANT.

It is unnatural; but for a Moment, my Lord, suppose the Americans should come into your Proposals, or agree with the Terms of your Motion, how, my Lord, can you make Reparation for the Injuries England and America, has sustained, or will it in any Degree lessen your Villainy, or atone for your Crimes; what Compensation can you make for the Loss of our Trade, to the Amount of near three Millions? What Compensation can you make for robbing the Nation of near one Million and a half of Money, to carry on your execrable Designs against your fellow-Subjects in America? you can make none; your Head indeed would be a pleasing Spectacle upon *Temple Bar*, but the Loss of that, and your Estates, would never atone for a ten thousandth Part of your Crimes and Villainy; still it is to be hoped the Minority in the House of Commons, and the People will never leave you, till they have both, till you are made a public Example, and brought to condign Punishment.

Every Measure, my Lord, of your Administration at home, has been cruel, arbitrary, and unconstitutional; and every Measure with Respect to foreign Affairs, has been weak, cowardly, absurd and ridiculous; unbecoming an English Minister, and only calculated to destroy the Honour and Interest of this Kingdom.

The Glory and Dignity of the British Nation, was never so infamously sacrificed both by you and the King, as in the Year 1770, by a scandalous secret Convention with Spain, concerning Faulkland's Islands.

With Respect to domestic Affairs, you have endeavoured to erect the Sovereign into a despotic Tyrant; you have made him trample under Foot, all Laws, human and divine; you have made him destroy the Rights and Liberties of the People, in every Part of the British Empire. You have made it apparently his Interest to promote Divisions at home; you have obliged him to quit the GLORIOUS title of Father of his People, and debase himself into the Head of a Party, whom he has invested with an absolute Dominion over him, and whilst he monarch's it in his own Closet, becomes contemptible in the Eyes of his Subjects, and the whole World; weak, timid, and irresolute; he deeply engages in all your Lordship's infamous Measures, and the Rest of his Ministers; and it is for this Reason we see every Act of ministerial Villainy and Murder, sanctified by Royal Authority.

A Parody, for your Lordship's Perusal, on the 3d Scene of the 5th Act of Richard the 3d.[2]

Enter NORTH, *from his Bed.*

'Tis now the dead of Night, and half the World is in a lonely, solemn Darkness hung; yet I (so coy a Dame is sleep to me) with all the weary Courtship

---

2. On the eve of the Battle of Bosworth Field in 1485, Shakespeare has Richard III's sleep disturbed by a nightmare. "Methought the souls of all that I had murdered," gasps Richard on awakening, "Came to my tent." The author(s) of *The Crisis* simply replaced characters in the play—including Richard's nephews, the two princes that he reputedly

of my care-tired Thoughts, can't Win her to my Arms; tho' even the Stars do Wink, as 'twere with over-watching.—I'll to my Bed, and once more try to sleep her into morning. [*Lies down, a Groan is heard.*

Ha! What means that dismal Voice? Sure 'tis the Echo of some yawning Grave, that teems with an untimely Ghost.—'Tis gone! 'twas but my Fancy, which ever, and anon, of late, conjures the People's murmurs to my Ear—no matter what, I feel my Eyes grow heavy.—[Sleeps.

Enter the Ghost of Britannia.

Brit. Oh! thou whose unrelenting Thoughts, not all the hideous Terrors of thy Guilt can shake; whose *Conscience*, with thy Body, ever Sleeps— Sleep on; while I by Heaven's high Ordinance, in Dreams of Horror wake thy frightful Soul: now give thy Thoughts to me; let them behold those gaping Wounds, which thy death-dealing Hand, from Time to Time, gave my anointed Body: now shall thy own devouring Conscience gnaw thy Heart, and terribly revenge my Murder.

Enter the Ghosts of those barbarously Murdered at Brentford, Boston, and in St. George's Fields, in the merciful Reign of the present King.

Ghosts. North Dream on, and let the wand'ring Spirits of thy butchered Fellow-Subjects grate thine Ear! could not the *cause* wherein we were em- barked; the *common, open birthright of a Briton,* persuade thy cruel Heart to spare our Lives? Oh! 'twas a cruel Deed! therefore alone, unpitying, unpitied shalt thou fall.

Enter the Ghost of the late Lord Chancellor.

Lord Chancellor. Could not the various wrongs thou didst thy Country's Weal, in CAMDEN, GRANBY, WILKES,[3] and many more, glut thy relent-

---

had slain in the Tower of London—who condemned him for what he had done with current figures in British public life. They echoed the characters demand for justice. Temporarily frightened, Richard III tries to convince himself that he could still prevail, though he falls to the sword of the earl of Richmond, who would take the throne as Henry VII—the outcome celebrated in Shakespeare's politically correct tale.

3. Charles Yorke, Baron Camden, and the Marquess of Granby all found themselves in the various controversies surrounding John Wilkes. Yorke, younger son of Philip Yorke,

less Soul? but thou and Grafton must aim thy Dagger at my Life—yes at my Life, unfeeling Man! for could'st thou think that after quitting every claim to Honour, Truth, or Right, I'd longer bare my hated Load, of Infamy—Oh! no! the Grave could only save me from myself! Wake then in all the Hells of Guilt! and let that wild Despair, which now does prey upon thy mangled Thoughts, be to the World a terrible example. [*Ghosts Vanish.*

North. Spare me my Life!—I do repent—your Wrongs shall be re-dressed.—Hah! soft—'twas but a Dream, but then so terrible, it shakes my Soul; cold drops of Sweat hang on my trembling Flesh; my Blood grows chilly, and I freeze with Horror: O! Tyrant Conscience! how dost thou afflict me? Fain would I re-assume my Walk; was it not terrible retreating? Who is there?

---

the first Baron, then first Earl, of Hardwicke, had seemed destined for greatness at the bar. Long expected to become lord chancellor, as his father had been under George II, he finally rose to the woolsack in January 1770 (and to be elevated as first Baron Morden), only to die less than a week later. He had succeeded Charles Pratt, Baron Camden, a longtime rival, with Pratt a strong Pittite and parliamentary leader but Yorke vacillating, too unsure of himself and too likely to give in to pressure and surrender his principles—as critics felt he did when it came to the various issues involving Wilkes and press freedom, the prerogatives of jurors, and Wilkes's right to be seated in the Commons. Similarly, Yorke's support of Stamp Act repeal as Rockingham's attorney general had made him popular with some, but pressing for a Declaratory Act to go along with it made him unpopular with them and others. For Pratt and Yorke as examples of how the constitutional could be caught up with the personal see Richard Pares, *King George III and the Politicians* (Oxford: Oxford University Press, 1957), p. 22. John Manners, Marquess of Granby, had similar problems in Parliament following a very successful career in the field as an army officer. Commander-in-chief and cabinet member under both Pitt (Chatham) and Grafton, he too struggled to find a place in politics that put him beyond controversy—he being targeted in a couple of early pieces by "Junius," an indication that he had failed (see infra VII.9 for "Junius"). For background on Granby see Alastair Massie's sketch in the *Oxford DNB*, 36:466–69; for Yorke, see John Cannon's entry in ibid., 60:831–33. Peter D. G. Thomas wrote the entry for Camden in ibid., 45:211–15. Thomas's *John Wilkes: A Friend to Liberty* (Oxford: Clarendon Press, 1996) is an excellent starting point for the times as well as the man. Also see Arthur H. Cash, *John Wilkes* (New Haven: Yale University Press, 2006).

Enter M U N G O, alias Jeremiah Dyson,[4]

Mungo. 'Tis I, my Lord,—the Morn is far advanced, and all your Friends are up, preparing for the House.

North. Oh! Mungo, I have had such Horrid Dreams!

Mungo. Shadows! My Lord—below the Statesman's heeding

North. Now, by my every hope—shadows to Night have struck more terror to the soul of North, than could the whole of ten *minorities*, armed all in proof and led by noisy Chatham.

Mungo. Be more yourself, my Lord; consider, were it but known a Dream had frightened you, how would your animated Foes presume on it.

North. Perish that thought!—no—never be it said that Fate itself cou'd awe the soul of North.

    Hence babbling Dreams you threaten here in vain
    Conscience avaunt, North is himself again!
    With this*, and with my gracious Sovereign's ear,
    I'll act determined—free from ev'ry fear.

*Producing the Key of the Treasury.

Printed and published for the Authors, by T. W. Shaw, in Fleet-Street, opposite Anderton's Coffee House, where Letters to the Publisher will be thankfully received.

---

4. Jeremiah Dyson was nearing the end of his career in the Commons with yet another safe seat, a reward for his support of government policy, from the Grenville ministry through that of North. Though trained in the law he had risen in politics as a result of his effectiveness as the Commons clerk, which made him an expert in House procedures and business. Isaac Barré had lampooned him as "Mungo," the lead character in Isaac Bickerstaff's immensely popular two-act comic opera, *The Padlock*, which had begun its run at the Drury Theatre in 1768. Mungo was the West Indian servant—or was it the slave?—of Don Diego and, though Mungo called Don Diego "Massa," he essentially ran the household. Peter D. G. Thomas wrote the sketch of Dyson that appears in the *Oxford DNB*, 17:513–15; there is also an entry for him in Namier and Brooke, *House of Commons*, 2:371–73.

THE

CRISIS

NUMBER VII   *To be continued Weekly.*

SATURDAY, MARCH 4, 1775[1]   [*Price Two-pence Half-penny.*

To the Right Honourable LORD APSLEY, Lord Chancellor of England.[2]

MY LORD,   *Feb.* 16, 1775.

I Was a Bye-stander this Day, when your Lordship and the House of Lords decided the very important Cause of PHILIP THICKNESS, Appellant, and PETER LEIGH and Others, Respondents: and though unconnected with the Parties, and consequently uninterested in the Event, I must own, I was forcibly struck—BY A SCENE SO NOVEL AND UNEXPECTED.—I stood, my Lord, with silent Awe, at the Bar of

---

1. Misdated as February 18, 1775 on the Bodleian Library copy used for this collection; correctly dated on the British Library copy. See supra I.1 for a comment on multiple printers.

2. Henry Bathurst was elevated to the peerage as Baron Apsley when he succeeded Charles Yorke as lord chancellor (see supra VI.3 for Yorke). Bathurst had been a member of the bar for three decades and earlier in his career had filled the family seat for the borough of Cirencester in the House of Commons. He had become a solid government man by the time of his elevation, though he began to doubt the wisdom of the American war as victory became more elusive by the end of 1777. N. G. Jones wrote the *Oxford DNB*, 4:351–52 sketch of him.

that Tribunal, which I had ever been accustomed to consider—as the Last Refuge of INJURED JUSTICE.[3]—I expected to hear a Question of Law, of infinite Nicety, discussed with Wisdom, and decided with Integrity.—Judge then, my Lord, my Astonishment, when, instead of that Decency in Debate, which ought to be observed, even in the lowest Courts of Justice, and which I had ever thought, in a Peculiar manner, characteristic of the House of Lords, I saw Proceedings that would have disgraced a POLISH DIET!—Yes, my Lord, in all my Experience of Courts of Justice, I never saw Judges, so avowedly corrupt, so indecently profligate, as YOUR LORDSHIP and LORD DENBIGH![4]—LORD CAMDEN delivered HIS Opinion on the Question, in an Argument, that will carry to the latest Times HIS FAME and Your Disgrace.

Your Lordship, in Answer to him, delivered your Sentiments, I cannot call them an Argument, because there was nothing that resembled a Chain of Reasoning; and indeed your Lordship seemed more to rely

3. Phillip Thicknesse had lost an inheritance case in the Court of Chancery in March 1774, which he also subsequently lost on appeal to the House of Lords. Later issues of *The Crisis* would return to the case as an example of the injustice (see nos. 10, 17, 23, 32, 31. 34, 53, and 59) that had come to typify the age. Thicknesse would write in his own defense as author of no. 30 (12 August 1775; see infra) in the series, the first of only two instances where an author is identified by name in *The Crisis*. The second would be William Stewardson, author of no. 67, on 27 April 1776 (see infra). For more on the contentious Thicknesse see Philip Gosse, *Dr. Viper* (London: Cassell, 1952); and Katherine Turner's sketch in the *Oxford DNB*, 54:242–46. A handwritten note on the page opposite the page with the Hope family crest for the Bodleian Library copy of *The Crisis* states that Thicknesse wrote issues 7 and 10 as well as 30. That is unlikely, as I explain in "George III, Tyrant," pp. 452–54.

4. Basil Feilding, sixth Earl of Denbigh, was a privy councillor and lord of the king's bedchamber, but he was not a leader in the House of Lords. That he and others like him had the ear of the king grated on those who longed for what some day would be called "responsible government," even if monarchy were to remain intact. There is no entry for Denbigh in the *Oxford DNB*, though there is in Valentine, *British Establishment*, 1:311–12 (under Basil Feilding, that is). Denbigh can be found, like all of the members of the House of Lords in 1775, in Frederick Barlow, *The Complete English Peerage*, 2 vols. (London: S. Bladon, 1775). The entry for Denbigh (see 1:321–24) is typical in reading like a precursor to Burke's peerage.

on the Letter you had received from Sir WILLIAM DE GREY,⁵ and the Conversation YOU SAID you had had with Sir Eardley Wilmot, and Sir Stafford Smythe, than on any Reasons you could advance in Support of your Decree!

When LORD CAMDEN, with a Decency becoming the Occasion, and the Place in which he spoke, reminded your Lordship how improper it was for a Judge—deciding so nice and difficult a Question of Property in the highest Tribunal of the Kingdom—to talk of Opinions of Men, not Judges in that Court, who had given their Sentiments in Private, probably, without much Consideration of the Subject, most certainly, without hearing the Facts stated, and the Question discussed by Council— *WHAT TREATMENT DID HE MEET WITH?*—LORD DENBIGH's Attack upon him was the Attack of a Ruffian, hired to carry through a profligate Measure, by assassinating every Man who should attempt Opposition.—YOUR LORDSHIP's Language was somewhat more decent:—it was the Language of Ignorance, delivered with that Insolence, which a weak and vain Man feels, confident in a corrupt Majority.

Has your Lordship still to learn, that the Opinion of a Judge, though delivered in the Course of a Cause in open Court, and handed down in Print; yet if it is on a Point NOT before Him, as a Judge, is never allowed to be cited even by Counsel in Argument? And wisely so established, my Lord: For the Law of this Country gives Credit to the Opinions of the Judges, only on those Points, which are necessarily brought before them in the Course of Judicial Proceedings. On these Points, when they have heard the Arguments of Counsel, they decide;—if erroneously, the Injured Party has his Remedy by Appeal;—if corruptly and iniquitously, the Decision of the Judge appears on the Record, and he is amenable to his Country's Justice.—Is your Lordship ignorant that this is the Law? or can your Lordship say—or will any other Man say for you—that in

---

5. A former solicitor general, as attorney general in 1770 he pursued the "Junius" prosecutions; before that he had been involved in the government's case against John Wilkes. Knighted for his long service to the crown, he had risen to become chief justice of the court of common pleas.

the Course of his Attendance on Courts of Law, he ever *before* knew a Private Letter, and Private Conversation, adduced by a Judge, not as ARGUMENTS, furnishing REASONS for an Opinion, but as AUTHORITIES IN LAW, to warrant his Decision?—My Lord, I will defy your Lordship, with all your long List of Advisers, from the hollow-hearted Lord, who made you Chancellor, down to the lowest Driveller who feeds your Vanity with Flattery, to say, that such a Sight was ever *before* exhibited in a Court of Justice.

From the Existence of Courts of Law in this Island, no Man ever, before this Day, saw a private Letter produced, read, and relied on, as Authority by a Judge, pronouncing Judgment.—Are the Arguments of counsel Mockery? or, are they supposed to suggest Matter, to be weighed by those who are to decide?—The Judgement of your Lordship, and the House of Peers, this Day, was avowedly founded on the Authorities of Men, who had never heard the Question discussed by Counsel.—If this mode of deciding is to prevail in Courts of Justice, Arguments by Counsel are useless: Your Lordship can decide, without hearing them: Nothing more is requisite, than for your Lordship to write a Letter to some Friend: His Answer, read in Court by your Lordship, will stand in the Place both of Authority and Argument.—Is this the Way, in which Justice is to be dispensed to the Subject, in the Supreme Tribunals of the Country—the Chancery, and House of Lords?

O. SEATS of TALBOT and of HARDWICK:[6] from whence those GREAT and GOD-LIKE Men, with a pure Heart, and Wisdom more than human, shed on this happy Land the fragrant Dews of Justice,— from whence the vanquished Suitor was wont to retire, satisfied, by the Arguments he had heard, that he had been mistaken in his Claim— *HOW IS YOUR GLORY FADED!*—The WRETCHED THING, who now fills the Place of your late bright Inhabitant, attempts not to give Reasons

---

6. Charles Talbot, first Baron Talbot of Hensol, served as lord chancellor under George II from 1733–1737; Philip Yorke, first Baron of Hardwicke (and father of Charles Yorke– see supra VI.3), succeeded him and held the post from 1737–1756. Both were considered fine jurists. Earlier in their careers, they had held seats in the Commons connected to family interests.

for his Decisions, but tells the Suitor in Plain Terms, that he decides the Cause, on the Authority of a Letter from one of his Friends, who had never heard the Facts openly stated, or an Argument from Council on the Subject!

My Lord, were I to tell a Man, bred up in the Courts of Talbot and of Hardwicke, that a Chancellor of this Country had decided a Question, on an Executory Devise, on the Authority of a Letter from Sir William De Grey, who had never heard an Argument on the Question—he would tell me, *IT WAS A LYE—IT WAS IMPOSSIBLE TO BE TRUE*;—It would be as repugnant to all his Ideas of a Chancellor's Proceedings, as if I was to tell him, That on the first Day of the Term I had seen the Chancellor carried round Westminster-Hall in Bacchalian Triumph, the Train, Mace, and Purse, borne by three drunken Trolls picked out of a Brandy-shop at Temple-Bar.

My Lord, Men's Minds are formed by what they have been accustomed to. Those who remember the polished Manners, and elegant Arguments, of former Chancellors, are shocked at your Lordship's Brutal Decision: Sic volo, sic jubeo.[7]—My Lord, I do not use these Expressions as merely similar to your Lordship's. I do aver, that since your Lordship has had the Custody of the Great Seal, I have heard you decide a Question at Law, argued by an eminent Council, in these very Words—*I AM OF A DIF-FERENT OPINION*—I heard your Lordship decide in these Words—*I HEARD THAT VERY DECISION REVERSED AS ERRONEOUS.*

My Lord, your Lordship's Conduct is become too glaringly despicable.— When the Great Seal had been taken from Lord Camden, for daring to speak his Sentiments in Parliament; and the ever-to-be-lamented Yorke[8] had, by a virtuous Death, atoned too severely for the Weakness of an un-guarded Moment, (for who can withstand the Persuasion of Kings, when they become Suitors?) the Gap was to be stopped—it was necessary that

---

7. "Sic Volo, sic Jubeo," from Juvenal's *Satires*, Book 6, commonly translated as "This I want, this I command," a phrase followed by "stat proratione voluntas" ("my will stands in place of reason"). See infra LXXX.2.

8. For Charles Yorke and his death see supra VI.3.

the Office of Chancellor should be filled;—your Lordship was pitched upon, by Lord Mansfield, as a Man who, being too weak to form Opinions of his own, would pay implicit Obedience of His Dictates, and, in the Character of the Great Law Officer, AVOW Legal Opinions, *his Patron might be unwilling to risque.*—This was the Ground on which your Lordship was made Chancellor;—The Nation saw it, and lamented, that an Office, of such infinite Importance, should be disposed of from such Motives, and to such a Man.—For, my Lord, do you think the World ever considered you as a Lawyer?—Those who had attended Westminster-Hall knew, that your Abilities as a Man, and your Knowledge as a Lawyer, were below Contempt.—They knew, that in the Character of an Advocate, you had never got 200 L. a Year in all the Courts of Westminster taken together:—They were astonished, when you were made a Judge;—but they were exasperated, when you were made Chancellor?—In the Discharge of the Duty of that Office, they saw that your Decisions were ever unsupported by Argument; from hence they were led to *suspect*, that your Decrees were made by Others.—My Lord, they *suspected* this: But they did not know it, till your Lordship, in the Debate of this Day, put the Matter beyond a Doubt:—You will say, perhaps, a Chancellor may ask the Assistance of those, whose Judgment he esteems.—True, my Lord; but then let him call on them in the Character of Assessors—that they may hear the Arguments of Counsel—that they may be answerable for the Doctrines they lay down—and, that the Suitor may know, by *whose* Opinion his Property is bound.

My Lord this is your Character; drawn with more Truth, than by those Sycophants, who tell you that you are greater a Chancellor than *Hardwick, Talbot* or *Camden!*—No Man ever doubted about your Head;—the Conduct of this Day has fixed Men's Opinions of your Heart.—My Lord, it was a foul Proceeding.

𝔍𝔱 𝔴𝔞𝔰 𝔞 𝔅𝔩𝔞𝔠𝔨 𝔇𝔞𝔶'𝔰 𝔚𝔬𝔯𝔨; 𝔍𝔲𝔰𝔱𝔦𝔠𝔢 𝔰𝔢𝔢𝔪𝔢𝔡 𝔦𝔫 𝔈𝔠𝔩𝔦𝔭𝔰𝔢:

The Suiter had seen with Grief, in what weak Hands the Great Seal was entrusted: but when he saw, that if your Ignorance led you to decide erroneously, a PACK'D HOUSE of PEERS might be brought together to sacrifice his Property to your Vanity, he was struck with Horror.—My

Lord, the Nation will not bear it,—and after the Scene of this Day, your Lordship cannot hold the GREAT SEAL.

JUNIUS.[9]

P.S. When the Decree was affirmed, there was not above five or six Lords in the House, besides Lords Camden and the *present* Chancellor.—Lord PAULET (to his Honour be it recorded) moved to have the Judges called in. This Motion was over-ruled, and he retired.—It was the Duke of Chandois, Lord Denbigh, Lord Cathcart, and Lord Galloway,[10] who took upon themselves to decide a nice Question of Law, which ought to have been argued with Wisdom and Discretion, but which was debated with Passion, and decided by Party-Zeal.—In short, what raised the Chancellor, ruined the Suitor,—THE TIMES.

Note, *When the House of Lords were met, to hear the Cause, a Message was sent to* Lord Mansfield *by the Chancellor,* to know if he would attend,— *but, the Chancellor very well knew, he would not attend:—He knew, that*

---

9. The author(s) may have turned to "Junius" for the nom de plume as an echo of the "Junius" essays that were published in London between 21 January 1769 and 21 January 1772 in the *Public Advertiser*, as well to make a connection to the legendary sixth century BCE founder of the Roman republic, Lucius Junius Brutus, or perhaps to Marcus Junius Brutus, the Roman senator who claimed to be descended from him and led the conspirators against Julius Caesar in 44 BCE. No essays appeared over the name "Lucius;" two (nos. 37 and 57) were written as "Brutus." Eighteenth-century British readers would have been familiar with the original Junius through Livy's *History* and the later Junius through Plutarch's *Lives*, both of which had long been translated into English. See John Cannon, ed., *The Letters of Junius* (Oxford: Clarendon Press, 1978), which includes a discussion of authorship and letters from "Junius" to various public figures as well as the essays themselves.

10. Harry Paulet [Powlett], sixth Duke of Bolton, was a classic example of rising through family connections, to admiral in the Navy and to a seat in the Commons before he succeeded his father into the peerage. A self-proclaimed king's man, he nonetheless became disillusioned with the American war after the French entered the contest. Charles Schaw Cathcart, ninth Lord Cathcart in the Scottish peerage, with a place in the House of Lords at Westminster, was also advantaged by family ties, from his promotions in the army (where he fought under the Duke of Cumberland at Culloden) to his stint as ambassador at the court of Catherine the Great. He died in the summer of 1776. John Stewart, seventh Earl of Galloway, was, like Cathcart, a representative Scottish peer at Westminster and a king's-man.

Lord Mansfield *could not resist the Arguments of Lord* Camden; *and that he must concur with him in* reversing the Decree:—*Lord Mansfield therefore stayed in Westminster-Hall, to decide the Property of* twenty-five Pounds, *and neglected his Duty to attend, where* Ten Thousand Pounds *were at Stake, as well as the Honour of the Nation*:—*He* well *knew the* honest Zeal *of Lords* Cathcart *and* Galloway, *the Villainy of Lord* Denbigh, *and the Folly of the cajoled* Duke of Chandois:[11]—*He knew that they* would *attend, constantly,* to take Notes, *in Order to* form a Determination, *they went into the House prepared for;*—*namely, To affirm the Decree,—and do for Lord* Mansfield *what he durst not do himself.*

Lord Mansfield's personal Dislike to the Suitor has long been well known.— When he appeared at the Bar of the King's Bench to receive Judgment for libelling Lord Orwell,[12]—*Lord Mansfield jumped from the* Seat of Justice, *and with Fury in his Eyes, and an Agitation of Body consonant thereto,—exclaimed* Commit him! Commit him!—*an Indecency of Behaviour which astonished the whole Court.*

*** Since writing the above, I have seen a Letter from Sir WILLIAM DE GREY, in Answer to one from the Appellant, requesting to know whether the Letter read by your Lordship in the House of Peers, was read with his Privity?—Sir William De Grey's Answer is in these Words:

> "*Sir,*—*I am entirely a Stranger to what has been passing in the House of Lords, upon the Subject of your Letter, not knowing till a Day or two ago, that there was any Cause depending there in which you were interested; and then, only in casual Conversation.*"

I am, Sir, &c.

WILLIAM DE GREY.

---

11. James Brydges, third Duke of Chandos, succeeded his father to the peerage in 1771. In earlier years he had sat in the Commons for two different constituencies but, tired of the haggling between rival factions, left Westminster in 1768, choosing not to stand for election anywhere.

12. Francis Vernon, Lord Orwell in the Irish peerage, had earlier used family ties to sit in the Commons for Ipswich.

On this Letter I will make but one Comment:—Either Sir William De Grey's Answer to the Appellant contains an Untruth, or your Lordship has practised on the House of Peers *an Imposition of the Blackest Dye.*

Printed and published for the Authors, by T. W. SHAW, in Fleet-Street, opposite Anderton's Coffee House, and by his appointment the Corner of Little Turnstile, Holborn, where Letters to the Publisher will be thankfully received.

THE

CRISIS

NUMBER VIII   *To be continued Weekly.*

SATURDAY, MARCH 11, 1775   [Price Two-pence Half-penny.

To the Lords *Suffolk, Pomfret, Radnor, Apsley,* and *Sandwich.*

> How Glorious the Æra, thrice happy th' Day,
> When Private Int'rest to Public gives way,
> When Bribes cannot tempt your Lordships to sell,
> Th' Birthright of Freemen to Tyrants of Hell.
>
> How Glorious th' Æra, thrice happy indeed,
> When TRAITORS, and MINIONS are sentenc'd t'bleed,
> When JUSTICE shall reign, and Heav'n's great call,
> The Proud Seed of Hell, Just Victims do fall.

My Lords,

YOU have a peculiar Claim to an Address from the Authors of the CRISIS, and it shall be our Business in this Paper, to preserve, if Possible, the preshiable INFAMY of your Names.

The Motion made by LORD RADNOR, on *Monday* the 27th of *February*, concerning NUMBER III of the CRISIS, was Unjust and Vi—us, the Paper contains nothing but the most SACRED TRUTHS, and therefore could not be a *false* or *scandalous* LIBEL: the amendment of the Epithet

Treasonable, proposed and supported by the Lords POMFRET, SUFFOLK, APSLEY, and SANDWICH was Infamous, and of a Piece with every other proceeding of the present Reign, and present Ministry; it shewed in a particular Manner, the BLOODY minded Disposition of prostituted Court-Lords, the instruments of MURDER and PUBLIC RUIN.[1] The *immaculate* Lord SANDWICH, insisted that the word Treasonable should stand Part of the Motion, as a proper Foundation for bringing the Author to *exemplary* and *condign* Punishment. Suppose, my Lords, this infamous Amendment to the RADNOR Motion, had been carried, and it had stood a *false, scandalous*, and *treasonable* LIBEL, could the mere *ipse dixit* of a few venal Lords, make that Treason, which in the Literal or constructive Sense of the Word, was not so.

The Author of NUMBER III, is perfectly well acquainted with the Statute of Treasons, passed in the Reign of *Edward* the Third,[2] and

---

1. George Fermor, second Earl of Pomfret, was a lord of the king's bedchamber, privy councillor, and keeper of Windsor Park (see infra XXXV.2). William Bouverie, first Earl of Radnor, had once sat in the Commons and, though not an opposition leader, supported Chatham's failed February 1st reconciliation proposal. Henry Howard, twelfth Earl of Suffolk, was a privy councillor long connected to the royal household. He held a cabinet level post as secretary of state for the northern department, but he did not play as forceful a role in policy making as John Montagu, fourth Earl of Sandwich, first lord of the Admiralty. Suffolk has more or less slipped through the historiographical cracks; not so Sandwich. See N. A. M. Rodger's sketch of him in the *Oxford DNB*, 38:744–48, and his full-length biography, *The Insatiable Earl* (London: HarperCollins, 1993). Also see infra XXV.5.

2. This 1352 statute still stood, with small modifications over the centuries, as the law in England and, by extension of acts passed by local legislatures, in the colonies. Although distinguishing between "high" and "low" treason, the 1352 act and those it inspired were still sweeping enough that practically any rebellious American–whether by word or by act—could have been arrested, prosecuted, convicted and hanged under them. The 1352 act is in Pickering, ed., *Statutes*, 2:50–53 (25 Edward III c. 2). For context see J. G. Bellamy, *The Law of Treason in England in the Later Middle Ages* (Cambridge: Cambridge University Press, 1970). And yet no colonist would be taken to court under that 1352 act or its subsequent revisions, an indication that Whitehall and Westminster wisely thought better of making an example of a rebel here and a rebel there. See my "Imperial Impotence: Treason in 1774 Massachusetts" *Law and History Review* 29 (2011):657–701, and Parliament's 1769 decision to apply a statute passed in the reign of Henry VIII to the colonists, so that colonists accused of treason in any of its forms could be prosecuted in England. Also see infra LXIV.1.

likewise with the various Expositions, and Interpretations of it; he well knew, the Paper was Written upon the true principles of the REVOLUTION, and that it could be justified by the Laws of the Land; he well knew, (though there is hardly any Villainy but what Court-Sycophants may do with ease) that it was not in the Power of Lord MANSFIELD, with all his Chicanery, with all his Artifice, with all his abuse of Law, with all his perversion of Justice, with all the aid of false Construction and forced Ineuendos, to bring it within the meaning of that Statute; he well knew the Disposition of the Sovereign and his Minions, and that nothing would, or can satiate Royal, Scotch, or Ministerial Revenge, but the BLOOD of those who oppose the present most horridly cruel, and most infamously wicked Measures of Government; and, my Lords, he well knew the shocking prostitution of Hereditary Peerage, and the bare-faced Treachery and Villainy of a purchased Majority in the House of Commons.

Has there not, my Lords, been INNOCENT BLOOD enough shed in this Reign, that your Lordships should still Thirst for more?

Why should your Lordships be so desirous of stopping every channel of Public information, the Infamy of your Actions are sufficiently known, and will be handed down to the last ages of Time, while your Names will stink in the Nostrils of Posterity.

The Statute of Treasons, my Lords, passed in the 25th Year of the Reign of *Edward* the Third, was an Act of vast importance to the Public Weal; for till then, there was hardly a Word spoke, or a Paper written, but what was deemed Treason; and the Parliament which passed it, was called *Benedictum Parliamentum*, the blessed Parliament.

The substance of this Statute is branched out by my Lord Cooke, into Six Heads, which we shall here give, with some Observations of our own, to shew your Lordships and the World, that NUMBER III of the CRISIS, is not within the meaning of either of these Heads, and that by your amended Motion, you designed to lay the ground Work of a Prosecution the most Cruel and Infamous, ever carried on in this Country, worse than those, which without Proof, or the Colour of Guilt, took away the Lives of the Great Lord Russel, and Algernon Sidney.[3]

The First Head concerning Death; by compassing, or imagining the Death of the King, Queen, or Prince, and declaring the same by some *overt Deed*. By killing or murdering the Chancellor, Treasurer, Justice of either Bench, Justices in Eyre, Justices of Assize, Justices of Oyer and Terminer, in their Places, during their Offices.

The Second is to Violate, that is, to carnally know the Queen, the King's eldest Daughter unmarried, the Prince's Wife.

The Third is, levying War against the King.

---

3. Sir Edward Coke, parliamentarian and jurist during the reign of James I, was celebrated by the American Revolutionary generation for rulings in "Calvin's Case" (1607) and in "Bonham's Case" (1610), when he was chief justice on the court of common pleas (as recorded in his *Reports*). In "Calvin" he reaffirmed the reality of an immutable law of nature; in "Bonham," where he cited himself in "Calvin," he also contended that the common law could be called on to negate an act of Parliament. Coke quoted as readily from the Bible as he did Aristotle and Justinian, mixing the Judeo-Christian with the classical and English. Allen D. Boyer offers a nice introduction to Coke in the *Oxford DNB*, 12:451–62; Catherine Drinker Bowen, *The Lion and the Throne* (Boston: Little, Brown and Co., 1957) is enthusiastically sympathetic to Coke, though Bowen did note that Coke, despite his attachment to the common law, would not let legal precedent stand in the way of what he considered justice when he ruled from the bench. William Russell, in line to succeed his father as Earl of Bedford, and Algernon Sidney were both executed (Russell beheaded and Sidney hanged) for their involvement in the so-called Rye House plot of 1683. In the years following the Glorious Revolution they would both be remembered as martyrs to the cause of limited government, respected for their defense of Parliament, their warnings against the royal prerogative, and opposition to the Catholic James, Duke of York, succeeding his brother Charles II to the throne. Sidney in particular would stand out because of his career that went back to the first Civil War and writings that made his reputation as a principled republican, part of a group that historian Caroline Robbins called "the commonwealthmen." His *Apology*, written between his conviction and execution, would prove a favorite Whig text. His primary writings have been gathered in Thomas G. West, ed., *Discourses Concerning Government* (Indianapolis: Liberty Classics, 1990). His role as symbol is discussed in Alan Craig Houston, *Algernon Sidney and the Republican Tradition in England and America* (Princeton, N.J.: Princeton University Press, 1991). Also see Jonathan Scott's sketch of him in the *Oxford DNB*, 48:50:537–44 ; Russell is also in ibid., 48:358–62, in an essay by Lois G. Schworer.

The Fourth is, adhering to the King's Enemies; within the Realm or without, and declaring the same by some *Overt Act*.

The Fifth is, counterfeiting the Great, the Privy Seal, or the King's Coin.

The Sixth and Last, by bringing into this Realm, counterfeit Money, to the likeness of the King's Coin.

First, To *compass and imagine*, is to contrive, design, or intend the Death of the King; but this must be declared by some *Overt-Act*, declaring by an OPEN Act, a design to *depose* or *imprison* the King, is an *Overt-Act*, to manifest the compassing his Death. I believe, my Lords, the Author of NUMBER III of the CRISIS, is not under the Predicament of this exposition.

Second, By the word King, is intended, 1. A King before his Coronation, as soon as ever the Crown descends upon him; for the Coronation is but a Ceremony. 2. A King *de Facto*, and not *de Jure*, is King within this Act, and Treason against him is Punishable, though the right Heir get the Crown.

Third, Note. It is very Strange, but in the printed Statute Books, it is there said, *probably attainted*, which is a gross Error; for the Words of the Record are, *et de ceo*, PROVABLEMENT *Soit Attaint*; *And shall be thereof* PROVABLY attaint: And it is amazing to me, that so gross a Mistake should be suffered, since my Lord Cooke has so expressly observed the Difference in these Words following. 3. *Instu. Fol.* 12. In this Branch, saith he, Four things are to be observed: 1. This Word (*Provablement*) *Provably*, that is, upon DIRECT and MANIFEST PROOF, not upon conjectural Presumptions, or Inferences, or strains of Wit, but upon GOOD and SUFFICIENT PROOF: and herein the Adverb (*Provablement*) *Provably*, hath great Force, and signifieth a DIRECT and PLAIN PROOF; and therefore the Offender must provably be attained, which Words are as Forcible as upon DIRECT and MANIFEST PROOF. Note, the Word is not *Probably,* for then *commune Argumentum* might have served; but the Word is *provably* be attainted. 2. This Word Attaint, necessarily implieth, that he be proceeded with, and attainted according to the due COURSE of LAW, and proceedings of Law, and not by

ABSOLUTE POWER, or by other Means, as in former Times had been
used. And therefore if a Man doth adhere to the Enemies of the King,
or be Slain in open War against the King, or otherwise Die before the
Attainder of Treason, he *forfeiteth nothing*, because (as that Act saith)
he is not attained: wherein this Act hath altered that, which before this
Act, in case of Treason, was taken for Law. And the Statute of 34 *Ed.* 3.
saves nothing to the King but that which was in Esse, and partaining
to the King at the making of that Act. And this appeareth by Ajudg-
ment in Parliament, in Ann. 29. H. 6. that Jack Cade being Slain in
open Rebellion, could no ways be punished, or Forfeit any thing, and
therefore was attainted by that Act of High Treason. 3. Of open Deed,
per *apertum Factum*,[4] these Words strengthen the former exposition of
(*Provablement*) an OVERT ACT must be alledged in every Indictment
upon this Act, and PROVED. Compassing by *bare Words*, is not an
Overt Act, as apppears by many temporary Statutes against it. But there
must be some *open Act*, which must be *manifestly proved*. As if divers do
conspire the Death of the King, and the Manner how, and thereupon
provide *Weapons, Powder, Poison, Harness,* send *Letters*, and the like, for
the execution of the Conspiracy. If a Subject conspire with a Foreign
Prince, to invade the Realm by open hostility, and prepare for the same,
by some *Overt Act*, this is a sufficient *Overt Act* for the Death of the King.
4thly. A Conspiracy is had to levy War, this is no Treason by this Act,
untill it be levied, therefore it is no *Overt Act*, or manifest Proof of the
compassing the Death of the King within this Act; for the Words are (*de
ceo &c. thereof*) that is, of the compassing of the Death. The Wisdom of
the Makers of this Law would not make *bare Words* to be Treason, seeing
such Variance commonly among the Witnesses, about the same, as few
of them agree together.

In the Preamble of the Statute of 1. Mar. (concerning the Repeal of certain Treasons declared after this Statute of 25. *Edw.* 3. and before that

---

4. A by-then common phrase in legal Latin, meaning an "overt act." In this instance
it appears to have been drawn from the introduction of *British Liberties* (London: H.
Woodfall and W. Strahan, 1766), p. 66, a compilation of important documents dealing
with the subject, beginning with Magna Carta.

Time, and bringing all things to the Measures of this Statute) it was agreed by the whole Parliament, that Laws justly made for the Preservation of the Common Wealth, without extreme Punishment, are more often obeyed and kept, than Laws and Statutes made with great and extreme Punishments. And in special, such Laws and Statutes so made, whereby not only the ignorant, and rude unlearned People, but also learned and expert People, minding Honesty, are often Times trapped and snared, yea many Times for *words only*, without other Fact or Deed done or perpetrated. Therefore this Act of the 25. *Ed.* 3. doth provide that there must be an OVERT ACT. 5. As to Treason by *levying* War against the King, we must Note, that though conspiring or compassing to levy War, without a War, *de Facto*, be no Treason, yet if many conspire a War, and only some few actually levy it, all are Guilty of the Treason. Raising a Force to burn or throw down a particular Inclosure, is only a *Riot*, but if it had been to have gone from Town to Town, to throw down all Inclosures, or to change Religion, or the like, it were levying of War, because the intended Mischief is Public. Holding a Fort or Castle against the Kings Forces is levying War. 6. Counterfeiting the Great, or Privy Seal, is Treason; but it must be an actual Counterfeiting thereof, compassing to do it is no Treason: affixing the Great Seal by the Chancellor, without Warrant, is no Treason: fixing a New Great Seal to another Patent, is a great Misprison, but no Treason, being not counterfeiting within this Act: but Aiders and Consenters are within this Act. 7. Treason concerning Coin, is counterfeiting the King's Coin; and this was Treason at Common Law, and Judgment only as of Petty Treason; but clipping, &c. being made Treason by other Statutes, the Judgment is to be Drawn, Hanged, and Quartered. Money here, extends only to the proper Money of this Realm. 8. As this Statute leaves all other doubtful Matters to be declared Treason in Parliament, but not to be punished as such, till so declared. So in succeeding King's Reigns, abundance of other Matters were declared Treason, which being found very Grievous and Dangerous, by the Statute 1. Mar. it is inacted that thenceforth no Act, Deed, or Offence, being by Act of Parliament, or Statute, made Treason, Petty Treason, or Misprison of Treason, by Words, Writing, Ciphering, Deeds, or otherwise however, shall be taken, had, deemed, or adjudged to be High Treason, Petty Treason, or Misprison of Treason, but only such as be declared and expressed to be Treason, Petty Treason, or Misprison of Treason, by this Statute of 25. *Ed.*3.

Here we rest the Matter, my Lords, convinced the Author of NUMBER III, is not within the meaning of this Statute, nor any exposition of it, and that the Design of your Lordships in adding the Epithet Treasonable, was wicked, base, and infamous, and will be sure to secure to you the Contempt and Detestation of every Honest Man.

To the People of ENGLAND and AMERICA.

On the 31st of *March* will be published, Price 1s 6d.
in Quarto, on a fine Paper and new Type,

The Prophecy of R u i n, a Poem.

Ense velut Stricto, quoties Lucilius ardens
Infremuit, rubet Auditor cui frigida Mens est,
Criminibus, tacita sudant Praecordia Culpa.

JUVENAL.

Sharp as a Sword Lucilius *drew his Pen,*
And struck with panic Terror guilty Men,
At his just Strokes the harden'd Wretch would start,
Feel the cold Sweat, and tremble *at the Heart.*

Printed and published for the Authors, by T. W. SHAW, in Fleet Street, opposite Anderton's Coffee House, where Letters to the Publisher will be thankfully received.

THE

CRISIS

NUMBER IX   *To be continued Weekly.*

SATURDAY, *March 18, 1775*   [*Price Two-pence Half-penny.*

The worst of all Tyranny
is that established by Law.

To the K I N G.

S I R,

YOU, Sir, ascended the Throne of these Realms with Advantages, which if properly improved, would have rendered your Reign, not only Glorious and Happy, but have made you the most powerful Monarch upon Earth; you might have kept the World in awe. Yet, O! shame to tell, though the Times demand it, you soon sacrificed your own Peace, the Tranquility, Honour, and Interest, of this Great and mighty Kingdom, to the Ambitious views, and Pernicious designs, of your infernal Minion Lord *Bute*, and his profligate, abandoned Adherents. Your Accession to the Throne, filled with Joy, the Breast of every Englishman; but alas, it was of short Duration, you soon convinced them of their Mistake, and the Compliments paid to your Understanding, the calm Hour of Reason soon convinced us, were ill founded.

No sooner seated upon the Throne of this vast Empire, than you, like all other Kings, as well as Tyrants, made the People many and fair Promises: you told your Parliament, that the suppression of VICE and IMMO-RALITY, the Encouragement of TRADE and COMMERCE, and the preservation of PEACE and HARMONY amongst your *People,* should be the RULE of your Conduct, and your principal STUDY. How far you have kept your Word, the sacred Pen of Truth shall now declare.

Scarce seated in regal Dignity, before you drove from your Presence and Councils, by the Advice of your *Scotch* Favourite Lord *Bute,* every Man of HONOUR and INTEGRITY, who was valued for Love to his Country, and affection for your Family. You implicitly followed the Advice of your Northern Minion, and in their Room, took those only, who were the most Conspicuous for their Vices, and the most abandoned in Principle, these are FACTS, which *Sandwich, Bute, Grafton,*[1] *North,* &c. will confirm.

These Men, you still continue to countenance, every scene of Iniquity, they have been concerned in, and every Act of Violence, Oppression, and Murder, they have committed, has been by you, tacitly approved, nay, Applauded. Adultery, Debauchery, and Divorces, are more frequent now, than in the corrupt and profligate Days of *Charles* the Second, these, Sir, prove incontestably, your religious Principles, and show how far you have suppressed VICE and IMMORALITY.

It will now be necessary to enquire how far you have encouraged TRADE and COMMERCE, was it by illegally imposing a STAMP Duty on the *Americans,* and taxing those Commodities which we supplied them with from this Country, which has stopped for near Six Years, a great Traffic between this Kingdom and the Colonies? Was it by suffering with the most shameful Impunity; the *Portuguese* to infringe upon the Privileges of the *English* Merchants at *Lisbon,* by

---

1. Augustus Henry Fitzroy, third Duke of Grafton, headed his own ministry (1768–1770) between those of Pitt (Chatham) and North. He was as often criticized as complimented for his attempts to steer a moderate political course—to not allow constitutional questions or divisive policy issues to disrupt the workings of government.

which many were not only Injured, but almost totally Ruined? Was it by blocking up the Port, and destroying the Trade of the Town of Boston; thereby reducing to a state of Miserable dependence, more than 30,000 People, and giving a vital Stab to the whole Commerce of America?

We will now examine, Sir, how far you have preserved Peace and Harmony among your people; was it by providing for all the Beggarly Relations, and miserable Dependents, of your *Scotch* Minion, in preference to your English Subjects, especially those who were the chief Instruments of placing your Family upon the Throne? was it by ordering the late Lord Hallifax to issue an ILLEGAL Warrant for apprehending Mr. WILKES? was it by rewarding that Delinquent after he had been found Guilty of a Breach of the English Laws? was it by screening your Minister behind the Throne, who violated the Rights of the Freeholders of England? Was it by rejecting the Petitions of your injured Subjects, and laughing at the Remonstrance presented to you from the first City in the World, the great Capital of the British Empire? Was it by NOT granting the Supplications of your People, and *meanly* referring those *Petitions* and *Remonstrances* to the Consideration of those very Men, whose Conduct they arraigned, and who were only the slavish Tools of your abandoned Ministers? Was it by sending Troops to *Boston*, depriving the People of their constitutional Rights, and contrary to all the Laws of this Free Country, enforcing the Tyrannical and oppressive Acts of your abandoned Parliament, with the SWORD, and laying America under a MILITARY GOVERNMENT?[2] Was it by rewarding the *Profligate,* the *Corrupt,* and the Plunderers of their Country, with TITLES and HONOURS? Was it by a *tame, dastardly* Submission, to the Insults of the *Spaniards,* and a

2. Technically speaking, the Massachusetts Government Act (see supra II.1) had not introduced military government and the troops sent to Boston in 1774 were in as nebulous a position as their predecessors had been in 1768. Major General Thomas Gage, as their commander—and as the Bay Colony's governor—found it virtually impossible to reverse the flow of power away from imperial authority and toward local control. For background see John Phillip Reid's *In a Defiant Stance* (University Park, PA: Pennsylvania State University Press, 1973) and *In Defiance of the Law* (Chapel Hill, NC: University of North Carolina Press, 1981).

sacrifice of the Honour of the British Nation? These, Sir, are the Means you have made use of, for preserving Peace and Harmony among your People. But, Sir, the greatest Piece of Ministerial Villainy, and diabolical Cruelty, is still behind, it is now going through the House of Lords, and you, Sir, will soon be called upon to sign it; it is a Bill for restraining the American Fishery, and starving to Death, or driving to a state of Desperation, more than 300,000 People; consider, Sir, the fatal tendency of this Bill, determine no longer to be the Dupe of an abandoned set of Men, act from yourself, and refuse to sign an Act of Parliament, which must involve one Part of the Empire in a CIVIL WAR, and reduce Thousands of your Subjects to Poverty and Want. Let no Consideration prevail with you to execute a Deed, at the Idea of which, Humanity revolts; consider, Sir, how much this will raise the Indignation of your People HERE, when they find you are Destitute of the common Feelings of Humanity, and that you can be so easily prevailed upon to sacrifice your Subjects to the Cruel designs of your Ministers and Favourites. Give some Proof of a determined Resolution, no longer to persue Measures, which must end in the destruction of your Kingdoms, and perhaps, in the Ruin of your Family.[3]

Consider, Sir, how despisable you appear in the Eyes of the World, who, instead of Governing, suffer yourself to be Governed; who, instead of being a Leader, are Lead; who, instead of being a King, are nothing but a mere Cypher of State, while your Favourite and Ministers, were all the Appendages to Sovereignty.

It has long surprized the Kingdom, to think how you could bear such Wretches to prey upon you, to think how you could Suffer them to ag-

3. The "fishery bill" was actually much more inclusive, restraining trade between the New England colonies and the rest of the empire as well as cutting off the Newfoundland fisheries. It was the first in a series of acts that Parliament would pass in 1775 and 1776 in an attempt to drive the colonies back into line through economic warfare. For the sequence (beginning with the "fishery bill") see Pickering, ed., *Statutes*, 31:4–11 (25 George III c. 10), 31:37–43 (25 George III c. 18) and 31:135–54 (26 George II c. 5). Patriot attempts to fight back through economic warfare did no better. See my *Mechanical Metamorphosis: Technological Change in Revolutionary America* (Westport, CT: Greenwood Press, 1985) for that side of the conflict.

grandize themselves and Creatures, to possess the greatest Wealth, and to hold the first Offices in the Kingdom; and all this by imposing upon you, by making you break your Coronation-Oath; by making you violate every Promise you made with your People, and by filling your Ears with Lies, instead of Truth; how is it possible YOU can bear such Usage, which no *sensible* Man in a private Capacity can bear? and be the Dupe of the Vilest of the Creation, is so much beneath the Dignity of the Man who *pretends* to Govern, that it is astonishing such Fiends should prevail as they do; indeed they never could, unless you, Sir, like them, was inclined to establish an Arbitrary System of Government, and to set up your own WILL in opposition to the Laws of the Land.

Let me advise you, Sir, as you regard your own Prosperity, and the Welfare of your Kingdom, let me conjure you, as you value your own Safety, to consider well the fatal and ruinous Measures your Ministers are persuing, and you sanctifying with the Royal Authority; consider the Miserable, the unfortunate Situation of this Country; think on the Dangers which threaten it on every side; consider, we are now upon the Eve of a Civil War with our Colonies; from the present Face of things, it is inevitable; Trade and Commerce is at a stand, and all the Horrors of Wretchedness and Want, stare them in the Face; consider, Sir, the feelings of Men, reduced in the short space of a few Days, through wanton Acts of Power, from a state of Ease and Plenty, to that of Misery and Famine, I ask, is it possible for them to set Bounds to their Resentment; consider, Sir, the French and Spaniards will not long remain idle Spectators, when once they see us deeply engaged in a War with the Colonies. Throw off then your supine Indolence; awake from your Lethargic State; and if you will not be excited by the desire of doing GOOD, awake at least to a Sense of your OWN DANGER: think when the general Calamity comes on, who will be the Objects of Public hatred. Will not the Advisers of these destructive Measures, be the first Sacrifices to the popular Resentment. When the Merchants, Traders, and Manufacturers, are starving; when the whole Body of the People are in Misery and Distress, what Security, Sir, can you expect to find? Where will your Ministers conceal themselves; they will not be Safe even within the Walls of your Palace?

Let these things, Sir, be well weighed, and no longer persuade yourself
the People was made for you, and not you for them; no longer believe
that you do not Govern for them but for yourself; that the People Live
only to increase your Glory, or to furnish Matter for your Pleasure: for
once, Sir, consider what you may do for them, and not what you may
draw from them.

The People, Sir, think it to be a Crime of the first Magnitude, to convert
that power to their Hurt, which was intended for their Good: and to
obey a King, while he Acts in this Manner, and tramples under Foot all
Laws, Divine and Human, argues not only a want of Sense in the highest
Degree, but a want of Love for our Country, and a disregard for ourselves
and Posterity.

Your Subjects, Sir, are under no Obligations to you, nor do they owe
you any *Allegiance*, any longer than you continue to *protect* them, and
make their Good, the chief end of your Government.[4] When a Prince
assumes to himself an extravagant, or an unlawful Power, then all Respect ceases; and he ceases to be a King: whilst he Protects and Pre-
serves his People in their just Right, and Governs them by the Laws
of the Land, all good Men will Love and Esteem him, and risk their
Lives and Fortunes in his Service; but when he begins to invade their
Liberties, to set up an Arbitrary Power, to impose unlawful Taxes,
raise Forces, and make War upon his People, and suffer Foreign States

---

4. By this point colonial protests had made it clear—see, for example, Thomas Jef-
ferson's [anon.] *A Summary View of the Rights of British America* (Williamsburg, VA:
Clementia Rind, 1774) and James Wilson's [anon.] *Considerations on the Nature and the
Extent of the Legislative Authority of the British Parliament* (Philadelphia: William and
Thomas Bradford, 1774)—that the ties that bound the empire could be unbound: that
the empire had been formed by compact, the colonists having returned to a state of nature when they settled on the far Atlantic shore, which they only left behind when they
voluntarily rejoined themselves to Britain. When they entered that political compact
they did so with the king, not parliament, and the king had as many responsibilities to
them as he had rights over them. For this view of the crown and empire see Richard L.
Bushman, *King and People in Provincial Massachusetts* (Chapel Hill, NC: University of
North Carolina Press, 1992).

to insult and injure them; then all Virtuous and Good Men, will detest and abhor him, and endeavour to remove him from a Throne, he unworthily fills.

In such cases, resistance is a Virtue, and to say that some should passively Suffer, lest by resisting they should cause the Ruin of many, is not a just Reason; because, in all Probability, they will be the Cause that Millions unborn, shall Live Happy and Free, and what can be a more Noble, Glorious, and Pious Motive for Suffering, than to transmit Liberty to Posterity: for this our Fathers bravely Fought, and many of them gloriously Fell, to preserve themselves and their descendants Free, and to destroy the Tyranny and Despotism of the *Stuarts*; and, Sir, let me beg you will reminder with Gratitude, to place your Family upon the Throne of the British Empire.[5]

The Author of this Paper, is far from advising violent Measures, upon every Error, or Misconduct of a Prince, but Resistance becomes a Duty, when they attempt the Ruin of the state, the subversion of Liberty, or overturning the Constitution of the Kingdom. It is notorious to the World, Sir, that your Ministers are Guilty of all these black, and deadly Crimes, and yet you Screen and Protect them; the Conclusions to be drawn from thence are obvious, and you, like *Charles,* may Live to see Your Favourites FALL.

---

5. The men behind *The Crisis* had almost certainly read about the right to resist unjust government in John Locke's *Second Treatise of Government*, sections 149, 155, 243, most accessible in Peter Laslett, ed., *Two Treatises of Government* (Cambridge: Cambridge University Press, 1960), pp. 149–50, 155–56, and 427–28, resp. Even Blackstone in his *Commentaries*, Book I, Chap. 1 (at 1:119–23) and Chap. 7 (at 1:243–44) had conceded the natural right to resist tyranny. Blackstone did not, however, consider that natural right as existing within the purview of English constitutional rights; thus his juxtaposition of the theoretical with the actual, thereby keeping the former and the latter distinct.

To the People of ENGLAND and AMERICA.

On the 31st of *March* will be published, Price 1s 6d.
in Quarto, on a fine Paper and new Type,

The Prophecy of R U I N, a Poem.

Ense velut Stricto, quoties Lucilius ardens
Infremuit, rubet Auditor cui frigida Mens est,
Criminibus, tacita sudant Praecordia Culpa.

JUVENAL.

Sharp as a Sword Lucilius *drew his Pen,*
And struck with panic Terror guilty Men,
At his just Strokes the harden'd Wretch would start,
Feel the cold Sweat, and tremble *at the Heart.*

Printed and published for the Authors, by T. W. SHAW, in Fleet Street, opposite Anderton's Coffee House, where Letters to the Publisher will be thankfully received.

THE

CRISIS

NUMBER X   *To be continued Weekly.*

SATURDAY, MARCH 25, 1775   [*Price Two-pence Half-penny.*

LETTER II.

To the Right Honourable LORD APSLEY, Lord Chancellor of England.

My LORD,   *March 6,* 1775.

I SHALL begin this letter to your Lordship, with an extract of a Letter, I addressed some Time since, to Lord Mansfield, because I knew how exactly your Lordship's *capacity is fitted, to think just as he thinks.*

To him observed;—to your Lordship I repeat it.—

"That in matters of private Property, we see the same byass and Inclination, to depart from the decision of your Predecessors, which you certainly ought to receive, as evidence of Common Law: Instead of those certain positive Rules, by which the Judgement of a Court of Law, should invariably be determined; you have fondly introduced, your own unsettled notions, of equity, and *substantial* Justice. Decisions given upon such Principles, do not alarm the Public, so much as they ought; because the Consequence, and tendency of EACH PARTICULAR INSTANCE, is not observed, or regarded." But the Day is now come my Lord;—the Public have taken the Alarm;—your Lordships lawless Decision, in the court of Chancery, in the Cause of THICKNESS and LIEGE, and the Mannner in which it was corruptly Affirmed in the House of Lords, has shook the Kingdom to its very Basis.—Till that fatal Day my Lord, the supreme Tribunal of this Country, stood un-impeached and un-polluted, as to Matters of Private Property: But that was a Day in which a Deed was done, that even *Lord Mansfield* durst not become a Partisan.

That Day, my Lord, was only a grievous Day, to the Appellant: but it will prove a fatal Blow to BRITAIN.

When the Foundations of Justice, are so corrupted, that the first Law Officer in the Kingdom, shall dare to stand forth, in the highest Court of Judicature, knowing that he has *assistant Judges,* determined to support him in reading Letters containing the Opinions of Men, not Judges in that Court; in order to affirm a Decree unsupported by Argument, and in direct contradiction to a former and recent Judgment of that House; the Day cannot be very remote, when the Nation, the Laws and the Violators of them, will all be involved in one COMMON RUIN.

You Lordship is now brought to a greater TRIBUNAL, than even the House of Lords.

The Tribunal of the P U B L I C.

You stand Charged my Lord, at that awful Bar, with setting at Defiance, those Laws you were so shamefully appointed to support, in order to confirm a wicked Decree, without Law to sustain it, or an Argument to give even a Colour to shade it. You did it my Lord, by the assistance, of that BUCKHORE BULLY, Lord Denbigh, who assassinated Justice, and stifled every Idea of Honor, or Humanity; till he had driven every honest Man, but LORD CAMDEN, out of the House! He, it is true, was not to be menaced from his Duty, by the grossest Language: nor frightened from his Post, by the foulest Fiend who ever appeared in human form.

Are you not afraid, my Lord, to lie down in your Bed, knowing—for you do know it; that you have sacrificed a whole Family to your Vanity, and thereby ruined a Gentleman, who has eight Children; the Eldest of whom, is next Heir, to a Seat in that House, you have so openly dishonoured, by plundering his Father, and Family, of their legal Property.

I have seen, my Lord, a Copy of this Gentlemans Letter, written to his Eldest Son, now at Giberalter, the Day after he was sacrificed at the Altar of *Ministerial Justice.*

In that pathetic Letter, my Lord, the highly injured, and deeply afflicted Father, after informing his Son with the foul doings of your Lordship, and your wicked Coadjutors,—adds;

"And now my dear Son, let me call upon you, as your affectionate Father, and as your faithful Friend, (for be assured I am both) never to enter the House of Lords, without casting your Eyes about you, and saying; IN THIS HOUSE MY FATHER WAS DEFRAUDED OF TEN THOUSAND POUNDS: and if ever you should be called to sit in Judgement there, never take your Seat in it, without looking up to Heaven, and calling upon GOD, in a short Prayer; to enable you upon every Occasion, to divest yourself of all Party-Zeal; all personal Pique; all private Resentment; and so to enlighten your Mind, and direct your Heart, that in all you say, or do, it may be conformable to that Godlike precept, OF DOING, AS YOU WOULD BE DONE BY.—If you do not this; then, to GOD, I offer up this, my fervent Prayer.—That you may never have any Voice where Justice ought to be Administered."

Can your Lordship sustain the horrid Reflection, of the Deed you have done? (OF THAT 𝕭𝖑𝖆𝖈𝖐 𝕯𝖆𝖞'𝖘 𝖂𝖔𝖗𝖐!) Can the SOOTHING GENTLE MANNERS of that flattering low born [†]*Perrin,* or the Smiles of your obsequious Register, divert you from feeling the most pungent Remorse? or do they, by telling you, *how much they approve your Decree,* make your pliant Mind easy? My Lord, I know they tell you so, but I will tell you, my Lord, that they durst not say so, to any LAWYER.

[†]He is the Son of an old Cloaths Man.

There is but one Opinion among them, and that is, (you shall hear it my Lord, while *Junius* can hold a Pen, and you the Seals) That Lord *Mansfield* singled your Lordship out, as a vain, weak, and wicked Wretch; to support the same false, and unsettled Doctrines in the Court of Chancery, which he has so long, and so shamefully practised, in the Court of King's Bench; and which he has Address enough to give sanction to, even *without appearing in Person,* to Appeals in the House of Lords.

When Lord Camden, with that gentleness of Manners, which ever accompanies solid Sense, and unshaken Integrity; told your Lordship, that no Mans Opinion, however high his Station, or however great his Abilities, if not a Judge in that Court, could be produced or Read, lest it should influence any of the Lords in their Judgments; you had the Boldness to stand forth, and casting down your Hat, with which you ought to have hid your Face;—you persisted in reading Sir *William De Grey*'s Letter; because your Bully, Lord Denbigh, said he would Read another to the same Purpose, if he had it.

Sir William De Grey's Letter was then Read by your Lordship! his Opinion *it seems, coincided with the Duke of Chandois's, Lord Denbigh's,* and the two Scotch Lords, *who sat for Lord Mansfield.*

By these *worthy Peers,* my Lord, and Two *silent Bishops,* your Lordship's (*I mean Sir William De Grey's*) *Decree*, was affirmed, without a Division!

The Weak and Feeble efforts of Lord Camden, *were over-powered, by your Lordship's great Abilities; and nobly sustained by Lord Denbigh, and your other auxilliary Troops.*

That Sir William De Grey's detection, has produced in him, both Shame and Fear, is very obvious; for he never suspected you would so openly Publish his *secret Instructions*; as his Letter to the Appellant THICK-NESS, will clearly Evince; and I make no Doubt, if I can *prevail* upon your Lordship, to attend to what the World thinks, and to understand what I say, you will be equally ashamed;—though I confess, not equally Criminal, with Sir William De Grey.—I say not equally Criminal, my Lord; for God forbid I should think the Crimes of so contemptable a Wretch as your Lordship, are equal to those of a Man as capable of Tortureing, at once, the Laws; and involving them, and a whole Family, in one common Ruin, as even Lord *Mansfield* himself.

Copy of Sir William De Grey's Letter, to PHILIP THICKNESS, Esq.

S I R,

I Am very Sorry that you press me so much to speak more explicitly upon the Subject of your Letter.

I do not think that I can, with Propriety, give an Answer to the Question you are pleased to ask me.

I am, Sir,

your most Obedient,

Februrary 21, 1775   humble Servant,

WILLIAM DE GREY.

In a former Paper (No. VII.) I gave your Lordship a Copy of Sir William De Grey's first prevaricating Letter, to the Appellant Thickness; on that Letter I made but one Comment; on this, I shall, at present, make only one other: either Sir William De Grey (I will not blot my Paper with calling him a Chief Justice) cannot Support Lord *Mansfield's Decree*, and is ashamed to repeat your Lordships unmeaning Jargon, about *substantive* Gifts; or, he has received *farther Orders.*

I shall conclude this Letter to your Lordship, by observing, that there are still a few People, disposed to think Favorably of you; and to impute the black Part of this Transaction, to Sir William De Grey; because they confess the Weakness of your Head, and Lament, as a National Misfortune; that a Man of such contemptible Abilities, as your Lordship's, and AT SUCH A TIME TOO, should disgrace the British Nation; in holding the highest Law-Department in it; without Talents to acquit yourself with common Decency, even in the Lowest; but some Men are still, willing to hope you are Honest.

Now, my Lord, for their Sake, and for your own also; either Answer the following Question, fairly, and openly, or for Ever decline holding out

Lights to dazzle the World with false Marks of your Virtue or Integrity. Would the selling a Living to Dr. Dodd, or his Buying it of you, have been Half so Criminal, as what you are now charged with?

Did not your late deceased Brother, Mr. Benjamin Bathurst, keep his Money, when he had any, at Messrs. Hoares, in Fleet-Street?[1] And did he not frequently over draw, on that very respectable House? My Lord he did;—you know he did: and did not you, his Executor, when you settled his Affairs, and possessed his Property, refuse to allow that House, a Sum of Money, your necessitious Brother, had over-drawn upon it, under the Shameful, Shameful! did I say?—under the Infamous pretence, that they could not recover it.—*The Time* being lapsed!

If this be true my Lord, and Facts *you know* are obstinate things. The World will then be as fully satisfied about the *rectitude* of your Heart, as they have always been about the extent of your Genius. They will then all be of one Mind, as to your Lordship, whatever they think of

J U N I U S .

I never yet knew a Man perfectly Sober, taking Pains to convince every Man he met, that he was so; but a drunken Man is always acting the Part of a Sober one: when you rung the Alarum about Dr. Dodd,[2] I violently suspected YOU, and soberly set you down for the Man, all the World will now believe you to be. And therefore I must repeat what I said before, the Nation will no longer bear with you; your Lordship cannot after such FOUL PROCEEDINGS, HOLD THE GREAT SEAL.

---

1. Benjamin Bathurst, Lord Apsley's older brother, died before he could succeed his father as Earl Bathurst. Apsley would inherit the Bathurst title in September 1775, when he was already lord chancellor (see supra VII.2). Henry Hoare ran the very successful family bank on Fleet Street begun by his grandfather, Sir Richard Hoare, over a century before.

2. William Dodd, Anglican reverend with an LL.D. from Cambridge, became a public figure through his popularity as a preacher and profligacy in his private life. His foibles proved fatal when he was hanged in May 1777 for forgery, a case that saddened some and infuriated others. Philip Rawlings presents him as a pathetic, even tragic figure in his *Oxford DNB*, 16:400–402 sketch.

*₊*CAMBYSES,[3] King of Persia, finding that his CHIEF JUSTICE, *Sisamnes*, had Pronounced an unjust Sentence, caused him to be Executed and Flayed, and with his Skin, covered the common Seat of Justice; then constituted *Otanes* his Son, Judge in his room, he sat My Lord upon his Fathers Skin; which probably put him in mind of his own: And *Perrin* will make the application for your Lordship, and if he is not ashamed, remind your Lordship, of the Fate of the two *time serving* Judges, EPSOM and DUDLEY, who were hanged in the Reign of Henry the 7th—of this Transaction, one of the greatest Lawyers and most upright Judges this Nation ever was blest with, makes this remarkable *Epiphonema*.

"Qui eorum vestigus insistunt, eorum Exitus prehorres cant.[4]

"Those that dare tread in their Steps, let them dread, or expect, the same dismal end."

In my next I shall lay before the Public some farther traits of your Lordships public and private Life, for be assured I will never drop my Attention to you, while you continue to hold the Seals.

☞ The Public are desired to observe, the cunning of that most artful, as well as most wicked of Men, LORD MANSFIELD. His Lordship first planned the affirming the Decree, made by his Chancellor in the above-Cause, in order to reak his private Vengeance on

---

3. According to Book 5 of Herodotus's *History*—available in a number of editions translated by Isaac Littlebury—Sisamnes had been a judge during the reign of the Persian king Cambyses II. The king had the judge executed for accepting a bribe in settling one case, after which his skin was flayed and attached to the seat where his successor sat. His successor was his own son, Otanes, now duly warned of the price of corruption.

4. This Latin phrase was copied (imperfectly), along with the English translation, from Philo-Dicaios, *The Triumphs of Justice over Unjust Judges* (London: Benjamin Harrison, 1681), p. 18. The comment had been offered originally by Sir Edward Coke in the fourth part of his *Institutes*, in reference to Richard Epsom and Edmund Dudley, judges who had vigorously enforced tax laws and collected fines at the instigation of Henry VII. They were arrested, imprisoned in the Tower of London and beheaded in 1510 by order of Henry VIII, essentially to silence critics and solidify the new king's hold on power. Richard Perryn, a judge who had risen to the bench through the court of chancery, was well-known for his preference toward lenity when deciding the fate of the guilty. He would rise to the court of exchequer the next year, as Sir Richard Perryn.

THICKNESS, and then, in a Matter in which he was totally indifferent about the Issue, he *affects to* correct Lords L.D. SPENCER,[5] and DENBIGH, for Interferring in nice points of Law.—This repremand, *was taken in good Part,*—the two Lords were *instantly convinced of their Error.* They made proper and public Acknowledgement, of their ignorance in the Tythe Cause; but Lord Denbighs Villainy in the former Cause, is to pass unnoticed.

J U N I U S.

On the 3d. Day of *April,* will be Published, (Price 1s. 6d.)

The Prophecy of R U I N, a Poem.

Printed and published for the Authors, by T. W. SHAW, in Fleet-Street, opposite Anderton's Coffee House, where Letters to the Publisher will be thankfully received.

---

5. Sir Francis Dashwood, son of a baronet, had been elevated as the eleventh Baron Le Despencer over a decade before. He was famous, even infamous, by then, as a rake, a hedonist rumored to engage in orgies and black magic rituals with friends in the onetime monastery at Medmenham that he had converted into the site of his romps, making his group one of the most notorious of these gentlemen's clubs. He took an active role in politics in the Lords, as he had in the Commons before, and he served for a time as chancellor of the exchequer in Bute's ministry. Patrick Woodland wrote the sketch of him in the *Oxford DNB,* 15:222–24. He is grouped with other pleasure seekers of his day in Donald McCormick's *The Hell-Fire Club* (London: Jarrrolds, 1958).

THE

CRISIS

NUMBER XI   *To be continued Weekly.*

SATURDAY, April 1, 1775   [*Price Two-pence Half-penny.*

THIS Country is now reduced to a Situation really Degrading and Deplorable, through the strange Obstinacy and weak Prejudices of the King, who is determined, even at the risk of his own SAFETY, the Preservation of the Kingdom, and contrary to the united voice of his People, to encourage and protect an abandoned set of Men in the DESTRUCTION of that Constitution, he was Sworn to SUPPORT and DEFEND.

History fatally informs us, that the English have been driven to extremes, by Causes of less Moment than those, which have shaken this Kingdom during the present Reign.

Since the last stupendous Revolution, it has been generally believed, that the nature of our Constitution, became clearly ascertained, and fixt on Firmer and more lasting Principles, than it had known before that glorious Æra; at least the obtaining these Ends, as well as redressing Grievances, are acknowledged to be the Motives to the transactions of those Times.[1] For had the exorbitant Power of the Crown been left *unlimitted*

---

1. For many on both sides of the Atlantic, the Glorious Revolution would mark the birth of Britain's modern political age, the point at which crown and parliament had been brought into proper alignment. It would be used by the authors of *The Crisis* as the

and *unsettled*, as before that event, and the Liberties and Privileges of the Subjects of England, in the same undecided State; it would have been only to change the Name of Masters, and not the Nature of their Sovereignty. And, if instead of removing the Causes of our Sufferings, and fixing our Rights and Liberties, we then gave to a House of Commons, an unlimited Power to dispose of the last according to their Inclination; it was only changing the Possessors of Arbitrary Power, by granting to a PROSTITUTED set of Representitives what was denied the King; and thus this illustrious Action of the Revolution, must appear to be the result of Faction, and aversion to one Interest, or unwarrantable Zeal for another. In what Manner can a Nation be more settled in its Freedom, by transferring ARBITRARY POWER from one Part of the Constitution to another.

It cannot be denied, but that the Laws, which were then enacted to establish upon a Foundation not to be again Shaken, the Freedom of the English Nation, and the Liberties of the People ought to be considered, as Unalterable, the very Basis and Boundary of the King's Prerogative, and the Rights of Englishmen, something in the Government like the Center *in* the Earth, the fixt Point, round which all Things move and to which they tend.

Those Acts which were made at the Revolution, relative to the Constitution, such as the BILL of RIGHTS, and afterwards in Consequence of it THE ACT OF SETTLEMENT,[2] which may be justly deemed the *com-*

---

benchmark for debates over excessive crown prerogative or constitutional issues such as the stationing of soldiers among civilians. Those who held true to the principles of that revolution—as they had been idealized after the fact—were understood to be true Whigs, dedicated to restoring the mixed and balanced government endangered by James II and his vestigial Stuart absolutism. For an ambitious take on what actually occurred then, as well as what has been said since, see Steven Pincus's *1688:The First Modern Revolution* (New Haven: Yale University Press, 2009)

2. These are two of the key texts in popular memory that justified the events of 1688–1689 as a "glorious revolution," and they are readily available in print and online. For both texts, in context, see E. Neville Williams, *The Eighteenth-Century Constitution* (Cambridge: Cambridge University Press, 1960), pp. 26–32 (for the 1689 bill of rights) and pp. 56–59 (for the 1701 act of settlement).

pact between the *House of Hanover* and the *People of England*, and which was preserved Inviolate, till broken by the *unhallowed* Hands of the Present SOVEREIGN and his Ministers; are undoubtedly of a Nature more SACRED than those which established a Turnpike Road.

Those Acts founded on our former Rights in MAGNA CHARTA, ought to be considered as the essential Authority by which the House of Commons exists, than Laws which a Parliament may Abrogate, through pure Inclination to indulge a King, or his Ministers, to make them Despotic, and the People Miserable; for it must appear strangely absurd in a Constitution, that the Representatives of the People who form a third Part of it, should be Authorised by them to destroy their Liberties, and thereby exclude them from the Rights which they possess in the Government of the Kingdom? Besides, it is contrary to the very Idea of a *free* State, that a People should have given a Power of *sacrificing* their Privileges, to Men chosen the Guardians of them.

Something must exist in a FREE STATE, which no Part of it can be authorised to alter or destroy, otherwise the Idea of a Constitution cannot Subsist; for unless we allow the Freeholders and Electors of GREAT BRITAIN to be *superior* to a House of Commons, we grant to them an ABSOLUTE POWER, a Power inconsistent with the Notion of a FREE PEOPLE, and destructive of the Principles of a MIXED GOVERNMENT.

Should it be acknowledged, that, though the Commons have exercised a power of annihilating many Privileges and Rights, belonging to the People, and, that they possess no legal Title to it; then all Laws subversive of Magna Charta, the Bill of Rights, act of Settlement, and spirit of the Constitution, are an excess of their Authority, and a Violation of their Trust; for which the present INFAMOUS PARLIAMENT, ought not only to be dissolved, but every MEMBER who visibly engaged in the Destruction of the Peoples Rights, should suffer DEATH, together with those Hellish MINISTERS who formed a design of enslaving the People; and it must be equally Just, as well as Necessary, to call to a strict Account the FIRST MAGISTRATE, who could be base enough to encourage the Destruction of our LIBERTIES and a SUBVERSION of the noblest Constitution in the World; as an Example to future Kings and Ministers.

If any Ministerial Hireling should assert that our Representatives after the Hour of Election, are no longer answerable for their Conduct, and are legally invested with Authority to Destory our Rights and Liberties at their Pleasure; then, what did King James do more than this by his Prerogative? and of what Advantage has the Revolution proved to us, if Subverting the Constitution be legally placed in the Hands of the Representatives? in what Sense does the Idea of a Free State, or the Liberty of the PEOPLE exist, when it depends upon nothing more permanent or established, than the vague, rapacious, or interested inclination of a Majority of FIVE HUNDRED and FIFTY EIGHT MEN, open to the insidious Attacks of a WEAK, or DESIGNING PRINCE, and his MINISTERS? surely it will be granted, that whether King, or Minister, who by undue influence should prevail in passing Laws subversive of the Statutes before mentioned, must be deemed an Offender against the most sacred of all Human Enjoyments, Liberty and the Constitution of his Country, and equally Criminal with JAMES THE SECOND and his Ministers.

The whole presumptive Title a Parliament can pretend to have of disposing of our RIGHTS and PREVILEGES can be but PREROGATIVE, which in many instances has been illegally carried beyond the Limits of Liberty and the Constitution. It is therefore necessary we should recur to the Spirit of the Constitution with the strictest Rigour and Perseverance.

The only Reason that can be given, why our Forefathers in the ancient Fundamental Statutes of the Realm, have delivered nothing verbally explicit on this Head; of limiting the Power of their Representatives, derives its Origin from the same Cause that the ROMANS had no Laws against Parricide: they never conceived that the thought of BETRAYING or SELLING a PEOPLES LIBERTIES, any more than MURDERING a FATHER could enter the Human Heart: they never imagined that the Representative could ever possess an Interest distinct from that of his Constituent, or that pecuniary Advantage could outweigh the Public good in his Breast: they did not foresee, that MINISTERS might have Occasion to OPPRESS US, for the Gratification of a WEAK or WICKED PRINCE; or that ENGLISHMEN no longer animated by the Soul of Public Prosperity, might Degenerate into granting OPPRESSIVE TAXES, till the NATION would be brought within ONE STEP of RUIN: Or that Laws essential to the Establishment of Freedom and Security of the State, could be made to burst at the Mandate of a Minister, by the Breach of a Majority of Five Hundred and Fifty Eight Men.

When the Representatives of the People Act contrary to the very Elements of the Constitution, betray and give up the RIGHTS, PRIVILEGES, and LIBERTIES of the PEOPLE, though nothing in the Fundamental Statutes literally prohibit so ignominious a Behaviour; the very Nature of their Station, the innate sense of Right, and Original Spirit of Government, directly contradict all possibility of their having Title for such proceedings; and whenever it is done, it is an unjust and wanton Exertion of Power, and not of Authority: add to this dreadful and heinous Crime the indignant and humiliating Consideration, that our Equals whom we chuse to save, have sold us like our Cattle to a WEAK (not to say worse) KING, and his accursed MINISTERS, who have paid our Betrayers with a Part of that Money which was most unjustly levied on us, not to Answer the NECESSITY of Government, but for the most Infamous and Villainous Purposes.

The Particulars mentioned in the Bill of Rights, at the Revolution, were then considered as so many Violations committed by King James, on the Previleges of the People, and necessary to be remedied, for the sake of securing our Religion, and reestablishing Liberty and the Constitution.

The Grievances at that Time complained of against the Sovereign, had their Foundation in Justice and the Rights of the People and the redressing them in the Nature of the Constitution: otherwise, by what Arguments could be assigned a Cause of Complaint against the Prince on the Throne or preserve those Men who accomplished the Revolution from the imputation of Traitors and Rebels to their King.

They considered the Constitution as the primary Object of an Englishman; and the King but as the Secondary; who by his attempts towards Despotism, became a Rebel against this superior Power. They justly reasoned, that as the People, who make a Third of the Constitution, are deemed Traitors, for plotting or attempting the life of, or taking up Arms against the King, who forms another Third of the Constitution, and doomed to Death in consequence of such Behaviour; in like Manner King JAMES rebelled against two Thirds of the Government, by attempting to subvert their Religion and Liberties: for our Constitution, supposes, that each Part of it has a Right to be preserved; that Two are more than One; and the Happiness of a whole PEOPLE to be preserved, in preference to the Ambition or pernicious Passion or Designs of a King.

Shall then the present Sovereign and his Ministers be exempted from a strict and nice INQUIRY into their Conduct, because they have effected in one Method, the very Despotism which was opposed in JAMES, who was deservedly drove into Exile, for attempting it in another. Forbid it Heaven! and every Thing that is Dear to ENGLISHMEN.

To the P U B L I C.

The POEM called the PROPHECY of RUIN, repeatedly advertised to be published, in Quarto, Price 1S 6d. the Author has been unavoidably obliged to postpone from Time to Time, through a severe Illness; in order therefore to make some Compensation to the Public, for the Trouble and various Disappointments they have met with, the ENTIRE POEM will be given next *Friday* Noon, in No.12. of the CRISIS, containing Three SHEETS in FOLIO, at the *reduced Price* of 6d.

Printed and published for the Authors, by T. W. SHAW, in Fleet-Street, opposite Anderton's Coffee House, where Letters to the Publisher will be thankfully received.

T H E

C R I S I S

NUMBER XII   *To be continued Weekly.*

SATURDAY, April 8, 1775   [*Price* Six Pence.

Ense velut stricto, quoties Lucilius ardens
Infremuit, rubet Auditor cui frigida Mens est.
Criminibus, tacita sudant Pracordia Culpa.[1]

JUVENAL.

Sharp as a Sword Lucilus *drew his Pen,*
And struck with panic Terror guilty Men,
At his just Strokes the harden'd Wretch would start,
Feel the cold Sweat, and tremble *at the Heart.*

The prophecy of R u i n,
A P O E M.

S HOULD e're a Prince the British Empire sway,
  (And I be doom'd by Heav'n to see the day)
  Who quite UNMINDFUL of that glorious state
To which he's rais'd, not by *desert*, but *fate*;
Should he be *base*, be *cruel*, and *unjust*,

---

1. A passage from Juvenal, repeated; see supra I.16.

FALSE to his friends. *unworthy* that great *trust*;
Should he, *unmindful* of the good that springs
From true *royalty*, and true *patriot* Kings;
By oppression (destroying like a flood)
Cause civil war, and fill the land with BLOOD;
Should he rebel 'gainst FREEDOM, LAW, and RIGHT,
And laugh at truths which honest men should write
With fair intent, write with no other view,
But to save HIM, and save their COUNTRY too;
Such deeds as these, would fire my soul with rage,
And make me e'en against my safety, wage
War with VILL'NY, and stamp the TYRANTS crimes,
That he might live and stink to after-times.

Thrice happy, NOW, *when ev'ry* blessing springs
From GEORGE *the* THIRD; *we boast the* BEST *of* KINGS.

Curs'd be the wretch who would support a plan,
Which must destroy the natural rights of man;
Perish the wretch, who *unconcern'd* would see
The LAWS DESTROY'D, a falling MONARCHY;
I could not, I am of another breed,
I ne'er should *tamely* see my *country bleed*;
Nor crouch to him, to *truth* and *justice* dead,
Or fawning compliment an *empty* head:
Let subtle knaves, to CANDOUR more inclin'd
Disguise the *truth*, I'd always speak my mind;
Perish the thought, the crime should ne'er be mine
To sacrifice at curst ambition's shrine
The RIGHT to SPEAK, and publickly display
In all it's hideous forms DESPOTIC sway;
I ne'er should understand those *prudent* rules,
Decorum call'd by PARASITES and FOOLS;
Discretion too, should with *decorum* fall,
I ne'er would be, what rascals *decent* call;
RESENTMENT should to *injuries* be shewn,

The people, by the language too be known,
'Tis *survile* wretches who are *decent* thought,
Such as are *sold*, and those that would be *bought*:
When FREEDOM calls, none should from *danger* start,
But take a NOBLE, a *decisive* part;
I'd in the cause of FREEDOM firmly stand,
And dare the stroke, e'en of that Tyrant's hand,
Confed'rate *villains*, and their pow'r defy,
Born *free* like my *forefathers*, I would die
In that great *cause,* which is the *cause* of *all*,
Or *free* I'd live, or *glory* should I fall:
While *truth* and *justice* did my lines support,
I'd fear no King, nor Minion of that court;
Nor King, nor Minister, should *then* escape,
But share alike, the *injur'd* people's hate:
Tho' minions talk'd, and lawyers set about,
To find the LIBEL, and the AUTHOR out;
Tho' one should stare, another rascal cry,
"'Tis TREASON all, the AUTHOR ought to die."
I'd laugh at them, nor care what they could do,
In honest rhime, each VILLAIN would persue.
Should such a PRINCE succeed to England's Throne,
(Tho' BORN a BRITON, they must BLUSH to own.)
Should he keep foes of FREEDOM, and of LAW,
Such foes as keep TRUE LOYALTY in AWE;
Pervert fair JUSTICE from her even course,
And know no LAW, except the LAW of FORCE;
Should he keep such as these, close to his breast,
(Striving the *Scepter* from his hand to wrest)
Should he keep such, and of the STUART race,
Who made this Empire tremble to her base;
Should *Scotsmen* be prefer'd to BRITON's brave,
And none but *Scotsmen*, or a *Scotsman's* slave
Appear at Court, and lord it o'er the land,
Keeping all pow'r from the sovereign hand;

Should he see only with a *Scotsman's* eyes,
Be taught to mock his *injur'd Briton's* cries;
Coop'd up at Court; (like sheep shut in a penn),
Little to read, and less to know of men;
To hear such men, as had no other ends
But to serve HIM, and be their country's friends
Call'd *disloyal*, and *rebels* made appear
By base-born *Scotsmen*, always rebels HERE;
This to believe, believe it as his creed,
And through those *traitors* make all *England Bleed*:
Coop'd up at Court, and there be made a *tool*,
The greatest *slave*, as well as greatest FOOL;
Should *England's Crown* be plac'd on such a head,
What mis'ry must the people *then* not dread:
Would they not curse the *cause*, the *secret* spring,
Whence all this dire oppression came, that King,
Would they not wish, the Day which gave HIM birth,
Had ne'er disgrac'd the records of the earth;
Would they not drag those *traitors* forth to view,
Who foes to him, sought England's ruin too,
And make them answer for such horrid crimes,
Which all their race, as well as future times
Should strive to equal, or exceed in vain,
Crimes, that would leave a long, a lasting stain
Upon the land, worse than the *Stuarts*; who
BORN SLAVES, tried to make slaves of FREEMEN too,
Who bound in chains, both LIBERTY and LAW,
Quite friendless then, but Heaven sent NASSAU;
He 'gainst Slavery, made a glorious stand,
And broke those chains, which had disgrac'd the land;
With tenfold terror hurl'd his Vengeance down,
And drove a *Slave*, and *Tyrant* from the Crown,
Founded the throne in *justice*, *truth*, and *right*,
And rescu'd FREEDOM from the shades of night,
Drove *superstition*, (with her bigot crew)

Far from this land, (*James* he run with her too,)
Drove *persecution* to her seat in *Rome*,
Whilst *Tyrants* wept at *Slav'ry's* bloody tomb:
Restored to *Britain*, all the *rights* of man,
First fixt by Heav'n, on wisdom's sacred plan.

Such deeds as theirs, wou'd fire my soul with RAGE,
And make me e'en against my SAFETY, wage
War with VILL'NY, and stamp their horrid crimes,
That each might live, and stink to after-times.
Would make me call forth ancient British rage
To just revenge, or mark the coward age,

Thrice happy NOW, *when ev'ry* blessing springs,
From GEORGE the THIRD, WE boast the BEST of KINGS.

Should such a King succeed to England's Throne,
(Tho' BORN a BRITON, they must BLUSH to own)
Should he succeed, when *France* and *Spain* are leagu'd
To shake the state, and make the nation bleed;
When *France* and *Spain* by COMPACT[2] shall engage,
To ruin us, with war's destructive rage,
When Heaven sees the lives UNJUSTLY slain,
By restless *France*, join'd with ambitious *Spain*;
Sees ENGLAND bleed, her blood UNJUSTLY shed,
And hurl's down vengeance, on each guilty head;
Bids ENGLAND'S arms pull lawless power down,
And with her conquests shake each TYRANT's crown:
Should he succeed, when ENGLAND rais'd above

2. The first "family compact" between France and Spain came in 1733, when Philip V of Spain entered into an alliance with Louis XV of France. Philip V (before then, Philip, Duke of Anjou) was the grandson of Louis XIV, Louis XV's father and predecessor. Philip had been invited to take the throne when Charles II, last of the Habsburg line in Spain, died, in 1700. The British only accepted the legitimacy of the accession in the 1713 Treaty of Utrecht ending the war that had subsequently erupted, on the condition that the two thrones never be formally joined under one monarch in that Bourbon family line.

All former times, and WISDOM join'd with LOVE,
In council sits, makes paltry factions cease,
And tho' at War, yet all at HOME is PEACE;
Whilst ENGLAND keeps one half the world in AWE,
And by her POW'R can give the other LAW;
When each new day, crowns Britons with success,
And Heaven seems some *Chatham*'s plans to bless;
Should he succeed, when war in dread alarms,
Calls forth the nation's WISDOM, with her ARMS,
Calls forth RESENTMENT from the BRITISH THRONE,
To make her VENGEANCE, and her POWER known;
Should he succeed, and roll SUPINE in state,
(And leave her GLORY and RENOWN to fate)
Would be a crime (that Heav'n could not forgive,)
To blast his name, and make his memory live:
Live, with recorded VILLAINS to that Day,
When time shall cease, and all the world decay:
Should he to make this crime still worse appear,
Turn out a Minister to ENGLAND DEAR,
Who'd rais'd his Country (from a SINKING state)
By WISDOM only, (not by chance or fate)
To POW'R and STRENGTH, not known in days of yore,
Known only then, and to be known no more;
At his command, like that great PATRIOT PITT,
Makes *France* to yield, and *Spain*, tho' proud, SUBMIT;
Makes British VALOUR, with just vengeance hurl'd,
Strike TERROR thro' each nation of the world:
Should he be (through a *Scotsman*'s base design)
FORC'D from his office, or MADE TO RESIGN,
And that same Scotsman of the *Stuart* race,
Mount in his seat, the nation's foul DISGRACE,
False to his King, give up those conquests won,
And fix in STRENGTH, both *France* and *Spain* undone;
Should he make war, DEFENSIVE war to cease,
On terms *inglorious*, by a *shameful peace*,

A peace which must from foul CORRUPTION spring,
Thro' that base *Scotsman*, but still BASER King;
Dead to all sense of England's *future good*,
To *sacrifice*, her *treasure*, and her *blood*.

Such deeds as these, would fire my soul with RAGE,
And make me e'en against my SAFETY, wage
War with VILL'NY, and stamp their horrid crimes.
That each might live, and stink to after-times.

Thrice happy NOW, *when ev'ry blessing springs*,
From GEORGE the THIRD, we boast the BEST of KINGS.

Should such a King succeed to ENGLAND'S Throne,
(Tho' BORN a BRITON, they must BLUSH to own)
Should he, (when by *Scots arts*, by *bribes*, and *fraud*,
A peace most *infamous*, is made abroad;
And, for *distinction* sake, at *Fontainbleau*,[3]
The curse of *England*, and of *Scotland* too;)
Should he, persuing still the path of shame,
Give up all pow'r, reserving but the *name*
Of King, let *rebel Scotsmen*, steer the helm
Of State, and sow *fell discord* in the realm,
Make tax on tax, (while England curst with peace)
Each year arise, each year to say increase;
Each year call loud, aloud for *new supplies*,
While ruin did, with double horror rise;
Should he, when such oppressions from those men,
Call'd forth some *Wilkes*, (a *Wilkes* may be agen;

---

3. The 1762 Treaty at Fontainebleau was negotiated secretly between France and Spain, as the conflict then raging between the great powers in Europe was winding down in what would be called The Seven Years War there, or the French and Indian War in the colonies. France and Spain not only renewed the "family compact" (see supra XII.2) first entered into in 1733 and renewed in 1743; France agreed to pass title of the Louisiana country, including New Orleans, to Spain to avoid having to surrender that territory to Britain, which had made it clear that it intended to keep New France from the Ohio country north.

Be sent by Heaven, his country to bless,
To rescue ENGLAND from each deep distress;)
Call'd forth some *Wilkes*, in *honour* to oppose
Their *measures*, and their *subtle arts* expose;
To shew the people ev'ry base design,
Their schemes to *thwart*, their plans to *undermine*;
To *speak* such *truths*, as some would fear to *think*,
And shew the *gulph*, where *Englishmen* must sink;
Sink and remain, till time would be no more,
In the *damn'd gulph* of ARBITRARY POW'R:
Thus to stand forth, and only with this view,
To save his COUNTRY, and her FREEDOM too;
To sound the alarm of danger in her ear,
Call forth her RAGE, and shew what she should FEAR
Make TRAITORS tremble at the strokes he gave,
Tremble and fear the nation to ENSLAVE;
To brand those villains with just marks of shame,
That each might live, live with a blasted name;
Thus to stand forth, with these, these noble views,
All DANGER to defy, and BRIBES refuse;
Would well deserve (altho' some TRUTHS might sting,)
Both FAVOUR and PROTECTION from that King:
Should he, (weak Prince, a surer hate to gain,
And make the people daily curse his reign,)
Dead to all sense, of HONOUR and of TRUTH,
The friend of SLAV'RY in his early youth,)
Drunk with PREROGATIVE, a *Scotsman*'s tool,
In MEANNESS bred, fond of DESPOTIC rule;
Should he in rage, exert a LAWLESS POW'R,
And order him, CLOSE prison'r in the TOWER;
(His friends REFUSE admittance to his room,
And cruel PRESECUTION be his doom;)
Immur'd within those walls for life must be,
Unless a PRATT should rise and set him FREE;
Yet in such times, and he once more at LARGE,

Some *Scotch Chief Justice*, may *renew* the charge;
Tyrannic pow'r not willing to RETRENCH,
And send him for TWO YEARS, to the *King's Bench*.
The people then would surely flock to see,
Fair FREEDOM'S friend, the friend of LIBERTY;
To shew their Love, (with well deserv'd applause)
To him, who tri'd to save their CHARTER'D LAWS.

A SECRETARY ready to fulfill,
The bloody mandates of a Tyrant's will;
Might send the cruel *Scots*, their swords to wield,
To gain fresh laurels in *St. George's Field*;
Should e'er the ENGLISH by the *Scots* be slain,
In such a cause, a TYRANT'S love to gain,
And I be doom'd by heav'n to see the day,
Some future year, and on the TENTH of MAY,
Should then a youth, thro' VILLAINY decreed
To fall, by SCOTSMEN there be MASSACRED,
(Whom for distinction sake, I'll ALLEN call,)
PERSU'D, and in his FATHER'S HOUSE TO FALL,)
An ONLY SON, and all his father's CARE,
His greatest HOPE, as well as only HEIR;
To see that father sunk in deep DISTRESS,
SUPPLICATE the Throne, begging for REDRESS;
Calling for JUSTICE, (distracted, undone,)
Justice, 'gainst the MURDERER'S of his SON
This REFUS'D, the MURDERER'S too be PAID,
A PRINCE for BLOOD, and from that KING have AID:
A Jury PACK'D, a JUDGE most ready too,
Obey that Court, and all its rotten crew;
'Gainst JUSTICE, LAW, and TRUTH, (cursed deed!)
To hear him say, "the *English* ought to *bleed*;"
"I have it in commission from the King,
"That not ONE SCOTSMAN, while he reigns shall swing;
"The SCOTS were SENT, the King he thus had will'd,
"They should have *butcher'd more*, nay, *thousand's kill'd*;

"There can no CRIME unto THEIR charge be laid,
"But by the KING, whom they have not *obey'd*;
"For by the world, this should be understood,
"'Twas his DESIGN, to fill the fields with BLOOD."

Such deeds as these would fire my soul with RAGE,
And make me e'en against my SAFETY, wage
War with VILLAINY, and stamp these Monsters crimes,
That each might live, and stink to after-times:
Would make me, if I had a hand to write,
Paint these foul deeds, dark as the shades of night;
Would make me call forth ancient British RAGE,
To JUST REVENGE, or mark the COWARD AGE.

Thrice happy NOW, *when ev'ry* blessing springs,
From GEORGE the THIRD, we boast the BEST of KINGS.

Should such a King succeed to ENGLAND'S Throne,
(Tho' BORN a BRITON, they must BLUSH to own;)
Should he, in meanness bred, LAUGH at all LAW,
The senate keep by BRIBES, and FRAUD and AWE;
That parliament to ROYAL MANDATE true,
Shall ruin England and her FREEDOM too;
Intestine war shall be at BRENTFORD laid,
(To which that King shall give his utmost AID;)
A war 'gainst TRUTH and HONOUR, horrid deed!
To root up FREEDOM, and make VIRTUE bleed,
To stab the *constitution*'s very *soul*,
That right destroy, which *now* supports the whole;
Elections right, that firm, that great support,
'Gainst *venal statesmen*, and a *slavish court*:
Yet none should suffer for such mighty *guilt*,
Nor all the *blood* which might that day be spilt:
Altho' by *hir'd villains* some should be slain,
The villains tri'd, condemn'd, 'twou'd be in *vain*,
In *vain* the nation should for justice call,

A *pardon* would be sent from *Surgeons Hall*;
That King should laugh, his minions should laugh too,
To think each day they *butcher'd one*, or *two*.

Such deeds as these would fire my soul with *rage*,
And make me e'en against my *safety*, wage
War with *vill'ny,* and stamp that TYRANT's crimes,
That he might live, and stink to after-times.

Thrice happy NOW, *when ev'ry blessing springs,*
From GEORGE the THIRD, we boast the BEST of KINGS,

Should such a King succeed to *England*'s Throne,
(Tho' *born* a Briton, they must *blush* to own;)
He would from *France*, to shameful insults *yield*,
And be afraid the *British* sword to *wield*;
Our cannon, *France* shall neither *fear* nor *dread*,
When known to her, a *Patriot* King was *dead*;
And he who reign'd, a scripture rule did know,
To strike him *once*, would turn for *t'other* blow;
The *terror* of our *fleets* should be no more,
Nor carry thunder to a *foreign* shore;
But piece, by piece, be left to rot away,
With BRITISH GLORY, *moulder* and *decay*;
The insulting *Spaniard*, *unchastis'd* shall dare,
To *seize* a ship, and off her *rudder* tare;
While *England*, neither dreaded, nor ador'd,
Stains with her *pen*, the lusture of her *sword*;
In cowardice gives up her *rightful claim*,
And blasts at once, her *honour*, and her *name*:
Curst be the time, the day, when that is told,
That *England*'s Empire of the sea is *sold*.

Such deeds as these, would fire my soul with *rage*,
And make me e'en against my *safety*, wage
War with *vill'ny* and stamp that TYRANT'S crimes,
That he might live and stink to after-times.

Thrice happy NOW, *when ev'ry blessing springs,*
From GEORGE the THIRD, we boast the BEST of KINGS.

Should such a King succeed to *England*'s throne,
(Tho' *born* a *Briton*, they must *blush* to own;)
Should he in *meanness* bred, *laugh* at all *law*,
The senate keep by *bribes*, and *fraud* in *awe*;
That parliament to *loyal mandates* true,
With *England*'s ruin, shall fix *Boston*'s too;
Her *charters* shall destroy, her *rights* invade,
Her *commerce* ruin, and the *town blockade*;
Shall fill that place, with men by *slaughter* fed,
To rob the *starving* people of their bred;
And fix by force, some curst *oppressive laws*,
Made through *Scots villainy,* (without a cause;)
In base compliance with that *Tyrant*'s will,
Her *freedom* to destroy, or *blood* to spill;
And step, by step, most infamous design,
Thus the whole *constitution undermine*;
First take from *Boston*, all the *rights* we gave,
Make each *American*, a *Scotsman*'s slave;
And next in *chains* the *English* shall be bound,
By that same King, in whom no *truth* they found;
Should I then live, I'd rather league with *Hell*,
Or rise in *arms*, and 'gainst that King *rebel*
Than be his *slave*, by all thats *just* and *good*,
I'd rather see *my children* roll in *blood*.

Such deeds as these, would fire my soul with *rage*,
And make me e'en against my *safety*, wage
War with *vill'ny*, and stamp that *Tyrant*'s crimes,
That he might live, and stink to after-times;
Would make me call forth *antient British rage*,
To *just revenge*, or mark the *coward age*.

Thrice happy NOW, *when ev'ry blessing springs,*
From GEORGE the THIRD, we boast the BEST of KINGS.

Should such a King succeed to *England*'s throne,
(The nation must, with *dire oppression* groan,)
Should he in *meanness* bred, laugh at all *law*,
The Senate keep by *bribes*, and *fraud* in *awe*;
That parliament to *royal mandates* true,
With *freedom*, shall *subvert religion* too;
The *Lords* and *Bishops*, shall that Senate join,
And with the State, the *church* shall *undermine*;
The *Protestant faith*, which for ages stood,
On *truth's* firm *base*, bought with a *sea* of *blood*;
Shall be *destroy'd,* and at that *Tyrants* call,
The *Laws* of *God*, shall into ruins fall;
The *English* then, to *Catholics* must bow,
And *worship Idols*, as they do *God now*;
Or else submit to *persecution's* rod,
Be burnt alive, (for owning of their God)
With shirt well *pitch'd*, to give a shocking light,
And *Smithfield* once more blaze, at dead of night;
Then as before, with *Hell* they may conspire,
To set our *churches*, and the *town* on *fire*:
(That *pious* King, at *pious* Priest's command,
May make *crusado's* to the *Holy-land*,
Thro' dangerous seas, to find the blessed spring
Of *holy water*, to which the *Pope* shall bring
Him safe, *purge*, and *absolve* him from *his crimes*,
As *Pope's* absolv'd our *King's* in former times,
And made them *devil's* on the *British throne*,
They reign'd in *blood*, and *Hell* was all their *own*.)
And Bishop's then e'en Satan shall out vye,
To please that KING will give their GOD the lie,
(But still they'll have a sure and certain hope,
And find at last a SAVIOUR in the Pope)
And no distinction could a SCOTSMAN bring,
'Twixt, DEVIL BISHOP's, POPE, and such a KING;
So far alike, (none should this disbelieve)

Their aim the same to ruin and deceive,
By oaths nor conscience neither would be bound,
Could worse on Earth, or worse in Hell be found.

Such deeds as these, would fire my soul with RAGE,
And make me e'en against my safety, wage
War *with vill'ny,* and stamp their cursed crimes,
That each might live and stink to after-times:
Would make me call forth ancient British rage
To *Just revenge,* or mark to *coward age.*

Thrice happy NOW, when every blessing *springs*
From *GEORGE the THIRD;* we BOAST the best of *KINGS.*

Through that dark gloom one comfort shall appear,
(And all the world own I'm a PROPHET here)
Altho' like crimes of old in SODOM's land,
Those might draw vengeance from GOD's righteous hand,
Yet for time, the AUTHORS shall not bleed,
Thro' one Just man, who then shall greatly plead;
One BISHOP shall be found, and only ONE,
Then true to *Man,* to *God,* and *Christ his Son,*
There shall be one, ASAPH⁴ that one shall sing,
Just to his *God,* his *Country* and his *King.*

Should that dread time to England e'er be known,
When such a Monarch sits upon the throne,
Her senate brib'd, and only kept for sport,
To aid the BLOODY measures of a court,
Should that e'er be, a few brave virtuous men,

---

4. Jonathan Shipley, Bishop of St. Asaph, a Welsh diocese, often sided with Chatham and Camden in the House of Lords in opposing the North ministry's American policies. Paul H. Smith, ed., *English Defenders of American Freedom, 1774–1778* (Washington, D.C.: Library of Congress, 1972), pp. 9–14, discusses Shipley before reproducing one of his sermons and a speech that he had written to deliver in the Lords. G. M. Ditchfield wrote the entry for him in the *Oxford DNB,* 50:369–70.

(A *Chatham, Burke,* a *Glinn,*[5] may be agen)
May try, with truth and justice on their side,
To stem the torrent of corruption's tide;
Like virtuous Romans they may firmly stand,
With some few more, to save a falling land;
May bravely struggle in their country's cause,
And nobly try to save her *charter'd laws*;
But try in *vain*, truth shall not find support,
From rascals brib'd, and by a rotten court:
Should honour rise, by justice call'd to tell,
How England bled, and how the *Romans* fell;
Should virtue honour join, at Heaven's call,
To shew that Britons must like *Romans* fall:
Should they, base villainy drag forth to light,
St. Stephen's troops, shall then prepare to fight;
And legions arm, against truth and virtue's laws,
Will there defend the blackest villain's cause;
And honour, justice, truth and virtue meet
This fate, shall victims fall at *powers* feet.

Dread EVILS these, yet they will surely spring,
From Lords and Commons, *join'd* with such a King.

In such a time, at FREEDOM'S glorious call,
Britons must strike, and make those TRAITORS fall,
A deed which would by ages be admir'd,

---

5. John Glynn, prominent London barrister and serjeant-at-law, had defended John Wilkes in court, and then again in the House of Commons after Wilkes returned the favor and helped him gain one of the seats for Middlesex. Peter D. G. Thomas wrote the brief entry for him in the *Oxford DNB*, 22:522–23. Paul Langford contributed the detailed, insightful essay on Edmund Burke that appeared in ibid., 8:820–41. Considering Burke a "friend" of protesting Americans is as complicated as thinking of Pitt (Chatham) in those same terms. Pitt had objected to the principle of Parliament's taxing the colonists; Burke, like his political mentor, the Marquess of Rockingham, objected only to the practice. Pitt had objected to the Declaratory Act from the moment it was introduced in 1766; Burke supported it and did not give up on it until 1778, long after it had become dead letter law.

A day kept HOLY, when their souls expir'd:
Then would, happier days, to Albion be restor'd,
By ANTIENT JUSTICE, with her PATRIOT SWORD.

In such a time would REVOLUTION stand,
Each Briton's boast, the glory of the land.

But should that time to England once be known,
When foul corruption stinks upon the throne,
And she has POPISH BISHOPS of her own.
When each other the THREE estates shall JOIN,
By force or fraud, the state to undermine;
When Britons do, and with INGLORIOUS ease,
SUBMIT to WRONGS, such curs'd wrongs as these;
When that shall be (quite dead to Heaven's call)
THE BRITISH EMPIRE MUST IN RUINS FALL.

N. B. The spirited letter signed CASCA, is come safe to hand, and shall be properly attended to. The Authors of the CRISIS will be extremely glad of the future favours of the Writer, which will be very acceptable, and the expence of postage, most readily paid.—They hope to hear from him soon, and would wish to have an addition in a few Days to the letter already received.

Printed and published for the Authors, by T. W. SHAW, in Fleet-Street, opposite Anderton's Coffee House, where Letters to the Publisher will be thankfully received.

THE

CRISIS

NUMBER XIII   *To be continued Weekly.*

SATURDAY, April 15, 1775   [*Price Two-pence Half-penny.*

With Rage from *Hell* the *Tyrant*'s Heart may glow,

But He's no *Briton* who can strike the Blow.

Every Englishman must deplore the ill Success, and abhor the unworthy Treatment which attended the *two* late *Conciliatory Plans* in relation to *America*. Pregnant with good Sense, Benevolence, and sound Reason; they will do eternal Honour to the Wisdom, Justice, Policy, and Humanity, of the *Heads* and *Hearts* that formed them. How different was the Plan of *North*? Crafty, Mean, Insidious, Impolitic, Irrational, Shallow, and (like himself and his Coadjutors) beneath Contempt.[1] This was not treating with *America*, but insulting her: every Step against *her*, hitherto, has been founded in the greatest *Inhumanity*, the grossest *Ignorance*, and the worst *Policy*. I will proceed to prove my Assertions, and defy the whole Cabal of *Ministerial Slaughtermen* to confute me. I do not call upon the *Master-Butcher*, because He can only be considered (after the Part he has acted by *asserting*) as an *executive*, and not as a *rational Monster* in this Business.—First then, for the *Humanity* of these Proceedings. Let it be granted only (as it

1. The sources for Chatham's and North's plans can be found at supra VI.1.

must) that the *Crown* stands in the same Relation to *America,* as a Parent to her Child, and my first Assertion proves itself. Have any *gentle, tender, sensible* Means, been used to reconcile *her?* Have not her humble Remonstrances, Proposals, Submissions, and Supplications, been treated with Contempt?—not suffered to lie upon the Table of a *British* House of Commons? Have they been deemed Worthy of a Thought by *her pious* Sovereign? Has *she* not been branded with the ignominious Name of *Rebel,* by Act of Parliament, for no other Reason (I mean no *true* one) than because she has *wisely and calmly* deliberated upon, remonstrated against, and steadily, but not tumultuously, resented the repeated *Injuries* she has received?—as to *Riots* by *Mobs,* they are not to be imputed to *her* as *Treason* and *Rebellion. America* (as a Nation most unconstitutionally oppressed) has hitherto only deliberated upon her Sufferings:—She has not *acted.*—My Lords *Suffolk, Pomfret, Radnor, Apsley, Sandwich,* they have not *acted.*—It is, as yet, no Treason, my Lords, to *think,* to *advise,* to *fear,* and to *prepare.* You cannot, you dare not, move to annull (as you may wish) the Statute of Treasons in *America.* The *Americans* have as good a Right to *that* as your Lordships. I mean as yet, my Lords, because I am not quite satisfied that (even in the Present *smuggled* and *corrupt* Parliament) the Boldest and most venal Prostitute, durst make so dangerous a Trial upon the Patience and long Suffrance of this Kingdom.—I will now inform your Lordships that it is contrary to the Law of Nations to attempt the Destruction even of the most inveterate Enemy by Famine, until he has been first solemnly summoned to *submit.* Have the Americans ever yet been (though, if Men, they shortly will be) in Arms? Have they yet had a Prospect of any other Terms than such as would make them Slaves? Will they be Weak enough to submit to such Conditions? the Preliminaries hitherto proposed, have been founded in Oppression, not in Reason: they are fit for Brutes, not Men. The *lenient,* the *compassionate* North, has treated America like the Assassin of an Alley—with his Knife at *her* Throat, he has *humanely* left it at her Choice to strip herself, for Fear she should be stripped by him.—Why have the Ministry had recourse *at first* to this inhuman Scheme of Famine? They fear the Army will *relent,* when they find they must Wade through the *Blood* of their own Country-men. Their present General (Gage) has, to his Honour, declined the Bloody Task. Even a foreigner, to whom the same Command was offered, has revolted at the Thought.[2] Is not this Stratagem of *starving* Freemen into *Slavery*, the most *Inhuman*, as well as the most *Cowardly*, of all others, especially when it is considered that all the Remonstrances of these unhappy Sufferers, have been rejected? I should insult the Reader's understanding by waiting for a Reply,—I therefore come to the next Ingredient in the American Persecution, *Ignorance*.—I must first Remark that some of their wise Lordships were for having Maryland and Virginia (very remote inland Countrys) prohibited from the FISHery.—Thus far have some of the great and sage Counsellors of this Nation been Ignorant even of the Situation of that Part of their Fellow-Creatures, whom they wish to involve in the most dreadful of all Calamities,—*Famine*. But the very Scheme itself is *Impracticable*; these wretched People cannot be totally destroyed either by Butchery or Famine: their Numbers are great and formidable; in such a vast extent of Country their resourses will be endless: they are not destitute of Arms already, and they will be supplied with more in spite of our *vigilant* Fleet. They have all the Materials necessary for War in the Bowels of their Country: they have Artists, Handicraftsmen, Manufacturers, and Mechanics of all Sorts; Cattle of all kinds; Fruit of the Earth in vast aboundance; fine streams and Rivers: though, no doubt, Administration (for the sake of Consistency) will give strict Orders, and pay highly for the *poisoning* of these; but that will not easily be effected: these People in General, know the use of Arms; they have Perseverance, Courage, Resolution,—and above all, (most *prophetic* Lord Sandwich) they have Virtue, which can never be overcome. Should our Army *strike*, and *fail*, the hatred, enmity, and revolt of America, is

2. It was only rumored that command had been offered to Prince Ferdinand of Brunswick. Among the interesting hypotheticals that would have followed that offer and his acceptance is the likelihood that Lord George Germain would not have been selected to succeed the Earl of Dartmouth as secretary of state for American affairs in November 1775. For Germain see infra L.5; for Gage, see John Richard Alden's sympathetic *General Gage in America* (Baton Rouge: Louisiana State University Press, 1948), and John Shy's brief sketch in the *Oxford DNB*, 21:256–58.

fixed for ever: they never will submit to lick the Tyrant-hand, which has once been raised against their Liberties, their Properties, and their Lives. Under the above Considerations, the Present scheme of Government must seem Impracticable; if so, or if from Rancour and Resentment, it has been viewed but Partially, it is the grossest Ignorance to pursue it. Should Heaven interpose on the Side of Justice, we shall perceive our Error too late; but were our Attempts by *Sword or Famine*, sure of Success, Government is only destroying its own Vitals.—What then is the Policy of this unnatural War? It is like the War between the Belly and the other Members; the whole State must feel is Consequences. Shallow North told his House of Commons (for it is his) that the Imports from the American Continent were inconsiderable. Now my Lord? You ought to know (and in Honour you should have declared) that the *Imports* of that Part of America into our Sugar Colonies were the very Life of them: neither Planters, nor Negroes, can Subsist without them; particularly in the prohibited, interdicted Article of Fish, which, when salted, is their general Food. Your Lordship by your War, and your intended Famine, has effectually starved and ruined all the Passive and obedient Sugar-Colonies, as well as your declared Enemies in America. Thus a most valuable Fishery, a considerable Sugar Trade, and Thousands (perhaps Millions) of Innocent and brave Lives will be sacrificed by a narrow-minded Ministry to wicked Views, and insatiable Resentments, in the Reign of a Monarch born a *Briton*! An ancient *Pict*, or a wild *Indian*, (Savage in their Natures) would Blush and Shudder at such Proceedings.—With the Colonies and Trade the Revenues must sink. If *roya*l Profusion, and Ministerial Corruption, were to sink likewise, it would be well; but they will still attempt to draw Blood from the most impoverished Veins. The Commerical, the landed Interest, the Public Bank, at last, must feel the Shock. Then, perhaps, when Famine threatens at our own Doors, the British Lion will be roused.— Then, (for I will *Prophecy* in my turn) comes a Revolution, fatal to Minions, Pensioners, Placemen, Knaves, and Tyrants; but happy for the Nation, if from the Ashes of all these Pests, the Rights of suffering and insulted Englishmen, can be once more established.—We shall find it to our Cost, in vain to send English Soldiers (none but Scotch will do the Business) against English Breasts. I am of Opinion (let the Wishes of the Ministry be what they will) that if every Officer who goes upon this Assassination were a Burgoyne,[3] he would be Disappointed of the Blood he pants for, his Command will be a *Sinecure*, and his Victory a brave and virtuous Desertion. All who deserved the Names of Soldiers, would throw down their Arms, and Embrace their gallant and unhappy Countrymen. An English Army will not, and a Navy cannot destroy the Liberties of America: the Ministry, who wish to deceive the Nation, are (as they frequently are) deceived themselves: they cannot execute their Plan without extraordinary and successive (almost perpetual) Drafts of Forces. Should the Patient Sprit of this Kingdom, rise at such a Time in Arms, and France and Spain add to the Horrors of a CIVIL WAR, even in the midst of these Calamities, it will be some Consolation that the Advisers, Abettors, and detestable Heads of these diabolical Measures, cannot long escape the Vengeance of an injured People.

C A S C A.[4]

Notwithstanding we have given almost the usual Quantity of Matter already, we cannot here omit without injury to our Readers and the Cause of Liberty, the spirited City Remonstrance which will do immortal Honour to the Heads and Hearts of those who framed it.

---

3. General John Burgoyne, who had distinguished himself in the previous war while fighting in Portugal, was a member of the Commons vocal in his support of the North ministry's punitive policies. Getting his wish to be sent to the colonies to help restore order there, his failed 1777 campaign, leading to his surrender at Saratoga, has become a stock tale of a war gone wrong. House of Commons hearings held in 1779 to evaluate his generalship provide excellent insights into the thinking of the time that led to the war's outbreak as well as its conduct. In the *Oxford DNB*, 8:807–809, Max M. Mintz returned to arguments that he had made in *The Generals of Saratoga* (New Haven: Yale University Press, 1990).

4. "Casca" appeared as the author of more essays in *The Crisis* than anyone else, first in this issue, last in no. 78, with twenty-seven others in between. At this point in Anglo-American memory the heroic Roman senator Servilius Casca of Plutarch's *Lives*, who joined with Brutus to assassinate Julius Caesar and save the republic, prevailed over the far more ambiguous figure in Shakespeare's "Julius Caesar," who is first to strike.

The ADDRESS, REMONSTRANCE, and PETITION of the C I T Y o f L O N D O N.[5]

"WE your Majesty's dutiful and loyal Subjects, the Lord Mayor, Aldermen, and Livery of the City of London, beg leave to approach the Throne, and declare our *Abhorrence* of the Measures which have been pursued, and are now pursuing, to the Oppression of our fellow Subjects in America. These Measures are big with all the Consequences which can alarm a free and commercial People. A deep and perhaps a *Fatal* wound to Commerce; the *ruin* of Manufactures; the *Diminution* of the Revenue, and consequent *increase* of Taxes; the *Alienation* of the Colonies; and the *Blood* of your Majesty's Subjects.

"But your Petitioners look with less Horror at the Conscquences, than at the *purpose* of those Measures. Not deceived by the *specious* Artifice of calling Despotism—Dignity, they plainly perceive that the real Purpose is—*To establish Arbitrary Power over all America.*

"Your Petitioners conceive the Liberties of the whole to be inevitably connected with those of every part of an Empire founded on the common Rights of Mankind. They cannot therefore observe, without the greatest Concern and Alarm, the Constitution fundamentally violated in any Part of your Majesty's Dominions. They esteem it an essential, unalterable principle of Liberty, the Source, and Security of all constitutional Rights—that no Part of the Dominion can be *Taxed* without being *represented*. Upon this great leading Principle, they most ardently wish to see their fellow Subjects in America secured in what their humble Petition to your Majesty prays for—*Peace, Liberty*, and *Safety*.—Subordination in Commerce, under which the Colonies have always chearfully acquiesced, is, they conceive, all that this Country ought in Justice to require. From this subordination such advantages flow, by all the Profits of their Commerce centering here, as fully compensate this Nation for the Expence incurred, to which they also contribute in Men and Money for

---

5. This appeal followed that of London merchants, and the merchants of other towns. See supra IV.2. *Lloyd's Evening Post*, 12 April 1775, had already printed it in full, on the first page.

their Defence and Protection during a general War; and in their Provincial Wars they have manifested their Readiness and Resolution to defend themselves. To require more of them would, for this Reason, derogate from the Justice and Magnanimity which have been hitherto the Pride and Character of this Country.

"It is therefore with the deepest Concern, that we have seen the sacred security of Representation in their Assemblies *wrested* from them—the Trial by Jury abolished—and the odious powers of *Excise* extended to all cases of Revenue—the sanctuary of their Houses laid open to violation at the will and Pleasure of every Officer and Servant in the Customs—the dispensation of Justice *corrupted*, by rendering their Judges *dependent* for their Seats and Salaries on the will of the *Crown*—Liberty and Life rendered *Precarious* by subjecting them to be dragged over the Ocean, and tried for Treason or Felony here; where the Distance, making it impossible for the *most Guiltless* to maintain his Innocence, must deliver him up a victim to ministerial Vengeance—Soldiers and others in America have been instigated to *shed the Blood* of the People, by establishing a mode of Trial which holds out Impunity for such *Murder*—the Capital of New-England has been punished with unexampled Rigour—untried and unheard—involving the Innocent and the suspected in one common and inhuman calamity—Chartered Rights have been taken away, without any forfeiture proved, in order to deprive the People of every legal exertion against the Tyranny of their Rulers—the Habeas Corpus Act, and Trial by Jury, have been suppressed; and *French despotic* Government, with the *Roman Catholic Religion*, have been *Established by Law*, over an extensive Part of your Majesty's Dominions in America; dutiful Petitions for redress of those Grievances, from all your Majesty's American Subjects have been fruitless.[6]

6. For various petitions to both crown and parliament, see IV.2 and the studies alluded to there by James E. Bradley. For petitions from the colonists in particular see Jack M. Sosin, *Agents and Merchants* (Lincoln: University of Nebraska Presss,1965); Michael Kammen, *A Rope of Sand* (Ithaca: Cornell University Press, 1968); and my case study, "Defining and Defending Colonial American Rights: William Bollan, Agent" *American Political Thought* 3 (2014):197–227.

"To fill up the Measure of these oppressions, an *Army* has been sent to enforce them.

"Superadded to this, Measures are now planned upon the *most merciless Policy* of starving our fellow Subjects into a total surrender of their Liberties, and an unlimited Submission to Arbitrary Government.

"These Grievances have driven your Majesty's faithful Subjects to despair, and compelled them to have recourse to that *resistance* which is *justified* by the great principles of the Constitution, actuated by which, at the glorious period of the Revolution, our Ancestors *transferred* the Imperial Crown of these Realms from the Popish and Tyrannic race of the *Stuarts*, to the Illustrious and Protestant House of *Brunswick*.

"Your Petitioners are persuaded, that these Measures originate in the *secret advice* of Men who are *Enemies* equally, to your Majesty's *Title* and to the *Liberties* of your People. That your Majesty's Ministers carry them into Execution by the same *Fatal Corruption* which has enabled them to wound the Peace and violate the Constitution of this Country—thus they poison the Fountain of Public Security, and render that Body which should be the guardian of *Liberty*, a formidable instrument of *Arbitrary Power*.

"Your Petitioners do therefore most earnestly beseech your Majesty to *dismiss immediately*, and *forever*, from your Councils, those Ministers and *Advisers*, as the first Step towards a full redress of those Grievances which alarm and afflict your whole People. So shall Peace and Commerce be restored, and the *Confidence* and *Affection* of all your Majesty's Subjects, be the *solid supporters* of your *Throne*."

The KING's ANSWER,

Which would do Honour to any
BUTCHER, MONSTER, or TYRANT *on Earth*.

"It is with the utmost Astonishment that I find any of *My* Subjects capable of encouraging the *Rebellious* Disposition which unhappily, exists in some of *My* Colonies in North America.

"Having entire Confidence in the *Wisdom* of *My* Parliament, the great Council of the Nation; I will steadily pursue *those* Measures which *they* have recommended for the support of the constitutional Rights of Great Britain, and the Protection of the Commercial interests of *My* Kingdoms."[7]

N. B. The Letter signed J. B. (Secretary) come safe to Hand. It is far from the Design of the Authors of the *CRISIS* to impose upon the Public, and they will allways think themselves obliged to those who promote the Sale of their Paper; but they beg Leave to inform J. B. that they cannot find UNDERSTANDING for him together with *Matter, Paper,* and *Printing* at the *Same Price*; however they faithfully Promise to stand *corrected* by *him* when he has learned to SPELL.[8]

Printed and published for the Authors, by T. W. SHAW, in Fleet-Street, opposite Anderton's Coffee House, where Letters to the Publisher will be thankfully received.

7. The king's response had been printed in the same issue of *Lloyd's Evening Post* (12 April 1775; see XIII.5 supra) that printed the City's petition. It was received by the townsmen on April 10th "with a mournful silence," according to that newspaper account.

8. It is not clear who "J.B." was—whether someone's real initials, or a nom de plume.

THE

CRISIS

NUMBER XIV   *To be continued Weekly.*

SATURDAY, April 22, 1775   [Price Two-pence Half-penny.

The present Necessary DEFENSIVE War on the Part of America, justified by the Laws of God, Nature, Reason, State, and Nations; and therefore no TREASON or REBELLION.

IT must be apparent to every Englishman, not blinded by Malice or Ignorance, that the Americans by raising Forces, and taking up Arms, have no Intention to offer Violence to his Majesty's PERSON, CROWN or DIGNITY, nor to draw any ENGLISH BLOOD; but only to defend themselves, their Rights and Liberties, against encroaching Violence and LAWLESS POWER, to rescue his Majesty out of the Hands of his present evil, malignant Advisers; to bring him back to a just Sense of his DUTY; and those Delinquents to condign Punishment; who are now engaged in a desperate Conspiracy against the natural Rights of Mankind. The *Americans* have endeavoured by every possible Means, to accommodate the present unhappy Dispute with the King and his INFERNAL MINIONS, upon *just, reasonable,* and *honourable* Terms; but hitherto in vain. His Majesty having contrary to his OATH, his DUTY, and the fundamental Laws of God and the Realm, sent an Army of mercinary Soldiers to *America,* against his Subjects, for the avowed and open

Purpose of robbing them of their PEACE, their RIGHTS, their LIBER-
TIES, their PROPERTIES, or their LIVES, and to impose UNLAW-
FUL TAXES by force of Arms; the *Americans* may Lawfully and Justly,
by the great Principles of the Constitution, without any *Treason* or *Rebellion*, take up Arms in Defence of their Privileges, Laws, Lives, Liberties,
and Properties; even if the King were present to assist and encourage his
Soldiers, in this *unnatural, bloody*, and destructive CIVIL WAR.

When a King throws off all restraint of Law, and is bound by no Principles of Justice or Humanity, when he Invades with open Force, the
Liberties and Persons of his Subjects in a hostile Manner, only to answer
the most *diabolical, arbitrary*, and *infamous* Purposes, the People of England, and every Part of the British Empire, will be justified in taking up
Arms, and resisting such Invasions and Violence; otherwise they must
fall a Prey to his insatiable Rapine, and become the absolute Slaves of
Arbitrary Power, by way of Conquest.

We have several Instances in the History of this Country, and in many
Ages, of the People of England resisting by *force of Arms*, the Oppressions,
Rapines, unjust Violence, and Armies of their Princes raised against
them; and they have even encountered their KINGS in open Battle, and
taken them Prisoners; sometimes expelled, and at other Times deposed
them from their Royal Authority, when they became Incorrigible, open
and professed Enemies to the Kingdom, and sought the Ruin and Desolation of their subjects when by *Office, Duty, Oath* and common Justice, they were Bound inviolably to protect them in *Liberty and Peace*.
Among many other Examples of such Proceedings, and the Bravery and
Virtue of our Ancestors, are the following; *viz.* the Case of *King John,
Henry* the *Third, Edward* the *First, Richard* the *Third*, and *Henry* the
Sixth; nor are these Examples singular, all Kingdoms, and in all Ages,
have done the same, when their King (like the present Sovereign on the
Throne of England) degenerated into Tyrants, of which there are infinite
Precedents in History: and such Actions in every Age and Nation have
always been deemed Lawful and Just; as warranted by the Laws of God,
Nature, Reason, State, and Nations; all which Instruct, not only par-
ticular Persons, but whole Cities and Kingdoms, for their own necessary

Defence and Preservation, the Support of human Society, and Liberty, to protect themselves against all unlawful Violence and Tyranny, even in the Person of their Kings, their Ministers, or Minions, to whom the Laws of God, Nature, Man, nor any civil Nation, ever yet gave the least Authority to murder, spoil, oppress, or enslave their Subjects, or deprive them of their Liberties or Estates: Resistance were it Unlawful or Unjust, (as the Pimps and Parisites of a Court would insinuate) a few ambitious, bloody minded, tyrannizing Kings, might, without Molestation, in a short space of Time, RUIN, MURDER, or ENSLAVE, the whole Race of Men; overturn the settled Forms of Civil Government, extirpate the Christian Religion, and destroy human Society at their Pleasure: this, and Worse, if possible, had been effected; nay, every State and Kingdom, had been totally subverted long ago, by the worst of Monsters, Lawless Princes; had not this just, natural, hereditary Power of resisting and opposing their illegal Violence, (inherent in the People) restrained and prevented, such bloody and destructive Designs, from being carried into Execution.

This necessary and defensive Opposition, and resistance against regal Violence, which has ever been held Lawful, and often practised in almost every Kingdom, will justify the *Americans*, in taking up Arms, and resisting the present Arbitrary, Cruel, and Bloody Measures, now carrying on against them, by an infatuated, obstinate, perverse King, his infernal Ministers, and their Agents, whose only Object in View, is the entire RUIN of this once GREAT, HAPPY, POWERFUL, and FLOURISHING KINGDOM, and the DESTRUCTION of PUBLIC LIBERTRY.

It is expressly declared by *Aristotle, Xenophon, King Edward the Confessor*, in his established Laws, the Council of *Paris* in 829, by *Bracton, Fortescue*, and even King *James* himself, that a King governing in a settled Kingdom, CEASES TO BE A KING, and degenerates into a TYRANT, *so soon as he leaves to rule by* LAW, much more, when he begins to INVADE his SUBJECTS, PERSONS, RIGHTS, LIBERTIES, to set up an ARBITRARY POWER, impose UNLAWFUL TAXES, RAISE FORCES, and make WAR upon his Subjects, whom he should PROTECT, and

Rule in PEACE;[1] to PILLAGE, PLUNDER, WASTE, and SPOIL his Kingdoms; IMPRISON, MURDER, and DESTROY his People in an HOSTILE Manner; this they severally declare to be the highest degree of Tyranny, condemned and detested by God, and all good Men. The whole State and Kingdom therefore, in such Cases as these, for their own necessary Preservation, may Lawfully, with FORCE of ARMS, when no other Means can secure them, not only Passively, but actively resist their Prince, in such his Violent and Tyrannical Proceedings; without resisting any Kingly lawful Authority, for that is vested in the Kings Person, for the PRESERVATION, not the DESTRUCTION of the Kingdom; because these illegal Oppressions and Tyrannical Actions, are not warranted, but prohibited by the Laws of God, and the Realm, (to whom he is Accountable, and by whom he is justly Censurable) he is no lawful King, nor Magistrate, but an unjust oppressive Tyrant, a mere Private Man, who by such Proceedings, hath denuded himself of his Just regal Authority: so that all those Laws made for the Defence of the Kings Person, and Sovereign Power, the Suppression of INSURRECTIONS, TREASONS, and CONSPIRACIES against him, while he Governs his People according to Law, as by OATH and DUTY he is Bound will yield no Countenance, Encouragement, or Protection to him; in such Tyrannical and cruel Oppressions, but more especially when he turns a public Enemy to his People, and proclaims OPEN WAR against them; invades their Laws, Liberties,

1. It is likely that the author(s) had in mind Xenophon's *Hiero: Or, The Condition of a Tyrant*, written ca. 370 BCE and available in various translations printed in London earlier in the eighteenth century. Xenophon was best remembered as an admirer of Socrates and chronicler of his adventures as a mercenary in Persia who fought his way home to Greece. Aristotle was revered as "the philosopher" in the Anglo-American world of this generation and his *Politics* had been translated into English for various London editions; a new one by William Ellis, *A Treatise of Government*, would appear the next year. Aristotle often came to American and British readers secondhand, and, in the case of law, through translations into English of Sir John Fortescue's *De Laudibus Legum Angliae*, which was reprinted a half dozen times in London during the eighteenth century. (Notably, though, as often as not, Fortescue read Aristotle through the lens of Thomas Aquinas.) Philosopher, jurist, chief justice of the Court of King's Bench under Henry VI, Fortescue, along with Henry de Bracton, was considered the most profound commentator on the English common law tradition, limited government, and popular rights under law. The reign of Edward the Confessor (1042–1066) had passed into lore as a golden age, before the Norman invasion, that preserved the vestiges of the ancient Saxon constitution.

and Persons, and exercises all Manner of Hostilities against them, the same as the most Barbarous and Foreign Enemy would do: It being contrary to common Sense and Reason, to suppose that our Laws, which strictly Inhibit and Punish the very smallest Violations of the Public Pease, in all other Persons, should COUNTENANCE, JUSTIFY, and PATRONIZE them in the King, the FIRST MINISTER, and supreme Fountain of Justice; and not permit the People under pain of *Rebellion* and *Treason*, so much as to defend their Lives, Liberties, Estates, and Religion, from the open Violence of the King himself, or his malignant plundering Ministers and Favourites. When as *Fortescue* and *Bracton* prove, Kings of all others, both by OATH and DUTY, ought to be more observant, and obedient to the Laws of God and the Land, than the very Meanest of their Subjects.

That Precept of *St. Paul, Romans* 13, 1–2–3. *Let every Soul be Subject to the Higher Powers.* &c.[2] Means no more than this, that as long as Kings legally and justly execute the Trust committed to their Charge, and conferred on them by God and the People, they must, and ought to be OBEYED and submitted to, without the least Resistance, Private or Public; but if they degenerate into Tyrants, and turn professed Enemies to their People, by Murdering, Imprisoning, or destroying them by open Violence; or endeavouring by FORCE of ARMS, to subvert their Laws, Liberties, or Religion, and expose them as a Prey to their merciless blood thirsty Soldiers; I dare confidently to affirm, it was never the Intention of St. *Paul*, much less of our Laws, to inhibit Subjects, under Pain of Damnation, High in conscience Treason, or Rebellion, by defensive Arms, to resist KINGS THEMSELVES, or any of their Mercinary Adherents.

It was certainly never the Intention of the Apostle, to establish in the World, any errisistable Lawless Tyranny, or spoil of Kingdoms, and Butchery of

---

2. "Let every soul be subject unto the higher powers. For there is no power but of God: the powers that be are ordained of God.

Whosoever therefore resisteth the power, resisteth the ordinance of God: and they that resist shall receive to themselves damnation.

For rulers are not a terror to good works, but to the evil. Wilt thou then not be afraid of the power? do that which is good, and thou shalt have praise of the same." Romans 13:1–3 (KJV)

Subjects, execrable to God and Man, in all Ages, and in all Persons who have resisted them, even unto Blood: he meant rather totally to suppress them. There being scarce any more pregnant Text, against the Tyranny, the boundless Prerogative, the illegal proceedings of Kings, and the higher Powers in all the Scripture, than that of *Romans* 13, 1st to 7th Verse, if properly understood, and rightly Interperted, as *Pareus*[3] and others prove: therefore the Resistance of the *Americans,* against our Present seduced, malignant, Popish King, is no Violation of any Law of God or the Land, but a *just* and *necessary* War, which they have by every Means, to the utmost of their Power, endeavoured to prevent, and therefore no *Treason* or *Rebellion* within the meaning of any Law, or Statute; they are only arming themselves, for their own necessary Preservation, and to prevent their inevitable RUIN, they mean not OPENLY to assault the royal Army of Butchers; and I believe, there is no Divine among the whole Bench of Popish Bishops, no Casuist among the whole Tribe of venal Lawyers, except a few prostituted Court Slaves, VILLAINOUS enough to affirm, that it is Damnation in Conscience, or Treason and Rebellion in point of LAW, for our injured and suffering Fellow Subjects in *America*, to take up Arms for the Preservation of their Lives, their Liberties, and their Property; but would rather deem it Just and Honourable, nay, a Duty for every *Englishman* to venture his Life, and his Fortune in their Defence; in Defence of the dear bought Rights of his Country, and rather than Live a *Slave*, to die Gloriously in the Cause of PUBLIC LIBERTY.

N. B. Two Letters from CASCA are received, they came too late for this Weeks Number, but shall be made the Subject of our next. The Authors of the CRISIS beg CASCA will accept their most grateful Acknowledgements for this Favour.

Printed and published for the Authors, by T. W. SHAW, in Fleet-Streer, opposite Anderton's Coffee House, where Letters to the Publisher will be thankfully received.

---

3. The king being bound by law was one of the many Reformist teachings of David Pareus, German theologian, most famously associated with the Collegium Sapientiae in Heidelberg early in the previous century. Some of his writings had been translated from Latin into English.

THE

CRISIS

NUMBER XV   *To be continued Weekly.*

SATURDAY, APRIL 29, 1775   [Price Two-pence Half-penny.

—Similis frondescit Virga.[1] —
A constant *Scourge*—still I'll renew the Charge,
And lash the *Tyrant* as his Crimes enlarge.

A *Foolish King* grasps at Wealth and Power, as the *Ends*, a *Wise King* uses them as the *means* of Government. With the *one*, they are Gorgeous, vain Appendages of Royalty; with the *other*, they are happy Instruments of *Benevolence*. A *foolish King* eyes LIBERTY askaunt, and execrates it as the bane of Greatness; a *wise King* knows that neither Kingdom, nor Sovereign, can be Great without it. The *Fool* endeavours to root up, what the *Patriot King* most assiduously Cultivates. A *weak Prince* is jealous of LIBERTY in its lowest Branches. Hence it is, that he not only strikes at the Rights and Privileges of his People, but

---

1. "Similis frondescit Virga," from Book 6 of Virgil's *Aeneid,* meaning, essentially, new leaves on a bough are like those they replace. In this instance, Virgil wrote figuratively of golden leaves.

is Mean enough to envy the IMMUNITIES of a CORPORATION.
He starts at *Shadows*. In such a Reign even COMMERICAL MEET-
INGS are ODIOUS, because they are composed of FREEMEN. Even
Common Halls are an UNLAWFUL CONGRESS; like that in *America,*
they are deemed REBELLIOUS ASSOCIATIONS. How sophistically
do *ministerial Scriblers* labour to draw an artful Veil over such Political Transgressions as SOVEREIGNS, without a Blush, avow? Can the
sagacious Doctor Johnson (that *ministerial Hackney)* any longer rally the
well grounded Jealousies of *England* and *America?*[2] Can he *now* ask these
Croakers of Calamity, how *Slavery* can be brought *from America* into *England?* If he dares, I refer him for his Answer to *Lord Hertford*[3] (one of the
State Nurserymen) who sowed a subtle Seed, *or two,* of *Slavery,* even in
our *Metropolis,* the other Day. I hope, however, that these Seeds will be
severely choaked by the rank and stubborn WEED of LIBERTY. A *Weed*
it is now deemed in the CABINET, and in the LEGISLATURE, and in
both condemned to be rooted up. A Crop far more promising is expected. The Experiment of raising it by SLOW DEGREES, has just been
made. His MAJESTY, sick of all ADDRESSES but those of his FAITH-
FUL PARLIAMENT, has just declared, *"That he will not receive on the
Throne, any ADDRESS, REMONSTRANCE, or PETITION, of the Lord
Mayor, and Aldermen of the City of London, but on their CORPORATE
CAPACITY."* Thus is the Notice worded by *Lord Mansfield,* Lord Chief
Justice (not of the *Ceremonies*) but of *England.*—The Reason, or rather
the DESIGN of this, is Plain. For all Acts done in their CORPORATE

2. The best brief introduction to Johnson is Pat Rogers' essay on him in the *Oxford
DNB*, 30:310–23; the best introduction to Johnson's pamphlet, *Taxation No Tyranny*
(along with the text of the pamphlet itself), is in Donald J. Greene, *Political Writings*
(New Haven: Yale University Press, 1977), pp. 401–54, the tenth volume in the Yale edition of Johnson's writings.

3. Francis Seymour-Conway, Earl of Hertford, was part of the King's inner circle. Then
lord chamberlain, he had in earlier years been ambassador to France and lord lieutenant
of Ireland. He supported the North ministry's American policy, at least at this point,
though he would later express doubts to his cousin and famous chronicler of the age,
Horace Walpole. His younger brother, Henry Seymour-Conway, would, in 1782, lead
the Commons in pushing the King to give up his American war. Presumably readers of
The Crisis already knew what the author(s) meant by their allusion to slavery.

CAPACITY, the City of London is Responsible as a CORPORATION. Neither the Proceedings, the Resolves, nor the CONGRESS of a COMMON HALL, can forfeit the CHARTER of the City; the *Offences,* (such as *Petitions)* of the *City,* as a CORPORATION, may. In the one Case, they act in their *Political Capacity*; in the other, they do not. The *Lord Mayor, Aldermen,* and *Liverymen,* are *Individuals;* but the CORPORATION has but one *Neck.* This *ministerial Mouse-Trap,* is baited by a Lord Chief Justice of *England,* whose Duty it most clearly is (for I will Teach it him) to carry the Balance *with an even and an equal Hand,* between the just PREROGATIVES of the CROWN, and the undoubted PRIVILEGES of the SUBJECT.

I make no doubt but a *Mansfield* and a *Thurloe* will conduct the intended Scheme as well as a *Jefferies,* or a *Sawyer.* The memorable Case of the SEVEN BISHOPS, in *James the Seconds* Time, is now forgot at Court, and PETITIONS are once more degenerated into CRIMES.[4]

Though the actual Annihilation of the CITY CHARTER may not be intended, as it cannot be the Interest of the Crown to check any Source of Wealth; yet the Menaces, and intimidating Prosecutions of a RAPACIOUS MINISTRY may be expected to have the same happy Effects, as *threatening Letters,* sometimes, have among *Thieves.* They found it so lately, in the Case of the *East India Company,* and it is not improbable that their Audacity may strengthen with their Hopes.

---

4. For Mansfield, see supra I.5. Edward Thurlow was, at that moment, the attorney general; he had been solicitor general before then. G. M. Ditchfield wrote the *Oxford DNB* 54:715–20 sketch of him. Thurlow and Alexander Wedderburn were often linked in criticisms of ministerial policy involving alleged legal abuses, committed against Americans as well as Britons. The seven bishops case lived on in popular memory as a victory against the absolutist ambitions of James II, though it revolved around his attempt to extend religious toleration for Catholics and Protestant dissenters and the resistance of high Anglicans, including the Archbishop of Canterbury. Charged with seditious libel for their written protest against the King's declaration of indulgence, all were acquitted. See William Gibson, *James II and the Trial of the Seven Bishops* (Houndmills: Palgrave Macmillan, 2009). For George Jeffreys (lord chancellor at the time of the June 1688 trial, which he had advised the King to avoid) and Sir Robert Sawyer (a lawyer for the defense, former attorney general, and leader in the House of Commons) see the *Oxford DNB* essays by Paul Halliday, at 29:882–90 and 49:146–49, resp.

Toys and Baubles must be bought, and *Baby Houses* must be crowded to amuse and divert VACANT SOVEREIGNS, and *Ravens* must have Food. The numerous Mouths of CORRUPTION must be stopped. Too many Stratagems for the Sake of WEALTH and ARBITRARY POWER, cannot be tried. For GOLD every Coffer; for POWER every Vein must BLEED. The Predictions of *America* in respect to *England herself,* are now verifying. They are coming forward *by slow Degrees,* at this Instant. Our *Ministers* of late have had a strange Appetite for CHARTERS. In *Wilkes's* Case they had the DARING IMPUDENCE to attack the GREAT CHARTER of ENGLAND for the sake of POWER. They have since been nibbling at the *East India Company's,* for the sake of *Wealth and Power both;* the Company compounded and acquiesed.[5] They are striking again at CHARTERS in *America,* (as their *retained* and *pensioned Advocate* Dr. JOHNSON says) for the sake of POWER, and they now have their Eye upon the Charters of London, for a Royal Reason,—for the sake of *pursuing the Commercial-Interests of this Kingdom.*

But are the PETITIONS of COMMON HALLS, or COMMON HALLS themselves, so dreadful? are the MEETINGS, (or more properely the GREAT COUNCILS,) of this METROPOLIS so *terrible?* are they not Meetings of MERITORIOUS Citizens and LOYAL Subjects? in both these Capacities they have ADDRESSED, and in both they have OFFENDED.

How harsh and grating is the Voice of TRUTH! how unhallowed are the Lips that dare to utter it before the THRONE! Approach it ye BRITISH SLAVES, upon the Knee; adore it with *prostration,* but profane it not with a PETITION! upon this *Mercy Seat* (alas!) the *Sovereign* will no more receive PETITIONS, from his FAITHFUL CITIZENS and *Friends,* from those who supply his WANTS, his SUPERFLUITIES, his EXTRAVAGANCIES, and his PLENTEOUS COFFERS, upon this *sacred Seat* he can only listen to the SYCOPHANTIC ADDRESSES of a CORRUPT and DESTRUCTIVE PARLIAMENT, those *Leeches* of the *Realm,* who so

5. For background see H. V. Bowen, *Revenue & Reform: The Indian problem in British politics 1757–1773* (Cambridge: Cambridge University Press, 1991) and the dated but still useful Lucy S. Sutherland, *The East India Company in Eighteenth-Century Politics* (Oxford: The Clarendon Press, 1952).

largely drain for their own abandaned uses, those Coffers, which his REPULSED CITIZENS so largely fill.

How like a GOD does a MONARCH look, encircled by TREACHEROUS MINIONS and RAPACIOUS FLATTERERS! How like a *mere* MORTAL, surrounded by Subjects MOST AFFECTIONATE, and SINCERE, who shower down at once both SUPPLIES and BLESSINGS, upon a Prince whom they HONOUR, ESTEEM, and LOVE!

But KINGS should quit the Track of MORTALS—they should disdain the *little Virtues* of HUMANITY! The *Spirit* of a *Monarch* should aspire at an ECCENTRIC CHARACTER, beyond the reach of MAN. This will nobly lead him not to *endure,* but to *repell* the humble Suits of his AGGRIVED SUBJECTS;—not to caress, but to detest his People;—not to sooth, conciliate, and appease; but to menace, insult, and exterminate: not to human Errors, but INHUMAN CRIMES: not to REFORMATION, but to MURDER. Not to JUSTICE, but to TYRANNY. Not to PEACE and HONOUR, but to REMORSE, HATRED, CALAMITY, RESISTANCE and the SCAFFOLD.

Let such Princes, like that unhappy Tyrant *Charles the First,* seek in Vain for Shelter, among the fawning Herds that idolize their Vices, for the sake of sharing their Prodigality and Profusion.

Let them try their faithful *Scots,* who as they have often received the Wages of CORRUPTION, will a *Second Time* receive the PRICE OF BLOOD.

Let them fly to the Arms of those *tender Tyrants,* their PRECEPTORS, who have thus carefully trained them to their IGNOMINY and RUIN from their Cradle.

Whilst they repulse a suffering and an injured Subject, let them fall for Consolation, upon the FRIENDLY Bosom of a *Mansfield* or a *Bute.*—Let them in their Frenzy fly for Succour to their CHANCELLOR,—not a *York,* alas!—but an *Apsley,* the poor SHADOW of a *Mansfield.*—Let them most deservedly taste all the Bitterness of *Despair,* and find Relief (though late) at last, in the generous CONDESCENSION and FORGIVENESS, of a DESPISED, INSULTED, and OPPRESSED PEOPLE.

ASTONISHED *then*, my Lord *Mansfield*, not at the Humble, just PE-
TITIONS, but at the LENITY of their PATIENT SUBJECTS, let them
deliver up their MINIONS to the BLOCK, with Shame and Contrition
resign the CROWN, and Sleep IGNOBLY with their Fathers; but let
their INFAMY be recorded, that succeeding Princes may profit largely
from such WEAK and GUILTY ANNALS.

C A S C A.

N. B. The Epistle to *Lord Mansfield* from CASCA is received, and shall
be made the Subject of our XVII Number. The Writer may depend, his
Directions will upon every Occasion, be implicitly followed—The Authors of the CRISIS wish to be honoured with a private Direction, how
to convey a few Papers Weekly to CASCA, for the Use of himself and
Friends, as a small Tribute of Gratitude for the repeated Favours he has
conferred on them. He may rest assured they never can betray PRIVATE
CONFIDENCE, nor abuse the sacred Offices of Friendship.

Printed and published for the Authors, by T. W. SHAW, in Fleet-Street,
opposite Anderton's Coffee House, where Letters to the Publisher will be
thankfully received.

THE

CRISIS

NUMBER XVI   *To be continued Weekly.*

SATURDAY, MAY 6, 1775,   [Price Two-pence Half-penny.

—Parcere *Subjectis*, et debellare *Superbos.*[1]—

VIRG.

To SUPPLICATION turn a *Princely* ear;

Nor MURDER Subjects you have SWORN to HEAR.

T HE Motto of this Paper gives a Specimen of *Roman*, the proceedings against *America*, of *English* Policy.—There is, and must necessarily be, a Compact, either *express*, or *emplyed*, between every *Sovereign* and *Subject*. PROTECTION and OBEDIENCE are the mutual Stipulations, if the ONE is WITHDRAWN, the OTHER CEASES. Now, PROTECTION is certainly withdrawn, when Subjects, guilty of no HOSTILE, or REBELLIOUS Act, (I defy

---

1. Another passage from Virgil's *Aeneid*, Book 6, translated: to spare the vanquished and subdue the proud.

the *Ministry* to prove *one* against them) are nevertheless treated (like the *Americans*) as ENEMIES and REBELS. *Administration,* most falsely and audaciously, stigmatize them with the Name of REBELS, merely to colour their own *base Designs*, and UNJUSTIFIABE HOSTILITIES against their Fellow-Subjects; in whom they discern an *odious* Spirit of LIBERTY, which sets (*for them*) a DANGEROUS EXAMPLE to the Mother Country. The NOBLE FLAME is dying HERE, and it would be fatal to *Ministerial designs*, that it should be cherished in any Part of our Dominions.

The SPIRITED AMERICANS feel this Truth, they foresee, and wisely guard against the Danger. They have *convened*, and *consulted* for the PUBLIC SAFETY, like TRUE BRITONS. What then? Is such a *national, political Congress*, a *traiterous Association?* At SUCH a Time too, and in SUCH a Cause? Is the Situation and Circumstances of *America* (a NATION in point of Territory and Numbers) to be compared to that of *Truro* (a rotten Borough) in *Cornwall?* *Buffoonery* in *serious Cases*, *Doctor Johnson*, dishonours human Nature, and degrades human Understanding. Not even the Example of your Master, Doctor, who played *Falstaff,* after he had deluded a late unhappy LORD CHANCELOR of *England* into *Suicide*, can sanctify *dramatic Pleasantry*, at the Expence of LIFE, LIBERTY, PROPERTY, and a whole COUNTRY.[2]

"Kill the next Piercy yourself," my Lord, is a species of *Drollery*, in a Case of BLOOD, unworthy even of a *Hackney Writer*; as to you, *Doctor Johnson,*—I do not expect you will write HONESTLY, but write *Sensibly.* Treat Subjects, (which might Affect even the Humanity of a

---

2. Whether Charles Yorke (see supra VI.3) died of a sudden illness or by his own hand in January 1770 was a matter of speculation then, and has been ever since. Most of the accounts about his demise are included in John Campbell, *Lives of the Lord Chancellors and Keepers of the Great Seal of England*, 5th ed., 10 vols. (London: J. Murray, 1868), 7:83–121. There is no hint there, however, that Mansfield–if he was the intended target as Dr. Johnson's "master"—had had anything to do with Yorke's death. Mansfield and Yorke had been associated through Lincoln's Inn and in various governmental capacities over the years, though they could hardly be considered political allies.

Scotchman) no more ludicrously, indecently, unfeelingly, and abandonly.[3]—With your leave, *Doctor*, I once more call *America* a NATION, and a great NATION; too far distant from her Mother Country, to receive from her either *immediate*, or *timely* Assistance on any sudden *foreign Attack*, SHE must, in such a Case, find Succour *within herself*, or PERISH. And shall SHE, whose ABILITIES we do not know, whose Country, on an emergency, we cannot Defend, shall SHE be denied the BRITISH RIGHT of Representation in our Parliament, if SHE must be TAXED by our Parliament: suppose it will not avail her, if she had it, and she would, notwithstanding, be borne down and overwhelmed (as *Doctor Johnson* tells us) by a Majority of CORRUPT VOICES: yet, let her have the Pleasure of seeing the UNCLEAN Hands, if not the TRAITEROUS HEARTS, of those by whom she is to FALL.—It is her BIRTHRIGHT.—Shall SHE, so situated, so circumstanced, be denied the INHERENT PRIVILEGE, that INDUBITABLE RIGHT, of MEETING, CONSULTING, and RESOLVING for herself, at all Times, much less when we have *wantonly assailed her*? Is this REBELLION, let me cooly ask, Who was the *first Agressor*? Did we *first consult*, *resolve*, nay, *act* against *America*, or *America* against us? Here *Administration* must be dumb.

If UNWARRANTABLE OPPRESSION may be RESISTED, upon Revolution Principles, the Tye between *England* and *America*, is actually dissolved, our PROTECTION is withdrawn, our TYRANNIC Sword unsheathed, and *Common Sense* proclaims aloud, that OBEDIENCE in *America* is no more.

Why have we thus attacked her with *unmerited* Hostilities? because SHE would not PASSIVELY hold out her Hands to receive our CHAINS.

---

3. The allusion is to a popular scene from Shakespeare's *Henry IV*, Part I, Act V, Scene 4. "There is Percy," boasts Sir John Falstaff, as he tosses down the body of Hotspur at the feet of Prince Hal as the Battle of Shrewsbury draws to a close. "If your father will do me any honor, so; if not, let him kill the next Percy himself." Prince Hal, not Falstaff, had in fact slain Hotspur, but he lets the boon companion of his misspent youth—so long an irritation to his father, Henry IV—continue with his ridiculous claim. Also see infra XXI.7.

SHE is wise,—SHE saw those CHAINS forging, and CONSULTED.—
SHE sees them now actually ready to be rivitted, and is RESOLVED.

The Memory of a *Cromwell* warms my soul! *America* wants *one* at this
Instant.[4]—Was there not a Period, long before those weak and wicked
Monarchs *Charles* the *First*, and *James* the *Second*, were RESISTED,
when *England* might have been truly said to have owed no Obedience
to those Sovereigns? This cannot be denied.—But, *Subjects* were then
to PRAY, and to APPEAL TO HEAVEN against TYRANTS, because
they styled themselves GODS VICEGERENTS upon Earth. We seem
to be coming round to the same Species of ADULATION and IDOLA-
TRY again. As a *Revolutionist*, and a *Whig*, I hold a KING to be no more
(upon Revolution Principles he is no more) than the HEAD CONSTA-
BLE of the Realm. If he is a PATRIOT KING, he ought to be HON-
OURED and REVERED; but if he *is less than that*, he is no more to be
WORSHIPPED than a CALF.[5]

In the Case of *America we* have been the Aggressors *clearly.* The Protection *stipulated* by the Sovereign AT THE ALTAR; extends to the LIVES,
the LIBERTIES, and PROPERTY of the Subject. ALL THESE have
been FIRST violated BY US, WANTONLY, WEAKLY, and WICK-
EDLY in *America.* Such a Violation is TREASON; (nay, start not, my
Lords *Bute* and *Mansfield*) I say it is TREASON by the Laws of England.—*Laws* (my Lord *Mansfield*) not so easily *erased* as a *Record.* Whilst

4. The author(s) may have been speaking ironically, or perhaps just sarcastically, here.
Oliver Cromwell was a fairly ambiguous figure, far more so than Charles I and other
figures from the Civil War of the 1640s. To some he was the English Caesar, corrupted
by personal ambition and a delusive sense of his own importance, but not to all. See,
for example, James Harris' *An Historical and Critical Account of the Life of Oliver Cromwell, Lord Protector of the Commonwealth of England, Scotland and Ireland* (London: A,
Millar, 1752), which tried to strike a rough balance, even as Harris decried Cromwell's
"illegal and tyrannical actions" and subversion of republican principles.

5. Readers would have known the basic story behind the allusion to idolatrous calf worship, even if not the precise scriptural sources in the Old Testament. The most notorious incident was recorded in Exodus 32, involving Moses, Aaron and Israelites losing
faith as they wandered in the wilderness; there were other incidents as well.

these Laws stand, every actual Breach of the COMPACT between King and People, committed by the SOVEREIGN, is TREASON AGAINST THE PEOPLE, and worse than TREASON; it is a Sin against HEAVEN, as well as against the SUBJECT. It is ROYAL PERJURY.

After *such* a *Breach*, does *Obedience* exist among Subjects? Answer me— not ye *Mansfields* and *Machiavels*, but ye *venerable Shades*, who bled for LIBERTY and JUSTICE; even the *fanciful* Montesquieu (as *Doctor Johnson* calls him) would turn a PERJURED MONARCH pale with his Reply.[6]—The Contention *now* (says the *Doctor*) is for *Power*. But is *Power* (before gentle Means are tried) to be maintained by FAMINE and by BLOOD! are *the earliest Supplications* of suffering Subjects to be *slighted*, *rejected*, and *derided?* Surely not.—Yet this has been the Fate of *America*. These humble Applications from *distressed America* have finally fallen down through the Fingers of MAJESTY, ADMINISTRATION, and the LEGISLATURE, to that consummate Politician, and Representative of the three great Estates of this Kingdom, *Doctor Johnson*; who has the *unparalleled-impudence* to treat them with low Humour, open Laughter, and Scurrility, in his late *patriotic* Publication, called *Taxation no Tyranny*. *Thus*, and *only thus*, have the *Americans* received a *verbal Answer*; received it from the *hackney Pen* of a *scribbling Prostitute*. They are, it seems, to re-

6. Latin editions of Machiavelli's works had long been available from London printers; a new English edition appeared in 1775. Countless Anglo-American writers referred to Niccolo Machiavelli whenever they urged readers—or policy makers—to "recur' to "first principles." Machiavelli looms large in Pocock's *Ancient Constitution* (see supra V.2); larger still in William R. Everdell, *The End of Kings* (New York: The Fress Press, 1983). Paul Sonnino's introduction to his translation of *The Prince* (Amherst, N. Y.: Humanity Books, 1996) serves as a caution to those who would use Machiavelli as the crucial figure marking a transition from the classical to the modern world. Charles de Secondat, Baron de Montesquieu's *Spirit of the Laws* was available in English translation as well as the original French. Montesquieu's place in the American founding, with his explication of separation of powers based on his understanding of the British "mixed" arrangement of king, Lords, and Commons, has long been a staple of the historiography of the subject. See, notably, Thomas L. Pangle, *The Spirit of Modern Republicanism* (Chicago: University of Chicago Press, 1988). Machiavelli and Montesquieu both figure prominently in Paul A. Rahe's magnum opus *Republics: Ancient and Modern* (Chapel Hill: University of North Carolina Press, 1992).

ceive a DECISIVE ONE in the FIELD.—Alas! had any TREASON been committed, *Bills of Attainder* would have passed? What? without hearing? Certainly. The consistent Spirit of Administration, and the MANLY PERSEVERANCE of their Sovereign, who confides *in a smuggled and corrupt Parliament*, would have requested it. *Government* now cannot be supported without *Injustice*. Besides, the *hungry Myrmidons*,[7] the *ministerial Bloodhounds*, are looking for their *Prey*. They are already gaping for *forfeited Lands in America*.—Had there been but a glimmering of *Treason*, Bills of *Attainder* must have passed. The *Fishery Bill* is almost as penal. *America* is at this Moment suffering without *an hearing*, and *without a Crime*.

The Means used by *Administration* are, most humanely, and sagaciously, *Preventive*. They are now carrying *Famine* and *Desolation* into *America*, for fear she *should resist*, and punishing her as a REBEL, for fear she should *Rebel*. Her Supplications spurned, all conciliating Measures rejected, *despotic Measures* alone pursued, what resourse has *She* now, but in *herself*? General *Gage*, the Commander first sent against them, has from natural Honour, Justice, and Humanity, exceeded his Commission: in his Heart he is more an *Advocate* than an *Enemy*.—He has *offended*—He has desired to be *recalled*.—*Administration* are *disappointed* in their Man; yet dare not discover and declare their *Disappointment*, by *recalling* him. This General, with a *handful of Soldiers*, was wisely commissioned to *bully all America*.—He *disdained it*.—It is a Task fitter for *Burgoyne*, who has learned it at the gaming Table, and practiced it at *Preston*. But this *favourite Commander* will make an admirable Figure for *Mat. Darley*, left, like a *solitary Quixote*, in the Field by his *honest Troops*, who will never sheath their Swords in the Bowels of their Countrymen.[8]

---

7. The "Myrmidons"—warriors who followed Achilles into battle at Troy—were probably familiar to Britons of this generation through Alexander Pope's translation of Homer's *The Iliad* and Ovid's *Metamorphoses*. Originally created from ants by Zeus at the request of Achilles' grandfather, Aeacus, they were famous for their swarming attacks and fearlessness in the face of danger.

8. Matthias Darly and his wife Mary ran a successful London printing and engraving shop on the Strand, where they also sold paper and pens, pictures and frames. They produced as well printed caricatures that were more about manners and fashion than politics, and Matthias became well-known as a furniture designer. See Timothy Clayton's essay on him in the *Oxford DNB*, 15:160–61.

Had we acted like a Parent, we should have *heard*, admonished, advised, and (if possible) reclaimed, *mistaken America*; but *still protected her*. Instead of this, we have not only withdrawn our Protection (without trying one lenient Measure) *but commenced War* against her.—She *sensibly* withheld her former commercial Intercourses with *England*, and threatened to do the same with the West India Colonies.—Thus (says *Doctor Johnson*) they have defrauded their Creditors *here,* and condemned our Merchants to Bankruptcy. If Creditors and Merchants suffer, if Manufacturers complain, they must recurr to the *first Cause*. These are the pernicious Effects of the wise Steps, taken first by the *ministerial* Aggressors in this Country. Nor is it to be wondered at, if the Consequence of these rash and unjust Proceedings by the *Harpies of Power,* should produce (in case of an approaching War with France and Spain) *a general Bankruptcy of this Nation.*—A Thought by no means *Chemerical*, but truly *Melancholy*; a Thought, which can neither be baffled by the buffoonery of *Hackney Scriblers*, the grave Sarcasms of *Statesmen*, or the *cruel Pleasantry* of *thoughtless Majesty itself.*

C A S C A.

Printed and published for the Authors, by T. W. SHAW, in Fleet-Street, opposite Anderton's Coffee House, where Letters to the Publisher will be thankfully received.

THE

CRISIS

NUMBER XVII   *To be continued Weekly.*

SATURDAY, May 13, 1775   [*Price Two-pence Half-penny.*

Casca's Epistle to LORD MANSFIELD.

*Uni æqures Virtuti atque ejus amicis.

To *Virtue* only just and *Virtue's Friends.*

CAN you, my Lord, who serve *despotic Ends*,
Can you be "*just to Virtue and her Friends?*"
To *wanton* † *Murders* when did She afford
Protection yet, or *alter a Record*?
Say, does your callous Soul receive no Shock,
When, *conscious*, in the Hall, you view the ‡ *Clock*?
Or can you fill *perfidious* ||*Scroges's* place,

---

*The Motto on Lord Mansfields State Coach.

†The two Kennedys—Balte and M'Quirke,—and the two Murderers of Young Allen.—The four last *pensioned*, as well as *pardoned*: with Lord Mansfield's Privity and Advice.

‡Judge Ingram. many Years ago, was fined for altering a Record; with that Fine, the Clock now in Westminster Hall, was erected.

||This Chief Justice was, of late Years, removed and punished for perverting Law, misleading and inviegling Juries, and other Crimes *in Lord Mansfield's way.*

Without a pressage of your own Disgrace?
Yes—Yes—to England's shame, you're out of reach,
And Laugh at him who Threatens to *impeach*.
If *Burke* should rise, the Farce no farther goes;
To one *just Aye*, *North* brings ten *impious No's*.
In Youth, before *dissembling* was your Trade,
To *James* Libations on your Knees you made:
Not *Loyalty,* but *Fear* has sheath'd your Sting;
No *Murray* can be faithful to his King.
From the black North in famish'd Clans you swarm,
And, *thawing*, feel how *Albion's* Sun can warm;
Your *Clime* you change, your *Sentiments* retain;
In *Scotchmen* Treason is an *innate* Stain;
Like *Itch* and *Scurvy*, in their Blood it reigns;
He who wou'd cure it, must exhaust their Veins.
Once against *Rebels*, 'twas your *Place* to plead;
Your *Mouth* condemn'd, your *Soul* approv'd the *Deed*.
Whilst round your *Heart* sad *Disappointmant* hung,
Dissimulation oil'd your *treach'rous Tongue*.
A *Murray* then (your Brother too) was found
In Arms, in secret Trust; in Duty bound,
And Principle *(like yours)* to aid a *Claim,*
Which you affected with a *Blush* to name;
A *Blush ill-acted*;—to thy *Ghostly pale*,
(Index of *Guilt*) soft Nature lends no Veil.
No—She, my Lord, disdains to serve *base Ends*;
She's "*only just to Virtue and her Friends.*"
On them She smiles, on CHATHAM'S Cheek she glows,
When *injur'd Children* are assail'd like *Foes*;
When *Famine's* call'd to aid the *coward-plan*,
And *North* completes what *Bute* and *You* began.
Perish your Names!—your *Thane* in fear is fled,
With ev'ry Curse, but *Scotland's*, on his Head;

*When Sollicitor General, in 1745.

In Shade, but not (alas!) in *Death* enshrin'd,
Whilst you, his *faithful Proxy*, speak his Mind;
And (to *weak George* from soothing Flatt'ry dear)
Pour your *Laird's* Poison in the *Royal-ear*.
Why do your treach'rous Actions shun the Light?
Why do *Back-stairs* feel *Mansfield's* Steps at *Night*?
To George your Councils and yourself convey,
Fraught with Infection, in the face of Day.
Let not the *royal Closet's* Whisper screen,
Your glorious Works; but let your Light be seen.
Conduct, avow, enforce your *Patriot-plans,*
Nor trust their Merits to *Subaltern Clans*.
Tho' *Bute* absconds, yet aid *your Joint-design,*
Yourself, my Lord; and help to spring the Mine.
Whilst *Grafton, Sandwich, Denbigh, North,* stand forth,
And to *astonish'd* Ears, proclaim their *Worth*;
Whilst, with rank Nonsense, *Suffolk, Pomfret,* dare,
Without a Blush, to make *Plebeians* stare;
Why, when your Sov'reign's pleas'd by *Law to kill,*
Step not *you* forth to guild the desp'rate Pill?
'Tis decent, sure, so pension'd, plac'd, and brib'd,
To recommend the Dose you have prescrib'd
But *Fear,* my Lord, mean, abject *Fear,* still gives
A Check—in you a *lurking Traytor* lives;
The worst of *Traytors*—you have Sense to see
Fair *Freedom's* Charms, yet blast the Soul that's *Free*.
Early and late, incessant in your Pains,
For brave *America* you forge vile Chains.
Yet meanly, in your House, or Court, take root,
When you should *Speak,* as *Deputy to Bute*.
He still lies Hid; perhaps, at *Clapham lurks,
Whilst *You* and *Apsley* carry on the Works.

---

*Whilst this Lord was thought to have been *abroad*, he was concealed at Mr. *Lovelace's* (the Banker) on Clapham Common.

To grant a *Nation's Claim* each *House* is loth,
But *You* have *Representatives* in *both*.
Strangely absurd!—yet this we know and see;
This Truth subdu'd your modest Member **Leigh*.
The Man had Sense, and felt his own Disgrace,
How well an †*Aston* wou'd supply his Place!
So *represented*, with such Leaders too,
(*North*—*George*—obsequious to your Lordship's Cue.)
This War *against ourselves* will soon be won,
Odious America be soon *undone*.
Remonstrances are vain, *Bute* won't relax,
But sternly bids *North* lay *another Tax*.
The Tax of *Death*, by Bayonet and Ball;
But *Famine* is the hardest Tax of all.
From *Scotland*, could that Thought derive its Source?
Where is *sharp Famine* felt with greater Force?
In all the Horrors *there* the *Fiend's* array'd;
There her shrunk Hand for ever chills the Blade.
There, with lank Sides, the meagre Cattle moan;
Their Keeper asks for *Bread* and gets a Stone.
From this distress *Bute* and *yourself* soon fled,
Yet pour it's plagues upon *a Nation's* head.
By *vilest means*, my Lord, you seek *vile ends*;
Thus are you "*just to virtue and her friends.*"
In all your strokes a master's hand appears:
Stand forth—claim all your praise, and banish *fears*.
If *Conscience* dictates every *ill* you do,
Frankly expose the *Knave* you hide, to view.
Plebeians scorn—to gain your King's applause,
Like base ‡*De Burgo,* fawn and wrest the Laws.

---

*The late Sergeant Leigh. Lord Mansfield on a *sudden Pannic*, got him into the House of Commons, by way of an Orator, to defend him in case of an Attack.
†One of Lord Mansfields *favourite* Judges.
‡A most iniquitous *Chief Justice*, who was *hanged* (like *Tresilian*) in Henry the Thirds Time, for *erasing Records*, as well as for other Villainies.—Good precedents both, and full in Point.

Dispise what faithful History shall say;
Full in your *Zenith now*, enjoy your Day;
Tho' in Times annals your foul Name shou'd rust,
Whilst *Fame* to *Holt's* erects lasting bust.
He had no **Smythe*; no bias *he* had shown,
But dragg'd *Assassins* from behind the *Throne.*
Guardian of England's Laws he gave 'em sway,
And held them forth for Sovereigns to *obey.*
Against the People's Rights he took no part,
But judg'd, and counsell'd,with an *honest Heart.*
Prerogative (*unpension'd* and *unbrib'd*)
He kept within the bounds that Law prescrb'd,
By *Freedom's* side he firmly took his stand,
Yet held the Ballance with an equal Hand.
Of that fair Plant he cherish'd ev'ry Shoot,
And, with a Parent's fondness, nurs'd the Root.
His Name, whilst Law endures, shall live in Praise;
Ashby and White, †no *Mansfield* can *erase.*
But you, my Lord, to *Infamy* still true,
Indulge your King's Caprice in all you do.
If *Citizens* their humble *Plaints* express,
You bid him spurn the *May'r,* and his Address.
With *pleasantry* your Sov'reign's heat asswage,
And arm him for the ‡*horned Cattle's* rage.

---

*This *godly* and upright Man, (Lord Mansfield's Favourite) tried the two Villains who murdered young Allen, and laboured their Acquittal; but they were found Guilty upon the clearest Evidence.—He then severely threatened any Person who should dare to print that Trial.—He has since been made one of the Commissioners of the great Seal, and Lord Chief Baron, as a Reward for his Integrity.

†In this well-known Case, Lord Chiet Justice Holt decided in Favour of the Right of Electors, in the Teeth of a menacing House of Commons, and in defiance of their pretended PRIVILEGES.

‡Soon after the memorable Petition in BECKFORD's Mayoralty, Lord Mansfield inserted a witty Stricture in the King's Speech, and made his Majesty talk of the Distemper which raged among the horned Cattle; under that indecent Sarcasm, coarsely alluding to the Discontents of the City of London. The Petition itself, the King took no farther Notice of.

Instruct him how to Speak, to Sneer, and Frown,
To try if *Tricks* will bear a *City* down:
To be *astonish'd* that one Voice shou'd sue
To turn a *Tyrant* from his *Bloody-view.*
Death is the Word—let loose the *Dogs* of *Prey;*
Burgoyne's the Man, my Lord; encrease his Pay.
Your *Heart's* well known; your Voice attention Draws;
Arise and vindicate your Master's cause.
In *Art* supreme, in *Perfidity* not weak,
Show bashful Lordlings what it is to *speak.*
Let not such Fools as *Suffolk,* when they rise,
Without a word of English, snatch the Prize.
Shall Peers, whose *Infamy* is scarce half-blown,
Vaunt *Mansfield's* Schemes, as if they were his own;
In Language, which no Grammar e'er equipp'd,
Language, for which a School-boy wou'd be whipp'd?
No.—Be *yourself,* my Lord; and unconfin'd,
Assert your Right of *ruining Mankind.*
Break forth in all your *Ciceronian blaze,*
And let your *Front* no more than *Heart* amaze.
Equal in *Private* and *in Public* shine,
And dare to be another *Cataline.*
Shou'd galling *Junius* make a new attack,
(Whose Lashes still are flagrant on your Back,)
The Libeller by some State blood-hound Trace,
And let him feel the Terrors of your *Place.*
Grafton in *Friendship* some sure Snare will lay,
As *Friend,* and *Spy,* he'll join him and betray.
If *precedent Injustice* can anoint,
John Wilkes's Case, will be a Case in point.
Then, make the Senate ring; like *Pomfret* rave;
And scorn by *pension'd Proxies* to *enslave.*
"*Pomfret!*—there's Weight in what *such Heads* advise;
Madmen in council are to *me* a Prize.
Since *Smith* is Dead, *Pomfret* may be endured:

We loose a *Vote*, shou'd the poor Man be *cur'd.*
Besides, he *Speaks*—in Sentiments *unites*,
He sometimes Raves and Stares, but never *Bites.*"
"Granted, my Lord"—but yet (unknown to yield,
As *your Troops* are) why don't you take the Field
In *Person?* Clear Suspicions, Doubts dispel:
No Lord *contrives, abetts*, or speaks, so well.
Does *virtuous Camden* talk your Spirit down,
Or *Chatham* awe you with a Roman frown?
When *Patriot Rockingham*, or *Richmond* rise,
Does *Freedom's* ray annoy your dazzled Eyes?
Does *Shelburne's* Boldness shake your dastard Soul?
Or *Temple's* perseverance want Controul?
Can you, with *Forces* so well paid, and fed,
Despond, unless your *Thane* is at your Head?
Can you, his staunch Lieutenant Colonel, fail
In *Senate*, as in *Council,* to prevail?
Or is your Courage check'd in it's Career,
Because you've lost *five thousand Pounds a Year?*
Long in *Commission* you had kept the *Seals;*
*Three Judges moving on your Lordship's Wheels;
Their Mouths pronounc'd, but your's prescrib'd the Law;
Thus have we *Kings* and *Judges* too, of *Straw.*
If *ten* such learn'd *Triumvirates* as that,
With all their Law will scarce make *half a Pratt;*
Who can behold (and not with Rage be stirr'd)
A *Prætor* †sliver'd from the *weakest Third?*
This Thought of yours, my Lord, your *Pow'r* ensures,
The *weaker* the Man is, the more he's *yours.*
In *Council, Court,* and *Parliament* we see
Your *faithful Shadow* moves as *you* decree;

---

*Smythe, Bathurst, (now Lord Apsley) and Aston.
†Lord Apsley.

witness the *Cause of *Thickness against Leigh*.]
This Project shows your *Machiavelian* skill,
You're † *Speaker* thus (and *more* than *Speaker*) still.
Profoundly *Politic* in all you do,
Thus are you *Chancellor* and *Speaker* too.
Yet, when you can foresee an *hard fought Day*,
Like *Falstaff,* from your post you sneak away.
The risque your *rag-o-muffin bands* may share:
You (like your THANE) make *Self* your dearest Care.
Boldly you counsel underneath the Rose;
But fly the Conflict when the Armies close.
A War of *Reason* gives your Lordship pain:
Virtue alone such Conflicts can sustain.
Too free, too pure, to serve *Oppression's* end,
She can't mistake a *Mansfield* for a *Friend*.
Some few hard fronts can stand the shock of Steel,
But none the Thunder of the Public-Weal.
Ev'n JOVE himself, GREAT JOVE, can't bear reproach,
Nor pass without a *pannic* in his Coach,
When to NORTH's smuggled Parliament he rides,
The *God* betraying what the Stoic hides.
Fain would he *smile*—shrill hoots his muscles check,
Then how he wishes *England* had one ‡Neck!
At ev'ry Hiss he feels a conscious Start,
And Groans re-echo'd pierce his Tyrant-Heart;
A Heart, in *infancy* too soon ensur'd:
To slight those *Ills* his People have endur'd;
Harden'd by *Female* Insolence and Pride;
To *Bute* entrusted as it's *only Guide,*
A *Guide* to what? not to the People's Love,
(The safest Ground on which a King can move)

---

*See JUNIUS's Letter to Lord Apsley, in the CRISIS, No. VII.
†To the House of Lords.
‡The Impious wish of that haughty Tyrant *Caligula*, in respect to *Rome*.

Nor to the Path of Honour, Truth, or Fame,
In which our *Edward's* won a glorious Name;
Not, with discernment, to enforce the Laws,
Or yield to Subjects in a *Righteous Cause;
To aid the just, to sooth the giddy Throng,
And wisely to distinguish *right* from *wrong;*
To temper Justice with an even Hand,
And drive *Corruption* from a sinking Land;
But train'd (alas!) to act the meanest part,
To speak a Language foreign to his heart,
To *promise* more than *Briton's* ever hear'd,
Trusting to have his †*sacred Lyes* rever'd;
To set his Honour and his soul to Sale,
As Water *false*, as courtly Sunshine *frail*;
In *Theory* well-School'd; in *Practice* taught
To be the sad reverse of what he ought.
Honour and Faith in *Falshood's*, Stream he laves,
And toil's to make a freeborn People Slaves.
Not so our great ‡ *Deliver'r* sought renown;
He knew from *whom*, and *why*, he had the *Crown.*
But *now,* the Globe and Scepter's held for show,
Bute, says that ‖*Craft* is all a King should know;
Quotes *bright* examples from each *Stuart's* reign;
To such a Scholar not one Hint's in vain.
A *Just Petition's* answer'd with a sneer;
And to secure his point, he drops a Tear.
Unhappy *York!* Too fickle to resist!
Alas! thy Death encreas'd the *Tyrants* List!
Not to be won by all that Sense could try,
You fell by water from the *weakest* Eye!

*Alluding to the City Remonstrances and Petition.
†For the Truth of this Assertion compare JOVE's Speeches with his Actions.
‡King William III.
‖What poor James I. pedantically called King-craft.

If *Hypocrites are *Murd'rers,* who shall dare
To excuse that *Guilt,* which bare-fac'd thanks declare?
When harmless Lives were lost, and *Rome* was burn'd,
NERO, in form his grateful thanks return'd;
Happy to have a cool, *obedient Scot*
Perform his *bloody Orders* to a jot;
Happy to find two more so bravely warm'd,
So hot for Blood, to stab *one* † *Youth unarm'd.*
O! when in British Annals shall this blot
Of Sanguinary Power be forgot!
Never whilst this corrupt and bloody Reign
Shall Furnish a Record of Slaves and Slain.
Never whilst brave America can feel
The Sense of wrongs, or the redress of Steel:
Never whilst Liberty and Right Divine,
Mark the vile *Stuart* from the *Brunswick Line.*
Behold! what *Bute's* long-labour'd Culture brings,
A King of Patches! And a shame to Kings!
A Baby! who is humour'd till he thinks
That Water sacred, which a Monarch drinks.
Taught that the height of Piety's to kneel,
He says his pray'rs and bids the Vulgar feel.
Let meaner Souls relent, forgive forget;
Such Weakness ne'er disgrac'd a *Stuart yet.*
No—let the *Slave* that thwarts US be undone,
Long live the *Mother* in the *Tyrant* Son!
Thus lectures *Bute,*—and this advice embrac'd,
All Sense of Virtue in the Bud's effac'd,
How shou'd King's see in infancy made blind?
Whose Manhood's watch'd, whose Knowledge is confin'd?
To whom no page in History's reveal'd,

---

*Must not a Man be a most notorious and cruel *Hypocrite*, who could say to the Duke of *Grafton* upon the above Melancholy Occasion, "Kill the next Piercy yourself my Lord." This is an actual Fact.
†Young Allen, in St George's Fields.

But where they find the Subject's Cause appeal'd
To Heav'n?—this same Redress *Carte's* Volumes teach;
These George may read—these *Bute* and *Mansfield* preach.
True to his trust the *Thane* his task begun;
He pleas'd the *Mother* and he *dup'd* the Son.
Taught him to fly above the legal Sphere,
And by sad *Charles's* Star his Course to steer;
To bear no Counsel, no sage hint, no Guide;
But think all Subjects born for King's to ride;
By *Famine brave resistance to entomb,
And (with *Macbeth*) to "leap the life to come";
To wait no Tide, attend no rising Gale,
But rashly spread *Prerogative's* full sail:
To heed no Subject in his bold careers,
But Passive Pensioners and rotten Peers.
To spare no Life, if poignant Satyr strikes;
To Plan the Death of him he most dislikes;
Waiting impatient for the setting Sun,
To hear good news from †*Martyn* and from *Dun.*
To give *in jest* a *Coronation Pledge,*
Nor think an *Oath* more sacred than a ‡*Wedge.*
Alas! that *Off'ring* shou'd suggest a Thought,
That *Charity* by *former* Kings was wrought;
That, from the royal Cradle to the Grave,
The *truest Piety's* to *guard* and *save.*
Such Acts as these to *Crowns* a Lustre lend;
This, Mansfield, this is being *"Virtues Friend."*
But, when *Destruction* is a King's *Command,*
And *Death* gains Passports from the *royal* Hand;
When *Carnage* is the Word—when gen'rous *Gage,*
Dreads that *his* Name shou'd blot th'historic Page,
And, with a Tenderness his Prince will *blame,*

---

*In America.
†Two Villains hired to murder Mr. Wilkes, for writing No. 45, of the North Briton.
‡A Wedge of Gold annually offered at the Alter by our King's.

Shrinks from *rank Murder*, and *eternal Shame*;
When Conscience and Remorse from *Court* is flown,
Nor dare sollicit a *despotic Throne*;
All must be *Slaves*, till *Spirit* shall return,
To fire those Bosoms where it us'd to burn;
Till we consider *Names* far less than *Things,*
Nor care from what *sound Stem* we take our Kings;
Till *scepter'd Pride* is taught to bless the Hand
That calls her to protect a *gen'rous Land*;
Is taught that *British Monarchs* owe their State,
To those who can *depose* them or *create;*
Provok'd, insult'd, spurn'd can spare, or try;
Or throw, with Scorn, their *royal Creature* by.
BUTE! MANSFIELD! These are Doctrines which appear
Horrid and *Harsh* to your *distemper'd* Ear;
But there will come a Time when you shall rue
That e'er you counsell'd with a Heart untrue:
When from those Counsels deadly Fueds shall rise
To force a *Tear unfeign'd* from *George*'s Eyes.
Truth ev'n on Kings in that sad Hour attends:
Charles found, *at last*, his *People* were his *Friends*;
To *Notions*, false as *Friends*, he bid adieu;
These had *deceiv'd*; the BLOCK spoke plain, but TRUE.
Ne'er may a BRUNSWICK taste such BITTER FRUIT,
But leave the AXE to MANSFIELD, NORTH, and BUTE.
These Lines, inspir'd by CHURCHILL's laurell'd Shade,
I write, unknown, unpatronized, unpaid:
Proud, if my honest Muse, by chance, has cropp'd
One Flow'r from that fair Wreath which *Churchill* dropp'd.
Let *Johnson* toil for *Hire*, with *Falsehoods* please;
(NORTH's FIAT feeds, and DUBBS him with DEGREES.)
His be the SHAME; the gen'rous Transport mine,
To goad a VILLAIN's Heart at ev'ry Line.
Disdaining Pidlers, who for FLOWRET's roam,
Like BRUTUS, ROUGH, I'll plant the Dagger HOME.

TYRANTS and TRAYTORS CASCA ne'er forgives;
Tremble SUCH Monsters whilst that CASCA lives.
The Blasts he blows their GUILTY Souls shall shock,
And drive them to PERDITION and the BLOCK.

Printed and published for the Authors, by T. W. SHAW, in Fleet-Street, opposite Anderton's Coffee House, where Letters to the Publisher will be thankfully received.

THE

CRISIS

NUMBER XVIII   *To be continued Weekly.*

SATURDAY, MAY 20, 1775   *[Price Two-pence Half-penny.*

Casca's Epistle to *L O R D   N O R T H*
—ita digerit omnia Cælchas.

VIR.[1]

If sad BRITANNIA wails, in deep Distress,
Her *Taxes* greater and her *Freedom* less:
She owes these Grievances to *Bute's* vile Tribe,
North's Dissolution, and a *Treas'ry Bribe.*

To you my Lord, these honest Lines I send;
To you the Sov'reign's not the People's *Friend.*
The Sov'reign's *Friend*? yes, when I think again,
A Friend like *Wolsey* in a *Harry's* reign.[2]

1. "So Coelebas [Calchus] interprets the omens," from Virgil's *Aeneid*, Book 2.

2. Thomas Wolsey rose in power as the king he served, Henry VIII, rose in stature. Even as a cardinal he remained involved in matters of state as well as church, wielding great power as Henry's lord chancellor. He fell from grace when he stood with Pope Clement VII against Henry's desire to divorce Catherine of Aragon so that he could marry Anne Boleyn. Wolsey would be remembered as an object lesson in the price of hubris, personifying the fate that awaits those caught up in their own ambition.

Harry, who gave his Royal Lusts full scope;
Commenc'd a *Devil* and renounc'd the *Pope.*
In *Bute* and *North* two *Devils* make us groan,
And at *Quebec* the *Pope* resumes his Throne.
Harry's despotic Frowns o'er cast us now;
Fate hangs on *Bute's* proud Will and *George's* Brow.
Below, *North* represents *absconding Bute,*
Above, a *Nation dyes by *Roy le veut.*†
Proud of *North's* Name Corruption wears no Veil;
At *North's* soft Bribe, no Senator turns Pale.
Shrew'd *Walpole* never went your Lordship's length;
But Boldness with supplies has gather'd strength.
Safe from Impeachments in this venal Time,
Each *Parricide* may triumph in his Crime.
Knaves in your Lordship's Numbers put their hope;
Lords fear no AX, and Commoners no ROPE,
Virtue's fair Dawn you've clouded with a Sum;
And check'd her *Test* for Seven Years to come.
ASSOCIATION is a dreadful Sound;
And *Bute* must dye if Virtue is not bound.
Shou'd *Tests* ensue; Impeachments wou'd take place,
And old *St. Stephen* wear an Honest Face.
What must be done?—"dissolve, crys *Bute* in Fits:
"*Dissolve*—and stab your Country with new Writs."
He spoke: and *North* obedient to his Voice,
With Gold prepar'd his Boroughs for their *Choice.*
Appriz'd his Members of the dex'trous Cheat,
And plac'd Corruption in her former Seat.
Crouching she licks the Hand by which she's fed,
And Joys to see *Sir Fletcher*[3] at her Head;

*America.
†Those Words are pronounced by the Clerk of the Parliament when the King passes the Bills.

3. Sir Fletcher Norton, then speaker of the House of Commons, had been solicitor general in the Bute ministry and attorney general under Grenville. Named speaker early on

To see *North* ape *Bute's* dictatorial Nod,
For *George* deserts his Country and his GOD.
To see her Sons alert when *North* Commands,
And at his beck lift up *Four Hundred Hands.*
But whence this mighty influence? whence this Pow'r?
All Virtue's delug'd in a golden Show'r
A *Treas'ry Storm* what Virtue can resist?
Ev'n *George* to drown her, dips his *Civil List.*
With Thirst hydropic all *North's* Patriots drink,
And *half* a *Million* scarce will make' em sink.
From craving more no Decency restrains,
At once they Poison and exhaust our Veins.
Let those, who feel the *Civil List* decrease,
Call on *Mountstewart* to restore his *Fleece.*
Father and *Son* are equally a Curse:
One dupes the *Sov'reign,* and one drains the *Purse.*
In Baubles and douceurs what Treasures fly?
How are the People *plunder'd* to supply!
Elegance lavish'd on a SCOT is vain,
A Hovel might content an *Embryo Thane.*
His Ancestors (this Truth is Wormwood now,)
Whose Hut contain'd their Wife, their Bairns, and Cow,
Thought e'er their Union taught their Pride to feel,
A Pounde in Siller was a muckle deale.
But since *Scots* felt the Blessings of that Law,
Which laid their *Thanes* on *Down* instead of *Straw,*
Bless'd them with Commerce, Arts, and all their Fruits,
And bade them herd no longer with their Brutes;
By Culture humaniz'd their Savage mind,
And plac'd them on a footing with Mankind;
Their *haughty Sons* who else had fed on Grass,

---

in North's ministry, he became increasingly disaffected with North's policies. He was forced out of the speaker's chair before the end of the American war but he kept his seat as a member of the Commons.

Or filch'd for hunger, Thistles from their Ass,
Shiv'ring on Mountains desolate and cold,
Strangers alike to luxury and Gold,
Forgetting, like their Sires, *Want's* bitter Sting,
Disdain the *Palace of an *English King*;
Demand supurb additions, vast expence,
To fit it for a Lordlings Residence.
O! Shame! where art thou fled!—ye Britons, rise!
Is it for *Bute's* pround Race you grant Supplies?
With just Resentment bid *Mountstewart* fly,
And feed his Pride beneath his *Father's* Sky;
There pinch on Rocks where barren Nature sleeps;
Yes—scourge him back to his *paternal* † *Nieps.*
Weak Sov'reigns, thus their artful *Minions* bless;
Ask what they dare their constant answer's YES.
When injur'd Subjects with Petitions go,
The Sov'reign, *low'ring*, looks an haughty NO.
Yet if his Kingship wants a fresh Supply,
Below—aye, aye,—above, Contents the cry.
Petitioners with Rebels are involv'd;
Let *Bute* but hint—the Parliaments dissolv'd.
This influence ‡BECKFORD labour'd to resist?
Corruption, was maintain'd, and HE dismiss'd.
Cities Petition, yet their Plague endures;
But *Virtue's* rage ‖*quick Dissolution* cures.

*Alluding to Kensington Palace lately ordered to be fitted up (in great Part) for the Reception of Lord MOUNTSTEWART, (Lord Bute's Son) and his Family—at a great Expence, out of the *Civil List Money.*

†Turnips are so called in Scotland. Before the Union they were the Wall Fruit of that Country.

‡Late Lord Mayor of London, who petitioned twice against Ministerial Tyranny and Corruption and was repulsed.

‖Alluding to the sudden dissolution of the last Parliament to avoid the Test and Association which were intended, but prevented by this surprize.

Say (for you know, my Lord,) the Cause of this,
You know who *Counsels* and who Acts amiss.
Disguise no Truth by Specious, trite harangue;
But say, at once your Parliament's a *Gang*.
If Truth's a Crime, and *George's* frown you dread,
Say in a Whisper who is at their Head?
That Question's home—your Lordship's silent still—
I'll answer it myself then—frown who will.

In ancient Days when simple Monarchs saw
No better means by reigning than by law,
When sages counsell'd with an honest Heart,
And Kings religiously perform'd their part;
E'er *Standing Armies* were a standing Curse,
Subjects were Children, and their King a Nurse;
No Suitor *unredress*'d then left the Throne;
The *Nurse's* Interest and the *Child's* were one.
The *three Estates* then us'd to coalesce,
With no Intention but to save and bless.
Now Kings, Lords and Commons, faithfully agree,
Like a Banditti, in Confed'racy.
Combin'd to plunge a Nation in distress,
To double Grievances without redress.
In vain to GEORGE the suppliant Knee is bent;
He enjoins silence, suffering, and content*.
With sullen gloom he arm's his sulky brow,
And tell us Slav'ry is our CHARTER now.
ASTONISH'D at his City's daring cries,
He tells 'em Kings and Parliaments are wise.
Tells 'em their *Constitution is controul*;
That of all *Trades oppression* is the *Soul*;

*See the Royal Answer to the City's Petition.

That their Protection hangs on Royal breath;
To Day 'tis slav'ry and to Morrow Death.
That all are REBELS, but that *Passive Tribe*,
Who kiss his *Chains*, his *Footstool* and his *Bribe.*
That ev'ry Subject's *Trayterous* in his View,
Who dares *petition*, *meet*, *consult* or *sue.*
These Sentiments are *Bute's* by *Mansfield* penn'd;
Mansfield who tells us *he is Virtues Friend.**
This Doctrine good my Lord, full scope affords,
To your *vile Commons and your supple Lords.*
Since ev'ry *Act* brings forth some Grievance *new,*
Enlarge the narrow bounds of *Treason* too.
Like *Mary's Minion* in her *Tyrant* Reign,
Enlarge Old *Edwards* †Act amend, explain,
Shew *Edward's* Sages they mistook the Case;
Declare new *Treasons*—'tis an *Act of Grace.*
Declare it *Treason* but to *wish Success*‡
To *Freedom's Arms*, or *Supplicate redress*;
Work your *new Doctor's* Insult into Fact;
'Tis *Johnson's* Thought, so call it *Johnson's Act.*
Go farther still, and stop the *teeming Press*;
If *wishing's Treason*, *writing* is no less.
Safe in your *Votes*, *Corruption* now invites:
This is your Time—Lop off the Hand that *writes.*
By *Libels* full of *Truth*, your *Mansfield* bleeds,
And *Bute* still dreads *Impeachement's* swelling Seeds.
Preserve your Sov'reign in *Tyrannic Health*;
Nor let him read the CRISIS but by *Stealth.*
No Quarter to that *whiggish* CRISIS give;

*See the Motto on Lord Mansfields State Coach.
†The Act of Treasons.
‡Dr. Johnson has the Impudence to declare this expressly, in his late Infamous Pamphlet, "Taxation no Tyranny."

But let the *Tory Patriot's* **Falsehoods* live.
Let *Johnson's Sheets* attract the *Monarch's* Eye;
There he may see how *Knaves well Paid can lye.*
In *Johnson's* Tenets let him read *his own*;
That Kings are born to *laugh* whilst Subjects *groan*;
That POWER is their's in *Supplication's* spite;
Whatever *They* and *Heav'n* inflict, is right.
When *Kings* for *wanton Slaughter* give the Word,
Subjects are bound to fall upon their Sword.
When *Kings* by *Famine* choose their *Slaves* shou'd dye;
Those *Slaves* must drop without an asking Eye.
So much for *Life*—to claim *our own* is vain:
Like *Montesquieu* they †*fancy* who *complain.*
What has a *Slave?* nor Fire, nor Cloaths, nor Meat;
Not for *themselves* they're warm'd, or cloath'd, or eat;
But to defend their *Master* in his *Pride*;
Their *Sov'reign*; who may *Tax* their very *Hide.*
Flay off their Skin in Wantonness and Sport,
Or send an Order for their *Heads* from Court.
Shou'd Freedom's odious Form presume to rise,
North makes a Motion, and the *Phantom* flies.
Mansfield and *Bute* the ‡*murd'rous Bill* invent,
North brings it in—'tis pass'd—and gains *Assent.*
No *Tax*, no *Pain*, no *Penalty's* too much;
All are *thrice hallow'd* by the *Scepter's* touch.
Thus by no *Tyranny* the *Slave's* oppress'd;
The Means are *sacred*, and the End is *bless'd.*
He's the best Subject who most *prostrate* lyes,
He's the *true Patriot* who submits and dyes.
Thus *Johnson* Writes:—at *Court* his Works have praise;
No *Resolution-Whims* in *George's* Days!

*Doctor Johnson's Paper.
†Doctor Johnson has the Assurance to call the great Montesquieu a fanciful Writer, see his Taxation on Tyranny.
‡Alluding to the Bill of *Famine*, against America, for prohibiting the Fishery.

Thus *frantic Savages* present their Breast,
To pointed Lightnings, with false Zeal possess'd;
Behold th' *Enthusiasts* all *Jove's* rage invoke;
And he's the Happiest who receives the *Stroke*.
O *mighty King! wise Council! righteous Throne!*
Where *Freedom, Property,* nor *Life's* our own.
Britons, adore *this Sun,* that gilds your Days;
Surround St. James's with new Songs of Praise.
Let WILKES no more, like BECKFORD'S GHOST,[4] arise,
And with PETITIONS sear his Sov'reign's Eyes.
For *wrong'd America* let Pity cease,
Let all her Sons be *massacr'd* in Peace.
Those Minds, says GEORGE, which *Sympathy* can stir,
In blackest *Treason* with his *Foes* concurr.
Those are his Foes; BUTE'S, NORTH'S, and MANSFIELD'S too,
Who of their *Actions* take too near a View.
Demand the Cause why *Sword or Famine* drinks
Bostonian-blood?—Crys *Johnson, Boston thinks*;
Thinks as her cursed Ancestors were us'd,
By whom our MARTYR CHARLES was so abus'd.
O glorious Martyrdom! henceforth appear
The Joyous Feast of ev'ry future Year.
Blest be those Shades! who taught our Kings to dread
No Loss of *Honour* like a Loss of *Head!*
'Tis that alone, my Lord, that can restrain
Kings and their *Minions* in a *Tyrant-Reign*.
The Good or Ill their Ministers may do,
Arises always from the Point in view.
Their darling Aim gives Life to their Designs;
Now *vacates Patents,* and now *watches Mines*.

4. William Beckford, a former lord mayor of London and member of the House of Commons, had died in 1770. He was a leader of the West Indies lobby, with lucrative sugar plantations in Jamaica. A devoted Pittite, he was also a champion of John Wilkes and defended him vigorously in the Middlesex election dispute.

To Day, supplants a BENTINCK in his Right,
And backs mean LOWTHER in a legal Fight;
The Board of Customs by Direction meet
To morrow, and pronounce SIR JAMES a Cheat.
For why? of late SIR JAMES too restive draws;
To scourge him NORTH pretends a PUBLIC Cause.
Now for SIR JAMES, in PATENTS *picking Holes,
And now against him for his Frauds in *Coals*.
Thus we discern the *Justice* of the State;
That Kings and Ministers breathe *Life* or *Fate*;
PETITIONS as rebellious are withstood;
Whilst Spleen is gratify'd for Public good.
Beware the Goal, my Lord, nor drive too high;
Kings dare be Tyrants, but they durst not dye.
'Tis a nice Conduct that can steer between
King's *Lusts*, Mens *Rights*, and *Ills* that intervene.
When godlike Kings (like ALFRED)[5] give Assent
To all that can relieve, assist, content;
When Justice by the royal Touch gains force,
And *Virtue* is supported in her Course;
When *regal Power* is for a *Blessing* us'd,
And *Mercy* like the Beams of Heav'n dissus'd;
Then *Righteousness* and *Truth* surround the *Throne*;
Then *Kings* are Ministers that *Heav'n* may own.
By Day their presence gives all Hearts delight,

*The infamous proceedings of the Crown, against the Duke of Portland, to gratify Sir James Lowther some little Time ago, is well known. All the Crown Patentee's were alarmed at it, and to secure themselves against their Masters faithful usurpations for the future, the Nullum Tempus Bill was passed.

5. Alfred the Great, who reigned from 871–899, was venerated as the greatest king of Saxon England. Laws that were implemented during his reign, laws that he himself may have authored, helped secure his posthumous reputation, though he was never able to expel the Danes who had invaded to his east and north, and unite the island into a nation.

And ev'ry Subject is their *guard by Night.
But when inflate with Pride they Ape the GOD;
Affect to damp Addresses with a Nod;
Check and o'er bear the humble Suiter's Claim,
And give to *Liberty*, vile *Treason's* Name;
When in their Face and Words the Tyrant's reigns,
And Free-born Subjects must receive their Chains;
When you, my Lord, behold this daring Scene;
With caution steer your little Bark between
The *Sov'reign's* and the *Subject's* side;
On a rough Sea behold each Vessel ride,
This mann'd by *Freedom*, that by *Tyrant Pride*.
Beware, my Lord; nor with a Bravo's boast,
Trust your small Pennace from the safer Coast.
Send Sandwich out, whose Tongue so vilely runs †
And bid *Clay Harvey*,‡ whip him to the Guns.
See what the *Mansfield, or the Bute* can do,
When *Freedom's Fleet* triumphant bears in view.
Hark!—*England* tells you that she will be *Free*:
Your servile Force turns pale; your Commons flee.
Mark well the Conflict, Lord; lament the shock;
If *England* conquers, you must kiss the BLOCK.
See, like a Coward, how the MANSFIELD flies!
At the first Fire, BUTE, and CORRUPTION, dies,
Against a Nation's Rage what Force can stand?
Your hirling Army's lessen'd to a Band.
Your venal Commoners, your vaunting Lords,
(How great a Change the fate of War affords!)
Your IDOL too, and IDOL now no more,
Kneel before those whose Suits they spurn'd before;

---

*Such a King has no Occasion for Sir John Fielding's Men about his Court.
†Alluding to that Lord's Scurrilous abuse of the *Americans*, in the House of Lords, calling them PALTROONS, &c.
‡See a Letter in that Name to Lord Sandwich, in Owen's Weekly Journal.

Not now insulting in *despotic Strains*.
But bound in wrong'd BRITANNIA's awful Chains.
Then her stern Lion rousing from her Den,
Shall treat pale *Tyrants* as they now treat *Men*.
MINIONS and TRAYTORS, in the Wreck be hurl'd,
And INJUR'D SUBJECTS see a better World.

C A S C A

No. XIX. will be addressed to the K I N G.[6]

Printed and published for the Authors, by T. W. SHAW, in Fleet-Street, opposite Anderton's Coffee House, where Letters to the Publisher will be thankfully received.

---

6. The next issue (No. XIX), as it turned out, is not addressed to the king. The one after that (No. XX) is.

THE

CRISIS

NUMBER XIX   *To be continued Weekly.*

SATURDAY, MAY 27, 1775   [*Price Two-pence Half-penny.*

—*Sero sapiunt Phryges.*[1]

False to *yourselves,* the *People* and the *State,*

Like *Foolish Phrygians,* you'll grow Wise too late.

ADMINISTRATION has now "*let slip the Dogs of War,* the hellish *Cerberus,* with her *three Heads,*[2] BURGOYNNE, HOWE, and CLINTON, is sailed. The dogmatic Goose Quil of the *sallacious* Dr. JOHNSON, that hireling Quixote of an *hireling Ministry,* has promulgated a solemn Sentence of Attainder against all Revolutionists in *Great Britain;*—Hear it ye WHIGS,

---

1. The Phryges (more correctly, their allies the Trojans) were wise too late, being fooled into bringing among them their enemies who had hidden inside the "gift" horse that they brought within Troy's city walls. From Cicero's *Letters,* but most likely by way of another source, since the phrase was popular as a warning proverb. Thus too the popularity of the now more familiar lines of "Beware Greeks bearing gifts," as adapted from Virgil's *Aeneid,* Book 2.

2. "Cry Havoc, and let slip the dogs of war," resolves Marc Antony, who had done nothing to stop the conspirators from assassinating Caesar in the Senate. Later lingering at the scene, he announces to the audience his plot against the plotters, his intention to

"And put in ev'ry honest Hand a Whip,
To lash the *Rascal* naked thro' the World."

This *pitiful Retailer* of Apologies for MINISTERIAL TREACHERY, has had the Impudence to declare with the Effrontery of a SANDWICH, or a DENBIGH, that whoever wishes Success to AMERICA is a TRAYTOR to his Country.

From this *patriotic Declaration*, I presume the *redoubted Doctor* is at length admitted into the *Arcana* of the Ministry. He pronounces with as much insolence as if he was assured of their Intentions to pass a Bill, (they have Voices enough to do it,) for declaring a *New Species of Treason*, namely, the *wishing Success to oppressed America*. I will venture to say, that every *Revolutionist* in *England*, *Ireland*, and the *Sugar Colonies*, have long since incurred the Pains and Penalties of this Law in Embryo, if such a One there be.

No *Englishman* can wear two Faces: Therefore if his MAJESTY, should for the future, see as much ill Humour and Contempt in the Faces of his *English and Irish Subjects*, as they observe in *his*, he must not be surprized. BUTE and MANSFIELD, will instruct him that the Aspects and Affections of a PEOPLE are beneath the Notice of a *Sovereign who inherits them*. But Conscience in the Depth of Night, will speak another Language, that will remind him, that he has rejected the Supplications of Millions in AMERICA, that has at length assented to their MURDER, that he has with an *Iron Tongue* and an *Iron Heart,* rung the *Knell* of *expiring* AMERICA.

It is a Maxim of our Law, (says the honest Chancellor FORTESCUE) that no Man was ever yet condemned or sentenced by the Mouth of the KING HIMSELF.—'tis not so now,—the *present Sovereign* has been advised to declare preemptoraly to his *Supplicating Citizens* of *London*, that, "he is *determined* to pursue the Measures which his *wise Parliament* have

---

wreak bloody vengeance in Shakespeares's *Julius Caesar*, Act III, Scene 1. Cerberus was a mythological three-headed dog with the tail of a dragon who guarded the entrance to Hades. Allowing the dead to enter but never to leave, this original hellhound had been a familiar literary figure since Homer's epics, returned to in Virgil's *Aeneid*.

recommended." We know that these are *not conciliating* but *destructive* Measures: Under these Measures AMERICA is either to be destroyed, or lost for ever to this Nation.

The late *Royal Answer* to the PETITION of the *City of London*, fairly interpreted, would run thus: Let it speak the Language of *Despotism* in *despotic Terms*: viz. "SLAVES, by daring thus to remind US of our OP-PRESSIONS in *America*, you are yourselves TRAITORS; by this *libellous Petition* you aid and encourage REBELS. It is the Duty of loyal Subjects passively to obey our *Will*. Our *Will* and *Pleasure* is REVENGE. This Resolve we think fit to notify by FAMINE and the SWORD: These are the lenient Measures, which our *Divan* has advised, and these we will pursue. Your Confidence and Affection we despise, we confide alone in the *Wisdom* of our *Divan*, by that great Council your fancied Rights and your despicable Commerce are wisely doomed, with our entire Concurrence, to DESTRUCTION."

Thus we see how easily a deluded *Christian Prince*, may speak the Language of an *Eastern Tyrant*; for this Purpose we have fairly cloathed an Eastern Spirit, in an Eastern Garb; we have given the *haughty Sovereign*'s plain Meaning in proper Words; we have not (like MANSFIELD, who penned the vile Harrangue) meanly suffered the Sentiments of an *insolent Mogul* to be cramped by the Poverty of Princely Diction.

Upon BUTE's and MANSFIELD's Plans, Sovereigns are Divine *Viceregents*, sent down from Heaven, not in Mercy, but in Wrath, to indulge their own *impious Lusts*, and *Scourge* Mankind. Let such Sovereigns, therefore, be consistent with themselves; let them equally disdain the Fetters of Language and Humanity—Let them speak DAGGERS to their PEOPLE, and *Salvation* to their MINIONS. But can such a Prince, conscious that his PARLIAMENT has been *infamously smuggled*, by a mean and execrable Stretch of the Prerogative, (a sudden Dissolution) For fear of a National ASSOCIATION against future Treachery; conscious that the Majority of his and his *Minister's* great Council (it is no *national Council*) are a Set of *Hirelings, filched into their Seats*, and *corrupted* to promote every despotic Lust of a deluded MONARCH; can such a *conscious Prince* pronounce the Doom of Millions, not only without Emotion, but with composed Stupidity? This is not *Fortitude*, but *Callosity* of Soul.

The whole European World is *astonished* at our Persecution of AMERICA, even Foreign, and despotic *Princes*, upon this Occasion, have different Feelings, from the FATHER of that People who are destined to *Destruction*: Even Princes, who can send forth *Sword* and *Famine by a* NOD, are ASTONISHED at our wicked Policy and abhor it; even the *natural Enemies* of GREAT BRITAIN presume to interfere with our INFERNAL ADMINISTRATION, they will not permit our Government (without *Reproaches, Insults, Threats,* and *animated Declarations*) to MASSACRE MANKIND: France, under the Mask of Humanity, presumes to make us sensible of her great Condescension, Magnanimity, and Moderation, in suffering AMERICAN MURDER to pass on freely and without Controul, She makes us understand that She connives at this *Slaughter* of our GALLANT SUBJECTS for the Sake of cultivating a good Understanding with the *King of Great Britain,* and the *whole English Nation*. But when *She* finds (as *She* shortly may) that this KING and KINGDOM are divided and trying the *Claim* of FREEDOM together in the *Field*, will FRANCE, who professes so much *Magnanimity* and *Moderation*, remain *Neuter?* Her *Humanity*, her *Honour* will not Suffer *her*. She will *retaliate* our former Interpositions in *her* Government with the like *Strokes of Political Humanity*. *Spain*, who has so lately felt the Force of *English Arms*, will not permit us to turn them so *unnaturally* against *oursleves*. *She speaks* in plainer Terms: Let his *persevering Majesty* hear her *Humane Menaces*; *She* tells him boldly, that *She* will not tye up her Hands from relieving *Fellow Creatures* suffering under *wanton unprovoked Oppression*. Alas! *Blind, infatuated Sovereign*. Canst thou not discern the Tendency of this *Artful Spanish Declaration?* Does not *Spain* already hold out Succour to AMERICA? Will not *Injured* and *Despairing People* embrace the Offer? Will they not rather submit to be *aided* by an *Enemy* than MURDERED by a PARENT? Will they not sooner Change their *Names*, their *Laws*, their *Government*, their *Religion*, in *just Resentment*, than enjoy these *flattering Modes*, these *Sounding Nothings* in a State of *Slavery?*—Think again, *Wise Sire*, before it is too late. Let me ask Thee, thou *Clement Pious* SOVEREIGN,[3] are not the *People,* in whose Favour *Spain* hath thus declared, *thy Fellow Creatures* also? Were they not under the *just Reign* of your *lamented Grandfather,* your *Fellow Subjects* too? Could *he* arise, one *Honest Frown* from *him,* would disperse your MINIONS, annihilate your *Pride,* blast your *execrable Politics,* and restore *Peace, Commerce,* and *Protection,* to the *tottering Constitution* of the BRITISH EMPIRE.

The *Spanish Nation* is brave, her *Pretext* for *interposing* is a noble one; tho merely Political, it is to be preferred to *that* which is *Tyrannical;* it has, at least, a plausible Appearance, for it speaks the Language of *Justice, Benevolence,* and *Humanity.* We find neither of these Ingredients in the *rigid Answer* which lately *repelled* the Petition of *the City. Fas est et ab hoste doceri.*[4]

Let BUTE and MANSFIELD, the Leaders of an INFAMOUS ADMIN-ISTRATION, let *their great Council their* Parliament (I say again it is not the *Nation's*) let the *Head Constable* of this Kingdom (the Dupe of all the *Herd*) for once receive *Instruction* from an *Enemy.* The *Spaniards* distinguish *justly* between a Sovereign's Right of reducing *refractory Subjects* to *just Obedience,* and making War upon *humble Supplicants* who Petition for their RIGHTS. They discern a difference (and there is a wide One) between *just Resistance* and *unnatural Rebellion.* They tell us in *Manly* (to AMERICA they are *tempting*) *Terms* that AMERICA shall not Suffer *unheared, unpitied, unredressed,* and *Innocent.* Tho'a *venal* and *Corrupt* Majority, to gratify *despotic Spleen,* have in a BLOODY ACT, styled AMERICA *Rebellious,* yet what Sanction

3. Most likely "Clement" (merciful in the use of power) and "Pious" (humbly devout) should have been separated by a comma, in a fairly common pairing. It is less likely that this was a veiled allusion to Clement of Alexandria, a famously pious Christian of the second century, once considered a saint in the Catholic Church but no longer by the eighteenth century. Some of his writings were available then, in both English and Latin. He is still venerated in the Church of England.

4. In effect, "one should be willing to learn, even from one's enemies," as reworked from Ovid's *Metamorphoses,* Book 4, available in a number of London editions, and also more generally as a familiar proverb.

can *such Laws* derive from *Venality* and *Corruption*? *Laws*, to be *Sacred* and *obligatory* must be consistent with the Laws of *God*, *Nature*, *Reason*, *sound Policy* and the *Constitution* of the Kingdom. If they err in these respects it is an Error in the first Concoction, they are absolutely Null and void in themselves, and are no more to be regarded than "*the Laws of a parcel of Drunken Porters*." I borrow this Elegant Comparison from the Mouth of a *Great Man*, who is, at one and the same Time, a *privey Counsellor*, a *Pensioner*, a *Placeman*, and SPEAKER of the House of Commons. *Situations* as *compatible* with that of SPEAKER, as *Obligatory Laws* are with *Venality* and *Corruption*.

I do not say that *Rebellious* SUBJECTS are not to be *chastised*; but they must first *Rebel*, all *Civil Chastisment* besides, must be inflicted by the Hand of *Wisdom* and *Justice*, not by the SCOURGE of the OPPRESSOR. The *Wanton Power* that *Aggresses* and *Afflicts* ought not to *Punish*, but *Redress*. What *Political Wisdom* is there in driving a whole *Territory*, a *Great Nation* of *Obedient* (tho' not *Passive*) Subjects to Despair? What *Wisdom* in *losing* or *exterminating*? What *Justice* in *refusing to hear* the *supposed Delinqnent* before *She* turned SUPPLICATION into RAGE.

AMERICA professes all *legal*, but like the BRAVE ANCESTRY from whence she Springs, difdains *passive Obedience*, she honours and revers KINGS, but despises and defys TYRANTS.

If she conquers she will continue to support the LIBERTY she wins, if she falls, (believe me ye WRETCHED, ye SHALLOW MINISTERIAL POLITICIANS!) she will not fall *unrevenged*, the Crowns of FRANCE and SPAIN, will not continue *neuter*, they will be the providential means of punishing our Iniquity to AMERICA; they will embroil a CIVIL WAR *here*, and assist it *there*, they will conquer ENGLAND in AMERICA, they will be received *there* with open Arms; in the last Agonies of AMERICAN DESPAIR, They will be received as CONQURERS, and *usurping* TYRANNY, will be *expelled for ever*.

AMERICA will never condescend to enjoy the *unessential Name* of ENGLISHMEN under the *Lawless Power*, of a GRAND MOGUL, and his *detested Divan*.

Printed and published for the Authors, by T. W. SHAW, in Fleet-Street, opposite Anderton's Coffee House, where Letters to the Publisher will be thankfully received.

THE

CRISIS

NUMBER XX   To be continued Weekly.

SATURDAY, JUNE 3, 1775   [Price Two-pence Half-penny.

To the K I N G.

SIR,

LIKE that fell Monster, and infernal TYRANT *Charles* the *First*, you are determined to Deluge the Land with INNOCENT BLOOD. Fired with Rage at the more than Savage Barbarity of your Mercenary Troops, your cursed Instruments of Slaughter in *America*, I can no longer keep within the Bounds of Decency; the Breast of every true Englishman must be filled with Indignation, and that Respect which is due to a King, will be lost in a noble zeal for the Preservation of our Country and Fellow Subjects.

Every Man must execrate a Tyrant, who can, without Remorse to satiate his Revenge, and gratify his lust of Power destroy Millions of his Subjects.

The *Americans*, Sir, are fighting for LIBERTY, the Birthright of every Man. they are fighting for the LAWS and the sacred CONSTITUTION of their Country, which you are, to your eternal Disgrace and Infamy, endeavouring to Destroy: Their Cause is just, it is the Cause of Heaven, and it never will be your Power, assisted by TEN THOUSAND Legion of TYRANTS besides, to fix your BLOODY Standard of Tyranny in *America*. *England* must take Part in this Bloody, this Unnatural CIV-IL WAR, brought on through your Baseness and Ingratitude, and the Treachery, Corruption, and Villainy of your MINIONS; unless she does this, she is lost forever, your unrelenting Cruelty, and desire of being Absolute, will never let you stop, and if once the *Americans* can be reduced to Slavery, we shall be no longer FREE; you will not, you cannot rest, till you have brought the whole Empire into the same State of Vassalage and Bondage: But I hope for the Honour and Valour of my Countrymen, all your infamous Designs will be frustrated, and that by a Noble Exertion, in defence of their persecuted Brethren in *America*, they will soon CONVINCE you, how Difficult, Unsafe, and Dangerous it is to ATTEMPT to enslave a Brave and Free People, and to establish your Throne in INIQUITY and BLOOD.

I hope fired with the noble Spirit of their Ancestors, they will speedily carry to the Throne, something more than Petitions or Remonstrances; I trust they will tell you in manly Terms, in Terms, worthy of Britons; in Terms that may shake your Tyrant S— that they are determined to be FREE, that you SHALL withdraw your Troops from AMERICA; that your Ministers SHALL be delivered up to Justice, as some atonement for the Blood that has been inhumanly shed in *England* and *America*; that they WILL have all their Rights confirmed to them; that they WILL be governed by the LAWS of the Land, and not by the Arbitrary WILL of you or your Minions; that without these JUST and NECES-SARY Requisitions are complied with, they are determined to appeal to Heaven, and OBLIGE you, as their Forefathers have other PRINCELY TYRANTS to govern according to Law and the SOLEMN OATH you took at your Coronation.

Englishmen, Sir, will soon be roused by the inhuman Slaughter of their Brethren and Fellow Subjects in *America*, from a state of Lethergy and Supineness; it will not be long in the Power of your infernal Tribe of Placemen and Pensioners, your Ministers and Minions, by all the Acts of Corruption and Debauchery to keep down the Glorious Spirit of LIB-ERTY; they will not, they cannot, if there is any Virtue in the Nation, longer remain idle inactive Spectators of such CRUEL and BLOODY Measures, in which they are so nearly, so deeply Interested; Measures which must end in the Destruction of LIBERTY and the Constitution, the Boast and Glory of this, and the Envy of every other Nation.

Your whole Reign has been one continued series of Tyranny, Oppression, Cruelty, and Injustice; the whole Business of your Ministers has been to deny right to the People, to sap the Constitution, to establish arbitrary Power upon the Ruins of PUBLIC LIBERTY in every part of the British Dominions; to feed your Avarice, to gratify your Ambition, and Satiate your Revenge against Individuals.

A King, weak, obstinate, perverse, and Cruel, deaf to the calls of Humanity, and regardless of the Sufferings of an oppressed, injured, and loyal People, disgraces the Dignity of human Nature; and is so far from possessing any of those Attributes which characterise Majesty, that he is only a Monster in human Shape, like the Devil, invested with Power, not for the Preservation, but the Destruction of Mankind.

The Breath of a TYRANT blasts and Poisons every thing, changes Blessings and Plenty into Curses and Misery, great Cities and flourishing Kingdoms, into Desarts, and gloomy Solitudes, and their rich Citizens into Beggars and Vagabonds. I could name Cities, which, while they governed THEMSELVES, could maintain Armies, and now enslaved, can scarce maintain the Poor proud Rascals who govern them. It is certain, that whatever Country or Place is subdued by a Prince, who governs by his WILL, is ruined by his Government.

You, Sir, like most other Princes, have been long introducing the *Turkish* Government into Europe; and have succeeded so well, that I would rather live under the *Turk*, than under the Tyranny of *George the Third*. You practice the inhuman Cruelties and Oppressions of the *Turks*, and want the tolerating Spirit of the Turk, and if you are not soon checked through the native bravery of Englishmen, the whole Polity of savage *Turkey*, will be established by you in all its Parts and Barbarity; as if the Depopulation which is already so quick, and taking such dreadful Strides, were still too slow.

TYRANTS are the common Destroyers of Mankind; they are for ever inventing now Machines of Cruelty, and will, till the Destruction of Mankind is completed. They seem to think they shall have Enemies as long as one Man remains, who cannot be made a SLAVE. But it is astonishing at first view, that ENGLISHMEN should have so long borne your Tyranny, Oppressions, and the unrelenting Slaughter of their Fellow Subjects:—But, alas! who knows not the force of Corruption, Delusion, and standing Armies.

Oh Liberty! Oh Servitude! How detestable are the different Sounds! LIBERTY is Salvation in Politicks, as SLAVERY is Reprobation; neither is there any other Distinction but that of Saint and Devil, between the Champion of the one and of the other.

No one can sufficiently shew the glorious Advantages of LIBERTY, nor set off the dreadful Mischiefs of raging, relentless, consuming TYRANNY.—A Task to which no human Mind is equal; for neither the sublimest wits of Antiquity, nor the brightest Genius's of late or modern Times, assisted with all the Powers of Rhetoric, and all the Stimulations of Poetic fire, with the warmest and boldest Figures in Language, ever did, ever could, or ever can, describe and highten sufficiently, the Beauty of the one, or the Deformity of the other: Language fails in it, and Words are too weak.

Those who do not Groan under the Yoke of heavy and pointed Vassalage, cannot possibly have Images equal to a Calamity which they do not feel; and those which feel it, are stupefied by it, and their Minds depressed; nor can they have Conceptions large, bright, and comprehensive enough, to be fully Sensible of their own wretched Condition; much less can they Paint it in proper Colours to others. The People of England, Sir, who enjoy the Precious, Lovely, and invaluable blessing of LIBERTY, know that nothing can be paid too dear to purchase and preserve it. Without it the World is a Wilderness, and Life a Miserable Burthen: Death is a Tribute we all owe to Nature, and must pay; and it is infinitely preferable, in any shape to an ignominious Life: Nor can we restore our Being back again into the Hands of our great Creator, with more Glory to him, more Honour to ourselves, or more Advantage to

Mankind, than in Defence of all that is valuable, religious, and praise worthy upon Earth.

How execrable then, and infamous are the Wreches, who for a few precarious momentary, and perhaps imaginary Advantages, would rob their Country for ever of every thing that can render Life desirable; and for a little tinsel Pageantry and survile Homage, unworthy of honest Men, and hated by wise Men, would involve Millions of their Fellow Creatures in lasting Misery, Bondage and Woe; such unnatural royal Parricides, unworthy of the human Shape and Name, would fill up the Measure of their Barbarity by entailing Poverty, Chains, and Sorrow, upon their own Posterity. And, Sir, you ought to remember such Tyrants have UN-PITIED, suffered in their OWN PERSONS, the sad effects of those cruel Councils and Schemes, which they intended for the Ruin of all but themselves and their Minions; and have JUSTLY fallen into that Pit they had TRAITEROUSLY digged for others.

> He that can levy WAR with all Mankind,
> Can cut his Subjects Throats, and fell his Friend;
> Ravish the Chaste, the sanctifi'd Prophane,
> Can pull down RIGHT, and wrong by FORCE maintain;
> Mortgage his FAITH, and trample on his WORD,
> And hew his Crown out by his LAWLESS Sword.
> Like *Nero* suck the Blood that gave him Life,
> And search engend'ring Nature with his Knife:
> Like *Cortez*, can a hundred Millions slay,
> Dream Death by Night, and finish it by Day:
> Like pious Peter, *cant* of Heaven's commands,
> Pray with his Lips, and Murther with his Hands.
> Can Sleep with BLOOD, and never start at CRIMES,
> And make his Mischiefs like his Pow'r supreme.
> By JUSTICE, sell OPPRESSION, bribe the LAW,
> Exalt the Rogue, and Keep the Just in awe;
> Embrace the GUILTY, Innocents Condemn,
> And Execute without pretence of CRIME.
> Can sacrifice WHOLE NATIONS to his Lust,

With Pleasure KILL, and think that Pleasure just:
Can Burn and Sing, dance to the waving Flame,
And in his country's Ashes raise his Fame;
Insult the Wretched, trample on the Poor,
And mock the Miseries Mankind endure;
Can ravage Countries, Property devour,
And trample Law beneath the Feet of Pow'r.
Scorn the restraint of OATHS, and promis'd Right,
And ravel Compacts in the Peoples fight;
With Indignation scorn to reign by Rules,
That King's a TYRANT, and the People Fools.

Printed and published for the Authors, by T. W. SHAW, in Fleet-Street, opposite Anderton's Coffee House, where Letters to the Publisher, will be thankfully received.

THE

CRISIS

NUMBER XXI   *To be continued Weekly.*

SATURDAY, JUNE 10, 1775   *[Price Two-pence Half-penny.*

To Lord N O R T H

My L O R D,

IN the fewest Words I can possibly use (for I will not waste many upon *you*, who are as CALLOUS as your *Tyrannic Master*) I most heartily congratulate your Lordship upon the *honourable Retreat* of your *unnatural and savage Mercenaries* under the Command of your Bully, Colonel SMITH.[1] I am told *your Master* LAUGHS *at the Event*; you, who *know him*, know to which of his *amiable Qualities* we are to impute this *heroic Merriment*; whether to his BRUTALITY, his STUPIDITY, or HYPOCRISY. Let

---

1. Lieutenant Colonel Francis Smith led the column of British soldiers that ventured into the Massachusetts countryside on 18–19 April 1775, precipitating the fighting at Lexington and Concord (and elsewhere along the line of march) that would mark the outbreak of a revolt that ended the next year in revolution—whose unfolding was so much the focus of *The Crisis*. Smith is remembered almost solely for this unrealistically planned and poorly executed expedition. By war's end he had risen to the rank of major general. See David Hackett Fischer, *Paul Revere's Ride* (New York: Oxford University Press, 1994); and Arthur B. Tourtellot, *Lexington and Concord* (New York: W. W. Norton, 2000; orig. ed. 1959).

him remember, and do *you* tremble, when I tell your Lordship, that neither of those Qualities will avail *him in the Field*, however they may be flattered in his *sycophantic Circle* at a *fawning Levee.*

In the subsequent Part of this Paper, I have given a true Reason for the early Prorogation of your *smuggled Parliament.* I have told how much your Lordship and your *Ministerial Gang* feared the Arrival of News from BOSTON, during the Sitting of Parliament.

But why has your Lordship stopped the Publication of this *pleasing News* in *your* GAZETTE? Why do you wait for the Arrival of the SUKEY? With what DELUSIVE LYE do you intend to cheat the People, who, even *in this Kingdom*, are upon the Eve of *taking Arms?* I tell your Lordship, peremptorily, that they will do so. Though I know, that neither *you*, nor any of your *impolitic, bloody Herd*, from the *Master Butcher* down to his lowest *Slaughterman*, can relent, yet, in the Name of the *People of England*, I charge you all to desist.

Forewarned, forearmed, my Lord, you have now, *most traitorously* opened a Scene of CIVIL WAR in *America*; let me conjure you not to risque one *here.* Turn over the Annals of that weak Tyrant CHARLES the First? lay them *fairly* (in Spite *of Bute* and *Mansfield)* before your deluded, infatuated SOVEREIGN, dare to be *honest* in this *dreadful* CRISIS, do not, like a Coward, consult *your own Safety*, but *your Country's.*—Let *Bute* and *Mansfield* perish; and, if there is a blacker *Parricide*, let *him* fall too; nay, rather fall *yourself*, my Lord, than lend a further Hand to extinguish *Liberty* in this *unhappy Empire.*

Your vain, your wicked Hopes of Conquest in *America*, will most assuredly prove abortive; your *retreating Troops*, your *mercenary Parricides* (*England* disclaims the Assassins) have drawn *Blood* from the *virtuous*, the *brave*, the *free Americans.* It is the Wish, my Lord, of every *true-born Briton*, that those *Military Hirelings* (who are *England's* BASTARDS, not her SONS) may fall a Sacrifice to the Justice of *America.* Rest assured, my Lord, that they will be cut in Pieces before *your murderous Reinforcement*, under that *necessitous Tool,* BURGOYNE, can possibly arrive.

That every Reinforcement for such *inhuman*, *unnatural*, and *unjust Purposes*, may share the same Fate, and that STRUGLING *America* may at last be *free*, or, if *enslaved*, that SHE may disdain to be *enslaved* by her *tyrannic Parent*, is the *pious Prayer* of every *virtuous Briton*, and the most fervent Wish of

C A S C A.

P. S. Though *his Holiness*, the POPE, may probably order *his Children* at *Quebec* to sing Te *Deum* upon your Lordship's late or future *Success* against your Fellow-Subjects in *America*, yet it may not be quite so prudent that it should be sung by the *hypocritical Choir at St. James's*, by Way of blinding People *here*, from whom the *Truth* cannot long remain a Secret:—Let me give your Lordship one more friendly Hint before we part; do not disgrace your SOVEREIGN AGAIN, by suffering him to return PUBLIC THANKS by his SECRETARY AT WAR,[2] to his *Military Cut-Throats in America*, as he did to those who murdered his *innocent* Subjects, for their foolish Curiosity in St. *George's Fields*.—And now, my Lord, "*To Dinner—with what Appetite you may.*"

Remarks on his Majesty's last *most Gracious* (I had like to have said infamous) *Speech*, to both Houses of Parliament.

Friday, May 26, 1775.

NO *Prince* can be more ASTONISHED at the humble Supplications of *injured Subjects* than I am at the shameful Negligence of *Charles Eyre* and *William Strahan*,[3] Printers to the King's most excellent Majesty. I am sorry to say that his *Majesty's last Speech*

---

2. William Wildman Barrington, second Viscount Barrington, had first been appointed secretary at war in 1755, during the reign of George II. He held that office for most of the years that followed until he stepped down midway through the American war. He was an effective administrator but he had little to do with making grand strategy, his close ties to George III notwithstanding; his was not a cabinet level post.

3. *His Majesty's most gracious Speech to both houses of Parliament, On Friday, May 26, 1775* (London: Charles Eyre and William Strahan, 1775). Strahan, a London printer for

is by far the fullest of *Typographical Errors* of any since the Revolution. These Errors will seem palpable and obvious to every Reader, who is not ignorant of the present *critical State of Great Britain* and *America*. The royal Printers are the less excusable for want of due attention, as a *Royal Speech* is no *ordinary Composition*, it originates from *Bute*, is trimmed up by *Mansfield*, adopted by *North* and pronounced by a *Royal Orator*; but as it is at last submitted to the Inspection of the Public, it must, like other Human Compositions, undergo the Public Censure.

Errata, Notes, and Queries.

"My *entire Satisfaction* in your Conduct."]—Quere, Whether there is one honest Man, in England *entirely satisfied* with the conduct of the Parliament except his *Majesty.*

"During the Course of this *important* Session."]—The Epithet *important* recalls to my mind a Passage in *Addison's* Cato—viz. ———"the great th' *important* Day,

"Big with the *Fate* of *Cato*, and of Rome.

"The *Rights* of my *Crown*."]—Here is an unpardonable Omission of the Printers,—after the word [*the*] insert the word [*despotic*;] alluding to the late assent to *illegal Taxation, Murder, Famine, Popery,* &c.

"Authority of Parliament"] before the word [*Authority,*] insert these words, [*legal and constitutional.*]

"You have protected and promoted the *Commercial Interests* of my King-doms"]—Namely by stopping by every *inhuman means*, the former intercourse between *England* and *America.*—by prohibiting, ruining, and losing, (perhaps for ever,) a most important Fishery, with all its Advantages to this Kingdom, and to Aᴍᴇʀɪᴄᴀ in general; without which

---

over thirty years, had won the contract as the king's printer some five years before and had likely been given a handwritten copy in advance. He had also secured a seat in the House of Commons in the September 1774 election condemned so roundly by *The Crisis*, no. II (pp. 13–20 supra).

none of our West India Colonies, or their Millions of Slaves can possibly subsist, without which, many Thousands of Souls, on the Continent of America, must perish.

N. B. This Royal Compliment to our *most virtuous* and *incorrupt Parliament*, is intended as a *second Snub* to the City of *London*, for their late ASTONISHING Petition. Here I detect the Pen of the Lord Chief Justice of England.

"As far as the *Constitution* will allow you"]—That is to say, as far as *Bute's* and *Mansfield's* unconstitutional Notions of the Constitution will allow; according to them, it allows only of these two alternatives, *Tyranny* or *Death*; *America* may take her Choice. Every Remonstrance, Petition, and Supplication of AMERICA, has been *spurn'd* by *King*, *Lords*, and *Commons*, two conciliatory Plans, upon *Constitutional*, *Free*, *just*, and *Honourable Principles*, have been rejected in each House. The inhuman *Ministerial Parricides*, should remember, however, that a conciliatory Plan may be gladly embraced again by *Tyrants*, when offered in the Field, like the *great one* in *Runny Mead*,[4] let them remember too, that upon the breaking out of a *Civil War*, in this Country, *Corruption* will not be able to secure to them the bravest Part, even of the *Standing Army*; not one of the *Constitutional Militia*; nor a single *General*, equal to those honourable Men, who have already refused to bathe their Swords in the Blood of the spirited Americans. Above all, let these *Tyrants* remember that the Hearts of the People throughout the whole *English Empire* are set against them.—BLOOD will have BLOOD, they say.

"Gratify *the* Wishes"] For [*the*] read *my*.

"Remove the *Apprehensions*,"] For [*Apprehensions*] read [*pretensions*,] namely, to *Liberty*, *Property*, and *Life*.

"Of my *Subjects* in *America*."] For *Subjects* read [*Objects*,]—i.e. Objects of *Indignation*, *Revenge*, and *Tyranny*, &c.—not of *Mercy*, or *Humanity*.

---

4. Runnymede, the meadow twenty miles to the southwest of London, where in June 1215 disgruntled barons forced concessions out of King John I in what, after various subsequent revisions, would be venerated as the Magna Carta (see n. V.2 supra).

"The most *salutary Effects*"] For [*Salutary,*] read [*Sanguinary*]

"The late mark of your *Affectionate* Attachment"] For *Affectionate* read [*affected.*]—This Passage alludes to the grant of *Somerset House* to the *King*, to reimburse his provident and frugal *Majesty*, for his *immense profusion* of the *Public Money*; dissipated with the greatest Taste, Elegance, and patriotic Pains, in the most costly puerile, superfluities of Toys, Baubles, Nick-nacks, Whim-wams &c. &c. in and about the *Queen's* Palace.—It looks like another Palace of Semiramis.—*Hoc novum est Aucupium!*[5] Supplies under such pretences, and for such Princely and Meritorious Purposes, is a new Species of Ministerial Gullery, not to say Impudence.

"I have great Reason to expect the continuance of Peace."] after the word [*have*] insert the word, [*no*]

"Nothing on my Part *consistent,*"] Instead of [*consistent*] read *inconsistent*.

"It gives *me* much concern"] after the word [*me*] insert the word [*not*]

"For the several *Services* of the current Year"] Instead of [*Services*] read *Devices*.

"Discernment of their *true* Interests"] Instead of [*true*] read [*new*] meaning the *new* and *defferent* Interests from what their *foolish Ancestors* had at the glorious Revolution. As the Crown and its Ministers have *new* Views, and *new* Modes of Government the People may well be supposed to have *new* Interests, since that *whiggish Period*, when the *true Interest* of the King and People were so much mistaken by a set of *wild Enthusiats* called *Patriots*. A Name which Doctor *Johnson*, in his Dictionary, says, is to be found in the Dictionary only; the Doctor at that Time little thought of writing an infamous Pamphlet under that Name.

My *faithful* and *beloved* People"] By this distinguishing and respectful Epithet [*faithful,*] must be meant the *faithful Majority* of Lords and

---

5. A passage from Act II, Scene 2 of "The Eunuch," by Terence (Publius Terentius Afer, a second century BCE Roman playwright) most likely from one of various compilations of his *Comedies*; meaning, "a new way to catch birds" or, by extension, to captivate.

Commons.—in the wheedling Epithet [*beloved*] this Majority is also certainly included—But the stiff-necked, patriotic Ministry, the plaintive *City of London*, the injured Subjects in general, and the brave *Americans* in particular, (not forgetting their truly noble Friend LORD EFFINGHAM,)[6] are most certainly excepted. As to the *firm Americans*, it is impossible that they should be comprised in these *tender Terms*; because his Majesty is most graciously pleased to intimate, a little before that if his firm and steady Parliament had not, with a firm and steady Resolution, devoted that Part of his Majesty's Subjects to Destruction, the Rights of his Crown, the Authority of Parliament, and the Commercial Interests of his Kingdoms, could not be maintained, protected and promoted.—The necessary Inference from these words is, that nothing can maintain, protect, or promote, the *true Interests* of the BRITISH EMPIRE, but *Popery, Sword*, and *Famine*, I may add TYRANNY, and TAXATION.—If the above *sugared Words*, [*faithful* and *beloved*] are extended generally, they must be looked upon as *Springs* to catch *Woodcocks*, they remind me of that shrew'd Reflection which SHAKESPEAR puts into the Mouth of *Hotspur*, upon *King Henry's* SWEET WORDS, to that young *Hero*, whilst his Majesty was *cajoling* him, (as he says,) like a fawning Greyhound—viz.

————what a deal of candied Courtesy!

"Gentle *Harry Piercy*! —and kind Cousin!

"O! the Devil take such *Cozeners*!"[7]

6. Thomas Howard, third Earl of Effingham, had protested North's hardline policies as they emerged by mid-1774. He resigned his officer's commission in the army on 12 April 1775, explaining that, loyal as he was to the king, he could not be part of any attempt to coerce the Americans into obedience, when their rights were so clearly being violated. The speech that he gave in the House of Lords on 18 May 1775 explaining his actions was printed in the *London Evening Post*, 27 May 1775, and the *London Chronicle*, 30 May 1775.

7. Part of a (slightly altered) speech by Hotspur, from Shakespeare's *Henry IV*, Part 1, Act I, Scene 3. Hotspur–that is Henry Percy, son of the earl of Northumberland and ferocious on the field of battle–vents his frustrations with a king (Henry IV) that he does not believe is worthy of his loyalty. Ultimately the Northumberlands and their

Q.—Whether this early *Prorogation* is not as truly symptomatic as the Minister's Fears, as the sudden Dissolution was of the last *infamous Parliament?* This early prorogation (by *Mansfield's* advice) shews, that after all the foul mouth'd, bullying, insolence, of a *Tyrannic Administration,* they dare not protract the Session of Parliament any longer for fear of hearing *news* from AMERICA (which they could not conceal) during that Session. This *Vacation,* therefore, is artfully contrived to give breath to a *confused, destracted,* and *trembling* ADMINISTRATION; at the opening of the next Session of Parliament, (if this vile ADMINISTRATION lives so long) we may (under *Bute's* and *Mansfield's* auspices) expect some curious State Manoeuvre, ready cut and dryed. I will venture to Prophesy with more certainty than Lord SANDWICH, Lord DENBIGH, or any other MINISTERIAL BULLY, in the GANG, that we shall, at last see, not a rational political Gratification of the wishes; but a pitiful, mean, contemptible, and dastardly SUBMISSION, (by downright COMPULSION) to the JUST DEMANDS of AMERICA. I call upon my Countrymen, to remember, that so insignificant an Individual as CASCA, now fortells that neither the present ADMINISTRATION, nor, (as I fear) the present REIGN will end till they have supplied Matter for a dreadful and most exemplary Record in the BRITISH ANNALS.

C A S C A.

Printed and published for the Authors, by T. W. SHAW, in Fleet-Street, opposite Anderton's Coffee House, where Letters to the Publisher will be thankfully received.

allies rise against the king. They are defeated at Shrewsbury in 1403, with Hotspur being slain by Prince Harry, the one-time reprobate son remaking himself into Shakespeare's future heroic Henry V. See n. XVI.3 supra.

THE
CRISIS

NUMBER XXII   To be continued Weekly.

SATURDAY, JUNE 17, 1775   [Price Two-pence Half-penny

BLOOD calls for BLOOD.

To the People of England.

Friends and Fellow Countrymen,

LET me conjure you by all you hold dear, HERE and HEREAF-
TER, by all the Ties of NATURE and JUSTICE, to rouse in Defence of your persecuted Brethren and Fellow Subjects in *America*,
who Daily fall Innocent Victoms to LAWLESS Power: let me intreat you
to rouse in Defence of your Rights and Liberties; those Rights and Liberties which Heaven gave, and for which your Fathers bravely Fought,
and Gloriously fell, to preserve themselves, and us their Posterity FREE;
be assured if BLEEDING *America* can be reduced to Slavery, all the
boasted Privileges of Englishmen must fall with her: let me therefore
beseech you to OPPOSE with uplifted Hands, and stretched out Arms,
the CRUEL, BLOODY, and UNNATURAL Tyranny of GEORGE the
Third, and his diabolical Tory Minions: Perdition, Destruction, and all
the Miseries of a tortured Death, attend the Wretch, who calls himself

an ENGLISHMAN, and yet can TAMELY see his BROTHER, or Fellow Subject, Perish through wanton Cruelty, Oppression, or the Sword.

No Tyrant was ever more Despotic and Cruel than the present Sovereign, who disgraces the Seat of Royalty in the British Empire; no Court ever more Corrupt than his, and yet, O my Countrymen, to this merciless and despotic Tyrant, and to his wicked and corrupt Ministry, you sacrifice your Rights, and yield a PEACEABLE Submission.

Consider the gloomy, the dreadful Prospect before you, the Plains of *America* are running with the BLOOD of her Inhabitants, the Essence of the English Constitution destroyed, and nothing but the Form, the mere Shadow of it remains; all the dear bought Liberties purchased and sealed with the BLOOD of your Forefathers, wrested from you by the polluted Hands of an abandoned set of Miscreants, supported and defended by a ROYAL TYRANT; and a dark cloud of Slavery, like a rising Tempest, overspreads the Land, it approaches Swiftly, and at this Moment threatens our Destruction; it is therefore high Time you should be roused and awakened to a sense of your Danger, and by an appeal to Heaven, by a glorious RESISTANCE, provide for your common Safety.

This is the only way, we have no other, to prevent the RUIN that threatens us, if we are inattentive or inactive at this Time, our Chains will be fast rivetted, and Liberty must expire; your Petitions and Remonstrances have been spurned by the King, and you have now no Remedy left but that of entering into an ASSOCIATION in Defence of your Common Rights, and the Rights of *America*. They have set you a noble Example, an Example worthy of Britons, an Example which you are Bound by all the Principles of Justice and Self-preservation to FOLLOW; he must be Blind that is not convinced of this, and he is an abandoned Wretch, an Enemy to Mankind, who will not pursue the Road.

Upon your Virtue and Resolution at this juncture, depends the SALVATION of England and America; it is now in your Power to prevent the farther Progress of Despotism, the Butchery of your Fellow Countrymen, and yourselves from Slavery and Ruin.

When the humble Supplications of an oppressed People are treated with Contempt, and a deaf Ear turned to their Complaints, when their RIGHTS are Daily invaded, their Property unlawfully wrested from them, and their Blood inhumanly shed, it is incumbent on them, it is a Duty they owe to God and their Country, to take the Field and resist their Oppressors, to shew themselves BRAVE, when Bravery is required, and dare to be Resolute in the Hour of Danger. Remember, my Fellow Countrymen, our Predecessors led the Way, the Americans have followed their noble Example, and we are Bound to follow them. Where would have been LIBERTY and PROPERTY, if it had not been for the Virtue, Bravery, and Resolution of our Ancestors? they stood FORTH in the glorious Cause, and many of them secured it to Posterity by their BLOOD. Shall we then, TAMELY submit to have those Privileges for which they FOUGHT and FELL, ravished from us by a Lawless tribe of Men, who call themselves Senators or Ministers, and who taking Advantage of their Prince, are laying waste their Country, and spreading Desolation through the Land? Shall it be said in after-Times, that the Year ONE THOUSAND SEVEN HUNDRED and SEVENTY FIVE, was less Glorious than that of SIXTEEN HUNDRED and EIGHTY EIGHT; and that as the Age grew more and more enlightened, it became more and more PUSILLANIMOUS. Forbid it Heaven!

Let me intreat you, O! Englishman, to rouse from that state of Supineness in which you have so long lain; open your Eyes to the Danger that surrounds you, and stand forth the Defenders of AMERICAN VIRTUE and PUBLIC LIBERTY. HAVOC is now the Cry at *St. James's* and the Dogs of War are let loose to tear out the Vitals of our Brethren; *America* through the abandoned Cruelty of an accursed Administration, and an unrelenting King, is become a FIELD of BLOOD, overspread with Desolation and Slaughter. It is in your Power to put an end to this horrid, unnatural CIVIL WAR, it must owe its extinction or continuance to you, if you are Virtuous, Brave, and Resolute, the Lives, Liberties, and Properties of your Fellow-Subjects, may be preserved, and your Country saved from Destruction; if on the Contrary, you should be irresolute and Pusillanimous at this Time, (unworthy the Name of Englishmen) Thousands, many thousand Lives must be lost; the Liberties of

England will be no more, and your Property taken from you at the Will and Pleasure of the King and his Ministers.

It can only be from the Virtue and UNITED efforts of England and America, that the Constitution of Great Britain, and all our invaluable Privileges can be preserved; should you remain quiet Spectators of the present inhuman Massacres, and destructive Measures, you will deserve the worst of Slavery, and the cruelest Punishment ever inflicted on a People.

If you have any Honour, if you have any Virtue, or any Bravery, you will now stand forth and resist the Tyrants, you will demand the Heads of those Men, who advised those sanguinary, fatal, and ruinous Measures; you will declare to the World, you will not consent to Arbitrary invasions of your Liberties, Arbitrary dispensings with the Laws, and Arbitrary governing by an Army; that you owe no Submission to a King, beyond the Bounds of Law; that your Lives, Liberties, and Estates, shall not be disposed of at his PLEASURE, and that you are Bound by the Laws of God and Man, to resist a Tyrant; that you will oppose all unjust Violence, and those who attempt the Life of the Constitution, as the great Enemies of their Country; this has been practiced in all Ages, and all Nations determine, that when Kings invade the Lives, Liberties, or Properties of their Subjects, that tear up the Foundations of Public Freedom, and the sacred Constitution of their Country, MAY BE RESISTED, either by calling in and joining with Foreign Assistance, or by taking Arms in Defence of the Law and common Liberty; this is what was declared at the REVOLUTION, and this is the Foundation upon which the People took Arms in the Time of *Charles the First*.

The Axe is now at the Root of the Tree; the overthrow of the Constitution is the great Design of the King and his Ministers, the open and avowed Enemies to the natural Rights of Mankind, who have already sufficiently proved to the World, that they mean the Subversion of the universal Right of Christians and of Subjects. Let those, my Countrymen, who plead for Tyrants, submit to their Power; but let us esteem Liberty, Religion, and Property, equally with our Lives, every Mans Birthright by Nature; no Government ever received a LEGAL Authority to abridge or take it away; nor has God vested any single or confederated Power in any Hands to destroy it; and it is in Defence of these glorious Privileges, these common Rights, I have written this Paper, and to preserve them unviolated by the polluted Hands of Lawless Tyrants, I would lay down my Life, for Life is a burthen in any other State than that of FREEDOM.

It is notoriously known, notwithstanding all the Royal and ministerial Falshoods which have been, and are Daily advanced, to our Disgrace, it is known that we do not enjoy, undiminished, one single Privilege purchased by the Blood of our Ancestors, and confirmed to us by MAGNA CHARTA and the BILL of RIGHTS. Every Man then, who remains passive at this Time, is an Enemy and a Traitor to his Country. I loose all kind of Patience when I reflect upon the melancholy Situation of England and America, and the villainous Principles of those Men, intrusted by the Sovereign with the Management of the Affairs of this once great, free, and powerful Kingdom. I am fired with a just Indignation against the Authors of our Misfortunes; and if I appear too Warm, I hope it will be imputed to my Zeal in the Public Cause, and not to any Malice or Resentment, against Individuals, for I here declare to have none, but I most sincerely wish to stop the further Effusion of Human Blood, and would willingly sacrifice my Life, could I rescue my Country from the Hands of PARRICIDES and TRAITORS, and from that Destruction which now threatens it.

To the P U B L I C.

THE Necessity, Utility, and National Advantage of a political Paper in Defence of the natural Rights of Mankind at this IMPORTANT ÆRA, must appear greater than at the last glorious Revolution. We now see, and with infinite Concern, the King and Ministry, the Lords and Commons, all united, and firmly resolved, on persuing Measures, which (without a noble Opposition from the People) must end in the Destruction of the Laws, Rights, and Liberties, of the whole British Empire, in *England and America*. It is therefore only necessary to say, this Paper will be carried on by two Gentlemen of literay Abilities, alike Enemies to the Arbitary efforts of ONE, or a *purchased Majority* of FIVE HUNDRED and FIFTY EIGHT TYRANTS, to whom they, and they hope, their Fellow-Subjects, never will submit.

Potior visa est periculosa libertas quieto servitio.

SALLUST[1]

The CRISIS will be continued with Spirit, in defiance of every exertion of Lawless Power, upon the true Principles of the Constitution, against the secret Machinations, and despotic Designs, of the present corrupt Court and Ministry. The Authors being determined, even at the risk of every thing that is dear to Man, to rescue the Liberty of the Press, the natural Rights of Mankind, and the Constitution of the British Empire, in *England and America*, from that Ruin, with which they are now threatened. In order with more Ease to accomplish these great Ends, they earnestly beg the Assistance of those, who are real Friends to the Laws, Liberties, and Constitution of their Country.

Printed and published for the Authors, by T. W. *Shaw*, in Fleet-street, opposite Anderton's Coffee House, where Letters to the Publisher, will be thankfully received.

1. This phrase by Sallust was used as the epigraph for the very first issue of *The Crisis*—see supra, n. I.1. Benjamin Franklin's sentiments, expressed in a letter of 11 November 1755, are reminiscent of Sallust's: "Those who would give up essential Liberty, to purchase a little temporary Safety, deserve neither Liberty nor Safety." In Leonard Labaree, et al., eds., *The Papers of Benjamin Franklin*, 39 vols. (New Haven: Yale University Press, 1959 —), 6:242.

THE

CRISIS

NUMBER XXIII   To be continued Weekly.

SATURDAY, June 24, 1775   [Price Two-pence Half-penny.

To his TYRANNIC MAJESTY.—the D E V I L.

Most *infernal Sir,*

D o not affect the utmost Astonishment at this Address; it comes not in the *tremendous* form of a PETITION; of these your SULKY MAJESTY shall have *no more* during the *short Time* you can hope to *Tyrannize* over us in a *regal Shape.* What I humbly offer now, concerns, not your *infested* and *afflicted* KINGDOMS, so nearly as your *dearer Self and Favourites.* Your MAJESTY's *best beloved Spirits, Bute* and *Mansfield,* the whole *astonished World* consider as the *blackest Imps* in all your Train; and *yourself,* as their *humble Executioner.* They advise, and you *most condescendingly* administer, *Destruction.* Their *Ascendancy* and your *Humility,* their *Patriotism* and your *Discernment,* their *Wisdom* and your *Humanity,* are Subjects of *universal Admiration.* But of all your *most diabolical Virtues, satanic Sir,* the most conspicuous is *Hypocrisy.* The Blaze of it, upon one Occasion, in particular, the Death of *Lord Chancel-*

lor Yorke. (as Milton says) *"far round illumin'd Hell."*[1] As you can practise it so successfully for the *Desolation,* let me intreat you, *gloomy Sir,* to assume it now (by way of Frolic only) for the *preservation* of Mankind; but, above all, for your own *precious Interest*, much dearer to you than the Salvation of an *inferior Universe.* Your *Majesty* has disported yourself amidst the *dangerous Indulgences* of three *most unprincely Passions*; *Pride, Anger,* and *Revenge*, for Fourteen Years past; ever since the Demise of our good King, George the Second; in whose Reign your *most hypocritical Highness* was *advised* to wear the Mask of *Decency* and *Circumspection*. You *then* cast a favourable Glance only at *Corruption*; but you have since spurned the Reign of *Policy,* and broke out into such uncommon Tyrannies, such Bloody Inhumanities, unprovoked, that your despotic Highness must now either desist, or expect to be deserted and deposed. My great Tenderness for two of your Highnesses dearest Friends, the Scotch Lords *Bute,* and *Mansfield*, obliges me to give you this timely Notice. Should you still continue, *dread Sir,* to "have entire Confidence in the Wisdom of your Divan," should you still "Steadily pursue those Measures which they have recommended"—your Reign can be but short; your animating Supporters *Bute,* and *Mansfield,* must surely fall. When these hellish Instigators of your Pride are gone, your unhappy Reign must end, when those *Arch Fiends* of Corruption and Iniquity, are no more, your *wise Divan,* will fall off from you like Water, they will neither support your *wanton Slaughter* in AMERICA, nor your pious Designs upon *Great Britain,* your faithful Pensioners will faint for want of these heartening supplies, with which they are now Daily refreshed in plenteous Streams, by your

1. The passage is from Book I of John Milton's *Paradise Lost*, and could have come from literally dozens of sources, from printings of the poem alone, to Milton's collected works, to various commentaries. It was lifted from this scene:

"He spake; and to confirm his words, out flew
Millions of flaming swords, drawn from the thighs
Of mighty Cherubim; the sudden blaze
Far round illumin'd Hell: highly they rag'd
Against the Highest, and fierce with grasped arms
Clashed on their sounding shields the din of war
Hurling defiance toward the vault of heaven."

Majesty's Feeder LORD NORTH, under the provident Eye of your best Subjects, *Bute and Mansfield*. When these Fountains of *Milk* and *Honey*, cease to flow, your *Majesty's* hired *Majority* will grow languid and relaps into what they once were, and ever will be, mere Dissemblers of patriotic Virtue, even your *Sovereign Tool* of all, who now audaciously plumes himself upon *their Support,* will then foreswear any further Attachment to them, or you. When your chief Agents *Lord Bute* and *Mansfield* are extinct, what must become of *Ways* and *Means, Arbitrary Taxation,* and most effectual Methods for carrying these pregnant Schemes into a daring Execution, by Sword and Famine. Your Angels, *Bute* and *Mansfield* are excellent at these Devices but their fervent Zeal for your Highness's Cause has, at last, transported them beyond the Bounds of Judgment. Call these *winged Hell-hounds* off in Time, great Sir, if you value the preservation of your despotic Power; and as you have hitherto played the Tyrant for your Pleasure, begin now to play the *Hypocrite* for your Safety. Should you permit these *Scotch Imps* of yours to proceed farther, you will hazard *all*. We now feel certain Stretches of your *persevering Powers,* too great for *human Patience,* or *human Nature* to support long; assume, therefore, *most steady Prince,* in this *dangerous Crisis,* a Virtue, to which you are, in Truth, a Stranger. Play off, once more, an appearance of *Clemency*; it will be better timed now, than it ever was in the Cases of *Sodomites, wanton Murderers,* and *military Cut-throats.* Dissemble your *causeless Anger,* and *effeminate Thirst for Blood.* By this Stratagem you may, probably, make the easy, long-suffering, passive Fools, whom you wish to destroy, believe that your Majesty is really sincere, when you condescend to call them (with inward reluctance and disdain) "Your faithful and beloved People."[2] Believe me, most *infernal Prince,* this is the only way to compass their utter Ruin, with the least probable Security to your gracious Self, your wise Divan, your faithful Minions, your obsequious Assassins, and pensioned Parricides. By these Means, and by these alone, you may still live in *prosperous,* and *plenteous Infamy.* Thus, and thus

---

2. Taken from the King's speech of 26 May 1775, which had already been dissected in *The Crisis,* no. XXI (supra, pp. 183–190) on June 10th.

only, can you hope to introduce, with Safety to yourself, that destructive plan of *Tyranny,* by which your beloved *Bute and Mansfield,* will immortalize your Reign. It must be introduced, my Prince, by gentle, slow Degrees. By your obdurate Steadiness, and precipitate Perseverance (Virtues not unworthy of a *Devil*) your darling Schemes may be suddenly extinguished, before you can have Time to declare again how much you are *astonished* at *those Sufferers,* who despise and detest *you* as much as CASCA.

To the Lords BUTE and MANSFIELD.

What Seas of *Blood* will *Civil Discord* shed?
Dire *Fiend!* by *George's Friends, Bute, North,*
    and *Mansfield,* bred.

My LORDS,

YOUR Lordships will Pardon me, and I am sure your Brother *North* will readily excuse me, if I pass *him* by, for the Present, as a mere expletive in your execrable Triumvirate. He is, in Truth, my Lords, (and the World sees it) no more than the ostensible Leader of that *fawning, false, corrupt Confederacy,* who arrogantly groupe themselves under the *specious* Name of King's Friends. Like *designing Traytors, they, and you,* my Lords, assume this *Mask* for the worst of Purposes; that of enriching your wretched *Selves,* by the Spoils of this unhappy Country; whilst your deluded, passive Sovereign, is but your stalking Horse. Poor, mean, obsequious, flexible Lord North, (like the rest of your servile Herd) is no more than the humble and callous Executioner of your infernal selfish Views, your inhuman Warrants, your destructive Bloody Policy. In a Word, my Lords, you are the *Subtiles,* and he is the *Face.*

To your Lordships, therefore, and to your Lordships only, as *Principals,* as the earliest and most indefatigable Deluders of weak and ductile Majesty; I now address myself, not in Terms of pleasing Flattery, but in the Rough, and odious Language of disgusting Truth. Such, my Lords, as the Sovereign is, the Nation has received him from your Hands. He was Born a BRITON; you, my Lords, have taught him not only to forget, but to shame his Birth. He was Born a Prince; you have levelled him with the worst, the most inhuman, and meanest of his Subjects. He became (too soon, alas!) a KING; you, my Lords, have debased him to a *Tyrant*. His *Mind*, though enlightened by no auspicious ray from Heaven, was yet capable of receiving some *moderate degrees* of Culture; it was, in its infant State, open at least to the impressions of HUMANITY; you, my Lords, in that early period, gave it a most *unnatural*, and *unhappy Bent*; you *moulded,* you *contracted*, you *steeled* it for your own wicked Purposes. To say the best of it, it remains, after all your painful Lectures, either totally unprincipled, or most atrociously perverted. Hence, my Patriotic Lords, have flowed (and still flow) all the Grievances of the present inglorious, ignoble, and inhuman Reign. Let me ring them in your Ears, my Lords:—Court—and Ministerial Assassinations, of which *Martyn*, *Dun*, and *Talbot*, can remind you, in Wilkes's Case. In the same Case, in Bingley's, and some others, Royal Persecutions, Star-Chamber Inquisition, erasing Records, inveigling, byassing, misleading, deceiving, overbearing, and even packing Juries, by Lord Mansfield.[3] Daring Corruptions and Perversions of Justice, by the same Hand, in the last Resort (the once righteous House of Lords) in the late Case of *Thickness* and *Leigh*, under the infamous, illegal, and unprecedented Conduct of *Lord Apsley*, *Lord Mansfield*, *Lord High Chancellor of Great Britain*. The unjust Proceedings in this Case will (to your immortal Infamy, Lord Mansfield) be handed down to the latest Posterity—even a *Jeffereys* would have blushed at them. As for your Shadow, *Apsley*; your dependant Scots, *Cathcart* and

---

3. Samuel Martin and the first Earl Talbot both believed that they had been maligned by Wilkes in *The North Briton* (their characters "assassinated," in effect), and fought pistol duels with him. Alexander Dun had threatened Wilkes's life. See *A Complete Collection of the Genuine Letters, Papers, &c. in the Case of John Wilkes, Esq.* (1769). William Bingley was imprisoned from 1768–1770 for printing *The North Briton* and refusing to testify at the Court of King's Bench about his involvement. He had begun his own weekly newspaper, *Bingley's London Journal* in August 1772, based in Falcon Court, off Fleet Street, where he would once again be under pressure for printing essays critical of public policy.

Galloway,[4] and your Bully *Denbigh*, they are but Tools in your Lordship's Craft, they live by the Breath of your Lordship's Nostrils, and are too inconsiderable to be named either by Historian or Reporter; but Lord Mansfield's Name and Doctrines will be faithfully recorded.—Now, my Lords, I returns to Grievances, the Offspring of your Scotch Politics. Among others, you may recollect the Violation of the Freedom of Election, and the Lives you have to answer for at the Middlesex Election, in Support of your Court-Tool, Sir *William Beauchamp Procter*.[5] Your Lordships, and your royal Pupil, countenanced a still greater Violation of the Rights of Election, which was most impudently and perfidiously avowed, and sanctified by a corrupt House of Commons, in the Case of that insignificant Time-server, Colonel Lutterell, the King's Brother in Law.[6] Let me now remind your Lordships (for you are too callous to be shocked with the Sound) of Murders (repeated, wanton Murders) at the Brentford Election, and in *St. George's Fields*, even of Women and

4. For Cathcart and Galloway see n. VII.10 supra.

5. Sir William Beauchamp Proctor, first baronet, had sat for Middlesex in the Commons for over twenty years, until he was defeated in the 1768 election by John Glynn (see n. XII.5 supra for Glynn). It proved to be a contentious and expensive contest, as both candidates sought to woo voters. Proctor had considered himself an independent, voting sometimes with the ministry, sometimes with the opposition. He had actually sided with Wilkes on the question of general warrants, but Wilkes and his supporters considered him too unreliable. He died in 1773. There is a brief entry for him in Namier and Brooke, *House of Commons*, 2:70–71.

6. Lieutenant Colonel Henry Luttrell, offended by John Wilkes, offered to run against him for one of the Middlesex seats in the House of Commons in the aftermath of the 1768 parliamentary election, despite having just been elected himself to represent a borough in Cornwall. In a 1769 by-election that followed, Wilkes beat Luttrell by a four to one margin, but a divided House declared the imprisoned Wilkes ineligible for the seat (as it had before) and awarded the seat to his opponent. When Wilkes finally secured a seat for Middlesex in the 1774 election, Luttrell returned to the seat for his Cornwall borough. He had been a favorite target of "Junius" (see n. VII.9 supra). He took little interest in affairs at Westminster and spent much of his time in his native Ireland, where he eventually succeeded his father to the peerage there as Earl of Carhampton. He was not George III's brother-in-law, but came close for a commoner; his sister had married the King's brother, Prince Henry Frederick, Duke of Cumberland. See Namier and Brooke, *House of Commons*, 3:65–66, and the *Oxford DNB*, 34:813–14 entry by A. F. Blackstock.

Children. The barbarous Carnage of young Allen (naked and unarmed) must be attoned for.——By whose Advise, and with whose Privity, my Lords, did your Pupil return public Thanks for this Slaughter of his Subjects; who in the one Case were but curious Gazers, and in the other, were discharging their Duties as honest, independant Electors, above ministerial Bribery and Corruption? Let me ask you, my Lord *Mansfield*, the Lord Chief Justice of England (whose Duty it was to bring these ministerial Cut-throats to condign Punishment) why were these guilty Miscreants screened, protected, pardoned, pensioned? Why, and by whose Orders (unless yours, my Lord) was so much affected Tenderness, Management, brow-beating of the Prosecutor's Council and Witnesses, such nice Caution in summing up the Evidence, such Menaces against those who should *dare* to print these public Trials, but particularly that of young Allen? Why did your Lordship's *upright*, *holy*, and *favourite* Judge, *Smythe*,[7] so signalize himself, and labour with such uncommon Partiality? Why were the known Laws of England, dispensed with in the Case of the military Scotch Ruffians, who spilled the innocent Blood of *Allen* in *St. Georges's Fields?* Who suggested the happy Thought of dissolving the last Parliament on a sudden, and of smuggling and packing (by means of private Intimations to the Court-Members) a corrupt Majority in the present House of Commons in support of the ruinous and despotic Plan laid by your Lordships, and carried on by your obsequious Instrument Lord *North*, and his pensionary Subalterns in both Houses of Parliament? How, and by whom, are the Seats of Justice to be filled for

---

7. Sir Sidney Stafford Smythe, Court of the Exchequer baron, heard the case resulting from the St. George's Fields "massacre" of May 1768 the following August at Guildford in the Surrey assizes. The soldier, Donald Maclane of the Grenadier Guards, was acquitted of the charge of murdering William Allen; the other two accused grenadiers were not brought to trial because the grand jury chose not to return a "true bill" against them. Smythe, who had sat briefly in the Commons for a Sussex borough some twenty years before, was reputed to pressure jurors to reach what he considered the correct verdict. In 1770 "Junius" would target him for just that reason in another trial. James Oldham wrote the brief entry in the *Oxford DNB*, 51:468. For an unofficial account of the August 1768 legal proceedings see *A Full and Impartial View of the Trial of Donald Maclane* (London: W. Harris, 1768).

the future, my Lords, and for what Purposes? I will not ask, what knowledge of the Laws, but what Interest, what private Reasons, made such a Man as *Hotham*, a Baron of the Exchequer?[8]—This is a new Grievance and a real one.

"I liacos intra muros *peccator, et extra."*

Within *St. Stephen's Chapel*, and without;
That *All's* one Scene of *Guilt*, we need not doubt.[9]

Perret sells out, *Hotham* buys in, and his Seat in Parliament is thus purchased and filled up by your Lordships.[10] I must interrogate your Lordships still further—Of all your other wicked Counsels, what impolitic, diabolical Spirit, could instigate you to advise your Pupil ever to con-

8. Beaumont Hotham, having sat in the Commons for a Lancashire borough, had been elevated to baronet and named to the Court of Exchequer just the previous month. His career rise within Britain's patronage system (Hotham's patron being the Duke of Portland, whom he had befriended as a boy at the Westminster School) in that sense made him an easy target for critics of the ruling order–and yet, note that *The Crisis* went after supposed abuses of the system, not the system itself. Hotham had joined the bar after terms at the Middle Temple and Trinity Hall, Cambridge and ,as it turned out, he performed credibly as a judge. He presided at the 1777 trial of the infamous arsonist "John the Painter." There is a fair amount on Hotham in my *Burning the Dockyard: John the Painter and the American Revolution* (Portsmouth: Portsmouth Papers, 2001); I also wrote the entry for Hotham in the *Oxford DNB*, 28:250–52.

9. A familiar passage from the second of Horace's epistles (that to Lollius), commenting on the Trojan War and human frailty: sin occurred within the walls of Troy as well as without; in other words, both sides were at fault for bringing on a tragic conflict. The authors substitute Parliament ("Within St. Stephen's Chapel") to find yet another way of making the point that Britain's leaders were failing in their charge to protect the people.

10. This appears to be a garbled reference to the recently contested election in Cricklade, a parliamentary borough in Wiltshire. The results of a by-election in December 1774 had been rejected by the House of Commons, a new election was held the following February, and John Dewar was declared the winner, after which he took his seat at Westminster. Samuel Petrie–written mistakenly as "Perrit"?–was one of the candidates who lost to Dewar. He apparently withdrew his name as the Commons reviewed the case and supported Dewar, with the other candidate (Samuel Peach) being disqualified, See the brief note under John Dewar in Namier and Brooke, *House of Commons*, 2:320.

sent to, much more to persevere, in the inhuman Massacre of *America?* Why were the Petitions of the City of London answered in your Reign, my Lords, with Sneers, Insults, Abuse, Menaces, indignent Frowns, and even with Accusations of High Treason? I refer your Lordships to your last Bashaw-like Answer to the City Petition, where you will find (to the general Astonishment) that you have almost impeached a part of his Majesty's faithful and beloved* People, of High Treason, for only making a constitutional Supplication to the Throne; for humbly remonstrating against the pernicious Influence of Corruption and your Lordships; and for expressing natural and just Feelings for their Fellow Subjects, doomed by your Lordships to Destruction in *America.*

These my Lords, are some of the most palpable Wounds which your Lordships have, by *Hirelings* and *Dupes,* already given, there are others in Embryo, which you are about to give to the *British Constitution.* For these Iniquities, when your Measure is full, my Lords, you must assuredly account at last, unless, like *true Cowards,* you fly from Public Justice, or disappoint the meritorious Executioner, by the timely Application of your own guilty Hands, to the *rottenest* and most *detested Hearts* that ever beat. It can be no Secret to your Lordships, that you are universaly considered as the CATALINES[11] of an *imperious Gang* of Ministerial Parricides, you must be sensible that the Nation has hitherto submitted with unexampled Patience, not, properly speaking, so much to the puerile Obstinacy of a *Brunswick,* as to the despotic sway of a *Bute*

---

*We are *coaxed* with these *sugard* Words in his Majesty's last Speech. What pity it is that *Words* and *Actions* do not agree.

---

11. To readers of *The Crisis,* Lucius Sergius Catilina (anglicized as Catiline) probably exemplified the danger of a public man corrupted by ambition. A Roman senator thwarted in his numerous attempts to be elected a consul, he conspired with others to clear his path to power. Decried by fellow senator and onetime friend Cicero, himself a consul at the time, Catiline raised a small army in early 62 BCE and was killed in battle. He was to some a sort of precursor to Caesar. Sallust chronicled the tale (under various translated titles) in his Catiline's conspiracy, which was sold in both English and Latin editions.

and *Mansfield*; at once the greatest *Tyrants*, and the greatest *Traytors*, and the greatest *Cowards* under Heaven. The truth of these Assertions is fully proved by your *banefull Councils*, from whence all the *Grievances* above mentioned have arose, and from whence more (I fear) will shortly spring. If murdering their *Innocence and Virtue*, in the Subject and extinguishing their influence in the Sovereign, is *Tyranny*, *Treason*, and *rank Cowardice*, I am no false accuser of your Lordships. The Instances I have already given, are such as would blacken the Reigns of a NERO, or DOMITIAN,[12] but they are such my Lords as sprung Naturally from those *infernal Institutes* which your Lordships have incessantly penned and preached, for the Edification of a *British King;* of a King; who neither does, nor possibly can, hold the Crown of England upon such Principles as your Lordships have laboured to instill, these Labours, my Lords, are crying Sins against the Liberties, and Majesty of this Nation, and the 𝕎𝕒𝕘𝕖𝕤 𝕠𝕗 𝕥𝕙𝕖𝕤𝕖 𝕊𝕚𝕟𝕤 𝕚𝕤 𝔻𝕖𝕒𝕥𝕙.

The present Generation (like that which called this Family to the Throne) are Revolutionists; your Lordships are, we know, of a contrary Perswasion. Under such Tutors our steady, persevering, unhappy Sovereign, must have imbibed the most unconstitutional, absurd, and fatal Notions. Your Lordships should have Taught him in his earliest Days, that Steadiness and Perseverance can never be maintained with Reason, but in the Cause of Truth and Virtue, Justice and Humanity. Cast your Eyes, my Lords, upon the black Catalogue of Crimes above enumerated, and say in which of them a Spark of Virtue can be seen? Turn over the political Institutes you have penned for your royal Pupil's use, and say in what part of that elaborate Manuel, you have, with Truth, delineated the Prince, the Politician, or the Soldier? Nay, the Man of Honour, Human-

---

12. Domitian (Caesar Domitianus Augustus, when in power from 81–96 CE) was the son of one emperor (Vespasian) and younger brother of another (Titus); thus the so-called Flavian dynasty. Fond of—and feared for—killing his rivals, he kept the army loyal by paying it well, but was brought down by a palace coup involving praetorian guards and even his wife, to the immense pleasure of many senators who were too intimidated to rise against him. Tacitus and Suetonius both wrote of Domitian, putting him in the same general category of others who led Rome badly, by their profligacy and brutality.

ity, or Common Honesty? It is too well known, it is most severely felt, that your Sovereign has from his Infancy proceeded, and still magnanimously persists, upon the Plan formed by your Lordships for his Direction. He opens his Ears and his Heart (if he ever opens them at all) to you alone. He cajoles his Parliament, he despises his People, but he confides in you. After all, my Lords, what is this Confidence in your Lordships likely to produce? A Snare to him, and Ruin to his People. Your Lordships have vitiated his Soul with every Quality of a genuine Scot, except true Valour, and Discernment. The one would, in your Opinion, have made England too Happy, the other would have made yourselves too odious. This would have blasted your impious Designs, and that would have crushed your pusillanimous and baneful Politics. The bitter Fruits of your political System, my Lords, begin now to ripen into a total Desolation, or, at least, an irrecoverable loss of a large, a valuable, a virtuous, (and therefore an obnoxious) part of the British Empire, into Foreign Wars; and intestine Commotions and Calamities; into universal Discontent and Slaughter; into Misery, Revenge, Anarchy, and a Revolution. Every feeling Man most devoutly wishes your Lordships an ample, and a speedy Share of that National Resentment, which you have in Season, and out of Season, laboured to deserve. That your pernicious and detested Lives may be prolonged, till your Lordships shall receive from the Hand of Public Justice, the Reward of all your indefatigable Pains to betray your King, and destroy your Country, is the Prayer of

C A S C A.

Y E S.

Printed and published for the Authors, by T. W. SHAW, in Fleet-Street, opposite Anderton's Coffee House, where Letters to the Publisher, will be thankfully received.

THE

CRISIS

NUMBER XXIV   To be continued Weekly.

SATURDAY, July 1, 1775   [Price Two-pence Half-penny.

—*Immedicabile* Vulnus
Ense recidendum, *ne pars sincera* trahatur.

Ovid.[1]

The prudent Surgeon, of a *Gangrene* sure,
By *Amputation* keeps the *Vitals* pure;
State Dissolutions thus effect a Cure.

A Disease of a venal Majority in the great Council of the Nation, may be truly called a Mortification in the Body politic. This desperate Case requires a desperate Remedy. A Patriot King[2] would neither delay, nor fear the application. It's Success depends upon the Hand that operates. The Operation of a wholesome and salutary

---

1. A passage from Book I of Ovid's *Metamorphoses*, advising that an untreatable or incurable wound needs to be cut out to prevent the healthy tissue from being infected. Thus the admonition in English that follows.

2. Bolingbroke's *Idea of a Patriot King* (1738) being the standard here, with which George III was familiar—and in some sense tried to emulate. See the Introduction.

Desolution has been wisely intrusted by our considerate Ancestors to the Sovereign. The Exertion of this great Prerogative was petitioned for, with the greatest Reason, during the Tyranny and Iniquities of the last venal Parliament, by the first, the most loyal, and respectable Metropolis in the Universe, the City of London. It was twice Petitioned for, and twice refused.

Several other Cities and Corporations in this Kingdom were not silent, they likewise supplicated the Throne, and met with the like Repulse. This Prerogative (a glorious one it is) is intrusted with the Sovereign by the People, to be by him exerted in the nicest and most critical Emergencies of State.

Of all the Prerogatives of the Crown, the most essential to the Constitution, the most salutary to the People, the most Honourable to a Patriot King, is that of dissolving Parliaments. In this respect a King of England is wisely invested by the People, with the Power of a temporary Dictator. *Ne quid detriment i Respublica capiat.*[3]

It is his Duty when either the two other Estates (the Lords and Commons) preponderate, to interpose, as a constitutional Moderator, and to keep the Ballance even, that the Common Weal may not suffer by Democratical Passions, or Aristocratical Ambition. This Power, however, (of Dissolution) never will be exercised by a Tyrant, and never can be exercised by a Fool, but for Purposes destructive of the Constitution; perhaps, to save a Minion, or to keep Corruption in the hopeful Channel prescribed for it by himself and his faithless Ministers. But the People's Hopes, Addresses, and Petitions, will be vain. What can they hope from a Tyrant, or a Fool? Either of these are equally unfit to Reign. The one will be duped by his Ministers and Favourites, the other biased by his Lusts. Ambition fires the Tyrant, and Geugaws captivate the Fool; the one is subdued by false Glory, the other by Flattery and Show.

---

3. Cicero's allusion to the charge given to consuls by the Senate that they should see that the republic received no injury during their term, in his oration defending the actions of Titus Annius Milo. For Cicero see n. LIII.2 infra.

Should the Majesty of Great Britain ever happen to be a compound of Fool and Tyrant, the National Misfortune will be equal. The Truth is, that so glorious a Prerogative cannot be justly exercised, or wisely conducted, without a discerning Judgment, and a good Heart; without Fortitude sufficient to throw off the Leading strings of presumptuous Favourites, and Sense enough to proceed without them; without Capacity to think, and Ability to act; without considering upon what Condition the Crown of England is now held, and by what Conduct alone it can be maintained; without adhering to Facts instead of Favourites; to Truth instead of ministerial Sophistry; to constitutional Principles, instead of unconstitutional Councils. A smuggled, venal Parliament is more properly a great Majority, than a great Council; it is certainly not the Constitutional great Council of this Nation. A King of England is a parliamentary King; he is wisely placed at the Head of that Parliament, as having in his Breast, the executive Power of the Kingdom. The other two Estates consult and propound, but he must approve; they advise, but he confirms; they prepare Measures, but he enforces them. If those Measures are salutary, his Assent promotes the Welfare; if pernicious, it may compleat the Ruin of his Kingdom. No English King ought, no PATRIOT KING will, be the subservent Fool of a corrupt, a wicked, or a bloody Parliament. He will judiciously, and righteously, withold his Assent to such Acts, as must inflict Dishonour and Infamy upon himself, and Destruction upon his People. The worst Consequence that can ensue, will be that this wicked, precipitate Parliament, must deliberate again upon their intended Measures. This wise Delay in a constitutional King, may be the saving of a great Nation. If a Tyrannic Parliament still persists, a PATRIOT KING, like an honest Dictator, will dissolve such Miscreants.

Thus Corruption will be extinguished, honest Representatives elected, and a good King enthroned in the Hearts of a grateful and affectionate People, whom he has thus constitutionally protected from Slavery and Ruin. What? (says some ministerial Scribler, a *Johnson* perhaps) shall a King of England detach himself from his Parliament? I answer, Yes; if that Parliament is corrupt, wicked, and tyrannical; it is then no constitutional Parliament, but an illicit Gang; nor is he a constitutional King, but a daring and unthinking Tyrant, who adheres to them. By so doing, he plainly shews that it is not his Intention to protect, but to enslave his People. That venerable Body alone can be called a Parliament, who are known, according to the im po⁴ of the Word, (*parler le ment*) to speak their Mind, to be above all human Influence. Can this be said of a servile, detestable, insidious, unconstitutional Majority, who come to the great Council, with a mercenary Gagg in their Mouths, their perfidious Names in the Court Calendar, and Lord *Bute's* (under the Colour of Lord *North's*) Instructions in their Pockets? Our Kings, it is true, are parliamentary Kings; but there is a wide difference between a Parliament and a Cabal; between Sages convened, and Voters hired, between free, constitutional States, and servile, ministerial Dependents.

When a Parliament is degenerated thus far, they loose their Honour, they ought to lose their former Name; they deserve no farther Confidence. They would find none, in a wise and good King. No Prince who is not under the Ideocy, Insanity, or the worst Passions, could adhere to such a Junto. Such Men are audacious in calling themselves a Parliament. They no longer Represent, but usurp; they are not faithful Servants, but assuming Tyrants, they are not Counsellors of the King, but Traytors to the People. A great Council (or rather a great Majority) composed of such Monsters, such Pests of a Community, cannot be said either to regard, or to represent, a People; their Views and Interests are different. The People sue for Protection, they for Places; the People wish to support the Constitution, they to supply their Luxury; the People are affected by the decay of commerce, they by the Largesses of the Minister.

Can a PATRIOT KING confide in, or cooperate with such a Mock-Parliament? When we hear a King talk of steadily pursuing the Advice of the great Council of the Nation, it must be taken for granted, that he knows and believes the Majority of that Council (whose Votes are decesive of the Fate of this Kingdom) to be incorrupt. Can such Faith as this

---

4. Apparently a typesetting error, the Bodleian Library copy being, in this case, the same as that at the British Library (see n. I.1 supra).

be found in Israel? If not, a King of England may well be asked, even by the Meanest of his Subjects, why he is wicked enough, or weak enough, to approve, sanctify, and confirm, the despotic Acts, not of such a Parliament, but of such a traiterous Convention? Is it his Duty in such a Case, to confide or to dissolve? In such a dangerous Crisis, the Constitution has given a judicial Power to Kings; they are Bound to exercise that Power, not for the Destruction, but for the Safety of the Commonwealth. They are not to consult the Views, the Wishes, the Interests, or Security of Ministers or Favourites, but the Salvation of the Kingdom. Our Laws, under which every King must submit to Reign, speaks plainly to the Sovereign, in open, intelligible, rational Terms, when it says, "*Cessa regnare, si non vis judicare.*"[5] "If you will not exercise those judicial Powers, with which the Constitution has entrusted you, resign your Crown, you are no longer fit to reign over a free People." The Word (*judicare*) in the Maxim above mentioned, extends not merely to the Exertion of a King's judicial Powers in civil, or criminal Cases, (though this would be the false Interpretation of a *Mansfield*) but it must be taken in it's largest, and most important Sense; it is allowed by every honest, learned Interpreter, to extend to the whole System of the King's executive Powers. In that large Sense it has ever been considered by such political Writers as *Locke, Sidney, Acherly*, and *Nathanial Bacon*, who Writes so admirably on Government.[6]

5. The notion, by then a principle captured in legal Latin, that a king who was unwilling to judge should cease to reign.

6. Unlike John Locke and Algernon Sidney, Nathaniel Bacon is now all but forgotten. Both he and Roger Acherley were well respected in their time and widely read as defenders of the ancient constitution. Bacon rose to prominence as a barrister and bencher at Gray's Inn before he was elected to the House of Commons and wrote a defense of Parliament's stand against Charles I in his *Historical Discourse* (1647). Acherley, of the Inner Temple, just as vigorously defended the Glorious Revolution in his *Britannic Constitution* (1727), which appeared in a fifth edition as recently as 1759. Janelle Greenberg wrote the *Oxford DNB*, 3:162–64, piece on Bacon; Matthew Kilburn contributed the entry for Acherley (at 1:435–36). And Acherley has not slipped entirely away: see Eric Nelson's "Hebraism and the Republican Turn of 1776: A Contemporary Account of the Debate over *Common Sense*" *William and Mary Quarterly*, 3rd series 70 (2013):787–88.

This Maxim is strong, and pointed; it comes directly home to my present Purpose, and opens a large Field for no very favourable Inferences at the present Juncture. A king of England must not, cannot live for himself (much less for his Minions) but only for his People. I speak an honest, constitutional Truth, when I say that he must not Indulge, but Toil. A King's Revenues, Magnificence, Splendor, Pomp, and Grandeur, are not designed to emblazon him, but to do Honour to his Kingdom. All his glittering rays of Majesty are reflected from the People. An English Throne is not like a Turkish Sophia, to be made the idle Seat of Slumber and Repose. It is erected for the Exercise of Mercy, Truth, and Justice. Neither of these Princely attributes is concerned in maintaining Corruption, or repelling just Suitors without Redress; nay, with ignominious Language and Contempt. It is a King of England's Duty to cleanse the Augean Stable.[7] He is the Argus of the Commonwealth;[8] his Eyes, his Ears, his mental Powers, must all be open to his People, whilst his royal Passions are subdued. He can acquire neither Honour nor Security by an injudicious Struggle with his Subjects. Truth and Liberty will prevail. Tyrants and Fools have been dethroned. Injured Subjects have triumphed and exulted in their turn. Minions, and abandoned Ministers have been guarded to the Scaffold; and Corruption itself, though not to be dissolved, may be, at last, extinguished, in another glorious and necessary REVOLUTION.

These are Lessons which English Princes should be Taught betimes in their Minority. By these, even King's themselves, may profit in riper

7. The Augean stables housed thousands of cattle and had not been attended to for years. Cleaning it in a single day was the fifth of twelve tasks assigned to Hercules so that he would humble himself before the Gods (most especially his father, Zeus). He performed them all successfully, despite their seeming impossiblity. In the case of the stables he diverted two rivers to flow through them, which flushed them quickly.

8. Argus, the one-hundred-eyed giant of Greek mythology, was also known as Argus Panoptes ("all seeing"). Since at least one of his eyes was always open he was the perfect guard. Caught up in one of the many little intrigues that pitted Zeus and Hera against each other, he was slain by Hermes at Zeus's command after Hermes had lulled him to sleep. His fate was recalled in Ovid's *Metamorphoses*, Book I.

Years. By these, the present obdurate, deluded Sovereign, whom Heaven has not been pleased to bless with any great share of natural Discernment, may be taught to avoid these Miseries, which must attend his rash and headstrong Perseverance, his unjust and guilty Confidence; his Tyrannic Pride, and an insolent Contempt of that People, through whose Patience and Indulgence, he most unworthyly holds the Crown of England.

C A S C A.

Printed and published for the Authors, by T. W. *Shaw*, in Fleet-Street, opposite Anderton's Coffee House, where Letters to the Publisher, will be thankfully received.

THE

CRISIS

NUMBER XXV   To be continued Weekly

SATURDAY, July 8, 1775   [Price Two-pence Half-penny.

Vis, Consili expers, mole ruit sua.

Hor.[1]

Be wise, ye Kings, nor to *mere Power* trust,
Without *sound Counsels,* Pow'rs *Tyrannic Lust*,
And brings it's *haughty Master* to the Dust.

W E have lately heard much, and too much, of the Wisdom of Parliament, the great Council of the Nation; that is to say, the corrupt Majority of that great Council, where the most Votes enforce the vilest Measures. We know what this great Council once was, and what it ought to be. Let us reflect upon what it now is. It is (alas!) no more at present than a Majority of Ay's and No's—Contents and not Contents. And what is this Majority? the Minister's—What is this Minister? The King's;—What is the King? my Lord Bute's.—What is Lord Bute? An Enemy to this Nation.—I had like to have said what I think, a Traytor; but I hope this will be said with more Weight in a future Impeachment, unless popular Revenge should

---

1. "Force without wisdom falls of its own weight," from Horace's *Odes*, Book 3.

justly make a less solemn, but a more dreadful Example of this public
Pest. Through these Channels of Wisdom flow all the Grievances, Oppressions, and Calamities, which are now so severely felt in England and
America. The Subjects of these Nations feel all the Power of this great and
wise Council, without a single ray of its Benignity. It shines upon it's Idols,
but lowers upon the Subject. Power, and despotic Power, is the great end
in view, and the Growth of it is cultivated with the greatest Boldness and
Assiduity. We now see the three great Estates of this Kingdom, which were,
in their Origin, wisely designed as salutary Checks upon each other, to
preserve the Constitution, in an amicable Confederacy to destory it. As to
the Peers, they are created by the Crown, not for Meritorious, but political
Reasons. Wealth, and a pliant Disposition, are essential Requisites. Some
Minion of the Crown becomes bound for their good Behaviour, and then
the Great Seal stamps them for the Tools of an audacious and corrupt Minister. But your Apostate *Chathams, Camdens, Richmonds, Buckinghams,
Temples, Shelburnes*, &c. are repudiated.[2] The virtuous Minority is too
thin to save their Country. They are out-clamoured, and out-voted. I have
heard Lord Chatham's manly Eloquence rudely drowned by a combined
Roar of the Minister's Majority in the House of Lords. I have heard that
great Orator answered by ministerial Mouths without Argument, without
Sense, without Grammar, and without English.

Their Lordships may well clear their House, and be as much ashamed of
their Speeches, as they ought to be of their Principles. As to the House of
Commons, it is filled, and fed, three Parts out of four, by the Minister.

Let me not forget, however, to congratulate them on a new Privilege,
which they acquired and established in *Wilkes's* Case, the rational and

---

2. William Pitt, first Earl of Chatham; Charles Pratt, Baron Camden; Charles Len-
nox, third Duke of Richmond; George Nugent-Temple, first Marquess of Buckingham;
Richard Grenville, second Earl Temple; and William Petty, second Earl of Shelburne.
Although all of these peers, at one time or another, led the opposition in the House
of Lords against one policy or another during these first years in the reign of George
III, they were hardly of one mind nor did they form some sort of solid political block.
Richmond, in particular, resented being lumped in with anyone as a political ally to be
taken for granted.

modest Privilege of electing themselves. This Acquisition is a great one. It is plain that honourable House esteems it so, because they have lately most iniquitiously refused to erase those base and daring Innovations upon the Rights of the People from their Journals. Thus they have industriously preserved the Infamy of the last detested Parliament to posterity. But they have likewise (which was the real Design) treasured up a vile Precedent to be produced in future Times of need, against the Liberties of their Masters, the People of this Kingdom.

There was a Time when this House of Commons was not too Modest to oppose the arbitrary Wills of Princes. There was a Time when they had the Honesty to refuse Supplies, when the Former had been ill-applied, and as ill-accounted for; when the old had been lavished in profusion and donceurs to Favourites, and new were demanded for the like Purposes, or worse, the insidious Purposes of Corruption. There was a Time too, when the Head of that House (the Speaker) had Integrity, though some Parts of that Body were Corrupt.

Whoever remembers Onslow, must respect his Memory;[3] whoever knew him must revere it. He respected his Sovereign, but he loved the People. He preserved the Dignity and Integrity of his Station. He distinguished nobly and justly between a Post of Honour and a Post of Profit. He was neither Pensioner, Placeman, nor Privy Councellor. He knew that it was impossible to serve two Masters. He rejoiced to be at the Head of a Free People. He had a thorough knowledge of their Rights, and was zealous in defending them. He knew that it was impossible for a Speaker of the House of Commons to be, with the least Consistency, a Courtier and a Demagogue at the same Time. He knew that if he held a lucrative Place, he could not hold his

---

3. Arthur Onslow had the distinction of being the longest serving speaker of the House of Commons to that point in British history, a post he held for nearly the entire reign of George II, from 1728–1761. Famous as a parliamentary proceduralist, admired for his commitment to the idealized Glorious Revolution, even political opponents respected him for his fairmindedness and integrity. Philip Laundy reviews his life in the *Oxford DNB*, 41:373–74 .

Integrity. He preferred his Duty to Trash. He preferred virtuous Liberty to ministerial Influence and Controul. He preferred Honour to Infamy, Sincerity to Duplicity, and Propriety to Absurdity. For what can be more absurd than a ductile Speaker, who is at the Head of the Commons in the Morning, and at the Ear of the Sovereign in the Evening? At one Hour in Character of a Speaker, at another in the Function of a Privy Counsellor. Now in the Peoples Chair, and now at a Ministerial Board. To Day collecting the Sense of the People, and to Morrow promoting the Intrigues of a Court. Cooperating with the People at one Instant, and forming Schemes against their Liberties at another. To crown all, let us suppose this Speaker an established Placeman for Life; to which Place an annual Income is appendant of 4000l. per Annum, and eventually twice that Sum, or more, in a Place which no subject had enjoyed for Years, till the present Speaker (*Norton*) broke the Ground anew. Why had it not been enjoyed for many Years before? Because it was for Life, and the Minister had not sufficient Confidence in the steady Perfidy, and superior Demerits of any one Hireling, to bestow it, till they were conscious that *Norton* deserved that, and more. Let us view this malleable Speaker, and patriotic Statesman, this political Proteus, this double-fronted Janus, in another Light, which will fully show the Compatibility of the two different Functions.[4]

Suppose a *Bute* or a *Mansfield* were to be impeached, as they well deserve, by the Commons of England ('tis but a Supposition, for Corruption at present makes it impracticable) suppose it only: Whose Duty would it be

---

4. Proteus was a figure from Greek mythology; Janus was one of the pantheon of Roman gods. Proteus had the power to prophesy, but did so only reluctantly. Able to change his form into that of ferocious beasts, those seeking knowledge of the future had to hold him fast as he writhed to get free. With tales that began with Homer and passed through Virgil, there were those who succeeded in getting him to speak. Janus presided over entrances and exits, real doorways and gates as symbols of passages through life. Represented on coins with faces looking in opposite directions, there also developed the more negative meaning of someone who could not be trusted because he was duplicitous in his dealings and disingenuous in his promises.

to carry up these Bills of Impeachment to the Bar of the House of Lords? Sir *Fletcher Norton's.* Sir *Fletcher?* What? a Placeman, a Pensioner, a Privy Counsellor? A Bird of the same Feather? Can *Jemmy Twitcher* 'peach?[5] I have said enough to be sufficiently understood, and to show how inconsistent and absurd it is for a Speaker of the House of Commons, to be amphibiously inclined.

Let us now return to the noble Lords—We see among them another Majority, not indeed with *Lord Bute* (for he absconds) but with his Deputy, *Mansfield,* at their Head.—No; 'tis *Lord Apsley;* those insignia upon the Table are his, true, the Insignia, (the baubles, the Purse and Mace) are *Apsley's;* but *Apsley* himself is *Mansfield's,* as *Mansfield* himself is *Bute's.* These three dance the Hay, like the Sun, Moon, and Earth, in the Rehearsal; though indeed it is *Lord Bute's* interest, at present to continue in Eclipse. At present that Thane is to all intents and purposes, by his two Proxies *Mansfield* and *Apsley,* at the Head of the House of Lords. He has his Majority of Myrmidons there, as well as among the Commons, where he is represented by *Lord North.* Where then shall we find a Patriot? in the Throne. This (alas!) would be a blessing "devoutly to be wished".

But the three great Estates of this Kingdom, are now not in a wholesome, but a dangerous Coalition; not in Harmony, but in Combination; not in Friendship, but in Confedracy. The House of Commons now shut the Doors against their Constituents, the Lords debate in private, they are ashamed, (as they well may) of their Harrangues, These Houses are now, in truth, a Divan, a Conclave, a Junto, a Cabal, a Gang; but they are no

---

5. John Montagu, fourth Earl of Sandwich, though never a naval officer, spent much of his public life in the Admiralty, and most of that as first lord. He worked diligently to institute a merit system of promotion within the ranks and he tried to reform the operations of the royal dockyards, with mixed results. The "Jemmy Twichter" nickname (from a character in John Gay's immensely popular satirical spoof, *The Beggar's Opera*) refers to his reputed lasciviousness, which government critics could use to great advantage when going after policies that he supported but may have had little real role in devising—very much like the Earl of Bute. For fine examples of Bute and Sandwich as targets of political satire see Michael Wynn Jones, *The Cartoon History of the American Revolution* (London: London Editions, 1977).

longer what they where, or what they ought to be; they will shortly feel the Consequences, of such an unnatural Coalition. The Body Politic can never be healthy, whilst it Functions are ill-performed; yet this is the great and wise Council of the Nation, in which Soverigns will confide.

I know that a Majority of Votes can save Minions and Favourites from the SCAFFOLD; but they cannot save them from PUBLIC VEN-GEANCE, nor can they secure the Sovereigns Peace, Affection, and Es-teem, they can augment the Civil List, from near a Million a Year to any Sum that royal profusion may demand; they can allow (without entering into pricise Accounts) what a King may expend for Public Uses, a Term of the largest the most vague and most indefinite meaning, including every Species of regal, domestic, political, and unjust Profusion; they can lay still heavier Taxes for this purpose, as well as for the carrying on the further ASSASSINATION of *America*; but they can neither force the united Subjects of this Kingdom to pay those unreasonable Taxes, nor heal the Wounds of a Civil War if they refuse. How will our com-mon Enemies France and Spain, embroil the Scene? at such a Crisis will an importation of Hanoverians, Hissians, and mercinary Troops from the little States of Germany avail? From Hanoverians no Assistance can be expected, they will not be able to defend their own State against the designing and ambitious King of Prussia. That great Monarch will not forget the ill Treatment he has received from England; Civil War here will afford him the long wished-for Opportunity.

Our Standing Army (if any Part should be base enough, to Fight for Tyrants, and the Benefit of being Slaves,) will be fully employed; Such Part of it as is truly English, will join their Countrymen, and put a final Period to Despotism and Corruption.

The constitutional, and the only constitutional Force of this Kingdom, the Militia, will not fail to signalize themselves in defence of LIBERTY, in this unhappy Period will the patriotic Spirit of Ireland be still? by what foreign Power, amidst this confusion at home, is *America*, at last, to be protected, or enslaved? By which of her Friends the French or Span-iards? Our standing Army will be too much wanted here to afford fresh Succour to *Burgoyne*.

Does that idle Notion prevail, any longer in this Century, which supplied King Charles the First with Forces and Recruits, in the last; when that *blessed Martyr*, endeavoured to subdue this Country to his Despotic Will by force of Arms? Is passive Obedience, non Resistance, and the Divine Right of Tyrants, of any weight even with the lowest of the People? Is not the Idea and Spirit of LIBERTY universal still? Is the Invasion of its Rights a Secret? It is true that we have long lived in an Age of Venality and Corruption, but we also live in an Age of Reason and Discernment. The meanest Individual among us knows that he has a Right to call his Life, Liberty and Property his own, and will die in their Defence.

A foolish and wicked King like the present effects, the Power of a Despot; a Patriot King uses the Authority of a Parent. A Sacrifice to Public Liberty could not be grateful to a Patriot King, it would sully his Glory, and disappoint his Views. To a weak or a designing Prince Liberty is odious, it is an Object of perpetual Terror and Alarm. Under the Reign of one, the Lives and Properties of the Subject are no longer valuable, then whilst they are employed to promote the wise Ends of paternal Government, Common Good; under the other, they are useless, unless they are exerted for the Public Safety. The People live in allegiance to the one, and in league against the other; the one reaps all the Fruits of National Confidence and Affection, the other feels all the Weight of general Distrust, and all the ignominy of individual Destruction, the one has no Favourites, and the other has no Enemies. The readiest Obedience waits upon the Father and the bitterest Execrations pursue the Despot of a Country.

C A S C A.

Printed and published for the Authors, by T. W. *Shaw,* in Fleet-Street, opposite Anderton's Coffee House, where Letters to the Publisher, will be thankfully received.

T H E

C R I S I S

NUMBER XXVI   To be continued Weekly

SATURDAY. July 15, 1775   [Price Two-pence Half-penny.

Molle Pecus, *mutumque* Metu.   VIRG.[1]

Mansfield derides and *George* such Suppliants Scorns;
You're a tame Herd; why don't you use your *Horns.

ADMINISTRATION dare not, as yet (or else they would) deny the Subjects Right of PETITIONING the King; but *Bute* and *Mansfield*, will not suffer even the Petition of the first City in the Kingdom, to be received upon the Throne. Can their supreme Lordships give a Reason why? I mean a solid Reason. It is an undoubted, and till now has been an undisputed Right, which this grateful City claims, a Right, which no ROYAL TYRANT in past Ages has controuled.

*Immediately after the Remonstrances in Mr. Beckfords Mayoralty, Lord Mansfield made the King in his Speech mention the Distemper which raged among the Horned Cattle, this was Cabinet-Wit, and a standing Joke at Court.

1. This phrase is pulled from a longer passage in Virgil's *Aeneid*, Book 9, lines 339–42, where a ravenous lion bites and claws its way through a flock of sheep, frozen in fear.

225

This late politic Display of Sovereign Insolence, has broke out, to dignify the present Reign; our Kings are still ready to receive a Petition from the greatest City in the Universe, but they are the Judges WHERE—at their Leveé—or in their Water Closet?—Be it ordained henceforth, that all Petitions for Redress of National Grievances, shall be received WHERE they may be most useful to the Sovereign, and least likely to rise in Judgement against the Minister.

Is it come to this at last, that one of the most essential Rights of a British Subject is to be treated with Indignity? Is it become a Farce that may be acted at a Sycophantic Levee, and attended to with as much affected Indifference as a Birth Day Ode? Is the Ground and Reason of this invaluable Right forgot? Or are the Rights of the Crown alone to be maintained, and those of the Subject trampled under Foot? Let us enquire into the Foundation of the Subject's Right to address the Throne; we shall then see with what Propriety, Policy, or Decency, this Satisfaction is refused now. Whilst the Sovereign has a Right to Allegiance, the Subject has an equal Claim to Protection.

These Essentials form the Bond of Union, the reciprocal Relation, between the Governor and the Governed; that the State may enjoy the Benefits arising from this Union, the King becomes the Head of the Body Politic, by the Suffrage of a Free People; the People remain Members of this Body Politic, giving up their Natural Rights, by Compact with the Sovereign, for the Sake of Protection and good Government. These are the two great Ends which every Subject has in View. A King of England, on the other Hand has not a single Prerogative which is not conducive to these two great Ends. This is the true State of an English Sovereign, and an English Subject: In consequence, a good Sovereign may well expect to be obeyed without Reluctance; a loyal Subject to be heard without Contempt; if the Sovereign's Dignity must be maintained, the Subjects Grievances must be redressed; the one is lessened by an insolent Deportment, and the other aggrivated by cold Indifference. The Prince who will not hear Information, is a FOOL; he who persists in Spite of it, is a TYRANT.

It is a Maxim with us, "that the King can do no Wrong;" the Result of every political Evil, is imputed to his Ministers, but the unthinking Prince who checks Petitions to the Throne, rashly takes every impolitic Transgression upon himself. To this injudicious Conduct that weak Tyrant Charles the First, deluded by his ministerial Sycophants, owed his Ruin, he foresaw the Storm approaching, when it was too late to take Shelter from its Fury, his Sufferings (and just they were) should be a perpetual Lesson for Crowned Heads, but alas! they are kept (if possible) in Infancy all their Lives, at their hazard their infamous Dependants are to rise; a wise King would not only open his Ears, but his Arms, to the Information of his Subjects, they are his Creators, and they ought to be his Guides, they are in Truth his only Friends.

Till Subjects commence Slaves, neither weak Kings, nor wicked Ministers, can stand before them, no Army is sufficient in a free Country, to encounter civil Indignation and Resentment, Iniquity never can prevail till Men have lost their Reason, those who dare to think, will dare to act. To injured Subjects the sharpest of all Incentives is Contempt, the happiest expedient is Redress, the sole Right of exercising this lenient Measure, lies in the Breast of the Sovereign; if Ministers are wicked he can discard them, if venal Parliaments, at the Back of a Minister, attempt to undermine the Constitution, he can dissolve them; without proceeding to this extremity, he can, and it is his Duty to withhold his Assent whenever any Act has improvidently passed the two Houses, which is likely to be pernicious to the Nation.

In such Times of Corruption and Iniquity, every Member of the Body Politic has a Right to inform the Head (the King) of the approaching Danger, in such Times, shall a great City be repulsed? if they are to be received with unusual Indignity, such an intended Reception is equal to an actual Repulse. That Prince wants Wisdom, who is not capable of reflecting that opulent Cities are the vital Parts of his Dominions, yet what Treatment has the City of London lately met with? have they not been charged with encouraging his Majesty's *rebellious Subjects* (as they are called) in *America?* Is it not TREASON to encourage TRAYTORS? Yet my *Lord Mansfield* knows that the Word (Encourage) is the Word used by his Majesty, in his Answer to the City-Petition. Now if Subjects have a Right, (and who dare deny it?) to Petition the Sovereign, they are intituled to some Degree of Decency, when they approach the Throne with a Remonstrance; because these Remonstrants are a most important Part, of those People to whom the Sovereign owes his Existence and Continuance. The Majesty of a People resides in the collective Body, not in a packed Majority of smuggled Representatives in a venal House of Commons, it is not from the Luxurious and Corrupt, but from the Industrious and Commercial Parts of the Kingdom, that this collective Body will take its Tone, they are the Sinews of the State. The rotten Commons, and still more rotten Peers, are but as Straws floating lightly upon the Surface of this great Community, these are the Bees that make the Honey, and those the idle Drones, that rob the public Hives; yet these alone are the Persons whom the "King delighteth to Honour," they alone are received with Smiles.

The incense of Flattery is grateful, the Voice of Truth an abomination, to the Throne, the Sovereign (tho' not to be surfeited with supplies) is grown sick of information; Petitions are therefore to be received at LE-VEES, there they will be handed to a Lord in waiting (one of the corrupt Gang) and neither opened nor heard of, afterwards, but when Petitions are received upon the Throne, a King cannot stop his Ears; their Contents, their Reception, and the Answer, are notorious, the whole World may then look on, and either applaud the Wisdom, or be astonished at the Justice of the Sovereign.

Can TYRANTS who violate the Laws of God, fear the sentence of this earthly Forum? Is it for this pusillanimous Reason, Public Remonstrances are to be treated like private Petitions, presented by indignant Individuals? Are the City of London to be received like Paupers in the Corner of a Levee? Do they come for Alms, or for Redress? Do they come to solicit a Pension, or to claim a Right? Do they sue for the Performance of a jobbing Contract made with a perfidious Minister, or for an Establishment and due Observence in future, of that Compact made between the Crown and the Subject, at the Revolution? If they come in the latter Shape, the Importance of their Suit demands all the Dignity and Attention of the Sovereign.

If Petitions of such a serious Nature, can be baffled by a careless, light Reception at a Levee of Idolatrous Placemen, and needy Mendicants, every Avenue of Honest Information is shut up by the false FRIENDS of deluded MAJESTY; the Sovereign is still kept in a State of Darkness and dangerous Perseverance, for the Sake of a Ministerial GANG of Public ROBBERS, at the Hazard of the Property, Lives, and Liberties of a whole Empire.

The iniquitons Proceedings of this *atrocious* GANG in the last, and present Parliament, which they packed, fully justify me in branding them with the Name of PUBLIC ROBBERS. Let them look into the Black *Journals* of their Guilty HOUSES—There they will find that Individuals, Corporations, Electing Counties in *Great Britain* (not to mention the vast Continent of *America* and the Colonies, Merchants, and Manufacturers, dependent on it) have been deprived of their Rights, their Liberties, and Lives, by that *Banditti,* who call themselves the KING's FRIENDS, yet act like ENEMIES to him, and to their Country.

Let me ask these National RAVAGERS, have no Royal Assents been given by their Procurement, to Bills most pernicious in their consequences to the whole *British Empire*? If so, are those Remonstrances, which seek a Repeal of these destructtive Acts, to be smothered in Oblivion? Are they to be stifled by those Guilty Parents to whom they owe their Birth? Are they to be crushed in the Pocket of some Lordly Lacquey, who attends a PRIVATE LEVEE? Shall those wicked Counsellors, who have brought on the Ruin of an Empire, stand for ever before the King? Shall *Bute* and *Mansfield,* with their dependent Shadows, *North* and *Apsley,* still be suffered to whisper at the Ear of Majesty? Whilst the Nation is justly alarmed for her Liberties, shall these domestic Spoilers be suffered to pursue their Triumph in Defiance of *Great Britain* and *America?* They have long trembled, and are now in hourly Fear of popular Petitions.

These would open the Way (should they at last meet with due Attention) first to their Removal from the King's Presence, and then to fatal Enquiries—To the Salvation of *Great Britain* and *America,* and to the Punishment of an Infernal GANG of *National Parricides.* They, on the other Hand, fearing only for themselves, wish to stop all Access to the

Sovereign's Ear, and every Appeal to his Understanding, or his Heart. *England* cannot look with Unconcern upon the Sufferings of *America*. Her Claim is just, she says, and she says truely, that Taxation (when it is for the single Purpose of taking Money out of her Pocket) and Representation are, and must necessarily be, *reciprocal.* In every other Respect She submits (as a Colony) to the Legislature of her Mother Country; She submits to all those Laws of *England,* which affect the general System of Policy throughout the *Empire of Great Britain;* but She says wisely, that the Money which She acquires by the Sweat of her own Brow, is not the Money of the People of *England*; and therefore cannot be given away by such Persons as represent the People of *England* only.[2]

It is no Objection, that all the People of *England* are not represented themselves; because it is well known, that they were once represented to a Man; but some of the poorer Counties petitioned the King (in the Infancy of Parliaments) that they might be excused from sending up Representatives to appear for them in the *Great Council* of the *Nation,* as they could not afford to pay their Expences and they were excused accordingly.

Thus stands the Case of *America*, whom Administration are labouring to bring under the absolute Yoke of their corrupt Parliamentary Majority: Unless they can compass this, they know that neither *America*, nor *Great Britain* (whom they keep like an Apple in their Jaw, as *Hamlet* says, first mouthed to be last swallowed)[3] can be effectually enslaved. Unless *America* can be massacred, and her refractory Numbers reduced,

2. The best starting point for the question of representation and colonial American rights is Jack P. Greene, *Peripheries and Center* (Athens, GA.: University of Georgia Press, 1986); but see also John Phillip Reid's magnum opus, *Constitutional History of the American Revolution,* 4 vols. (Madison, Wisc.: University of Wisconsin Press, 1986–1993); and the one-volume abridgement published in 1995 under the same title by the same press.

3. "Take you me for a sponge, my Lord?" Rosencrantz asks Hamlet. Duped by Claudius, he and Guildenstern are warned by a disgusted Hamlet that they are unwittingly headed for doom—though he, because they choose to do Claudius's bidding, will be the one to seal it. From *Hamlet*, Act IV, Scene 2.

by Sword and Famine, within a Possibility of Controul, She will set a terrible Example of SPIRIT to her MOTHER COUNTRY, for whom a Net is likewise already spread. Till America is totally subdued, the Liberties of *Great Britain*, cannot be finally extinguished. The Aim of the present despotic Administration, and their servile MAJORITY, is plain: They wish to bring *America* not only under the Yoke of our Legislature, but of their standing Army, with which they will keep them under Foot for ever, should they conquer now. Should they fail in this Diabolical design; *America* rising from her Ruins, will erect an Empire of her own; an Asylum for the distressed Subjects of her MOTHER COUNTRY; who, as they seem at present careless about the RIGHTS, will at last retain the Name of ENGLISHMEN. But should our Parricides succeed, and *America* be once subdued, the whole *British Empire* will in due Time be Slaves.—Then will the Patriotic Scheme of our present Virtuous Administration be compleat; their Friendship to their KING, their Affection for their COUNTRY; the vain Confidence of the one, the well grounded distrust of the other, will appear. The secret Machinations of the Cabinet, the superior Wisdom of the *Great Council of the Nation*, will be disclosed, to the eternal Shame and Infamy of those, who must neither presume to call themselves *Britons* nor Men, if they long continue thus tamely to PETITION when they ought to ACT. Then shall We all deserve the Ridicule of the Sarcastic *Mansfield*, and be, in very deed, a tame Herd of Animals, among whom the worst of all Distempers (Slavery) may be said to rage; whilst we dare not avail ourselves either of our HOOFS, or HORNS.

C A S C A.

N.B. The Authors of the CRISIS acknowledge with gratitude, the various Favours received from their able, judicious, and sensible, Correspondent CASCA, which will be carefully attended to.

☞   The Authors of the CRISIS present their respectful Compliments to CATO, and return him Thanks for his Spirited Address to the KING, which shall be made the Subject of our next Number; the Authors fear no TYRANT, nor the Instruments of TYRANY, and they will always pay particular attention to the future Correspondence of CATO, who breaths the Godlike Sentiments of FREEDOM. They embrace this Opportunity of contradicting a most Infamous Report, no less INDUSTRIOUSLY than FALSELY Propagated by the Emissaries of the present infernal Administration. "*That the* CRISIS *was set on Foot, and is countenanced by the Ministry as a Pretence for laying a Restraint on the Press.*" The Authors beg Leave to declare in the most solemn Manner, before God and Man, that such Assertions have not the least Foundation in Truth, and that they are circulated by a Tribe of PENSIONED RAS-CALS, who are employed to write down Truth, and establish Falshood, only with a View to DECEIVE and MISLEAD the People, and to draw their Attention from the true Channel of FAITHFUL Information, and from that DESTRUCTION with which they are now threatened. The CRISIS was set on Foot with a Design to support and defend the CON-STITUTIONAL RIGHTS and PRIVILEGES of *England* and *America*, which the Authors hold equally dear with their LIVES. It was set on Foot at a Time when the LIBERTY of the PRESS was nearly destroyed, or rendered useless, by Ministerial Prosecutions; a *Scotch* CHIEF JUS-TICE, and the Dastardly Souls of narrow-minded Printers, who were afraid to give a TYRANT his true Appellation. The Authors are deter-mined to Write like ENGLISHMEN unawed by FEAR, or Prosecution, to SPEAK bold Truths, such Truths as some would fear to THINK. Freedom of Speech and Writing is one of the FIRST, and most Glorious PRIVILEGES of a FREE People; this the Authors Claim as a RIGHT, and this they are firmly Resolved to use and Defend; for to this Privilege we may again stand indebted, for another REVOLUTION.

Printed and published for the Authors, by T. W. *Shaw,* in Fleet-Street, opposite Anderton's Coffee House, where Letters to the Publisher will be thankfully received.

THE

CRISIS

NUMBER XXVII   To be continued Weekly

SATURDAY, JULY 22, 1775   [Price Two-pence Half-penny.

To the K I N G.

Each *British* Ghost by *Thee* depriv'd of Breath,
Now hovers round, and calls *Thee* to thy *Death*.

Pope's Homer.[1]

REFORM thy Conduct, Monarch, or attend,
The Doom denounc'd, by Virtu's constant Friend,
Heav'ns awful God, his Mandate 'tis I bear,
And call on GEORGE's callous Soul to hear.

Reform thy Conduct, or expect that Heav'n,
By whom thy delegated Pow'r is giv'n,

---

1. With the authors of *The Crisis* having substituted "British" for "Grecian," so Achilles taunts Hector in their duel to the death outside the walls of Troy. Achilles, assisted by Athena, prevails, as Hector, abandoned by Zeus, meets the fate brought on by his own hubris—as would Achilles not long after. Alexander Pope, *The Iliad of Homer*, 5 vols. (London: J. Whiston, et al., 1771), 5:77 (Book 22, lines 346–47).

Will rouse in Wrath; and hurl *thee* from the Throne,
Unworthy Prince, whom Britons blush to own.

See Civil Rage torment the bleeding Land,
Rais'd and supported by a Monarch's Hand;
Permit me Prince, t'unfold the dreadful Scene,
And Actions that disgrace the Name of Men,
See British Legions reeking from the Sword.
Of worthless Britons, and their misled Lord,
The orphan'd Son, the helpless Mother see,
Plung'd in the depths of awful Misery;
Youth and hoary Age lie whelt'ring on the Plains,
And Desolation and Destruction reigns:
Such Scenes as these must sure your Soul appall,
Thou art th' Occasion, *thou* the Cause of all;
Whate'er thy cursed Minions can design,
Thou giv'st Assent, and the *whole Guilt is THINE*;
See Britain wasted by her Father's Sword,
And France and ev'ry foreign Aid implor'd;
Suppose they shou'd be conqur'd, what remains,
What can be had from CAPTIVES and from CHAINS;
What large Revenues can your Coffers Boast,
From ruin'd CITIES, and a wasted Coast,
From Nations slaughter'd, and from Seas of Blood,
What Gain to make the *MIGHTY MISCHIEF GOOD.*

Remember Prince, on what precerious ties,
The uncertain Safety of a TYRANT lies;
What poor Defence will Guards, and Armies yield,
When long insulted Subjects take the Field;
What Safety then can Parasites bestow,
Or how elude the long deserved Blow;
When Justice rises and demands the BLOOD
Of haughty TYRANTS, and their fawning Crowd;
Ah, blush, deluded Prince, with conscious Shame,
That GEORGE should merit that detested Name.

Search British Annals, and let them declare,
Those Truths too harsh to wound the Royal Ear;
See brave *Fitzwalter* lead the Barons on,
And force the unwilling Deed from Coward (1) JOHN;
With Iron Sway the blustring Dastard rules,
The constant Dupe of swarming Knaves and Fools.
(2)"The weakest Athiest Wretch all Heav'n defies,
Who shrinks and shudders when the Thunder flies."
So shrunk the TYRANT, when *Fitzwalter* led,
His warlike Cohorts on to *Runny* (3) *Mead*
Then Ancient *Windsor*'s lofty Tow'rs beheld,
The blazing Standards waving o'er the Field,
The shining Jav'lins glittering from afar,
The moony shields and all the pomp of war;
Sheath'd in bright Steel then Britains *SAVIOURS* stood,
Undaunted, firm, and resolutely good;
Forth in the midst the frowning *TYRANT* came,
And viewed with FEAR and RAGE each Godlike Name;
The Coward shrunk at Britains brave array,

(1) The despicable Character of this Monarch will sufficiently appear, if we consider the mean and extraordinary Oath he took before all the People, kneel-down upon his Knees, and putting his Hands between those of the Legate.

"I, JOHN, by the Grace of God, King of England, and Lord of Ireland, in Order to expiate my Sins, from my own free will, and the Advice of my Barrons, give to the Church of Rome, to Pope Innocent, and his Successors, the Kingdom of England, and all other Prerogatives of my Crown; I will hereafter hold them as the Pope's Vassal. I will be faithful to God, to the Church of Rome, and to the Pope my Master, and his Successors legitimately Elected, I Promise to him a Tribute of a Thousand Marks yearly, to wit, 700 for the Kingdom of England and 300 for Ireland.

(2) Two Lines from Pope's Homer's Illiad Book 20.

(3) Runny Mead, a Field between Stains and Windsor, when King John signed Magna Charta, the grand Basis of English Liberty.

And MAGNA CHARTA (1) crown'd the glorious Day,

Search further yet how Edward's (2) Minions fell,
That galling Truth, to BUTE and MANSFIELD tell.
May every Curse, vindictive Heaven can pour,
Descend on them, in one destructive Shower,
Perish their Names, O! let the *TRAITORS* Bleed;
Justice demands, the Realm approves the Deed.

Proceed and be by faithful Hist'ry taught,
How *Essex* labour'd, and great *Cromwell* fought;
When haughty CHARLES disgrac'd the British Throne
And trod our Freedom and Religion down.

That dreadful CRISIS big with loud alarms,
Call'd every Briton to assert in ARMS
The dear bought Rights, the violated Cause,
Of their dear Country and its SACRED LAWS;
They came obedient to the glorious call.
One generous Spirit animated all:
Such generous Souls may Brittain yet afford.
And own again a CROMWELL's *Saving Sword*;
An *Hampden* (3) yet, *an Essex* (4) yet may rise,

(1) This Charter gave the Barons, a definitive Judgment upon whatever they thought proper to represent as a Grievance; they were to prefer their Complaints to the King, and he was in Forty Days to give them Satisfaction, or they were legally impowered to Command it, by every Method the Circumstances of Time or Place could suggest.

(2) These were Gaveston and the Two Spencers, Gaveston's Pride, (says an impartial Author) his being a foreigner, his Insolence, soon raised a Strong Party against him. An Army was formed to oppose his Administration (a Noble Precedent) he was taken and beheaded, without even the Formality of a Trial. Quere is not the conduct of the present King Obstinate and Irresolute as John's and that of his abandoned Ministry Effeminate, Debauched and Wicked, as Gavestons. This Truth let Sandwich, Denbigh, Dartmouth, North declare.

(3) John Hampden a private Man of Courage, and Integrity, who stood forth as a Champion for the People, and refused to pay a Tax not authorised by Parliament (the

And *TYRANTS* yet may fall as Sacrifice.
Illustrious Shades the faithful Muse shall Crown,
Your glorious Names, with Honour and Renown,
Long as this World with all its Splendor stands,
Stupendous Frame, rais'd by Immortal Hands,
Long as the Annals of Eternal Fame,
Record each Hero's and each Patriot's Name,
Long as a Briton lives t' assert the Cause,
Of Heaven, of Freedom, and the British Laws;
So long shall *Cromwell*'s, *Hampden*'s, Name remain
And Times erasing Vengeance prove in vain.

Inspire your Children, O ye Patriot Band,
To rush on Death, and save a sinking Land;
You who could haughty Tyranny repell,
Protect the Cause, in which you nobly fell,
That glorious Cause, which Heaven eternal owns,
And fires to Vengeance your too tardy Sons:
They rise at length, t' assert the Freedom given;
T' assert the Cause of Liberty and Heaven;
Tremble thou *TYRANT* at the awful Day,
When injur'd Britons give their Vengeance way;
Tremble ye Minions who your Prince misled,
Uncommon Wrath remains for you to dread,
The Traytors who your Sovereign's Heart have steel'd,
And cur'st him with a Soul that cannot yield,

---

famous Ship Money Tax) the Sum at which he was rated, amounted but to Twenty Shillings, yet he refused to contribute even this, and brought his Cause before the Court of Exchequer. Never was a greater Cause argued in any Court before. The Judges were by this Sentence to determine, whether the Nation, and their Posterity, were to be Subjects to Arbitrary Power, or to enjoy Freedom. The Judges determined in Favour of Servitude, and Hampden was Cast. Hist. of Eng. in Letters. Letter 40.

(4) The Earl of Essex Chief Commander of the Parliamentry Forces against the King, an honest Man, (says an Noble Author of the English History in series of Letters) who fought from Principle only.

Eternal Vengeance must your Crimes pursue,
Justice demands you, as the Public due.
Unfeeling Man, if e'er thy Soul can know,
Steel'd as it is, the touch of Human Woe;
If generous Pity can a thought impart,
To shake the horrid Purpose of your Heart,
If Pity harbours in that Iron Breast,
Call back your CUTTHROATS, give your People rest;
Withdraw your Fleets, send no more Armies o'er,
But bid the Martial Thunders cease to roar,
Do this, and Britain may again forgive,
Again consent to let a TYRANT live.

But dare not triffle with a Moment given,
Presumptous Prince, nor sport with awful Heaven,
Think not that Britons passive will remain,
Hug the vile Yoke, and Smile upon the Chain;
They have not learnt the Faith which Cowards own,
(1) "Th' enormous Faith of many made for one,"
Far nobler precepts Fire the British Breast,
Then yielding FREEDOM for INGLORIOUS REST;
Far nobler ends their Free-Born Spirits own,
Then basely crouching to a TYRANTS Throne;
Such base Concessions stain'd not BRITAINS FAME,
When (2) *Charle's*, DEATH IMMORTALIS'D their Name;
Or Guilty *James* (3) his injur'd Subjects fled,
Lay hid in France and trembled for his Head;
Remember this, O Monarch, nor presume;
On tir'd out Faith and Lenity to come.

(1) See Pope's Essay on Man, Epistle.

(2) This, says the great Milton, was the most glorious Deed ever done in this or any other Nation under Heaven, whereby an odious and obnoxius Tyrant was made a Public Sacrifice to the injured Justice of his Country.

(3) James the Second who meanly abdicated his Crown, and fled to France, on the approach of our great Deliverer the Prince of Orange.

The Sword is drawn and hellish Discord roars,
Let loose by MANSFIELD on *North Am'rick's*, Shores;
The trait'rous Thane t' enslave a Nation joins,
And blust'ring North avows their cur'st designs;
(1) *George* too consents and Signs the horrid Deed,
By which unnumber'd INNOCENTS must BLEED.
With tenfold Rage, inspire, O Muse, the Strain,
To Paint the Horrors of this Guilty Reign;
Young ALLEN dies in his paternal Field,
And murder'd Laws, audacious Murderers shield,
The Sovereign too t' enlarge the mighty Guilt,
Thanks his dear Scotsmen for the Blood they've spilt,
Petitions spurn'd at, with a sulky Frown,
The Monarch drives his Subjects from the Throne,
(2) *Astonish'd* that those Subjects dare to sue,
For Fellow Subjects, Rebels in his view,
Tells them his firm, his steady Soul retains
Its iron Purpose, and his Heart remains
Inflexible, determin'd to enslave,
And Murder Thousands he had Sworn to save.
Remember Prince the Throne to GEORGE was given,
T' Assert the Cause of LIBERTY and HEAVEN,
But when he ceases FREEDOM to maintain,
And dares attempt, unaw'd by LAWS to Reign,
When Heavens great Cause is spurn'd at and forgot,
And horrid Popish Superstition taught, (3)

(1) Alluding to the several oppressive and unconstitutional Acts lately past, to the Disgrace of a British Parliament, against the injur'd Inhabitants of North America, but particularly that called the New England Fishery Bill, which occasioned the spirited Remonstrance of the uncorrupted Livery of London, with their noble Chief Magistrate. April the 10th 1775.

(2) See the last Royal Answer to the City Petition.

(3) As they evidently are in Canada, commonly called the Quebec Bill, passed in 1774, against which the unshaken Livery of London, also Remonstrate, under the Conduct of their late worthy Mayor, Mr. Bull.

The Cause that gave the Scepter them demands,
The same again from his unworthy Hands.
Resign, Proud Man, with Shame resign the Throne,
And let Contrition for your Faults attone,
Or once again the call of Heaven attend,
And be your Peoples, not your Minions Friend,
Do this and Britain may again forgive,
And let a Tyrant thus repenting Live.
Your hopes of Conquest on *North Am'ricks* Coast,
Are blasted, and your Expectations lost,
Your Armys routed, and your Generals driven
Back to their Fleets, the Sport of angry Heaven;
(1) When they embark'd, what storm's convuls'd the Pole,
What Light'nings flash'd, what awful Thunders roll;
'Tis GOD against you in his Wrath declares,
Their are his Omens, and his Thunder theirs,
Say can your Madness stand the dire Alarms,
Say can you meet *OMNIPOTENCE* in Arms.

But hark they call you from the Realms of dead,
The dauntless Souls that for their Country BLED,
At *Concord* (2) SLAUGHTER'D, lay the glorious Train,
That met the British TYRANT with disdain,
The call for Vengeance from the Shades below,
And Point at you the Author of their Woe.

My Soul's on fire, distinctions are forgot,
I'll speak to Tyrants, as a Briton ought;
By THEE our plains lie steep'd in HUMAN BLOOD,
By THEE our rivers pour a PURPLE flood
By THEE the British glories are no more,

(1) On the Night the three Generals Burgoyne, Clinton, and *How*, embarked for America, one of the most dreadful Storms of Tunder and Lightning, took place, that has shaken the *British Channel* in the Memory of Man.

(2) See the dreadful Engagement at that Place, on the 19th of April.

And vast destruction whelms th' *Atlantic* shore;
By THEE our cities dread the dire alarms,
And horrid slaughters of fraternal arms;
Thy trait'rous ministers the deed design,
THOU giv'st assent, and the whole GUILT is THINE:
Wave after wave, the mighty mischiefs flow,
Thick and more thick, the threat'ning dangers grow;
Impartial ages yet to come will read,
With secret horror each *infernal* deed;
Rend THEE, like *Stuart*, from the rolls of fame,
And unborn millions curse a G——'s name.

C A T O[2].

Printed and published for the Authors, by T. W. *Shaw*, in Fleet-Street, opposite Anderton's Coffee House, where Letters to the Publisher, will be thankfully received.

2. "Cato" is the pen name used here and in issue no. XXIX infra. Marcus Cato preferred suicide to accepting Julius Caesar's subversion of the republic. A dutiful veteran of the legions before he rose to the Senate, he was revered in the eighteenth-century Anglo-American world as a martyred defender of Rome, in part because of his depiction in Plutarch's *Lives*, but more especially because of Joseph Addison's 1713 play *Cato*, a recurring presence on the London stage and even a favorite of George Washington. See Christine Dunn Henderson and Mark E. Yellin, eds., *Cato: A Tragedy and Selected Essays* (Indianapolis: Liberty Fund, 2004).

T H E

C R I S I S

NUMBER XXVIII   To be continued Weekly

SATURDAY, JULY 29, 1775   [Price Two-pence Half-penny.

By his Excellency THOMAS SHAW, PROTECTOR and
DEFENDER of MAGNA CHARTA,
and the BILL of RIGHTS.

A P R O C L A M A T I O N.

WHEREAS the infatuated Multitudes, of Royal Neronian Dependants, Catamites, Pimps, and Parasites, too many to be enumerated; have long conducted themselves as PARRICIDES and TRAITORS in a fatal Progression of Crimes, against the Constitutional Liberties of the British Empire, and have at length proceeded to avowed and open Rebellion against the Laws of the Land, and the LIVES of Englishmen in *England* and *America,* and the good Effects which were expected to arise from the PATIENCE and LENITY of the People, have been often frustrated, and Remonstrance proved ineffecttual and now rendered hopeless, from the Obstinacy and Cruelty of the SOVEREIGN, by the Influence of their infernal Counsels, and Confederacy, it only remains for the PEOPLE, who have the SUPREME POWER, as well for the Punishment of those guilty Parricides, as for the Protection of the Innocent, to prove they do not bear the SWORD in VAIN.

The Infringements which have been committed upon the sacred Rights of MAGNA CHARTA and the People of *Great Britain* and *America*, are too many to enumerate on one Side, and all too atrocious, too infamous, and too diabolical to be palliated on the other. All un-prejudiced, un-pensioned, and un-placed Englishmen, who have been Witness, (or even heard) of the late Transactions, in this *Kingdom* and *America*, will find, upon a transient Review, Marks of Premeditation and Conspiracy to destroy the CONSTITUTION of the *British Empire*, that would Justify the fullness of CHASTISEMENT; and even those who are least acquainted with Facts, cannot fail to receive a Just Impression of the Enormity, in proportion as they discover the Arts and Assiduity, by which their Bloody Designs have been falsified and concealed. Those Parricides, the Authors of the present BLOODY Measures and un-natural Revolt from the Laws, never daring to trust their CAUSE, or their ACTIONS, to the Judgment of an impartial Public, or even to the dispassionate Reflection of their Followers and Adherents, have uniformly placed their chief Confidence in the Suppression of TRUTH; and while indefatigable and shameless Pains have been taken to DESTROY the real Interest of the People of *England* and *America*, the grossest Forgeries, Calumnies, and Absurdities, that ever insulted Human Understanding, have been imposed upon their Credulity, by the KING, and those Miscreants. The Press, that distinguished Appendage of Public Liberty, and when fairly and impartially employed, its best Support, has been invariably Prostituted by those Pensioned Rascals, *Hume, Johnson, Kelly, Shebbeare*, and other Ministerial Hirelings, to the most contrary Purposes.[1] The animated Language of Ancient and Virtuous Times, calculated to vindicate and promote the just Rights and Interests of Mankind, have been ap-

---

1. David Hume and Samuel Johnson were of course not simply "ministerial hacks;" nor, for that matter, were Hugh Kelly and John Shebbeare, with Kelly enjoying a fair amount of success as a playwright. Of the four, only Shebbeare truly struggled to earn a living and his seeking a government pension caused critics to dismiss him as a pen for hire. See XLII.2 and LXVII.2 infra.

plied by the KING'S MINIONS, to countenance the most abandoned Violations of those sacred Blessings, and not only from the flagitious Ministerial Prints, but from the slavish Harangues of prostituted Peers, and venal Senators, Men have been taught to depend upon Activity in SHEDDING of BLOOD, for the Security of their PLACES, PENSIONS, and PERSONS, till to complete the horrid Profanation of Terms and of Ideas, the Name of GOD, has been introduced in ADDRESSES and in the Pulpit, by a Groupe of rotten Popish Bishops, to excite Devastation and Massacre.

The Minds of Men, such as *Gage, Percy, Burgoyne, Clinton* and *Howe*, and the KING's Mercenary Soldiers,[2] having been thus gradually prepared for MURDER, a Number of armed Troops to the Amount of *Eighteen Hundred*, and upwards, on the 19*th* of *April* last, at CONCORD, cowardly attacked about SIXTY peaceable Americans, who not expecting so consumate an Act of Savage Barbarity, unprepared for vengeance, and willing to decline it, made use of their Arms only in their own DEFENCE.[3]- Since that Period, the MERCENARIES, deriving Confidence from Impunity, have added Insult to Outrage; have repeatedly fired upon, and barbarously killed many of their Fellow Subjects, with Cannon and small Arms; and with a preposterous Parade of Military Arrangement, they try to frighten, and mean if possible to enslave *America*, while Part of their Body make daily and indiscriminate Invasions upon Private Property, and with a Wantonness of Cruelty, peculiar in this REIGN, and ever incident to LAWLESS POWER, carry Depredation and

2. To dismiss Major Generals Thomas Gage, John Burgoyne and William Howe, along with Brigadier General Hugh Percy, as "Mercenary soldiers" might hardly seem fair, but the men behind *The Crisis* had in mind as their standard the Earl of Effingham, who would resign his commission before leading troops into battle against American colonists—to him, they were fellow Britons (see n. XXI.6 supra). Of the four, only Gage, a true career soldier, played no role in making public policy. Burgoyne and Howe had borough seats in the Commons; Percy, who sat for Westminster in the Commons, always had doubts about using force against dissident colonists. He eventually succeeded his father as Duke of Northumberland.

3. For the fighting in the Massachusetts countryside on 19 April 1775, see n. XXI.1 supra.

Distress where ever they turn their Steps. The Action of the 19th of *April*, and the Cruel, Bloody, and Inhuman Circumstances attending that Day's CARNAGE, are of such Notoriety, as must baffle all Attempts to contradict them; and the Flames of Buildings, the Cries of helpless infirm Old Men, Women, and Children, wantonly slaughtered in COOL BLOOD, spread, and will for ever stand a Melancholy Confirmation of the subsequent Assertions.

In this exigency of *Neronian Cruelty* and complicated Calamities I avail myself of the last Efforts, within the Bounds of my Duty, as a peaceable Subject, to spare the Effusion of Blood; to Offer, and I do hereby, in the Name of the WHOLE PEOPLE of *England* and *America*, Offer and Promise a most gracious PARDON, to all the Mercenaries who shall forthwith lay down their Arms, and return to the Duties of Peaceable Subjects and Faithful Englishmen, loyal to the Laws and the Constitution, excepting only from such Pardon, *John Stuart*, *Earl of Bute*, and *William*, *Lord Mansfield*, the Authors and Promoters of Bloodshed and Cruelty, whose Crimes are of too Flagitious a Nature to admit of any other Consideration than that of Condign Punishment.

And to the End that no person within the Limits of this proffered Mercy may plead ignorance of the Consequences of refusing it, I by these presents proclaim not only the Persons above named and expected, but also their Adherents, Associates, and abettors, meaning to comprehend in those Terms, all and every Person and Persons, of what Class, Denomination, or Description soever, who have appeared in arms against the SACRED LAWS and CONSTITUTION of the British Empire, and shall not lay down the same as aforesaid; and likewise all such as shall so take Arms after the Date hereof, or who shall in any wise protect or conceal such Offenders, or assist them with Money, Provisions, Cattle, Arms, Ammunition, Carriages, or any other Necessary for Subsistence or Defence, or shall hold secret Correspondence with the MERCENARY MURDERERS, by Letter Message, Signal or otherwise, to be Rebels and Traitors to the British Constitution, and as such to be treated.

And whereas during the continuance of the present BLOODY and UN-NATURAL CIVIL WAR in America, Justice cannot be obtained by the common Law of the Land, the Course whereof has for a long time past been violently impeded, and wholly interrupted by the King and his Paracidial Minions and Military Cut-throats, from whence results a necessity, in Order to preserve the dear bought Rights of Englishmen and hallowed Constitution of the Empire, for using and exercising the *Lex Talionis*, or Law of Retaliation;[4] I have therefore thought fit by the Authority invested in me by MAGNA CHARTA as a FREEMAN, to Publish, and I do hereby Publish, Proclaim, and order the use and exercise of the *Lax Talionis*, or Blood for Blood, within and throughout Great Britain and America, so long as the present unhappy occasion shall necessarily require, till the Sons of Freedom shall gain a decisive victory over TYRANNY and LAWLESS POWER, till each Parricide and Traitor shall be brought to the BLOCK or the GALLOWS, or otherwise fall a sacrifice by the Hands of a much injured and enraged People, and till the Liberties of England and America are settled upon a sure and lasting Foundation, not to be again shaken by any Tyrant of the House of *Brunswick*; whereof all true Englishmen are hereby required to take Notice, and ARM themselves—with a Resolution as well to maintain their Rights, as to resist encounter, and subdue the Merconaries and Traitors above described.

To these inevitable, but I trust Salutary measures, it is of a far more pleasing part of my duty to add the assurances of protection and Support to all who in so trying a Crisis shall manifest no allegiance to Tyrants, but an Affection for the sacred constitution of their Country;—So that such Persons as may have been induced to join in the present Royal and Ministerial Measures for destroying the Laws, Liberties, and LIVES of their fellow Subjects in America, may return to their respective callings and professions, be no longer the Instruments of MURDER and PUBLIC RUIN, but stand distinct and separate from the Parricides of the Constitution, till God in his mercy shall turn the Hearts of Tyrants, and restore Peace to this distracted Land, now polluted with INNOCENT BLOOD.

4. Under law, the right of retaliation, commensurate with the offense committed, a perpetuation of the Old Testament (Exodus 21:24) notion of an eye-for-an-eye.

Given at London, the 28th Day. of July, in the 15th Year of the Tyrannical Reign of his Merciful M——— G——— the T——— Defender of the Romish Faith, Traitors, and Murderers, &c. Anno Domini, 1775.

T H O M A S   S H A W.[5]

By his Excellency's Command,

Thomas Bradshaw, Secretary.

God Save AMERICA.

Notwithstanding the Royal lying Gazette has given us an Account, signed by that BLOODY Monster in Human Shape, *General Gage*, of another Massacre in *America*, on the 17th of June last, wherein this modern *Kirk* extols his Officers and Mercanary Soldiers, stimulated by Liquor, and Promises of Plunder, to slaughter their Fellow Subjects, for their Valour and Bravery, and boasts his having gained something like a Victory, over the brave and virtuous *Americans,* fighting for LIBERTY, whom that Wretch calls *REBELS*; yet the public may depend this *pretended* Superiority of his Troops, Conduct of his Officers, and Mighty Victory is a LYE; and it will soon be proved, from unquestionable Authority, that he has lost some Hundreds of his men, more than is mentioned in the *Gazette* of *Tuesday* last, which contains the most notorious Falshoods, and infamous Impositions on the Public, calculated to deceive the People here, and to *Spirit* up the few remaining Troops we have in England, to embark with the greater Readiness to the field of *Slaughter* in *America,* there to fall a just Sacrifice to the injured Laws, and glorious Liberties of the *British Empire*: it will likewise appear that General Gage's Army, with all the Advantage of Artillery, and the Assistance of several Ships of War, and armed Vessels. was obliged to retreat to their Barracks and sneaking Holes in Boston, under Protection of the *Men* of War.

5. T. W. Shaw appeared as the printer of every issue of *The Crisis*, from beginning to end. This is the first instance where Shaw is author as well as publisher; the second is in issue no. XXXV infra, 16 September 1775 (see pp. 319–325 infra), where as Thomas William Shaw he writes an impassioned defense of freedom of the press.

If it was ever necessary to rouse the sleeping Genius of England, to excite a generous Emulation of our warlike Forefathers, and to animate every Briton, by their Example, to fight valiantly, to conquer nobly, or perish gloriously in Defence of his Country—This is certainly the Time.

If it was ever necessary for the People of England to rise altogether as one man, and fall like a torrent on the Bloody Tyrannical invaders of their Lives and Liberties, and overwhelm them in the midst of their fancied insolent security—it is surely at this time.

If it was ever necessary for the People to enter into an association, to express and fully explain in a MANIFESTO the causes of their discontent; and to declare they take up Arms to put a stop to the encroachments of those who Govern in the King's name; to bring to condign Punishment the betrayers of their Country; to preserve their Rights and Liberties from farther violations; to restore the Laws and the Constitution now tottering to its base, to their pristine rigour; to prevent the inhuman Slaughter of their fellow Subjects in America by the Hand of Lawless power; to enforce a due obedience to MAGNA CHARTA from the King and his Ministers; to oblige his Majesty to dismiss those Parricides and Traitors who surround his Throne, and to restore the Ancient independence and freedom of Parliaments: If such a measure was ever necessary to preserve the People and Kingdom from Slavery and Ruin—it is NOW. But alas! It is (I fear) in vain to appeal to the reason or to the passions of Englishmen, they seem to have lost their very nature and Genius they seem to have forgot the arts of War, and the blessings of Freedom; they have fatally degenerated into Luxury and Vice, and at last become insensible to every generous Sentiment of Public Liberty; they have lost the Virtue, the courage, and Bravery of their glorious Ancestors; and are now looked upon by surrounding Nations, as a Herd of pusillanimous Drones, devoted to slavery, or doomed to Destruction.

N. B. The Authors of the CRISIS are anxious for the Welfare of their much-admired and spirited correspondent CASCA, and hope to remove their Fears of his indisposition, to hear from him soon.

Junius's Address to the King has been fetched from the Place he directed.—The Apprehension *Junius* mentions in his private Letter to *T. W.*

Shaw is groundless.—The Authors of the CRISIS are but too sensible, of the many shameful Blunders, and gross Mistakes, that have appeared in several Numbers of their Paper, entirely owing to the Carelessness and inattention of the PRINTER.

Printed and published for the Authors, by T. W. *Shaw*, in Fleet-Street, opposite Anderton's Coffee House; where Letters to the Publisher, will be thankfully received.

THE

CRISIS

NUMBER XXIX   *To be continued Weekly.*

SATURDAY, *August* 5, 1775   [Price Two Pence Half-penny.

To the K I N G.

Grasp not at Sceptres, which may turn to Rods,

To Day is your's, To-morrow is the God's.

Lee's *Sophonisba*, Act V. Scene I.[1]

S I R,

ONCE more to stay the Fury of the Sword,
Cato addresses Britain's misled Lord;
Grasp not at Sceptres, by a Tyrant's Rules,
A servile Empire is the Curse of Fools;
Freedom to Man did Heaven's great God ordain,
Shall Man presume that Freedom to restrain;
Vain Mortal, can'st thou bid thy Light'nings fly,
Or hurl like him, thy Thunders thro' the Sky;

---

1. Nathaniel Lee's *Sophonisba: Or, Hannibal's Overthrow. A Tragedy* was first performed in London in 1675, and enjoyed periodic revivals through the next century. The play's

And dar'st thou then annul the Gift of Heaven,
And strive t'abridge the Freedom God has giv'n:
Cease, cease, presumptuous Prince; nor longer dare
'Gainst God and Man to Wage unequal War;
'Tis Heaven asserts each individuals Right,
Oppressing them, 'gainst Heaven itself you fight.
Think not 'tis Malice that incites the Pen
Of Cato, thus t'address the first of Men;
Heav'n knows my Heart, and knows it is sincere,
And Heaven is Witness while I solemn swear;
Thou hast not on the glorious British Shore
A single Subject that reveres thee more;
I love the Name of George, I love my King,
But hate the Traitors, whence these Evils spring;
Call'd forth in Arms t'assert my Country's Cause,
I'd dye with Joy for Brunswick and the Laws;
Those Laws for which your Family has fought,
And Principles your God-like Grandsire taught;
Tenets avow'd by him, from whence you came,
(What Glories wait on his all-honour'd name)
Illustrious Frederick, how each Briton glows,
To see his Prince a Minister oppose;
Walpole shrunk back, when foremost Frederick came,[2]

---

text was often reprinted as an individual title and had been included in *The Dramatic Works of Mr. Nathaniel Lee*, 3 vols. (London: W. Feales, 1735); 3:61, for the passage quoted as an epigraph. The two lines above came from a meeting that legend said took place between Hannibal and Scipio before the Battle of Zama outside Carthage in 202 BCE. Hannibal offers to live in peace, with the Carthaginians pulling out of Spain, Sicily, Sardinia, and Italy, leaving all to Rome in exchange for peace. Sophonisba was a Carthaginian noblewoman who poisoned herself rather than suffer the humiliation of being taken back to Rome as part of the victorious Scipio's triumph. The ever-popular Plutarch did not feature her tale, but it was mentioned by both Livy and Polybius. See the *Oxford DNB*, 33:93–95 for the essay on Lee by J. M. Armistead.

2. Robert Walpole was a lightning rod for controversy during his years heading ministries under both George I and George II, and ever after as a symbol of a "stock jobber" in office—someone who played the game of public politics to further his private

And glorious Pitt supported every claim;
When (*)Pultney rose to t'assert the injur'd Laws,
And Wyndham Argued in his Country's Cause;
On Frederick's Heir impatient Britons wait,
And hail great Great George, the Savior of the State:
Your glorious Grandsires Conduct Prince review,
And be the Father of your People too;
But are you so, can God-like Truth declare,
"You are not (answers the dire Pow'r of War)
My Reign extends along the frighted Shore,

(*) Pultney, Earl of Bath. And we can still I hope, boast some honest Names whom no Tyrant can drive from their Country's glorious Cause, among the Foremost, may we not rank *Rockingham, Shelburn, Camden, Effingbam, Torrington, Asaph, Abergavenny, Manchester, Portland, Richmond, Devonshire, Leinster, Abingdon, Archer, Berkeley, Cholmondeley, Fitzwilliam, Ponsonby, Stanhope, Tankerville, Temple,* Fred, *Exon. Spencer, Craven,* and *Wycombe.* These are thy Saviours, Britain, after failing to succeed in the Preservation of *American* Liberty, by the most forcible and constitutional Reasons, gave their silent Negative (their glorious Names only) as the last Proof of their own Virtue, as well as a contemptuous Record against their Opponents, for Want of Humanity and Love of their Country. Can Britons be so degenerate? Can they be so base as to desert a Cause wherein so many glorious Names are embarked? Forbid it every Idea of Honour! Forbid it every Idea of Shame! Let it unanimously concur in this Request to misled Majesty, "To dismiss, immediately, and for ever, from his Counsels, these Ministers and Advisers, as the first Step towards a full Redress of those Grievances which alarm and afflict your whole People." The noble, the unprejudiced Livery of London, generously did their Parts; and shall we, because a mean dastardly Common Council deserted the Standard of Freedom, shrink from the glorious Cause; and when the Trumpet sounds the Charge, ignominiously leave the Field.—No, let us, in the Language of Resolution and Fortitude, "Tell our Dictator this," That Britons will be FREE.

---

interests, incapable of distinguishing between his personal desires and the needs of the people. The best starting place for him is Stephen Taylor's long essay in the *Oxford DNB*, 57:67–90, which notes his place in the historiography as well as the history of his era. The men behind *The Crisis* joined many other critics of public policy who used the long-dead Walpole for their own presentistic purposes, as they did Caesar from Roman history and Cromwell from their own to stress an analogy. While gibes at Walpole may have resonated with readers in London, colonial Americans had no ax to grind against Walpole; under his second ministry came the so-called era of "salutary neglect."

Witness you Hills of Slain, you Seas of Gore;
The Plains of Lexington dire Prospect rise,
And call for Vengeance from the frowning Skies."
Let's try the Cause from whence these Evils spring,
And view the TYRANT and the PATRIOT King.

See the pale Wretch sit trembling on the Car,
Greatly unhappy 'midst his Crouds of War,
Hem'd in with Arms, beset with Swords and Spears,
His very State acknowledging his Fears;
Marching amidst a Thousand Guards he shows,
His secret Horror of a Thousand Foes,
'Midst all his Triumph, trembling at the Guilt,
And shrinking from the BLOOD his Hands have spilt,
The Cries of injured Innocence prevail,
And Justice sternly lifts her broken Scale,
Vengeance stands by and points th'eternal pow'r,
And stifled Conscience arms the dreadful Hour;
(*) Some Voice of God close whispering from within,
"Wretch., this is Villany, and this is Sin,")
Each rustling Wind the haughty Tyrant hears,
Fills him with conscious Dread and Causeless Fears;
Though Thousand Guards around his Chariot wait,
And Kings in Triumph led proclaim his State;
Though crouding Laurels wreath his conqu'ring Brow,
In every Face the Tyrant fears a Foe,
Greatly unhappy in his Breast he feels,
Torments surpassing Flames, and Racks and Wheels.

O how unlike him is the Patriot Name,
Fear march'd before where'er the Tyrant came;
Here LOVE alone prepares the Hero's Way,
And Joy and smiling Pleasure ever gay,

(*) Two Lines from Pope's Translation of Homer's Odyssey. Book 20.

Around his Triumph the glad nations wait,
And hail him home, the Father of the State;
Chearful, serene, the tranquil Monarch moves,
His People's LOVE a constant ARMY proves;
He needs not Guards, the Sword, or brandish'd Spear,
Nor all the Dreadful Habiliments of War;
A sacred Calmness lulls his conscious Breast,
With sweet Composure, and with heartfelt Rest,
Secure in Heaven bred Innocence he stands,
The Sire belov'd of the surrounding Bands,
The general Voice proclaims him o'er the Rest,
At once the first, the wisest, and the Best;
"From Conscious Virtue strong Assurance flows,
Whose CAUSE is RIGHT can brave a THOUSAND FOES,
Such conscious Virtue fires the Patriot Mind,
Devoid of Ill, to every Good inclin'd,
He Lives but for his Country's Good, his Care
Still points at that, his Soul is center'd there.

Say, which of these can Britain's Monarch claim,
Th' Tyrant's hated, or, th' Patriot's honour'd Name,
May Heaven, indulgent for our Errors past,
Forgive, and George again assume the Last.
See Heaven consents, AMERICANS still sue
To GEORGE, and once more beg their Peace from you;
Slight not their Overtures, offend not Heav'n,
Nor trifle with the precious Moment given,
United firm, in honourable Peace,
May every Woe, with Civil Discord cease;
Now is the Time, now is the important Hour,
And Peace is yet within a GEORGE'S Power;
To Day attend, attend your Peoples Pray'r,
Call back your Armies, and consent to spare;
To Day attend, the next may be too late,
To save a Nation from impending Fate.
To Day is yours, the gracious Call attend,

And bid AMERICA be BRITAIN'S Friend;
Peace with its Blessings, to these Realms restore,
And bid the Martial Thunders cease to roar,
Do this, and grateful Thousands shall revere,
The Name of GEORGE, and Love as well as Fear.

Remove, for ever, from the British Throne,
The Traitors who their Country have undone,
The titled Villains, whose protracted Fate,
Just Heaven delays, to make their Ruin great,
Let not imploring Millions sue in vain,
But hope from thee this Justice to obtain;
Rise, rise, vindictive and with dreadful Ire,
Bid the Black Traitors back to HELL retire,
Do this, and GEORGE'S ever honour'd Name,
The foremost Place 'mongst Britain's Chiefs shall claim.

This precious Moment, Heav'ns indulgent Pow'r
In Mercy gives, embrace the auspicious Hour,
Behold the Genius of *North Am'rick* stand,
The SWORD and OLIVE waving in her Hand,
Chuse WAR or PEACE, the great Decision lies,
On THEE, the World attends with anxious Eyes;
By YOU must Peace with all its Blessings reign,
or CIVIL RAGE embroil the British Plain;
Weigh well the Importance of this trying Hour,
And seize the Moments, yet within your Power;
Do this, or hear an injured Nation say,
VENGEANCE is theirs, and they will sure repay;
Can pension'd Rascals, who your Throne surround
Protect that Throne, when tott'ring to the Ground,
Can MANSFIELD when much injur'd Subjects rise,
Or BUTE, Protect you with fallacious Lies;

Can JENKINSON and RIGBY Realms engage,[3]
Or Wav'ring NORTH support a People's Rage;
Will bullying then, their Monarchs Cause sustain,
When gasping Britain bleeds at every Vein;
When her brave Sons those very Traitors bring,
Dragg'd from the Arms of their deluded KING,
To Public JUSTICE,—see the Villains come,
'Midst JOYFUL MILLIONS, trembling at their Doom.

Let Britons try this Justice to obtain,
Nor longer hear the Nation sue in vain.

Grasp not at Scepters, let not Lust of sway,
Perswade thee Prince, the Laws to disobey,
The LAWS I say, from whence our Monarchs SPRING,
The sacred Laws, Britannia's GREATER KING;
We owe no Faith to Brunswick's empty Name,
Nor any Monarch can obedience claim,
Who ceases sacred Freedom to maintain,
And dares attempt unaw'd by LAWS to reign,
Not any King can force us to OBEY,
Who dares from Britain's sacred Laws to stray.

Curst be the Man, whom Danger can perswade,
To sell his RIGHT, and dares a DESPOT Aid;
Curst be the Man, unworthy of the Light,
Who aids a Monarch, 'gainst his Countrys Right;

---

3. Charles Jenkinson sat in the Commons and eventually (long after the American crisis) became first Earl of Liverpool; Richard Rigby held a seat in the Commons as well and, like Jenkinson, was considered a solid ministry man, supporting North's hard-line policies against the colonists. At this moment in time Jenkinson was also a member of the privy council, vice treasurer, and reputedly had the King's ear; Rigby was serving as paymaster general. For Jenkinson see John Cannon's *Oxford DNB* entry (at 29:973–76); and, for Rigby, Roland Thorne's entry at 46:75–76. Also see Namier and Brooke, *House of Commons*, 2:674–78 and 3:355–60, resp.

Curst be the Man who draws or dares to draw,
His Trait'rous SWORD against the British LAW.
What Scenes of Woe, beyond the Atlantick lie,
By GEORGE the THIRD, whole Nations doom'd to die,
Can Heavens just God, his Vengeance long restrain,
Or let his aweful Thunder sleep in Vain;
When Crimes like these, with proud Defiance look,
And dare the Arm Almighty to the Stroke;
A Moment Prince, their Magnitude survey,
And blush to own them in the Face of Day;
Thy Subjects BLOOD by thy Direction SPILT,
In vain on GAGE's head transfer the Guilt;
The Deed was acted by the Sovereign's Hand,
The Sword was pointed by the King's Command;
THINE was the dire Design, 'twas *THINE* alone,
Years of Contrition must the crime attone;
Nor can your guilty Soul expect Relief,
But from a long Sincerity of Grief;
To Lust of Arbitrary sway inclin'd,
That cursed Poison, to a Prince's Mind,
In Paths of Error, daily dost thou rove,
And loose thy great Defence, thy Peoples Love;
Ill counsel'd, vanquish'd, fugitive, disgrac'd,
Thou hence shalt mourn the British Strength defac'd,
Perhaps the King diminish'd, and the Crown,
With lessen'd Rays, descending to thy Son;
Shalt see the Wreaths thy Grandsire knew to get,
By active Toil, and Military Sweat,
Pining, incline their sickly Leaves and shed
Their falling Honours from their giddy Head;
By Arms or Prayer, unable to asswage
Domestic Horror, and intestine Rage,
Shalt from the Victor, and the Vanquish'd fear,
From Britain's Arrow, and North Am'rick's Spear.

May gracious Heaven avert this Scene of Woe,
Nor thou, O! Prince, these various Evils know;
If yielding to an injur'd Nations Prayer,
You call your Cut-throats back, and bid them spare;
If wrong'd America can pity claim,
As you again assume a Fathers Name;
Your People's Love, your Remnant Life shall crown,
And be the firm Supporter of your Throne,
Dire slavery Clank no more her horrid Chain
But God-like Liberty smile o'er your Reign,
Wars hateful Fiend, besmeard with human BLOOD,
Start back, and cross again the Stygean Flood;
You then distinguish'd, in the bright Rolls of Fame,
Shalt stand; and Millions bless a GEORGE'S Name.

Printed and published for the Authors, by T. W. *Shaw*, in Fleet-street, opposite Anderton's Coffee House, where Letters to the Publisher, will be thankfully received.

A

CRISIS

EXTRAORDINARY.

WEDNESDAY, *August* 9, 1775   [Price Two Pence Half-penny.

Projicit *Ampullas.*   Hor.[1]

On *Souls*, of Slav'ry more than Death afraid,
Gage wastes his *Pardons* and his *Gasconnade.*

GENERAL GAGE'S *Proclamation*[2] lies before me, tho' it is not a Subject for Criticism, yet it deserves Notice, we may overlook the Style, but must detest the Doctrine; with what Judgment the General may Command, with what Spirit he may Fight, with what Prudence he may Retreat, is yet unknown; but if his Conduct in the

---

1. As taken from Horace's "The Art of Poetry" meaning, essentially, pompous or in-flated language (projicit ampullas et sesquipedia verba; often translated as "he throws away his inkwell in foot-and-a-half long words").

2. *A Proclamation* "By His Excellency The Honourable Thomas Gage, esq." appeared as a broadside in Boston on 12 June 1775, the day it was issued, and was widely reprinted thereafter—in other American towns and in London newspapers as early as July 18th in the *Public Advertiser, Lloyd's Evening Post,* and the *London Evening Post.* "Regulus" took Gage to task for it in the *London Evening Post,* 22 July 1775, two weeks before *The Crisis* turned to the proclamation, just one more reminder that *The Crisis* was part of a much

Field is equal to his Composition in the Closet, the Success of his Majesty's Arms must be owing more to Fate than Judgment. This *murderous* Proclamation opens with great Solemnity, bold Assertions, and notorious Falsehoods, it proceeds with the *presevering* Spirit of the *Times*; but alas! its imperious Offers of Clemency, and its conceited Menaces, are vain alike. The one will make no Converts for Want of *Confidence*; and the other can make no Cowards for Want of *Power*, to subjugate AMERICA *entirely* by Means of our Fleet and standing Army, is impossible, the Thought only proves, that *Administration* is as weak as it is wicked, should they be determined, like their misguided *Master*, to *persevere*, they will, e'er long, find it impracticable either to go forward, or to retreat, they will (let them *mark the Words* of an unknown Writer) oblige the PEOPLE, throughout the Empire of GREAT BRITAIN, to take the Power again into their own Hands, even *Anarchy* is preferable to DESPOTISM, especially while the Government is in the Hands of *Fools*, *Madmen*, *Knaves* and *Tyrants*; hard Usage justifies hard Names:—Let us now proceed to this *alluring Proclamation*; this flimsy, political Trap for antiquated *Roman Virtue*.

The *General* thought fit to arraign the Conduct of *the Americans* as *Incendiaries* and TRAITORS against the *Constitutional Authority* of the State; if the Word *Incendiary* has any Meaning in the English Language, it can only be applied with Propriety to One who is the first Kindler of Commotions in a State; according to our Constitution, the very Head that wears the CROWN may be an *Incendiary* by encouraging a FACTION, which may as well originate in the *Court*, as in the *Cottage*, if the KING and his Parliament, devoted to a vile *Administration*, combine to persevere in carrying any one Point against the *Constitution*, they are from that Moment, a *Faction*, (*Incendiaries*) and not a GOVERNMENT; they are TRAITORS, TRAITORS to the PEOPLE. Let me now ask, whether FACTION first took rise in AMERICA, or the *Mother Country?*

---

larger conversation in the press, with a truly transatlantic character. John Trumbull offered a parody of it as *A New Proclamation* (Hartford, 1775). For context see my essay, "Imperial Impotence," pp. 693–96.

In that Spot (wherever it may be) we must look for these INCENDI-ARIES and TRAITORS, I have put the Question fairly; it is simple, plain, and determinative,—I pause for a Reply,—not from the Mouth of a haughty Pensioner, a Scotch Placeman, or a fawning Courtier; but by the Decision of a true Constitutionalist, I am willing to abide; in the Interim, I shall declare my own Opinion. That the Mother Country, represented as she is, by a *corrupt Majority*, first formed a *Faction* herself, against the Laws and Liberties of AMERICA; nay, she has done more; she has artfully formed even a *Religious Faction* (the worst of all others) upon that great Continent; Her Government has of late been administered upon such mistaken, narrow, rotten Principles, that she did not think herself secure, till she had established POPERY by *Act of Parliament* at *Quebec*, by Way of fomenting Dissentions and Enmity in those Dominions she would enslave; or Administration knew and feared the Principles of the People upon that Continent, they had read that their Ancesters were *Puritans*, and no Friends to TYRANNY or POP-ERY; they knew their Designs, and planted *Papists* in their Rear, to keep their REBELLIOUS SUBJECTS (as they call them) between two Fires, and to deter them from taking refuge in the back Settlements; but they have Numbers and Virtue sufficient to enable them to keep, or at least to recover their Ground. Thus have a corrupt Majority, (falsely called the *Great Council* of the Nation) themselves departed, and encouraged Government to depart, in this as well as numberless other Instances, from the Line of Right laid down at the *Revolution*; a Period but little reverenced by our State-pilots, BUTE and MANSFIELD, these two Men, with their Lacqueys in and out of Parliament, are the real and only INCENDIARIES of AMERICA. The wretched Americans (unjustly branded by every *Hireling* with the Name of TRAITORS) are only busied, and justly busied, in extinguishing those Flames, which such a Government, (if it deserves the Name of one) has kindled; whether the Americans are *Traitors*, or unhappy Subjects making a lawful Resistance to repeated *Tyrannies*, must be determined, not by Hirelings, who assassinate for Pay, but by those who pay them with Reluctance by the collective Body of the People, in whom all Power virtually resides, from whom it originates and to whom it must, perhaps, shortly dissolve again. What the General calls *Treason* this collective Body (an awful Tribunal) will pronounce *Constitutional Resistance.*

The Americans are next accused of a fatal Progression of Crimes against the Constitutional Authority of the State.—By the Term *Constitutional,* if the *General* means an Authority *constitutionally* exercised, I deny his Assertion; it is as little founded on Truth, as our Ministerial Measures are upon sound Policy, Justice, and Humanity; when the Principles of the Constitution are abandoned (as they have lately been) the State may proceed authoritively, or rather despotically, but it cannot be said to act *constitutionally*—That the Americans avow REBELLION, I deny likewise, that they avow RESISTANCE (as their brave Ancestors once did, and as all true *Revolutionists* will do) every *Briton,* as an Enemy to Slavery, must Rejoice.

For the Patience and Lenity of the King's (in Truth of Lord *Bute's* and Lord *Mansfield's*) Government I appeal to FACTS. Those, who are Masters of the Disputes between *England* and *America*, and stand unbiased by Corruption, will pass an impartial Judgement between the Oppressors and Oppressed; we doubt not but the Sovereign's Patience is equal to his other God-like Attributes; but we know that the Patience of AMERICA has been severely tried, among other Invasions, she has been stripped of the most valuable Privilege, the Birthright of a British Subject, *Trial by Juries.* In many other Instances Government has attempted to enslave them; and shall the Aggressors presume to boast thus of their Patience and Lenity? at what Time, in what Particulars, were they exerted? were the humble Supplications and Remonstrances of AMERICA received by either, and by which of the three great Estates of this Kingdom? If so, a *Norton,* and *Apsley,* or some Ministerial Parricide, can inform us; but if they were (and they really were) rejected with Contempt by ALL, what Pretence, what Effrontry have the Tools and Sycophants of Power, to insult the Understandings of Mankind with SOUNDS? What HOPES (for such the *General* talks of) could AMERICA ever entertain of such an Administration, such a Parliament, and such a Sovereign? She has, (alas!) been driven to Despair, by all; nay, her Supplications have been finally answered by those divine effects of *Patience* and *Lenity*—FAMINE and the SWORD. Thus are those who are entrusted (as the General says) with supreme Rule; manifested to all the World, that they bare not the Sword in vain. Could GEORGE the THIRD, that Mirror of *Perseverance,* that *Idol* of an abandoned Ministry, present the Sword of Justice, like the old Heathen Emperor, to the People, and bid them use it for HIM, or against HIM, according to his *Deserts?* if he could, he then bears not the Sword in vain, but in Defiance of Heaven and Earth; in Defiance of all Laws, Human and Divine; nor can he bear it long.

But the most sacred Rights of the Crown, and People of *Great Britain* (says the General) have been infringed—It is a most audacious Piece of Military Insolence; after the late Act of *Tyranny* assented to by the *Steady Sovereign*, to join the Names of Crown and People together, as if their Views and Interests were still (as in Truth they ought to be) the same. Blind to its own Interest, to its Honour, to its Establishment, to its sacred Engagements, at the Altar, has the Crown (whose sole Aim is plainly Despotic Power) consulted the Interest of the People, in its Disputes with AMERICA? the Rights of the *Crown* and *People* were stipulated anew, at the Revolution; But has the Crown kept its Compact, with the People of *America?* if not, by whom have the Rights of the People been infringed?—As to the Rights of the Crown as stipulated at the Revolution, they are well known, and have been religiously submitted to both at home and abroad, even in *rebellious America*, but when it begins to stretch out the Arm of Usurpation, it is Time that its Despotic Sinews should be shrunk.

That the *Americans* have been guilty (and bravely guilty) of *Premeditation* and *Conspiracy*, is most true. They have been provoked to *Action,* and they were too wise to act without *thinking*. They have most virtuously *conspired* against *Tyrants*, and disdain to wear the Chains of the *most pious King*, the *wisest Administration,* and *most incorrupt Parliament* that Great Britain ever knew.—For these Demerits the *Fullness of Chastisement* is threatend. But suppose the *Chastisers* should be *Chastised?* I have always understood that true Courage was ever accompanied by the greatest Modesty. History is full of these Examples, But our Ministry (like their *Sandwich* and their *Denbigh*) have idly thought that *America* may be subdued *by Gasconnade*. Such corrupt Wretches are Strangers to the great Effects of Virtue. Sad Experience will inform them soon that all human Souls are not as abject as their own.

The *Americans* are next accused of an *unnatural Revolt*. If by this Expression is meant a Revolt against their *natural Allegiance*; I answer, that when *Protection* is first unjustly withdrawn on the *Sovereign's* Part, all *Allegiance* ceases on the *Subject's*. The *Subject* must then recur to the Rights of Nature; *Resistance* may ensue but no *Revolt*; for the *Sovereign*, by breaking his Compact has set the *Subject* free. A Politician would reason thus; but a *Soldier* has no Idea of any Mode of Government but by the Sword.—We are then told that our Colonists *dared not trust their Cause to the impartial Judgment of the Public, or even to the dispassionate Reflection of their Followers.*—But with what Truth? Were not the general Congresses throughout the Continent of *America* so many open Appeals to the Judgment of an impartial *Public?* were not the flagitious Prints, the popular Harrangues, the Declamations from the Pulpits (which the General complains of) so many Incitements to the cool, dispassionate Reflection of their Followers? indeed, *General*, you should always reason Sword in Hand.—The Pen is not your Fort.—You are lost upon Paper, and must at last submit to be vanquished in the Field. PUTNAM is in earnest.[3]

The Poor Americans are charged in the next Place with a Suppression of Truth.—with obstructing every Appeal to the real Interest of the People; with the grossest Forgeries, Calumnies, and Absurdities—To say that the Americans have been guilty of suppressing Truth, forging Falshoods, venting Calumnies and imposing Absudities, upon their Party, is but a kind of petulant Recrimination; these dishonourable Proceedings (if true) are but the common Stratagems of War, they are not peculiar to one Side only—The King's Party has practised them; all the insidious

---

3. Israel Putnam of Connecticut, veteran of the French and Indian War who would distinguish himself in the fighting at Bunker Hill on June 17th, had captured London's attention with his riposte to Gage's proclamation of June 12th (see supra *Crisis Extraordinary*, 9 August 1775 n. 2), which the *Morning Chronicle*, 25 July 1775 called "a consummate piece of manly elegance."

Spies of Government have practised them; General *Carlton*,[4] has practiced them most basely; you yourself, General *Gage*, have practised them
as dishonourably, but after all this malicious, splenictic Recrimination,
a Proof of *Treason* and *Rebellion* against these injured People? In Spite of
all this foul Language, the World will think that there is as much Verac-
ity, Virtue, Candour, Honour, and true Courage on the Part of Freemen
who defend, as on the Part of *Tyrants* who invade their Liberties.—I
now wish to be informed of these APPEALS which have been made (if the
General says true) to the real *Interest* of AMERICA.

Through what Channels have they passed? Have either of the three great
Estates of this Kingdom, or has the Minister, or even a single Tool or
Lacquey, of Administration, has a *North*, a *Sandwich*, or a *Denbigh*, once
condescended to advise, admonish, or expostulate, with America? Has
the Secretary of State for that Department ever had Orders to write in
such a Strain? Have not all Lord *Bute's* servile Clan, endeavoured, on the
contrary, to carry every Thing with a high Hand, and a menacing audacious Front? Have they not shut their Eyes, Ears, and Hearts, against
every humble Approach, every filial Intercession of *America?* These insolent Invaders of Royal Charters, human Rights, and established Laws,
have been too much flashed with the Hopes of *Conquest* to wish cordially
for a *Reconciliation* with *America*. They have industriously stopped up
every opening towards it. The Mouths of our Patriots and our Citizens
have been stopped by *corrupt Votes*, and *Majestic Insults*; as to the Proposal made by Lord *North* in his House of Commons, it was calculated
for the Contempt it met with. His Lordship was not quite Fool enough
to think it could take Place. By whom, then, has any *Appeal to the real Interest of America* been made by those who would exterminate the People?

The *Prostitution of the Press* makes the next Item in the *General's* Catalogue of Complaints; If the *American* Press has been prostituted, I pray

4. Governor Guy Carleton's declaration of martial law in Quebec on 9 June 1775 made
its way across the Atlantic as quickly as Gage's proclamation in Boston three days later.
It was, if anything, even more widely reprinted in the London press than Gage's proclamation, often without direct comment, but, in the case of the *London Evening Post* on
1 August 1775 and the *Morning Chronicle* the next day, with the wish that the spirit of
resistance to tyranny shown in Massachusetts had spread north.

that *Doctor Johnson* may be called upon to declare, upon the Honour of a Court-Pensioner, how gloriously the *English Press* has been employed in the Cause of Truth by his Brother Garreteers; even the Eloquence of the Laity and Clergy has been exerted (says the *General*) to *excite and justify Devastation and Massacree.*—Can a Soldier, who should be a Man of Honour, assert so gross a Falshood? It is notorious that no one *popular Harrangue* (as the General calls them) has been made in *America,* with any other View than that of animating their gallant Countrymen to a just Defence of their Liberties, Properties, and Lives; the noblest Purpose of which the distinguished Gift of Speech can serve. That the brave and virtuous *Americans* have animated each other in Support of their National Rights, will be recorded in History to their immortal Honour; that our perfidious Government has armed the *Papists*, whom they patronize at *Quebec*, with a View of destroying their Protestant Subjects, is a Circumstance which will make a Figure of a different Cast in History; and will most assuredly bring the Advisers of that Measure to an ignominious Death, in Spite of the standing Army, employed and paid at present, for no other purpose than that of protecting TYRANTS; whether *popular Harrangues* made it one Case, or *Arms* supplied in the other, is most Characteristic of National Honour and Virtue, may easily be determined.—And to this the *base*, the *cowardly*, the *traiterous* Design of Government (after all their Parade and Military Bluster) of surrendering *Canada* to the *French*, a vast Province acquired last War, at the Expence of so much Blood and Treasure. This pusilanimous Thought has been suggested to gratify a despairing TYRANT.

I now accompany the *General* to the Account he gives of the Action of the *Nineteenth of April last*, respecting an Attack upon the KING's Troops from *behind Walls, and lurking Holes.*—Be it so; yet, who can believe that the KING's Troops should have been unprepared for *Ambuscade,* or any Acts of hostile *Frenzy*, as the *General* calls it? Have not the *Americans* been driven to this *Frenzy*? Is it not common for an Enemy to take every Advantage? Is it not uncommon, nay, impossible, that Troops, charged with *Vengeance*, should be *unprepared* to take it? They could not be *unprepared* for taking it, if they were *armed*; nor would they *decline taking it*, if they were *Scotchmen*: Their not taking it, therefore, must be owing, either to a Want of Spirit, a Want of Conduct, or a Want of Power. Since that Period (of the *Nineteenth of April*) says the *General*, the *Rebels have derived Confidence from Impunity.*—Is it a Matter of Merit, then, with a mercinary Soldiery, that they did not execute what they were unable to effect? This is talking like a Driveler *General!* But these *Rebels*, these *Traiterous Revolutionists* in *America,* have dared *to fire upon the KING's Ships and Subjects*—Granted—but have not these *Ships* invaded them, have not these *Subjects* (why did you not say, *Soldiers* and *Marines*) threatned their Destruction? Is the Doctrine of passive Obedience, and Non-Resistance to the Divine Will of TYRANTS, to be observed by the insulted and enslaved *Americans,* till they felt their *Sovereign's* Bayonets in their Bosoms?—These *Rebels* have proceeded even further; they have *affected* (says our *General*) to hold the KING's Army *besieged*— Have they? May Heaven prosper such a glorious Piece of *Affectation!* Every *Constitutionalist* throughout the British Empire, hopes they will not only *affect* it, *but effect* it: Every true-born Briton longs to see the final Triumph of *America* marked as an *Epocha* in the future Annals of his Country; nor would their Joy be checked by the Appearance of another *blessed Martyrdom* in the Calendar. *Tyranny* and *Martyrdom,* like *Representation* and *Taxation,* should go together.

The Charge of *Invasion upon private Property,* and a *Wantonness of Cruelty,* is not only indecent, but imprudent, from that Mouth which commands the KING's *Banditti* in *America,* who have so daringly themselves invaded the Liberties, the Properties, the Laws and Lives of free People, with the Sword; merely, because they claim, and will maintain, the Rights of *Englishmen.*

As to the Actions of the *Nineteenth of April last,* which so often haunt the *General's* Mind, they ought to stand for ever recorded in the Calendar, to the eternal Honour of *America,* who that Day not only totally disappointed, but bravely resisted, no inconsiderable Party of the KING's *military Assassins.* If any Improprieties were committed on that *Nineteenth of April* by the *American* Troops, which cannot easily be pardoned by so consummate a Soldier as *General Gage*; yet, their gallant Behaviour on the *Seventeenth of June* following must surely have deserved his Admiration. They did not fire then from *behind Walls* and *lurking Holes*, but bravely faced, attacked, and defeated, the TYRANT's Forces. This appears sufficiently, even from the Letter which has been artfully imposed on the Public for *General Gage's* genuine Account of that Action; but let the *Minister* shew forth the *General's* real Letter, if he dares. His Master lost his Colour when he read it; and I verily believe that even Lord *North* (the ostensible Minister) is not himself entrusted with the true Contents of it. His Lordship is but the Drudge. He has the Name without the Confidence of a *Minister*; and meanly submits to be responsible for Iniquities *not his own*. The real genuine Letter (so dreadful are its Tidings) is a Secret to all but the TYRANT, and his *Gemini*, the *Castor*, and *Pollux*,[5] of his Cabinet, *Bute* and *Mansfield*,—They *dare* not publish it.

I am now come to the *last Effort* within the Bounds of the *General's* Duty, to spare the *Effusion of Blood*, which he is strictly charged to shed without Mercy or Reluctance. The *General*, according to his Orders, most dutifully dispatched his blustering Colonel *Smith* to commence the intended Carnage. This Bully failed; yet Blood was unnaturally and unjustifiably drawn by our *hireling Cut Throats* at *Concord*; and then the *General*, in Commiseration of the *Calamities* which his *murderous* Army had occasioned, most humanely offers, two Months afterwards (when he found himself unequal to the Task of *Conquest*) his Majesty's *most gracious Pardon* to these unhappy Sufferers. Your treacherous Offer is disdained—away with it!—and *massacre* (if you can) but without an Insult the bravest Men in the British Empire. Did not the Ancestors of these brave Spirits spurn the insidious Proclamation of that *Tyrant Charles*, and shall their Sons fall a Prey to the delusive Orders of a weaker TYRANT, and a more consummate *Hypocrite?*—Will not the gallant ADAMS, and the meritorious HANCOCK fall with their Country, if it is

---

5. Castor and Pollux were famous as the twin brothers or "Gemini" of Greek (and later Roman) mythology. They were a mixed pair, honorable, even heroic, in some tales, base and disreputable in others. With Pollux inconsolable when Castor dies, Zeus allows the brothers to be reunited, spending half of their time in Olympus, half in Hades, later to be immortalized as a constellation in the night sky.

her fate to fall?[6] Or, should they be unfortunately taken Prisoners, will they not cast an indignant Smile upon the Wretch, who should affect to pardon them, after he had enslaved their Country? The proclaiming all *America* (except the KING's *Roman Catholic* Subjects, and good Allies at *Quebec*) TRAITORS, is but a contemptible Echo of that Act of Parliament which declared them so long since, for consulting and preparing, only against an intended *Massacree* by Sword and Famine.—*America* despises your Threats, your Clemency, and all naval and military Terror and Parade, thou impotent TYRANT! This *General* concludes his *Gasconnade* with a most notorious Falshood, by asserting that the present *unnatural Rebellion* of the *Americans* (as he calls it) has stopped the *Administration of Justice* in that Country—For Shame, For Shame! *General*; a *Soldier!* and guilty of a *Lye!*—Your *Master* knows, you know, the whole World knows, that the rotten Parliament of this Nation not only stopped the Course, but extinguished every Benefit of the *Common Law* (the Subjects great Inheritance) when they dared take away the Privilege of *Juries.* The Design was base, atrocious, glaring, perfidious, and tyrannical; but why does this unthinking Tool of military Power call the *Royal Charter* of the Province to his Aid; that *Charter*, which his *Master* and his *Parliamentary Junto* has so grossly violated? Is that *Charter* unfavourable to *Freedom,* and can it now serve the Cause of *Slavery?* Has it hitherto been slighted, and is it now made Use of to *betray* the People for whose

---

6. Samuel Adams and John Hancock, leaders in the extralegal Massachusetts provincial convention, a shadow government that called for the people's loyalty as an alternative to royally-appointed officials like Gage. Thus, there was revolutionary action long before there was avowedly revolutionary rhetoric, a willingness to move outside the imperial governmental structure before there was denunciation of the crown and renunciation of the empire—for which see William Lincoln, *The Journals of the Provincial Congress of Massachusetts in 1774 and 1775* (Boston: Dutton and Wentworth, 1838). Only Adams and Hancock were exempted from the pardon offered in Gage's proclamation of June 16th (see supra *Crisis Extraordinary,* 9 August 1775 n. 2) to those who had incited unrest—indeed, committed treason, in the eyes of the king. Adams and Hancock had in fact been on a February 1774 list of eight Bay colonists who Attorney General Edward Thurlow and Solicitor General Alexander Wedderburn believed could have been tried for treason because of their supposed involvement with the Boston tea party two months before. See, again, my "Imperial Impotence," pp. 671–74.

Protection it was granted? Has it been so often disallowed, with an indignant Sneer, when *America* petitioned for *Redress*, and is it now set up against her by the shallow Tools of Power, when she is defending those Rights and Liberties which it gives her? Is this *Royal Charter* now called in Aid of *despotic* Measures, through Weakness, Insolence, or Inadvertency? Why, General, General! Your haughty, unrelenting *Master*, tramples on the *Royal Charters* of his wiser Predecessors. I tell thee, *Homicide,* that the Faith of KINGS is now no more. Our very *Laws* must shortly truckle to the *Sword*. The *Law Martial*, which you have just proclaimed (and of which you may shortly taste yourself) will, if you succeed in *America*, be at length the only Law of *England*. *Mansfield* is an Advocate for summary Proceedings. The Die is cast in the *Great Divan* (the *wise* Council of this Nation) and those who would rise again to the State and Liberties of *Englishmen*, must rise through BLOOD. The *Parricides* of this *Constitution*, General, are to be found in *England*, not in *America*; unless among the *established Papists* at *Quebec*; nor can *Happiness*, *Peace*, *Liberty*, and *Law*, be now restored (unless *Providence* miraculously intervenes) but by another *Revolution*.

C A S C A.

Printed and published for the Authors, by T. W. *Shaw*, in Fleet-Street, opposite Anderton's Coffee House, where Letters to the Publisher, will be thankfully received.

THE

CRISIS

NUMBER XXX   To be continued Weekly.

SATURDAY, August 12, 1775   [Price Two-pence Half-penny.

To the K I N G.

From Philip Thicknesse, Esq.

BEFORE the Contents of this Paper is communicated to your Majesty, the Writer of it will have taken an everlasting Farewell of *your* Kingdom, and his *own* Native, and *once* beloved Country. He will consider himself a Citizen of the whole World; who has been defrauded of his Fortune, by a Combination of your Majesty's *wicked and corrupt Judges*, and supported therein, by your Majesty's *own, Domestic Servants* and *Friends*.

He will consider himself, (and so Sir will all your Majesty's *honest* Subjects) as a Man grown Old in your Service, driven from your Dominions, with *Eight Children in his Train*, to seek his own Subsistance, and their Fortune, at an Age that he might reasonably have expected to have been in Possession of a comfortable Support, as a Reward for his long and faithful Services; instead of which, his own private Property has been wrested from him, by a most unheard-of Proceeding, in a House, *called the House of Lords*; but whose shameful Conduct to him, justifies his calling it a *Den of Thieves*; and that too, of the worst Sort; because the Robbery they committed, was done under the *Sanction* of the Law; though he really fell a Sacrifice to the wretched Politics of your Ministers, and to the Personal Pique, of that worst of Men, Lord *Mansfield*.—He will consider himself as a Man, owing Allegiance to no Prince upon Earth, till he has found one, who will afford him an Assylum, for himself, and his large Family; and who will protect his Person, and maintain his Property, *by the established Laws of his Country.*

Sir, I have served in the Armies of your Majesty, and your Royal Grandfather, from the Age of Fifteen, to Fifty. I have served in almost every Part of the Globe, and have spilt some of my Blood in severe Services; and now Sir, before I quit my Native Country, I am determined to stand forth, with that Boldness which Truth inspires, and Injuries provoke, to tell your Majesty some alarming and wholesome Truths;—Truths, which the Men *now* about your Person, durst not tell you, and which your real Friends *cannot*. It is needless to inform your Majesty of the scandalous Behaviour of your present Chancellor, Lord *Apsley*, in the House of Lords; on the 16th Day of *February* last; but it seems *Necessary*, to remind your Majesty of the *Virtues of his Predecessors*.—I need not repeat all the shamefull Misdoings of the former, because I know your Majesty has seen the VII and X Number of this PAPER; and if your Majesty condescended to read the Petition, I had the Honour to deliver into your Hand, by the favourable Assistance of the Earl of *Oxford*,[1] you are equally as well informed with my unhappy and singular Situation.

But neither the Injustice which has been done me in the *House of Lords*; my long and faithful Services; my large Family; nor the humble Petition of a Man who has a eight Children, (the eldest of whom is the presumptive Heir to an ancient Barony) has proved sufficient to induce your Majesty to attend to my humble Prayer.

Permit me, Sir, to remind your Majesty, that it is not for *your Sake* only, but for the *Sake of your People*, that you are appointed *their Chief Magistrate;* for surely, Sir, if you had considered this, you would not have

---

1. Edward Harley, fourth Earl of Oxford, was a lord of the king's bedchamber, so he did have access to George III.

removed from the Highest, and most important *Seat of Justice*, a virtuous and an able Man, whose *equitable Decisions*, gave even the *vanquished Suitor* Satisfaction; and have placed in his stead, a Man, whose Name I am ashamed should blot this Paper.

Does your Majesty know, that the Chancellor of this Country decides, in the Course of a few Years, half the Property in your Kingdom?—You certainly do:—and does your Majesty believe, that your people will be satisfied, now they know that your present Chancellor has neither Abilities to discern, nor Integrity to decide, honestly, even when *the Law is pointed out to him.*

All the World acknowledge the Abilities of Lord *Camden* as fully as they esteem him for his *Integrity.*—He is confessedly the first and ablest Lawyer in Your Majesty's Kingdom, and allowed by all *Parties* to be *an honest Man.*

Why then, Sir, at a Time his eminent Abilities were so essentially necessary in your private Councils, was he dismissed from his *high Office?*—I, Sir, above all Men, have a Right to ask your Majesty this Question; because *his Dismission* has been *my Ruin*; and take Care, least his Successor, and his Abettors, do not ruin a *greater Man.*

Is the Property of your Majesty's Subjects to be sacrified to his Vanity or Support?—Must his Decrees be affirmed right or wrong? Does not your Majesty hear of the constant Appeals from his Decisions? and does your Majesty think the Confirmation of them by Lord *Denbigh*, and your Bedchamber Lords, will satisfy the injured and plundered Appellants? who, instead of gaining their Property, are ruined by Expence, and rendered wretched by unnecessary Delays. Surely, Sir, if not for their Sakes, you will instantly for *your own*, put the Seals into the Hands of an able Man.—You cannot put them into weaker, or more dishonest Hands.

Is the Man, who took the Advantage of Mr. *Hoare's* Generosity to his necessitous Brother, by an Act which a Petty-fogging Attorney would have blushed at, a fit Person to administer the *Law*, even if he knew it, to the Subjects of *Britain?*—Forbid it *Justice*;—forbid it *Truth*:—*I tell you plainly, Sir, the Nation will not bear it.* Your Majesty knows, that the

Seals were given to Lord *Apsley*, because no other Man but his Lordship would accept them on Lord *Mansfield's Terms*; who knew him to be a vain, empty Creature, who would implicitly obey *his Mandates*.

What must your Majesty's Subjects think of a Man, who said in the House of Lords;—"My. Lords, I *pride* myself in asking, and obtaining, the *Private Opinions* of my Brother Judges:" Yet his *priding* Lordship stood silent, and looked sullen, when Lord *Pawlet* moved the House to have the *Public Opinion of all* his Brother Judges."

And when his infamous Abettors (your Majesty's Bedchamber Lords) had over-ruled that honest Motion, what did he do? stood forth and read a *Private Letter* obtained from Sir *William De Grey*, for the wicked Purpose, and imposed that Man's pretended Opinion, in order to sustain Lord *Mansfield's* and his own, though he was previously told by Lord *Camden*, "That it was *contrary to Law* to read it, and that, if it had been otherwise, the Opinion of a Man, *not a Judge in that Court*, ought not to weigh, even as a *Wafer in the Scale.*—Nor, said his Lordship, should *such an Opinion* be even whispered in this House."

I appeal, Sir, to your Majesty's Justice, and to the good Sense and Candour of all your Subjects, whether *such Proceedings* as *those,* had any Resemblance of the benign Face of *Equity* or *Justice*. No, sir, every Bystander saw, with Concern and Pity; and many of the more feeling Part, with Astonishment and Horror. The Day my Ruin was effected, the Contest was not *for Justice* to *either Party*; but whether your Majesty's *present* Chancellor, and his wicked Abetters, could bully down and defeat the irresistable Arguments, and good Sense of that good Man, Lord *Camden*.

This, Sir, is the Sense of the whole Nation, and it is NOW, *their Misfortune, more than mine. This*, Sir, is a Truth, told you by an unfortunate Man, who is no longer your Servant, nor your Subject, nor any longer interested in the Welfare of a Kingdom, which has treated him with such repeated Acts of Injustice, for he has long before this, been a *Mark* to be *shot* at.* He has asked *Alms* of your Majesty since this fatal Blow; but his

---

*See his Trial at a Court-Martial, published about ten Years since, and his Letter to Lord *Bute*.

Prayer has been made to *your Majesty* without Effect! perhaps without Pity.

Do not therefore Sir, suffer it to be said, that void of a due Sense of the Duty I owed to your Majesty, or a natural Love to my native Country, that I forsook *both*, from interested Views, or Want of honest Principles: No, Sir, I forsook my Country, like an honest, but injured Man, owing no one any Thing; and having a *large*, and *just Demand* upon it.—I have forsook it, Sir, in the 56th Year of my Age, and the 35th of my faithful Services, to seek an honest Subsistance, for myself, and my large Family, because the little Pittance *I have left*, is insufficient to maintain them; and because my legal Property, has been *violently* wrested from my Hands, by your Majesty's three first *Law Officers*.

Oh, Britain! how is thy Glory faded! Art thou the *Nation*, so lately renowned through the *World*; for its Valour in *War*; its Wisdom in *Council*; and its equitable Distribution *of Justice!*—Thy Inhabitants now behold, with Astonishment and Horror, Lord *Denbigh* become the chief Prop to the first *Law Officer*; Lord *Sandwich*, to the Archibshop of *Canterbury*; and Lord *Le Despencer* to the *Propagaters of the Christian Religion!* And yet, strange to think, all these Things are come to pass, during the Reign of a *Religious King*, and the *best of Princes*.

The Day, Sir, my ruinous Cause came on before the House of Lords, a Report was as artfully, as wickedly, propagated *at St. James's*, "That Lord CAMDEN was going down to the House of Lords, to commit *Hostilities* against your Majesty's Chancellor."—*Hostilities* was the *Parole*; it was whispered about till it was *thought necessary* to send some *Household Troops* down, to sustain LORD CAMDEN's *wicked Attack upon Justice*. Lord *Denbigh* was the Ruffian, to whom the Command was given; and he executed his Business with such Alacrity, that he soon drove Lord *Pawlet* from his Post; Lord CAMDEN sustained the Attack singly, for an Hour and twenty Minutes, but was at length, obliged to give Way to *Numbers*.—Thus, Sir, a *complete Victory was obtained* over Lord CAMDEN's *wicked Intentions*; and *My Ruin* was accomplished. I confess, Sir, I fled from the Field of Battle, during the warmest Part of the Conflict; but it was the *first Time*, and I was *deeply wounded*. I thank GOD, however, I left *Lord* CAMDEN, fighting singly on my Side.—He fought Sir, *valiantly*, and fell *nobly*; *for he fell with vanquished Justice by his Side*; fighting for the Honour of his Country, and a friendless Stranger: His Honour, Sir, and his Pity, has been my Support. I say his Pity; for though I am unfortunately an utter Stranger to that great and good Man; I know he has almost dropped a Tear in Pity to my Misfortunes; and I have seen, under his own Hand, a Letter, in which are these Words:

"I am glad I did not know the distressed Situation of Mr. Thickness, before his Cause came on; I am sorry to be acquainted with it now, because my Heart bleeds for him, and I can give him no Relief. His Case would have been hard, had the Law been against him. &c. &c.*"*

These, Sir, are the Sentiments of your Majesty's *late* Lord Chancellor; and as your Majesty knows, what Sentiments the whole Nation entertain of your *present*; remove him, I beseech you, from that once chaste Seat he has so infamously defiled, and no longer disgrace your own Dignity, nor risque your Subjects Property, to the Controul of so contemptible a Person; for a Knave in that Station, would be more acceptable to your People, than a Fool; and even Lord *Mansfield* is much more fitting for that Employment, than Lord *Apsley*; but if you wish to recover the Affection of your People, restore *Lord* CAMDEN to a Seat he will fill with so much Honour to your Majesty, and so much Satisfaction to the whole Nation.—I am sure the Day is not very remote when you *must* do it; and I hope you will spare yourself that *Mortificaton*, and do it *now, because it ought to be done.*—I know not how to subscribe myself, for I know not who, or what I am; but this I can with Truth say, that I *was* your Majesty's faithful Subject, and devoted Servant; but am now driven into Exile, by being plundered of my private Property, because your Majesty's Ministers thought it better to sacrifice me to their Prejudice and Politicks, than expose the Weakness and Wickedness of your Law Officers; or to Countenance even the *Laws of the Land*, while they are in *the Custody only of Lord* CAMDEN.

I shall conclude this Address to your Majesty with an Extract, from the Writings of the *great* Lord *Bacon*; who says, "When *any* of the *four Pillars of Government* are mainly shaken, or weakned, which are

*Religion,—Justice,—Council,—*and *Treasure.—Men had Need to Pray for fair Weather.*"—And speaking of Sedition, his Lordship says, "The Matter of Seditions is of two Kinds:—Much *Poverty*, and much *Discontent*. *Lucan* noteth well the State of Rome *before* the CIVIL WAR."

Hinc usura vorax, avidumque in tempore foenus.

Hinc concussa fides, & Multis utile Bellum.

"This same *Multis utile Bellum*, is an assured, and infallible Sign of a State disposed to Seditions and Troubles; and if the Poverty, and broken Estates of the better, be joined with Necessity in the mean People, the Danger is imminent and great; but the main Causes of Seditions are, he says, *Innovations* in *Religion,—Taxes,*—Alteration of *Laws* and *Customs*, breaking of Privileges, general Oppression, and *Advancement of unworthy Persons*, &c."[2]

Now, if any of that great Man's Remarks are worthy of your Majesty's Royal Attention, it behoves you to obtain better Information, than Lord *Denbigh can*, or Lord Mansfield *will* give you. I shall conclude this Address to your Majesty, in beseeching you to consider, what my Sentiments and Sensations were, while I stood a full Hour at your Closet Door, in Order to throw myself on my Knees, at your Feet, to ask a bare Support for myself, and for my Family, when I saw that painful Hour, chiefly employed by your Majesty, in familiar and gracious Conversation with a Man, who has been on *his Knees* to call down Destruction on your Family; and indeed, *upon them*, for even a Prostitution of a more *unnatural Crime*. However Sir, the Sun shall not go down upon my Anger, and may it long shine upon your Majesty, and all your *real Friends*.

N. B. A Citizen of London, of the *Drybutter Family* (with whom he had been *closely connected*) left him a Legacy of Ten Thousand Pounds, and

---

2. The author(s) were quoting from and paraphrasing Francis Bacon's essay "Of seditions and troubles," available in various editions of his *Essays, or Counsels, Civil and Moral*, in this case the 1755 London edition published by A. Millar, from pp. 42–43. Bacon, for his part, had borrowed from Lucan's *Pharsalia*, Book 1, and Lucan's observation that Caesar's ambition had unleashed voracious usury, the destruction of credit, and the pursuit of war by many who found it to their advantage.

that it was, which first raised this Man from Obscurity, to be a Scourge to *this* Country.

A CARD to *LORD* ———.

Mr. T——— presents his Compliments to Lord ———;, and desires his Lordship to consider, that his voluntary Offer to recommend him to the King's Favor, when he had no such Design, was Cruelty in the first Degree.—Has his Lordship forgot, that Sir RICHARD LYTLETON, and Mr. COLLETON,³ were Mr. T———'s Acquaintance and Friends, as well as his Lordships? and does his Lordship think, that a certain *singular Transaction before he was married* to Miss ——— died with those two Gentlemen?—Surely his Lordship does think so, or he would not have been so *wantonizing* cruel.

₊ Shortly will be published, a Letter to Lord ———.

On Wednesday the 9th of August, instant, at Ten o'Clock in the Forenoon, was published, by T. W. SHAW, *in* Fleet-Street, *Price Twopence Halfpenny,*

A C R I S I S Extraordinary,

Proving, unanswerably, that the KING supports a Faction against the Laws and Constitution, that the AMERICANS are not REBELS, and that those who would rise to the State and Liberties of ENGLISHMEN, must rise thro' BLOOD.

Printed and published for the Authors, by T. W. *Shaw,* Fleet-Street, opposite Anderton's Coffee House, where Letters to the Publisher, will be thankfully received.

---

3. The author(s) could have been referring to Sir Richard Lyttelton, baronet, an army officer who also held a seat in the Commons; he had died in 1770. His older brother George, who died three years later, had been one of Pitt's political allies early in his career, before he was elevated to the peerage. It is not clear who Colleton was or the "Mr. T———" alluded to in this card to Lord ———, also a question mark.

THE

CRISIS

NUMBER XXXI   To be continued Weekly.

SATURDAY, August 19, 1775   [Price Two-pence Half-penny.

To the K I N G.

For Seas of BLOOD which your mad Fury shed,

God soon will hurl his Veng'ance on your Head;

Struck as when SATAN from his Glory fell,

Your CONSCIENCE must be one continu'd Hell.

S I R,

WHILST News-paper Scribblers, in the PAY of your Ministers, are varnishing over the Actions of a *Nero*, or a *Dioclesian*,[1] and others who pretend to be Friends to the natural

---

1. Diocletian, Roman emperor from 284–305 CE, rose through the ranks of the army
to become emperor. He mixed autocratic tendencies and ambitious projects (including

Rights of Mankind, and the Constitution, disguise their real Sentiments, or Write more like effeminate Distards of the East, than Englishmen, and the Descendents of Britons, against your MINIONS ONLY.—The Authors of the CRISIS will not be afraid to expose TREASON and PERJURY, though covered with the Robes of Royalty; they are determined, at every Hazard, to speak the boldest and most galling Truths, although they should offend the Ears, strike deep into the Heart, or excite the Rage of the most despotic Tyrant.

One Part of your Subjects, that is, your Ministers and their Creatures, call you the BEST of KINGS; the Authors of the CRISIS, and more than *Nine-tenths* of your People in every Part of the British Dominions, not only think, but know you to be the worst of T——ts.

Let your Flatterers and Sycophants, who surround your Throne, point out ONE single Act you have done in the Course of a FIFTEEN Years Reign, worthy of a KING, *i. e.* a FATHER of your People; and the whole Nation will that Moment, make a solemn Sacrifice of their Liberties, at the Altar of DESPOTISM which you have erected: but alas! on the contrary, how many damning Proofs have we already upon Record, sufficient to stagger the Belief of Posterity, of your cruel and perverse Will, of your Tyrannical and obstinate Disposition; in a Word, of the Weakness of your Head, and the Badness of your Heart. It is not necessary for you, Sir, to be guilty of one more Act of Cruelty, you have reached the Summit of Human Greatness; you have gained the glorious Appellation, the immortal NAME of *St. George's Fields, Brentford*, and *America*, will remain (though Stone and Marble might decay) lasting Monuments to your Memory, and will be sufficient to perpetuate your Ingratitude, your Treachery, your Hypocracy, and your Savage Cruelty, to succeeding Ages.

You may, Sir, be able to manage the Nursery, to guide the principal Wire of a Puppet Shew, (with which you often amuse yourself) to smile at

---

splitting the empire into eastern and western halves for a time) with a desire to secure the frontier and stabilize finances. He left no lasting successes but he was astute enough to avoid assassination and stepped down to live over a decade in retirement.

little Pinchey's Gew-gaws, at *Breslaw's* Slight of Hand, and Automaton Figures, and to laugh at *Foote's Theatre;*[2] whilst the BLOOD of Thousands, the Widow and the Fatherless, plunged in the Depths of Misery, are calling for Vengeance of YOU and your MINIONS.

But, Sir, notwithstanding all those amiable Qualities (which might do Honour to a *Hottentot*) you are by no Means fit to govern one of the petty States of Germany, much less this great and powerful Kingdom.

Although the Hands of the BEST of KINGS are besmeared with HUMAN GORE.

Although the infernal Designs of your abandoned Ministers to enslave America, have been frustrated at the Expence of the Lives of many brave and virtuous Men, who preferred DEATH to SLAVERY.

Although the Futility and Impracticability of reducing the Western World by Force of Arms, to a State of abject Dependance on your WILL, a State more horrible than that of Egyptian Bondage, has been sufficiently proved.

Although you have forced more than THREE HUNDRED THOUSAND of your Subjects into a just Resistance to your Tyranny, to preserve all that is held dear by great and good Men, their Lives, Liberties, and Properties, from the cruel Invasions of an infamous Majority in both Houses of Parliament, notoriously corrupted with Bribes, Places, and Pensions, to do the dirty Work of your Court, to raise a Revenue for the avowed and ONLY Purpose of paying such Bribes, Placemen, and Pensioners, and to aid the bloody Designs of your Ministers, to carry into Execution, at the Point of the Sword, (contrary to the Sense of every

---

2. Pinchey is most likely a derisive reference to Christopher Pinchbeck, who kept up the London clock-making business begun by his father. George III was one of his patrons, known to favor Pinchbeck's clocks and other mechanical curiosities that he designed and built himself. Philip Breslaw was a London stage magician, famous for his sleight-of-hand tricks, who also claimed to be able to read minds. Samuel Foote was a contentious actor and playwright, by then part of the London theatre scene for the past forty years.

independent Man in England) the most unjust and sanguinary Laws that ever disgraced a British House of Commons.

Although your Kingdom is defenceless by sending out Ships and exporting Troops to America, to massacree their Fellow Subjects, (or to be slaughtered where Glory cannot be obtained, but Dishonour and eternal Infamy must attend their Fall) and this at a Time when you are meanly crouching to France and Spain, and trembling for FEAR of their vast and powerful Armaments, ready to sail at a few Hours Notice, should these our natural Enemies invade this Kingdom, which there is but too much Reason to expect from your weak and bloody Politics; England must be destroyed, or become a tributary State to the combined Power of the House of Bourbon.

Although your People HERE are oppressed to the last Degree by enormous Taxes, to feed the Luxuries of your corrupt rotten Court, whilst Thousands of Manufacturers are out of Employ, and, with the Poor, starving for Want of Bread.

Although your Treasury, and your Exchequer is empty, your Servants five Quarters in Arrears, and your Tradesmens Bills unpaid.

Although the People of England labour under Grievances little inferior to those the Americans justly complain of, and will soon take up Arms to redress their Wrongs. I say, Sir, notwithstanding all these existing and impending Dangers, which evidently threaten a Destruction of the Empire, yet you seem determined, by obstinately denying Right to your People, and pursuing Measures big with Public Ruin, to drive your Subjects into a State of Desperation, and all the Horrors of a CIVIL WAR, as well in England as America; that you may glut your Rage and Thirst for Blood, by issuing illegal Proclamations, declaring every Man who shall defend the LAWS and the CONSTITUTION a Rebel; for WE have no Alternative left but to be REBELS or SLAVES, it being the general Opinion of Mankind, that you would rather risque your Crown, and wade through Seas of BLOOD, than drop your present Design, aided by a corrupt Senate and a profligate Ministry, to establish an absolute Sovereignty over the Nation, and Reign a merciful DESPOT on the Throne of England.

There may, Sir, possibly be some Men, (and that there is no doubt your Ministers have made you believe) so superlatively LOYAL, that rather than not live under the blessed Tyranny of George the Third, they would give up all the glorious Privileges of ENGLISHMEN. It is possible there may be a few such Wretches, their Number, however, cannot be great, nor does it consist of any but those who are well paid for their Servility; remove them from their Places, cease to bribe, and let them no longer have an Interest in calling you the BEST of KINGS, in being loyal, and submitting to your Mandates and your Bondage, and they will the next Moment (as they do already in their Hearts) execrate and condemn you, your Impolitic, and Bloody Measures.

The Transactions, Sir, in this Kingdom, since you imbibed the Principles of the *Stuarts*, espoused the Interests of the Church of Rome, and pursued the persecuting Spirit of the Catholics, are so full of Wonder and Astonishment, that were the Facts not well attested, I am persuaded Posterity would not believe them.—But what is the most alarming now, and will be hardly credited hereafter, is, that so GOOD and WISE a King as George the Third, should give himself up to the Guidance of so BAD a Set of Men, as *Bute, Mansfield, Jenkinson,* and *North,* though *Born* a BRITON, and *glorying* in the Name, he should be a SCOTSMAN, though bred a *Protestant*; he should be a *Catholic*; though SWORN to preserve the Rights, Lives, and Liberties, of the People, and the Constitution of the Kingdom in Church and State, as by LAW established, he should violate that solemn Engagement made before God and Man; be the Murderer of his Subjects, the Destroyer of their Rights, Liberties, and Properties; the Subverter of the Constitution in Church and State, and the Instrument of general Ruin.

The Astonishment of our Descendents will not end here; they will be more surprized still, to find such horrid Masacres, inhuman Laws, and cruel Plans, for the Destruction of a People and Kingdom, as disgrace the present Reign, were suffered in ENGLAND, without RESISTANCE, with a Stoical cowardly Patience; nay, almost Insensibility.

Non-resistance may keep Fools and Cowards in AWE; but, Sir, what Man can be so lukewarm as even to DOUBT, when a Nation is falling, (as England now is) from the greatest Height of glory, into the most despicable Condition, that the COMMUNITY has a RIGHT to COMMAND his Services. That the Right is founded upon NECESSITY. He ought to know by the Principles of the last Revolution, that every FAITHFUL SUBJECT is bound to resist the Prince, who endeavours to ruin and enslave his People, and that he may push this Resistance to the dethronement and exclusion of his Race. It was, Sir, by an Exertion of those Principles, that YOUR FAMILY came to the Throne of these Kingdoms. The LAWS and CONSTITUTION are the general Property of the Subject—not to defend, is to relinquish; and who is there so senseless as to renounce his Share in the common Benefit, unless he hopes to profit by a new Division of the Spoil. The highest Station, Sir, and the greatest Glory that any Mortal can aspire to, is to be during the whole Course of his Life, the Support of GOOD, the controul of BAD GOVERNMENT, the protector of Virtue, the Patron of Industry, and the Guardian of PUBLIC LIBERTY. When our Rights are invaded, our Feelings ought to tell us how long we ought to submit, and at what Moment it would be Treachery not to RESIST. The present Situation of his Country and America. (*Thanks to you, Sir, the best of Kings*) is alarming enough to rouse the Attention of every Man, who pretends to have a Concern for the Public Welfare. Bad as it is, Sir, there is no Extremity of Distress, which, of itself ought to reduce a GREAT NATION to Despair. A Luke-Warm Conduct is always odious; in Times of National Ruin, highly CRIMINAL. We owe it to our Ancestors to preserve entire those Rights which they have delivered to our Care; and we certainly owe it to our innocent Posterity, not to suffer their DEAREST INHERITENCE to be destroyed. If we are sensible of these sacred Claims, we shall find there is an Obligation, binding upon OURSELVES, from which nothing can acquit us.—A PERSONAL INTEREST, which we cannot SURRENDER.

Every Man is apt to delight in his own Country. I am proud to confess a particular Predilection for mine, and would give ample Testimony of my Love for it, by spilling the last Drop of my BLOOD in its Defence. The Authors of the CRISIS, Sir, only think favourably of YOU, as your ACTIONS correspond with the known Laws of JUSTICE, and the Principles of the CONSTITUTION. No Man, Sir, will be be more faithful and Loyal to you than they, while they are sensible you make the Good and Prosperity of the People, your Glory; none more your Enemies, when we are convinced you do the contrary.

It would be well for you, Sir, not to plume yourself on the Security of your TITLE to the CROWN, but recollect, that as it was gained by ONE REVOLUTION, it may be lost by ANOTHER.

On *Wednesday the 9th of August at Ten o'Clock in the Forenoon, was published by* T. W. SHAW, *in* Fleet Street, *Price Twopence Halfpenny.*

A   C R I S I S *Extraordinary,*

Proving, unanswerably, that the KING supports a Faction against the Laws and Constitution, that the AMERICANS are not REBELS, and that those who would rise to the State and Liberties of ENGLISHMEN, must rise thro' BLOOD.

Printed and published for the Authors, by T. W. *Shaw*, in Fleet-Street, opposite Anderton's Coffee House, where Letters to the Publisher, will be thankfully received.

THE
CRISIS

NUMBER XXXII   To be continued Weekly

SATURDAY, AUGUST 26, 1775   [Price Two-pence Half-penny

A ROUGH SKETCH
For the ROYAL ACADEMY.

SHUT not the Door, good *Hertford*, I'am but One,
  A single Sufferer can't alarm the THRONE.
  No *Mayor* am I, no Sword and Mace I bring;
No *Suit prefer*, to terrify a KING.
No rude *Petition* in my Hand I bear;
I grieve in Silence, I prefer no Pray'r
Nor want the *Mouth-piece* of *Recorder Eyre*(1)
with no bent Knee I'll worship THRONES and STOOLS.
They who repeat this *Farce*, are *passive Fools*;
No *Lyes*, on my account, shall *Hertford* forge;
I'll wring (like *Beckford*,) no *Reply* from GEORGE;

(1) This Man pitifully deserted that patriotic Lord Mayor *Mr. Beckford*, when he went up with his first spirited Remonstrance to the Throne, for which he has since been made a Baron of the Exchequer.

Let him reply above, when Heav'n demands,
Thousands of murder'd Subjects at his Hands,
Let him erect th' *impaling Stake* and *Wheel*;
Then seem *astonish'd* that his SLAVES can *feel*,
I'll force (like WILKES) no (1)Lines from *Mansfield's* Pen,
Which he's asham'd of, when he thinks agen:
And courts his *pliant Master* to *disclaim*
Mean *Hertford's* Pride—e'en let him take the Blame.

Let *Laureat Whitehead*[1] his Invention rack,
And deify a DOLT to earn his SACK;
Let *pension'd Johnson* toil, with aching Head,
To burnish up in *Gold* a *Lump* of *Lead*;
In Verse, or Prose, I'll make no TYRANT vain,
Nor praise the Virtue of a NERO's Reign.
Sooner shall *Whitehead* in his Butt be drown'd,
And *Johnson* be ador'd on (2)*Salem's Ground*;
Sooner shall *Bute* renounce the Name of Scot,
And *James's Claim* by *Mansfield* be forgot;
Sooner from *Court* shall Guilt and Vice depart;
KING, *Lords*; and *Commons* wear an honest Heart,
SOLOMON's Wisdom in a FOOL be known,

(1) Lord *Hertford's* late Letter to the *Lord Mayor*, penned by *Lord Mansfield*, and since appologized for, explained away, and in a Manner disavowed by the Court, who in this Instance over-shot themselves.

(2) In New England, where he was lately most deservedly burnt in Effigy, for his infamous Pamphlet, *Taxation no Tyranny*.

1. William Whitehead had been poet laureate for nearly twenty years. His skill at play writing matched his talent for verse, and he had at least a couple of successes on Drury Lane, with the help of his friend David Garrick. I should note here an interesting omission: *The Crisis* says nothing in this issue or the next about the King's August 23rd proclamation denouncing "many of our Subjects, in diverse parts of our Colonies" for rising in rebellion. The *London Evening-Post*, the *Morning Chronicle* and *Morning Post* had all printed it two days before, on the 24th.

And genuine TRUTH be utter'd from the THRONE.
No Slavish Doctrines from my Pen shall spring,
I'll *strip* no Subject to dress out a *King*;
But ev'ry *Villain, pension'd, plac'd, or crown'd*,
Shall on my Canvas, *like himself*, be found.
Burke, Saville, Barre, in my faithful Tints,
Shall see how *Meredith* and *Conway* squints;[2]
Not with a Cast which Nature gave their Eye,
But at round Sums, which on *North's* Table lie:
Let *these* but speak, no Want of Votes appears:
They win the *Commons*, and secure the *Peers*.
Charm'd by these Spells see *Conway's* Vigour flag,
And frail Sir *William* grasp at *Treas'ry Bag*,
The *Baronet* for Wealth quits Honour's Course;
The Soldier takes but a *Regiment* of Horse.
Pension'd and Plac'd these *Quandam-Patriots* laugh;
One shakes his Purse, and t'other wave's his (1)Staff,
Of every hopeful Plant are these the Fruits?
Can *North's* Breath blast *Britannia's* strongest shoots?

(1) As a General Officer.

2. Edmund Burke, Sir George Savile, Isaac Barré, William Meredith and Henry Seymour Conway were all, in one way or another, opposed to elements of North's get-tough colonial policy of 1774. That they did not always agree on what they supported as well as what they found objectionable is a good reminder that the opposition did not present a united front. Burke and Savile were closely linked with the Marquess of Rockingham, while Barré was more closely tied to Pitt (Chatham), with Meredith and Conway vacillating between this position or that—though, notably, Conway would be the one to introduce a proposal in the Commons calling for an end to the fighting in North America after Cornwallis's debacle at Yorktown. For Conway, as with many others, ending the hostilities was a way of avoiding, not recognizing, American independence. See my "Ending the War and Winning the Peace: The British in America and the Americans in Vietnam" *Soundings 70* (1987):445–74; and, for the fractured nature of oppositionist political factions, Frank O'Gorman, "The parliamentary opposition to the Government's American Policy 1760–1782" in Dickinson, ed., *Britain and the American Revolution*, pp. 97–123; which summarizes much of what O'Gorman had argued in *The Rise of Party in England* (London: George Allen & Unwin Ltd., 1975).

The fairest Virtue with Infection tinge,
And catch our *Eagles* in *Corruption*'s Spring?
Safe from *North*'s Lure can no firm *Patriot* fly?
Abroad, at *Home*, must FREEDOM *crouch* or die?
Crouch, like a patient Camel, at a Beck,
Till *George* ascends his *Zenith* from her Neck?
Or else, in sulky State, her Back bestrides,
Whilst *Bute* admires, how well his Scholar Rides?
How rich his Trappings! By shrewd *Grenville* vamp'd;
Supurb in (1)Rags and Sheep Skins duly stampt,
Permits and *Cockets*, in huge Holsters swag;
What Elephant so overwhelm'd could wag?
Tho' Taxes upon Taxes load the Pad,
Bute adds his Weight to make the Creature mad.
To all her plaints affecting to be blind,
Th' *unfeeling Thane*, trys to get up behind.
But finding how she Kicks and Flings for Ease,
Bids *North* unload full *half an Ounce* of TEAS(2)
North to his Charge repairs with nimble Feet,
But GEORGE with Turkish Firmness keeps his Seat;
Persists, tho' *gen'ral Ruin* shoul'd incurr,
And as a Test to Spirit, adds the (3)Spur.
Not *Mars* himself, not *Moloch* ever made
So grim a Show, in *Human Blood array'd*
On ev'ry side, behind him, and before,
His dull Ears pierc'd with Groans, he rides in GORE;
Smiling he views *Destruction* raging round,
And *brave Bostonians* biting *Freedom's Ground*.
How is *this God* in Extasy dissolv'd,
To see ev'n Infants in Death's Snares involv'd!

(1) The Materials of Paper and Parchment—Alluding to Mr. *Granvile*'s *Stamp Act*, which created the first ill Blood in America.

(2) Alluding to the ridiculous Reduction upon that Commodity, by Way of Lenitive.

(3) The Spur of Famine, Slaughter, and Desolation.

Th' *expiring Babe* cling to it's *Mother's* Side,
To find those milky Streams which FAMINE dry'd
Famine let loose on ev'ry Sex and Age,
To sooth a TYRANT'S Impotence and Rage,
Himself a Father, yet wants Sense to feel,
And in the Suppliant sheaths his murd'rous Steel.

Thus are you Drawn, Great Sir, but not by (1)*Dance*;
By Royal Hands—by *Prussia*, *Spain*, and *France*,
The *first* to *Hanover*, extends his Eye,
Some Kings are born to fight and some to (2)CRY.
The *other Pow*'r deludes *you* till the Time,
Comes to supplant *you* in the Freer (3)Clime
The *Third* perceives you're *cruel*, *proud*, and *dull*,
In Heart a *Pidgeon*, and in Wit a *Gull*;
She laughs to see you throw the Sov'reign by,
To feed through Optic Tubes your vacant Eye;
To see you spurn God's Laws, on Subjects War,
Yet pry into those Laws which guide a Star,
To see you gape at Planets while they stray,
And take Old Saturn, for the *Milky Way*;
To think how little that poor Prince must know,
Who bays the *Moon*, when he should look below.
To see how KINGS in privacy appear,
When *Baubles* claim the Heart, their Eye, their Ear;
When Wisdom's Fruits in Royal *Toyshops* grow;
Pictures for Study plac'd, and Books for show.
At *Kew* the World admires your great Designs,
Where (4)Cielings glory in your Princely Lines;
Not Lines which speak a Genius for rude Wars,

---

(1) The Painter.

(2) Lord Mansfield and Lord Hertford can explain this.

(3) America

(4) A Fact.

But such as *Mimic Wheaten Straws* and *Stars*.
Thro' *George*'s Works what splendid Fancy roves,
Adorning shady Temples, and Alcoves!
Not less he charms amidst a Levee full;
So stalks among tame Sheep the surly Bull.
Tho' *France* trips neater round the courtly Ring,
France can't display such *Buttons* as *our* KING.
Buttons by no inferior Genius wove,
Or plann'd—divinely wrought—and fit for Jove.
Buttons, projected by *Great Britain*'s Sire;
He drew the Model, and *he* chose the *Wire*,
Minerva's Self close by the Artist lurk'd,

And secretly inspir'd him as he work'd.
Let *Prussia*'s Hero ape the God of War;
We boast a greater *Mars*, a bolder *Tar*,
With *Prussian* Camps *Blackheath*, *Hyde Park*, shall vye,
At *Portsmouth-Fights*, our *Neptune* scorns to fly.
Does *Sandwich*, or a God, the Trident hold?
How *British Fleets* stream (like Twelfth Cakes) with Gold!
The Cannon's touch'd—what Soul unchill'd by Fear,
This prelude to a dreadful Fight can hear!
What earthly Prince can stand the furious shock,
Without a *cold Collation*, and *Old Hock*!
Yet GEORGE, serenly calm, in Smoak and Blaze,
On *Sandwich*'s pale Cheek with smiles can gaze;
Breathes Courage into *Talbot*, and cheers up
His *Bully Denbigh*, with another Cup.
Tho' in the Midst of Battle's fiery Flakes,
No Terrors check his Royal Gust for—Cakes.
O happy *England*! did you know your Bliss,
When to your Sov'reign, no Toils come amiss,
Now, in *Hyde-Park* in Battle's heat he rides;
To-Morrow, within Shore, a Navy guides;
Bids his *First-Rates* disdain all Thoughts of *Fear*,

Nor strike—unless a *Spanish Frigate*'s near.
Since thus in hair-breadth Scapes *George* draws his Breath,
For *Public Good*, what *Tears* must wait his Death!
Ev'n such as *He* for (1)*Yorke*'s Destruction shed;
So weeps the *Crocodile* on *Nilus* bred.
The *Crisis* then shall mourn in *fun'ral Verse*,
And hang with *Elegies* her *Patron's Hearse*.
The *Nation* then usurping (2)*Garter*'s Place,
Shall in mute Scutcheons *blazon forth* her *Case*.
See, in just Colours, what a Piece displays
The State of *England*'s Bliss in *George*'s Days!
Here *standing Force* all *Civil Power* confounds,
And *naked Allen*'s cover'd o'er with Wounds;
Corruption there her unmask'd Visage shews,
And tries to make *Elections free* by *Blows*.
Balf and *M'Quirk* adorn Sir (3)*Beauchamp*'s Side,
Their *Courage* cooly view, their *Laws* decide;
Secure of *Pardon* ere their Work began,
With *royal Leave*, they *murder* all they can.
A *Treas'ry Bribe* gives their *hir'd Rage* an Edge,
And for their *Pensions North* becomes a Pledge.

A *warmer Canvas* shews *Bute's rising Sun*;
A *vicious Mother*, and a *Prince* undone;
She smiles at Postures *Aretino* gives;
He's taught to lisp "*a King's Prerogatives*."
The *Baby* learns to *weedle*, *weep*, and *lye*;
And with a Frown, puts *Magna Charta* by.
These are the Fruits of *Perfidy* and *Lust*!
Thus *Bute* proves true to *England* and his *Trust*!

(1) "*Kill the next Piercy yourself, my Lord.*"
(2) *King at Arms.*
(3) Sir *W. Beauchamp Procter*—at the Middlesex Election.

Nor in the Story is *sly Mansfield*'s Plot
Against our *Laws* and *Liberties* forgot;
(Mansfield) who moulds a *Jury* till they please;
Who in a *court of Law* makes *Scotch Decrees*;
Who bids the Criminal (1)HIMSELF BETRAY,
And makes *Records* (2)speak what he'd have 'em say.
Brave Wilkes confronts him with a *Patriot-Face*,
And in strong Colours tells his Country's Case.
In the *back Ground* see the STAR CHAMBER plac'd,
Hung round with *Hands, Ears, Tongues, Records eras'd*.
Envenom'd MANSFIELD at the CRISIS spits,
And Smiles whilst *Ketch* the Writer's Nostrils (3)slits.
There *Fame* reports the Wrongs that *Thickness* feels(4)
And *servile Apsley* weeps to lose the *Seals*.

Now see where *Lust of Power* wild Havock makes,
And every Frame, but *pious Nero*'s shakes!
The Artist, finishing what *Bute* first plann'd,
Pursues his subject with a trembling Hand;
Rolls thro' the Piece *sad Massachusett's* Flood,
Her ruins smoaking, and her Fields in Blood.
Driven to Despair, see *Bostonian's Genius* rise!
To wipe the Fear from all her Children's Eyes.
Liberty leads 'em to the tented Field,
And *Virtue* guards 'em with a heav'nly Shield.
Behold her Troops their dastard Foes surprize!
And at her Head *another Cromwell* rise.
How long will *Gage*'s flimsy Force endure!

(1) By administring *Star Chamber Interrogatories*.

(2) In Wilkes's Case *he* had the *daring Assurance* to erase and alter a *Record* upon *his own Authority only*, without *Writ of Error*.

(3) The Court of *Star-Chamber* often ordered these Numbers to be cut off.—Nostrils to be slit, &c.

(4) See the *Crisis* No. VII. and No. X.

Ticonderoga(1) and *Crown Point* are sure:
Freedom's awake, whilst *Tyranny*'s secure.
(2)*Christ's Vicar* triumphs in this fruitful Wreck,
And arms his *pious Children* at *Quebec*;(3)
Not with vain Weapons of *corporeal* Steel,
But with *Anathema*'s, which *Souls* may feel;
With *Pardons* to those Babes of heav'nly Stamp,
Who shall contrive to Poison (4)*Putnam*'s Camp;
Within the Laws of *Holy War* shall keep,
And bravely murder *Hereticks asleep*.
His Holiness thinks *England* may be won,
And hopes to make of *George* another (5)*John*.

Whilst thus disturb'd th' enrag'd *Atlantic* flows,
Britannia too is plung'd in *Civil Woes*.
Sound Policy her Streets with Slaughter fills,
And *Perseverence* multiplies her *Ills*;
Corruption pulls the Work of Ages down,
And *Justice* from a *Tyrant* tears his *Crown*.

Powr's furious Storms, *Wars, Famines*, Terrors past,
America's bright Sun breaks forth at last.
With *Vict'ry* see the closing Story fill'd;
Bostonians free, their fertile Fields re-still'd;
Their *Senate* seated—not *in Tears* to save
Their *suppliant Sons* from *Famine* and the *Grave*;
But *independent*—to pronounce that *Law*,
Which shall, in Times to come, keep *Kings* in Awe;
Their native Kings—no more to *Britain bound*,
But Masters of *themselves* on happier Ground;

(1) These important Places were taken by the brave *Americans*, whilst their Enemy were asleep in their Beds.

(2) The *Pope*.

(3) Where we have established *Popery* by Act of Parliament.

(4) An American General.

(5) K. *John*—an abject Dupe to the *Pope*, and a Tyrant to his Subjects.

Not gall'd by Chains beneath a *Tyrant*'s Gripes,
Nor meanly crouching under *slavish Stripes*;
No more insulted by a *butchering Band*,
But Guardians of their *Rights* and *native Land*;
America no more shall bend the Knee,
Bless'd in a State that's *virtuous*, *rich*, and *free*,
And well divided from *her Foes* by Sea.
No longer for a *British Vassal* known,
But boasting *Laws*, *Fleets*, *Armies*, *Kings*, *her own*.
In Pray'r *she* turns to Heav'n her thankful Eyes;
To Heav'n, that bids *her* now to *Empire* rise;
Lays at her Feet the *Tyrant*, and his *Tax*,
A Body *headless*, and a wreeking *Ax*.(1)

C A S C A.

Printed and published for the Authors, by T. W. *Shaw*, in Fleet-Street, opposite Anderton's Coffee House, where Letters to the Publisher, will be thankfully received.

(1) If the *American* Scene should close *thus*, it will be fullest and *best* Answer that can be given to that *vile ministerial Pamphlet, Taxation, no Tyranny*; written to please a *foolish Tyrant*, justify an *impious trembling Ministry*, and delude an *insulted, patient, Nation*.

THE

C R I S I S

NUMBER XXXIII   To be continued Weekly

SATURDAY, September 2, 1775   [Price Two-pence Half-penny

*** Whilst the News Papers are Daily FILLED (in compliance with a rediculous Proclamation, and to the eternal Disgrace of the Printers) with the laboured Performances of Ministerial Writers in favour of DES-POTISM; the CRISIS will be found to contain the most spirited Essays in support of the CONSTITUTIONAL LIBERTIES of ENGLAND and AMERICA, and the natural Rights of Mankind. The Authors are determined to proceed at this dangerous and alarming Crisis, even at the hazard of their Lives; regardless of any STAR CHAMBER Proceedings of the King's Attorney General, or Ten Thousand PROCLAMATIONS, fabricated by the infamous Minions of an arbitary DESPOT, and issued from the Sink of Corruption. Firmly persuaded they shall meet with the Assistance, Support, and Protection of those who are the real Friends of their Country.

———How short of reason he must fall,

Who thinks *all* made for *One*, not *One* for *all!*———Pope.[1]

1. From "Epistle III" of Alexander Pope's still popular *Essay on Man* (dedicated to Bolingbroke), which the author(s) could have pulled from numerous sources. In this

MY two last Papers, described the *morbid State* of the *Ministerial Majority* of the *great Council* of this Nation, pointed the only Cure by *Dissolution*, and shewed the Reason and Necessity for applying that Cure in time. I shall still pursue my Thoughts upon that Subject. And here I must averr, that a *Patriot King* can neither Think nor Act with a venal and corrupt Parliament. The *Brunswick Family* were called to the Crown of this Kingdom as *Patriot Princes*, in favour of Liberty and the Protestant Cause. Has Liberty been supported by the Violation of the Rights of Election, as in *Wilkes*'s Case? Has the Protestant Religion been maintained by the late *Quebec Bill*, for establishing Popery in that Part of his Majesty's Dominions? But the Father of our Church, the Primate and Metropolitan of all England, has not hesitated to declare lately in the House of Lords, that, in his Opinion, the *Quebec Bill* had not established, but only tolerated Popery in that Province,—Fye, Fye, my Lord!—read the Bill again:—your Grace's Character should be more sacred than that of a *Mansfield*, a *Denbigh*, or a *Sandwich*. Permit me to assure you, that it can be no Honour to your Grace to resemble your Predecessor *Laud*, in any Part of your ecclesiastic Character.

If our Norman Conqueror, *William*, thought it Wise to pay some respect to the National Constitution, will a *Brunswick* ever set his Face against it? Could that Patriotic Legislature, to whose paternal Care we owe our present happy Establishment in Church and State, could they have supposed that any future King would connive at the most dangerous Innovations in both? Would a Patriot King have suffered so wicked, so anti-constitutional a Parliament, to have sat another

---

case I went to the *Collection of Essays, Epistles, and Odes* (London: J. James, 1762), p. 30. The full stanza reads:

"Know, nature's children shall divide her care;
The fur that warms a monarch warm'd a bear.
While Man exclaims, "See all things for my use!"
"See man for mine!" replies a pamper'd goose:
And just as short of Reason he must fall,
Who thinks all made for one, and not one for all."

Day? Could such a King have been afraid of wanting Supplies, when he had gained the Hearts of his People? Could a Dissolution of one of the most iniquitious Parliaments that ever infested England, have been productive of any other Consequence, than that National Happiness which was the primary Object at the glorious Revolution? It is true this Parliament was dissolved at last, but for no Patriotic Reason; the Administration saw, and feared a glimmering Spark of Virtue, not yet totally extinguished by Luxury and Corruption. They feared a Test and Association.—Shall we say that our Sovereign feared it too? Were all the three great Estates of this Kingdom in league against the Rights and Liberties of the People? I could wish that a Statesman of Lord *Mansfield*'s acknowledged Abilities, would give an Honest Answer to this Question. If either, or both of the inferior Estates were culpable (as they most certainly were) a Dissolution of that arbitrary Body was but national Justice. This Justice was not only delayed, but denied, in defiance of Magna Charta, the great Bulwark of the English Constitution. If that sacred Act of Parliament is yet in force, and not erased or destroyed, it will Support me in asserting, that Justice has been withheld, by not dissolving, at the Suit of the Subject; and the most flagrant System of Iniquity has been promoted by dissolving the last infamous Parliament at the instigation of the Minister; who is really, and truely, Lord *Bute* still. To that detested Influence we owe every national Grievance since the Commencement of the present Reign. Two of the greatest of these Grievances are the long Continuance of the last, and the Smuggling of the present Parliament. The Consequence of which will, most probably, be a Civil War in *England* and *America*; nor will that War remain unembroiled by the hostile Powers of *France* and *Spain*. By the sudden and artful Dissolution of the last Parliament, Corruption was not only connived at and tolerated, but (like Popery by the *Quebec Bill*) it was encouraged, propagated, and established.

When the People petitioned for a Dissolution of that execrable Parliament, they were answered with Contumely and Frowns. At that Tyrannic Period, when the Lower House was Rotten, were not Twenty-five found Peers in the Upper, who had Courage and Honesty enough to do their Duty by procuring Justice for the People? Had they all forgot the Seventy-third Clause of Magna Charta?[2] or, is that glorious Statute obsolete? Perhaps, a Repeal of it is to be attempted by the corrupt Majority in the present Parliament. Till that Charter is annihilated, the Peers of England (I mean the Honest Part of them) are bound to see Right and Justice done to all the People. Though they are not the Representatives of the People, they are the Guardians of the Realm, and as such they are answerable to the People for all the bad Effects of any unjust Conduct in the Sovereign, against which they did not oppose all their Weight. It is not enough that they protest in their own Journals against Arbitrary and unjust Proceedings; they ought also to demand, and as far as in them lies, to procure Redress. I will not (in the insolent and gross Language of Lord *Denbigh*) say that far honester Men than his Lordship were wicked and traiterous Men for not doing this; but I will say that their courtly Modesty has betrayed them into a Breach of national Trust; for which Breach they are accountable to the whole Realm. Though they are not Delegates of the People, they are, like constitutional Eyes in the Body Politic, bound to be watchful and observant over the other two Estates for the Public Good; that no Innovations may be made, that no Strides towards Despotism may be taken by either. They are Part of the great Council of the Crown by Birth, when in Parliament assembled; but they can neither live, nor act with Dignity, in such Times as these, unless they live and act for their Country. What pernicious Effects to the whole British Empire have flowed, and are still likely to flow, from their Modest and passive Silence, at a Time when the whole Kingdom was

---

2. The author(s) meant clause 63, the last in the 1215 great charter, rather than 73 (or, more likely, it was a printer's error): "Wherefore we wish and firmly command that the English church shall be free, and the men in our realm shall have and hold all the aforesaid liberties, rights and concessions well and peacefully, freely and quietly, full and completely for them and their heirs of us and our heirs in all things and places for ever, as is aforesaid. Moreover an oath has been sworn, both on our part and on the part of the barons, that all these things aforesaid shall be observed in good faith and without evil intent." From the translation in Holt, *Magna Carta*, Appendix 6, p. 473. John disavowed the charter—which had been written for him, not by him—as soon as he felt it was safe.

alarmed, and just supplicating the Throne for a Redress of Grievances! to be relieved against the daily Oppressions of a corrupt Majority, stood foremost in their Prayers. They prayed (and well they might) above all Things, for a Dissolution of the last perfidious Parliament. It was denied them in prejudice of Justice and the Constitution, to be granted shortly afterwards in favour of Tyranny and Corruption.

Let us now mark the Consequences of this Denial in the one Case, and of this ready Compliance in the other. Here We too may be well astonished in our Turn, and astonished with much more Reason than a Constitutional King could be, at the just Petitions of an injured and aggrieved People.—We are astonished at an impious attempt to change the Constitution of England by violating the Rights of Election. We are astonished at the Tyrannic Treatment of *America*, who has an equal Right to the same Constitution. Nor can we agree with Lord *Mansfield*, (who as Chief Justice of England, ought to be the Guardian of English Liberty) when he declares in an illiberal, servile, and sycophantic Tone, that a bad Constitution is better than no Constitution at all. Yet his Lordship, like another *Drances* (whose Character he remembers)[3] is not ashamed to declare this in a *British Senate*. I Answer, that (whatever an eloquent Coward may think) it is better not to exist at all, than to exist a Slave! His Lordship, I presume, is of a very different Opinion. His late Sentiments on this Head respect America, whose Religion our Parliament are endeavouring to subvert in derogation of the royal Word to our settlers at *Quebec*; and whose Pockets they are picking, not by legal Taxation, but by Tyranny. For who will affirm that the Money of the Americans is the Property of

---

3. Drances was an aged leader of the Italians fighting against Aeneas and the Trojans who fled with him to a new land, as Virgil told the tale in Book II of *The Aeneid*. Drances suggests that they declare a truce so that both sides can bury their dead and find a more peaceful way to settle their differences. Whatever his motives, his suggestion is not followed and the fighting resumes, with the result being determined more by the gods than by men, Virgil emulating Homer in describing the outcome of battles. *The Aeneid* had been translated into English for London printers, all or in part, more than a dozen times in the eighteenth century.

the People of England? If not, how can it be legally disposed of by the Representatives of the People of England only, in a British Parliament, to which no *American Representatives* are admitted? The Civil Law says, your *Scotch Law, Lord Mansfield,* says, and our English Law says, nay common Sense says, *Nemo dat quod non habet.* "No one can give and grant what is not his own."—Had the last fatal Parliament been dissolved when they first attempted to Tyrannize, England might have escaped a Civil War, and America Desolation. I flatter myself that She will yet escape the Chains of English Tyrants; and if She must fall, that She will surrender Herself to some foreign Power, who cannot use her with more despotic Severity than her natural Parent. *Lord Denbigh* asked some Time ago in the House of Lords, what End Administration could have in enslaving *America*? I will Answer him without reserve.—Administration hopes for Plunder from *America.*— Corruption cannot be supported without Means.—They are grasping at the Treasures of *America,* not to defray the Expences of American Government, but for their own vile Uses. A free Parliament which alone can save this Nation, would destroy them. Traytors would be impeached and suffer. When the civil Counsellors of the Sovereign were called for, to what Asylum must *Bute* and *Mansfield* fly? *North's* Servility might, perhaps, be pitied; and the blustrings of a *Denbigh* and a *Sandwich* would be heard no more. Should the Hopes of these Men succeed, we should soon see them and their Dependants reaping the Spoils of their flagitious Labours. An arbitary and rapacious System of Government would ensue, and we should soon see a new Exchequer, and a new Treasury, arise out of the Ruins of *America.* To these there must be necessary and unnecessary Appendants, swarms of official Locusts; and those industriously multiplied, for the further Advancement of Corruption and Tyranny, not only in *America* but (as *America* has foretold) in *Great Britain* likewise. Nor would ministerial Providence be remiss in planting a standing Army in *America* to secure their virtuous Conquest, they would, like true Patriots, extend their Paternal Care still further; they would never rest till they had fixed their despotic Government upon a respectable and permanent Foundation. A Vice-Roy, a Bashaw of seven Tails, must be appointed to silence the Murmurs of his Captives with a Frown.—Thus have I reminded Lord *Denbigh* of the Ends which he and his corrupt Fraternity most certainly have in endeavouring to enslave *America*.

I now proceed to enumerate the further Consequences of not dissolving the late execrable Parliament in due Time, and of procuring another Parliament, by the basest Means, equal, if not superior in Merit to the Former. One of the most alarming Consequences will be, the destruction of our Liberties by the constituted Representatives, and fiduciary Guardians of the People; for such are the Lords and Commons of this Realm, in Parliament assembled. One Innovation in the System of political Government, will ever produce another. Thus will artful Tyrants effectuate a total Change of a national Constitution by degrees. Such a Change we must expect to see. The bloody and inhuman Scene is already opened in *America* to be closed in *England*. Had a former Parliament been dissolved at the Suit of the Subject, instead of the Minister, and had a subsequent Parliament not been smuggled, and infamously packed by a treacherous Surprize upon the People, the present wicked ministerial System had been broke; *England* had regained her Constitutional Freedom, (particularly as to her Rights of Election) and *America* had regained that State to which She is intitled to by the Laws of God, of Nature, of *England*, of Humanity—by the plighted Faith of Sovereigns, and by her own Merits and Virtues; the greatest of which is, not that She has bravely by her own Arm, subdued our savage Enemies, the Indians: not that She has as bravely assisted in subduing our more polite Enemies the *French*; but that She disdains to be subdued herself, by her more inimical and perfidious Parent.

Had that accursed Parliament been dissolved, and the Wicked taken away from before the King, then had his Throne been established in Righteousness; then had a most infernal Groupe of Traytors gained their Reward in this World, upon the Scaffold and the Gibbet; perhaps, their Holy Father, the Pope, (whose Power they are now establishing in *America*) might have ensured their Souls, for a valuable Consideration, in the next. Then had a deluded Sovereign once more recovered his own Honour, and the expiring Affections of his People; then had this Reign been no longer marked for Dissimulation, Hypocrisy, Perfidity, Prodigality, Cruelty, Injustice, Tyranny, and BLOOD. Then would the Descendants of the trayterous Thane, and his ministerial Herd, (the most Infamous and daring that ever yet made the Reign of a British King truly odious to his People) be taught by the recorded Punishments of their detested Ancestors,

——How short of Reason he must fall,

Who thinks *all* made for *One*, not *One* for *all*.

C A S C A.

N.B. In No XXXIV. we propose to DISSECT the Master Butcher, Lord Bute, Lord Mansfield, and the *Proclamation*.

Printed and published for the Authors, by T. W. Shaw, in *Fleet-Street*, opposite *Anderton's Coffee House*, where Letters to the Publisher will be thankfully received.

THE

CRISIS

NUMBER XXXIV   *To be continued Weekly.*

SATURDAY, *September* 9, 1775   [*Price* Two Pence Half-penny.

To Lord BUTE.

My L o r d,

I Shall address your Lordship with as little Ceremony as you have met with Occasionally, from certain great Personages, whose Names and Memories are odious to you, because they knew your Baseness and abhorred your Principles. The singular Iniquity of your Lordship's moral and political Character, makes all Apology unnecessary. Your Loyalty as a Subject, and your Virtues as a Man, are equally conspicuous. The Mischiefs which your baneful Influence has wrought throughout the British Empire, will endure perhaps, for Ages after your detested Person is mingled with the Dust. Your pernicious Counsels have destroyed our Commerce, checked and discouraged our Manufactures, distressed our Colonies, impoverished our Merchants, injured Public Credit, impaired our Trade, promoted Corruption, dishonoured the Nation, and plunged the most Virtuous part of our Dominions, in all the Horrors of a *Civil War*, which you most impudently affect to call *Rebellion*. Your Lordship should remember that what *Jacobites* call *Rebellion*, we *Revolutionists* term constitutional *Resistance*. We detest the Principles of the *Stuarts*, renounce their slavish Doctrines, and hold that Wretch to be an Enemy to this Kingdom, who shall attempt (like your Lordship) to revive them. Such Principles instilled into the Mind of a weak King, must be productive of another Revolution. Yet, in spite of this Reflection, your Lordship, in Combination with your Associate *Mansfield*, continues still to *persevere*. Under your united Efforts the *Crown* has lost its Dignity, the *Parliament* their Honour, the People their Security, and the Nation its Importance.

The grand Tribunal of *English Justice* is biassed by Pique and Prejudice; perverted by the crafty Insinuations of your pliant *Mansfield*, bullyed by the empty Blusters of a *Denbigh*, and betrayed into Acts of the most iniquitous Partiality by the outnumbering Votes of mercenary *Scotch Lords*, purposely sent down by your Lordship's Agents, to countenance the Lord High Chancellor of England, in a servile and base Compliance with the Commands of his Creator *Mansfield*.

In Proof of these Assertions, I refer your Lordship (though very needlessly) to the late Case of *Mr. Thickness* in the House of Lords, and to No. VII. X. and XXX. of the *Crisis*; where you will see (to your Shame) a true and striking Picture of *national Justice*, under the wise Government of *Bute* and *Mansfield*; which it is now become *Treason* and *Rebellion* (though the three Great Estates of this Kingdom are misled by you) to oppose. I again averr, my Lords, that under your united Efforts, the *State*, and every Appendage of it is a Snare for the People; all its *Councils* act in Subversion of our Rights and Liberties and the very *Cabinet* is become a *Pandæmonium*.

As your Lordship's *carnal* Sins were happily lessened by the welcome Death of your imperious *Mistress*, so your *political* Sins are like to find a speedy End, either in your *Master's* Ruin, or your own.

Your Lordship must not take this Epistle as *admonitory*, it is only meant as *declaratory* of that Sense which the whole British Empire has of your Lordship's Merits, and supreme influence and Power over the Property, Lives, and Liberties of *Englishmen*. Let me likewise add, that though I address your Lordship by Name, I neither wish for your Attention, nor your *Reformation*. Not for the First, as I mean to use you, at present (as you constantly use your *Sovereign)* merely as a *Vehicle*; not for the Second as I hope to see your Lordship shortly on the *Scaffold*. For these Reasons, my Lord, I make free with your execrated Name, for the single Purpose of conveying my Sentiments to the People; as your Lordship frequently makes use of your Sovereign's, for the sake of dispensing your corrupt Munificence among your Slaves, gratifying your Avarice and Ambition, or indulging your Malice and Revenge. Were your *Master* penetrable, I might wish that these Lines could find their Way to him; but your Lordship's Agents carefully guard every Avenue of Access either to his Person or his Understanding The one you have rendered Odious, and the other Contemptable. However, before the Executioner holds up your devoted *Head*, I will undertake to dissect your treacherous *Heart*; this will afford a useful Lecture to a deluded King; and *that* will be a joyful Spectacle to an injured People. Upon inspection of that Pernicious Organ, we shall be sure to find the blackest Ingratitude, the most atrocious Perfidy, the foulest Lust, the rankest Disloyalty, the meanest Duplicity, and the most dangerous Ambition. The three first of these *Virtues* discovered themselves long since, against your *former Master*, who raised you from the Obscurity of a *Scotch Lairdling*, to the Notice of an *English Court*. His generous Friendship first placed your Lordship on the lowest round of that Ladder, which you have since ascended with such impetuous Strides. He drew you forth (in an ill Hour) from a *little private Residence* which your Pride has now forgot. As soon as your Lordship gained Courage to look *upwards*, you basely rewarded his Benevolence by doing him repeated Injuries in the tenderest Point; In a Point, where not only his Honour, but a *Nation's*, was concerned. You fawned, you flattered, you insinuated, and at length effected your treacherous Designs, upon the Weakness and Vanity of a lascivious Woman. You had the audacions Villainy to hope for the production of another Reign of *Scots*. Your abandoned Principles, conjoined with more than *German* Lewdness, prompted your insatiate Vanity to a *Deed* which might lay the Ground-Work of your impious Designs upon this Kingdom. Whether your perfidious Wish succeeded, you best know; but your Lordship's Influence is as great as if it had. Not content with the humble Character of a Schoolmaster, you have most impudently assumed the *Father*, where (conscious of your unpardonable Guilt) you should have trembled to have interposed. But *Ambition* (the Vice of *Scotchmen*) would not suffer you to check your insolent and aspiring Hopes, by a Moment's reasonable Reflection. To your native Virtues, you added those of a *Bothwell* and a *Rizzo*.[1] Thus did you most ungratefully, most perfidiously, and most audaciously, requite your first princely Benefactor. After the period of your impious Hopes of producing a suppositious Burthen upon a People were at an End, you still submitted to endure your former loathsome Connection, for the sake of Rank and Lucre; and in hopes of preserving your Mock-paternal Authority during the inglorious Life of an unhappy Pupil, intrusted to your Care; whom you wished to fashion (and have fashioned) for your Purposes. Under the filthiest Yoke of female Lust, for which both Agent and Patient should have suffered Capitally, your Lordship most servilely condescended to maintain your *Power,* not at the Expence of *Honour,* (for you lost that upon your first perfidious Contact) but even at the Expence of *Health*; a Blessing, which is, for the sake of divine Justice, often granted to the worst of Men. Your Lordship is a striking Instance that Impurity of Mind and Body go together.

Though you have (to the general Joy) lost your guilty Paramour, though you have obtained more Riches and Honours than a wise Man would have wished, and far greater than a wicked one deserves, yet your Lordship still continues Restless and Dissatisfied; you still affect to *govern*; you still blindly and fatally persevere in your pernicious Counsels, at the hazard of your Life, and to the Ruin of the English Nation. Your hopes

1. This is yet another anti-Scots historical allusion. David Riccio had been an adviser to Mary Queen of Scots before court intrigue led to his murder. James Hepburn, fourth Earl of Bothwell, was Mary's consort before becoming her third husband, in a tempestuous relationship that ended with their estrangement and his eventual death in exile. Most of what readers of *The Crisis* knew about Mary before she was imprisoned in England and eventually beheaded probably came from William Robertson's *History of Scotland*, 2 vols. (London: A. Millar, 1759), or a later edition—there were six published in London by 1775 (where Riccio is rendered "Rizio"). Robertson, a Church of Scotland minister as well as widely respected historian, if indeed the basic source, would not have appreciated being put to such partisan use.

of greater Honours must be over. You are so generally detested by all Ranks, that you durst not ask, or receive them. Though you are Mean enough still to share the royal Bounty, and permit your Family to beg and pillage from your Sovereign, yet one might hope (since every Man's Hand and Heart is against you) that universal Hatred, conscious Guilt, Shame, Fear, and Contrition, for your past Offences, would induce, or rather impell your Lordship, to withdraw your baneful Influence before it is too late.

I am no Stranger to your Lordship's false Pretence for interfering still.— You say, you cannot in Honour refuse your Counsels to your Sovereign—nay, you dare to add, that purity of Heart is your Motive, and Innocence your Shield.—But would your Lordship chuse to own, even in your present House of Lords, the Discovery made by the late Duke of York? The Contempt and Indignation you was treated with by the late Duke of Cumberland?[2] The stinging Truths you heard, and the gross Contumelies you received from the deceased Duke of Bedford? Why did your Lordship, with so much of the *Stuart Blood* in your Veins, decline the *Challenge* of that fiery Duke? Why did you tamely receive the *Lye* from him? Was it merely in compliance with the long established Custom of a Court, which allows one political Knave to deceive and abuse another with Impunity? However this might be, to the last mentioned Duke you crouched; nay, you hid yourself from his Resentment, and contrived to sooth him by scattering Douceurs and Places amongst his *Gang.* To the two other Dukes your Lordship was most deservedly Odious, as you were well known by them to owe your rapid Rise to servile Lust, and secret Treason. They saw you live to be a stain to their Family and a pest to the Kingdom. They then feared, as we now feel, the Conse-

---

2. The author(s) resurrected all three men to underscore George III's perceived inadequacies: Prince Edward Augustus, Duke of York, the King's now-deceased younger brother, who, in the early days of George III's reign had struck many as brighter and more charming; Prince William Augustus, the Duke of Cumberland, hero of the Battle of Culloden and George III's uncle, now a decade gone, who did not hold his nephew in high regard; John Russell, the fourth Duke of Bedford, who died in 1771, his disdain for Bute and his frustrations with George III barely hidden.

quences of that fatal Ascendency which you have completely gained over the weakest Man in England. Were that Man's Sensations delicate, his Resentments Manly, or his Understanding moderately good, your Lordship had long since been wiped out of that Rank which you continue to disgrace. But (unhappy for England) the *Traytor* is suited to the *Tyrant*, and the *Tyrant* to the *Traytor*. Your Lordship has artfully thickened the Ignorance, fed the Pride, created and confirmed the Prejudices, imposed upon the Weakness, cherished and even administered to the Vices of your dull Superior, till he is become as a Lump of kneaded Dough, under the plastic Hand of your Lordship and your crafty Agent *Mansfield*.

As a convincing Instance of this Truth, let me ask your Lordship, Whether a late *Proclamation* might not with more Propriety, have been Published on the *First of April*, than on the *Twenty Third of August* last? It was calculated by your Coadjuror *Mansfield* plainly with a View of deluding the English Soldiers, who begin now to revolt at the Thought of *murdering* their Fellow Subjects. This Massacree must be attempted by none but *Scotchmen*. What Soldier (not an Ideot, or in Liquor) will be brought to think that the *Americans* (as this *Proclamation* declares) withstand the Execution of the *Laws?* Every Man of the meanest Capacity must see that they mean only to oppose the Execution of *Themselves and Families*, and to prevent the illegal Extinction of all Law; which it is not in the Power of a corrupt Legislature to effect.

Have the *Americans* levyed War against the *King*, my Lord? Or has your Lordship, in the King's Name, levyed War against them? Have they, in Truth, acted any other than a *defensive* Part? Is an *English* Subject bound, since the *Revolution*, to act a *passive* Part? At that memorable and blessed Period, were not certain *Rights* confirmed to them and their Posterity, which they are bound most Religiously to maintain and defend, even against a *corrupt Government?* Let us, for a Moment, suppose the worst of Cases that can happen; a corrupt and desperate Combination of the Three Great Estates of this Kingdom to enslave the Subject. Are the People to crouch in passive Obedience to such *Tyrants?* If *the Americans* have been guilty (as the *Proclamation* says) of disturbing the *Public Peace*, will Breaches of the Peace by *Mobs* in a Colony, warrant a Breach of royal Charters, an infringement of constitutional Rights, a Perversion of Justice, or alteration of the established Modes of Trial, in the *Vicinity*, and by *Juries*; are these Offenders (which were but few, and the lowest of the People) to be dragged out of the *Territory* to be tried by Persons who cannot be supposed to have the least knowledge (as a Jury should) of the Facts committed? Is this the Law of the Land? Or can that Law, the Birth-Right of an English Subject, be altered or taken away, even by an Act of Parliament? Most clearly not. The greatest and honestest Lawyers (Lord Chief Justice Holt[3] among the rest) have declared that even a Man's *right of Action* cannot be taken away by an Act of Parliament. Yet our *virtuous Parliament* not only annihilates their established Rights (the Inheritance of every Subject) but has sent out Fire, Sword and Famine, throughout a whole Country, because Breaches of the Peace have been committed by *Mobs*; and because the People justly and bravely claim a Repeal of all those unconstitutional and tyrannic Acts of a *venal Parliament*, which have robbed them of the clear Rights and Privileges of English Subjects; have sported with their Lives, their Liberties and Properties, and given them perpetual *Slavery* for their Charter.

Such Innovations, Impositions, and Oppressions, the *Americans* are expected to bear under your Lordship's Government, or they are proclaimed *Rebels*. If your Lordship should succeed in your present Stratagem, your pliant Parliament will shortly annihilate the *English*, as they have lately the *American* Constitution. They will crouch, like Spaniels, to have the Net drawn over themselves and their Posterity. That all Subjects are bound by Law to aid and assist in suppressing a *real Rebellion*, I agree, but are they also bound to aid and assist in

---

3. Sir John Holt, chief justice of the court of king's bench under William III, then queen's bench under Ann, was regarded in the 1770s—and even now by some—as one of England's greatest jurists. *Ashby v. White* (1704), where he put the rights of electors before any "privileges" claimed by the House of Commons, is usually cited as his most famous and controversial case. He had been celebrated in a biography (attributed to John Rayner) published in London just a decade before *The Crisis* made its debut. See Paul D. Halliday's essay on Holt in the *Oxford DNB*, 27:830–34.

suppressing lawful, *revolutional Resistance?* If the Rights of the Subject have been violated (as they clearly have) in *America*, can a flimsy Proclamation, or even a tyrannic Act of Parliament, sanctify these Breaches of English Liberty? Is the Defence of constitutional Rights, Rebellion, because a ministerial Parliament, or a depending Privy Council stiles it so? Falsities are not to be thrust down the Throats of *Englishmen* by a *Proclamation*. They, and the *Americans* have *Magna Charta*, the Bill of Rights, the Establishment at the Revolution, and they ought to have the CORONATION OATH, in protection of these, to depend upon. If either of these are violated, after dutiful Petitions have been proferred, and those Petitions have been refused, denied, or slighted by the Sovereign, it is with a very ill Grace, and entirely without Reason, that the *Crown* betakes itself to calling Names in a studied *Proclamation*. Let me now ask what *Attempts* have been made against the *King*, unless by repeated Supplications that he will remember his solemn Engagements, attend to his own Interest and that of his People, which ought to be but *One*; and listen to the Dictates of Reason, Justice, sound Policy, and Humanity? As to his *Majesty's* Crown and Dignity, are they endangered by any of his Subjects except your Lordship and your *Chief Justice?* Can your Lordships then (for I suppose you clubbed for this *Proclamation)* be in Sober, serious Earnest, when you charge all loyal Subjects to transmit full Information of all Aiders and Abettors to one of the principal Secretaries of State? If so, it may be Misprision of Treason[4] in me to conceal your Lordships. Had I the Dishonour of being a Member of the present House of Commons, I would impeach your Lordship of High Treason the earliest Day of next Sessions; for you yourselves, my Lords, have, by your wicked Counsels, excited this *Resistance*, which you nick-name *Treason*; and therefore you are yourselves the only *Trayters* in this Kingdom. Can your Lordships really wish to be brought (as you certainly deserve) to condign Punish-

---

4. "Misprision of treason" referred to those who could be accused of treason who, although not actively involved themselves, did nothing to stop or report what they knew to be a treasonous plan or act. For more on treason under English law, going back to a parliamentary statute passed in 1352, see n. VIII.2 supra.

ment, and to make your Exit upon Tower-Hill? Alas! you are too Circumspect, too Designing, and too Cunning, even for yourselves.

The Eyes of the *Military* begin to open, they now discern not only the Inhumanity, but the impracticability of your Lordship's intended Massacree in *America*. Passively obedient as Discipline hath made them, they yet feel they are *Men*. The Valour, Virtue, Generosity, and Humanity, of their Fellow-Subjects in *America*, have touched their Hearts. The compasionate and tender Terms offered to the poor Remains of the King's Troops, shut up in *Boston* by the brave *Washington* at the Head of a most powerful Army, not of *Mercenaries*, but of *Volunteers*, have convinced the simplest of his *Majesty*'s deluded Soldiers, that they are sent to *America* as so many Sacrifices to your Lordship's infernal Schemes. Reflection and sad Experience have now taught them that if they Conquered, they could be but dishonoured *Murderers*. If twenty thousand Men would be (as your Lordships Generals say) but a feeble Reinforcement in *America*, I have Charity enough to doubt whether your Lordship could find even *Scots* enough to compleat the Business; for your Lordship must know that the Lives of your Countrymen have been much more valuable to them since the *Union*. If you cannot muster a sufficient Number of *Scotchmen*, I flatter myself that your Lordship will hardly find a Body of English Troops to serve your Purpose. The latter are a kind of People not easily cajoled, deluded, or intimidated into a Service they dislike. They will not submit to be made use of as *Assassins*, or to be sent on such inhuman Expeditions as would disgrace the Cut-Throats of an Alley. How vain then is your Lordship's late delusive *Proclamation?* To what Purpose has your Lordship stooped to bribe the Publishers of a late occasional Paper called the *Remembrancer?*[5] Will the Suppression of such

5. *The Remembrancer* was a monthly published by John Almon, beginning in June 1775 and carrying into 1784, with a focus on American affairs. The allusion to a "bribe" is the author(s)' insinuation that Almon was paid by the ministry to steer a middle course, not to editorialize in any way and not to reproduce anything that would cast too harsh a light on imperial wartime policy. Almon's *Remembrancer* should not be confused with a weekly of the same title that appeared in the 1740s; for which see Jeremy Black, *The English Press in the Eighteenth Century* (Philadelphia: University of Pennsylvania Press, 1987), passim.

Truths as that Publication might contain, assist your Lordship's Hopes, or allay your Fears? Can your Lordship's Plans be disconcerted by every Information which the People of Great Britain may receive? Does the Success of your Lordship's Politics depend upon their being kept in profound Ignorance? If your Lordship's Zeal is real, and your Heart is truly loyal, instead of silencing the Voice of Truth, and poaching for Generals who will be base enough to receive the Price of *Murder* at your Hands; go forth yourself with your desperate Clans, and let us hear with Joy, that you have expired like a wounded Monster, in the Dust. Skulk no longer from the Public Eye, but quit your lurking-Place, and make the *cowardly Americans* fly at the Name of *Bute*. Prefer Destruction in the Field, to Death upon a Scaffold. Rather face the Vengeance of *America*, than wait till you receive the Dagger of a *Felton* in your perfidious Bosom. Should your Lordship, when your pernicious Soul is fled to the World of Spirits, have yet a Sense of what passes in this sublunary Globe, what a Change of Men, of Measures, and of Circumstances will you then observe? You will not then behold your Descendents (as you vainly Hope) enriched by the Plunder of vanquished and distressed *America*. You will not see her crouching, like a Vassal, under a *Scotch Vicegeneracy*, or lamenting her Calamities amidst the Ruins of her depopulated Cites. No—You will view, with a malignant Eye, the Ocean covered with her Fleets, and Sovereigns of great Nations suing for her Friendship, or dreading her Displeasure. You will not then see *Famine* preying on her People, her Habitations laid waste, her Empire filled with Slaughter, Desolation, and Distress; but you will admire the Richness of her Fields, the Industry of her Inhabitants, the Plenteousness and Opulence of her Cities, the Magnificence of her Palaces, the Abundance of her Commerce, the Strength of her Fleets and Armies, the Wisdom, Policy, Virtue and Stability of her Government; and, above all, the unerring Justice of her Laws.

With such a Scene of Happiness, your Lordship may contract that lamentable Period wherein you and your *Minions* governed, dishonoured and distressed *Great Britain* and *America*; when the Laws were violated, Justice prostituted, Liberty invaded, Subjects massacreed, the great Charter of the Nation and all its established Rights derided, *Corruption* openly admitted into Church and State, and suffered to take her Seat even in the

last resort of Justice; the three Great Estates of this Kingdom most venally united against the Constitution, the sacred Compact between Sovereign and Subject broken, Public Faith expiring, Civil Discord raging;
Weakness, Perfidy, and Tyranny, at length Dethroned; a discontented
People emigrating, and the Seat of Empire changed, after a necessary
Revolution, from *England to America.*[6] These will be the sure Effects of
your impolitic and inhuman *Perceverance*; the Vice not of brave, wise,
and *pious* Kings, but of dastardly, wicked, weak, and unfeeling *Tyrants.*
Then will the senseless *Idol*, which your Lordship Worships, (the Work
of your own Hands) be thrown down; then will your Lordship's Poster-
ity feel the Weight of all your political Iniquities, visited upon them and
theirs, and lament in deserved Poverty and Contempt, the complicated
Crimes of their ambitious Ancestors to the latest Generations. THUS
MAY DIVINE JUSTICE AVENGE THE SUFFERINGS OF AN IN-
JURED PEOPLE.

C   A   S   C   A.

Printed and published for the Authors, by T. W. SHAW, in *Fleet-Street*,
opposite *Anderton's Coffee House*, where Letters to the Publisher will be
thankfully received.

6. Benjamin Franklin had predicted that so many Britons would emigrate to the colonies that, combined with population growth through natural increase, North America
would become the true heart of the empire within a century. See his 1751 "Observations Concerning the Increase of Mankind," in Labaree, et al., eds., *Papers of Franklin*,
4:225–34. The failure to use that projected growth as a source of strength is reflected
in the inability to come up with a satisfactory system of governing the empire at that
moment, as imperial reformers considered seating Americans at Westminster, creating
an inter-colonial congress, or allowing colonial assemblies legislative autonomy. See my
"Federalism and the Failure of Imperial Reform" *History* 86 (2001):155–79. Immigration
as a source of strength for the newly independent nation caused Franklin to return to
the subject in the 1780s, as he encouraged immigrants to come but cautioned them
against delusive dreams of easy wealth.

THE

CRISIS

NUMBER XXXV   *To be continued Weekly.*

SATURDAY, *September* 16, 1775   [*Price* Two Pence Half-penny.

> Splendide *mendax*——   Hor.[1]
>
> What will not *artful Ministers* devise?
>
> O! how they triumph in their *glorious Lies!*

To the AUTHORS of the CRISIS.

GENTLEMEN,

AS one of your Correspondents, I beg leave to call upon you, and hope you will take this short Hint into Consideration: nay, I flatter myself that you have Interest enough to invoke the Assistance of Junius upon it. Unable to check the Progress of your *constitutional Paper*, either by *Prosecution*, or *Persecution*, the *Runners* of

---

1. A phrase from Horace's ode to Mercury, referring sarcastically, in this case even ironically, to ministers being "nobly untruthful."

Administration have been industrious lately in scattering oblique Hints abroad, that the *Ministry themselves* have set *your Paper* on Foot, by Way of laying a *sure Ground* for stopping the *Liberty of the Press.* Their Drift is easily perceived. They wish, by every, and any Means, to stop your Channel of *popular Information.* The Light of *Truth* is too strong for them. The weekly Product of *your Press* is too alarming.

In the name of *England* I call upon you, Gentlemen, not only to stand forth in print, in Defence of your own Cause, and that of your Country, but to chastise this *abandoned and artful Ministry,* for their *insolent Aspersions.* Should they ever *dare* (but what will they *not dare)* to attack the *Press,* no Hand that can hold a Dagger ought to rest, whilst there is a Heart among *this hellish Gang* that can be perforated. They ought to be pursued, and dragged from behind the *Throne,* to *instant and immediate Justice.* Their mangled Limbs should be scattered throughout the Palace of any *Tyrant* who shall presume to interpose between the *Temerity of Minions,* and the *just Revenge* of an *insulted Nation.*

Administrations in such a Government as *Ours,* act at their *Peril.* They are always, and always ought to be, accountable to the *People.* They are bound not only to *ensure,* but to *hear, to pay Attention* to, the *Sentiments of the People,* and to *redress their Grievances.* Under a *Whiggish King, Ministers* of *State* are *Servants of the Public.* Under a *Tory King* (who must be an Enemy to *Revolution Principles)* they are Instruments of *Despotism* and *Destruction.* Under the *First,* they will hear *patiently,* proceed *justly,* and *redress wisely.* Under the *Latter,* they will act *tyrannically* (like our present Ministry) and endeavour to stifle the Voice of *just Complaint;* first, by stopping *Pens,* and then by stopping *Mouths.* They will proceed from the *Press* to the *Person;* they will take away *Life* as well as *Liberty;* and for every *popular Libel* (that is, for every *popular Truth)* which is *published,* there will, at length, follow a *ministerial Assassination.*

A *wicked Administration* may well be jealous of the *Press.* It is like a national *Alarum bell,* wisely placed in the *Palladium* of British Liberty, to proclaim the approaching *Enemy* by Day, and to deter the undermining *Thief* at Night.

As for the *respectable* (for it is ignorant and ridiculous to say *sacred*) Character of a *King*, it will ever be *revered*, whilst it continues *amiable* and *good*: When it is *warped* by the *wicked Advice* of *designing Men*, it must ever be *stigmatized* and *detested* by a *Free People*.

This is the Condition of that painful Pre-eminence called *Sovereignty* in all Nations, which are not, and will not submit to be, *enslaved*. Upon this Condition is the *Crown* received among *Us*; upon this Condition, only, can it be held, with *Dignity*, *Peace*, and *Safety*. There is a *Majesty* of the *Sovereign*, but there is, also, a *Majesty* of the *People*. If the *Sovereign* cannot brook *Offence*, he must neither countenance nor offer *Violence*. Such Attempts cannot pass without *due Notice* from the *People*. They must be *undertaken* with the greatest Hazard; they cannot be *enforced* without the *Severest Censure*, and, perhaps, *at last*, without *exemplary Punishment*.

C A S C A.

***One of the greatest Blessings this Nation enjoys, superior to any other, is, undoubtedly, the *Liberty* of the *Press*, that noble Freedom of venting our Compliants, and speaking our Mind in Print. In most other Countries, no Man dare to open his Mouth on Religion or Politics, but in Conformity to Government, nor dare to publish his Sentiments, but at the Hazard of his Safety—What is this but perfect *Slavery?*—There was a Time when it was so with Us, when nothing could appear without an *Imprimatur*—But some Men, of more Resolution than others; dared to open their Mouths against arbitrary Proceedings, and tyrannical Encroachments; They shewed their deluded Countrymen the great Advantage of Public Spirit, convinced them of their former Vassalage, and urged them to stand forth in Defence of their Rights and Privileges; they did so; and by a noble *Resistance*, a *Resistance* well timed, secured Freedom to their Posterity, and immortal Honour to themselves.—This Freedom we have long been in Possession of;—it is now become the Birth-right of Englishmen—and this Freedom the Authors of the CRISIS are determined never to relinquish, but with their Lives.—The Establishment of a FREE PRESS, and the under-written Address to the Public, will, the Authors doubt not, be a sufficient and satisfactory Contradiction to all the ministerial LIES that have been fabricated against the CRISIS, by a Tribe of pensioned Rascals, who are employed to write down Truth, and establish Falshood, only with a View to *deceive* and *mislead* the People, and to draw their Attention from the true Channel of *faithful* Information, and from that *Destruction* with which they are now threatened.

A

FREE PRESS.

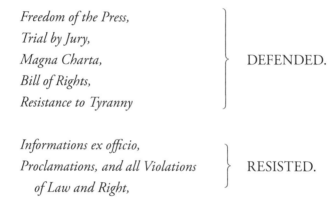

Freedom of the Press,
Trial by Jury,
Magna Charta, } DEFENDED.
Bill of Rights,
Resistance to Tyranny

Informations ex officio,
Proclamations, and all Violations } RESISTED.
 of Law and Right,

To the P U B L I C.

FLEET STREET, *September* 16, 1775.

THE LIBERTY of the PRESS is inestimable, it is sacred, and shall not be destroyed by the arbitrary Efforts of a *Pious* King and Tory Ministry.—Whilst most of the NEWS PAPERS are Daily filled with the laboured Productions of MERCENARY Writers, employed to gloss over the infernal Measures of the present Reign; the CRISIS will be found to contain the most spirited Essays in favour of PUBLIC LIBERTY and the NATURAL RIGHTS of Mankind—I am determined at every Hazard, to support the FREEDOM of the Press, I shall never be intimidated by, nor submit to, any STAR CHAMBER

Summons from the king's ATTORNEY GENERAL, and by that Means leave myself at the Mercy of a *Scotch Chief Justice,* and sacrifice at once, the most glorious Privilege of my Countrymen, TRIAL by JURY.—I shall never pay any regard to PROCLAMATIONS, fully convinced they are issued at this Time, only to answer the infernal Purposes of DESPOTISM, and are a most daring and violent INFRINGEMENT on the established RIGHTS and LIBERTIES of the People of ENGLAND. Whatever Essays may be sent to me (fit for the Public Eye) in defence of the CHARTERED RIGHTS, and CONSTITUTIONAL LIBERTIES of the BRAVE *Americans,* who are nobly struggling in the Cause of FREEDOM, against the TREACHERY, FRAUD, and FORCE, of impolitic, cruel, bloody, and unfeeling TYRANTS, shall be immediately inserted in the CRISIS.—The Spirit and extensive Sale of this Paper, exceeds, perhaps, any Periodical Publication of the kind, since the last GLORIOIUS REVOLUTION. It was set on Foot at this IMPORTANT ÆRA, to open the Eyes of the *deceived, abused, betrayed,* and almost *enslaved* People of *England* and *America,* and to put them upon their Guard against the fatal Designs of the *Three* Estates of this Kingdom, most venally united to DESTROY the CONSTITUTION. The Authors, conscious of the rectitude of their Actions, and convinced of the Utility, the Necessity, and Advantage of such a Paper, are determined to persevere, and hope for the ASSISTANCE of those who are Friends to LIBERTY, and wish to transmit the blessings of FREEDOM to SUCCEEDING AGES; for this Purpose they will *enlarge* their Paper as *occasion* shall require, that every Essay through the Channel .of the CRISIS, may be conveyed to the Public AS SOON AS POSSIBLE.—Letters will be gratefully received,

By the Publicks most obliged,
and most obedient Servant,
THOMAS WILLIAM SHAW.
Printer and Publisher of the CRISIS.

N. B. Thirty-four Numbers of this spirited Paper, are already Published, and will be sent to any Part of England, CARRIAGE FREE, by directing as above.

HINTS for the AUTHOR of the CRISIS.

AS soon as the Queen became a Mother, the Carleton House Troops chose her for their Chief. Lady Mansfield's Sister, Lady Charlotte Finch, was, under the Denomination of Governess to the Prince, placed under the King's Roof, to prevent any but the Scotch and Germans getting Access to the Queen. The Lords Mansfield and Bute stipulated with her Majesty to cause her Family to be naturalized, and make them considerable in England; and she, on her Part promised to keep the king in their Hands, and abet all their Schemes. The Duke of York opposed the Importation of the Germans with so much Vehemence, that the King, refused to enter into the Queen's Measures: It was agreed she should have the Electoral Dominions for her Family. The King had promised the Government of Hanover to the Prince of Brunswick; but broke his Royal Word with him. The King of Prussia seeing the Spring of the King's Conduct, not only threatened to seize Hanover, and obtained a large Sum of Money, but two Years ago he laid Claim to the miserable Principality of Strelitz, which had long been mortgaged to the House of Brandenbourg, and the Queen's Friends discharged the Debt from England. In Germany all the unaccounted Millions center; and the Scotch have a Claim to the Places of Honour and Profit, as the Price agreed upon for the Services they have rendered the Queen. Several Scotch and Germans are employed to deceive the Public by false Representations in the public Papers, where most they feared Detection. The King's Brothers are banished [from] the Court, the only Means by which the King might know the Truth. The Duke of Gloucester will soon resign his Life, which has long been a Burden from the cruel Treatment he has received. The Queen revenges upon him the Opposition she found from the Duke of York. The Queen of Denmark solicited, when living, but in vain, to return to her native Land, whilst the Princess of Brunswick declares she will never see England, till governed by ENGLISHMEN.

The King is rather the Dupe, than the Knave, of the Faction, and would relent in Favour of America, if the Queen would let him; but her Party drives her on, and she wants the King to be absolute, to carry her Point of transplanting her own Family. Prince Ernest is ever at the King's Ear, pleading his own Cause, and Lady Charlotte Finch does her Duty by her Brother's Patron Lord Mansfield.[2]

These Facts may be of Use to your Pen, which, alone, can do Justice to an injured Country, by dragging forth the vile Crew who govern the King and ruin America. Expose them to the World, and you will have the Thanks of all true Patriots.

I am your constant Reader,

D E T E C T O R.

N.B. No.36 will be addressed to his *Pious* Majesty *GEORGE THE THIRD.*

Printed and published for the Authors, by T. W. *Shaw*, in Fleet-Street, opposite Anderton's Coffee House, where Letters to the Publisher, will be thankfully received.

---

2. Prince Ernest Augustus, the eighth of George III's children, was only five at the time; he would some day rise to the throne of Hanover. Lady Charlotte Finch was governess to all of the King's children, and had been for nearly thirty years. George Fermor, second Earl of Pomfret, was her older brother (see n. VIII.1 supra). Barlow's contemporaneous *Complete English Peerage*, 2:9, offered this description: "His lordship is an excellent scholar, and a man of fine understanding, but somewhat precipitate and flighty in his conduct."

THE

CRISIS

NUMBER XXXVI   *To be continued Weekly.*

SATURDAY, *September* 23, 1775   [*Price* Two Pence Half-Penny.

The *best of Kings* destroys us like a Flood,
Each Morning washes in fresh Streams of BLOOD;
Like PIOUS *Nero* mounted on a THRONE.
Thinks he's a GOD, and all Mankind his OWN.

An Ideal S C E T C H of a F O O L I S H   K I N G.
——Let the stricken Deer go weep.——

SHAKESPEARE.[1]

To the K I N G.

S I R,

LORD Bolingbroke has drawn a masterly Picture of a *wise King* in Idea, never, perhaps, to be realized in any Nation. As the contrary Character often has appeared, and may again, it seems a much easier Task to sketch out the Portrait of a *foolish King*. I will attempt to

---

1. "Why, let the stricken deer go weep, The hart ungalled play; For some must watch, while some must sleep; So runs the world away"—Hamlet's comment to Horatio, after the play within a play proved to his satisfaction that his father's ghost had told the truth

delineate this *Phantom*; but Woe be to the Kingdom it infests! —Indulging, Sir, my Imagination as an ideal Limner, I should. represent such a "*King of Shreds and Patches*" at the Head of a limited Monarchy, totally ignorant of the Constitution, fond of Government, but a Stranger to the Means. Trained in his Childhood to Hypocrisy, an early and habitual Practice would make him consummate in the Art. He would be told, no doubt, (as you have been) by his Preceptors, that the Operations of this Vice, in the Day of Affliction, may be of sovereign Use; but it can be of Use only to a *weak*, a *wicked*, and *designing Prince*. It may, indeed, at a desperate Juncture, (like the present) supply its narrow-minded Master's Purpose; but Artifice is the meanest Tool of the meanest Politician; and Hypocrisy (which you glory in, and daily practice) the meanest of all Artifices. Its inward Workings, when its Professor is a Genius, may, at a dead Lift, fill the Eyes of distressed Majesty with Tears.

Tears, well timed, and flowing from a Prince, are, perhaps, the happiest, and most powerful, of all Resorces, to subdue, at once, the stubborn Virtue of the firmest Patriot. But, Sir, such dramatic Stratagems, which you have too often made use of, are beneath a King. He must be a *Machiavel*, indeed in practical Hypocrisy, who can thus basely toil to seduce the fairest Virtue, and yet be capable, the next instant, of boasting (as you once did) with a smiling Sneer,* of the Conquest his infamous Duplicity had made. A Conquest which might perhaps, be followed by Remorse, Despair, and Suicide. Such a Prince, acting under such a Mask, would be, as the dissembling Richard says, "*Himself alone.*"[2]

---

* *Kill the next Piercy yourself, my Lord, said your Majesty to the Duke of Grafton, soon after the Victory obtained over the late Mr. York.*

---

and that his plan to exact revenge should proceed. From Shakespeare's *Hamlet*, Act III, Scene 2.

2. The "dissembling Richard" apparently refers again to King Richard in Shakespeare's *Richard III*, Act V, Scene 3, though the lines "Himself alone" do not appear here (or anywhere in a Shakespeare play, except in Act I, Scene 4 of *Coriolanus*). Richard not only hid his real self from others (hence the "dissembling"), but from himself, when

For the Honour of Mankind, it is to be hoped, that his equal never did, and yours never will, exist.—Such a Prince might be a *Native* of his Kingdom, but he would be an *Alien in Sentiment.* By the mere Accident of Birth, he might, probably, gain the Love of a generous People, without Merit or Attention; (as you have done) but, by his untoward Cast of Mind, he would lose it again, without Regret. A Want of Sensibility, joined to a natural Perverseness, but poorly marks the Father of a Country. Unacquainted with the Character, the Genius, the true Interests of his People, he would view them, Sir, through the false Medium which Ministers and Favourites (under the insolent and insidious Name of the King's Friends) hold out to his Majesty. Thus he would, assuredly, become the most unpopular Man in his Kingdom, except his prime Favourite. To this Minion's Tutelage, joined, perhaps, to that of a proud, vain, imperious, Mother, he might owe his Weakness, his Ignorance, his Misfortunes, and, at last, his Ruin. Despised by his People for his Folly, he would hate them for their discernment. Conscious that he had lost all Popularity, he would affect to scorn it, without reflecting, that the Contempt of a limited Monarch for the Affections of his People, must be the first and surest Step to his Destruction. Educated Sir, as you have been, like a *Stuart*, in despotic Notions, he would think (if he thought at all) and act accordingly. His very Vices would be idolized by his Flatterers, and dignified with the Name of Virtues. In the Language of *Court-Flies*, Hypocrisy would be Policy; Kneeling would be Piety and Religion. Even a daring Attempt in the most distant Parts of his Empire (by Way of Prelude) to subvert the established Religion of his Country, *which he had sworn at the Altar to maintain*, would pass, among these fawning Seducers of Majesty, for a splendid Instance of Moderation, and a tolerating Christian Spirit. The most bloody Acts of TYRANNY would be applauded, and encouraged by Addresses from a few mean, base, ignorant, slavish, bankrupt Merchants, and worthless Wretches in the Towns of

---

after his disturbing dream he blurts out "I am a villain: yet I lie, I am not." He tried to reassure himself that "conscience is but a word that cowards use." See *The Crisis,* nos. VI and XXXII supra, which sports with Lord North by casting him in the role of the disgraced and soon to be slain King.

Manchester, Lancaster, Leicester, and *Liverpool.* Partiality, Injustice, Slavery, and Death, and a manifest Neglect and Violation of the Laws, would usurp the Name of Mercy.

I can easily suppose such a King guilty of the greatest Breach of Justice, Trust, and Duty, by pardoning willful and wanton Murderers, ministerial Affassins, Sodomites, &c. &c. He would be merciful, at one Time, to oblige a Favourite, or a Whore, and, at another, merely (like a Baby) to shew his Power, not from any just, humane, or solid Reason, which, alone, can justify the Exertion of that amiable and God-like Part of the Prerogative. Let such Kings know, and you should know, that Mercy shewn to the greatest Pests of Society, is Cruelty to the Kingdom.

Nor is this the only Error which servile Adulation would countenance in *such* a Government, or Nick-name in *such* a Court. Meanness, there, even in Point of Royal Hospitality, would pass for Œconomy. Abstemiousness, practiced, not rationally, or philosophically, but timidly, merely to prolong an useless, invaluable, and detested Life, would be honoured with the Name of Temperance. An unrelenting, implacable, and Female Spirit of Resentment, (infinitely beneath a Prince towards his Subject) would be extolled as an Instance of Fortitude, Magnitude, and Resolution. But if a *Martyn,* a *Dun,* or a *Talbot* could be procured to dispatch the Object of his Hatred, his fawning Courtiers would applaud the murderous Principle, and procure a *Johnson* to record it in all the Bombast of *Scottish* Pedantry, as an Achievement worthy of an *Alexander,* a *Cæsar,* or a *George.*—From a puerile Fondness for military Exhibition and Parade, this Royal Baby would be celebrated for the Love of Arms. In short, these Court-Magicians would give to every Vice of their deluded tyrannic Master, the Semblance of Virtue. Perpetual Flattery wou'd teach him to look upon himself as a *Proprietor,* not as a *Father* of his People. From this Nation, a sullen, gloomy Pride (except in the varnished Moments of Hypocrisy) would over-cast his Countenance, and diffuse, not a placid Dignity, but an illiberal, haughty, and forbidding Air, over his whole Deportment. Far from being affable and gracious, he would seem to overlook his Subjects, as Beings of an inferior Species. Should Custom ever force him to take some Notice of them, he would do it, like you,

Sir, with all the empty Elevation of a Bashaw, who senselessly rates his Dignity according to the Number of his Tails; he would do it, not only with a supercilious Air of Self-distinction, but with manifest Reluctance and Contempt. The least Inclination of the Head to the Authors and Supporters of his Royal Pride, would be thought a most degrading Condescension.

In these Points of liberal Decency and Regard, he would be governed, not by parental Feelings, but, probably, like you, by a Scotch Preceptor, and French Dancing-master.

Instead of viewing his People with the easy Complacence of an affectionate Parent, he would scowl upon them with the haughty and contemptuous Brow of a disdainful Tyrant.

With him, as with you, (ever mindful of the Principles he had imbibed from his virtuous Tutors) his Subjects would pass for Slaves and not for Children.

He had, long ago, perhaps, been taught that his narrow and wicked Purposes could be only answered by the Representatives, and not by the collective Body of his People. Those false Guardians of the public Safety he would first corrupt, and then adore. To them he would basely offer up all the servile, and insidious incense of Hypocrisy, sure that it would be wafted back again to the Throne in the shape of dutiful Addresses, and bountiful Supplies.

He had, perhaps, been taught to mistake those Addresses for the real Sense of his People, and those Supplies for the Sinews of his Government; duped by the Treachery of perfidious Tutors, wicked Ministers, and his own Passions, he would distrust the plain Evidence of his Eyes and Ears. He would be weak enough to ask how it happens that the general Voice drowns that of Hirelings, upon all Public Occasions saluting the Monarch with repeated Hisses, Execrations and Reproach? How comes it that the enraged Populace presume even to spit in the Face of Majesty? Let the haughty, self-willed, cruel, and unfeeling Prince, who is most deservedly held in such Contempt, thank the traitorous Authors and Abetters of his *vile Principles*, and *viler Actions*, for his present *Infamy*, and future

Sufferings. By them he has, perhaps, been taught to slight, and he is weak enough to show that he slights, the Sense of his People. He has, perhaps, been led to collect it from the sycophantic Addresses of a corrupt and detestable Majority of a rotten House of Commons. Can human Ears be deaf to the public Voice, crying even in the Streets, and hallowing out the Substance of the Remonstrances and Petitions of the first City in the Kingdom? Has not such a King been dangerously advised, to look upon the Bulk of this Nation as Mob? Has he not been advised by Traytors, who tremble for themselves, (should real Grievances be redressed) not only to reject, but deride the Petitions of the Subject? Do such Advisers counsel upon Revolution-Principles? Does their deluded Sovereign hold his Crown upon any other?—I grow warm—but should such an ideal King (such a royal Log) as I have here fancifully described, ever Reign over a Free People, by what greater Curse can they be visited? May not such a King be truly said to be given them by Heaven *in it's Wrath?*—But I must proceed to delineate further, this Monster of my Brain, under whom every Evil and Oppression of bad Government would be severely felt. Among others, the heaviest and most enormous Taxes would not be the least. These too would be considerably increased by various and ingenious Modes of Profusion and Corruption. Without these endless and unconscionable Exactions, royal Prodigality, and childish Fondness for Toys and Superfluities, could not be gratified. Nay, the rapid Course of Despotism itself (the sole Aim and End of such a Government) must stop. Profligacy and Poverty, Rapacity and wicked Policy, will oblige a King, who governs by such vile Acts, to drain the Vitals of his Kingdom by grievous and superfluous *Taxes.* His own insatiable Appetites must be gratified, and the craving Mouths of his Dependants and Accomplices must be filled.

C A S C A.

[To be continued, and addressed to the present PIOUS King.]

Printed and published for the Authors, by T. W. SHAW, in *Fleet Street*, opposite *Anderton's Coffee House*, where Letters to the Publisher will be thankful received.

THE

CRISIS

NUMBER XXXVII   *To be continued Weekly.*

SATURDAY, *September* 30, 1775   [*Price* Two Pence Half-Penny.

Curst be the Man! What do I say, as tho',
The Wretch was not already so?
But curst on let him be, who thinks it brave—
Or great his Country to enslave.—

COWLEY.[1]

To the PEOPLE of ENGLAND.

THE CRISIS is at length arrived when Truths are branded with the opprobrious Name of TREASON, and constitutional Resistance to the unjust and bloody Commands of a *pious* King, and an arbitrary and abandoned Ministry, is called REBELLION—When Men are deemed Rebels who have bravely and honestly refused to plunge their Swords into the Breasts of their loyal Fellow-Subjects—and have

---

1. From Abraham Cowley's "Discourse" on Oliver Cromwell, taken, most likely, from *The Complete Works of Mr. A. Cowley*, 2 vols. (London: W. Bowyer and J. Nichols, 1772), 2:22–23. Cowley, a successful dramatist as well as poet, had been a royalist in the civil war of the 1640s. There is a nice entry for him in the *Oxford DNB*, 13:288–91, by Alexander Lindsay. The "Discourse," which had been published originally as a separate

had Resolution to oppose the oppressive Measures of an infernal Gang of Parricides.

When Petitions and Remonstrances avail not—When the first City in the World is repulsed, and treated with Contempt by Hirelings and TRAYTORS; when they are denied Access to the Ears of a deluded and weak Sovereign; whilst the once virtuous Throne is surrounded by German Beggars, and Scotch Rebels.—When our Trade and Manufactories are at a Stand; when our Commerce is ruined, our Liberties and Properties invaded, and the industrious Tradesman starving in our Streets.

At such a CRISIS an Appeal lies only to the PEOPLE; they, and they only, are proper to be addressed.—The Right of a King exists no longer than he acts as a King.—With his Honour falls his Power, and with his Justice his Prerogative. We owe him no Obedience as Subjects and Children, when he throws by the Parent and usurps the Tyrant.—When a King breaks his Coronation Oath, his Subjects are absolved from their Oath of Allegiance.

Resistance to such a one (notwithstanding PROCLAMATIONS, fabricated by a Lord Chief Justice) is not Rebellion; but justifiable by the Laws of God and England—It is a Duty we owe to God, Ourselves, and our Posterity.

Rouse, then, my Countrymen, from your Lethargy; let not the Sycophant and Syren Voice of an abandoned Ministry lull you asleep, whilst they forge Fetters, nay rivet them, on the expiring Remains of Liberty.— Revenge your own, and the Wrongs of injured America. Preserve, uncontaminated, those Rights and Privileges which cost your virtuous and brave Ancestors such Seas of Blood, and hand down to your Children, in its original Lustre, the glorious Blessing of English Liberty.

---

title soon after the Restoration, was a combination of prose and poetry, Cowley writing as if he had been in a dream. The stanza goes on:

"Who seeks to overpoise alone
The balance of a nation:
Against the whole but naked state,
Who in his own light scale makes up with arms the weight."

Drag from behind the Throne, the Traytors who dared to advise those destructive Measures now pursuing in America. In despite of Royalty itself seize them, and bring them to immediate and condign Punishment. Let not the Coronet, or Robe of Crimson, intimidate you; they deserve Respect no longer than the Wearer proves himself worthy of them.— Pull off the one and expose the Weakness of the Head: Draw back the other, and display the Treachery and Wickedness of the Heart.

Present yourselves to his Majesty, not as Petitioners, introduced by Lord Hertford, or some other servile Courtier, but as ENGLISHMEN; as Men who know their Rights, and are resolved to defend them.—Let a deluded Sovereign see there are still some Men, who however ungrateful to his Ears, have a Spirit left to tell him his Faults; who, unawed by a false glare of Royalty, are resolved to tell their Wrongs and seek Redress.

Tell him Treason lurks within his Palace: within those Walls he will find more Traytors than in America; paint her Wrongs, and present her bleeding Sons expiring by the Hands of infatuated and mercenary Soldiers; Represent, if possible, the Distresses of her Inhabitants. The loving Wife mourning with her orphan Children, over the dead Body of their Father.—Parents bewailing the Loss of an only Son, who was sent by Heaven as a Blessing in their declining Years. The Scene grows too affecting; it is too much for human Nature, and Humanity recoils at the Recital.

With a manly Fortitude and a Spirit becoming Britons, impeach those cursed Minions, who advised these wicked and fatal Measures, who now enjoy the Smiles of Royalty, and bask in the Sun-shine of Court Favour.

Bring to this View America, as a ruined and depopulated Nation.—Let him behold in Recital, the Distresses occasioned by the late bloody and inhuman Acts of Parliament.—Tell him the fatal Effects occasioned by his refusing the Petition of the City of London, and his heedlessly signing the Bill for restraining the American Fishery; only to please an abandoned Ministry, who advise the Destruction of Millions by FAMINE and the SWORD, and the Ruin of Kingdoms, that they may share in the Spoil. Nor will they ever want Wretches to carry their Measures into Execution, whilst they can bribe them with the Money of the PEOPLE;

such Assassins as Gage, Burgoyne, Clinton, and Howe, will always do any dirty Work Lord Bute, Lord Mansfield, or Lord North shall order them, when they are well paid.

Point to his Majesty the Father, who, before the passing that cruel Bill, earned an industrious and honest Livelihood by the Fishery; now surrounded by a Wife and Children craving for that Bread his Majesty and a corrupt Parliament has robbed them of.—He must, if he has one Spark of Humanity left: acknowledge, that the Americans draw not the Sword without Provocation. If his Soul is not moved with Pity, he is unworthy the Name of a Man; much less (the Title he once declared he gloried in) a BRITON; and it is an Insult on Religion to call him pious or merciful, Epithets which his hireling and pensioned Writers frequently bestow on him.

His Majesty, out of his great Mercy and Piety, lest an innocent Person should suffer, can pardon even hired Ruffians, the Violators of the Right of Election, who were clearly convicted by an honest and impartial Jury.—And will the same pious Sovereign, who could save the Lives of detested Murderers, persevere in the Destruction of the innocent, brave, and loyal Americans.   .

Can he whose tender Conscience would not permit a Malefactor to be executed; lest he should prove innocent (though there was no reason to believe him so, unless his being hired by Sir William Beauchamp Proctor, and murdering Subjects with a Promise of Pardon, can be construed into Innocence). Can such a Prince consent, I say, (or rather will the People of England suffer him) to punish Thousands, for the Fault of a misguided Rabble. Even Women and Children, nay, even Children unborn, have already been destroyed in the general Slaughter.—Blush, O Prince, at the Cruelties committed, with your Consent, by your Minions and Ministers, and let your Reign no longer be marked in Characters of BLOOD.

My Blood boils at the very Thought! with what Abhorrence and Grief will succeeding Generations read (and Read they must and will, for Truths are not like a judicial Record, to be erased by a MANSFIELD; and what is engraving in the Hearts of *Americans,* will be handed down to

Posterity with every cruel Circumstance) and in the black Annals of our Time, learn that this and more, was acted under, and by the Command of GEORGE the THIRD.

Is Slavery become less Hateful under a Prince of the House of Brunswick, than it was during the Reign of a Stuart; or are we less Virtuous and fond of Liberty, than our glorious Forefathers; who brought to the Block, the Tyrant CHARLES the FIRST? are we not the Descendants of those Men, who brought about the last happy and glorious Revolution? I call upon you NOW, my brave Countrymen, in the Name of those Ancestors, to DEFEND and RESIST, even till you Perish, any TYRANT who shall offer to trample upon the Laws which he is bound, and was solemnly sworn to preserve.

Proclaim, O my Countrymen, in the Ears of Majesty (which have long been Strangers to Truth) "These are thy Doings, misguided Prince, thy Laws, like those of DRACO,[2] are written not with INK, but in BLOOD. Repent ere it is too late, and hearken to the Advice of your faithful Subjects and real Friends, not to an abandoned Ministry, who are interested to SEDUCE you, lest by attending to Truths, you should find out their TREASONS. Dismiss the Traitors from your Confidence, and give them up to justice.—Be persuaded to follow the Inclinations of your People, and fulfill the solemn and sacred Oath you took at your Coronation.—It still is though it will not be so long in your Power to reconcile yourself to America, by an immediate Redress of their Grievances you may gain their Affections for ever; but should you still persevere in oppressive, cruel, and bloody Measures; the Time perhaps, is not far distant, (though Heaven retard the Hour) when the Sword of Liberty which is now drawn in America, will be unsheathed in England.

At that dreadful Period, a deluded King will call in vain for Assistance from Lord Mansfield, Bute, or their Instrument North and his Gang.—

---

2. Draco was the source for the later appellation of "draconian" as being needlessly harsh. He devised the first written legal code for Athens in the 7th century BCE. It included a death sentence for many crimes, minor as well as major, and was in effect until replaced by a more reasonable code under Solon in the next century. Solon was still revered in the Anglo-American world of *The Crisis* as a great lawgiver.

The whole infernal Crew, conscious of their Crimes, will hide themselves, if possible from the Vengeance of a justly enraged Nation; put an End to their detested Lives by SUICIDE; or be brought to the SCAFFOLD to the great Joy and Happiness of every true Friend to his King and Country in England and America.

B R U T U S.[3]

Instructions from the FREEHOLDERS of the COUNTY of Middlesex, to the Right Honourable JOHN WILKES and JOHN GLYNN, Esquires, KNIGHTS of the SHIRE for the COUNTY of MIDDLESEX.[4]

"WE, the Freeholders of the County of Middlesex; summoned here by Public Advertisement of the Sheriff of this County, acknowledge our Approbation and grateful Sense of your Conduct as our Representatives, during the last Session of Parliament; and though we have no Reason to doubt your steady Perseverance in the true Interest of your Country, yet we think it our indispensable Duty to acquaint you with our Sentiments at the present awful Crisis, big with the Fate of this great Empire, and the Happiness, Glory, and Prosperity, of the whole People.

"We behold, with all the Horror and Grief natural to a Free People, the fatal Stab given to our excellent Constitution, by a Majority of the last

---

3. This is the first of two pieces with the "Brutus" nom de plume; the second would be no. LVII (17 February 1776). For a brief comment on the identity of Brutus see n. VII.9 supra.

4. Passed on 25 September 1775, at a gathering of five hundred or more. Notes about the meeting, along with the instructions, were widely circulated in the London press the next day, as in the *London Evening Post,* the *Middlesex Journal and Evening Advertiser,* and the *St. James Chronicle,* and the day after that in the *Morning Chronicle* and the *Gazetteer and New Daily Advertiser.* The "doctrine" of instruction, as it came to unfold when demands for parliamentary reform became more pronounced, is discussed in J. R. Pole, *Political Representation in England & the Origins of the American Republic* (London: Macmillan and Co., 1966), which Pole revisited in *The Gift of Government* (Athens: University of Georgia Press, 1983). Also see H. T. Dickinson's *Liberty and Property* (London: Weidenfeld & Nicolson, 1977) and *The Politics of the People in Eighteenth-Century Britain* (New York: St. Martin's Press, 1994).

VENAL Parliament, whereby the most sacred and unalienable Right of the Freeholders of this County, the Right of Election, was in the most impious Manner wrested from the Electors, and assumed by the Elected, who placed a Person as our Representative in Parliament, contrary to the Sense and Will of the County, expressed by a great Majority of legal Votes, thereby establishing a PRECEDENT of the most dangerous Tendency to the Rights of all the Electors of Great Britain; which Injury has been again confirmed, by the Malice of our inveterate Enemies, in the present Parliament (chosen by Surprize under a National Delusion) suffering that Vote to appear in their Journals, a standing Record of the INJUSTICE, VENALITY, and CORRUPTION of their Predecessors.

"We are called upon to redouble our Attention and Zeal for the Defence and Preservation of ALL our constitutional Rights, from seeing the iron Hand of Oppression extended to our Fellow-Subjects on the other Side of the Atlantic; POPERY, that Bane of civil and religious Liberty, established in an Extent of Country infinitely larger than all our Possessions in Europe, thereby arming, as it were, many of our Fellow-Subjects with the CRUCIFIX in one Hand and a DAGGER in the other, against our Protestant Brethren; a POPISH BISHOP appointed, and the greatest Comfort and Encouragement given to the Clergy of that Church, while the Pastors of our own pure and excellent Faith, are suffered to remain without Support or Provision, but what ROMISH Priests and ROMISH Counsels shall deign to afford them; other cruel and oppressive Acts passed against our Fellow-Subjects in AMERICA, wholly repugnant to the ancient, just, and generous Proceedings of British Councils and British Assemblies, destructive of that Glory of the ENGLISH Law, the Trial by Jury, and many other undoubted Rights and Privileges of English Subjects; in Violation of Charters and royal Covenants of the most solemn Nature, which Acts and Oppressions, under the Influence of the present Ministers, have been productive of a most impolitic, unnatural, cruel, and destructive CIVIL WAR, against our suffering and much injured Fellow-Subjects in America.

"We lament as a commercial People, the inevitable Injuries that must be sustained by the Loss of a most valuable Branch of our Commerce, the decay of Trade and Manufactures, and consequent Distress of the industrious Poor.

"To remedy all these Evils, the melancholy Experience of past Times evincing, how insufficient the removal of a Ministry, while their Maxims and Views are entailed upon the Government. We desire that you will not only continue strenuously to oppose them, but endeavour to procure us such constitutional Security, by shortening the Duration of Parliaments, and enacting such other Laws as may prevent the Nation from suffering by the like Errors and Iniquities for the future.

"And we instruct you to exert yourselves in procuring that Vote of the late House of Commons to be rescinded, which in the most injurious and unconditional Manner, deprived the Freeholders of this County, of their undoubted Right of Election.

"We also instruct you, to forward an enquiry into the Expenditure of the Public Treasure, so peculiarly necessary at this Time, and in a Nation burdened with Taxes, and oppressed with Debts; that you will not suffer the People to be imposed on by the flimsy Artifices of a Minister pretending to lessen, while he is, in reality, encreasing the Public Burthen.

"Should any additional Land-Tax, or new Imposts be proposed, in the ensuing Session, we expect that you will not assent to them without a previous Redress of Grievances; and that you will strenuously oppose all Votes of Credit or taking any Foreign Troops into the Pay of Great Britain unless another Attempt should be made by TORIES and JACO-BITES, against his Majesty's Person, Family, or Government.

"The state of the Navy, the great Bulwark, Safety, and Protection, of the Commerce of this Nation demands, and we hope, will engage your serious Attention; and that you will enquire by what fatal Mismanagement and corrupt Influence, after such immense Sums have been voted during a Peace-establishment, that it is in its present deplorable Condition.

"We particularly instruct you to exert yourselves in preventing the further effusion of the BLOOD of our innocent Fellow-Subjects in America, and to put a speedy end to the present-unnatural and ruinous CIVIL WAR.

"We also desire you to use your unwearied Endeavours to assist and support the Representatives of the City of London, for obtaining a repeal of every obnoxious and unconstitutional Act, and in bringing to the Justice of their Country, the Advisers of such nefarious Measures, as have been adopted during the last Fourteen Years, tending to SUBVERT the Constitution of this Country, and which we are convinced will very soon effect the Ruin and Destruction of the British Empire."

No sooner were they Read, than Mr. *Justice Pell* with great dignity arose, and declaring, "That as he could not separate the STRAW from the WHEAT, he should object to every one of the Instructions."

The Motion for instructing the Members was carried, like every other Motion, in behalf of Public Liberty, by a prodigious Majority. It was then moved, "That a Letter should be addressed from the Freeholders of Middlesex to those of Great Britain." Objected to by Mr. *Justice Pell,* on the Principle "That it was sounding the Trumpet of Sedition throughout the Camp of Israel." Mr. Staples, the Lighterman objected to the Motion on a Ground not quite so Scriptural; he said, "It would be making fast the Chains of Tyranny." Mr. Rutson echoed the Denunciation of a PROTEST. The Letter, however, was read, and the Motion "That it be addressed to the Freeholders of Great-Britain" passed by an immense Majority. The Letter is verbatim as follows:"

A *Letter from the FREEHOLDERS of MIDDLESEX,*
to the FREEHOLDERS of GREAT BRITAIN.[5]

"The perilous Situation of public Affairs, and the Calamities which threaten the whole Empire, are the Reasons, and, we hope, will be a sufficient Apology for our addressing you.

"The Vote of the late House of Commons, by which a Representative was forced upon us, to the immediate Violation of our Rights, and the eventual Injury of those of all the Electors in the Kingdom, remains

---

5. This too was well circulated, such as in the *Gazetteer and New Daily Advertiser* and the *Morning Chronicle,* 27 September 1775.

yet on Record. It remains as a Precedent against the most sacred and fundamental Franchise of the People, to authorise the same Violence, by Ministers, as ARBITRARY and Representatives as CORRUPT.

"We trust, Gentlemen, that you will not cease to co-operate with us, till that dangerous and shameful Record be condemned and done away, in the most solemn and effectual Manner.

"The present state of America is such, as ought to give the deepest Alarm and Concern to every Man, who regards the Rights of human Nature, the Liberties of Englishmen, and the Happiness and Safety of the whole Empire. The arbitrary and inhuman Conduct of the present Administration, has driven our most affectionate American Fellow-Subjects into Despair and Resistance. Seven Years Supplication for a Redress of their Grievances, has been answered by AN ARMY to enforce them. Their Petition last Year to the King, implored— Peace, Liberty, and Safety. In Return they received Acts of the most inhuman Restraints; and open Hostilities, in the Desolation of their Country, the Destruction of their People, and the Conflagration of their Towns. They have again besought his Majesty," in a late humble Petition, "to stop the further Effusion of Blood; and to direct some Mode by which he would be pleased to receive the united Proofs of their Devotion, as most dutiful Subjects, and most affectionate Colonists." They declare their most "ardent Desire that the former Harmony between them and the Parent-State, may be established upon the most lasting Foundation." They expressly declare they do not "request such a Reconciliation as may be, in any Manner inconsistent with the DIGNITY or WELFARE of this Country." We cannot conceive what can be offered, fairer, or fuller, on their Part.

"But the Ministry, it seems, have advised his Majesty to give this Petition no Answer; and thereby to deprive the Petitioners of every Hope of Redress and Reconciliation. They are farther making the most open and extensive Preparations for War. Even Roman Catholics are allured and incited to take up Arms against their Protestant Fellow-subjects. Thus we see these most pernicious Measures, prosecuted by the worst and most dangerous Means.

"The immediate Injury of such a War to our Commerce and Manufactures,—the Consequence of that to the Produce of the Land—the additional Taxes necessary for such distant and expensive Operations, must sink this unhappy Country, already over-burthened with the enormity of her Debt, into unavoidable Ruin. Upon the LAND must the whole Expence ultimately fall. Upon the LANDHOLDERS, then, it is especially incumbent to use their utmost Influence in stopping the Course of this unnatural and fatal War.

"The Americans have repeatedly appealed to the Justice and Humanity of their Fellow-subjects in Great-Britain. We hope such an Appeal will never be made in vain. We lament the Fate of those brave British Soldiers who have been sacrificed in so inglorious and hateful a Contest. We are persuaded our Fellow-subjects in America, are contending in the Cause of Liberty; and are cruelly oppressed. We will never, willingly, aid in urging the Oppression, or trampling upon the Rights of any Part of the Dominions. We cannot see any probable Consequence from the Prosecution of this ministerial War, but Misery, Shame, and Ruin to the whole Empire.

"Upon these Principles we have instructed our Representatives in Parliament; upon these Principles, Gentlemen, we wish for your Co-operation, in establishing Liberty, Peace, and Harmony through all his Majesty's Dominions."

Printed and published for the Author's by T. W. SHAW, in *Fleet Street,* opposite *Anderton's Coffee House*, where Letters to the Publisher will be thankfully received.

THE

CRISIS

NUMBER XXXVIII   *To be continued Weekly.*

SATURDAY, *October* 7, 1775   [*Price* Two Pence Half-penny.

—Tu ME etiam, Nebulo, ludificabere?

TERENT.[1]

Shall *Dunning* by revolt ensure renown,
And *Bute* not take away his silken Gown?

ANONYM.[2]

S INCE every Truth is now considered, by the King's Friends, as a Libel upon Government, I do not remember ever to have seen a truer, and, consequently, a more atrocious Libel than that which was lately uttered by Mr. Dunning in his Charge, as Recorder, to the Grand Jury at the general Gaol Delivery in the City of Bristol on the 5th of September. Before I proceed further, I think it right to apprize

---

1. A farcical exchange from Act IV, Scene 4 of Terence's "The Eunuch," where one character sends another away for mocking him.

2. "Anon." being most likely the author(s) of this issue of *The Crisis* (see n. XLII.1 infra for another example). John Dunning was a very successful barrister who sat for Calne in the House of Commons. He and his friend John Glynn had acted as counsel for John Wilkes; he was also close to Baron Camden and the Earl of Shelburne. Not comfortable as solicitor general under the Duke of Grafton, he was more at ease in the

my Readers that I intend to display much Star-Chamber Learning in this Paper, by Way of preparing them for what they may soon expect; a laudable Exertion of the united Abilities of Administration to construe all Publications founded in Truth into Libels against Government, and to punish them accordingly.

They will want no Juries. They will have a Star-Chamber.—The Star-Chamber was a motley Kind of Court, like those in Scotland, compounded of Law and Equity, (or, at least, what they called Law and Equity) where a Board of Inquisitors came, predetermined, in the double Capacity of Judge and Jury.—[3]

Now, before such Judges, Libel, or not Libel, is a Question depending upon Construction only. I will shew my Readers, immediately, the Mode of Interpretation in such Cases. For that Purpose I shall exhibit Part of the Recorder of Bristol's Speech by Way of Specimen.—That Gentleman told the Grand Jury, that it had always been his Custom (and a laudable one it is) to inform them of any Acts of the previous Session of Parliament, which related to the Civil Liberties of the People, or to the Administration of Justice. But he observed, most truly, and, therefore, most libellously (for Truth, it seems, is the greatest Ag-

---

opposition and sharply critical of North's 1774 hardline American policy. Bute, ever the easy target, would not have been in a position to remove Dunning's "silken gown"— that is, to disqualify him from arguing the government's case in any of the king's high courts. For Dunning see Namier and Brooke, *House of Commons*, 2:367–68; and John Cannon's entry for the *Oxford DNB*, 17:333–35.

3. Remembered as a sobering example of law being twisted to suit political purposes, the Court of Star Chamber as it was used by Charles I (and Henry VIII before him) became a symbol of royal prerogative run wild, subverting English freedoms. Parliament abolished Star Chamber in 1641. It dated from the 14th century and, as the English court system evolved, had been seen by some as a necessary supplement to common law and equity courts. With its ability to act more directly as an extension of the royal will and its secretive proceedings, Star Chamber prosecutions had proven an effective way of bringing the high and mighty to heel—but at a cost to the sanctity of justice under law. The best brief discussion of Star Chamber and other conciliar courts and their relation to common-law and equity courts is J. H. Baker, *An Introduction to English Legal History*, 3rd ed. (London: Butterworths, 1990; orig. ed. 1971), pp. 135–45.

gravation of a Libel) that the Proceedings of the late Session furnished no such Information; Business of a very different Nature (meaning the late American business) having engrossed the Attention of the Legislature.—He then expresses, with the most pathetic Sensibility, his first Wish to be the Union of the British Empire; that it might, once more be happy and flourishing; and declares the Crime of that Person who indulges a contrary Wish to be infinitely more heinous than any that stained the Calender then before him.

This Gentleman's Observations are just, and his Assertions true; but for that very Reason a Court of Star-Chamber must condemn him.

Truths make the strongest and most lasting Impression upon the People, and are, therefore, held in the greatest Detestation by the present Ministry. To them every Man who thinks is an obnoxious Subject; but the Hand that writes must be disabled. Under the Sway of a Bute and a Mansfield, Information is no less criminal than Resistance. All Freedom of Speech and Pen will shortly be condemned by Proclamation, and suppressed by Inquisition.

The King's Friends (as they call themselves) cannot do their Duty if they omit to censure, resent, and punish the late opprobrious Behaviour of the Recorder of Bristol; a Man whom they hate, with great Reason, for his free Spirit, Abilities, Integrity, Discernment, Inflexibility, and public Virtue; and, therefore most righteously, displaced him as Solicitor General, to make Way for one who would suit their Purposes. Lord Bute did right—he smelt a Rat.—The Name of Junius made him start.—The Man who dares to publish free and virtuous Sentiments, in Times like these, who is too proud and stubborn to receive either Insults, Bribes, or Orders from the Minister, deserves to wear the King's Gown no longer. Let him be stripped of his silk Robe, and, to his immortal Honour, let him wear Shalloon for Life; but let him not presume to vent his galling Truths in public. Shall he be suffered to spread Jealousies and Discontents among the People, to play the Constitutionalist before a Grand Jury; to scatter malignant Hints and seditious Insinuations throughout a City, and to lead Men (who might otherwise be tame and quiet) into political-Inquiries and national Resentments? Can a Mansfield be blind to such Audacity as this? Is the great inquisitor of the Nation slumbering? Have the mouldy Precedents of his favourite Court of Star-Chamber, no Pains, no Penalties, no Maims in Store for such Offences? When the Heads of a virtuous Administration are plotting against the Liberties of the Press, shall Freedom of Speech, or Pen be allowed to any but the pensioned Friends of Government your Johnsons, Maduits, Shebbears, and Kellys?

This Recorder is not only a free Speaker, but he is suspected of being a free Writer, and shall he not be punished in those Members which offend? Ought he not to be examined upon Interrogatories? If he should (like Bingley) contumaciously refuse to accuse himself, let such Refusal be taken for full Proof against him, and let his guilty Hand and Tongue pay the Forfeit of his Temerity. This Procedure has been held just and legal in Reigns no less virtuous and constitutional than the present; nor can Lord Bute's System of Government be supported, unless this summary Mode of Trial is restored.[4]

If Americans have no Right to be tried by Juries, no more have the other Subjects of Great Britain. Juries are said to be constitutional, but they are dangerous. They are no Friends to Government. They listen too much to Conscience. They know they have an undoubted Right to judge of *Law* as well as *Fact,* and that every Judge is a *Liar* and a *Knave* who tells them to the contrary, and dares to dictate, controul and overbear, when it is his Province only, to assist and inform.[5] How can Juries swallow the ministerial Doctrine of our Day? Let them be at once abolished.—With

---

4. John Dunning held the post of recorder of Bristol from 1766 until his death in 1782. The author(s) essentially paraphrased Dunning's speech as it was reported in the London press-such as, for example, in the *London Chronicle*, 5 September 1775. It would indeed be difficult to find anything libelous about administration policy in it.

5. Juries were increasingly ruling on questions of law as well as matters of fact in libel cases—that is, determining whether a libel had been committed (the question of law), not simply establishing the accused's role in writing or printing it (the matter of fact). They would not be officially empowered to do so by statute until 1792. See Pickering, ed., *Statutes at Large*, 36:627–28 (32 George III c. 60).

the present Administration whatever *is*, is *right*: A glorious Maxim!—
pregnant with unerring Justice. The great Sir Thomas Filmer has wrote
a Volume in its Praise.[6]

The conscientious, pious, amiable and God-like Family of the Stuarts (to
whose Principles our Ministry most religiously adhere) pluming themselves; on their manifest Vicegerency under God, did singular Honour
to this Maxim, by adopting it as their great Rule of Government. It
made that divine Being, Charles the First, a blessed Martyr, and will,
probably, beatify and canonize more anointed Fools. Such short-sighted
Dupes of wicked and designing Ministers and Friends, have ever found
a Way to Heaven through Inquisitions, Massacres, Tyranny, and Blood.
Those who are Friends to the People are ever treated as Enemies to such
a Government, and have generally been attempted either by private Assassination or judicial Iniquity. I shall not, therefore despair of seeing
this free speaking Recorder brought to the Bar of the Inquisitor General
of England.

If Truth makes a Libel more criminal, (as every Star-Chamber-Lawyer
from Coke to Mansfield has declared) can Thurloe want sufficient Matter for an Information against Mr. Dunning? Will not our Sollicitor
General (our little Scotch Lord Chancellor in Embryo) be ingenious
in supplying necessary Inuendoes and bold Averments, which are the
Quintessence of such State-Proceedings? Can any Aspersion upon the
great Council of the Nation (in whose Wisdom our Sovereign has so
repeatedly declared he would confide) be more gross and virulent, and,
what is worse, more true, than that which Mr. Dunning has thrown out
upon it? Has not this Great Council, has not the Privy Council, has not
our most pious King, has not the great Lord Bute himself (that infallible
Consistory of George's Soul) shewn of late the noblest Instances of Perseverance? Does any human Virtue bid so fair for the Promotion of Civil
Liberty and Justice, as tenacious and obdurate Steadiness?—What if no
Acts have passed, relating to Liberty and Justice, in the late Session of

6. For Robert Filmer see n. I.12 supra.

Parliament, has not that Session nobly avowed supported and persisted in all the salutary Provisions made before for the Advancement, Protection and Prosperity of Religion, Commerce, the Lives, Liberties and Properties, nay, for the Preservation and lasting Happiness (in Heaven) of all his Majesty's dissatisfied petitioning Subjects in America? And shall Government be upbraided, or discouraged, because a little Recorder of a little Corporation dares to arraign the Assiduity, Vigilance, Justice, and Attention of the late Session of our incorrupt Parliament? Does this little Man presume to be wiser than the whole legislative Body?—

What contributes more to the Preservation of Civil Liberty, than to suppress Licentiousness? And what Licentiousness is so great as that of Subjects who shall dare to meet, consult, deliberate, and at last, to act in Defence of themselves, and their pretended Interests, against the Proprietors of their Liberties, Lives and Fortunes? Shall a Set of Men, who have thrown themselves under the Protection of the Crown, from whose Grace and Benignity they received a Charter in their Infancy, presume to withstand their Owner's Will? Has not this modest, patriotic Doctor Johnson most learnedly and convincingly amplified, expounded and explained, stipulated Subjection into passive Obedience, rational Subordination into real Slavery? And durst any loyal Subject dispute the Doctrine and Authority of his magesterial Goose-quill?—So much for Civil Liberty.—As to the Administration of Justice, can that be more effectually provided for than by the Prevention of political Injustice? And what can be more unjust than that those whom the wisdom of the Great Council of this Nation has branded as Rebels should escape Famine, Sword and Gibbet? What could be wiser and more just than to call in the Aid even of Famine, in such a righteous Cause? What more laudable than the abolishing Trials by Jury in Cases of *meum* and *tuum*, in such a detested Country? What more equitable than the transporting such traytorous Children hither, where they will be sure to find a Judge, a Jury, and a Halter ready for them?—But the most obnoxious and severest Insinuations against the State, are couched under the Recorder's next Observation, that "Business of a very different Nature from the Civil Liberties of the People, or the Administration of Public Justice had engrossed the Attention of the last Session"—

Now what is so contrary to its natural Civil Liberty, as established Slavery, what so foreign to the Administration of Justice, as the promotion of Corruption, Oppression, and Iniquity? These may be truly said to be Businesses of a very different Nature from those which in all well-governed States, engross the perpetual Attention of a good Prince and a wise Legislature. Such a Prince and such a Legislature would endeavour to multiply the Benefits and mitigate the Sufferings of the People. They would have no Resentments to gratify, no Vices to indulge, no Dependants to support, no Confederates to bribe, no private Ends to serve, no Wish but what tends to the Welfare, the Honour, the Happiness and Preservation of the Realm and its Dominions. But, by saying that Business of a different Nature employs the Thoughts of Government, what does this Recorder mean, but that the Administration must be wicked which Promotes, the Legislature corrupt and venal that Assists, the People stupid who endure, and the Sovereign more Fortunate, than he deserves, who does not Suffer for so gross an abuse of delegated Power.

Such Insinuations as these, are fit for the Consideration of a Court of Star-Chamber.—But this keen Libeller, this Apostate to a Pious King, this Deserter of a virtuous Administration, this zealous Opponent of an incorrupt Majority, has presumptuously formed a Wish for the Happiness, the Prosperity of America in a lasting Union with Great Britain.

Does he remember that the great Lord Bute has declared by his Amanuensis Doctor Johnson, that whoever wishes well to America, is a Traytor?

Does he not know that our Sovereign has set his Face against America? That our all-wise and almighty Majority are determined to gratify the Rage of disgusted Royalty? That the Extinction of that detested Race of Subjects is determined? Who then shall dare to wish for an happy Union with that devoted Territory, which is doomed to Desolation. Such a Trayterous Wish is equal to a Trayterous Act, and deserves no less a Punishment.

But our wild Recorder stops not here; in a loose of frantic Zeal, he proceeds to rank the Three Great Estates of this Kingdom, with the worst of Felons; asperses and calumniates the whole virtuous Gang, from Bute to Jerry Dyson. He involves them with Pick-Pockets, Cut-throats, and

Assassins. Nay, I suspect by his using the Word (Person) in the singular Number, that he points at the Master-Butcher.—This is ungenerous. He, (poor Man) is but a mere Puppet, and is moved upon the Wires of his two Scotch Governors.

Mr. Recorder, to enflame the Minds of the Public, insinuates farther, that "the End of this American Business cannot be clearly seen."—But here I suspect him of the most artful Dissimulation for some secret and pernicious Purposes; for every Man may see the End of this Business; who knows the Temper and Fortitude of the Americans better than Lord Sandwich, or Lord Denbigh? and reflects that Virtue and Magnimity always go together and are invincible.

This Recorder then, does not scruple to declare that he intends still to give his Opinion firmly on all Questions relating to America.—Upon this, a late made Baron may remark, that Mr. Dunning does not intend to barter his Seat in the House of Commons, for a Fur-gown, or to give up the National Interest, and his own Honour, for a larger Perriwig.— But the higher Monkies climb—the Reader knows the rest.

Let me not forget the grossest of all this Recorder's Insults: it is well known, and felt, that the Government, abetted by the wise Council of this Nation, have thought fit to declare themselves Enemies to America; they have thought fit to withdraw their Protection from Her; and have bravely and justly resolved by all Means, Human, and Inhuman, to exterminate those Rebels: and shall this puny Gownsman dare to proscribe so illustrious, so august a Body as King, Lords and Commons, and hold up a Calendar of Thieves and Murderers as their Betters? Unparralleld Assurance! audacious Insolence! unpardonable Contempt!—But let this daring little Bully of a King's Bench Bar, mark and tremble at the End of these licentious Outrages against a pious King, an upright Parliament, a righteous and unspotted Administration, and a godlike Thane, the great and first Mover of our political Sphere of Government.

Let every Anti-Revolutionist rejoice that the great and glorious Day of Reformation is at Hand, when the now-teeming Press shall be Free to none but Johnson and his Subalterns; when literary Publications from every other Quarter shall be supervised and punished under a new constitutional Inquisition; when the Tongues of perjured Revolutionists shall be rooted out, and the impious Hands that spread their Doctrines, shall be severed; when more Writing shall (as it was in Sidney's Case) be again pronounced Acting; when Petitioning shall be Death, and lifting up a suppliant Eye towards the Throne, shall be punished as an High Crime and Misdemeanor.—Then shall the glorious Suns of Bute and Mansfield, break forth in Scottish Splendour, and eclipse the puny Majesty of England; then shall rebellious America be abandoned to her Fate; no more protected and sustained by her affectionate and indulging Parent; but spurned, with Indignation and Contempt, as an odious Prodigy of that monstrous and enormous Virtue, which is not to be subdued by Luxury, Corruption, Perfidy, Treachery, Famine, Ministerial Assassination, royal Perseverance, or a Breach of Magna Charta and the great Compact between King and People.

C   A   S   C   A

*₊*The Authors of the CRISIS present their respectful Compliments to Casca, and beg he will excuse their not having printed some of his Words which were scored for italic in that Character:—They have a new Font of the various Sorts of Letter nearly finished, when they will be able to comply with the particular Requests of Casca and their numerous Correspondents.—The Authors hope to hear from Casca soon.

Printed and published for the Authors, by T. W. SHAW, in *Fleet-Street*, opposite *Anderton's Coffee House*, where Letters to the Publisher will be thankfully received.

THE

CRISIS

NUMBER XXXIX   *To be continued Weekly.*

SATURDAY, *October* 14, 1775   [*Price* Two Pence Half-penny.

An Ideal S C E T C H of a F O O L I S H   K I N G.

Continued from Number XXXVI.

To the K I N G.

S UCH a King would occasion innumerable Distresses to his People, but feel none. The greatest he could be apprehensive of, and the only one he would regard, would be a deficiency of Votes. Perhaps a TEST, or ASSOCIATION, on the side of Liberty, might alarm him for a Moment, but Inequity is ever fruitful in Expedients. One Parliament may easily be dissolved, and another smuggled by surprize So many Years are now elapsed since the Revolution, that its Principles are almost forgot. They are showy in *Theory*, but obsolete in *Practice*. Besides, a hopeful Majority may always be obtained by multiplying *Placemen*, *Pensioners*, and even *Tax gatherers*. An *honest Parliament* is the Representative and Servant of a *free People*, a *corrupt Parliament* is the *Creature* and *Slave* of a *foolish King* and a *knavish Minister*. This is governing not by *Policy*, but by *Stratagem*. Hence it comes that *such* a Prince need only ask and have. The Wretches who form this patriotic Majority, and give away the public Treasure thus profusely, share a Part, proportioned to their Merits in the public Plunder. This is not a System like that formed at the glorious Revolution, which introduced the present Family, from a contemptible Electorate, to the noblest Empire in the Universe, but it is such a one as originated under that great Corruptor and vile Minister (Sir Robert Walpole) and has shot up lately into most luxuriant Infamy, under the fostering Hand of Bute. It is a System under which the Prodigalities, Vices, Crimes, and Tyrannies of a foolish King will hourly increase. Till this raging Pestilence (Corruption) can be subdued, it will be the mutual and perpetual Interest of the faithless Majority to grant, and of the profligate Sovereign to remunerate the Benevolence and dutiful Attachment of his Myrmidons. Surely such a Pestilence as this in any State is far more dangerous in its Consequences than that among the Horned Cattle, which was once lamented with a fatherly Concern, at a Time when a great City petitioned, and exerted all it's Zeal to destroy (among other obnoxious Pests) that many headed Monster Corruption. The horned Cattle was then a happy Thought, suggested by some sly Court Sycophant (perhaps a Mansfield) in derision, and indecently adopted by his sneering Master. The Allusion (like the Wit) was Low and Vulgar, fit only for the Mouths of the lowest Rabble. As the first Citizens in the Universe were buffooned under this unmanly, coarse Allusion, it is to be wished that Firebrands had been fastened to the Horns of that tame Herd, whose greatest Offence was an humble, constitutional, and just Supplication to the Throne.

These Horned Cattle (my Lord Mansfield) yielded daily Nourishment and Supplies to the Wants, Superfluities, Vices, and Profusion, of all the royal ministerial pensioned, placed, and bribed Blood-suckers of an oppressed and injured Nation. At the same Time, I must confess, it is an Instance of the greatest Condescension and Humility in your Lordships (whose Duty it is to bear the Standard of Liberty before the People to submit to be the first Buffoon in a sycophantic Drawing-Room.) From this Disgression I return, and must observe that when Grants are in any State too easily obtained by a foolish and profuse Prince, from a venal and corrupt Majority, upon Grounds hardly Colourable, (without a due inquiry into the real Applications of so much Treasure) immense yearly Revenues will be squandered in royal Baubles, courtly Superfluities, and national Corruption. Nor will these stipulated Largesses be sufficient of themselves, but further supplemental Supplies will modestly be asked, and most dutifully granted to eke out the small annual Revenue of near a Million, as often as that enormous Sum proves too scanty to answer the frugal, pious, munificent, and wise Purposes of a Monarch, whose Magnificence, Oeconomy, and Zeal for the Happiness and Prosperity of Himself, his Minions, and his People may be notorious.

A Revenue less than one Million was more than sufficient to defray all the Expences of the Crown, the Fleet, and the Army, in the Days of the renowned Elizabeth, embarrassed as she was both at home and abroad. At a far less Expence did that illustrious Princess support her Kingdom's Honour, and her own Magnificence and Splendor, in the midst of the most formidable Attack that was ever made upon this Kingdom; not against the puffing Menaces of a few French flat-bottomed Boats, but against a real approaching Invasion of the whole Power of Spain with her invincible Armada. At that Period, the Hand of Providence was seen, but the Hand of Wisdom, Prudence, and true Patriotism was not idle. At that Period it pleased Heaven to give Understanding to the Sovereign, Abilities and Integrity to the Ministry, and Virtue to the Parliament. The amiable, revered, and beloved Sovereign of that Day, saw with her own Eyes, and heard with her own Ears. She had Sensibility, Spirit, Fortitude, true Magnanimity and Discretion. She had Penetration and Sagacity. Her Piety, like her Courage, was unaffected: She disdained Hypocrisy, and upon all important Occasions she spoke and acted from an upright Heart. In her Reign (and it is not to be equaled in our Annals) the public Treasure was not lavished, but applied. It brought back Honour, Peace, Security and Freedom to the Nation. In worse Reigns, and under worse Administrations, it has been, and will continue to be, pusillanimously and treacherously applied, to purchase Infamy abroad, and Slavery at home. In every Reign the continual and repeated Cravings of royal Dissipation and Corruption, ought to be suppressed. This Evil grows by feeding, and will at last prey upon the exhausted Vitals of an expiring Country. A weak and wicked Prince, makes the wealth of his Kingdom, an Object of his Thoughts, no farther than it serves to supply his insatiable childish Appetites, or tyrannical Designs. Were the Treasures of a Nation inexhaustible, and the dispensing Hand ever profuse, such a Cut-purse of the Realm, such a Royal Prodigal, would in six Months sink an imperial Revenue to a Farthing, and still remain in Debt to the meanest of his Tradesmen and Domestics. At the same Time (so inconsistent is the Spirit of Profusion with pretended Æconomy) that the Current of all laudable Hospitality would be stopped in the very Kitchen of the Royal Palace; where even the menial Servants would stinted to Board-Wages, and the Houshold Expences of a great Monarch pitifully curtailed to that of a Pound of Bread and an Inch of Candle. Under this Mask of domestic Prudence and Frugality, a venal and corrupt Set of Wretches (to whom the public Honour, the public Treasure, and the public Freedom were entrusted) would be exorbitantly bribed by this excellent Oeconomist, with the Money of the Nation, to betray their Masters. A patriot King would exert his Talent of Oeconomy in Matters of greater Honour and Importance. Instead of pinching the Bellies of his poor Domestics, he would save, not to dishonour, but to aggrandize the Nation. He would be sparing in all unnecessary Impositions upon his Subjects. Safe in their Affections, his Fears would not suggest to him the Necessity of a most expensive, useless, and unconstitutional standing Army. That it is immensely expensive the annual Estimates will evince. When I call it useless, no wise Man will affect Surprise till he has heard the following Questions fairly answered,—In an Island can such an Army be kept up against foreign Enemies?—No.—Islanders can fear none whilst their Marine is attended to. Let foreign, continental Powers be ever so ambitious, let them combine, unite and threaten; yet how can they invade? The Ballance of Power (so idly talked of by crafty Politicians) is to be kept, not by a tyrannic standing Army; but by a respectable Navy only.—Is this Army maintained for Shew and for

Reviews? Hardly—turning, or making Buttons would be an Amusement less expensive to the Kingdom. But, is it maintained against the People? The most audacious Tyrant, or most abandoned Minister, would tremble to affirm it. Yet this, alas! is the real Truth.—It may be useful to protect an odious Sovereign and his corrupt Adherents against the Cries of Justice and an injured Nation. As soon as Corruption was found necessary for the Support of the political System, standing Armies were embodied, to maintain if possible, by Force, what Oppression and Tyranny must loose, I mean the Submission of an insulted People. Their Affections, in our new World of Politics, are not regarded. Is this a constitutional Army? No.—The national Militia is the only one, and the only one that ought to be endured in this Kingdom.—We have a national Militia, says my Lord North, by an Act passed in the Reign of his present patriotic Majesty.—It is true, my Lord, but this Act passed, not with the Wishes of Ministry; it was (in the military Phrase,) a March stolen upon them. I refer to your Lordship's Recollection for the History and Truth of what I now assert. The Digression would be long, and foreign to my present Purpose, or I would give the History of this Piece of patriotic Condescension in the Ministry. Another Opportunity may disclose it, together with some valuable Anecdotes, and interesting Remarks upon the Subject.—

It is now Time that I should pursue my ideal Scetch of a foolish King. Imperious, ignorant, self-willed, and self-sufficient, no wise and honest Counsellor would approach him. His Weakness would shut up every Avenue to good Advice. He would listen only to that fawning Herd who might, probably, have the unparalled Impudence to embody themselves under the arrogant Appellation of the King's Friends, (a new Order of Sycophants) as if the Wiser and honester Part of the Nation were his Enemies. The Advice of such Men alone would be relished, as most grateful to his vitiated Appetites. Hence would arise real Grievances at home and in his Colonies. If the injured and oppressed Subjects remonstrated in an humble, constitutional Manner, they would be derided; if they received the Chains and Badges of their Slavery with any Shew of Manhood and Resistance, they would be treated as factious and rebellious. Such a Sovereign would not relieve, conciliate and appease—No—He would still oppress, irritate, insult, and, at last, endeavour to exterminate them. This would be his pious and parental Conduct in his Colonies.—At home, his Myrmidons, his mercenary standing Army, would surround his Throne.—These, instead of the constitutional Civil Power, would be employed, under a needless Pretence, of assisting the Civil Magistrates in the Execution of the Laws; and, it is most probable, that these military Assistants would be guilty of military Murders. I can easily suppose some Parts of the Army (as well as of the Senate) not quite free from Infection in so corrupt a Reign. What if a simple Youth, drawn by indiscreet Curiosity, to approach too near the Scene of Confusion and Riot (which the unconstitutional Appearance of the Military, instead of Civil Powers had occasioned) should be singled out, pursued and butchered, though defenceless and unarmed? Let us suppose (for such a Case has happened) that two military Scotch Ruffians most maliciously pursued this unarmed Straggler. till he had taken Shelter in a Hovel, where, defenceless as he was, he might have been taken without a Blow, and brought to Justice, if culpable. Instead of seizing him (for he was inclosed, and the Door of the Hovel shut) these two military Executioners of our Laws perforated him most inhumanly in several Places with Bayonets fixed, till the unhappy Youth fell dead at their Feet, a Victim to the Janissaries of a standing Army. Can it be imagined that a wise or Christian Prince could not only approve, but applaud such a Massacre as this? Ought the royal Thanks to be publicly given to the commanding Officer in such a Scene? Ought the murderous Villains themselves to have the Means of an Escape provided for them? Ought Justice itself to be tampered with in their Favour? Ought such Cut-throats to be pensioned for their good Services? Ought there to have been a Sham-trial of two Persons who did not actually commit, but were Accessaries to the Murder, whilst the real Murderers were conveyed away privately? Ought a Judge to have laboured the Acquittal of these guilty Accessaries, knowing and well knowing, that the Principals had escaped? Ought a chief Justice of England to connive at such iniquity? Ought a Sovereign to patronize, protect and reward it? Ought he to go still further, and give formal Thanks to the Commander of this Atchievement so honourable to the British Arms? What could a NERO or a DOMITIAN do worse?[1]

C A S C A.

[To be continued, Addressed to his PIOUS Majesty George III.]

Printed and published for the Authors, by T. W. SHAW, in *Fleet-Street*, opposite *Anderton's Coffee House*, where Letters to the Publisher will be thankfully received.

1. The readers are being returned to the scene of the St. George's Fields "massacre" and the "murder" of young William Allen. See n. III.1 supra.

THE

CRISIS

NUMBER XL   *To be continued Weekly.*

SATURDAY, *October* 21, 1775   [*Price* Two Pence Half-penny.

An Ideal S C E T C H of a F O O L I S H K I N G finished.

Continued from the last Number.

To the K I N G.

THUS fall by standing Armies, innocent Individuals unrevenged?—Thus, and only thus, can they be useful—to a wicked Administration, and a Tyrant. In such a Scene as I have just supposed, the most pusillanimous Prince (without half the Spirit of his Mother) may stab by Proxy. In such a Reign neither Liberty, Property, nor Life, are safe. Religion (though he has sworn at the Altar to maintain and defend it is as little so. Suppose a Foolish King (so tender of the Blood of his Subjects) should still, through the Patience and long sufferance of his People, remain unshaken in his Throne; could it be adviseable for him to lay himself still more open to the just Resentment of a brave, a spirited, and feeling People? Would he be wise (though he practised all the outward forms of sanctimonious Piety in his Palace) to risque a change of the established Religion in any part of his Dominions? Could any political Pretences reconcile such a Step as this, either to his People or his Conscience? Could such a rash Attempt be considered in any other Light than as a daring Prelude to a more extensive and decisive Stroke? Suppose such a Prince had not the Capacity to plan, but only give his dumb Assent to such a Scheme, would he be less culpable than the other Parts of a corrupt designing, treacherous Legislature, who ventured to enact it? Might not such a foolish, such a wicked King, be truly said to be at the Head of a Faction! Or might he not (upon Revolution-Principles) be stiled a Traytor to his People?—The consequence of such Treason must, and ought to be, as fatal to the Sovereign (upon those Principles) as to the Peasant.

A King of England holds his Crown, at this Time of Day, upon a strict Conformity to the Principles of Government, established at the Revolution. This Engagement makes a part (and a most essential part) of his CORONATION-OATH. If he suffers these Principles (this mode of governing by Law established) to be violated in any Part of his Dominions, he is clearly guilty of wilful Perjury; of a more corrupt Species of Perjury than the low Villain who is suborned to commit it in a Court of Justice. The importance of the Case aggravates the Crime. He breaks the solenm Contract made with his People at the Altar. This People are the whole collective Body of Subjects throughout his whole Empire. By breaking this Contract he becomes a Deceiver of his People, and a Betrayer of their Rights. When I say a Betrayer, I mean a Traytor. The words are synonymous. In this Case of Contract (for there always must be one, either express or implied, between Sovereign and Subject) the Obligations on either Side must be reciprocal; and, consequently, if a Subject is guilty of a Breach of Allegiance on his Part, he becomes a Traytor to his King; on the other Hand, if a King is guilty, on his Part of a Breach of Contract, he must necessarily be a Traytor to, or Betrayer of his People. If such a Subject ought to die, such a King ought not to reign. A Nation may better endure another Saint, or Martyr, in the Calendar, than another Fool or Devil on the Throne. Such a wretched Shadow of Royalty, might chance to suffer, not for his own proper demerits, but for confiding too far in a corrupt Set of Men whom he thought his Friends;

he might even happen to suffer for confiding in the Wisdom of a corrupt Parliament. Such a Prince, meanly content with the flattering Name of King, would, in a delirium of Confidence, leave the actual Sovereignty to be exercised by those who duped him. Unacquainted with Men and Things, however impatient of the Leading String, he must endure it, because he would feel himself in a perpetual State of infancy. Natural Pride must, in this Instance, and in many others, yield to natural Weakness. With an Education too narrow to enable him to think or act like a Man, he would still stand in need of Lectures from his Tutor, like a Child. If a mere Machine might be said to act, so might he.

Unapprized, or stupidly inattentive to the Fate which has constantly attended those unhappy Princes, who have been the Dupes of Favourites, under the specious name of Friends, such a King would persevere in lavishing Honours upon the most odious Person in his Kingdom. To him, alone, or to his Under-Agents, would such a Prince open his Eyes, his Ears, and his Heart. From that baneful Quarter, only, would he receive Advice; under that pernicious Influence he would act, and upon such insidious Counsels would he risk the Dignity of his Crown, the happy Establishment of his Family, the Welfare of his People, and no small Portion of his Empire. He would be taught to look upon the Laws as the Instruments of his Pleasure not as the Rules of his Actions. Made thus a Tyrant in Theory, the happiest Circumstance of his Reign would be, his wanting Courage to attempt the Practice, at least near the Seat of Empire.

The Necks of his Subjects (by that Advice which he confides in) would first be bowed to the intended Yoke in the remotest Parts of his Dominions. If they, after the necessary Intimidations had been used, received it tamely, he would piously hope that the Contagion of Slavery might be artfully and gently diffused, till it made its Appearance as well in the Senate as the Palace. Sure from such a Conduct, to meet the Hatred and Contempt he justly merited, he would anxiously shun the public Resentment, and lead, as much as possible, a Life of domestic Obscurity, like his Brethren, the Tyrants of the East. This, by the Sycophants of his Court, would be called a Love of Retirement, a Sign of conjugal and parental Happiness; perhaps a pious Retreat for the Performance of religious Duties; at least, a necessary Relaxation from the Weight of Government.

But, alas! in this splenetic and sullen Refuge from the greatest Happiness of a Patriot King, the grateful Acclamations and reiterated Blessing of a happy People, even in this remote Asylum from the public Eye, such a pent-up-Monarch (if native Stupidity did not blunt Reflection) would count the bitterest Moments of his Life.

Look in upon a foolish Prince in these Hours of Seclusion, sacred (as his Minions would insinuate) to public, conjugal, parental, and religious Duties, and he will, probably, be found, like another DOMITIAN, catching Flies, and giving them the Torture; or in some Amusement no less puerile.

Instead of turning his Mind, like the King and Father of a Country, to political and princely Studies, behold him intensely busied in disposing the Pictures in his Baby-house in new Lights, or shewing his Abilities, as a military Draftsman, in sketching out a new Pattern for a Button to a Birth-day Suit.—Turn your Eyes hither, ye Potentates and Princes of the Earth! Behold here a Blaze of Majesty! Admire such Magnanimity, and tremble at *such* an Enemy!—

Let us now view this Solomon in the Zenith of his Glory, encircled by his Flatterers, and receiving, greedily, the humble Offerings of courtly Incense in his Palace. Even here he will seem to want Dignity in his Manner, Grace in his Address and Affability, though he may affect to smile. The sparing Tinge of a generous Education will appear through all the Trappings of Royalty. Poverty of Mind is not to be concealed beneath a gorgeous Habit. Even a Crown must first receive the Lustre it reflects.

When a princely Education has been designedly and wickedly withheld, Nature must be liberal indeed, or the Character of Majesty must be strangely inconsistent. Such an unfinished Scrip of Royalty must be hot, precipitate, perverse and overbearing in Council; cold, pusillanimous, and inactive in the Field; averse to receiving any advice himself. Uxorious, yet not constant; sanctified, not religious; avaritious, yet profuse; sullen without Spirit; obstinate without Fortitude; rigid without Virtue; tenacious without Reason; assuming without Abilities; longing to be absolute, yet timid in effecting it; trembling to invade, yet basely undermining public Liberty, by the mercenary Endeavours of every Tool he can corrupt; wounding, like a dastardly Assassin, in the dark, that Constitution which he has not the Courage to destroy, or even boldly to attack. An Adept in the mean Arts of Perfidy and Treachery; but a mere Novice in the kingly Art of Government. A nominal and pretended Guardian of the Laws, yet a secret Abettor of those Traytors who, at his own Instance, daily corrupt the Source from whence they flow. Of a Character too equivocal to be feared as a Tyrant, or beloved as a King, he is the first at Heart, and the latter only in Appearance. Perpetually mistaking Men and Things, Means and Ends, his Government would produce Anarchy and Confusion; his tyrannic Principles, Resistance and a Revolution. With a Mind busy, yet pusillanimous, he would, probably, pursue mechanical and artificial, more than military Knowledge; but his Patronage would discourage, his very Name disgust and damp all Genius. If he affected the liberal Arts, and should be prompted, not by Taste, but Vanity, to encourage, or to fancy he encouraged them, he would, most assuredly, mistake the Means, by meanly patronizing one Party of Artists against another. His despotic Disposition would break forth even in the slightest Instances, and thus absurdly would he blast and cherish with the same Breath. Royal Academies might be instituted, Royal Professors might make sycophantic Orations in Honour of their ROYAL MECENAS, but still the Arts wou'd droop, if not die. Under the Auspices of so weak a Patron, should they unexpectedly preserve their Vigour, it must be owing merely to public Taste, not to Royal Affection and Caprice. What if he should take it in his Head to study Stars more than Men, and busy himself more about the planetary than the political System? What if he should lend a patient Ear to the nauseous Flattery of Painters, Fidlers, Mechanics and Buffoons, yet reject with Scorn and Insult the repeated Supplications of the first Metropolis in his Kindom? What Name, what Censure, what Contempt, what Ignominy, would he not deserve?

But I am tired with the irksome Contemplation of this Mass of Royalty; born alas! to grasp, not to sway, a powerful Scepter; to squander, not to apply, an immense annual Revenue. Too much a Child to know an End of Prodigality, too little of a Man to set Bounds to his Revenge. As the one has no Object, so the other has no just Cause.

I want Patience to dwell longer upon the Portrait of this ideal Monster. If Nature ever furnished its Original, his Kingdom must be distressed indeed.

However, before I quit this motley Character, this vile Compound of heterogeneous and unprincely Qualities, I will try to penetrate this lumpish Mass of indigested Majesty with one short Word, and then plunge it in Oblivion, with Contempt.

If this vain Idol hath Ears, and heareth, let it hear this honest and wise Precaution, given to crowned Heads by the discerning Lord Bolingbroke: "Let not Princes flatter themselves," says that great Statesman, "they will be examined closely, as well in private, as in public Life, and those who cannot pierce further, will judge by the Appearances they give in both."[1]

C A S C A.

***No. XLI. will be addressed to the People of England, upon the Meeting of Parliament (alias the Conspiritors) to register Edicts of an ungrateful Tyrant.*

Printed and published for the Authors, by T. W. SHAW, in *Fleet-Street*, opposite *Anderton's Coffee House*, where Letters to the Publisher will be thankfully received.

---

1. This passage from Bolingbroke's "Of the Private Life of a Prince" can be found in *The Patriot King* (London: T. C., 1740), Letter Three, p. 22, and various other editions published over the intervening years, most commonly in the combined edition *Letters on the Spirit of Patriotism.*

THE

CRISIS

NUMBER XLI   *To be continued Weekly.*

SATURDAY, *October* 28, 1775   *Price* Two Pence Half-penny.

Rome, *Sparta*, and *Carthage* PERISHED, and without there is some COURAGE in Englishmen, *Britain* must be DE-STROYED.

To the PEOPLE OF ENGLAND.

Men and Britons, Friends and Countrymen,

YOUR LIVES are to be sacrificed, your LAWS destroyed, your RELIGION changed, your LIBERTIES annihilated, and your ESTATES taken from you by a corrupt House of Commons, a Blood-thirsty Administration, and a tyrannic p-----d King. With YOUR Money FOREIGN Troops are to be paid, to cut the THROATS of your Brethren and Fellow-subjects, and to carry Slaughter and Desolation through the wide extended Continent of America. The most savage Means have already been made use of to reduce an industrious, brave, free, and loyal People, from a State of Affluence, to that of Poverty, Want and Slavery, only because they have nobly resisted TYRANNY and LAWLESS POWER, and defended their own, and the natural Rights of Mankind, with a Firmness and Resolution (not to be equalled in History) that will do immortal Honour to their Names.

The Cruelties exercised upon our Brethren in America by mercenary Soldiers, would disgrace the most barbarous Nations upon Earth, and will for ever mark with indelible Infamy, the present Sovereign and his Ministers. Illegal and unjust Taxes have been levied upon them, by a House of Commons smuggled for the Purpose; their Property wantonly and arbitrarily seized; several People inhumanly butchered without Provocation or Offence; their Charters destroyed; new made Judges, and new modes of Proceeding appointed, unknown to the Laws and Constitution, an Act was passed the last Session of Parliament for the horrid, the diabolical Purpose of destroying, by FAMINE, more than TEN THOUSAND Souls; since that, their Towns and Properties have been destroyed by FIRE AND SWORD, when aged Men, Women, and Children perished in the Conflagration.

The House of Commons are now met, for the avowed Purpose of imposing illegal, heavy, and unjust Taxes upon you, to carry on the present bloody, unnatural, ministerial War against the Americans, and to take into the pay of Great Britain a certain Number of foreign Troops, who are to plunge their Swords into the Bowels of our Fellow-subjects, and to carry Devastation, Slaughter, and Massacre through the Land. Should the King and his Ministry succeed in their diabolical Design to enslave one Part of the Empire, and you can be base enough to give them Assistance in this horrid Work, by paying UNJUST Taxes, and tamely complying with such Measures, you will be the next Victims at the Altar of Despotism.—It is, therefore, a Duty you owe to God, to your Country, to yourselves, and to Posterity, not only to REFUSE the Payment of any Taxes that may be levied upon you by the present venal Senate, for the Purpose of paying foreign Troops to carry Fire, Sword, Famine, and Desolation through the Colonies, but you ought to OPPOSE and RESIST the Execution of any such Laws: unless you have Virtue and Resolution enough to act in this Manner, you will entail upon yourselves, and Millions yet unborn, Misery, Oppression, and Slavery. Petitions and Remonstrances have been spurned with Contempt. Your Prince is weak and obstinate;

he is a Slave in his Palace, the mere Tool of a Scotch Junto in the Council; ignorant of the Laws and Constitution; a Stranger to military Affairs, and the whole Art of Government—Under the Pretence of supporting a SUPREME parliamentary Authority over the most distant Parts of the Empire, NOT REPRESENTED, they design to establish Tyranny and arbitrary Power by Act of Parliament in America, and as a Majority in the present House of Commons is notoriously bribed with the public Money to betray their Trust, every Englishman may soon have the Honour of being made a Slave by Law, for if this uncontroulable Supremacy of Parliament is once admitted, and not opposed and resisted, the Life, Liberty, and Property of every Man will be at the Mercy of a few venal Representatives, a royal Tyrant and his Minions.—Let me advise you then, before this Doctrine, so fatal to the natural Rights of Mankind, gains Ground to make a noble Stand.—Nothing can be more dreadful than for a Nation to be involved in the Horrors of a Civil War; but when the common Welfare of ALL is willfully neglected, the most SACRED RIGHTS of the People OPENLY INVADED, the repeated Petitions for Redress of Grievances, not only thought undeserving of Consideration, but the Petitioners made the Jest and Mockery of a corrupt Court, thereby adding Insults to their Injuries, every GOOD MAN will steadily unite in the COMMON CAUSE, and use his utmost Endeavours to wrest the POWER of GOVERNMENT out of Hands that have exercised it WEAKLY and WICKEDLY.

It were much to be wished, that the EVILS of a NATION might be cured without Violence; but when it is evident that the PUBLIC LIBERTY and SAFETY is not even tolerably secured, and that Mischiefs, and those too of a more lasting Kind, daily arise from the Continuance of the present Men in Power, than are to be feared from the vigourous Efforts for an ALTERATION of them, it is LAWFUL and HONOURABLE, and it is OUR DUTY, to oppose and defeat their System of Government, which apparently tends to the utter Subversion of the RIGHTS and LIBERTIES of a FREE PEPOLE. By the Law of Nature every Man has a Right to defend himself against the Abuse of Power, and by the singular Constitution of this Kingdom, when KINGS and MINISTERS break through the Bounds prescribed by LAW, the People's Right of RESIS-

TANCE is unquestionable: for as the End of all Civil Government is the SAFETY and HAPPINESS of the whole Body, any Power not naturally conducive to this End, is certainly unjust. The Prince and People enter into a Compact, or Engagement, one with another; the Prince to govern well; and the People, so long as the Contract is religiously adhered to on his Part, to honour and obey him. If he regards his own Interest, or the Interest of his Minions, in Preference to that of his People, he necessarily forfeits every Claim to their Affection and Esteem.

In Times of national Decay—when Trade is rapidly declining—when the POOR are groaning under the Oppressions of the RICH—when the ancient Rights and Liberties of the People are daringly attacked, and openly violated—when that Land which used to be esteemed a PARADISE, is made a Stage of Cruelty and Injustice—when Merit is wholly neglected, and those only advanced at this Time, who are willing to be Instruments in the horrid Work of DESPOTISM—when PUBLIC DUTIES engage not the least Share of Attention; but senseless Ostentation, Profuseness, and Dissipation, are the sole Objects of Delight amongst the GREAT, whose pernicious Examples tend to draw all Ranks of Men to a base Uniformity of SPIRIT with THEMSELVES—when our Court is slavish, our Parliament corrupted, and those who formerly brought Kings and Ministers to a Sense of their Duty, submit themselves, in the midst of Affluence, to a mean, servile Dependance upon the Crown—when Bribery at Elections, which utterly destroys the Morals of the People, is publickly avowed, as the necessary Expedient of Government—when all Manner of Profaneness, Looseness, Luxury, and Immorality are set up and countenanced, instead of Piety, Modesty, and Justice—when the SWORD is employed by a Blood-thirsty implacable Administration to massacre our guiltless Fellow-subjects abroad, and is surely destined, in the End to butcher those at home—when rascally INFORMERS are employed by the Ministry, as in the infamous and corrupt Reign of Charles the Second, to swear away the Lives of those few brave and virtuous Men, who are the tried friends of their Country.—What Joy can an Englishman receive when the true Face of our Affairs carries such a miserable Aspect? What Heart is there so unfeeling with Respect to the Public Welfare, as not to sympathize with the Distresses and Calamities of his Country.

It is, therefore, the indispensible Duty of every Man, at this Time, who has Virtue enough to prefer the general Good of the Community, and who pretends to a Concern for its Interests, to consider well the PART he ought to take, in a Scene so pregnant with MISCHIEF, RUIN, and DISTRESS. He must either shamefully relapse into an indolent Indifference about every Thing that ought to interest him as an ENGLISH-MAN, or be animated by a just and honourable Purpose of obtaining a Satisfaction to the LAWS OF HIS COUNTRY, equal, at least, to the Violation they have suffered.

Unless the present infernal Ministry is removed, the present Parliament dissolved, the Septennial Act repealed, Placemen and Pensioners not suffered to sit in the House of Commons, a more equal Representation of the People, and the present Measures of Government entirely changed: I say, unless these Things are accomplished through the intrepid Firmness and spirited Resolution of the People, the Life and personal Liberty of every Man who may ACT, WRITE, or SPEAK in Opposition to the Corrupt and Bloody Court of George the Third, must be in danger from Ministerial ASSASSINS and INFORMERS. The Orders for apprehending STEPHEN SAYRE, Esq; and seizing his Papers, upon a ridiculous, futile Charge of TREASON, ought to alarm every Man in the Kingdom.[1] The best and worthiest Men in England may fall a Sacrifice to those PARRICIDES, those TRAYTORS, those BLOOD-HOUNDS of Power, and their suborned Evidences, if a speedy Stop is not put to their infamous Proceedings by a general ASSOCIATION of the People. The sagacious Fielding, and the Cyclops Rochford, ought to have known,

---

1. Stephen Sayre was a New York merchant and banker who moved to London and, like William Lee of Virginia, had been elected a sheriff there. He spent a harrowing if brief time in the Tower of London on a trumped-up charge of plotting to seize the King on his way to open the new parliamentary session on October 26th, incite the people of the city to support the conspirators, and oblige the King to renounce North's policies toward the colonies. See John Richard Alden, *Stephen Sayre* (Baton Rouge: Louisiana State University Press, 1983), pp. 67–96, which Alden characterized as "bizarre proceedings;" John Sainsbury, *Disaffected Patriots* (Montreal and Kingston: McGill-Queen's University Press, 1987), pp. 100–103; and Julie Flavell, *When London Was Capital of America* (New Haven: Yale University Press, 2010), pp. 143–63.

that the Information given against Mr. Sayre, by RICHARDSON, who was paid for the Purpose, did not authorize them to commit him, under the Statute of Treasons passed in the Reign of Edward the Third.—The Informer did not prove, as the Statute requires, any OVERT ACT of Treason, which ought to have been done; as it was not, the Commitment is arbitrary and illegal. NO WORDS can amount to TREASON.—If a Subject conspire with a foreign Prince to invade the Realm by open Hostility, and does not PREPARE for the same, by some Overt Act, it is no Treason, by the before-mentioned Statute. A Conspiracy to levy War is no Treason, by the same Act, until it be levied, for without that it is no Overt Act, or manifest Proof of compassing the Death of the King. To compass and imagine, is to contrive, design, or intend the Death of the King; but this must be declared by some OVERT ACT. Indeed Lord Mansfield, with the Assistance of Chancellor Apsley, may make Treason of the Lord's Prayer, or the Ten Commandments, by CONSTRUCTION. However, if a grand Jury should find a Bill there surely is not Twelve Englishmen to be got in the Kingdom who would, even with all the Sophistry and all the Chicanery of a Mansfield, convict Mr. Sayre of Treason; besides, there must be TWO Men of the same CONDITION with the Prisoner, to prove an OVERT ACT of Treason; but if all Sir John Fielding's Thief-takers and himself, together with Lord Rochford and his INFORMER, should swear, that Stephen Sayre, Esq; SAID, he would seize the King's Person, and take the Tower of London, it would not make these bare WORDS Treason. There is no doubt, however, but Lord Rochford, and the rest of the Ministry, as they could suborn one Wretch to inform, will be able to procure another, equally infamous, to swear they shall desire.

Many brave and virtuous Men, the Champions of Liberty, have been villainously dispatched to the other World in former Reigns, by illegal Trials, suborned Evidences, corrupt Judges, and infatuated Superiors, and why not at this Time? what has been, may be again. The great ALGERNON SIDNEY fell a Sacrifice in the Time of Charles the Second, a Reign equally infamous and inglorious with the present: In those Days, as in these, the scattered Remains of English Liberty were attacked on all Sides, and no Man who was distinguished for a Love of Freedom, could escape Destruction. The SPYING and INFORMING Trade was carried on with great Success, and encouraged by Charles the Second and his Ministers, as it is now by George the Third and his Ministers. Charles was blessed with the bloody-minded, the inhuman JEFFERIES, as CHIEF Justice: George is equally happy in a MURRAY. Sidney, with the true Spirit of an Englishman, when he came before the Council, told them, with a Boldness which Innocence inspired, that if they had any PROOF against him, he should make the best Defence he could; but they were not to expect he would fortify their Evidence by any Thing he should say: By this Means his Examination was very short, besides there being no Sort of Evidence against him, his Commitment like that of Mr. Sayre's was illegal and against Law; for he was not taken up as a Plotter, or Traitor, but, like Mr. Sayre, for being a Republican. However there was no Crime at that Time more capital, nor is there a greater at this, than to be an Enemy to unlimited Monarchy, and despotic Power. Mr. Sidney was committed to the Tower, but not denied the Use of Pen, Ink and Paper, or the Sight of his Friends, as Mr. Sayre now is, to the eternal Disgrace and Infamy of the present Ministry. The Trial of Mr. Sidney was certainly a Master-piece in its Kind, and will transmit the Infamy of the Judges and Juries which were employed, to latest Posterity. A Jury was picked out, agreeable to the Desire of the Court: They consisted of the meanest of the People. Sidney objected to a Number of them because they were not Freeholders; but Jefferies (the Mansfield of our Days) told him, that had been over-ruled in Lord Russel's Case, and therefore it should be so in his. JEFFERIES, like MANSFIELD, was for making PRECEDENTS, and as no Witnesses could be produced, not even the unpardoned WEST, and the to be pardoned Lord Howard, that proved any Act of Treason, and as Jefferies was resolved to condemn him right or wrong, he had Recourse to his Papers, and though no one could prove the Hand-writing, yet by the singular Sagacity of Jefferies, they were found to contain sufficient Proof for Conviction. Not to mention a Number of other Particulars equally infamous and disgraceful, the Court concluded, that SIDNEY was not only guilty of being concerned in a PLOT which was charged upon him, but that he could not have been otherwise, because his PRINCIPLES led him to it, to which Jefferies added, that he was born a Traytor. O! glorious Times, renewed again by George the Third: Now for Plots and Counter-plots, which Mansfield shall make out.

Printed and published for the Authors, by T. W. SHAW, in Fleet-street, opposite Anderton's Coffee House, where Letters to the Publisher will be thankfully received.

THE

CRISIS

NUMBER XLII   *To be continued Weekly.*

SATURDAY, *November* 4, 1775   *Price* Two-Pence Half-penny.

. The Authors of the CRISIS propose, in their next Number, to DISSECT the last BLOODY Speech of the present Pious, Hypocritical Sovereign; the Operation would have been performed this Week, but the CALM ADDRESS of the canting, jesuitical *Wesley*, agreeable to the order of Time, claimed our Attention first.

Whilst servile *Wesley's* Pen with *Johnson's* vyes,
Enforcing all his Sophistry and Lyes;
Enlisted in the Service of the *Press*,
His *passive* Soul breaths forth a *Calm Address*.
This *Saint* from holy Toils how *Mammon* draws!
Truth his pretence, but *Gain* the latent Cause.
A *Mitre* tempts; and *North,* not slow to thank,
Returns the *Priest* his Compliments in *Bank*.
North knows Saints fight, but never think, nor yield;
And thus secures the Myriads of *Moorfield*.

Mad Hosts, who drown with Hymns the Trumpet's Sound,
And purchase Heav'n by dunging hostile Ground!

ANONYM.[1]

T HE trumpet sounds in *Zion*; the sons of *Whitfield* are alarmed,
and *John Wesley* himself hath taken up the arms of the spirit.[2]—
How wretched a cause have *Bute* and *Mansfield*, when the very
Tabernacles must be ransacked for advocates, and field-preachers are inlisted in the service of a ministerial *press? General Gage* complains (I think
in his proclamation for enforcing military law in *America*) that the *presses*
there teemed with sedition, and that the very *pulpits* were prostituted to
that service. Is not every imposition, every means of blinding and deceiving the good People of *England* practised in our metropolis both by clergy
and laity, in the pulpits, in the public papers, in lying pamphlets, in public
Coffee Houses, nay, in private families, as often as ministerial hirelings
can gain admittance? Do not the corrupt lackques of a corrupt *Admin-*
istration, insinuate themselves, like evil Genii, into every company, in all
shapes, and characters, labouring to taint the principles of every honest
Revolutionist? Are not the pastors of every *sect* pressed into the trammels of
government, to aid, defend, or palliate the pernicious schemes of *Bute* and
Mansfield, those *Empsons* and *Dudleys* of the Nation?[3] The very enthusiasts of Moorfields, are now wrapt in political reveries, their Tabernacles
resound with *anti-revolution* Doctrines, whist their holy pastors are drawn
aside by the *Mammon* of unrighteousness. Paradventure, a pair of *lawn*

---

1. I suspect this is another instance (see n. XXXVIII.2 supra for the first) of the author(s)
doggerel, composed as an epigraph just for this occasion, to ridicule Samuel Johnson
and John Wesley.

2. John Wesley's efforts as a pamphleteer in *A Calm Address to Our American Colonies*
(London: R. Hawes, 1775), which appeared in numerous printings, are first targeted
here and would be again in subsequent issues (no. LVIII, on 24 February 1776, then nos.
LXI–LXIII, 12 March through 30 March 1776), with Samuel Johnson and newspaper
essayist John Shebbeare being condemned in the same breath for their views as well. For
Johnson see n. XV.2 supra; for Wesley and Shebbeare, the *Oxford DNB*, essays by Henry
D. Rack, and M. John Cardwell, at 58:182–93 and 50:143–46, resp.

3. For Empson and Dudley see n. X.4 supra.

slaves is promised (and only promised) to *John Wesley*, if he will work up his *thousands and ten thousands*, to roar, like bulls of *Basan*, in the cause of *falsehood*, *corruption*, *tyranny*, and *blood*.

By the acquisition of this leader of the *elect*, how are the secular arms of *Johnson* and his scribbling *Garretteers* strengthened and enforced? How is the *ministerial* cause supported? With what awful pomp will the *royal standard* be hoisted, when these *maddening zealots*, with *John Wesley* at their head, shall dance before it, and all the furious hosts of *hot-heads* shall shout *Amen*, to the bloody Purposes of a pusillanimous driveling King, cloathed in *purple and fine linen*!—However this new captain of our *political salvation* may have escaped unanswered from his *Tabernacks*, he must, in this worldly warfare of the *press*, submit, not only to a reply, but, perhaps, to some rebuke. When he takes up the pen, he must re-member that he wields a weapon of the *flesh*, and must sometimes stoop to kiss the rod.—In his late *Calm Address* to our *American* Colonies, I find but little to applaud, though much to reprehend. This preacher treads in *Johnson's* steps; but without the least abilities or knowledge, as a *hackney writer*. He is a mimic of his master; he apes his *sophistry*, and almost equals his *audacity*. He sets out by likening a body of *Colonists*, settling under the royal charter, to a trading *corporation*, or the *vestry of a parish*. Proceeding upon this infectious mistake (among others which he has copied from his master *Johnson*) all he advances must be wrong. He will pardon me if I submit to him my notion of a *chartered Colony*, by observing, that emigrants from civilised states, who have the settlement of a *colony* in view, though they leave their native country, do not mean to abandon their natural allegiance. They change their place without a change either of their national or social principles and attachments. In consequence of these sentiments and affections, the first act of notoriety where they fix their settlement, is generally to hoist the colours of that state from whence they come, claiming, by proclamation, the vacant territory for their lawful sovereign, whose charter they receive, of course, as an assurance of his protection, in return to their loyal declaration of allegiance. Thus foreign territories, discovered by Englishmen, (and the same rule holds among all civilized nations) belong to the crown of England. I say, to the crown of England, to the sovereign only, and not to king, lords, and commons. It is the undoubted prerogative of the sovereign to grant a *charter*, which may, if the king thinks fit, be a charter of *incorporation* to his *colony*. By the word *colony* I understand a body of emigrants who separate from one *community* to form another *distinct one* where they please, still professing allegiance to, and, in return, receiving protection from, their natural or lawful sovereign, by virtue of his royal charter. Now where is the least similitude between such an emigrant body, though *incorporated* (as some have actually been) for the purpose of settling a *colony*, and a trading *corporation*; except that both have received the royal charter? At the same time, it must be observed, that it is not in the *king*'s power, whatever he may intend, to *abridge* the rights and liberties of his subjects by any restrictions in such charter. Though the chartered body thereby acquires a new *politic* capacity, yet it still retains, in all its *individual* members, its *natural* capacity. A mere *fiction* of law cannot extinguish the rights of a subject. To such a *fiction* every corporate body owes its *politic* existence. Taken *collectively* it is the creature of the *king*, and its rights are circumscribed (as the ministerial scribblers insist) by *charter*; but taken *individually*, they are so many members, or (permit me to say) *heirs*, of the British constitution, whose rights were clearly settled at the revolution, as far as that settlement extends; for it is not perfect; it is confessed on all hands, (not inimical to the constitution) that some necessary stipulations are omitted. Be that as it may, the rights of all *corporate* bodies, acting in their *natural* capacities, can be limited only (as the constitution stands at present) by the compact between sovereign and subject at the *revolution*. We do not find *there*, that subjects can be *taxed* without their *consent*, as parson *Wesley* asserts. We do not find there that the *king* can annex his *colony* (his own *demesnes)* to the realm of England by other means than the policy of the English law allows, that is, by act of parliament; for to such acts as concern the whole realm, the whole realm, all its *three* estates, king, lords, and commons, must be parties. By these, and these means only, can a colony, *out of the realm*, be *taxed* constitutionally by our parliament. The colony cannot otherwise be either *virtually*, or *actually* represented; and therefore all the flimsy *Tory* arguments respecting *virtual* representation must fall to the ground; and the mercenary troops of ministerial *pen-men* are laid on their backs, as it is devoutly wished their *swordsmen* may be on the plains of distressed, insulted, and dragooned *America*.[4]

If the pockets of *America,* like those of *Great Britain,* must be picked, for the worst of purposes, that of undermining the constitution, let them be picked *in due form*, and with some shew and colour of decency; let them be picked according to the established precedent for annexing the sole property of the crown, in *foreign territories,* to the realm of England: they will still be picked no less by *act of parliament*, without letting loose *famine, fire, massacre*, and all the miseries of war upon subjects whom neither *king* nor *parliament* have a right to *pillage*, but in a *legal way.*—Let me pursue this disquisition a little further. In that community which English colonists have left, they were either *actually or virtually* represented, or they could not have been bound by any law of the legislature which they left behind them. In the new community, also, of which they are now become a part, they must be represented likewise, either actually or virtually, before they can be bound. But in the legislature of that community which they have left they cannot be bound (in respect to pecuniary taxation) because they are now no longer, either actually or virtually represented there. How can the commons of *England* give and grant the money of a distinct community of another realm or territory, not yet annexed to the realm of *England?* In a territory which is the *sovereign's demesne*; for whatever some hireling scribblers have asserted to the contrary, yet all territories newly discovered still belong (as they did at the time the several settlements were made and granted on the *American* continent) to the crown. They who deny this know, or ought to know, that in order to avoid an unanswerable difficulty, they have the impudence to deny an undoubted truth.

4. Edmund S. and Helen M. Morgan made the dispute over "virtual" representation an essential component of their *The Stamp Act Crisis* (Chapel Hill: University of North Carolina Press, 1953). Also see, more ambitiously, Gordon S. Wood's *The Creation of the American Republic, 1776–1787* (Chapel Hill: University of North Carolina Press, 1969). The notion of virtual representation had not been contrived by Thomas Whately in 1765 at George Grenville's behest, for the debates of the moment; it had been posited any number of times over the years, in the Irish Parliament as well as the British Parliament.

As the king's prerogative stands at present (for it still stands as it did in the reigns of our worst kings, the *Stuarts*) all new colonies must hold their lands (as the old ones originally did) of the king, as tenants, in *capite*. It is, indeed, in the sovereign's power, if he pleases, to grant these *demesnes* of his in *capite*, to be held of him for the future as *free socage*; in such case the kings of England have ever received some valuable consideration for such grant. King Charles the second received a subsidy of four and a half per cent on the sugars of that island from the colonists of Barbados, on this consideration. There are other instances of this in the other Carribbee islands. Now who were parties to this grant? The parliament of England did not, nor could, interfere with the least propriety (though jealous of prerogative at that time a-day) in a matter which concerned the king and his property alone. Who granted this revenue to the king, this *internal tax* (for so it was) the parliament of *England*, or the legislature of Barbados? It was the latter, who thought then, as *America* thinks now, (and rightly thinks) that they had an exclusive and peculiar right to give and grant the monies which they earned by the sweat of their own brows in a community distinct from that of *England*. This *tax* was, in the strictest sense, *internal*; for it was to be paid before their own sugars could be permitted to be shipped from their island to their mother-country. Though king Charles the second (who by turns duped, and was again himself the dupe of parliament) in his charters to Connecticut and Rhode-Island, and Pensylvania; though *William and Mary* in their grant of Maryland to Lord Baltimore, expressly reserve to the parliament of England (merely out of complaisance) their full power of taxation, &c. over those colonies, yet that reservation can confer no new powers on the parliament, much less can it enable them to tax unconstitutionally, and without either actual or virtual representation, persons who had quitted their territory for a distinct community, and who had acquired in that new community a new property of their own, of which they cannot legally be stripped but in due and legal form, either by the law of nature, the law of nations, or the common law of England, which every emigrant to an English colony takes with him, though he leaves his former legislature together with the local privileges and benefits of England behind him.

Now, tell me, thou *calm addresser*, thou echo of thy master *Johnson*, in what respect is such a chartered body of emigrants like a trading *corporation*, or like the *vestry of a parish*, neither of which bodies are (like foreign colonies) out of the Realm, or unrepresented either actually or virtually in our parliament? No argument can be fairly formed, no just and true conclusions can be drawn between cases which are totally dissimilar. Though this corporation of colonists may subsist (as Mr. *Wesley* says) by a grant from *higher authority*, yet that *high authority* to which, he says, they still continue subject, cannot *tax*, (and most of our royal charters declare that the King will not *tax* them himself) nor can the King give the parliament of England a power of taxing them, and therefore the reservations of such a power in the royal charters to our parliament, is vain and nugutory, mere courtly froth, as I said before.

Having thus, with more attention than Mr. *Wesley's* whole performance deserves, overturned his corner stone, I leave all his first eight plain inferences, as so many baseless superstructures, to fall to the ground. Whatever his designs may be, is no less a *visionary* in politics than in religion. His first eight paragraphs are a mere abridgement of the futile arguments which have been retailed by all the ministerial scriblers, from their Captain, Doctor *Johnson*, which to himself, and have been confuted again and again.

I come now to his ninth paragraph, where he declares his opinion freely, upon his own *virre dire*,[5] assuring his readers that he is quite unbiassed, and that he was nothing to hope or fear on either side. I congratulate him upon this christian spirit of self-denial, so highly becoming a man of his sacred function; should he hope for a *bishopprick*, or even for a *deanery*, he must know that no confidence can be put in princes, nor in the sons of men, for they will deceive him; should he fear that his numerous flocks (from whence alone, perhaps, his hope cometh) should return to their sober senses, awakened, as from a dream. by the tyranny of their

---

5. Presumably a corruption of the older meaning "voir dire," which meant the promise of jurors to tell the truth.

rulers; his fears are groundless; such holy poisons as priest-craft can instill prevent all recovery.—But let us hear him—He says, there are a few men who are declared enemies to *monarchy*—true—all *revolutionists* are enemies to every monarchy which is *unlimited.* Now, if the *king,* lords, and commons were to form a mere *cabal,* a *junto,* a *combination,* and *confederacy;* if the *king* had a venal *majority* of his own in the two houses, he would then be to all intents and purposes, a monarch *unlimited.*—Such a *monarch,* and such *monarchy* a *Briton* will always hate.—As to *personal* hatred, we see it sometimes even in the animal creation. Why does the generous horse hate the *ass,* as much as a wise man hates a *fool?*—As to the kingly *office,* it will ever be revered in England, while exercised upon *revolution principles,* and for ever opposed (perhaps to its destruction) when it proceeds upon principles of *usurpation, tyranny,* and *blood.* Every *kingly* act which exceeds the limits of *humanity* degrades the *kingly office* beneath the office of the *common hangman.*—As to a *common-wealth,* which Mr. *Wesley* dreams of, I believe it is no wise man's thought, much less his *idol;* yet Mr. *Wesley* seems as if he was deep in this secret—He has discovered these *Guy Fawke's* with their dark lanthorns.[6] This good man certainly pictures out (like his predecessor *John Bunyan*) what he has seen in some spiritual trace.[7] Let him enjoy his vision, and penetrate, if he can, to the very bottom of a design which seems to be secret to all beside himself.—As to *foreign assistance,* England has good reason, *of late,* to be sick of it, and *America* can have no occasion to call it in; she is a nation of warriors; and is fully able (to the sorrow of our *Machiavels*) to effect her virtuous purposes by her own intrinsic strength.—Mr. *Wesley's* tenth paragraph contains the gentle, comfortable, sage, emollient admonitions of—an old woman.—His eleventh paragraph is altogether

6. The infamous Guy Fawkes of the 1605 Gunpowder Plot, whose name and memory were invoked for countless political purposes; in this case, for a little political sarcasm. See Mark Nicholls' *Oxford DNB*, 19:190–94 essay, which draws on Nicholls' book, *Investigating Gunpowder Plot* (Manchester: Manchester University Press, 1991).

7. John Bunyan, of *The Pilgrim's Progress* (1678) fame, used by the author(s) this time, like Guy Fawkes above, sarcastically. For Bunyan see Richard L. Greaves, *Oxford DNB*, 8:702–11.

dehortatory—it is a master-piece of rhetoric in that style. Dissuading *America* from a final breach and disunion with Great Britain, he apprizes her that the *remedy will be worse than the disease*; that is to say, that truly *patriotic revolutional resistance* will, in its effects be more pernicious to brave and virtuous subjects than the worst of miseries which war can enforce, or tyrants can invent: for, O! says the preacher, what convulsions must poor *America* feel before any government is settled?—*Poor America*, Mr. Wesley? What, do you pity her? It is all over with you then; take my word for it, you will never be a *bishop.*—But, to be serious; why must *America* be so horribly convulsed before a government is settled there? What settled government upon earth ever proceeded upon sounder policy, greater deliberation, wisdom, fortitude, and good conduct, (I hope shortly to be able to add *success*) than the several *American* states. If to see a virtuous individual struggling with afflictions is a spectacle worthy of the Gods, as the devine Socrates declared, with what adoration would that greatest of all heathen philosophers have looked upon such a nation as *America,* united to a man in the noblest cause that ever justified *resistance?* What *yoke* can such a nation of heroes fear, but that which already galls them; that which they are wisely and bravely resolved to shake off, casting the cords of *England* from them? Should this resolve be crowned with the success it merits, out *spiritual pastor's* fears for the *poor Americans* will be eased.—The man of God in his twelfth paragraph discovers, that his *American* brethren are dupes and tools to the designs of certain *Achitophels,*[8] who are in league to overturn the *English government* in *America.* I suspect a most unpardonable *erratum* of the printer here. I am pretty confident (if Mr. *Wesley* is an honest man, for he does not want understanding) that instead of the words *English government,*

---

8. Achitophel personified the warning against listening to friends who offer bad advice, as played out in the second book of Samuel in the Old Testament. It was he who persuaded Absalom to rise in revolt against his father, King David. Readers of *The Crisis* likely knew the tale; they may have also known John Dryden's much reprinted 1681 reworking of it as a satirical allegory, in the midst of the Exclusion Crisis (the failed move to prevent James, Duke of York, a Roman Catholic, from being designated the successor to his brother Charles II).

we ought to read *English usurpation*. Let the true reading of this passage be restored, and these *Achitophels* will be *Absaloms*;⁹ these designing incendiaries will become saviours of the constitution.

I am now arrived at the spiritual exhortation to peace and *passive obedience*, with which this holy advocate for regal tyranny concludes his *Calm Address*. I shall dismiss it with this short observation: that if the *City of London* would but take their cue from this preacher-up of *non-resistance*, this divine joiner of borrowed arguments for *slavery*, their next address would be music to the *sovereign*. But, be the success of Mr. *Wesley*'s little labours what they may, as he professes to write from the *heart*, a priest of *such principles* most certainly deserves a *mitre*.

I cannot, however, pass over his appendix to this *pastoral catch-penny*, wherein he passes many strictures upon *Dr. Smith*'s sermon at Philadelphia.¹⁰ Mr. *Wesley*, like all other enthusiasts, is a very bold asserter, but a very weak opponent. What he endeavours to shew in his appendix is, that the *American* complaints of unconstitutional taxes, violated rights and infringed, or, as he calls them, *mutilated* charters, are vain and groundless. But hear, ye sheepish volunteers, for whom this preacher is beating up, how little this holy man knows of the English constitution; as it stands since the *revolution*. Dr. *Smith* has asserted, and most truly, that no power on earth has a right to *give and grant* away *American* property without *American consent*.—Then, says Mr. *Wesley*, you have no *sovereign*: because, every *sovereign* under heaven has a right to *tax* his

---

9. One of the Old Testament's most tragic figures. Son of King David and Bathsheba, he had his servants kill David's oldest son, his half brother Amnon, for raping his sister. He flees, is forgiven, plots against his father, leads an uprising against him, and proclaims himself king. Defeated in battle by his father's forces, he is slain, despite David's wishes that he be spared. "Oh my son Absalom," sobs a grief-stricken David; "would God I had died for thee, O Absalom, my son, my son!" (2 Samuel 18:33, KJV).

10. William Smith preached *A Sermon on the Present Situation in American Affairs* (Philadelphia: James Humphreys, 1775) on 23 June 1775, at Christ Church, in the heart of Philadelphia, at the request of the city militia battalion. It was reprinted twice in short order by Edward and Charles Dilly, London publishers sympathetic (Edward especially) to the patriot cause.

subjects, that is, to grant their property either *with* or *without* their consent.—So, peremptory, so audacious, so ensnaring an assertion should have dropped from him only in the *pulpit*, where he could neither have been confronted, contradicted, or exposed. This assertion, in a *general* sense, is false, in a *confined* one, as relative only to an *English* sovereign, not only false, but *treacherous*, nay *traiterous*. It is a capital treason against the sacred compact between king and people at the blessed *revolution*: it is poisoning the ductile minds of his implicit believers with that exploded doctrine which cost *Charles* the first his head,

> Hail *Wesley*, hail!—thy *Brass* the prize secures:
> Ev'n *Johnson*'s front's a bashful front to yours.

But this *ecclesiastic tool* does not blush even to repeat his monstrous assertion—"Am I, or two millions of Englishmen, made *slaves*," says he, "because we are taxed without our own consent?"—Tell me, then, thou shepherd of the *elect*, thou inspired teacher of that faithful remnant which shall be saved, thou great surviving luminary of the *tabernacle*, if this is not *slavery*, what is the difference between *slavery* and *freedom*?—I pause for a reply,—Take your time for it, even till the last trump shall found.—In the interim, let us hear this reverend deceiver again, this *unbiassed* imposter, who has nothing to hope or fear from siding with an anti-revolution ministry, and thus basely offering up the grateful incense of a court-sycophant to the weakest, if not the wickedest of men. This *divine* observes, that one of the *American* charters exempts the colony from the payment of taxes for *seven years*: this implies, says he, that taxes are to be paid after the expiration of that term; and remember, too, says he, that the *Pensylvania* charter says, in express terms, that you are liable to taxation. These are the resonings, observations, and opinions of all our Tyrants and their scribblers in respect to all the colonies, whether the royal charters speak or imply any thing upon this head or not. But neither the royal charters themselves, nor those sycophants who are paid for their mis-interpretation of them, can annul *right*, or sanctify and establish *wrong*. The nature of these two contrarieties will continue the same eternally, let a venal majority confound them as they will. It is well known, that no colony ever was taxed *internally*, but by their own assemblies, till the ingenious Mr. *Grenville* suggested that happy mode,[11] which was soon dropped by our parliament in a *panic*, but afterwards resumed, and is now to be maintained and enforced by every pitiful ministerial stratagem at home, and by famine, sword, fire, and all the plagues, calamities, and devastations of a most inhuman war abroad.—This righteous scribbler runs back, even to the early days of William the Conqueror, another confessed Tyrant,[12] for arguments to support the despotic measures of a slavish, arbitrary majority of parliament, in the pious reign of *George* the third.—But to say the truth, our pamphleteer seems at all neither to understand himself, nor to convey his meaning clearly to the reader. I will, therefore, only remind him, that all earthly power, if communicated to a sovereign, must necessarily be communicated by the people, and by the people only, in whom alone it can reside.—Why should this *Calm Addresser* fly, in his concluding word from the exhortatory to the accusatory style? why should he leave his *American* sheep in a fume? why should he so uncharitably; and so groundlessly, condemn them as so many wicked confederates against their rightful *sovereign* and the *fundamental* laws of their country? Is every rightful sovereign so divine a being that he cannot commence a *tyrant*? And are the laws relating to *American taxation,* the *fundamental* laws of England? the truth is, that this clerical plagiary,

11. George Grenville still serves as a scapegoat for Britain's failed imperial policies leading to war, since the 1765 Stamp Act had been so much an extension of his desire to pull dissident Americans back into line, combining the financial and political in a single piece of legislation that was in turn part of an ambitious program of imperial tightening. Grenville never saw himself as anti-American; if willing to send troops in 1765, he opposed any such move in 1768 and did not object to seating Americans at Westminster to mollify them—though he would not have allowed them enough seats in the Commons to matter. John Bullion attempted to paint a revisionist view of his program in *A Great and Necessary Measure* (Columbia: University of Missouri Press, 1982), which prompted Thomas Slaughter's rejoinder, "The Empire Strikes Back: George Grenville and the Stamp Tax" *Reviews in American History* 12 (1984):204–10. Also see J. V. Beckett and Peter D. G. Thomas's sketch for the *Oxford DNB*, 23:723–27.

12. The authors anticipated by several months Thomas Paine's condemnation of William the Conqueror as a "usurper," as nothing more than "a French bastard landing with an armed banditti," in *Common Sense*, a pamphlet to which they never referred in *The Crisis*. See n. I.10 supra.

for his arguments are all pilfered, is either totally ignorant of the English constitution, or else he prostitutes a good understanding, and a sacred character, with selfish, or worse than selfish views, to serve the worst purpose of the worst administration that ever ruined a weak and deluded prince, or disgraced the annals of a free country.

CASCA.

Printed and published for the Authors, by T. W. SHAW, in Fleet-street, opposite Anderton's Coffee House, where Letters to the Publisher will be thankfully received.

THE

CRISIS

NUMBER XLIII   *To be continued Weekly.*

SATURDAY, NOVEM. 11, 1775   *Price* Two Pence Half-penny.

Of meaner Crimes we scorn to mention more,
But of a M--------R CROWN'D, besmeared with GORE.
What Seas of BLOOD? What desolated Lands?
What murder'd Nations? by his base Commands,
Curst Mischiefs which his greater Crimes procure,
RESIST, O! Britons, only THAT can CURE.

FROM the advancement of the present Sovereign to the throne of these realms, to this hour, his government has been one perpetual exercise of rage, malice, cruelty, treachery, deceit, falsehood, fraud, injustice, madness, and folly.

The WORST and most infamous of men have been armed with powers, for the purpose of destroying the BEST, and reducing the people, by gradual steps, from a state of PROSPERITY and FREEDOM, to that of MISERY and SLAVERY; and to the disgrace of the people of England, they have been suffered QUIETLY to carry their diabolical designs so far into execution in one part of the British dominions, that nothing can now save the Empire from ruin, but THEIR DESTRUCTION.

The People HERE do not seem to consider, that, by arming the Sovereign and his minions with a power over their country, they rob themselves of all title to their LIVES and ESTATES, help to overthrow the constitution of the kingdom, and are not only the parricides of their country, but the murderers of their own children and posterity by putting lawless daggers into the hands of TYRANTS, to execute their murders; thus they sell their own blood and posterity, to these IMPERIAL BUTCHERS, whose great delight, and chief employment, will be to shed it.

O! degenerate Englishmen! your illustrious ancestors never thought of this vile subserviency of their descendents, to SLAVES and TYRANTS, the first they despised, the latter they bravely resisted, and generously shed their BLOOD to secure FREEDOM to their posterity, who it is greatly to be feared will leave to their children and all succeeding ages, the terrible inheritance of servitude, exile, tortures, and massacree.

The speech of the king to the Lords and Commons, and of course to the whole people of England, on *Thursday*, the 26th of *October*, is the speech of a TYRANT, it abounds with the most notorious falsehoods, impotent menaces, rediculous offers of mercy, and the daring impudent assertions of a despot, firmly resolved on the destruction of his subjects, and busily employed in forging chains for his country.[1]

In the subsequent part of this paper, we will detect the falsehoods, and expose the artifice of this piece of state-craft, fabricated in the sink of corruption at *St. James's,* and designed to deceive, mislead, and ruin the people of England. This merciful father of his people (who destroys them according to act of parliament by thousands, with FAMINE, FIRE, and SWORD) begins his false, hypocritical, bloody harrangue, in the following words.

---

1. The King's speech of 26 October 1775, opening the second session of the fourteenth parliament, can be found in Simmons and Thomas, eds., *Proceedings and Debates,* 6:69–70, and had been printed the next day in the *Daily Advertiser,* the *Morning Chronicle,* the *Morning Post,* and the *Public Advertiser.* For the Lords' "dissentient" led by the Duke of Manchester, see n. XLV.2 infra.

"The present situation of *America*, and *my* constant desire to have your advice, concurrence, and assistance, on every important occasion, have determined me to call you thus early together."

Notwithstanding the present situation of America (which is deplorable indeed) and this pious King's constant desire to have their advice, concurrence, and assistance, yet his Majesty could garrison Gibraltar and Minorca with Foreign troops, which is contrary to law, illegal, and unconstitutional, without their advice or assistance, and afterwards call HIS bribed, obsequious Senate, who immediately sanctify this notorious violation of MAGNA CHARTA and the BILL of RIGHTS. We can no longer boast of a free constitution, and a limitted Monarchy, the King is arbitrary, and we may soon expect to find the Sovereign and his privy council, levy taxes on the people, like Charles the First; this he may do with safety, and the present rotten House of Commons will directly declare the infamous INJUSTICE and TYRANNY to be legal.

"Those who have long too successively laboured to inflame my people in America, by gross misrepresentations, (*that is, BARNARD HUTCHINSON, and the rest of your infamous ministers*) and to infuse into their minds a system of opinions repugnant to the true constitution of the Colonies, and to their subordinate relation to Great Britain, now openly avow their revolt, hostility, and rebellion."

It is not a rebellion, but a just, legal RESISTANCE to your arbitary laws and tyranny, which is warranted by all the laws of God and man. "They have raised troops," *which you are very uneasy about; yes, and they have lawfully, (not illegally, as you have done;) raised them to defend their lives, liberties, and estates, which you want to destroy,* "and are collecting a naval force, they have seized the public revenues," *that is their own property, which you intended to rob them of, with the assistance of your bribed parliament, contrary to every principle of law and justice,* "and assumed to themselves, legislature, executive, and judicial powers," *as you had abused your trust, destroyed their constitution, and instead of exercising the deligated powers of a legal government, you had erected a tyranny, they had a just and legal right to take those powers which were originally theirs, into their own hands again;* "which they already exercise, in the most arbitary manner, over the persons and properties of their fellow subjects;" *this is an absolute falshood, purposely designed to deceive the people of England, that they might the more readily join in the bloody measures now carrying on against the Americans;* "and although many of these unhappy people may still retain their loyalty," *O rediculous, every man that is loyal to a tyrant, or a tyrannical government, must be paid for it,* "and may be too wise not to see the fatal consequence of this usurpation, and wish to resist it. (*what a desception*) yet the torrent of violence has been strong enough to compel their acquiescence, till a sufficient force shall appear to support them." *It is notorious to the world, that there is not one thousand people in the whole continent of America, that wish to support the present bloody measures of administration, and what force will be SUFFICIENT to support the dependants of his tyrannical Majesty, must be left to his sagacity, and the villainy of his ministers to discover.*

"The authors and promoters of this desperate conspiracy have, in the conduct of it, derived great advantage from the differene of our intentions and theirs." *This is literally true, the intentions of government have been, and still are, VILLAINOUS, and the intentions of the Americans JUST.* "They mean only to amuse, by vague expressions of attachment to the parent state;" *this is not true, but it is an absolute fact, that by such artifice, YOU always meant to RUIN and DECEIVE,* "and the strongest protestations of loyalty to me, whilst they were preparing for a general revolt." *It is only to be lamented, that they should profess or exercise any loyalty to an unfeeling Prince.* "On my part, though it was declared in your last session, that a rebellion existed within the province of the Massachusett's Bay, yet even that province we wished rather to reclaim than subdue." *Surely his Majesty must think the people are as credulous, as his system of government and ministers are infamous, to believe such falshoods.* "The resolutions of parliament breathed a spirit of moderation and forbearance;" *what a misfortune it is, that Kings seldom or ever speak truth*; "conciliatory propositions accompanied the measures taken to enforce authority." *How daring, impudent, insulting, and false, is this assertion, when it is known to the world, that those propositions were not concilatory, but deceitful, treacherous, and ruinous.* "I have acted with the same temper;" *yes, you have acted with a temper that would disgrace a savage,* "anxious to prevent, if it had been possible, the effusion of the blood of my subjects, and the calamities which are inseperable from a state of war." *When a criminal at the bar of the Old Bailey tells a wilful lye, to save his LIFE, he is, in my opinion, excusable, but nothing can extenuate the crime of a Sovereign, who for the worst, and most infamous purposes, publishes notorious falsities to the world. The inattention, disrespect, and contempt, shewn to all the petitions from America to the throne, as well as to those delivered by the people of England in their behalf, will for ever stand upon record to all succeeding ages, a flat contradiction to the above assertion*; "still hoping that my people in America would have discerned the traiterous views of their leaders." "They have sufficiently discerned your traiterous views and designs, but those of THEIR LEADERS are just and honourable, and have been convinced, that to be a subject of Great Britain, with all its consequences, is to be the freest member of any civil society in the known world. Yes, and of this they were not only convinced, but satisfied, till your inglorious reign. The rebellious war now levied, is become more general, and is manifestly carried on for the purpose of establishing an independant empire," the various solemn declarations of the Congress, and the several petitions from America, sufficiently refute that assertion. "I have also the satisfaction to iuform you, that I have received the most friendly offers of Foreign assistance," "there is no doubt but mercenary cut-throats, assassins, and savages, may be procured for money, and must; or will the people of England be base enough to assist you, by submitting to heavey and unjust taxes, for the horrid purpose of paying those murderers to massacre their fellow-subjects in America, surely not, such guilt would call from Heaven, vengeance on their heads; and if I shall make any treaties in consequence thereof, they shall be laid before you, great condescension indeed, to let the people know in what manner they are to be robbed and slaughtered. and I have, in testimony of my affection to my people," who can doubt his affection for his people, when he only makes use of FAMINE, FIRE, and SWORD, to destroy them, "who can have no cause in which I am not equally interested, sent to the garrisons of Gibraltar and Port Mahon, a part of my electoral troops, yes, in direct violation of the Bill of Rights, in order that a larger number of the established forces of this kingdom, may be applied to the maintenance of its authority; and the national militia, planned and regulated with equal regard to the rights, safety, and protection, of my crown and people." The rights, safety, and protection of the people will certainly be secure, under a military government, and any power, however dangerous, may be put with safety, into the hands of so pious and good a King.

"When the unhappy and deluded multitude, against whom this force will be directed, shall become sensible of their error, I shall be ready to receive the misled with tenderness and mercy;" may God of his infinite goodness, always keep the people of this nation, from the tender mercies of a tyrant; "and in order to prevent the inconveniences which may arise from the great distance of their situation, and to remove as soon as possible, the calamities which they suffer, I shall give authority to certain persons upon the spot, to grant general or particular pardons and indemnities, in such manner, and to such persons, as they shall think fit." The Americans will treat this piece of foolish King-craft, treachery, and artifice, with the contempt it deserves. they want no pardon from you, and will despise your insidious offers, 'tis you, and your blood-thirsty ministers, who stand most in need of pardon, both from God and them, "and to receive the submission of any province or colony, which shall be disposed to return to its allegiance; it may be also proper, to authorize the persons so commissioned, to restore such province or colony, so returning to its allegiance, to the free exercise of its trade and commerce, and to the same protection and security, as if such province or colony had never revolted;" amazing kindness (if the Americans will quietly submit to slavery and chains, they are to be restored to their trade and commerce; this Scotch chicanery will not do, the Americans are not to be deceived or enslaved, Bute and Mansfield must find out some other scheme.

"I have fully opened to you my views and intentions which are to destroy the LAWS, RELIGION, and CONSTITUTION of the Empire. The constant employment of my thoughts, and the most earnest wishes of my heart, tend wholly to the safety and happiness of all my people; this infamous falsehood, must surely raise the indignation of every honest Englishman who reads it, have not the lives of many thousand people in this abandoned reign, been wantonly and wickedly sacrificed? Have not the most sacred rights of the people been openly violated, and these violations sanctified by the king; not to mention a thousand tyrannical oppressions besides; is not then the above sentence the greatest insult and provication ever offered to a suffering people, and a shameful public sacrifice of truth, made in the face of the world."

. On Monday last, at noon, was published, (*Price Two-pence Halfpenny*) the SPIRITED PROTEST of the minority Lords, and his Grace the Duke of Manchester's animated speech, against an address to the King, and taking foreign troops into the pay of Great Britain, without consent of parliament.

To the P U B L I C.

For COUGHS, COLDS, HOARSENESSES, &c.

The PECTORAL DECOCTION, *an infallible Remedy.*

A Gentleman, who, at this Time, when COUGHS and COLDS are no less dangerous, than general, has destributed to his Friends, Neighbours; and the Poor round him, the above Remedy GRATIS, is, by their Persuasions, and from motives of Humanity, induced to make it Public, as the Community at large could receive no Benefit from it, while confined to a private local Distribution, indeed it would have been an act of the greatest INHUMANITY to have with-held this valuable SPECIFIC from the Public, when more than fifty People have been cured by taking it, within these few Days, and one who had quite lost his Speech.—The Proprietor expects this Tribute of Gratitude from the Public, that ATTESTATIONS of its Efficacy may be left at the Places of Sale by those who receive Benefit from it, as the greatest Pleasure he enjoys is in being useful to his Fellow Creatures. This DECOCTION is sold in Bottles of

Two-shillings each, with Directions, at Mr. T. W. SHAW's, opposite Anderton's Coffee House, Fleet-street; Mrs. KINGMAN, the corner of Sweet-
ing's Alley, Royal Exchange.

*N. B. The PECTORAL DECOCTION may be given to Children of the
tenderest Age.*

Printed and published for the Authors, by T. W. SHAW, in Fleet-street,
opposite Anderton's Coffee House, where Letters to the Publisher will be
thankfully received.

THE

CRISIS

NUMBER XLIV   *To be continued Weekly.*

SATURDAY, Novem. 18, 1775   *Price* Two Pence Half-penny.

His *Pupil*'s Tongue, how *Mansfield*'s Brain supplies,
Teeming with Mischief and *majestic Lies!*

ANONYM.[1]

I Have just observed how one of the weakest and wickedest men in England was lately escorted, *trembling*, where no fear was, under an unusual *civil* and *military* parade, to the most *corrupt House* in the British empire, amidst the secret curses, open hisses, and bitterest reproaches of a free people; who will not long brook the repeated insults, treacheries, barbarities, and treasons of a venal combination of TYRANTS, under the specious names of *King*, *Lords*, and *Commons*. The assassins of *government* have placed *me* beyond the further reach of *royal* or *ministerial* vengeance. My *massacre* was but a prelude to what will shortly follow; that of thousands, by the hands of *foreign* troops, most *kindly and parentally* called in (as the *parliamentary addresses* say) for the

---

1. An anonymous epigraph, again (see *The Crisis*, nos. XXXVIII and XLII supra) most likely by the author(s) of this installment.

399

constitutional necessity of cutting the throats of ENGLISHMEN. From *me* let ENGLAND receive a timely caution. Let not the sons of liberty be deceived by the vile artifices of traytors, and the only traytor to their country.[2]

This combined gang of venal parricides, in order to take off the attention of the people from their villainous designs, and to impress them with false fears, are now pretending PLOTS against the *government*; a *government*, for which (as it is now administered) the people need not be very anxious. The fruits of it can only be enormous taxes, despotic edicts, bloody massacres, and final *slavery*. A temporary *anarchy* is far more eligible than these. In the *pious* reigns of *Charles, and James* the second, there was an *Oates* and a *Bedloe*.[3] The present reign, more *pious* still, has produced a *Richardson*, who will be damned, I hope, to equal infamy with his two *courtly* and *ministerial* predecessors.[4]

---

2. Isaac Barré had used this phrase in House of Commons debates on 6 February 1765 to describe those patriots in the colonies who banded together to defend American rights and protest unwise, even unconstitutional, imperial policies. See Simmons and Thomas eds., *Proceedings and Debates*, 2:16. Pauline Maier, *From Resistance to Revolution* (New York: Alfred A. Knopf, 1972), pp. 81–82 noted that Barré's statement was reported in the colonies and that Barré was not the first to use that phrase. I will only add here that he most likely borrowed it from Anglo-Irish opposition leader Charles Lucas, whom Barré was known to admire. See my *Neither Kingdom Nor Nation*, pp. 85–86.

3. Titus Oakes was remembered as a shameless liar who warned of a non-existent conspiracy among English Catholics, guided by Jesuits, to assassinate Charles II. Arrests were made, men were tried and dozens were executed, and all the while Oates had the ear of the king as the "Popish Plot" ran its course. Charles II eventually came to regret having listened to Oates, but Oates was not prosecuted until James II (who also was supposedly a target) succeeded his brother. Oates was convicted of perjury (not a capital offense) and sentenced to life in prison, so the many enemies he had made and people whose lives he had damaged did not have the satisfaction of seeing him hanged. He managed to get himself released in the aftermath of the Glorious Revolution, though thoroughly discredited. William Bedloe was one of Oates' cronies, whose duplicity and ability to conflate the truth with a lie was almost as sharp. He died before he could be prosecuted. John Dryden wrote Oates into his *Absalom and Achitophel* as the "monumental brass" (see n. XLII.8 supra). There are entries for both Oates and Bedloe in the *Oxford DNB*, 41:335–40 and 4:787–89, resp., by Alan Marshall.

4. Francis Richardson, an American-born British army officer, had offered evidence in the specious charges brought against Stephen Sayre. See n. XLI.1 supra.

This latter villain has been palpably set up merely for a pretence of inspecting Mr. Sheriff *Sayre's* private papers. The scheme was *Mansfield's*. A *stale* stratagem to alarm the people, whilst the *Ministry*, at a venture, poached for crimes in the cabinet of the only *city magistrate* they *dared* attack. Such *ministers* (like those of *Charles* and *James*) will even precipitate base and needy wretches into eternal perdition to serve their own pernicious purposes. With them the subornation of *Perjury* against the lives and fortunes of innocent men, is no more than the subornation of *votes* from a guilty and corrupt *majority*. These shallow devices may excite the contempt and resentment of a discerning people, but never can procure a single hand or heart in aid of a perfidious and designing *government*.

The next *royal speech*, may, perhaps, promise to unravel *horrid plots* against the constitution: but it's only enemies, its only traytors surround the throne, engross the *cabinet*, and instill infectious principles into the head and heart of ductile and deluded *Majesty*. Let *Bute* and *Mansfield* be instantly dismissed; let them depart in time, to the world of spirits, nor be suffered longer to mislead a *peevish baby*, to the ruin of himself and the whole empire of *Great Britain*; let them know, that their repeated attempts to deceive and enslave a free people, are capital offences, and demand immediate vengeance from an injured nation.

If they suffer the *infernal author* of the last delusive *speech*, to write another, they deserve to fall the tame victims of all his MACHIAVELIAN plans, for the establishment of despotic power, and the destruction of the British constitution. Hear how this *Scotch traytor* dares to scatter his studied delusions from the throne, and make his SOVEREIGN an instrument for palming his crafty, but shallow impositions on the public!—He opens with the (*situation of America*)—a miserable one indeed!—To this *situation* is *America* reduced, by the pernicious counsels of himself and his colleague *Bute*, who durst reside no longer at his own habitation, but skulks about in holes and corners of the Palace, the *David Rizzio* of the present Æra.

Let us now attend to the (constant desire of having the advice, concurrence, and assistance) of whom? Of a corrupt majority, bribed and pensioned to betray those for whom they pretend the most disinterested and paternal care.—A whining insinuation next succeed against (those who have long laboured to inflame). That is, against all the true constitution-alists and honest revolutionists throughout the empire. These *incendiar-ies*, it seems, have (infused a system of opinions repugnant to the true constitution of the colonies.) Does the true constitution of the Colonies differ, then, from the established constitution of England? Let the saga-cious *Mansfield* declare in what particular, and learn to blush (if possible) at his own LYE. This courtly PROTEUS⁵ talks in the next breath of *Ameri-can (usurpation.)*—Good my Lord, in candour, in honour, and in truth, ingenuously confess, that *resistance* and *usurpation* are very different in their natures. The noble Lord winds his paragraph up with a threat of (*a sufficient force to support*) the weaker and more loyal part of *America*. This menacing assertion must be received with laughter and contempt. There is no part of *America* so weak as to crouch passively under the tyrannic rod of an arbitary unfeeling government. If this be loyalty, may they still glory, to the honour of humanity, in being most virtuous and illustrious rebels; such rebellion is true constitutional resistance; nor has the uni-verse a sufficient force to subdue the combined virtue of a nation; though an inundation of parliamentary assassins may destroy the works of ages, ruin commerce and cultivation, lay waste cities and whole provinces, and leave their brave inhabitants expiring on the earth. But this noble union in the cause of liberty, is called by Mansfield (*a desperate conspiracy*).

The (*authors and promoters of so desperate a conspiracy*) if your Lordship, in your great zeal for the public good, really wishes to detect them, men bribed and pensioned with the public-money, to form a destructive ma-jority in parliament, and sheltered behind the throne, I do not say in it, are by no means fit for the purpose, and well may the (*intentions of the two parties differ.*) But the lenity of government was such, that it *wished rather to reclaim than subdue.* Indeed! Why then did these mild reclaim-ers, in all the petty impotence of their despotic vengeance, send forth

---

5. A second allusion to Proteus; see n. XXV.4 supra for the first. For Mansfield, see n. I.5 supra.

FAMINE, FIRE, SWORD, and all the horrors of WAR, in one hand, whilst they stoped their parental ears against the repeated supplications of their children with the other?

Thus did a mild government, and a christian parliament, breathe (*the spirit of moderation and forbearance.*) His Lordship adds, that (*conciliatory propositions, accompanied the measures taken to enforce authority.*) Tis true, the benevolent alternative held out to oppressed *America*, was an easy and a generous choice, between the poison and the dagger; between a lingering and an instant ruin. The coercive acts against *America*, was adapted, says Lord Mansfield, to cases (*of criminal combinations, among subjects not then in arms).* The ground upon which the fishery (or famine) bill was brought in and defended by Lord North, against the *Americans*, was, that they were rebels, and then actually in arms; though the real truth was, that they had at that period, proceeded no farther than consulting in what manner they should defend themselves against a siege of ministerial oppressions, enforced by an obedient Parliament.

How Lord Mansfield, with all his jesuitical precaution, makes his Majesty give the LYE to his ostensiable minister! If the *Americans* were not *then in arms*, they could not have been rebels and traytors, as Lord North and his ministerial clan, then called them; and it was the height of savage barbarity to treat them as if they were so, and instead of endeavouring to reclaim them, (as the ministry now pretend they wished) to set out against subjects and children with every hostile means of extirpation. His Lordship (finding now, that Americans are not to be bullied) pretends, after the loss of a large army, (*an anxiety to prevent, if possible, the effusion of American blood.*) Was it not possible then, my Lord, to have adopted any conciliatory measures, but those which were replete with death and desolation against subjects, who, you say yourself, were not in arms at the time of passing your favourite coercive acts, for yours they were? Before they had acted, did they deserve to be called traytors by your parliament, and to perish by FAMINE and the SWORD? Are these the boasted consequences of being a subject of *Great Britain?* Are those subjects thus made (*the freest members of any civil society in the known world?*) Is freedom to be found under a government where your Lordship presides in consular dignity, together with your colleague Bute? Does your Lordship think that the people of England are to be gulled by words, or the people of America duped by declamation? Let me attend your Lordship now, in your political fears, that America is setting up (*an independant empire.*) If your lordship, and your colleague, will not suffer her to be free, she is too powerful, too high spirited, and too wise, to be a slave. But will your Lordship condescend to listen to America even at this moment; after she has been in some degree victorious; after your military assassins have been worsted, and the poor remains of them blocked up, disheartened, dying daily, and averse to further murders; after all this, America tells your Lordship, in the humblest terms, that she does not wish to be independant, she only wishes not to be enslaved. But it seems she tells you so in congress; an unlawful assembly, whom you cannot stoop to hear. Proceed then, my Lord, at your peril, (prepared as America now is) to draw more blood: but know, that the *spirit of the British nation is indeed too high, the resources with which God has blessed her, are too numerous, to give up so many colonies*, to the pride, the ambition, the rapacity and tyranny of *three* men, for there are but *three* in the whole empire, who wish for the destruction of America, in their heart; the rest are but the venal echoes of this accursed triumvirate. But I find your Lordship's wisdom and clemency, at length induce you (*to put a speedy end to the disorders in America.*) Be not too confident, my Lord, before the disorders in America end, disorders in England will begin, such as neither your wisdom, clemency, nor all your Foreign assistance can allay.

What hopes can your Lordship's party have in the national militia? They will not draw a sword but upon national principles. They will not serve your turn. They will not do the business of mercenary cut-throats, like those employed in St. George's Fields. In the next paragraph, your Lordship (smoothing your warlike front) is pleased most graciously to extend pardon and indemnity, not only to deluded individuals, but to whole provinces and colonies; they are to be restored upon submission. Restored! to what? To their slaughtered friends and families? To the enjoyment of their habitations, towns, and cities, laid in ashes? To the enjoyment of their best inheritance, their laws, which have been wrested from them? To their charters, given upon royal faith, which have been infringed and violated by tyrannic perfidy? To the liberty of using, giving, and granting, their own distinct property, acquired by the sweat of their own brows, in their own distinct community? O! righteous administration! O! pious Sovereign! O! godlike dispensation! O! unparalelled instance of royal munificence and justice! But alas! to what must these pardoned penitents submit? Name it not, my Lord, in the hearing of a single Englishman. To passive obedience, to established slavery; to the despotic yoke of men, who instead of fostering parents, have already proved themselves unfeeling tyrants; of men, who have shut their eyes, their ears, their hearts, against the repeated cries, and humble supplications of their injured children. No, my Lord, your sagacious accomplices may despair, America will never sue; she never will accept your proffered pardons and indemnities, whilst she has a single tongue, with which she can demand redress, or one faithful band, unsacrificed in the cause of freedom. Call in your Ruffians, let them loose like a deluge on your colonies, and let them become masters, at last, of that soil which they have fattened with the bravest blood in your Dominions. Like a true Scotchman, make a wise advantage of the virtue of America, receive the price of blood, and sell your depopulated empire in America, to those warlike savages. Add this jewel you despise, to the Ruffian crown, and let us see the purchase-money piously bestowed in subduing the liberties of *Great Britain*, and bowing her stubborn neck beneath the yoke of Bute. This with you, my Lord, would be true constitutional dependance.

Here I will dismiss your Lordship's speech, struck (as I am) with the deepest admiration of your two addresses; I make bold to call them yours, my Lord, because I am satisfied they were likewise penned, or at least, perused, settled, and approved by your lordship, whom I hold to be the fabricator of every ministerial machination and iniquity. These two addresses (servile echoes of your Lordship's speech) shame even the slavish sycophant of court and parliament, in the more magnanimous reign of James the First; who, (like another royal coward in the present age) was in hourly fear of a life so truly precious to his kingdoms. That anointed fool was equally suspicious of momentary plots against his sacred person. That celebrated heroe, zealous to preserve God's vicegerent upon earth, used to search the very pockets of his courtiers, nay, of the

Queen herself; for knives, scissars, bodkins, and crooked pins; yet, in that pusillanimous reign, a crouching, hired majority in parliament, offered up the liberties of the people at the shrine of prerogative, a shrine erected then, and since, in breach of the coronation oath, by an ignorant, perjured, weak, and tyrannic hypocrite. Our present addressing majorities, with an audacious and a rapid hand, are opening all the ancient, stagnated sluices of prerogative, to overwhelm anew, that glorious constitution, which they artfully espouse in words, but traitorously undermine in practice; uniting in one confederate body, with another Stuart, to destroy the laws and liberties of their country.

ALLEN'S GHOST.[6]

. On Monday last, at noon, was published, (*Price Two-pence Halfpenny*) the SPIRITED PROTEST of the minority Lords, and his Grace the Duke of Manchester's animated speech, against an address to the King, and taking foreign troops into the pay of Great Britain, without consent of parliament.

To the P U B L I C.
For COUGHS, COLDS, HOARSENESSES, &c.
The PECTORAL DECOCTION, an *infallible Remedy*.

A Gentleman, who, at this Time, when COUGHS and COLDS are no less dangerous, than general, has destributed to his Friends, Neighbours; and the Poor round him, the above Remedy GRATIS, is, by their Persuasions, and from motives of Humanity, induced to make it Public, as the Community at large could receive no Benefit from it, while confined to a private local Distribution, indeed it would have been an act of the greatest INHUMANITY to have with-held this valuable SPECIFIC

---

6. Another reference to William Allen, slain in the "massacre" of St. Georges's Fields (see notes III.1 and XXXIX.1 supra).

from the Public, when more than fifty People have been cured by taking it, within these few Days, and one who had quite lost his Speech,—The Proprietor expects this Tribute of Gratitude from the Public, that AT-TESTATIONS of its Efficacy may be left at the Places of Sale by those who receive Benefit from it, as the greatest Pleasure he enjoys is in being useful to his Fellow Creatures. This DECOCTION is sold in Bottles of Two-shillings each, with Directions, at Mr. T. W. SHAW's, opposite An-derton's Coffee House, Fleet-street; Mrs. KINGMAN, the corner of Sweet-ing's Alley, Royal Exchange.

N.B. The PECTORAL DECOCTION may be given to Children of the tenderest Age.

Printed and published for the Authors, by T. W. SHAW, in Fleet-street, opposite Anderton's, Coffee House, where Letters to the Publisher will be thankfully received.

THE

CRISIS

NUMBER XLV   *To be continued Weekly.*

SATURDAY, NOVEM. 25, 1775   *Price* Two Pence Half-penny.

May the Name of that Wretch; be for ever blotted from the Annals of this once happy Nation, who shall dare to attack the Rights and Liberties of free-born Subjects; or lay a restraint upon the Trade and Commerce, by which the Dignity of the Nation is supported, and the Poor made Comfortable and Happy.

To the Earl of D A R T M O U T H,

Late Secretary of State for the Colonies.[1]

My Lord,

I Shall not address you in the flattering stile of a pensioned courtier at *St. James's*; or with the wild enthusiasm of a pliant preacher of *Bunhill-fields*, or *Tottenham-court Road*; the one I despise for his treachery and meaness; the other I pity for his ignorance and superstition: I shall therefore, lay aside all respect, (for you deserve none) and endeavour

---

1. William Legge, second Earl of Dartmouth, succeeded the Earl of Hillsborough as secretary of state for American affairs in 1772; he had just been succeeded by Lord George Germain (see n. L.5 infra). Hillsborough had shown little patience for colonial

409

to speak to you in the language, and with the boldness of an honest English-man.—Hitherto you have escaped (through your insignificancy) the notice of *the Authors of the Crisis*.—But flatter not yourself, or think, my *dissembling Lord,* to remain any longer, hid from the eyes of PUBLICK JUSTICE. "You have been weighed in the balance and found wanting." Your crimes are of so black a dye, that nothing short of your *pious* life, can satisfy the manes of the murdered *Americans.* The part you have already taken, in the unnatural *civil war* in *America,* is not only uncon-stitutional, but irreligious and inhuman. The BLOOD of peaceful sub-jects, already shed in *England* and *America,* pleads to heaven, and calls for immediate JUSTICE; not only upon your Lordship, but upon the whole infernal gang of *ministerial* PARRICIDES and MURDERERS.

The earth cannot cover those seas of innocent BLOOD, which has been wantonly spilt, by mercenary and infatuated soldiers; to please an aban-doned, BLOODY MINISTRY. At that awful day, when the secrets of all hearts shall be opened, it will rise up in judgment against you, and call for vengeance. Then, my Lord, titles and honours will avail nothing; the conscious wretches, standing at the bar; not of a *Mansfield*; but of a just God; self-accused, and self-condemned; who will pronounce this dread-ful sentence; *depart from me,* ye *cursed, into everlasting fire, prepared for the Devil and his Angels.* Repent therefore before it is too late.

Your Lordship has been represented (by your emissaries) as religious; indeed the same epithets are now bestowed upon our *virtuous* Sovereign, as well as your Lordship. But can your *religious* Lordship, lay your hand upon your heart, and say that the measures now pursuing in America, are either virtuous or just? You may answer yes; (for what will not vil-

---

protests, though he was not the doctrinaire hardliner as some have painted him. There were imperial reformers on both sides of the Atlantic who had hoped that Dartmouth would be more flexible. That he seemingly did nothing to fend off the coercive poli-cies of North, his stepbrother, proved disappointing to those who expected the mild-mannered Earl to chart a less confrontational course. See B. D. Bargar, *Lord Dartmouth and the American Revolution* (Columbia: University of South Carolina Press, 1965); Peter Marshall's brief *Oxford DNB* sketch at 33:198–201; and my "Federalism and the Failure of Imperial Reform," pp. 157–72.

lainy do or say, when supported by power) but if you had one spark of honour, honesty, or humanity left, you would answer in the negative; nay, you must acknowledge they are cruel, unconstitutional, scandalous, and a disgrace to the name of Englishmen and christians. If so my Lord, what must be the opinion of the world concerning your Lordship. They must look upon you with *abhorrence* and *detestation*, and despise you, as a man destitute of every principle of virtue, honour, justice, religion, and humanity; as a wretch, who basely betrays his country, to gain a *paltry pension*, and prostitutes his honour and conscience, to enjoy a little court-favour.

The time is not far distant, my Lord, when an enraged people will demand justice on the authors, promoters, and abetters of the present CIVIL WAR. When an insulted people, will drag to punishment, without the form of a trial, not only the projectors, but the meanest instruments now employed, to carry their measures into Execution.

Happy day, when the spirit of freedom shall rise into action, and the PEOPLE determine to do themselves justice, and make the authors of their miseries feel their vengeance; when they shall drag forth to public execution, the whole tribe of PARRICIDES and TRAYTORS.

The *British Lion* now slumbers; but the spirit of Englishmen will not suffer them to receive many more insults, before it rouses them to a just, and glorious REVENGE. It will then be too late to repent, or alter your conduct. When the people are up in arms, it will be no excuse that you acted only as *secretary of State.* They will receive no excuses, no equivocations, but convinced of your guilt, bring you to punishment. It will be in vain to plead for mercy, for mercy must give place to JUSTICE. Even the present misled, royal cypher, will not be able to save you. His greatest FAVOURITES and dearest MINIONS, will then be brought to the SCAFFOLD, amidst the triumphs, joy, and insults, of a long oppressed people.

Hear this my Lord, and tremble! Consider it, and resolve speedily to alter your conduct!—Be no more the tool of Lord North; nor of those ARCHTRAYTORS, Bute and Mansfield; shake off all dependance upon such wretches, and if you have virtue enough left, endeavour to atone for your past conduct, by immediately informing your foolish Sovereign, of the real state of affairs in *America*. Stop, as much as lies in your power, the further effusion of human BLOOD. If his misguided and PIOUS Majesty still remains obdurate; forsake a Court devoted to destruction, aud follow the noble example of a RICHMOND and a CAMDEN, by protesting against its measures.

Your Lordship cannot plead ignorance of the state of affairs in America; the dispatches which daily pass, (or at least ought) through your hands, must inform you of the loyalty of those people. Notwithstanding the worst of slaves, *ministerial scriblers*, are hired to blacken the Americans in the eyes of England, your Lordship knows the peaceful disposition of that People. Even *General Gage's* letters, bloody and false as they are, contain so many truths in favour of America, that they are not given to the publick, until they have undergone a revisal and alteration by the *junto* in *Downing-Street*; nay, so fearful is our coward ministry, least their black deeds should come to light, or that things in America should be known in their true state, that every clerk, from the menial to the highest, in your Lordships office, is sworn to secrecy. This, my Lord, you know for a fact, nor can your *pious* and *religious* Lordship deny it.

In what light then, must we look upon your Lordship, either as a *fool* or a *knave*; as a mere *puppet*, who move and act as your master, Lord North, pulls the wires.—Fye, my Lord! retire and hide yourself from the scorn and redicule of mankind, and no more attempt to mislead and deceive your King. If you have not honesty enough to inform him of the trnth, forbear to call down the vengeance of heaven, by forging lies.

Leave the court, and indulge your *pious* self, as heretofore, in lolling over your garden wall, at *Lewisham*, to hear the ravings of a methodist preacher. But dare not any longer to conspire against the liberties of America; least the sword of justice, which now hangs impending o'er your guilty head, be seized before its time, and you fall the first victim, to the injured laws of England and America.

At this time, my Lord, when men in power are, through views of interest and ambition, sapping the constitution, and undermining the foundations of the Empire, it is incumbent on, nay, it is the DUTY of every man boldly to stand forth in its defence. I know it will be said, indeed it has been said, that Senators in opposition, are no other than incendiaries, who set fire to a house, in order to plunder it during the general distress, and riot in the confusion; but, my Lord, when we consider that such persons have by a timely and spirited conduct, often roused the people from a state of insensibility, in which they supinely lay for ages before and led them on to LIBERTY, that glorions prerogative of Britons; when we consider, my Lord, that it is to THEM we owe the first and greatest blessings we enjoy; the idea of *incendiary* immediately brightens into that of PROTECTOR, and where we dreaded an enemy, we find a friend.

Under this notion of things, my Lord, shall I be afraid to say, that unless some bold, some resolute, nay, some DESPERATE step is taken, and that immediately, the constitution of this country, that constitution which received its birth from the virtuous struggles of our ancestors, will inevitably expire? Shall I be afraid to say, that unless we all to a man, instantly put forth an arm to support the falling fabrick, it will be presently too late, its towering top will be leveled with the ground, and all that is dear and valuable to us, be buried in its ruins? No, my Lord, the people will look upon themselves as men, equally interested in the public cause, with your Lordship, and other parracides, who are, to the eternal disgrace of the nation, intrusted with the management of our affairs; they will not fear to approach the throne and pour out their complaints; they will not fear to tell their ungrateful Sovereign that he is willingly deceived, nay, duped by such pious hypocrites as your Lordship, and the rest of his infamous ministers, that though smiling in his face, you are secretly putting the knife to his throat; they will not fear to remonstrate, and *make* him know, that 'tis the duty of a King to see with his *own* eyes, and to hear with his *own* ears; that the end of Sovereign power is, that *all* may be happy under the vigilance of *one*, and not that *one* should prey upon *all*, that *abuse of power* betrays *a baseness of soul*, and that 'tis an act of *cruelty* to oppress the wretched, who have nothing but their cries or their tears to defend them; that nothing is so *noble* as greatness and goodness united, and nothing so *ignoble* as that savageness of disposition, which often prevents greatness from respecting human nature, when not disguised by some worldly pomp. In short, they will not fear to tell him, that if the nobles of the realm owe their greatness to him, he owes *his* greatness, power, and dignity to the PEOPLE.

If all this will not do, they will have no alternative left, 'tis incumbeut on them to take the field, and shew themselves *brave*, where bravery is required, and *dare* to be resolute in cases of necessity. Our *predecessors* led the way, *we* have nothing to do but to *follow*.

Shall we, my Lord, put it in the power of a *child*, to say, when our heads are low in the grave, "Such and such privileges, my great-grandfather purchased with his life, and bequeathed to his son; that son preserved them pure, and left them to my father, but he, confusion to his memory, sat quietly by his fire-side, while the ravager plundered him, and entailed beggary and slavery upon his offspring." No, my Lord, it must not be, we have some *virtue*, and I hope as much *resolution* as our forefathers, as great, if not greater privileges to contend for, and as great a necessity for doing it; and nothing, my Lord, but such a resolution at this time, can save the nation from destruction, or prevent the present Sovereign, and his infernal Ministers, from any longer tyrannizing over a brave and free People; a people who pride themselves in their LOYALTY, while their Prince is *gracious*, but who glory in REBELLION, when REBELLION is necessary to tumble down a TYRANT.

*** On Monday last, at noon, was published, (*Price Two-pence Half-penny*) the SPIRITED PROTEST of the minority Lords, and his Grace the Duke of Manchester's animated speech,[2] against an address to the King, and taking foreign troops into the pay of Great Britain, with out consent of parliament.

---

2. George Montagu, fourth Duke of Manchester, after well over a decade in the House of Lords, had only recently become a vocal member of the opposition, more often in line with Rockingham than with Chatham (Pitt). As the crisis deepened, he warned that the use of force would drive Americans to seek independence; he also warned that France and Spain would join in the struggle, assisting the rebels to hurt their old enemy. Rockingham, Richmond, and Effingham were all listed as having joined Manchester in the "dissentient" against the King's speech opening Parliament on October 26th (see n. XLIII.1 supra). Manchester's speech, to which this issue alluded—and which T. W. Shaw, publisher of *The Crisis*, printed—appeared as *The SPEECH of His Grace,*

To the P U B L I C.
For COUGHS, COLDS, HOARSENESSES, &c.
The PECTORAL DECOCTION, an *infallible Remedy.*

A Gentleman, who, at this Time, when COUGHS and COLDS are no less dangerous, than general, has destributed to his Friends, Neighbours; and the Poor round him, the above Remedy GRATIS, is, by their Persuasions, and from motives of Humanity, induced to make it Public, as the Community at large could receive no Benefit from it, while confined to a private local Distribution, indeed it would have been an act of the greatest INHUMANITY to have with-held this valuable SPECIFIC from the Public, when more than fifty People have been cured by taking it, within these few Days, and one who had quite lost his Speech.—The Proprietor expects this Tribute of Gratitude from the Public, that AT-TESTATIONS of its Efficacy may be left at the Places of Sale by those who receive Benefit from it, as the greatest Pleasure he enjoys is in being useful to his Fellow Creatures. This DECOCTION is sold in Bottles of Two-shillings each, with Directions, at Mr. T. W. SHAW's, opposite Anderton's Coffee House, Fleet-street; Mrs. KINGMAN, the corner of Sweeting's Alley, Royal Exchange.

N.B. The PECTORAL DECOCTION may be given to Children of the tenderest Age.

Printed and published for the Authors, by T. W. SHAW, in Fleet-street, opposite Anderton's Coffee House, where Letters to the Publisher will be thankfully received.

---

the Duke of Manchester, and the SPIRITED PROTEST of the MINORITY LORDS. A copy of the pamphlet was bound in with *The Crisis* that eventually ended up in the Bodleian Library; it was not with the print run that is now housed at the British Library. See John Cannon's sketch of Manchester in the *Oxford DNB*, 38:727–29.

THE

CRISIS

NUMBER XLVI   *To be continued Weekly.*

SATURDAY, Decem. 2, 1775   *Price* Two Pence Half-penny.

Go on vile Prince by lawless strides, and try
How soon your Crown will fade, your Empire die.
By your base arts, AMERICA shall RISE,
The name of *Slave* and *George* alike despise.
Great Britain's sons, will fight in freedom's cause,
And gladly bleed, to save their rights and laws.

TO THE KING.

SIR,

EVERY age has produced Heroes and Politicians, and every age has produced COWARDS and TYRANTS; among the latter, succeeding generations will rank you the first; they will read with horrour and detestation, the annals of your reign (for you and your ministers, like *Cataline* and his accomplices, seem to have drank a cup of HUMAN BLOOD, as a pledge of your UNION) the faithful Historian will paint you in your true colours, as a weak, wicked, insidious Prince, enflamed with rage, and with an impious and daring hand, overturning every thing held sacred amongst men, and destroying with unceasing fury, the natural rights of mankind, and the constitutions of Empires.

He will represent you at the head of a bribed, corrupt, abandoned, hellish Parliament, and a diabolical House of Lords, persuing measures, and framing laws (under all the forms of a constitution once held sacred) equally unjust, cruel, and bloody; laws designed for the horrid purpose of destroying, or enslaving mankind; laws which none but those who poisess the qualities of a Dæmon could suggest; and laws which none but parricides and Tyrants, could either assent to, or carry into execution.

He will represent you with a groupe of robbers and murderers, cowards and traitors, always round your throne, whose ruinous and destructive advice you implicitly followed, contrary to the general sense of the Nation, and sent FAMINE, FIRE, and SWORD, into every part of the Empire, where your lawless will, and arbitrary mandates were not obeyed; that you violated all the laws of God and man, of nature and nations, and made a cruel and unprovoked war upon your country and people; laid towns in ashes, depopulated whole provinces, slaughtered indiscriminately and without mercy, men, women, and children, by means of an army of foreign and domestic mercenaries, and involved in all the dreadful calamities of CIVIL WAR, more than THREE MILLIONS of innocent people; that your most solemn promises were calculated to *deceive*, that your *Coronation Oath* could not bind you, and that the sanctity of religion was made a cloak for the greatest iniquities, to this black catalogue of crimes; he will add the crying sins of ingratitude, treachery, and baseness. He will declare you broke, outragiously broke, every tye, that could bind a human soul; honour, virtue, religion, law, trust, humanity, and every thing that is sacred amongst men; that you was chosen first magistrate over a brave and free people; greatly honoured and supported in all the pomp of regal state, and trusted by them, with the military and naval force of the kingdom, and the executive power of the laws; that all this power and credit, and all those forces by sea and land, you turned, ungratefully, barbarously, and traitorously, against the people your masters, and made, or wanted to make, a prey of them, with their own money and arms.

Reflect, Sir. in time, resolve at once to alter your conduct, and it is possible you may yet redeem your character; a system of tyranny and blood seldom succeeds, and when it does, it always proves fatal, not only to the Tyrant, but to his race; of this we have many instances, not only in the *Roman* and *Grecian* history, but in our own; it is true you may now go great lengths, with the assistance of those archtraitors *Bute* and *Mansfield*, and the *Officers* of the Devonshire Militia who have addressed you for that purpose;[1] but, Sir, you will certainly meet with some opposition in England, though I fear, not with so severe a *chastisement* as you have *already* met with from our brave and virtuous brethren in AMERICA, who equally despise your *power* and your *chains*. Indeed your savage mercenaries, *next spring*, by Lord North's account, are to do wonders, and that old letcher *Sandwich*, your first Lord of the Admiralty, who is remarkable for not speaking *truth*, has confirmed his assertions; this is one of the most ruinous and villainous plans that has disgraced the present reign; ruinous, because it will for ever separate the Colonies from Britain, and deprive England at once, of the whole commerce of America, and one half of her natural strength, besides making the Americans our rivals in *trade* as well as *empire*; villainous, for it has its foundation in *felony*, because it is done with no other view or design, but that of robbing the people of England of their money, as ten times the number of Foreign *Slaves*, more than what is, or may be proposed, will never answer any good purpose, it is impossible for them to fight with success, against FREEMEN and BRITONS; this, Sir, both you and your Ministers are convinced of, but when you have fixed upon a scheme of *Blood* and *Plun-*

---

1. "None can hold in greater Detestation than we do the unnatural Behaviour of your American Subjects," proclaimed the officers of the First Regiment of the Devonshire militia. Printed in the *London Gazette*, 14 October 1775, and noted in the Commons on November 2nd (Simmons and Thomas, eds., *Proceedings and Debates*, 6:172–74) by John Dyke Acland, who presented the address. The political implications of this action were few, compared with what militia on the American side of the Atlantic did. In Massachusetts, notably, most militia regiments and companies had been reconstituted by the end of 1774, swearing allegiance to the extra-legal provincial convention rather than the crown. They would muster in response to local, not imperial officials—as Gage found out on 19 April 1775, which had been foreshadowed by near misses, such as what occurred at Salem the previous February.

der, it is never given up. Next year, Sir, you may possibly find yourself, your Ministers, your Generals, and your Soldiers, not crowned with *laurels* and *victory*, but covered with *disgrace* and *infamy*.

The *Americans*, Sir, whom you have by cruelty and oppression forced into arms, to defend their lives, their liberties, their property, their wives, and children, are fired with the noblest of views, the love of FREEDOM and their COUNTRY; they will fight with an ardour unknown to *slaves*, and conquer whilst justice and Heaven is on their side, ten thousand legion of mercenary men. They know, Sir, what the people of England seem to have forgot, that if all the privileges and impunity belonging to a just Prince, who protects his people, and rules himself and them by *law*, and their own *consent*, do also belong to a public *oppressor, scourge; executioner*, and *plunderer*, then these blessed consequences follow; that there is an utter end of all public and private right and wrong, every King may be a Tyrant, and every Tyrant a just magistrate; if it is *unlawful* to resist the greatest human evil, the necessary means of SELF-PRESERVATION, are *unlawful*; and though it is lawful to destroy *little* robbers, who have as *much* right, and *more* innocence, than great ones; yet it is *impious* and *unlawful* to oppose *great* robbers, who, out of lust, avarice, revenge, rage, cruelty, or wantonness, take away liberty, life, and property, and destroy nations at pleasure: That real, great, and general mischief, is defended by giving it a good name, by which he who commits it is protected; violence, fraud, and oppression, may be committed with security, if they be but called *Magistracy*; and the execrable authors of them are not only *safe*, but *sacred*, if they be but called Magistrates. Though it is unlawful to be a public *destroyer and murderer*, yet it is unlawful to destroy him, or his instruments; that is, it is unlawful to prevent or punish that which is most impious and unlawful; and, finally, that any man who can oppress and enslave the world, and destroy nations, may do all this with *impunity*.

The AMERICANS, Sir, know, and they are determined to let *you* know, that is the most wicked and absurd position, to assert, that a whole people can ever be in such a situation, as not to have a RIGHT to *defend and preserve* themselves, when there is no other power in being to *protect and defend* them; and much more, that they must not oppose a TYRANT, a TRAITOR, an universal ROBBER, who, by violence, treachery, rapine, infinite murders, and devastations, has deprived them of their legal protection.

It was, Sir, a known maxim of liberty amongst the great, the wise, the free ancients, (which the *Americans* seem well acquainted with) that a TYRANT was a beast of prey, which might be killed by the *spear*, as well as by a fair chace, in his *court* as well as in his *camp*, that every man had a right to destroy *one* who would destroy *all men*; that no *law* ought to be given him, who took away *all law*; and that, like *Hercules's* monsters, it was glorious to rid the world of him, when ever, and by what means soever, it could be done.

If we read, Sir, the stories of the most celebrated heroes of antiquity (men of whom but very few of the present generation are worthy) and consider the actions that gained them their highest reverence and renown, and recommend their names to posterity with the most advantage; we shall find those in the first rank of glory, who have resisted, destroyed, or expelled Tyrants and Usurpers, the pests, the burthens, and the butchers of mankind. What, Sir, can be more meritorious, what more godlike and beneficient to the world, than the saving *millions* of men at the expence of one GRAND MURDERER, one merciless and universal plunderer? And can there be any better or juster reason given for the opposing, nay, killing of a Tyrant and his Instruments, than that of preserving the *innocent?* Indeed an action so great, glorious, and advantageous to mankind, is highly noble and praise-worthy; and can never be censured, but by abject flatterers, and survile creatures of power, who are always ready to sanctify and abet, any, the most enormous wickedness in Kings, whilst it is attended with *profit* to themselves.

By the maxim, Sir, before mentioned, and the first law of nature, self-preservation, the *Americans* are determined to act. They have likewise on their side, the spirit of the British Constitution, and of those laws of liberty which have subsisted for many hundred years.

They have already shewn a firmness, intrepidity, and bravery, in the cause of FREEDOM and their COUNTRY, against the *tyranny and oppression* of your MAJESTY, and your Ministers, which have already gained them the love, esteem, and admiration, of all just and good men throughout the world. They are, Sir, the open and declared enemies to TYRANNY, and all the artful shackles of a TYRANT, your ridiculous scheme of sending Commissioners to America, to treat with the brave, virtuous, and godlike Americans, whilst the sword is at their throats, is futile and absurd, and will be treated by them with the contempt and detestation it deserves; the deception and artifice is too thinly disguised not to be seen. They will act, Sir, to your cost, like Britons of old, they have, and will, prefer *death* to *slavery?* It is a true British spirit, that scorns an ignominious life, held at the mercy of a TYRANT, or to flatter his villainy and abet his TYRANNY; a spirit which those who want it can never admire.

Never, Sir, will eloquence, with all its pomp, never will the greatest genius be able to express the *grandeur* of *your exploits*, much less to add the least lustre to them, by the manner of relating them. I dare, however affirm, that among the many illustrious actions of GEORGE the THIRD, none will be more glorious, than those in *America*. I often reflect, and find a real pleasure in publishing, that the noble actions of our most celebrated Generals, those of the most renowned Princes, or of the most warlike nations, cannot be compared with *yours*; whether we consider the *greatness* of *wars*, the *multitude* of *battles*, the *different countries*, the *rapidity* of *conquests*, or *diversity* of *enterprises*. By *your* victories, you have subdued a great *number* of *regions*, vastly distant from one another, and these you conquered as *expeditiously*, as another would have traveled through them. And I should be void of all sense not to own, that such exploits are almost superior to any idea we can form to ourselves of them. The advantage of *commodious posts*, and *encampments*, the assistance of allies, naval forces, and *seasonable* convoys, contribute very much to victory. But in this war, you have no companion, no competitor to dispute glory with you; how *bright*, how *august* soever it be, (*and nothing can be more so*) tis all *your own*. Fortune herself, that haughty disposer of human events, cannot rob *you* of the least part of that *honour*; she yields it intirely to *you*, and acknowledges it wholly *yours*; for *temerity* and *chance*, are never found where WISDOM and PRUDENCE preside.

Your *conquests*, Sir, will be read in our annals, and those of almost all nations; nor will they be forgot by the latest posterity. But when we read or hear of relations of wars and battles, it so happens, I know not how, that the admiration they excite, is in some measure interrupted by the tumultuous cries of *orphans* and *widows*, and the universal cry of unprovoked *murder* and *massacree*. But you, Sir, whom we have the happiness to see; you whose *heart*, whose very *soul* we *know*; you who have no designs, but such as tend to *preserve* the common-wealth, at least as *much* as has escaped the *rage* of *war*; what *praises* shall we pay *you?* What *zeal* and *respect* shall we shew *you*; the whole kingdom is sensible of your generosity; even the walls of *St. Stephen*, express their joy for the design you have of restoring the nation to its ancient SPLENDOR and AUTHORITY.

₊ On Monday last, at noon, was published, (*Price Two-pence Half-penny*) the SPIRITED PROTEST of the minority Lords, and his Grace the Duke of Manchester's animated speech, against an address to the King, and taking foreign troops into the pay of Great Britain, without consent of parliament. See End of No. XLVII. pag 310.

Printed and published for the Authors, by T. W. Shaw, in Fleet-street, opposite Anderton's Coffee House, where Letters to the Publisher will be thankfully received.

THE

CRISIS

NUMBER XLVII   *To be continued Weekly.*

SATURDAY, DECEM. 9, 1775   *Price* Two Pence Half-penny.

'Tis I that call—remember MILO's END.

Wedg'd in that Timber which he strove to rend.

Ld. ROSCOMMON.[1]

E VERY wicked *ministerial* stratagem, every human and inhuman
mode of distruction has been tried; even POPERY itself, has been
called in to check the glorious spirit of true *revolutional resistance*
in *America*. In the midst of this infernal struggle for despotic power, tho'

---

1. These are the final lines in a stanza that begins: "Learn, learn, *Crotona's* brawny
Wrestler cries, Audacious Mortals, and be *timely* wise!," from "An Essay on Translated
Verse," in this case from the *Poems of the Earl of Roscommon* (London: J. Tonson, 1717),
which is just one of many editions featuring this author and other "minor" poets. The
"Essay" was originally printed in 1684 with a tribute to Roscommon offered by John
Dryden. Wentworth Dillon, fourth Earl of Roscommon in the Irish peerage, was remembered as a classicist determined to bring to modern readers the best verse translated
from Greek and Latin. He hoped that their own thoughts would become more elevated
and their personal lives more moral as a result. When he died in 1685 he was interred in
Westminster Abbey. Milo, the mighty wrestler of Croton, turned up in various classical
sources, from Herodotus to Cicero, often as an example of hubris: a great man undone
by his own pride.

425

the British Constitution shakes from its foundations, tho' we are upon the very brink of loosing more than two thirds of our whole empire, yet the history of experience of past ages, still administer a drop of consolation. They teach us that *ministerial* and *tyrannic* artifices and iniquities, have ever been attended with glaring inconsistencies, *providential disappointments,* and at last, with a certain distruction of their authors, and diabolical abettors.

Impressed with these reflections, who can hear the united outcries of the present ministerial hirelings, without smiles of indignation and contempt? without the warmest expectations of exemplary justice, against these superior malefactors, who are in hourly combination against their country? These Vipers advised and carried through both houses, by dint of corruption the *Quebec Bill,* not barely for the *toleration,* but for the entire *establishment* of *Popery,* in those settlements. Our pious sovereign, does not only *connive* at, but *cultivate this odious Religion* there, with the greatest assiduity; this is *moderation*—Even a *popish* bishop is supported there, whilst our *protestant clergy* are discountenanced, oppressed, neglected and starved; these patriotic guardians of our constitution, have the unparalleled assurance, to call *resistance* by the name of *rebellion,* in the frontiers of *America*: whilst they themselves are audaciously raising innumerable seminaries of *treason* and *rebellion,* in the back settlements, under licenced missionaries of the *See* of *Rome*; these absurd wretches declaim against the disloyalty of brave and wise *protestants,* in the colony of *Massachuset,* whilst they encourage *popish priests,* to cultivate doctrines subversive of our empire in *Canada.*

Fools, (even *anointed fools*) have sometimes tried intervals, in these they have sometimes been prevailed upon, to adopt the language of reason and common sense; to such an interval, we owe some sharp and wise reproofs from *James the first* to the *Irish agents,* who came into *England* in order to remonstrate against the proceedings of parliament, "you (said his *scholastic* Majesty) are but *half subjects,* and you ought to have but *half privileges*; you that have an eye to *me* one way and to the *Pope* another way; your bodies bend one way, and your souls another,.—you send your children to the seminaries of *Treason,*—your priests teach you such grounds of doctrine, that you cannot follow them with a safe conscience, but you must cast off your loyalty to your king.—"I would most humbly ask his *present majesty*, whether this is not good sense, wise policy, sound reason, and unanswerable truths? Is not this mode of reasoning, equally applicable to the present state of religious policy at *Quebec* in the happier and wiser reign of *pious George the third*? In this absurd instance, we are a most rediculous exception, to all civilized nations upon earth. Where can one be found, whose government does not make a wise distinction between the national *religion* and other professions? In what other governments in the known world is the practice of foreign religions indulged, otherwise than by convenience? have the professors of them any share in civil preferments? do they (like the *papists* at *Quebec*) enjoy *offices of truth and profit*, in the state? Are they (like *them*) admitted into the government of the state? are *our pious* government endeavouring how to nurse up all *Canada*, in *popish* religion, for the satisfaction of massacreing so many *rebellious* subjects hereafter, for they will *rebel* at a convenient period? Or do they foster them as so many *Corps de reserve*, against their *protestant* subjects upon that continent? Are they reared and destined, to compleat the wished for massacre, of that offending people, who will not tamely wear the yoke of a *misguided Tyrant* and his *Minions*? Or is the propagation of *popery* in those remote parts of the British dominions really *legal?* perhaps the multitude are mistaken, and the *revolution compact* and its principles may extend in truth, no further than *Great Britain*, as Mr. Attorney General *Thurloe* asserted the other day in the House of Commons; shall such a prostitute ever have the *great Seal of England* in his custody? shall such a man become the keeper of the King's conscience? for such a barefaced, daring, impious LYE, an honest *House of Commons* would have expelled the servile ministerial reptile, with every mark of detestation and indignity.

Leaving *this official drudge*, with disdain, to pace in the trammels of a guilty administration, let me now persue my subject, by avering and proving the weakness and iniquity of government, in planting a *popish* colony at *Quebec*, Yet there are slaves at the head of the church, and on the seats of justice, who extoll the lenity, the piety and charity, of this proceeding replete as it is, with absurdity, inconsistency and folly. The sovereign is made in his late speech to complain heavily of a want of subordination, nay *of usurpation, revolt, hostility and rebellion*, among his English subjects in *America*; yet he adopts the astonishing plan of propigating the *Roman catholic religion* in his province of *Quebec*; a religion which flatters its votaries with eternal happiness, if they venture their lives in the destruction of an heretical prince and his detested government; the priests industriously sow the seeds of *rebellion* in the very cradle.

So inconsistent are these measures of government, if they mean to retain *Quebec and their Dominions in Canada*, that we may well suppose they have bargained for the sale of them, to their old masters the *French*; and are now, by means of their obsequious tools in parliament, performing their part of the agreement, by restoring that country to the influence and spiritual dominion of the *Pope*—Thus we see that no honour can arise to the crown from false policy, no safety from *papists*, no credit from a Breach of the most solemn and sacred *obligation*, nor will the sale of *Canada*, (as I conjecture,) be as tamely suffered by the nation as that of *Dunkirk*, in the reign of *one* who had rather the advantage of our present *pious* sovereign; for he had not only all the detested principles and vices, but he had the odious name of *Stuart*.

The least pernicious consequence, that can possibly flow from this most *gracious* indulgence at *Quebec*, will be innumerable swarms of ecclesiastic and religious drones, whose only occupation (like that of our present government) will be the affectation of righteousness, and the practice of *iniquity*.

Under the present auspicious government *England* feels the worst effects of *Luxury, prodigality, corruption* and *ministerial selfish perseverance*, from the parliamentary establishment of bishops, priests, monks, friars, monasteries, nunneries, and mass-houses at *Quebec*, all *America* (unless our troops should annihilate her with a *look*,) will feel too soon, a dead weight upon her industry, manufactures, and cultivation; for to all these (I prophesy) she will soon restore herself by her own arm—But should she *condescend*, under her present apparent advantages, to a *re-union* with *Great Britain*; let me ask, with what face, with what pretence, with what justice or humanity, can our wise government (when they come to feel

the inconveniencies of their new popish establishment) attempt to evacu-
ate and expel these holy drones, these spiritual locusts, these real enemies
to the prosperity, peace, and safety of every *protestant* community? must
that valuable part of the British Empire still be doomed to nourish and
support those crafty serpents, which will at length destroy her? or, will
our charitable godlike *sovereign* and his ministers (who are now bringing these vermin into life for the worst of purposes) crush them in the
shell?—if the present establishment of popery, in those parts is founded
in good policy, its sudden dissolution must be founded in caprice. But the
imputation of mere caprice, can reflect no disgrace upon a government,
already stained with the *innocent* blood (if self-defence be innocent) of
the best and bravest of subjects in its whole dominions. Permit me to
mention a probable consequence more alarming to a guilty, perservering
administration; would not an expulsion of these holy adventerers, whom
we have invited over from *Rome* to *Quebec*, be justly deemed a piece
of sportive inhumanity? As such should it not be resisted; with some
colour by a confederacy of the Roman Catholic States? might not this
resentment involve *England* in a most unnecessary and expensive war?
Have not our *commercial* and *landed* interest, our colonies in general, our
manufacturers, and the flower of our army suffered yet sufficiently, for
the errors and iniquities of a revengeful government, deceived in point
of information, and soild, (as she will ever be,) in a needless contention
with her own children, who own the superiority of a *parent*, but will
not brook the insolence of a *tyrant*; are not the misfortunes of a civil
war, *abroad* and the daily expectations of one *at home* sufficiently alarming to an almost *Bankrupt–Nation*, but must the probability of a *foreign
war*, be added to the number of our fears? Need *France and Spain* be
furnished by our own bad policy with a plausable pretence for breaking
with us? Our folly and cruelty have hitherto gone hand in hand, they
have produced an *American* war.—Be that the last.—It will of itself be
sufficiently fatal in its consequences. Those *rebels* will guard their estates
from forfeiture and themselves from slavery. They will rise in defiance of
us or crush us in their fall.

I have proceeded thus far, to shew the *weakness* of our state-politicians,
who, instead of conniving at, and *bravely tolerating* the *Romish Religion*

in our settlements, have armed the *French* there, with such privileges, immunities, and powers, that the *Protestant religion* itself, may be truly said to be only tolerated in those parts, and its ministers universally discouraged, and wholly unprovided for.

I will now shew the *iniquity* of government, in the respect already mentioned; the iniquities of that government which boasts of *planting, nursing, encouraging* and *defending*, her English colonies in AMERICA, like a *parent*—These are the *furbelow terms* of the late royal speech—Even this *patential* government is, at this moment, *planting, nursing, encouraging, protecting* and *defending*, (under the blessed sanction of an act of parliament,) a colony of romish priests, monks, friars, &c. with a *popish*, bishop, and all his trumpery at their head; what a *royal* tribe is here of spiritual enthusiasts, tutored from their cradles to procure and effect, by every means the dethronement, destruction. and massacre, of all heritic princes and their subjects, who may fall within their power! To these *loyal* manifestations of allegiance are all orders of *papists*, regular, and secular, moved and encouraged by decrees of council, rescripts, bulls, and dispensations of their *Popes*; in this point of *loyalty* to sovereigns who differ from them in religious sentiments the decree of the council of *Lateran* is express: neither local nor natural allegiance must restrain them; it does not become me to enquire what are the religious sentiments of his most pious majesty *George the Third*. He has (thank Heaven) been so well guarded since that *wicked and tremendous plot* of sheriff *Sayre* has been discovered, that his precious life is beyond the reach of any danger, but what may arise from the nursery or the petticoat. But we know that the brave *Americans* after their laudable resistance to tyranny, has proved *successful*, must still guard against the *popish Hydra's* in their back settlements, where they are planted and cherished, by the humane and generous policy of our *nursing government*, to supply the deficiencies of their military *cut-throats*; by such a blessed *nursery of papists* fell forty or fifty thousand naked *protestants* in Ireland, before they suspected the least danger, in the memorable year 1641; this was a similar stroke of state-policy, in the *pious* reign of *Charles the First*, who was *himself* (it is supposed) no stranger to the design, it was a heavenly piece of King-craft, and seems to have afforded an useful hint to our BLOODY ADMINISTRATION: This Irish carnage (where the Roman Catholic children killed the English children) was the happy fruit, not of an actual establishment, but of a bare toleration *of popery in Ireland*. if it be true (as it has been ever found) that like causes, will have like effects, there cannot be a doubt with our government, but that the same hellish spirit will break out hereafter among the *papists* in *Canada*; under the tender nature of such an administration as the present; it cannot fail.

I must confess, it is a far wiser and honester policy to endeavour to draw off the senseless parts of the *American* army, from their gallant leaders by a fruitless offer of *pardons*, and *indemnities*, then to nurse up *papists* with paternal tenderness, to cut the throats of *Englishmen*; but these vain ministerial schemes will succeed alike.

Let us grant, for argument sake only, that the past suppositions are injurious to our present *administration*; yet they must be answerable *above*, for every bad effect which may chance to flow from their patriotic conduct; even in times to come. I would suppose that this colony, of these new planted *papists*, will encrease according to common calculation, 7-8ths every Twenty years; what multitudes of intestine *Enemies* and *Rebels*, will shortly be produced from the diabolical feed of jesuits, monks and friars. Quebec will be an asylum for the sons of Loyola. What an ample provision have our ministry and parliament made for the certain, designed destruction of AMERICA hereafter! this was a noble stroke of policy, to effect their revenge on the colonies they hate, even in after-ages, but *Providence*, perhaps, aiding the cause of oppressed *America*, will prevent their hellish designes from taking place, she must otherwise fall a prey, at last, to the worst of savages; assassins, armed and commissioned by the See of *Rome*, who dye *saints and martyrs* in every conflict with heritics, and are taught to purchase salvation by massacreing mankind. With such hopeful colonies as these, impressed with a deep sense of *allegiance* to an *heritical* prince refuse to open their arms to a *French Invasion*, and to surrender the dominions of a credulous british government to their old sovereign the grand monarch, a son of *Holy Church?* Answer me ye *Mansfields*, and ye *Norths*! answer me thou Thane of *Bute*; or rather help your royal master to answer me *himself*, bid him, like his brother

William, to encrease the number of royal authors; teach him to rival his learned predecessor, *James* the First in literary merit, in immitation of that great *Solomon's* blast against tobacco, assist your lesser *Solomon*, in writing a *blast* against the *protestant religion,* against the *revolution, Cor-onation-oaths*, and *limited* monarchy, you may add a little appendix in defence of mental reservation, jesuitical equivocation, perjury hypocrisy, prodigality, tyranny. falsehood, and corruption. His holiness the *Pope*, in return for such glorious efforts in the cause of truth, and ever mindful of the late blessed indulgences at *Quebec*, would undoubtedly compliment his *new-ally* with every necessary dispensation, absolution, benediction &c. conveyed by one of the most faithful of his holy legates, his *holiness* might condescend, in honour of such a convert, to treat our *dilitanti senators* with a raree-show, in the recess of parliament, and exhibit the *beatification of George* the *Third,*—but, to be serious on a serious subject by the late establishment of *popery* at *Quebec*, one should almost suspect that the sovereigns solemn engagements at the altar, to maintain and defend *the religion by law established*, did not, as Mr. attorney *Turloe* elegantly expresses it *embrace* his majesty's whole dominions, or else one should imagine that his *Majesty*, by some secret *prerogative,* could dispense with his own *oath*, as easily as his faithful majority have dispensed with the established laws and religion of their country; let us examine the dangerous effects of this *Quebec-Bill* a little further. By an act in the reign of the late *good* king, an *alien* residing seven years in any of his majesty's *American* plantations, became a *denizen* of *Great-Britain*; consequently, in seven years from the passing of the late *pious Quebec-bill*, all the legion of *Holy-cheats* dispatched from *Rome*, for the propagation of *popery* in those parts are justly intitled to all the privileges of the English subjects, so will their offspring be, how welcome must an importation of such holy vermin be in England? they may swarm here legally in eight years by virtue of their derivation in America, in defiance of every law made in better and wiser reigns, for their perpetual expulsion. *By* that time, perhaps it may seem expedient, to repeal all the acts in support of the reformation—Shall I add, the revolution too? let these acts stand, or fall, yet how can these catholic *denizens*, (who will infest Great Britain in legions) be expelled from thence, or from America, by an honester and wiser parliament than the last? In such a case, how must the memory of the late treacherous parliament, be damned to eternal infamy? how must the name of the head of that vile patliament (who assented) stink in the nostrils of posterity? That pious head which (if speeches may be credited more than acts) declares from the throne, *"that the constant imployments of its thoughts, and the earnest wishes of its heart, bend wholly to the safety and happiness of the people.* A little flattery, (as the Tyrant Richard says,) sometimes does well—But good trees are known by their fruit,—quere,—what is to be done with a bad tree? in a reign which abounds with so'many horrid plots and conspiracies (of which Mr. Sheriff *Sayre's* is not the least) this must be a most alarming question, and will justify the sovereign, in calling forth Lord *Barrington's** paper-forces; not a single man of which can now be safely sent to *Boston.*— Alas the security of the sovereign's person requires that they should all be formed into a body-guard, without delay.

C A S C A.

---

*This Lord (as secretary at war,) exhibited the other day in the House of Commons a most tremendous list of *military forces* which were to be dispatched to *Boston*, for the reduction of the *Rebels* there; but his lordship ingeniously confessed that they were, as yet, only *upon paper,* and could not hitherto, be raised, tho' the bounty had been enlarged and the standard lowered, and all means whatever had been tried.:—What wonder? what *wretch*, what *savage* would be hired for such bloody aud tyrannic purposes? Let the *butchers* lay on their *Ruffians if they dare.*

Printed and published for the Authors, by T. W. SHAW, in Fleetstreet, opposite Anderton's Coffee House, where Letters to the Publisher will be thankfully received.

THE

CRISIS

NUMBER XLVIII   *To be continued Weekly.*

SATURDAY, Dece. 16, 1775   *Price* Two Pence Half-penny

When Kings are base, when Tyrants they are grown,
May Britons hurl them headlong from the Throne.

IT will I am convinced be allowed this is not a time for ceremony, the necessity of speaking in plain terms, must be obvious to every one. It shall therefore be the grand subject of this paper (however dangerous) to point out to the English nation, the *lawless power* assumed by the prince and to shew that he has commenced tyrant in the strictest sense of the word. To obey him then whilst he acts in this manner, and tramples under foot all laws, divine and human, argues not only a want of sense in the highest degree, but a want of love to our country, and a disregard for ourselves and posterity. It would eternally brand us as SLAVES and VASSALS, and we should no longer deserve the name of *free Britons*, of *Englishmen*, names which for ages have been a terror to the world. The King at his coronation, took a SOLEMN OATH to observe and cause all the laws to be kept. The ceremony of that day was scarcely over, before the sovereign broke that most sacred promise; and directions as well as encouragement was given to the ministers, to act in open violation of the laws of the land and the personal liberty of the subject; redress was sought for in vain, the King has a Scotch rebel at the head of the law, ready to support all his measures, who is defending the cause of his abandoned *minions*, and trampling under foot the laws of England, those laws which were purchased by the blood of our ancestors, who placed his family upon the throne of this great *empire*, extirpated the whole race of Stuarts, and preserved themselves and their posterity free. But the grand question at present is, whether we got any thing by the swap.

The authors of the CRISIS declare it would make no difference to them whether they lived under a tyrant of the house of *Stuart* or a tyrant of the house of *Brunswick*, names and families are meer sounds; and they can conceive no reason, why we should quietly submit to the chains that are *now* forging for us under *George* the *Third*: unless the nature of slavery is altered, and become desirable; the many *virtues* which the minister tells us the King is possessed of, may perhaps make it light and easy, but the people are rather inclined to think, that those virtues so much talked of, are only a MASK for many *crimes*, and till their *ipse dixit*[1] will pass with mankind; let them rest assured that the English nation will always judge by the actions and inclinations of the Prince. Oppression has succeeded oppression, and the people have been deprived of their share in the legislature, they have complained, they have petitioned, they have presented remonstrances to the sovereign, and he has absolutely refused to grant them any relief or redress, notwithstanding the power is in his own hands, and he *solemnly swore* to preserve the rights of the people, he has not only done this, but he has sent slaughter and disolation through the land, and butchered his subjects, with the most savage and unrelenting cruelty. This then is tyranny in the extreme, it is despotism in the Prince; and a perseverance a few months longer may perhaps oblige the brave and much injured people, of this island as well as the Americans, to seek that redress with their own hands, which their ungrateful monarch has denied them. *James* the second was requested to call a free parlia-

---

1. "He himself said it," which had passed into legal Latin, to mean that the speaker (or writer) himself made an otherwise unsubstantiated claim, or that, having said it, he should be held to it.

ment, he refused to comply with the requests of his people. The virtue of our fathers, however, soon made his throne shake, and the crown totter on his head. He, coward and tyrant-like, deserted the kingdom. The prince who now sways the British scepter, was called upon, by the majority of the nation to dissolve the last house of commons, and to send the electors to a choice of new representatives; HE insolently refused to comply with their request, as he has with every other just and equitable requisition from his subjects in every part of the Empire, it is the general wish of the whole kingdom, that he may take warning by former times, before it is too late and reflect upon the consequences of his conduct. The tyranny of this reign, however, does not end here, the laws upon many occasions have been suspended and dispensed with, as at the time of the revolution, to answer the vile and wicked purposes of a corrupt court; the people have been murdered in an inhuman manner, by a lawless military force, and those very murders sanctified publickly by the King's authority; the murderers pensioned and suffered to escape the punishment due to their crimes; these are the blessed effects of the boasted virtues, and mildness of a Prince of the house of *Brunswick*, but the brave and sensible part of the English nation call it the wicked and absolute tyranny of George the Third.

I shall now proceed to point out to the nation the steps that are necessary to be taken in order to bring the King to reason, and a *just sense of his duty* as well as the obligations he is under to the People of England.

In every state where the people enjoy liberty, resistance to all unlawful acts of government, and every kind of violence and oppression, is warranted and justified, by all the laws of God and Man, of reason and nature, or with what shadow of truth, could it be said this or any other nation is *free*.

Now both the legislative and the prince having acted contrary to their trust, the legislative by invading the property of the subject, and making themselves arbitrary disposers of the lives, liberties, and fortunes of the people; the prince by employing the force, the treasure, and offices of the kingdom, to carry on bloody and inhuman *CIVIL WAR*, and to corrupt the *representatives*, in order to bring them over to his cruel and wicked purposes. This then is, according to Mr. *Locke, Grotius, Puffendorff*[2] and other great writers against unlimited power, an actual dissolution of government; the king having set up the declared abettors of his own will, for the true representatives of the people, and the law-makers of the English nation: which is as great a *breach of trust*, and as perfect a declaration of a design to subvert the government, as is to be met with in history.

The people sensible of the injury, petitioned their sovereign, without effect, they remonstrated, but to no purpose, in terms too respectful, to a man whose ingratitude could carry him beyond the bounds of humanity; whose weakness and ambition could make him treat with contempt the very men who were the benefactors of his family, and had raised them to the imperial dignity of this realm; nay they were made the jest of those *slaves* and *sycophants* who surrounded him. This behaviour of the prince, is in the opinion of all thinking men, a most convincing proof, as well as a confirmation of a design to establish an *arbitrary* system of government.

Resistance to those measures is therefore not only necessary, but it is become the duty of every man in England to save us from a state of lasting slavery, as a nation, nay, it is become the duty of every individual, in order to preserve himself and children from *lawless violence*, from the hands of merciless *tyrants, and bloody monsters. Lord Mansfield* and other time-serving Judges, may perhaps declare this doctrine of resistance and this paper to be the standard of rebellion; it would not be at all surprising, but they must however, at the same time destroy the King's right and title to the throne, the constitution of England, and the principles upon which the last revolution is founded, and by which the house of Hanover was elevated to three crowns. If they should be able to make out that the King can do no wrong, which is the most rediculous absurdity

---

2. The Dutch legal theorist Hugo Grotius (1583–1645); Samuel Pufendorf (1632–1694) of Saxony, in what is now Germany; and the Englishman John Locke (1632–1704). All three philosophers were advocates of the notion of natural rights being antecedent to positive law; all three also contributed to the emerging body of international law, with their writings about the justice *of* war and justice *in* war; all three were respected in the British Atlantic world as seminal thinkers.

that can be conceived in politicks, nor is punishable or blameable by our constitution, but the *ministry*; then the people acted in a very strange and unjust manner at the revolution, in which the KING who must be INNOCENT only suffered, and the *ministry who must be guilty*, were not only excused, but intrusted and employed. In a word, whoever attempts to establish the above maxim, or a doctrine contrary to what is here advanced, does *ipso facto* overturn the constitution, and destroy the foundation upon which it stands.

The good of the People governed, is the end of all government, and the reason and original of governors; and upon this foundation it is that, It has been the practice of all nations, and of this in particular, that if the mal-administration of governors, have extended to *tyranny* and *oppression*, to the destruction of *right* and *justice*, overturning the constitution, and abusing the people, the people have thought it lawful to reassume the right of government, in their own hands, and to reduce their governors to reason. Now they who say it *lays a foundation for rebellion*, to tell the People they are absolved from obedience, when illegal attempts are made upon their liberties or properties, and may oppose, the unlawful violence of those who are their magistrates, and invade their rights contrary to the trust reposed in them; and that therefore this doctrine is not to be allowed, being so destructive to the peace of the world; They may as well say upon the same ground, and with the same reason, that honest men may not oppose robbers, or pirates, because this may occasion disorder or bloodshed. If any mischief happens in such cases, it is not to be charged upon him who defends his own rights but upon him who invades others. If the honest innocent man must quietly quit all he has for the sake of peace, to him who will lay violent heads upon it; the peace of the world would then consist only in violence and rapine, and be maintained only for the benefit of thieves and oppressors, As this would be the case should the vile, the destructive doctrine of *passive obedience and non-resistance* ever gain ground again in this island. We will then ask this question, which is best for mankind, that the people should be always exposed to the boundless will of tyranny or that the rulers should sometimes be liable to be opposed, when they grow exorbitant in the use of their power and employ it for the destruction, not the preservation of the people.

No one can with the least shadow of reason say that mischiefs must arise from hence, as often as it shall please a busy head, or a turbulent spirit, to desire the alteration of the government. It is true, such men may stir, whenever they please, but it will be only to their own just ruin and perdition. For till the grievances of the nation are general, and the wicked designs of the rulers become visible, as they most evidently are at this moment to the whole kingdom, the people, who are more disposed to suffer, then right themselves by resistance are not apt to stir. The examples of particular injustice, or oppression of here and there an unfortunate man moves them not. But if they have a perswasion grounded upon manifest evidence, that designs are carrying on against their liberties, and the general course and tendency of things, cannot but give them strong suspicions of the evil intention of the prince, or his ministers, who is to be blamed for it? who can help it if they who might avoid it bring themselves in to this suspicion? are the people to be blamed, if they have the sense of rational creatures, and can think of things no otherwise, than as they find and feel them? I grant that the pride, ambition, and turbulency of private men, have sometimes caused great disorders in common-wealths, and factions have been fatal to states and kingdoms. But whether the mischief hath oftener begun in the peoples wantonness, and a desire to cast off the lawful authority of their ruler, or in the rulers insolence, and endeavours to get and exercise arbitrary power over their people; whether oppression or disobedience gave the first rise to the disorder, let impartial history determine.

Whosoever uses force without right, as every one does in society, who does it without law, puts himself in a state of war with those against whom he uses it; and in that state all former ties are cancelled, and all other rights cease, and every one has a right to defend himself, and to resist the aggressor. This is so evident that *Barclay* himself,[3] that great

3. William Barclay, a contemporary of fellow Scotsman James I, studied and taught law in France, and defended the doctrine of the divine right of kings. His most important

asserter of the power, and sacredness of kings, is forced to confess, that it is lawful for the the people, in some cases, to resist their Kings: and that too in a chapter wherein he pretends to shew, that the divine law shuts up the people from all manner of rebellion. Whereby it is evident, even by his own doctrine, that, since they may in some cases resist, all resisting of Princes is not rebellion.

Printed and published for the Authors, by T. W. SHAW, in Fleet-street, opposite Anderton's Coffee House, where Letters to the Publisher will be thankfully received.

---

treatises, first published in Latin, were also translated into French and English, though none in London during the eighteenth century. No doubt the author(s) of *The Crisis* lifted the phrase describing Barlcay as "that great asserter of the power, and sacredness of kings" from John Locke's *Second Treatise*, which was readily available in Locke's combined *Works* or under separate title—such as in *The Two Treatises of Government*, 5th ed. (London: J. Bettesworth, 1728), p. 298.

THE

CRISIS

NUMBER XLIX   *To be continued Weekly.*

SATURDAY, Dece. 23, 1775   *Price* Two Pence Half-penny

When Kings the Sword of Justice first lay down
They are no Kings, tho' they possess a CROWN.
Titles *are Shadows,* Crowns *are empty Things*;
The GOOD of Subjects is the End of Kings:—
To *guide* in WAR, and to *protect* in PEACE,
Where Tyrants once commence, the Kings do cease:
For Arbitrary Power's so strange a Thing,
It MAKES the TYRANT, and UN-makes the King.

THE last news from *America* is of the most shocking and alarming nature; but nothing can either convince the judgements, or divert the intentions of the *infernal* Ministers of George the Third. They have formed in conjunction with the BLOODY-minded COWARD and TYRANT their Master, a FACTION and CONSPIRACY against the Laws and Liberties, the Lives and Properties of the PEOPLE in every part of the wide extended Empire of Britain.

THEIR plan is ROBERY and MURDER; and although they are fighting against the natural Rights of Mankind, and all the Laws of God, Justice and Humanity, yet an obstinate perseverance (which none but Demons

443

possess) marks their steps; altho' their measures are reprobated by every honest man in England, and the TYRANT's Forces worsted in every Battle with the brave and virtuous *Americans*, (who to their immortal honour are now struggling in the great cause of freedom and their Country) yet all this cannot make those Plunderers and Butchers desist from their RAPINE and VIOLENCE.

THE last advices which arrived here a few days since from *America*, brought to the infinite satisfaction of all GOOD Men, a circumstantial and particular account of the Americans being in possession of FORT CHAMBLEE, and FORT Sт. JOHN's in the Province of *Canada*, with little loss or bloodshed; that General Carleton had been defeated by the Provincials, and was very near being taken Prisoner of War. The Ministry, however, strictly adhering to their original plan of delusion and villainy, thought fit to suppress the Publication of these Accounts in the last *Gazette*, published by AUTHORITY, a Gazette known at this time, only for the most notorious LIES, and the most shameful Misrepresentations; in short, every circumstance relative to the present royal and ministerial CIVIL WAR in *America*, which most sensibly and fatally affects the people of England, has either not appeared in that paper, or been scandalously MIS-represented and falsified by ministerial artifice and King craft. How long the people here will suffer themselves to be thus imposed upon, and their money to be unjustly wrested from them to carry on a cruel and unprovoked War against their Fellow Subjects, Time only can determine: But it is to be hoped for the honour of the Nation and humanity, their present TAME ACQUIESCENCE will not be of long continuance; and that they will soon convince both the Sovereign and his Ministers, that they are determined not to be the infamous SUPPORTERS of TYRANNY, nor the QUIET Spectators of the Ruin and Butchery of their Friends and Countrymen, in whose Destruction must be involved in their OWN: That rather than see the Constitution overturned, their Liberties annihilated, their Property unlawfully and wantonly torn from them by a rapacions King, and their Posterity enslaved; they are resolved to make the Throne of Tyranny shake, and like their Forefathers prove to the World that no Prince shall tyrannize over them, and sacrifice the dear bought Rights of Englishmen with IMPUNITY.

The Orders lately sent by the Ministers of the grand MASTER BUTCHER at *St. James's* to DESTROY ALL THE TOWNS on the Coast of *America*, and to leave the innocent and defenceless Inhabitants, infirm Men, Women, and Children, exposed to the inclemency of the Weather, WITHOUT SHELTER, and all the horrors of Poverty and Want, is such an Exercise of wanton Cruelty, as cannot be paralleled in the History of the most SAVAGE Nations upon Earth; and will (if any thing possibly can) surely rouse the Indignation and Resentment, the noble Spirit, and generous Feelings of Britons, against the Authors of such till NOW unheard of Barbarities, altho' the Head of the First MONSTER in this inhuman Business should be encricled with a DIADEM.

Every good Man must condemn these Measures, and the hellish Spirit of the Conspirators, it being evident to the World, that their whole Aim and only Design is PLUNDER and PUBLIC RUIN, should they be suffered to proceed further, the whole Empire must be thrown into Convulsions, and the People submit to slavery, OR, all the dreadful Calamities of intestine War; nay, (dreadful to behold!) we shall see, like the brave Americans, our Houses ransacked, our Villages plundered our finest Cities encompassed with Foreign Armies, and our firuitful Fields cloathed with Desolation; and still more horrid to relate, we must be shocked with the more frightful Images, of Garments rolled in Blood; and of a Ruffian's Blade REAKING from a BROTHER's Heart! What amends can the present Tyrant and his Ministers make for the Property they have already plundered in America, for an Immense Commerce ruined or lost, for Cities laid in Ashes, for contending Armies, Bloodshed, Slaughter, and Battles; for general Desolation, innumerable Murders, and universal Destruction; much less for the Evils just before mentioned, which must happen in the BOWELS of THIS COUNTRY, should the People of England remain as they now do, supinely negligent of their own PRESERVATION, and not RESIST their Oppressors, the common Enemies of Mankind.

To the black Catalogue of Crimes and mischiefs they have committed, the present merciful, pious Tyrant and his Ministers, are about to make a glorious Addition, that of PROHIBITING all Trade and Intercourse from every Part of the World with North America. This Bill is now passing through the British Senate, a Senate which like that in the Time of *Henry* the VI. has deservedly obtained the Appellation of *the Parliamentum Diabolicum*, or the Devilish Parliament.[1]

This Method of declaring War on the Americans, instead of answering the Ends which the Tyrants designed, has a direct Tendency to Effect and will forever separate the two Capital Parts of the Empire. Nothing can certainly be more rediculous than to behold a Nation making a Separation of its Parts by LAW, with a View of re-uniting them by a TREATY. The Clauses of this wicked, absurd, and impolitic Bill, consign ALL to Punishment, whether Friends or Enemies to Government.— Yet the Preamble only declares, that MANY are Guilty. The English on both Sides of the Ocean are now taught by ACT of PARLIAMENT to look on themselves as separate Nations; Nations susceptible of general Hostility, and proper Parties for mutual Declarations of War, and Treaties of Peace. The Tyrant and his Ministers, are by THIS ACT, preparing the Minds of the Americans for that Independence, which they have been falsely charged with affecting, whilst they are drove to it, by repeated Injuries.

The Framers of the Bill, not satisfied with making predatory War upon the Trade of the Colonies, thought it necessary to stimulate particular avarice and rapacity to an activity in such service, by rendering captures of North American Vessels, and Goods, the Property of the CAPTORS. This must be considered (for the *first* Time) as holding out the Spoil of their Fellow Citizens, for the Reward of ALACRITY in Civil War, as a source of the most dangerous Corruption that can be conceived, in the first instance to our Navy, and in its consequences to the Army. A number of bold, desperate, enterprizing

---

1. See n. IX.3 supra for the sequence of parliamentary acts cutting off the rebellious colonies from trade with the larger world.

men trained to the profession of Arms are naturally lovers of War; and when they have once tasted of emoluments from domestic Spoils they will no longer look on the Commerce of England as an Object of PROTECTION, but of PLUNDER. They will see the prosperous State of peaceful domestic industry, not with Pleasure, but with Envy. The greatest Republic, of which History gives us any Knowledge, was subverted by this Licence of DOMESTIC PLUNDER. The Navy of England, (curse on the Traitors) want no such unnatural and impious Encouragement, towards the performance of any Duty which their known Public Spirit, and as yet uncorrupted Honour, may make it necessary to perform. And it is a Matter of the most serious concern to the Nation that a service always looked upon (and hitherto most justly) not only without fear or jealously, but with the greatest Affection in every Part of the Empire, should be unnecessarily exposed to the lasting ODIUM which must attend those who are enriched from the SPOILS of Citizens, amongst whom they may be obliged to spend their Lives, and form their Connections.

This Bill equally unjust and villainous in every Part, by anticipating the legal Judgment of the Offences of those whose Goods are forfeited, overturns one of the most Fundamental Parts of the BILL of RIGHTS, which declares, "that all Grants of Fines and Forfeitures of particular Persons BEFORE CONVICTION, are ILLEGAL and VOID."—This Provision was expressly made, lest rapacious Ministers seeking confiscation, or rapacious Soldiers allured by the Lust of Plunder, should be induced to enrich themselves out of the Public Disorders.

The whole scheme of this nefarious Bill, and predatory War for private Lucre, is put under the direction of certain COMMISSIONERS, Men not even known by Name; who are to have a Power to give such continuance to the Ravages Authorized by this Bill as their Blood-thirsty Wills shall suggest; to Pardon or except from Pardon, any number of description of Persons, and with such Exceptions as THEY shall see fit, without any other Rule than their own private Opinion, Fancy, Caprice, Favour, or Resentment; This Power is not only unjustifiable and unconstitutional, but the greatest that can be given to any Tyrants, and ought not to be in the Hands of any Man or set of Men.[2]

The farther we examine this Bill the more infamous and diabolical it appears, that Clause of it, which by a Refinement in Tyranny, and in a Sentence worse than Death, obliges the unhappy Men who shall be made Captives in this predatory War, to bear Arms against their Families, Kindred, Friends, and Country; and after being plundered themselves, to become Accomplices in plundering their Brethren. By this Clause which none but DEVILS could suggest, not only common Seamen, but Masters of Vessels, are, without regard to Age, Circumstances, or Condition, to be ignominiously turned before the Mast, and subjected to the austere Discipline of the Boatswain. Persons, in that subordinate Station, not being animated with the liberal and ingenuous Spirit which distinguishes our Officers in the Navy, and taught to consider these *forced Volunteers* as REBELS, will be but too apt to aggravate the Miseries of Captivity by INSULT and OUTRAGE. The Prisoners among the Comrades they are obliged to live and serve with, may probably be often forced to behold the Spoils of their honest Industry, and the natural Support of their sober Families, squandered in riot and profligate Debauchery before their Faces. This every Man must look upon as the last Degree of Wretchedness and Indignity, to which human Nature can be subjected. These Cruelties, (O! Shame to Britain) unknown to the most Savage Nations are to be practised, (if they can stoop to the hateful Task) by Englishmen on Englishmen. Such Examples of Barbarity were never known or heard of, except among Pirates, the Out-Laws and Enemies of human Society.

---

2. George III had finally decided on December 9th to send peace commissioners, and then only reluctantly. For his hardening attitudes as the crisis had deepened see Andrew Jackson O'Shaughnessy, "If Others Will Not be Active, I Must Drive" *Early American Studies* 2 (2004):1–46. There was no point in the Continental Congress attempting to send negotiators; the King would not have received them. As the King's commissioners the Howe brothers were to seek reconciliation even as they waged their 1776 campaign to seize New York. They were not to treat directly with any rebel government, the Continental Congress included, and were to use North's February 1775 resolution as the basis of discussions with any interested parties. See my *Turning the World Upside Down* (Westport, Conn.: Praeger, 2003), pp. 131–42. What the Howes began in 1776 would be kept up by others through the end of war in 1783, with no success.

N. B. CASCA's LETTER is received, and shall be made the Subject of the next Number.—The AUTHORS of the CRISIS owe him many Obligations, for his spirited and sensible Essays in Support of Civil and Religious Liberty. They have always given particular Directions to their Printer to set every Word scored for *Italic*, in that Character, and to be, in the Composition of his Epistles, exceedingly careful—but *Ex nihilo nihil fit.*[3]

Printed and published for the Authors, by T. W. SHAW, in Fleet-street, opposite Anderton's Coffee House, where Letters to the Publisher will be thankfully received.

---

3. From nothing comes nothing.

THE

CRISIS

NUMBER L   *To be continued Weekly,*

SATURDAY, *Dec.* 30, 1775   *Price* Two-pence Halfpenny.

—*Dolus*, an *Virtus*, quis in *hoste* requirit?[1]

Whether by *Valour*, or *Deceit* we tame
Our *hostile Children*, 'tis to *Bute* the same.
Let *Bute's Commission Scottish Treachery try*;
The want of *Force Bute's Treaty* will supply;
Freedom and *Bute* are Foes.—let *Freedom* die.

I N my last I shewed that our *virtuous administration*, by their accessaries in a corrupt parliament, had laid a plan for the secret, and (as they hoped) effectual destruction of *America* by *Popery*—by the intended *restraining Bill*, now passing with the greatest rapidity through both houses, at the thinnest season, two fresh nets are spread for the ruin of oppressed *America,* by *treaty* upon land, and *captures* at *Sea.*— Thus are *policy* and *piracy* like *war*, and *conciliation*, jumbled together, with most profound wisdom in one and the same Bill. The British arms,

---

1. Taken from Virgil's *Aeneid*, Book 2: who asks (or what does it matter) whether an enemy was defeated by strategy (even subterfuge) or valor?

like the British policy, have hitherto been foiled, disgraced, dispised and providentially disappointed in *America*. No sufficient *land forces* can be raised, *administration* are now going to try their fortune upon *Sea,* at the same time craftily equiping, not an *army* (for they they cannot) but a specious commission for the land-service; whose business is, *not to invade*, but to *undermine*, not to *attack* but to *betray*, AMERICA; in this and in this alone, *administration* are consistent, in endeavouring to accomplish the basest ends by the basest means. *America* is not to be *enslaved* by arms, she must therefore be attempted by restraint, perfidy, snares, stratagem and proscription. *England* at the very outset of the dispute, withdrew her protection from AMERICA, and bent upon *enslaving* her, not only spurned her supplications, but treated her with the earliest and most unjustifiable hostilities; not wishing to *reclaim* her as a refractory *child*, but to *extirpate* her as an odious, because she was a virtuous enemy; because she boldly and bravely claimed the undoubted rights and privileges of a *British colony*; because she insisted, with the greatest truth, that *subordination* and *slavery*, were terms of a very different import, and disdained to be degraded from the rational state of a *subject* to the servile, tame, and helpless condition of a *Brute*. Not yet convinced of her erroneous notions either *by famine, fleets*, or *armies*, it remains for her to be attacked by *privateers* and *state-commissioners*. Every English Vessel on the American Seas, from a first rate to a pinnace, is to be armed against her, and every *Scotchman*, is exerting his interest to be nominated in this *muckle gude* commission, (now in contemplation,) every *Sawney* pretends to some knowledge of *juris prudence*, and therefore thinks himself equal to the Business.[2] But this kind of learning will be useless, for Sir *George Hay* has told us lately in the House of Commons, that the *Laws of Nations* are not to be obeyed in a *treaty*, with *rebellious* subjects.[3] The

2. Anti-Scots sentiments, with a softer even though sardonic edge: "muckle gude"—much good—from the Scottish vernacular, and "Sawney," long familiar slang for a Scotsman or any simpleton or fool.

3. Sir George Hay had sat for a number of boroughs in the House of Commons over the previous twenty years. His politics could vary, though on American affairs he was predictably a government man and he supported North's new policies. As an Admiralty judge he even hoped the prosecution and conviction of those who violated the

Doctor (like a true *court-civilian*,) took much learned pains to establish this position, in order to justify (if possible) the flagrant inhumanity of government, which has hitherto treated the AMERICANS, (contrary to the *law* of *nature*,) without the least regard to humanity, charity, christianity, and reason, under sanction of the omnipotent law of *Parliament*, which has conformed throughout, with the steadiest perseverance, to the pleasure of the *minister*. The *doctor's forensian declamation* interlarded with latin quotations, unintelligible to more than half the house, might have been well spared.

Under the present ministerial influence, (the baneful influence of BUTE) no treaty with *America*, can proceed in earnest; the *commission*, the *treaty*, the *conciliation talked of*, are mere pretexts, blinds and mockeries; a real *conciliation* will not answer the purposes of the present patriotic *administration*, they are bent (like true *tories*) upon obtaining despotic sway, and illegal plunder throughout the *Colonies*.

These glorious *prerogatives*, having once taken root in *America*, are by degrees, or perhaps at once (when *Bute* and *Mansfield* shall give the nod) be transplanted hither, and naturalized under the fostering wings of a *Scotch administration*, a *corrupt parliament*, a *standing army*, and a *tyrannic baby*, who is sufficiently pleased if he can purchase childish toys and baubles, empty power, and prerogative, with the BLOOD of MILLIONS. Will such a hopeful *junto* ever treat in earnest with *America?* never.—They have not, they cannot have, a thought of reinstating that injured country in all her undoubted rights, upon other terms they know she will not treat, upon other terms she will not exist. These are the fixt resolutions of her *patriotic Congress*. But with this *general Congress*, our *Commissioners* will be forbid to treat. No.—they are to regain each province *separately* by the dint of superior wisdom and delusive declarations, but above all, by the great electrical shock, which they intend to give these *Rebels*, (as they call them) by this impious *preliminary*: First

---

Prohibitory Act would help drive rebellious colonists back into line. Matthew Kilburn offered a quick review of his career in the *Oxford DNB*, 25:997–99; there is also an entry for him in Namier and Brooke, *House of Commons*, 2:599–600.

lay down your arms.—This first word of *command*, is a compleat key to *Doctor Haye's* late learned speech in the House of Commons. Upon this previous requisition, I will venture to foretell, that the *American treaty* will break off immediately. This is the expectation and hope of our present ministry, who are born and formed, for acting upon no other than the most destructive principles. for this reason they will arm their *commissioners* with articles of *treaty* in one hand, and a *restraining act* in the other; *America* may then take her choice, whether she will he shackled by *land,* or pillaged and dismembered upon the *ocean*; all her effects will be lawful *prize*, and all her seamen will be *rebels*. This will be the result of the pretended *treaty*, and the contemptible fruits of the new *restraining bill.*

Contemptible I call them for they will soon be blasted by the wisdom, vigilance, and spirit of *America*; Our state-politicians have already roused a *Lion* in the field, and they will shortly find a *Leviathan* in the waters, instead of healing the breach they have already made, they are most injudiciously calling forth all the powers of a vast territory, against us both by sea and land.

Mis-informed and ignorant as these *ministerial miscreants* are in every point, they do not know, they have not the least conception, that *America*, whom they are now enraging till she puts forth all her strength, has it in her power, to be great and terrible, even unto the *ocean*. I aver and it is well known by those who know her, that there is no one requisite for this purpose which she has not within herself. Add to this, as we have lately felt to our sorrow, (the miserable remains of our defeated army there will witness it) she wants neither discipline, activity, nor courage, whatever men can effect by these, has already been effected by *America* upon *Land*. Will she be less industrious with every advantage of art and nature on her side, to make a figure worthy of her upon *sea?* She is no stranger to the art of building or navigating ships.—will she be unable, or afraid to fight them? I should not credit *Lord Denbigh*, no, nor *Lord Sandwich*, who holds the *trident* at our board of admiralty, were they to assert it.

I believe these *bablers*, these perpetual *yelpers* in the *ministerial pack*, have now sufficient reason to run silent, since the last advice from *America*.

The *Americans* have not proved paltroons and cowards, (for so their lordships prophesied) upon land, nor will they disgrace their country or their cause upon the deep. Till they are called into action there, I shall amuse myself with the conjectures I have formed upon this *mock-commission*, and its success by *treaty*.

Upon this subject I will pronounce boldly, in one decisive word, that without a change of *men* and *measures* at the helm, there can be no reunion with *America*. I need not consider articulately what demands she may reasonably make, let me only suppose, in one word, with every warlike advantage on her side, she submits to a *reconciliation*, even now, upon being put in *statuquo* and upon having those rights restored to her which have been wrested from her, together with the liberty, so justly claimed by her, of *giving* and *granting* away her own peculiar property acquired (as I have often said and say again) by the sweat of her own brow, in a *distinct community,* subordinate indeed (and so she owns) to the *equity,* but not to the *tyranny,* of English *Lords* or *Laws*. Suppose *victorious America,* should ask no more after her towns and cities have been wantonly laid in ashes, and her young men and maidens given up to FIRE, FAMINE, and the SWORD? Will the present humane *administration* sign a *treaty* upon these terms? no, all they mean is to *dis-unite* the provinces, procure the *American army* to be disbanded, and then their point is gained.

This *tory administration* have begun like *butchers*; they will *treat* like Foxes, and keep their faith like *devils,* their principles are *despotic,* with a *treaty* in their hands, *extirpation* and *extirpation* only, is in their hearts. Tho' *Bute* rules no longer, (thank heaven) *within* the curtains, yet he still rules *behind* the curtain. Under such an accursed influence *freedom* must be blasted, a *Stuart* near is like a *Stuart* in the throne. Under this malignant influence, no *addresses* have been *graciously* received but such as have most constitutionally solicited our *pious sovereign* to draw blood enough from the noble veins of distressed *America*. *Administration,* in the vanity of their hearts, had devoted her as a certain victim to their despotic Views, their murderous machinations have been foiled, the united forces of *Great Britain* are not sufficient to guard us at home, and at the same time massacre our gallant colonies abroad. No *recruits* for such bloody and inhuman purposes can be raised, *administration,* therefore, are now attempting to eke out the Lion's skin with the Fox's tail. They are calling *stratagem* in to aid *tyranny.*

The first pretence of these *negotiating despots* will be, that it is not consistent with the dignity of *Great Britain,* to treat with *rebels under arms,* if *America* on any pretence, lays down her arms, till she is *secure* she is no more, let her, who can baffle *arms* beware of *snares.* let injured and oppressed *America* remember, that her *cause* dignifies her measures, and put her on an honourable level, with the greatest potentates upon earth, she has been oppressed, disowned, abandoned as a *child,* let her therefore treat with her unnatural and hostile *parent* with the greatest caution, nay, with some degree of prudential distrust and jealousy, the measures of a *tyrannic government* will justify her; let her treat, not as an helpless, passive *Colony,* but as an injured, insulted, and offended *Nation.* Let her hear of no alternatives, after such an impious *assassination,* but ample *restitution,* or total *extirpation.* In a word, let her consent to remain a *subject* but still disdain to be a *slave.* Unless she can share the *Rights* of a British Subject, let her despise the *name.* Should her fortune (after treachery, war and tyranny have done their worst) be only equal to her glorious spirit, she must be *free.* Should she, in spite of all her fortitude and virtue, prove unsuccessful, she may at length become a *slave*—but not to *England.* Alas! our shallow *Ministry* (though aided by their conceited politician *Mansfield*) are but little aware of the *American recources* and *revolts.* They have felt the arm, but are as yet, strangers to the internal strength and native magnanimity of such an *enemy,* if she survives, she will set them a Roman example of true policy and superior greatness, if she falls, she will astonish, confound, and crush them with her ruin, their insolent menaces are but air, their iniquituous acts of parliament, like their arms, are impotent; their miditated *treacheries* under colour of a pretended *treaty,* will be at once (as they themselves are) the scorn of *America* the redicule and detestation of mankind.

What man of real honour will sanctify a *mock-commission* with his name, or a perfidious *treaty* with his presence? Not *Sir Jeffery Amhurst* surely?[4]— The honest part of the nation has better hopes of him. A man of honour will not be made a *tool.* Lord *George Germaine* has been spoken of for this *honourable* service.[5] His talents, which were *before* mistaken, may now, perhaps, be useful. His *sword* will not be wanted, and *training* may be his Lordship's *fort.* But he must still treat as a *Subaltern* under *orders.* Can we suppose his Lordship will understand the *orders* of Lord *North* better than he did the *orders* of Prince *Ferdinand?* Will Lord *George Germaine,* behave more to the satisfaction of his *commander* at the *treaty* of *Boston,* than Lord *George Sackville* did at the *battle* of MINDEN? Upon

4. In December 1774 Sir Jeffery Amherst had made it clear to ministry insiders that if he were offered command of his Majesty's army in North America he would refuse, not because he opposed North's policies, but because he had no desire to return to the colonies. It is also possible that he did not want to replace and thereby embarrass Gage, his successor and onetime comrade-in-arms, even if Gage stayed on as governor of Massachusetts. Amherst no doubt foresaw that he could end up in the same situation as Gage, blamed for an all-too-likely failure—whether it be renewed attempts to conciliate that led nowhere, or attempts to coerce that produced even more intractable behavior. Admired as the major general who had forced the surrender of New France in 1760, he had also been criticized for not handling the Indian uprisings that followed as well: reputations, he knew from experience, rose and fell, and masters could be fickle. Midway through the war he did accept the post as commander-in-chief but he had little talent or patience for the politics involved in a cabinet-level post. Elevated to the peerage as Baron Amherst, he left the debating to others. William C. Lowe offers a brief overview in the *Oxford DNB,* 1:48–51.

5. Lord George Sackville made Germain his surname with an inheritance in 1771. As Sackville he had been court-martialed in the aftermath of the 1759 Battle of Minden. Prince Ferdinand, the allied commander there, had ordered Germain to bring forward the British cavalry under him; Germain delayed in executing the order, causing Ferdinand to believe that his victory was less complete because of it. Piers Mackesy tried to remove the tarnish from Germain's name in *The Coward of Minden* (London: Allen Lane, 1979). Mackesy also wrote the entry for Germain in the *Oxford DNB,* 21:957–62. For Germain and the colonies see Gerald Saxton Brown, *The American Secretary* (Ann Arbor: University of Michigan Press, 1963); O'Shuaghnessy, *Men Who Lost America,* pp. 165–203; and, more generally, Margaret Marion Spector, *The American Department of the British Government, 1768–1782* (New York: Columbia University Press, 1940).

the whole, is a man so *stained* (let his *courtly-merits* be what they will) fit to be a *Commissioner* of a *Turnpike?* Unless the *conciliating minister* can find men of *seeming* honour to execute his purpose, his attempts on *America* by *treaty* will be vain.

In that *commission, Knavery's* plain face must not appear. An aspect so malignant would frustrate all hopes of prevailing by *deceit*, even before the opening of the COMMISSION.

Therefore all Ministerial Lacqueys, Pensioners, Placemen, Tories, Scotchmen, and Cowards, should, in good policy, be kept at home. The names of such servile wretches may dishonour the Great Seal of England, but such slaves of power cannot be properly qualified even to *deceive America.* They will help to swallow part of the *national Supplies* indeed, but if our *yielding* Administration with (and it is their only wish) to amuse, betray and ensnare *America;* they must send *Instruments,* who have, at least, the *semblance* of some virtues. Even Sir *Grey,* (the quondam Mr.) *Cooper,* tho' lately *dubbed* and *dignified* for the purposes of carrying and managing the *Commission,* even this *Sir Trusty,* this *Ambidexter* to Lord *North,* will (if his Lordship is wise) be ordered, upon second thoughts, to stay in England.[6] The *Man* smells too strong of the *Master* for *America.* She can have no confidence in *apparent Tools.* Such *supple* Delegates as these from the very sink of *corruption,* will give the *Americans* just reason to suspect the intended cheat before it can be played off. Set *Sir Grey* aside, and prick me down, in his stead, the *rhetorical* Mr. INNIS.[7] He cannot *speak,* but

6. Sir Grey Cooper, a recent baronet, had been a successful barrister for twenty years and a member of the Commons for ten. The "Ambidexter" label was often applied to those, lawyers especially, who seemed to be driven more by ambition than principle, able to switch sides at their convenience and causing critics to accuse them of double-dealing. There is an entry for Cooper in Namier and Brooke, *House of Commons,* 2:250–51; and a note on him in the *Oxford DNB,* 13:253–54, by Hallie Rubenhold.

7. William Innes, a London merchant, won a Commons seat in the 1774 election, argued vigorously for the use of force against American rebels once the shooting started, then lost his seat in December 1775 after the election results were challenged. There is a brief entry for Innes in Namier and Brooke, *House of Commons,* 2:666.

he can *read*, to listening *America*, (as he lately did to an admiring *House of Commons*) the most *enlarged* and *purest* notions of *Civil* LIB-ERTY. *Hear him! hear him!* his two best and and strongest arguments against *American Liberty* are these: 1st, Because there is a variety of claimers among them who cannot all be as they pretend, *Descendants* of the First Settlers; namely, Scotch, Irish, Indians, and even Trans-ported Felons. But, Mr. INNIS will permit me, with all the deference of a modest Opponent, to ask him, Whether Scotch and Irish, by *Transplantation*, lose their *Birth-right?* Whether the Tawny *Indian* is less free than the fairer subjects of *Great Britain,* because he has a copper-cast of countenance? and whether the *transported Felon* is not *free,* after his term of punishment is expired, as the *Sovereign* who signed his warrant?—Now hear Mr. *Innes*'s second objection to the *freedom* of *America*; it is, because many, if not most, of her natives draw their first sustenance from the bosom of *Slaves*, let me remind Mr. *Innes* here, that wiser Englishmen than he, have, in their infancy, been nourished by Goats, Cows, and Asses, are they therefore to be numbered with the beast of the field?

One should think, that the learned *Dr. Haye*, (who has lately laboured with *Mr. Innes* in the same oral drudgery, as a mouth-piece for the min-ister) had helped Mr. *Innes* to a false position; viz. partus sequitur—*mammam*—instead of—*Ventrem.*[8] Be this as it may, Mr: *Innes*'s mode of reasoning will secure him from all suspicion of design, and therefore he will be the better qualified to act a part, under a *proper Instructor,* in this national-commission, the mode of its proceedings will be perfectly agreeable to the narrowest soul that can be employed in it; it will be di-rected by BUTE, and settled finally by MANSFIELD; the two great patrons of Civil Liberty; to whom AMERICA will at last owe a glorious *Independent Empire,* and GREAT BRITAIN, in all probability, another glorious *Revolution.*

C A S C A.

8. Latin as applied to law, with "Partus sequitur Ventrem" meaning that a child's legal status follows that of its mother; the informal "mammam" presumably meant that sta-tus was determined by whoever provides nurture.

Printed and Published for the AUTHORS by T. W. SHAW, in Fleet-Street, opposite Anderton's Coffee-House, where Letters to the Publisher will be thankfully received.

THE

CRISIS

NUMBER LI   *To be continued Weekly,*

DURING THE PRESENT BLOODY CIVIL WAR IN AMERICA.

SATURDAY, JANUARY 6, 1776   *Price* Two-pence Half-penny.

It is an Act of PUBLIC JUSTICE not only to RESTRAIN, but to DESTROY TYRANTS

DIOCLESIAN, the Emperor and Tyrant of *Rome*, was so full of Vanity, Folly, and Wickedness, that he would be worshiped like a GOD; and have his Subjects kiss his Feet. He was an Enemy to public Freedom, and hated the Christians to such a Degree, that he began the most cruel Persecution against them, that ever polluted the Earth with Blood; however, their Numbers increasing daily, he was at last obliged to abdicate the Throne, and seek Shelter in a foreign Land, and died of Despair and Rage, because he saw Feedom and Religion triumph over Idolatry and Oppression. Had not this bloody Monster been RESTRAINED and drove from the Empire, Rome had been enslaved and Christianity trampled under Foot: And unless the present BRITISH TYRANT is resisted and restrained, in his attempts to destroy the Religion, Liberties, and Property of the *Americans*, the Constitution of this Kingdom in Church and State must be overturned, and the Nation enslaved.

461

DOMITIAN the last of twelve Cæsars, (what will not Tyrants do) poisoned his BROTHER to be made Emperor: at first he governed well, but soon became both cruel and impious, and put to death many of the first and best Men in Rome, he began the second Persecution against the Christians, debauched his own Niece, delighted in Sodomy, took the Name of God and Lord, and would have destroyed all the human race, but he was at length murdered by the Hands of one BRAVE and FREE Roman: May every Tyrant meet HIS FATE. This merciful Emperor used to divert himself in Catching of Flies, and Piercing them with a Bodkin. The present Sovereign of England is often not much more usefully employed in examining little Pinchy's Gew-gaws, Baubles, and Trinkets, and many Times more cruelly with his Ministers in forming Plans for the universal Destruction of Mankind.

NERO succeeded Claudius in the Empire of Rome: at the begining of his Reign, like most other TYRANTS, he made fair Promises, and not to lose any Occasion of evidencing his Liberality and Clemency, he eased the People either by taking away, or diminishing the Taxes and Impositions and by great Liberality to the Poor.[1] When the Sentence of a Person condemned to death was presented to him to be signed, "*I wish,*" said he, "*that I could not write.*" At another Time when the Senate made him a public acknowledgement of his just Administration, he answered with great Modesty, "*Pray let me deserve it first.*" In short, during the first five Years of his Reign, he made many excellent Speeches, and did Honour to the Seat of Royalty. But from that Time forwards his Life was spent in the most extravagant Enormities, horrid Crimes, and monstrous Abominations, that ever entered the depraved Imagination of Man. He caused his Mother to be murthered, his Wife *Octavia* to be put to death, and his Wife *Poppea* he killed with a Spurn of his Foot; the same Cruelties he exercised against his Relations, Friends, and the best Men in *Rome*; he wished all Mankind had but one Head, that he might have the Pleasure of Cutting it off. To have the Glory of Rebuilding *Rome*, and having it called by his Name, he set that famous City on Fire, and to Insult over it

---

1. For Nero and Claudius as emperors see II.5 supra.

the more, got on a high Tower, and thence taking a View of the Flames, in a Comedians Habit, SUNG a SONG of the Burning of *Troy* to his Harp. At length he justly became the common Detestation of Mankind, as the most execrable Monster that ever disgraced human Nature: His Armies in *Gaul* declared against him, and *Galba* revolted in Spain, which News threw him into such Despair, that he designed to have poisoned himself, or to have demanded the PARDON of the PEOPLE; but as he was pursued on every side, and found he must be justly sacrificed to the Resentment of the Public, he was forced to turn his own Executioner, nor could he have found a more infamous Hangman. Such is generally the Fate of all Tyrants, the common Destroyers of Mankind.

The History of this Country, like that *of Rome*, will furnish us with many Instances of such Monsters, seated on the Throne of Royalty. It is true his present Majesty, was always very *dutiful*, and too much of a BABY and SUCKLING to kill his Mother, but he drove into Banishment, and was instrumental in the death of a BROTHER, because he had given Offence to his *Mamma*'s favourite, and since that, he has driven from *St. James's,* the common Sink of Corruption, two other Brothers, because they are virtuous and have each a Wife, and also his best Friends, with many of the greatest Men in this Kingdom.[2] His Majesty too, by means of his Instruments of Destruction, has set one Part of the Empire on FIRE, and he no sooner heard of the BURNING of *Charles-Town* in AMERICA, and the Slaughter of more than THREE THOUSAND of his Subjects, but he set off in HIGH SPIRITS with two venal Lords in waiting, for *Foot's Theatre*, to whom he was observed to be Whispering and Laughing during the Performance, thereby shewing to a TAME DASTARDLY English Audience, the Satisfaction he felt on Receiving the horrid News of that CONFLAGRATION and MASSACRE.

---

2. In *George III* (London: Viking, 1998) Christopher Hibbert wrote a great deal about royal family dynamics and far less about the King's public policy. But in terms of George III's greatest concerns, that may have been the best approach, with George III worrying more about his household than affairs at Whitehall or Westminster, which he worried about more than he did general English affairs, but then he was also more concerned about England than Britain, and more about Britain than the larger empire.

From the Instances already mentioned of Roman Tyrants, the necessity of opposing and resisting such Monsters, must be apparent to every Man; and no wise Nation in the World, ever yet trusted to the sole Management, mere Mercy, and absolute Discretion of its Magistrates, when it could help doing it; and no Kings ever had absolute Power over any Nation, but they turned the same to its Ruin, and their own vile Gratification. As long as Men are SUFFERED to govern by their Passions, their Passions will always increase with their Power; and therefore, whenever the People cross the Passions of any Man who governs them, he will turn all the Power they put into his Hands against them, and will destroy them unless timely resisted and restrained. This is evident in a Thousand Instances, but in none more fatal than in that of *America*, where THREE MILLIONS of People are to be sacrificed to the private Lust aud cursed Ambition of ONE TYRANT.

A Nation has but two Sorts of usurpation to fear; one from their Neighbours, and another from their own Magistrates; and the *Americans* rightly and sensibly Judged, a domestic one was far the most dangerous of the two, proceeding insensibly by Degrees, till those Chains which had been secretly forging for them, were fast riveted; they therefore early and nobly resisted, and happily frustrated every Scheme that had been formed, and every Snare laid for their Destruction, and with a Firmness and bravery, that will immortalize their Names, preserved those Rights, which a Tyrannic King meant traiterously to have seized.

The present Sovereign not convinced by fatal Experience, the continual defeat of his Armies, and the Loss of more than One Half of his Empire, but he is still determined to persue his diabolical Plans of devastation and Massacre, to gratify his rapacious and unrelenting Fury; with this view TWENTY THOUSAND Russians are to be added to the present Number of English Mercenaries, that we may be the better enabled to Butcher with the greater cruelty the Virtuous, and as yet Free *Americans*, still exulting in the Luxury, of DYING, where we forbid them, longer to live FREEMEN, and with their last Breath, indignantly devoting us, the venal Sons of Britain, to a willing Thraldom and Perdition.

An unrestrained Power in ONE Man, or in a FEW, over ALL, is such an extravagant Deviation from Reason and Nature, that neither *Briareus* with his many Hands, nor the *Hydra*, with its numerous Heads, nor the *Centaurs* half Man and half Beast, were things more unshapen monstrous and frightful; nor would these Fictions appear more fabulous and Improbable, than such Power would be to a FREE PEOPLE, who never heard of it before.[3]

What could seem to common sense a wilder *Chimera*,[4] than that ONE Man, not created with Features and Endowments different from other Men, should have a lasting RIGHT from his Blood, his Pride, or his Madness, to domineer over ALL Men, and to rule, kill, starve, famish, banish, and imprison as many as he pleased, (which the present King of England, and all other Tyrants would do if not restrained and resisted.)

Only the Checks put upon Kings make Nations FREE, and the want of such Checks make them Slaves. Thus by a criminal Patience unworthy of Englishmen, and for want of a strenuous Opposition HERE, to the Measures of a foolish, weak, wanton, wicked, insolent Tyrant and his Ministers, thousands of our American Fellow Subjects have been butchered, and the Nation nearly enslaved.

3. Mythological creatures, all: Briareus, one of three Hekatonkheires, a son of Uranus and Gaia, so huge that he could throw immense stones, and did so on the side of Zeus in his battle against Kronos and the Titans; the many-headed Hydra, destroyed by Hercules in the second of his twelve labors, its one immortal head buried under a great rock; and the often savage centaurs, who were half men, half horse.

4. "First, dire Chimaera's conquest was enjoined:
   A mingled monster, of no mortal kind;
   Behind, a fiery dragon's tail was spread;
   A goat's rough body wore a lion's head;
   Her pitchy nostrils like flaky flames expire;
   Her gaping throat emits infernal fire."

Thus the Chimera, a terrible beast, but cleverly slain by Bellerophon from above, with an arrow that he fired from the back of the winged horse Pegasus. From Pope's *Iliad of Homer.* 2:168 (Book VI, lines 219–224).

The Americans have certainly been guilty of the horrid Crime of distinguishing between PROTECTION, and OPPRESSION, between FREEDOM and SLAVERY, and they have already convinced the World, how truly sensible they are of the DIFFERENCE, and how much they prefer the former to the latter; and to the utter Confusion, eternal Disgrace, and lasting Infamy of the King and Ministry; they have hitherto gloriously triumphed over Fraud and Violence, and all the Instruments of Hell and Despotism; like the true Descendants of Freemen and Britons, they are determined to check, and if possible destroy the Lawless Power of a Tyrant, who has broken his Coronation-Oath, and all the Bonds of human Society, and is at this Time, by the Aid of his Ministers and the infernal Spirits of Darkness, endeavouring to enslave, or extirpate from the Face of the *Earth* more than *THREE MILLIONS* of People; but they, fighting in the Cause of Truth and Freedom, Justice and their Country, and preferring *DEATH to SLAVERY*, will be crowned with Victory and never-fading Laurels, whilst the vengeance of Heaven, will persue and destroy the *Enemies* to universal Liberty, and the natural Rights of Mankind; and *America* shall rise like the *Phenix* out of her *Ashes*, and erect an *INDEPENDENT EMPIRE* of *HER OWN*, the Terror and Admiration of the World.

In this Manner did our Forefathers check the enormous Power of the Crown, and resist the Tyranny of their Kings, and left to their Children, (the present degenerate race of Englishmen) purchased with their BLOOD, the glorious Inheritance of LIBERTY and FREEDOM.

Thus did the *Romans* (and all Free States) restrain Power, and those who had it; and when any Power was grown quite ungovernable, they abolished it. Thus they expelled *Tarquin*, and the kingly Government, having first suffered, much by oppression and injustice; and they prospered as eminently without it. That Government too was extremely limited: the first *Roman* Kings were little more than Generals for Life: they had no *NEGATIVE* vote in the Senate (as our Kings have), and could neither make War nor Peace; and even in the Execution of Justice an Appeal lay from them to the *PEOPLE*. By confining the Power of the Crown within Proper Bounds, their Kings gained Power without Bounds in the

AFFECTIONS of the People. But the insolent *Tarquin* broke through all Bounds, and acted so openly against Law and the People of *Rome* that they had no Remedy left but to *EXPELL* him and his Race, which they did with glorious success.[5]

What does that Tyrant deserve who can deliberately order the Burning of Towns, and the Ruin of Thousands. Who can read the horrid Recital of the Destruction of Charles-Town, and Falmouth in America,[6] without feeling his Mind agitated by a Mixture of pity, horror, shame, indignation, and resentment? To burn a Town and ruin its Inhabitants in COLD BLOOD, surpasses every Idea of savage Barbarity and Brutality! If I, who am an Englishman (unconnected with *America*, except by the ties which ought to bind Fellow Subjects) not even known to an American, am thus agitated by the Contemplation of such an infernal Scene, what effects must it have produced in the Breasts of those who saw their Habitations Smoaking in RUINS! Must they not have been raised to a pitch of Fury; to a Madness not to be equaled in the Regions of Bedlam? And perhaps ere now, the same inhuman, cowardly Revenge of a despicable Tyrant and his Ministers has involved every Town on the Coast of America in one COMMON RUIN? The Americans will think,

5. There were several Tarquins in the morality tales that doubled as the early history of the Roman republic. This final Tarquin was in some sense the worst of these throwbacks to the Etruscan era. He was driven from the throne by the heroic Lucius Junius Brutus, legendary founder of the Roman republic in the 6th century BCE (see n. VII.9 supra). The report that, in protesting the Stamp Act during House of Burgesses debates in May 1765, Patrick Henry had alluded to Tarquin and Caesar both having their Brutus, with listeners to infer what that meant for their own time, made its way across the Atlantic to London's *Public Ledger*, 13 August 1765. For the controversies over what, exactly, Henry said, see Henry Mayer, *A Son of Thunder* (New York: Franklin Watts, 1986), pp. 81–98; and Eran Shalev, *Rome Reborn on Western Shores* (Charlottesville: University of Virginia Press, 2009) for the larger context.

6. Much of Charlestown, Massachusetts, burned as a result of the fighting at the Battle of Bunker Hill on June 17th; Falmouth (now Portland), in the Maine country of Massachusetts, had been shelled by a small British squadron on October 18th. At Falmouth the British justified their actions as retaliation for an earlier confrontation there between militiamen and naval personnel. The townsfolk had been given notice beforehand, which did nothing to assuage local opinion.

it was the Act of the English NATION,—but how unjust their Supposition! The English Nation recoil with horror from the view, which even to their imagination is dreadful! They execrate the Tyrant and his Ministers who commanded the Shocking Devastation, and easily foresee that unless he is soon restrained, and brought within the bounds of Law, in the DESTRUCTION of AMERICA must be involved THEIR OWN.

Printed and Published for the AUTHORS by T. W. SHAW, in Fleet-Street, opposite Anderton's Coffee-House, where Letters to the Publisher will be thankfully received.

THE

CRISIS

NUMBER LII   *To be continued Weekly,*

DURING THE PRESENT BLOODY CIVIL WAR IN AMERICA.

SATURDAY, January 13, 1776   *Price* Two-pence Half-penny.

SCOTCH REBELS,

AND

Traitors Triumphant;

OR, *LORD LOVAT*'s Son, who with his Father, in the Year 1745, would have dethroned GEORGE the SECOND of Glorious Memory; and extirpated the whole Race of BRUNSWICK, now the Firmest and best Friend of George the Third.

> *O! REBEL* where is thy *Blush.*
> *O! KING* where is thy *Shame.*

The following Bill which has been stuck up in every quarter of the Town, clearly proves } That { BUTE and MANSFIELD } Reign.

T O
All A C T I V E and S P I R I T E D
V O L U N T E E R S,

Who are sensible of GLORY, and desirous of serving the BEST of Kings, in support of the best of Constitutions, for THREE YEARS, or during the REBELLION; in that choice Body of *HIGHLANDERS* now Raising, to be commanded by

MAJOR GENERAL FRASER,

With the PARTICULAR ADVANTAGE of being distinguished by that becoming and Martial Garb, the HIGHLAND DRESS, which never failed to strike an Enemy with Terror, are desired to apply, &c. &c.[1]

N. B. Several Men fit for Serjeants and Corporals; also TAYLORS and HAIR-DRESSERS are much wanted.

˙ *In case this famous Regiment of Scotch Highlanders should be raised, and sent over the Atlantic, the Americans who are BRAVE and FREE, and justly despise these REBELS and TRAITORS, will soon find some other employ for them than, that of making Cloaths or Dressing Hair; or, they will presently put it out of their Power to do EITHER.*

---

1. Unlike his father, Simon Fraser, the eleventh Lord Lovat, the younger Simon Fraser escaped execution for his involvement with the Scottish uprising of 1745. Though the family lands and title were attainted, Fraser was granted a pardon, returned to public life, then raised and commanded a Highland regiment in the French and Indian War where he served dutifully at Louisbourg and Quebec. Promoted to major general before the American rebellion, he commanded the 71st Highlanders through much of the conflict. And yet, for some, there was always that cloud that hung over him as a once rebellious Scot, which of course *The Crisis* could turn to its advantage. Stuart Reid wrote the sketch of Fraser for the *Oxford DNB*, 20:869–70.

A PARODY on the above BILL.

T O

All A C T I V E   and   S P I R I T E D
S C O T C H   M E R C E N A R I E S,

Who are sensible of INFAMY, and desirous of serving the WORST of Kings, in DESTROYING the BEST of CONSTITUTIONS, for Three Years, or during the RESISTANCE: in that choice Body of HIGHLAND TRAITORS, now Raising and to be commanded by that known REBEL,

MAJOR GENERAL FRASER,
SON of the REBEL LORD LOVAT,

With the particular Advantage of being distinguished by that becoming and Martial Garb, the REBEL HIGHLAND DRESS, which never failed to strike an *Old Woman* with Terror.

Through the Influence, Artifice, and Cunning of the two great Criminals, and infamous Traitors BUTE and MANSFIELD, the above proscribed REBEL, has recovered by an Act of the last ruinous Parliament, and the Baseness of the King, all those Estates belonging to Simon Fraser, Lord Lovat, his Father, which were justly and for ever forfeited to the Crown of England, at the Time of the last unnatural SCOTCH Rebellion in the Year 1745, when he was taken in Arms against the late Good old King, and beheaded on Tower-Hill. His Son however, is now become a FRIEND to the present Royal BABY, because he is found to be a proper Instrument to cut the Throats of our American Brethren and Fellow Subjects; yet this same *General Fraser*, 30 Years ago commanded a Regiment of Scotch Rebels at the Battle of *Culloden* against the late gallant Duke of Cumberland.[2]—It must be confessed indeed, that this Miscreant Son of the old Traitor Lovat, inherits the principles at this Hour, which he did in SEVENTEEN HUNDRED and FORTY FIVE: He was *then* OPENLY in Arms against the

---

2. George III's uncle, Prince William Augustus, the Duke of Cumberland, who had died in 1765, was still admired as the hero of Culloden, victor over the uprising of '45. See the entry for Cumberland in the *Oxford DNB*, 59:105–13, by W. A. Speck.

present Royal Family, and the British Constitution in Church and State, with a design to seat upon the Throne of England the Pretender's Son, and to introduce the Roman Catholic Religion. He is *now* SECRETLY carrying on the same design in conjunction with BUTE and MANSFIELD, under a pretence of Loyalty to the present Royal Cypher (who is weak and wicked enough to believe any thing) and a veneration for the Constitution he aimes to destroy.

S C O T C H   P O L I C Y.

Old Lovat, Father to the Rebel just mentioned, about the Year 1737, became greatly suspected of some treasonable Designs; and an Information was given to one of the Secretaries of State, that his Lordship, under pretence of providing Arms for his independent Company, had bought up a considerable Number of Fire Arms, Broad Swords, and Targets.

This was represented to a certain great Man at Court, who thereupon wrote to Lord Lovat upon that Head, desiring from him an Account of the Truth of those Matters, and that he would satisfy the Government with respect to the Charge; and the more effectually to quiet the apprehension that some People had entertained of his Conduct, and as it was generally reported that his Lordship proposed to send his sons to France for their Education, he advised his Lordship to send them up to London; and to encourage him thereto, he offered to have a particular Regard in their Education, and undertook to be at the Expence thereof out of his own Pocket: Such was this Nobleman's generous Care and Concern to preserve the Rebel Fraser Family from Destruction: But the old Traitor was deaf to his Counsels and Admonition, and contented himself with sending him long Letters in his own Vindication, stuffed with shuffling Evasions and flattering Speeches, and Boasting of the great Services he had done in the Year 1715,* which he pretended ought to free him from any false imputation of disloyalty.

---

*Before the Rebellion in 1715, there was a sentence of the Court of Justiciary against him for a Rape, and he was also found guilty of High Treason, in Levying War in Scotland, against Lord Salton, and Mungo Murray, a younger Son of the Marquis of Athol. On which Account he was forced to fly his Country, and with true Scotch Policy in order to obtain his Pardon (which he did) he opposed the Rebels in 1715.

SCOTCH GRATITUDE.

Lord Lovat was under many and great Obligations to the Government for the fortunate Turn in his Affairs after the Year 1715. His Majesty George the First, frequently heaped Favours upon him; made him Lord Lieutenant of the County, and Governor of Inverness, gave him a Pension, and the command of a Highland Independent Company, there being several of those Companies raised after the Rebellion to preserve the Peace of the Highlands.

The King knew this old Traitor's Character, and that he appeared in Arms against the Rebels purely to serve himself; and therefore his Majesty resolved, if possible, by loading him with Favours, to let him see that his chief Interest lay in serving the Government faithfully. *But it is not all the ties of Honour or Gratitude that can bind a Scotsman.* It was not long before his Lordship plainly shewed, and by his Conversation discovered, that he only wanted an Opportunity to break out into Rebellion.

SCOTCH TREACHERY.

This treacherous Scotsman made an offer to a Person at Court, that if TWENTY FIVE THOUSAND POUNDS was put into his Hands, to be distributed among the Chiefs of the Clans, he would engage one Part of Scotland should be quiet, and the Highlanders obliged to join the King's Forces.

His Proposal, however, (as it deserved) was rejected with Disdain, and his Designs suspected, so that he engaged with the greater Spirit in support of the Pretender, whose Cause he had, like a TRUE Scotsman, about 40 Years before notoriously BETRAYED, and strenuously OPPOSED in the Year [17]15.

The Lord President, who, after the breaking out of the Rebellion in [17]45, was exceeding active in the Service of Government, out of a sincere Concern for Lord Lovat, the common Betrayer of all Parties, wrote him a Letter, expressing his unfeigned Friendship for his Lordship; but at the same Time intimated, that he was not unacquainted with his secret and disloyal Practices, entreating him to relinquish an enterprize, the certain and unavoidable Consequence of which would be Ruin and Destruction to himself and Family.

It was in vain to think of reclaiming his Lordship; (*indeed a Scotsman with whom the Principles of Rebellion, Treachery, Baseness, Ingratitude, and Meanness are INNATE, never can be reclaimed*) for he still continued more daring and open in his Proceedings; which determined the Earl of Loudon, who was then at Inverness, to put a stop thereto. He marched with some Hundreds of his Men to Castledowny, (his Lordship's Seat) and sent Lord Lovat a Message, in the King's Name, to attend him to Inverness, and to deliver up what Arms he had in his Possession. The old Rebel not finding himself in a Condition to resist, submitted to go along with Lord Loudon, and remain at Inverness as a Security for his peaceable Behaviour; and accordingly stayed there for some Days; but upon some sham Pretence or other delayed to perform his Promise, as to delivering up the Arms; and notwithstanding he was strictly watched, and Centinels placed at his Lodgings, yet he found Means to break through the back Part of the House in the Night Time, and made his escape. After which, he was the first and greatest Instrument in fomenting and carrying on the Rebellion, by Raising and Arming the Highlanders, and alarming them with Fears of being extirpated and destroyed by the King's Troops, with Fire and Sword, and persuading them there were no other Means left for their Preservation, but having recourse to Arms to defend their Lives, Properties, and Families, from the Rapine and Violence of their Enemies.

In order to enforce this Matter he published a Manifesto, or Declaration, which he caused to be publickly read in the Kirks on a Sunday.

S C O T C H   L O Y A L T Y.

His Son the present Major General Fraser, in whom there is undoubtedly as much FAITH to be put as in his Rebel FATHER, and who is NOW so TRUE and LOYAL to GEORGE the THIRD, commanded a Regiment at the famous Battle of Culloden-House, and was defeated.

R O Y A L   G R A T I T U D E.

Our present wise, just, virtuous, and magnanimous Sovereign, has taken into his Favour, pensioned, and placed all the Enemies to public Liberty, and every base, beggarly, Rebel Scotsman, who has been in Arms against his Family, and the Religion of this Country. And he has dismissed from his Counsels, and treated with Contempt, every Englishman who is a known Friend to the Laws and Constitution of the British Empire; and particularly those brave and virtuous Men, who were the chief Instruments in RAISING his Family to the Imperial Diadem of these Realms. This GRATEFUL Prince, O! my injured Countrymen, is called by *Scotsmen* the BEST OF KINGS.

Printed and Published for the AUTHORS by T. W. SHAW, in Fleet-Street, opposite Anderton's Coffee-House, where Letters to the Publisher will be thankfully received.

THE

CRISIS

NUMBER LIII   *To be continued Weekly,*

DURING THE PRESENT BLOODY CIVIL WAR IN AMERICA.

SATURDAY, JANUARY 20, 1776   *Price* Two-pence Half-penny.

—————————————We are in *Blood*
Stept in so far, that should we wade no more,
Returning were as tedious as *going on*.

Shakesp. Macbeth.[1]

To LORD MANSFIELD.

My Lord,

YOUR Lordship's late Speech in the House of Lords upon the *Restraining Bill*, has opened a large Field of Contemplation to the Moralist, the Politician, and Divine: I might say, indeed, to the whole *Christian World*, who view your Lordship's Principles as the *English* do your Person, with the utmost Horror and Detestation. Of

---

1. Unnerved by having just seen Banquo's ghost, King Macbeth has an inkling of his dark fate; even so, he knows that it is too late to turn back. From Act III, Scene 4 of Shakespeare's *Mabeth*.

your notable Harangue the Motto at the Head of my Paper is a concise, but just Epitome. I admire your Lordship's Magnanimity. You despise the narrow Principles of sound Philosophers, honest Politicians, and orthodox Divines. The groveling Maxim, "*Nihil utile quod non honestum.*" (permit me to translate it by our vulgar Proverb, "*Honesty* is the best *Policy*,") a Maxim to which the greatest Nations have owed their Power and Prosperity, is too trite and old to find a Patron in your Lordship. Though it had long prevailed in the *heathen*, though it hath been since adopted in the *Christian* World: nay, though your favourite *Tully*[2] labours in it's Praises, yet has it never biased your Lordship's *political*, or *judicial* Conduct. Great Souls are not to be confined by Tenets to which the Generality of Mankind subscribe; No,—They make, and hold *their own*. With such a singular and peculiar Spirit your Lordship plans, co*unsels*, *acts and speaks*. In the same House, where your Lordship, by your *judicial Proxies* (for you feared the Eye of the equitable *Camden*) effected the Ruin of an injured *Individual*,* you have lately owned yourself an *Accomplice* in the Destruction of an *injured Nation*. In the case of *Mr. Thickness* you absconded, you neither dared to show your Teeth, nor espouse your own pitiful Resentments; the Dread of engaging in a *legal* Question with a *Camden* over-awed you; you worked then *underhandedly*, by *Proxies*: you had your *Chancellor*, your *Denbigh*, and your *Scotch Lords*, upon that Occasion, for your *Agents*. But in the Case of *America*, you have ventured to appear in *Person*. Like a Great Soul, you can lend your Hand openly to *Murder*, though you scorn to be detected in a *Larceny*. I must

*Mr. *Thickness*, See Crisis No. 7, 10, 30.

---

2. Popular as Cato was as the symbol of the Roman as republican (see n. XXVII.2 supra), Cato could not match "Tully"—the anglicized nickname for Marcus Tullius Cicero—in terms of posthumous fame. Like Cato, Cicero was venerated in Plutarch's widely read *Lives*. Unlike Cato, many of Cicero's orations continued to be reprinted in Latin and translated into English, so much so that countless public men in the British Atlantic world learned their Latin and had their basic grounding in the classics through Cicero; indeed, some of what they knew of Cato came from Cicero. Even so, Cicero's murder by Marc Antony's supporters followed many political twists and turns, making his martyrdom in the republican cause less clear-cut than Cato's choice to take his own life rather than live under Caesar.

confess that your Lordship, when you delivered your Sentiments upon the *Restraining Bill*, had screwed yourself up to such a surprising pitch of political Effrontery, that you pronounced the Speech of a *Parricide* with all the mimic boldness of another *Cataline*. Your Lordship's known Principles will preclude you from the *Esteem*, but your late desperate Avowal of such Principles has drawn upon you the *Wonder* of Mankind. The *Tories* applaud your *persecuting* Spirit; the *Whigs* are amazed at your *Machiavelian* Doctrines in a free Country, whose *Liberties* are fixed (as they conceive) on the solid Basis of a just and happy *Revolution*. On the other hand, *Administration* congratulate each other, that the timid, the reserved, the circumspect Lord *Mansfield*, should lay himself so open, even in the Face of Parliament, as to declare in the most explicit Terms, his full Assent and Concurrence with them in every despotic and destructive step, which they have yet taken against *America*, that he should not only vindicate, but *father*, such unconstitutional Devices against *Revolutional Resistance* as must, sooner or later, draw down the just Vengeance of this Nation upon the Heads of the whole *Confederacy*. These *Tyranic Traitors* rejoice to see a Man of your Lordship's great and fatal Abilities added to their guilty Number; for on the Number and Importance of their foul Adherents they place their Safety and Defence. These your *Accomplices*, my Lord, hope to derive Strength, Support, Protection and Security, from your Lordship's late unlimited Professions in open Senate. If such were your Lordship's Opinions, the World can have no doubt but they must have influenced all your *Counsels* in relation to *America*. Your Lordship's Word's (I do not mean the *Tenor*, but the *Purport* of them) I shall take Leave to repeat by Sentences, because they are too remarkable to pass without a separate Comment. In doing this, your Lordship will pardon me, if I consider one of the greatest Men in Europe, for a Moment, as an obsequious *Proxy*, *Tool*, and *Echo*, to one of the worst; I mean Lord *Bute*; not presuming, however, to insinuate that your Lordship is, in any respect *inferior* to the *Thane*.

Your Lordship was pleased to open (as it was supposed) your whole Heart upon this Occasion in the House of Lords: If you did, Your *Counsels* (ruinous to Great Britain) must have corresponded with your Declarations; and then the whole Empire will owe its Declension, and perhaps its Fall, in an eminent Degree, to the superior Abilities of Lord *Mansfield*. If you did not, your Lordship was guilty of the grossest *Falshood* and *Deceit* in that august Assembly. On the other hand, if your *Counsels* to your *Sovereign* varied from your real Sentiments promulgated in Parliament, you must have been guilty of *Perjury* in the *Cabinet*. But the whole Nation are ready to acquit your Lordship of both these dishonourable Charges. They believe (and with the greatest Reason) that your *Counsels* have ever been agreeable to your late Declarations, and your late Declarations to your *Principles*. I shall therefore select such Parts only of your Lordship's Speech in *public* as discover the evil Tendency of your Advice in *private*. Thus I freely exculpate your Lordship of *Deceit*, tho' I must, in justice to my Country, impeach you of *High Treason*. Yes, my Lord; *Counsels* built upon such unconstitutional, unjust, and pernicious Principles, as you have just disclosed, must mark your Lordship as an Enemy to this Country. If your Lordship can hear them without a Blush, and a strong disposition to recant, I shall be induced to think that Learning and uncommon Abilities are Curses to Mankind.

I touch upon your Leadership's *Exordium*,[3] merely because one Expression in it, (I mean that of *Rebel Army* opposed to *royal Army*) leads me to take notice of one of the most pernicious Errors which could have been implanted in the infant Breast of an *English Sovereign*; yet by your Colleague *Bute*, and yourself, my Lord, it was not only implanted, but impressed. I will remind your Lordship of it as I proceed.—That a *Royal Army* should be so employed against valuable, brave, and loyal Subjects, driven (for *ministerial purposes*) to the last Despair, is a Disgrace to England, to the Sovereign, to English Councils, to an English Parliament, and to human Nature. This *Army* is, in Truth, a *ministerial Army*; it is Lord *Bute*'s, and Lord *Mansfield*'s Army. By calling it *royal*, your Lordship throws the blackest Imputations on your *Sovereign*. By this Appellation you insinuate, that in all the outrageous *Murders* and *Desolations*

---

3. That is, in the introductory part of the speech, where Mansfield was endeavoring to impress and win over his listeners—following the rules of effective rhetoric, within the classical tradition.

it had (before its providential defeat) committed, its savage Operations were directed by the Will and Pleasure, nay the strict Command of the *most pious* Prince in Christendom. Thus your Lordship most jesuitically turns the public Eye from the *ministerial Accessaries*, to the *royal Principal*. That such a *Principal* exists *America* has felt. That the *Heart* of this unhappy Homicide is no less guilty than those of his ensnaring *Accessaries*, every *Whig* in England believes. I will tell your Leadership upon what grounds they have fixed a Belief so unfavourable to every Quality which should adorn and endear a *Father of his people*. They have founded it, my Lord, upon that Basis which your Lordship and your Colleague *Bute* most industriously laid almost in the Cradle of your *Sovereign*. Lord *Bute*, like a *true Scot* would have formed his mind (if possible) to his own purposes in the very Womb. He took, however, the earliest Opportunities of bending the *royal Twigg* himself. The first Rudiments being laid, your Lordship was, in due Time, admitted to *assist*. What was, for the worst of reasons, practiced upon that *Solomon, James the First*, your Lordships, for the like reasons, successfully perpetrated upon *pious Geogre the Third*. The principle, of all others, infixed the deepest, was traitorous and destructive to the last Degree. This it was: "That *Kings* are made, not by the *People*, or for their *sole Benefit*, but that they derive their Right and Title from *above*, as *God's Vicegerents upon Earth*." The Consequence, my Lord, is plain; *oppressed America* has felt it: Against such *Divinities-regent* all *Resistance* whatsoever must be *unlawful*, and every oppressed Subject so *resisting* must be a *Rebel*. Thus I account for the propriety of your Lordship's Term, *Rebel Army*, and for your applying it (as every *Court-Sychophant* does) to the *Americans*, who have been driven into Arms by such impolitic and pernicious *Councels* as your Lordship's.—A brave and loyal People whose Ancestors left this Country because they justly abhorred, and therefore sensibly renounced, *passive Obedience* to one of the weakest and worst *Tyrants* (except *one*) that ever sat upon the Throne of *England*. If your Lordship and your *Colleague* have (and we know you have) infused the same false and detested Principles into another Prince, as infected *James*, and broke out to the Ruin of *Charles* the *First*, he must necessarily look upon every Species of *Resistance* as *Rebellion*. As such he must have been taught (like *Charles*) to

call and treat it. Like *Charles* he must at length succeed. Your Lordships
will probably be Joint-Figurers in the *closing Scene*. The Day will come
when your Lordships must be answerable for every ruinous Consequence
that may ensue from the Superiority of this *Rebel Army*, as you and your
abettors, affect to call them: an *army* provoked by yourselves to stand
forth in defence of their Liberties, Properties, and Lives, which have
been attacked by every Species of Cruelty which Tyranny could invent,
or Inhumanity inflict.—I now pursue your Lordship's Sentiments again;
which you declared to have been in disfavour of the *Americans*, ever since
the Commencement of that unhappy Dispute—From this Declaration I
may fairly collect that your Lordship's *Advice in Council* has gone hand
in hand with these *liberal Sentiments* of your's from the very first. If
so, your Lordship lent your patriotic Aid betimes to the bringing on
of national Misfortunes.—Your Lordship, in the next place, upon no
better Evidence than that of *Montcalm's Letters*, declared your full persuasion that *America* had *concerted* a Scheme of *Independence* ever since
the Peace of Paris.[4]—If your Lordship, as a *Statesman*, dived no deeper
for Evidence than *Montcalm's Letters*, you are neither a *Burleigh*, nor a
Walsingham.[5] Could your Lordship *advise* that a whole Nation should
be proscribed, his Majesty's Protection withdrawn, and the Standard of
Tyranny erected against her, upon no better grounds than these? For
Argument's sake only, I will suppose she really had *concerted*, nay began

---

4. The Marquis de Montcalm had purportedly written on 1 October 1758 from Montreal to an official back in Paris that "All these informations, which I every day receive,
confirm me in my opinion that England will one day lose her colonies on the continent
of America." This letter was not actually published in London until 1777 by John Almon, with others, as *Lettres De Monsieur Le Marquis De Montcalm Gouverneur-General
en Canada*. But the Earl of Mansfield referred to them during debates in the House of
Lords on 20 December 1775 on what became the Prohibitory Act (see the *Public Ledger*
and *St. James Chronicle*, 21 December 1775; and Simmons and Thomas, eds., *Proceedings
and Debates*, 6:380–81). They were written by Pierre-Joseph-Antoine Roubaud, who for
a time had worked in the office of the secretary of state for American affairs. He eventually admitted that they were forgeries. A most curious character, there is a brief sketch
of him in the online *Dictionary of Canadian Biography*.

5. Sir William Cecil, Lord Burghley, and Sir Francis Walsingham, were masters of real-
politik and astute advisers to Elizabeth I, not easily duped by anyone.

to *execute* this Scheme of *Independence*; was *Slavery* on the one hand, or *Annihilation* on the other, to be her Doom? Yet such was the Tendency of the rash and fatal *Measures* taken against her; which *Measures* your Lordship does not hesitate to *approve.* As your Lordship has confessed that you *approve* them, you most certainly *advised* them. How successful these have proved, your Lordship and the whole Kingdom by this Time know, upon better Evidence than the *Letters* of *Montcalm*, or than those, which have been first garbled, and then published by ministerial Orders in the *London Gazette*; that infamous Vehicle of weekly *Lies*, fabricated and uttered under the *Royal Sanction* to deceive the *Public*.

In one instance only your Lordship seemed to differ with your *Party,* let me rather say, your *Faction*; as to the Necessity and Propriety of making the *Declaratory Act*, which (as your Lordship said) so fully *asserts* the Supremacy of our Parliament over *America in all Cases whatsoever.*—I will admit, that *Declaratory Acts*, made in an *independent, honest, unsmuggled Parliament*, are clear and certain Evidences of Original and Constitutional Existence of such Rights as they would still support; But, in *passive, fawning, corrupt*, and *venal Parliments, Declaratory Acts* have often introduced *State-Persecutions, new Prerogatives, National Oppression, and Tyrranic Usurpation*. Your Lordship must allow this Observation to be just, unless you discredit ancient Records, Faithful History, and the Journals of both Houses of Parliament.[6]

Your Lordship was aware of this Truth, you knew that *such an Act* must call up dissentions, debates, and murmurs, within doors and without; and therefore *wisely* wished your *Faction* had proceeded boldly, without the Aid of any Act at all, as if those Rights, and that universal Supremacy of Parliament, had been clear and indubitable, which that DECLARATORY ACT pretended to assume. This, my Lord,

---

6. The 1766 Declaratory Act is too often written about sloppily, as a clear assertion of parliamentary supremacy (it was not) and an application to the American colonies of what had already been in place for Ireland since 1720 (again, it was not that simple). For the former, see my "When Words Fail," pp. 361–64; for the latter, my *Neither Kingdom Nor Nation*, pp. 86–87 and 87 n. 26.

I own, is the true Spirit of ARISTOCRATICAL TYRRANY, perfectly consistent with your Lordship's Principles and Counsels, and would have
been more consistent with those MINISTERIAL MEASURES which your
Lordship so heartily approves.

[To be concluded in our next.]

Printed and Published for the AUTHORS by T. W. SHAW, in Fleet-Street,
opposite Anderton's Coffee-House, where Letters to the Publisher will be
thankfully received.

THE

CRISIS

NUMBER LIV   *To be continued Weekly,*

DURING THE PRESENT BLOODY CIVIL WAR IN AMERICA.

SATURDAY, January 27, 1776   *Price* Two-pence Half-penny.

To L O R D   M A N S F I E L D.

[Continued from our last.]

I Come now, my Lord, to that *Emphatic Question,* which your Lordship put to the House with all the phlegmatic Composure of a *Machiavel,* whose Prince had been plunged, like yours, into the worst of Difficulties by the worst of *Counsels.* Your Lordship exclaimed, *"Where* are we now, my Lords, and what are we to do? We are engaged in a *War,* which we must pursue, or *run away from*: We cannot do the latter: If we do not get the better of *America, America* will get the better of us."—Let me intreat your Lordship here to cast your Eye, for a moment, upon the Motto (in Number Fifty Three, the beginning of this Address to you) you will there admire the like kind of reasoning put into the Mouth of one of your own Countrymen, by a Poet who knew every secret Spring and movement of the human Heart. How strikingly does your Lordship's *Question* confirm to us the propriety of *Shakespear*'s Language in the Character of an ambitious and inhuman *Tyrant?* How do the political *Mansfield,* and the murderous *Macbeth* agree in Sentiment? When I

485

touch upon your Lordship's political Abilities, (your Fort in your own conceit) with which you so successfully fascinated the late Duke of Newcastle, long before he made you *Sollicitor General*: when I reflect on these, my Lord, and your pretence to the deepest Knowledge in every branch of *Civil Law*, but, in particular, in those of *Nature* and *Nations*: Permit me to inquire, whether any approved Writer upon the Law of *Nations* concurs with your Lordship in asserting (for in effect you do assert) that an *unjust War*, once entered into, ought, at all events, to be prosecuted by the *Aggressor* for fear he should be obliged, at last, either to *submit*, or to *run away?* Will your Lordship deign to consult *Grotius, Puffendorff, Voet, Bynkersboek,*[1] all Writers of the first Class? Nay, search your favourite *Suarez*, the most *jesuitical* of all Writers; I think I may venture to affirm, that even *Suarez*[2] hesitates at sowing such inhuman Doctrines, as your Lordship, without a Blush, avowed. Even your own *Machiavel* apologizes for suggesting such bloody Instructions as must of Necessity be pursued in a desperate and uncommon Crisis, when a whole Empire is at Stake.[2] Nay, he does more, he confesses most ingenuously, that they are not agreeable to the Principles of Morality, Religion, or Humanity. Yet your Lordship gives the Spur to a *desperate and bloody Administration*, without Apology, Hesitation, or Remorse. The best Writers upon these Subjects agree that there is a wide distinction between a *foreign* and a *domestic* War: They mark the Conduct which the *Sovereign Power* ought, in Justice and Humanity, to hold in each. They all repeatedly declare that an *unjust War* is not to be pursued on any Consideration or Pretence. Those who obstinately *persevere* in such a War, they number among *Tyrants* and the *Enemies of Mankind*. In this detested Class the whole *Christian World* beholds the *pious Sovereign* and *Great Council* of the British Nation. The latter has by solemn *Acts* adopted and sanctified all the political Sins of a

1. Johannes Voet (1647–1713) and Cornelius Bijnkershoek (1673–1743) were Dutch jurists whose works were written and printed in Latin, sold in London, or ordered through any number of booksellers.

2. Francisco Suárez (1548–1617), Spanish theologian and philosopher, a Jesuit and Thomist who, as a jurist, helped lay the foundation of modern international law. His works had not been translated into English, which was not a problem for Mansfield, who could read them in their original Latin.

wicked *Administration*; the former has strictly executed all their *savage Edicts* without Reluctance. They have concurred with ardour in laying a Plan of future *Despotism* among the Subjects in *America*. They have answered the *Supplications* of those Subjects by laying their Country waste, and have tenderly redressed their *Grievances* by the *Sword*. These are the *Measures* which your Lordship so much *approves*. *Measures*, which every able Writer upon *War* and *Peace* not only dis-advises, but abjures. In the Case of an *alien Enemy* they censure them as cruel and inhuman, unless the War is *just*; in the Case of a *Subject* they hold them *impious*. But your Lordship and your Adherents have, by the Wisdom of your *Councils*, brought a Period of unsurmountable Calamity upon this Nation. You have forced the assassinated *Americans* into a *defensive* War, which has at last in some Degree broke out (in preservation of themselves) into an *offensive* one. In this State of the Case your Lordship asks your Brother Peers, "What is an *honest* Man to do? Are we to sit still with our Hands before us, because they tell us this is an *unjust War*, till *America* has fitted out an *Expedition* against this Country?"—The ruinous Effects of your own sage *Counsels* have at length, I find, given your Lordship a palpitation at the *Heart*. After reminding your Lordship that neither you, nor your Associates, stand in the Predicament of *honest* Men, I shall refer your Lordship once more to your Closet; examine there what the best (not the *jesuitical*) Writers say upon the Subject of an *unjust War*, and then examine your own *Heart*: Remember that you are a *Man*.— Throw off the *Privy Counsellor* and all his views, attachments, and prejudices for a while, and assume the *Christian*. You will then be able to solve your own alarming Question, with satisfaction to yourself, and justice to your Country. Let me only add, that such a *formidable* Nation as our *hectoring Administration* have at last, found in *America*, should not, from a State of peaceable and profitable *Subjection*, have been roused by *desertion*, *insult*, *oppression*, and causeless *Desolation*, into a State of unavoidable *Resistance* and final *Enmity*. These, my Lord, are the natural Fruits of *steady Perseverance* in those despotic and cruel *measures* which your Lordship honours with your warmest *approbation*.—Fired by those *Principles* which have secured your attachment and Affections to the worst and weakest *Ministry* that ever practised upon the Patience of this Nation, your Lordship closed your *patriotic* Speech like an hopeless Partizan of a disappointed *Faction*. You are convinced in your own Mind that *America* is lost for ever, and therefore you declared, that *"in the present situation of Things*, you considered the *Restraining Bill*, which the House was then about to pass, not only as a *just*, but as a *necessary Bill."*—By the *present situation of Things*, your Lordship means the present situation of a desponding *Administration*, who, with your Lordship's Advice and Assistance, have planned this hopeful *Bill* in the last Agonies of political Despair. By an impotent attempt to *subdue* those Subjects, whom they ought, in justice, to have *redressed,* they have most imprudently disunited two thirds of the British Empire (perhaps for ever) from Great Britain. Their *military Expedition* has been defeated, partly by the Hand of God, and partly by the Powers of *America*. No *Reinforcements* can be raised. *America* has gained Strength and Spirit. She is become (contrary to all Expectation) too formidable an Enemy to be either extirpated, or opposed. Armies which cannot be raised, cannot be sent. An immense one is now become necessary; a considerable one (in the prime of Life too) has already been destroyed. They so far from being strong enough to bear down all before them (as our Politicians thought) were not able to procure Subsistence for themselves in one of the finest and most plentiful Countries in the World. All further attempts on Land are vain. The *Government*, (however willing) dare not, for many solid Reasons, pour in a Deluge of *Russian Troops* upon their Subjects in *America*, yet they still keep up the Shadow of a Land-War upon that Continent, where our *doughty Generals*, with an handful of Men, remain (for ought we know yet to the contrary) pent up in *Boston* merely for the sake of *military Form*. In this *Situation of Things*, my Lord, the hellish Spirit of *Revenge* is let loose against *America* upon the *Ocean*, having hitherto proved ineffectual upon *Land*. The last efforts of *ministerial* Despair must be gratified; and this Consideration makes the *Restraining Bill* (the Offspring of your Lordship's inventive Brain) a *just* and *necessary* Bill. For this purpose the Navy of Great Britain are to dwindle into *Privateers*: They are to plunder their Fellow-Subjects in the Atlantic Ocean like Pirates, by *Act* of Parliament. They are to stop the Commerce of *America*, and by so doing to deprive all the innocent Colonies in the West-Indies of the only means of Subsistence which they have for Millions of Slaves, without whom the *Sugar-Manufactories* are no more. The Sugar-Works must drop, the Cattle, at certain Times, perish, and the very Planters starve without such Supplies as the Continent of *America* alone can yield in proportion sufficient for their Wants. Thus your Lordship's *just* and *necessary Restraining Bill* is calculated to bring effectual Ruin on all the British Colonies at once. Has your Lordship considered cooly what difference this may make, not only to the *Revenue*, but to the commercial Interest of Great Britain? Does your Lordship dream of subduing *America* by *Sea*, or even of checking her Commerce to any great Degree? Alas! my Lord, you and your *Confederates* are deceived. Neither your *Thane* nor you, may live to see it, (unless *Justice* should be very slow indeed) but *America* will shortly make no disgraceful stand against her Enemies even *upon Sea*. She has all the means of becoming powerful upon that Element within herself, and *OPPRESSION* will make her active. In the interim, she will be able (she is so at present) to face many, and to out sail most of your Sloops and Frigates armed for her Destruction. To prevent her Commerce will be as much impossible, as to prevent her future Greatness. The very attempt will create us *foreign* Enemies. Your Lordship will see what a *Trade* she will soon open, and *with whom*: For, by this Time, in all probability she has expelled the miserable Reliques of our vanquished Troops. She will be sufficiently prepared against future Invasions, and betake herself to *Agriculture* (the Basis of all Commerce) in a Soil capable of producing all the Necessaries, and even the Luxuries of Life. She will now be indefatigable in drawing from the Produce and Bowels of her fruitful Country, whatever can be necessary for her Felicity in Peace, her Defence in War, a successfull extension of her Commercial Views, and the final Aggrandizement of her *Empire*; a great and *Independent Empire*, to which the Children of her present *Tyrants* will see her rise, by the very means which their Fathers have concerted for her Depression. Nay, those *guilty* Fathers may live to see her rising *Empire* augmented by a numerous *Succession* from this Kingdom; not (by *Hundreds* but by *Thousands*). These, and these only, can be the Fruits of your Lordship's *Counsels*, and that *just* and *necessary Bill*, which will lift up *America* among the Nations, and hasten the Declension of *Great Britain*.

When an universal Spirit of *Emigration* has prevailed, and it will too soon, will Agriculture or Commerce flourish long among us? Can we continue Masters of the Sea without a Navy? Can the Navy be built without Materials? Can those Materials be furnished without *America?* What foreign States (jealous and envious as they all are of British Power) will supply us? Has his *Majesty* any Forests of Oak in his *Electorate* which he can sell to the Commissioners of his Dock Yards in Lots, as he did his Forest of *Whittlebury?* Will not the Exports and Imports of all our American Colonies in general (including the great Northern Continent) be missed at the Custom-House? Will the crafty *Minister*, when this Kingdom is upon the point of depopulation, still continue to deceive us by *fallacious Entries?* Will these be any Evidence for our subsisting Wealth? Are our late unwarrantable Acquisitions, or even our established Settlements, in the *East Indies* permanent Funds of Treasure to this Country? Or, if they were, (though the Man must be Moon-struck who affirms it) can the Gold of *Ophir* be transported hither without Ships? Can a venal Parliament any longer be *corrupted*; a wicked and traitorous Gang of *Counsellors* and *Ministers* protected; despotic Government supported; a prodigal *Sovereign*, and his rapacious *Friends*, kept in necessary *Contact* without *Gold?* Regardless as your Lordship must be of your Country (*People*, my Lord, were made for *Kings*) I grieve to think how much your ministerial *Faction*, your supple Parliament, your god-like *Thane*, and your wise and *pious Sovereign*, must be distressed by the certain Effects of your *just* and *necessary RESTRAINING BILL*.

C   A   S   C   A.

P. S. *Quere.* Whether the AMERICANS will not make *Reprisals* on our EAST INDIA *Ships?*

Printed and Published for the AUTHORS by T. W. SHAW, in Fleet-Street, opposite Anderton's Coffee-House, where Letters to the Publisher will be thankfully received.

THE

CRISIS

NUMBER LV   *To be continued Weekly,*

DURING THE PRESENT BLOODY CIVIL WAR IN AMERICA.

SATURDAY, FEBRUARY 3, 1776   *Price* Two-pence Half-penny.

A candid Appeal to every true Lover of GOD,
his Country, and Himself;

FRIENDS and COUNTRYMEN;

IN Matters of the utmost Importance, we are bound to use the greatest
Caution. No good Man who has the Welfare of Mankind at Heart,
will hastily involve his Fellow Creatures in Calamities and Troubles,
Civil Wars and Commotions, for such trifling Injuries, or wrong Conduct
of our Rulers, as may sometimes be incident to Persons of the fairest and
most upright Intentions. But when the common Welfare of all is wilfully
neglected, the most sacred Rights of the People openly invaded, and their
repeated humble Petitions for the redress of Grievances, not only thought
undeserving of Consideration, but themselves made a Topic of Jest and
Mockery by the Court, thereby adding Insults to their Injuries, every
good Man will steadily unite in the common Cause, and use his utmost
Endeavours to wrest the Power of Government out of Hands, that have
exercised it weakly and wickedly. It were much to be wished, that the Evils
of a Nation might be cured without Violence: But when it is evident that

public Liberty and safety is not even tolerably secured, and that Mischiefs, and those too of a more lasting Kind, daily arise from the Continuance of the present Men in Power, than are to be feared from the vigorous Efforts for an Alteration of them, it is our Duty, as it is lawful and honourable, to oppose and defeat their System of Government, which apparently tends to the utter Subversion of the Rights and Liberties of a free People. By the Law of Nature, every Man has a Right to defend himself against the Abuse of Power, and by the singular Constitution of this Kingdom, when Kings and Ministers break through the Bounds prescribed by the Laws, the Peoples Right of Resistance, is unquestionable. For as the End of all civil Government is the safety and Happiness of the whole Body; any Power not naturally conducive to this End is certainly unjust: And what our worthy Ancestors (perhaps rashly) granted, we may contract or abolish, whenever we find it necessary for our Preservation so to do. If they had a Right to constitute, we have a Power to abrogate.

The Prince and People take, in Effect, a sort of Engagement one with another, the Prince to govern well, and the People, so long as the Contract is religiously adhered to on his Part, to honour and obey him. If he regards his own Interest in preference to that of his People, he necessarily Forfeits every Claim to their Affection and Esteem.

Let the Calm, the Dispassionate, the rational Man, survey with his own Eyes the present Situation of our Affairs, and regulate his Conduct upon Principles of Reason.

In Times of National Decay—when Trade is rapidly Declining—when the Poor are groaning under the Oppressions of the Rich—when the ancient Rights and Liberties of the People are daringly attacked, and openly violated—when that Land which used to be esteemed a Paradise, is made a Stage of Cruelty and Injustice—when Merit is wholly neglected, and those only advanced at this Time, who are willing to become Instruments in the horrid Work of Despotism—when public Duties engage not the least Share of Attention, but senseless Ostentation, Profuseness and Dissipation are the sole Objects of Delight amongst the great, whose pernicious Examples tend to draw all Ranks of Men to a base Conformity of Spirit with themselves—when our Court is slavish,

Parliament corrupted; and those who formerly brought Kings and Ministers to a Sense of their Duty, submit themselves in the midst of Affluence, to a mean servile Dependence upon the Crown—when Bribery at Elections (which annihilates all due Regard to Conscience, and utterly destroys the Morals of the People, the sure Basis of national Felicity) is publickly avowed, as the necessary Expedient of Government—when all Manner of Profaneness, Looseness, Luxury, and Immorality are set up and countenanced, instead of Piety, Virtue, Modesty, and Justice—when the Sword is employed by a blood-thirsty implacable Administration, to massacre our guiltless Fellow-subjects Abroad, and seems destined in the End to butcher those at Home, what Joy can an Englishman receive, when the true Face of our Affairs carries such a miserable Aspect? whose Heart is there so unfeeling with respect to the Public Welfare, as not to sympathise with the Distresses and Calamities of his Country?

It is the indispensable Duty of every Man, who has Virtue enough to prefer the general Good of the Community, and who pretends to a Concern for its Interests, to consider well the part he ought to take, in a Scene so pregnant with Mischief, Ruin, and Distress. He must either shamefully relapse into an indolent Indifference about every Thing, that ought to interest him as an Englishman, or be animated by a just and honourable Purpose of obtaining a Satisfaction to the Laws of his Country, equal at least to the Violation they have suffered.

Our Duties in this Life, if we are sensible, that we have any to perform at all, stand in a regular Subordination: Our Duty to God; Mankind; our Country; our Family, Friends, and Neighbours; and our Duty to ourselves; these several Distinctions ought to be carefully considered, and religiously observed. Whoever pursues his own Interest at the Expence of his Neighbour or Family, commits a Breach of Duty, not only in that, but in every superior Degree. This is a most certain Rule in Religion, Virtue, and Morality: The Luxurious, as well as the Avaricious, will do well to attend to it.

Our Ancestors evidently appear not only to have intended well, but to have taken a right Course to accomplish what they intended. They were convinced that no System of Government was practicable in this Country, but that which, after a most generous Profusion of their precious Blood for many Ages, was established at the last glorious Revolution. By that Settlement, all the Blessings of Freedom which can consist with kingly Rule, the People have; and all the Prerogatives of Royalty which can consist with civil Fceedom, are indulged to the King. From this just Intermixture of popular and regal Forms, when kept within their due Bounds, they might, as they did reasonably expect, that both Prince and People would be too wise to violate this excellent Constitution. In the present Reign, and at a shorter Distance than a Century, we have to lament—the decay of that Fabrick, which they thought; would last till the End of Time. We live to see Parliaments, which in former Days were the best Defence of our Lives, Liberties, and Estates, sell and destroy the Interests they were chosen to preserve.

Miserable People! to be cheated and sold by them they trusted: Infamous Traffic! by Men, who (to the Disgrace of Human Nature) have crept into the Government of a Nation, and who intend nothing by their Offers to the Publick, but to feed their Avarice, their Vanity, and their Luxury, without a Sense of any single Duty they owe to God, their Country, or Mankind. Those who used to bridle Kings, and were instituted purposely to keep the Balance equal between them and the People, are now become the Instruments of all our Oppressions, and a Sword in the Hands of Mad-Men to destroy us. Here pause awhile—consult our own Understandings, and convince ourselves of the Duty we owe to our Forefathers, Ourselves, and our Posterity, as Englishmen.

The Voice of Freedom calls us, as our very Security demands it of our Hands, to repair the Breaches that are already made, and are increasing daily in the Constitution; we must fortify those Parts, which Time and Experience have proved to every thinking Man, were left too Naked, Open, and Defenceless.—Shorter Parliaments—An utter Exclusion of Placemen and Pensioners from our House of Commons—Contracting the enormous Revenue of the Crown, with a more fair and equal Representation of the People, are what Necessity must convince us all, ought in our Time to be accomplished. In a Work so conducive to our future Happiness, no Time should be lost. We should remember, that the Evils of a Nation, like many Diseases of the Body, through Inattention and Neglect, frequently become Incurable; that the Constitution lives in

Pain, continues in Langour, and, if not relieved, must die soon—That the Means of Redress are in our Possession, and we are shamefully degenerated if we are wanting in Spirit—And that our Fathers who left the most valuable Inheritance of any in the whole World, A FREE GOVERNMENT, in their last Prayers beseeched Almighty God, that their Posterity might enjoy the Blessings of Freedom, no longer than they had Sense to value, and Virtue to deserve them.

Liberty is to the collective Body, what Health is to every Individual; without Health, no Pleasure can be tasted by Man: without Liberty, no Happiness can be enjoyed by Society. The Obligation, therefore, to maintain and defend the Constitution, will appear most sacred to every rational Understanding. Men who are sensible of themselves, of their Dignity and Rights, will never shrink from the Service of their Country, or promote its Interests cooly and uncertainly, but on every Occasion, be ready to risque every Thing in its Defence. They will behold, with the utmost indifference and unconcernedness, the Ridicule and Censure of those Tools of Power, who would drown the Voice of Freedom in the Clamours of a Faction. For the false Glare of Integrity, and supposed Abilities of many, who would be the Instruments of a wicked Administration, rather than have no Employment at all; Honest Men will shew much well-grounded Contempt; and against the real Immorality of such, as are so wicked to prefer the basest Service, to the Re-establishment of a Free Constitution, they will ever have a just Indignation. Such Slaves ought to be treated as they deserve, because they are avowed Enemies to Freedom, from that Antipathy, which private Interest, and the Lust of Power for selfish Ends, will ever bear to true Patriotism and Public Virtue.

Let them please themselves with making a King Absolute, who thinks a whole Nation may be justly sacrificed for the Interest and Pleasures of a Man, and a few of his Followers. Let others rejoice in their Subtlety, who, by betraying their Trust, have advanced themselves in these dangerous Changes; perhaps, they may one Day find, that they have, with much Pains, purchased their own Ruin; that the King's Power, is their Shame, His Plenty, the Peoples Misery: and that the gaining of an Office for the Sake of enriching themselves, is but a poor Reward for destroying a Nation, which if it were preserved in Liberty and Virtue, would be the most glorious of any in the whole World.

What Man can even doubt, when a Nation is falling from the greatest Height of Glory, into the most despicable Condition, that the Community has a Right to Command his Services. That the Right is founded upon Necessity. He ought to know by the Principles of the last Revolution, when the present Family was called to the Government of this Kingdom, and its Dominions, that every faithful Subject is bound to resist the Prince who endeavours to ruin and enslave his People, and that he may push this Resistance to the Dethronement and Exclusion of his Race. The Laws and Constitution are the general Property of the Subject—not to defend, is to relinquish; and who is there so senseless as to renounce his Share in a common Benefit, unless he hopes to profit by a new Division in the Spoil. The highest Station, the greatest Glory that any Mortal can aspire to, is to be during the whole Course of his Life, the Support of Good, the Controul of bad Government, the Protector of Virtue, the Patron of Industry, and the Guardian of Public Liberty. When our Rights are invaded, our Feelings ought to tell us how long we ought to submit, and at what Moment it would be Treachery not to Resist. The present Situation of this Country, is alarming enough to rouse the Attention of every Man, who pretends to a Concern for the Public Welfare. Bad as it is, there is no Extremity of Distress, which of itself ought to reduce a great Nation to despair. A luke-warm Conduct is always odious; in Times of national Ruin, highly criminal. We owe it to our Ancestors to preserve entire those Rights which they have delivered to our Care; and we certainly owe it to our innocent Posterity not to suffer their dearest Inheritance to be destroyed. If we are sensible of these sacred Claims, we shall find there is an Obligation, binding upon Ourselves, from which nothing can acquit us—a Personal Interest which we cannot surrender.

Printed and Published for the AUTHORS by T. W. SHAW, in Fleet-Street, opposite Anderton's Coffee-House, where Letters to the Publisher will be thankfully received.

THE

CRISIS

NUMBER LVI   *To be continued Weekly,*

DURING THE PRESENT BLOODY CIVIL WAR IN AMERICA.

SATURDAY, FEBRUARY 10, 1776   *Price* Two-pence Half-penny.

A candid Appeal to every true Lover of GOD,
his Country, and Himself;

[Concluded from our last.]

Every Man is apt to delight in his own Country. I am proud to confess a particular Predilection for mine, and would give ample Testimony of my Love for it, by spilling the last Drop of my Blood in its Defence. My Thoughts as to King and State depend entirely upon their Actions. No Man shall be a more faithful and loyal Subject to him, than I, when I know he makes the Good and Prosperity of his People, his Glory; none more his Enemy, when I am convinced he does the Contrary. It would be well for him not to plume himself upon the Security of his Title to the Crown, but recollect, that as it was gained by one Revolution, it may be lost by another.

As an Englishman, I admire the excellent Constitution of my Country, its wise System of Laws, and prefer no Form of Government to a Monarchy so qualified and limited, as ours was intended to be by the last Settlement of our Ancestors. And although I sincerely wish it may for ever preserve its original monarchial Form, I will always entertain the Manners of a strict Republican—I will ever shew a general Attachment to the Common-Weal, distinct from any partial Attachment to Persons and Families—an implicit Submission to the Laws only, and an Affection to the Magistrate, proportioned to the Integrity and Wisdom, with which he distributes Justice to the People, and administers their Affairs at Home and Abroad.

The best Form of Government may be tamely given up, and surrendered into the Hands of a Master, but English Spirit hath always hitherto been answerable to the Constitution. The most insidious Attempt on their Liberties, never failed to awaken the Resentment of our generous Forefathers. The Jealousy, with which Englishmen have ever yet guarded national Freedom, is a convincing Testimony of their Right, and of their constant Possession of it.

How can I see all that I love in the World destroyed? As a Briton, I have an Interest, equal to the proudest Noble in the Laws and Constitution of my Country; and am equally called upon to make a generous Contribution in Support of them. Can I submit to serve a Government, that seeks the most detestable Means of establishing itself? Ah! No. I must live by just Means and serve to just Ends, or not at all. My Duty, as a Subject, truly loyal to the Magistracy, is neither to advise or submit to Arbitrary Measures. As a rational Being, distinguished by the peculiar Goodness of God, can I degrade the Dignity of my Nature, by a Tame Surrender of my Freedom, for the base Shackles of Slavery? No. If Life be the Gift of Providence, I will not renounce the Blessings of Freedom, without which, Life is not only miserable, but contemptible.

After such a Manifestation (which the whole of the present Reign has afforded) of the Ways by which it is intended the King shall govern, I do, in the most solemn Manner, resolve never to become a Slave. I cannot learn the vile courtly Arts of these flattering Times; I will not betray my Brethren. I hope to die in the same Principles in which I have lived, and I will live no longer than they can preserve me. Less than this, I think cannot be dispensed with in an honest Man. I have ever had in Mind, that, when I should be cast into such a Condition, as that I cannot save my Life, but by the surrender of my Liberty, which is far dearer to me, the Hour is come, wherein I should resign both.

There have been Monsters in other Ages, and in other Countries, as well as ours, but they never continued their Devastations long, when there were Heroes to oppose them.

I have ever wished for Peace, Safety, and good Government, which I trust under God, from a firm Union of the true Friends to their Country, will be established. Let us remember, that the more Genius, Industry, and Spirit are employed to destroy, the harder the Task of saving our Country becomes; but that our Duty increases with the Difficulty. God, who knows the Hearts of all Mankind, will vouchsafe to sanctify the Pursuits of all those who intend fairly and honestly by the People.

Vice and Folly, will do much to defeat the Ends of the best Institutions; what Effect they have had in our Time, is visible to all. Every legal Method for redress of Grievances, has been repeatedly tried without the smallest Hope of Success. The first Appeal was to the Integrity of our Representatives—the Second to the Justice of our King—the last Argument, which is our Duty to have recourse to, will carry more than Persuasion to Parliament, or Supplication to the Throne. The Multitude in all Countries are patient to a certain Point. On that Day, which Almighty God of his infinite Goodness, will set apart from all other Business, for the Vindication of his own Honour, and the Redressing of our Wrongs, let us beseech him to have Mercy on his People, and that he will save and defend them, and avenge the Blood of those who have already perished, upon the Heads of those, who in their Pride, think nothing is able to oppose them. And likewise, that he will animate us, with a firm, temperate Zeal, so as to prevent the Constitution itself from falling a Victim to enraged Fury, in the Moment that we risque our Lives in Opposition to Tyranny and lawless Ambition.

Truly happy must that Man be, whom God shall make an Instrument of his Justice, in so blessed a Work, as the Maintenance of Truth and Reason, Liberty and Virtue.

If Governments arise from the Consent of Men, and are instituted by Men according to their own inclinations, they did therein seek their own good; for the Will is ever drawn by some real good, or the Appearance of it. That is that which Man seeks by all the regular or irregular Motions of his Mind. Reason and Passion, Virtue and Vice do herein concur, though they differ vastly in the Objects, in which each of them thinks this good to consist. A People therefore that set up Kings, Dictators, Consuls, Pretors or Emperors, do it not, that they may be great, glorious, rich or happy, but that it may be well with themselves and their Posterity. This is not accomplished simply by setting one, a few, or more Men in the Administration of Powers, but by placing the Authority in those who may rightly perform their Office. This is not every Man's Work: Valour, Integrity, Wisdom, Industry, Experience and Skill, are required for the Management of those military and civil Affairs that necessarily fall under the Care of the Chief Magistrates. He or they therefore may reasonably be advanced above their Equals, who are most fit to perform the Duties belonging to their Stations, in order to the public Good, for which they were instituted.

Marius, Sylla, Cataline, Julius or Octavius Cæsar, and all those who by Force or Fraud usurped a Dominion over their Brethren, could have no Title to this Right;[1] much less could they become Fathers of the People, by using all the most wicked Means that could well be imagined to destroy them; and not being regularly chosen for their Virtues, or the Opinion of them, nor preferred on Account of any Prerogative that had been from the Beginning annexed to their Families, they could have no other Right than Occupation could confer upon them. If this can confer a Right, there is an End of all Disputes concerning the Laws of God or Man. If Julius and Octavius Cæsar did successively become Lords and Fathers of their Country, by Slaughtering almost all the Senate, and such

1. Roman generals Gaius Marius and Lucius Cornelius Sulla, like Catiline (see n. XXIII.11), Julius Caesar and Octavius (before he was Caesar Augustus), were stock characters in the literary world of *The Crisis*, which is obvious in the way their names are simply tossed out—the meaning attached to them apparently needing no explanation, with Plutarch's *Lives* the primary source.

Persons as were eminent for Nobility and Virtue, together with the major Part of the People, it cannot be denied, that a Thief, who breaks into his Neighbour's House, and kills him, is justly Master of his Estate; and may exact the same Obedience from his Children, that they render to their Father. If this Right could be transferred to Tiberius, either through the Malice of Octavius, or the Fraud of his Wife; a wet Blanket laid over his Face, and a few corrupted Soldiers could invest Caligula with the same.[2] A vile Rascal pulling Claudius out by the Heels from behind the Hangings where he had hid himself, could give to him. A Dish of Mushrooms well seasoned by the infamous Strumpet his Wife, and a Potion prepared for Britannicus by Locusta, could transfer it to her Son, who a Stranger to his Blood. Galba became Heir to it, by driving Nero to despair and death. Two common Soldiers, by exciting his Guards to kill him, could give a just Title to the Empire of the World to Otho, who was thought to be the worst Man in it. If a Company of Villains in the German Army, thinking it as fit for them as others, to create a Father of Mankind, could confer the Dignity upon Vitellius; and if Vespasian, causing him to be killed, and thrown into a Jakes less impure than his Life, did inherit all the glorious and sacred Privileges belonging to that Title, 'tis in vain to inquire after any Man's Right to any thing.[3]

2. Tiberius succeeded his step-father Caesar Augustus (Octavius) and, as Tiberius Julius Caesar, ruled as emperor from 14–37 CE as part of the (loosely defined) Julio-Claudian dynasty. A successful army general, he had not sought to become emperor–hence the comment by the author(s) above. Surviving a plot against him by Sejanus, he all but withdrew from public life and was reportedly smothered by his successor Caligula, whose reign would be wrapped in infamy (see n II.5 supra). The most popular sources for Tiberius and Caligula for readers of *The Crisis* would have been the English translation and London printings of Tacitus's *Annals* and Suetonius's *Twelve Caesars*.

3. The Roman allusions continue, with the author(s) assuming that each individual alluded to is already familiar to readers: Britannicus (son of Claudius), Locusta (perhaps his poisoner, and that of Claudius before), and the emperors Galba, Otho, Vitellius and Vespasian are all arrayed here in the same order that they could be found in Suetonius's *Twelve Caesars*. As I commented above, the author(s) of *The Crisis* clearly expected readers to already know their basic Roman history, and the correct lessons to be learned from it.

If there be such a thing as right or wrong to be examined by Men, and any Rules set, whereby the one may be distinguished from the other; *these Extravagancies* can have no *Effect* of Right. Such as commit them, are not to be looked upon as Fathers; but the most mortal Enemies of their respective Countries. No Right is to be acknowledged in any, but such as is conferred upon them by those who have a Right of Conferring, and are concerned in the exercise of the Power, upon such Conditions as best please themselves. No Obedience can be due to him or them, who have not a Right of Commanding. This cannot reasonably be conferred upon any, that are not esteemed willing and able rightly to execute it. This Ability to perform the highest Works that come within the reach of Men; and Integrity of Will not to be diverted from it by any Temptation, or Consideration of private Advantages, comprehending all that is most commendable in Man; we may easily see, that whensoever Men act according to the Law of their own Nature, which is Reason, they can have no other Rule to direct them in Advancing one above another, than the Opinion of a Man's Virtue and Ability, best to perform the Duty incumbent upon him; that is, by all Means to procure the Good of the People committed to his Charge. He is only fit to conduct a Ship, who understands the Art of a Pilot: When we are sick, we seek the Assistance of such as are best skill'd in Physick: The command of an Army is prudently conferred upon him that hath Industry, Skill, Experience and Valour: In like Manner, he only can, according to the Rules of Nature, be advanced to the Dignities of the World, who excels in the Virtues required for the Performance of the Duties annexed to them; for he only can answer the End of his Institution. The Law of every instituted Power, is to accomplish the End of its Institution, as Creatures are to do the Will of their Creator, and in deflecting from it, overthrow their own being. Magistrates are distinguished from other Men, by the Power with which the Law invests them for the Public good: He that cannot or will not procure that Good, destroys his own being, and becomes like to other Men. In Matters of the greatest Importance, Detur digniori is the Voice of Nature; all her most sacred Laws are perverted, if this be not observed in the Disposition of the

Governments of Mankind: But all is neglected and violated, if they are not put into the Hands of such as excel in all Manner of Virtues; for they only are worthy of them, and they only can have a Right who are worthy, because they only can perform the End for which they are instituted.

Printed and Published for the AUTHORS by T. W. SHAW, in Fleet-Street, opposite Anderton's Coffee-House, where Letters to the Publisher will be thankfully received.

THE

CRISIS

NUMBER LVII   *To be continued Weekly,*

DURING THE PRESENT BLOODY CIVIL WAR IN AMERICA.

SATURDAY, FEBRUARY 17, 1776   *Price* Two-pence Half-penny.

To the K I N G.

S I R,

With a Heart truly sensible of the many Blessings which the People of this Kingdom have enjoyed ever since the happy Accession of your Family to the imperial Throne of these Realms; Blessings which were bequeathed to the present Generation pure and untainted, by your royal Predecessor. Permit one of the most faithful and most loyal of your Subjects, born in the great Capital of your Kingdom, and who had the Pleasure to join in the loud Acclamations of a grateful People, when your Majesty ascended the Throne of your royal Grandfather, with all due Submission to approach you, and to expostulate with your Majesty on the various Causes which have contributed to damp that universal Spirit of Joy and Exultation, which diffused itself throughout your extensive Dominions at that happy Period; and to account for the many disagreeable Events which have since arisen to disturb your royal Breast; and to interrupt that Repose and Tranquility, you might expect to enjoy; after having terminated (but suffer me to say infamously and ingloriously) the most successful War, that was ever carried on by this or any other Kingdom, a War, that must have humbled in the Dust (had it continued but one Year longer) the old inveterate enemies of this your native Kingdom.

No Expression shall be found in this Remonstrance to wound the Ear of Majesty, nor shall one unfavourable Sentiment tending to infringe on the just Prerogatives of the Crown, or to lessen the Dignity of Government, escape me,—but at the same Time I will be bold enough to assert and maintain such Truths, as a *good* King will ever listen to with Attention, and with no other Emotion, than such as may proceed from a firm, spirited Resolution to remove from his Councils, and from the Administration of Government every set of Men, without *exception*, however dignified, distinguished or *allied*, through whose Inability, Venality and Servility, the Fame and Honour of Great Britain has been sullied on the CONTINENT, by whom the Revenues of this Kingdom have been exhausted and brought into such a deplorable Situation, as to endanger that very delicate Foundation PUBLIC CREDIT, on which is built the Power, commercial Strength, Riches and Happiness of your Dominions. By whose dastardly and imbecile Conduct, Faction and its constant attendant Corruption, has risen to such a Height, that you Sir, have been under the Necessity of lessening yourself in the Eyes of your whole People, by submitting to disgraceful mercenary Proposals from different Parties, who have boldly seized the Reins of Government for a short Time, with the sole View of extorting from your Majesty such Pensions and Reversions, in Case of Removal, as argued at once a conscious Inability to continue long in Office, and a premeditated Resolution to have as large a Share as possible, in the Plunder of an almost ruined Country,—by whom every rapacious Dependant on your contending Courtiers, has been amply provided for, at the Public expence—who have dared on every Occasion to make use of the royal Name as a Sanction for every illegal and unconstitutional Measure, and have presumed to express an Approbation, *you* could never give of a most unwarrantable, and cruel Exertion of the *Military Power*, against your innocent Subjects; such an Exertion as would have entitled the Offenders to condign Punishment, in many States which are stiled absolute, despotic Monarchies, as I shall soon convince you in the sequel of this Remonstrance; from recent In-stances,—who have spread Consternation, Terror and Dismay through the Land, Violating the most sacred Rights of the People, interrupting the Freedom of Elections, rendering the Attendance of the Freeholders dangerous to their Persons, ransacking the Coffers of Public Trading Companies, to supply the Deficiencies from a Mismanagement of the public Revenues, in a Word,—who have withheld from you Sir, the true State of the Nation, and have construed every Complaint, every mod-est Representation of the Subjects, both at Home and in the Colonies, against the arbitrary, and oppressive Measures of an unstable, wicked Administration into Sedition; and every Defence of their Rights and Properties against the Exertion of lawless Power (sanctified in the Name of Majesty) into overt Acts of REBELLION till they have at length roused the public Spirit of the People throughout your whole Domin-ions; the Alarm is become general; the Constitution of the Kingdom is now deemed at a CRISIS, and if your royal Name is still made use of to stamp an Authority on public Measures, diametrically opposite to the Welfare of the Nation, the Consequences must prove fatal to both.

Sir, wonder not, that I have preferred the Stile of Remonstrance to that of Petition; having no private Favour to ask, I have presumed to consider your Majesty as a Man, endued with a rational Soul, capable of distin-guishing, between sound Reasoning, and artful Sophistry; such a Mode of Expostulation therefore, as might be persued in Conversation by a modest Dependant, or an affable, generous Patron, seemed to me the most eligible for conveying my Sentiments with manly Firmness, and to enable me to steer clear of that abject Submission, and disgustful Adula-tion which debases almost every Address that is offered to Sovereigns.

I shall therefore, Sir, take the Liberty to represent to you, that under the several Administrations which have governed this Kingdom, from your Accession to the present Hour, some one or more of the enumerated Evils already delineated, have taken Place, and that they seem to be all gather-ing to a Head under the present Ministry: and as it cannot be consistent either with your Honour or your Interest, to suffer universal Discontent, popular Animosity, and CIVIL WAR to be kept alive in your Dominions, let me advise you to effect that by their Removal, which all the military Force of this Kingdom, with the superaided rigour of penal Laws, will never accomplish; I mean the Restoration of Harmony, Unanimity, and zealous Attachment to your Person and Government. Be assured, Sir, whenever under a Prince, blessed with native Goodness of Heart, and a benign Disposition, the People feel the Weight of an undue Exertion of the royal Prerogative, they will naturally ascribe it to ministerial Influence, and in spite of every Exertion of the military Power, they will loudly and incessantly exclaim against such Influence, nor will they desist, till their Complaints are listened to, and their Grievances redressed by a total Change of Men and Measures.

Forbid it Heaven, that you Sir, who ought to be the political Father of your People, born and educated among us, should be any longer accused in our Streets, or insulted at our public Spectacles, for a supposed Tolleration of, or Connivance at the arbitrary Principles and destructive Practices of your Ministers; or that your Subjects should tremble with the Apprehension that large Strides are making towards a State of SLAVERY, or a servile Dependance on Ministers, and their Tools; under their native Prince, which was never experienced in the Reigns of those Kings who were born and educated in a foreign Land, and who openly avowed the most despotic Principles. Let it never be believed Sir, that you will of your royal Motion, give Orders to punish with Fines, Imprisonment, inquisitorial Persecution, Fire and Sword, every innocent Subject, who shall dare to assert his native Freedom and Independence, in Opposition to weak, or wicked Ministers.

Your People Sir, are not disposed to judge from Appearance, they expect to see a full display of those political Virtues which constitute the Character of a great King: in expectation of this happy Event, they patiently wait, and *passively* submit, resting assured you will be inspired with a speedy and just Abhorrence of those Men, who first spread Murmur and Discontent through the Realm? and covered the Land with BLOOD; a Ministry, whose Weakness, Cowardice, and Cruelty, whether they are considered separately in their respective Departments, or collectively in a Body as an Administration, is not to be paralleled in the Records of the History of England.

Let us now great Sir, turn our Eyes from this disgraceful Picture of the Times, the odium of which your Ministry in vain endeavour to fix on the People, since their Lives and Conversation alone stamp a Character in the Manners of the Nation, and examine with Attention, the Characteristics of a sound permanent Administration, as they are described to us by the best political Writers, and take some one or other, or all of your present Ministry by the Hand, while we make this fair Scrutiny.

"The Administration of public Affairs, in a limited Monarchy, such as England, ought to be committed to several Men, illustrious by Birth and Education, possessed of ample Fortunes as collateral Security for their Integrity and Incorruptibility, of virtuous, unsullied Characters, and arrived to such a Period of Life, that experience may have matured early acquired political knowledge: such may be found in every State, and must be chosen independent of all Regard to Family Connections, or party Leagues.—Such a select Band of great and able Men jointly engaged in one Administration, with any preponderating Weight thrown into the Scale of the chief of any Department; and acting independent of one another in their different Stations, though with mutual Confidence at the Council Board is the only Model of Government suited to the Legislature, and to the very Genius of the English Nation.

Ministers on such a Plan are a mutual Check on each other, each of them has his distinct set of Adherents, but his principal Support must be, the Character he bears in his Country.—Such a Ministry must act upon popular Principles, for it is built upon the only Basis likely to secure the People's Affection, and to render it permanent, the just Fame such a Ministry must acquire, will set them above every foolish Temptation of Pageant Honours, of Power, or Wealth, if to be purchased only by making a Sacrifice of their Character. In short, as Example is more efficacious, and has more Authority than the rigorous Exertion of penal Laws, or even military Execution, the People being animated by the pious Character of their Sovereign, exhibited, not only in his own private Life, but in his public Capacity, by the prudent Choice of his Ministers; all Ranks of Men would come into the Fashion of leading virtuous lives, the Scale would preponderate in Favour of Morality, there would be little or no Temptation to Bribery and Corruption, Men being chosen to high Offices for their Virtues and Abilities, would not be necessitated to support themselves in them by such low Means: the Law would have less Occasion for Officers, Executioners, Gibbets, Proscriptions, and Outlawries to enforce its Decrees, and the Empire of Love and Reason would be universal throughout the British Dominions. I shall here leave your Majesty for the present. I find the sensible Pleasure which this Representation has given you; it ill becomes me to interrupt your important Meditations on this pleasing Scene, and the less so, as I must demonstrate to your Majesty that Birth and Education misapplied alone excepted, your present Ministry cannot find one single Qualification to which they can put in a just Claim.—I therefore quit the Subject till a more favourable Opportunity offers of resuming it.

B R U T U S.

Printed and Published for the AUTHORS by T. W. SHAW, in Fleet-Street, opposite Anderton's Coffee-House, where Letters to the Publisher will be thankfully received.

THE

CRISIS

NUMBER LVIII   *To be continued Weekly,*

DURING THE PRESENT BLOODY CIVIL WAR IN AMERICA.

SATURDAY, FEBRUARY 24, 1776   *Price* Two-pence Half-penny.

This *galling Truth* to GEORGE let BRITONS tell,
When *Kings* grow TYRANTS Subjects will REBEL:
It must be so, and Monarchs *strive* in vain
'Gainst FREEDOM's Sons, who will their RIGHTS maintain;
The People have by RIGHT, and by CONSENT,
DETHRON'D a MAN, to SAVE the GOVERNMENT:
The LAWS to their own Channel DID restore,
And yet the Crown was SAFER than BEFORE.

To the K I N G.

S I R!

AS a dutiful and loyal Subject, who wishes your Majesty's Person protected from the Rage of an incensed People; I warn you of the impending Ruin, which every Moment threatens your Crown and Dignity: If you have a Wish to preserve your own safety, dissolve your present corrupt Parliament; discard your Pensioners; abandon your present set of Privy Councellors; and turn your Resentment on

511

those, who have advised your Majesty to adopt such Measures, the Event of which now (too late) betrays the abominable Wickedness; and desperate Designs of the Advisers.

Will any set of Men presume to advise your Majesty to dispatch Forces to America, to spill the Blood of their own Countrymen; and at the same Time tell you, what none but Traitors could dare to utter, and what none but Fools can be simple enough to believe; that England is nevertheless in a defensive Situation against France and Spain. For Heavens Sake put not so obstinate a Confidence in the Wisdom of those Men, who in the Opinion of every Man who dares to think, speak, and act for himself, (Pensioners and bribed Lords excepted) are aiming at the Destruction of your Majesty's Crown, and the Introduction of a Spanish or French Government.

Gibraltar is certainly in Danger, it totters to its Base.—What Fate may not England then expect. And yet this alarms you not, you repose such Trust in your diabolical Parliament, that you are determined to persevere in the grossest Ignorance, under the Conduct and Direction of the most wicked, artful, and designing set of Men in all your whole Dominions. Everybody, nay, your very Ministers tremble for, and dread the Event. North, Mansfield, Bute, and Apsley advise (with quivering Tongues, and reproaching Consciences) such Perseverance, barely to secure their own HEADS; for they well know, that were they at this CRISIS to confess the Measures adopted, had better be declined, it would betray their whole System of traitorous Villainy; and they must meet the Fate of a JEFFRIES or a LAUD.—No Sir, never expect those Ministers to advise conciliatory Measures, who having advised the present, would assuredly be held up to public Infamy, and Example, as TRAITORS to their Country.

America offers the most just and honourable Terms, which your Inhumanity and Thirst for Plunder, to gratify the avaricious Views, and raise upon the Ruins of American Property, immense Fortunes for your Creatures and Slaves, will not suffer you to accept.

Every one of your Majesty's Well-Wishers avow the present proceedings to be inconsistent, not only with Humanity, but sound Policy; and consequently ought not (by your Majesty) to be pursued. I rank not your Ministers amongst your Well-Wishers, because by their Conduct they are shewn to be otherwise; which, is what a blind obstinacy, and fatal Perseverance, peculiar to TYRANTS, will not let you see.

Men, Societies of Men, the most respectable, and the farthest distant from any of your Majesty's Favours, have advised, have petitioned, have remonstrated; and yet they are with Scorn rejected, while every Lesson of a Court Favourite is strictly enforced, though it tend to the most destructive Ends.

If your Majesty is determined on Obedience to arbitrary Government, expect something worse than to see the Citizens of London approach your Majesty with a Petition or Remonstrance. To avoid the Fate of Charles, flee in Time from the Wrath to come: or if you have not Wisdom enough to govern a People, like JOHN RESIGN your CROWN.

I have never, Sir, been conscious to myself, that the Temptation of any base Interest, or the apprehension of any threatning Danger, could corrupt me to betray, or force me to decline, that which I well knew to be the true Interest of my Country; and therefore I have constantly looked upon those, who made it their Business to break in upon the just Rights of the People, as the wicked Instruments in the Hands of a weak or designing Prince, to involve the Nation in Tyranny and Confusion, which is always attended with the most destructive Consequences to the Subjects Lives, Liberties, and Property.

It is therefore with great Indignation I have observed, how strenuously this vile Design, has been laboured, from the fatal Moment you mounted the Throne of these Kingdoms, to this Hour. Under the screening Shelter of your affected Piety, Popery, and arbitrary Power have been favoured, nay cherished with all the Art and Industry, which Men of slavish Principles, and profligate Consciences could devise, till the twin Monsters are at length arrived to their fullness of prodigious stature.

As a good Preparative for the Introduction of Slavery and arbitrary Power, pernicious Pamphlets have been published by *Shebbeare*, *Johnson*, and the Jesuitical Hypocrite, *John Wesley*, wherein it has been magisterially asserted, that the Realm of England is such a complete imperial Sovereignty, that you, Sir, have FULL, PERFECT, and entire Jurisdiction from GOD ALONE; and that the People ought rather to suffer DEATH *wrongfully* than resist you. It has been indeed speciously granted, that there were *political Laws* to secure the Rights of the Subject, but it was stiffly maintained, that the *imperial Laws*, which ascertained the Rights of the Prince, were SUPERIOR to the *political*, and might and ought to determine when the *political Laws* should be *observed*, and when *not*. Which is no more than saying the Rights of the Subject should be secure from all Invasions, but that of their King, a pretty Security indeed; what Sophistry! Why did not these Advocates for Despotism and Murder, these common Enemies to the Peace and Liberties of Mankind? ingenuously and boldly assert what they really meant, that your WILL, Sir, is the LAW. No—the Design is so wicked and odious, that to have owned it in *plain Words*, would have been to overthrow it. But by subtle Distinctions and treasonable Sophistry, the People are to be juggled out of their Liberties; indeed they would be no longer a People, but a PLUNDERED and ENSLAVED Rabble, left only *Tenants* at *Will* for their Lives, Religion, Rights, and Estates.

The Design, Sir, (whether first formed by you, or your Ministers, or both, is not material, but that one has been formed is notorious to the World) of changing our legal, into an arbitrary Government, and it was certainly copied from the *French*. in *France* it was laid in the Reign of *Lewis* XI. and took Effect to the Destruction of the Rights of the People, by destroying as you and your Ministers have done, through Corruption and Bribery, the Power of *Parliaments*. This was carried on by the most easy and modest Encroachments, that a People weary of their Liberties could have wished for. The King did not pretend to raise MONEY when he pleased, by himself without his Parliament. All that he *desired*, was only to be *permitted* to raise MONEY—*now and then*—upon OCCASION—in the intervals of Parliament; and not that neither, but in Cases of *mere* NECESSITY, when the safety of his *good* Subjects absolutely required it. And how could it be denied him, who (like YOU) *loved* his People so well, to judge of Cases of NECESSITY. But the Power of raising MONEY being once gone, the deluded People presently perceived, that they had purchased their SLAVERY with it; for then all Power fell into the Hands of the King. It was in vain to dispute with him any *civil Rights*, not yet parted with by name; (as the Americans have experienced from you.) The French King became by the above artifice (as you have by foul Corruption) at perfect Liberty to be, or not to be a TYRANT, which he pleased. Let no one ask how he governed; for did ever a Man grasp at the Power of doing Mischief, without the Purpose? If there has been such mysterious Riddles of irregular Virtue, yet the *French* Kings after *Lewis* XI. were no Instances of it;—nor can I, Sir, have Faith enough notwithstanding all your hypocritical Piety, to believe you will be one. In them it appeared plainly how effectually the Temptation of unlimited Power works on ambitious Nature. It was not enough for *Lewis* XIV. to be the LAW, but he must be the RELIGION also of his SLAVES; and this ought to be a fatal Warning to the People of England at this melancholy Æra, when all Laws divine and human are trampled under Foot, and made the jest and mockery of a slavish and corrupt Court. With many it was Argument enough to be of the same Religion as *Lewis*, because it was his: while his spiritual Dragoons disputed more forcibly with those of a more backward Faith; the Priests had stood altogether idle, and unconcerned in this Conversion, but for the Merit of that flattering Doctrine: A King is accountable to none but GOD, but to make amends for their being less serviceable than the *military*, their *unaccountable* King they stiled the VICEGERENT of GOD, nay the very IMAGE of the Most High. It is much to be wondered at, they did not maintain that their King was accountable to none but himself; for if he prescribed their Religion, and dictated their Law, he was their IDOL GOD, as well as their ROYAL TYRANT.

This Sir, is an exact Picture of the French Original of arbitrary Government, and the Manner and Methods made use of to destroy the Liberties of that once free Country; which you and your Ministers, and your present Bench of Anti-Protestant Bishops, seem to have had before you, and to have copied with such a Masterly nicety, that it is really difficult to be distinguished from the Original, unless by some few adepts well skilled in the Art of Tyranny.

There is, Sir, another original Draught of a Tyrant, set forth in that excellent History of the Revolution in *Sweden* wherein many Particulars bear a perfect resemblance of the present Times, as to the Transactions in AMERICA, which most clearly proves that all Tyranny is alike; for though the Streams from the same Fountain may run in several Ways, and various Channels, yet they all tend to the same OCEAN of BLOOD.

Many advantages however, will raise from the glorious Designs of those two trusty and well-beloved Ministers of Belzebub, BUTE and MANS-FIELD, and the Preparations you are making for the triumphant Entry of POPERY and SLAVERY. You will bind Sir, firmly to your Interest, three most FAITHFUL and POTENT ALLIES, The TURK, the POPE, and the DEVIL.

Printed and Published for the AUTHORS by T. W. SHAW, Fleet-Street, opposite Anderton's Coffee-House, where Letters to the Publisher will be thankfully received.

THE

CRISIS

NUMBER LIX   *To be continued Weekly,*

DURING THE PRESENT BLOODY CIVIL WAR IN AMERICA.

SATURDAY, March 2, 1776   *Price* Two-pence Half-penny.

"For the Sake of the miserably convulsed Empire sollicit Peace, repeal the *Acts*, or Britain is *undone*."

Dr. *Church's* (Gen. Gage's *Spy's*)
Letter to Maj. Kane of the King's Army.[1]

HAD I the honour of knowing Lord *Mansfield*, I should not hesitate to tell him that the hint conveyed in the motto of this paper, might prove far more useful to our precipitate *adminis-tration*, than any in *Montcalm's* Letters, which seem to be the basis of his Lordship's politics. Dr. *Church* (one of his *Majesty's* spies *royal*) has

---

1. Dr. Benjamin Church spied for General Thomas Gage at the same time that he served as a physician with the American troops laying siege to Boston in the summer and fall of 1775. Ardent in his defense of American rights in the years leading up to the fighting, he delivered the third annual Boston Massacre oration and had been active in the extralegal Massachusetts provincial convention formed in October 1774. Brought before a board of inquiry for what was considered duplicitous behavior by communicating (in code) with British contacts in Boston, he was jailed, temporarily released because of

advised like an intelligent and *honest* counsellor. The *ministry* must credit him because he is a villain of their own. The intelligence of the *spy*
must have been received with confidence at *St. James's,* where the petition
of the subject has so often been repulsed. That Dr. *Church's* advise deserves the most serious attention, the late spirited, wise, and deliberate
resolves in *America* have fully shewn. Their articles of *perpetual union* do
honour, not only to the cause of liberty, but to the dignity of man. Since
the renowned union of the free states of Greece against the haughty tyrant *Phillip,* no human coalition in support of civil liberty (unless I may
except our glorious *revolution*) has deserved equal admiration and applause. I do not mean to sound a panegyric, but to assert a truth, when I
declare that history can hardly produce its parallel. In what records can
we find a single instance of national defence founded on clearer principles of justice? On the other hand, with what indignation, with what
execrations, must posterity read of an *English* invasion upon *English subjects,* supported by a detestable combination of daring ministerial tyrants?
tyrants, who are prompted not by policy, but by rapine; not by wisdom
but revenge, not by the love of order, but by the lust of power, not by a
goldlike effort to *reclaim,* but by an infernal (though a vain) resolution to
exterminate. I write, with a copy of the *American Confederacy* before me,
penned with the greatest deliberation, wisdom, justice, moderation and
magnanimity; breathing a spirit of true patriotic zeal, and *independent
empire.*[2] As an Englishman I honour them for the one, as a citizen of the

---

illness, jailed again in Boston after the British evacuated it, and once again released in
1778, then perished at sea. For the problem of his "treason" see David James Kiracoffe,
"Dr. Benjamin Church and the Dilemma of Treason in Revolutionary Massachusetts"
New England Quarterly 70 (1997):443–62.

2. The proposed outline for an "American Confederacy" that "Casca" was so pleased to
have in hand had been widely circulated in the London press, first in *Lloyd's Evening
Post,* 8 December 1775, which reprinted a copy that had appeared in the *North Carolina
Gazette,* 6 October 1775. The *Public Advertiser* printed it on 3 January 1776, to be followed the next day by the *Gazetteer and New Daily Advertiser,* the *General Evening Post,*
the *Middlesex Journal and Evening Advertiser,* and the *St. James Chronicle.* It would be
June before the Continental Congress formed a committee to draft Articles of Confederation for an independent nation, the so-called Dickinson draft that became the

world, and a friend of *freedom*, I revere them for the other. The wise provision, however, which they have made for future independent empire, is, even as yet (I call upon the suspicious *Mansfield* to observe it) but *conditional*. They have, with the greatest moderation, left their unnatural parent room to return to her duty; but if neither shame, nor honour, nor a sense of justice can lead her to repentance, she must at last fall a victim to her own rapacious views and insatiable resentments, unpitied at home, and despised abroad; no longer the queen of commerce, the mistress of the ocean, the mediatrix between contending nations, dreaded in war, admired in peace, the palladium of civil and religious liberty. Posterity indeed may view her thus pourtrayed in history; they may feast their imaginations with ideas of past blessings: but this country, almost unnerved already by luxury and corruption, if it once crouches (as I fear it will) beneath the iron grasp of *tyranny*, will revive no more. Its inhabitants (if they dare even to wish for liberty) must seek it where alone it can be found, among their brethren in *America*, whose massacre they once tamely viewed without attention, pity, or revenge. They must sue like hopeless dastards, to be united with those whom they once deserted in the glorious cause of liberty; nay betrayed, invaded, murdered, and would (had it pleased heaven to favour their intended parricide) have

---

basis of the final text approved in November 1777. Dickinson had drawn on an earlier proposal drafted by Benjamin Franklin, a conditional Articles of Confederation that would produce a "perpetual union," including the West Indies as well as Britain's North American mainland colonies (and even Ireland, in a first draft), but only if Britain failed to repeal the 1774 legislation that, in American patriot eyes, had caused the fighting to begin. That was the text to which "Casca" referred. Franklin's proposal had been discussed by Congress on 21 July 1775, then was put aside, never again to be formally reviewed. It is nevertheless a significant proposal, especially for showing an ambivalent American state of mind—rebels who were not yet revolutionaries. *The Crisis* could endorse this position, but not what followed, when full independence rather than reconciliation became the Patriots' goal. For Franklin's plan itself see Labaree, ed., *Papers of Franklin*, 22:120–25; Ford, ed., *Journals of the Continental Congress*, 2:195–99; and the Papers of the Continental Congress, 1774–1789 (Washington, D.C.: Government Printing Office, 1959; 204 reels microfilm), Item 9, pp. 1–6 (reel 22); and for context Burnett, *Continental Congress*, pp. 90–91; and Jack N. Rakove, *The Beginnings of National Politics* (New York: Alfred A. Knopf, 1979), pp. 136–39.

swept from the face of the earth, for daring to assert the rights, the privileges, the dignity of mankind. Yes, they must petition to become *confederates* with the brave *Americans* against the insupportable *tyranny* of *Great Britain*. Into this illustrious *confederacy* I will venture to foretell (my prophesies have hitherto proved true) that impatient *Englishmen* will at last secede, leaving the dregs of this unhappy country under the vassalage of a *corrupt majority*. What a capacious, what a fruitful bosom will *America* open to receive them? She has already erected the standard of virtue and liberty in her *union*; she has displayed the sword of magnanimity and justice in the field. She wields the latter in the noblest cause; she founds the former on the noblest principles. I have asserted, and I assert again, in the face of a rotten-hearted ministry, a venal parliament, and a lumpish *despot*, that this *perpetual union*, is in the highest degree wise, just, dispassionate, and magnanimous. To this deserved encomium the proceedings of the British government have furnished a *vile antithesis*. It is true they have (under the execrable influence of *Bute* and *Mansfield*) *persevered*, but they have *persevered* in folly, cruelty, injustice, tyranny, and blood. They will have their reward. From the innocent blood thus spilt in *America* will arise a *hydra* with many heads: not a *monster*, but (hear it ye wise counselors of the royal cabinet!) an opulent, a splendid, a powerful *Commonwealth*. Its outlines (and noble ones they are) are now before me. The most contemptible *tyrant* that England has ever known, (if his mind were sufficiently enlarged) might survey them with admiration, confusion, and remorse. Their virtuous and spirited contents would sit heavy on his guilty soul. They present all true Britons with a subject worthy of their contemplation. They speak the language of our wisest and our bravest ancestors, in calm defiance of a wicked gang of traitorous placemen, pensioners, and ministerial sycophants, basely combined to enrich themselves by the ruin of their country. If a Tory hackney scribbler (like *Johnson*) should rebuke me for writing a *panegyric* on *America*, and a *libel* on his masters; I will prove the former to be *just,* by referring him to the several wise and virtuous resolutions, the pious, necessary and intrepid oppositions of *America*: I will prove the latter to be *true* by reminding him of the repeated *supplications* rejected, the outrages, murders and depredations sanctified, *in suppression of civil liberty*, by a venal majority, under a flagitious administration. I forbear to take notice of the still weaker *pilot,* whose duty it was (had he known it) to have kept the *ship* from rolling; but she ought not to be lost (if the passengers are wise) for want of better conduct at the *helm.* Having thus replied to the supposed, and natural impertinence of this ministerial scribler, I would take notice, before I leave him, of a passage in his infamous pamphlet, called *Taxation no Tyranny:* the purport of his words is this; I speak upon memory: "What confusions, what convulsions must poor *America* feel before her government (supposing her *disunion*) can be settled?" I am inclined to think, *doctor,* nay, permit me to say, I sincerely hope, her worst pangs are at an end. If you will deign, most learned *doctor,* to cast your magisterial eye upon the *American articles,* you will presently discern the great out-lines of a *Commonwealth;* the offspring of your *Thane's* patriotic *perseverance.* They are as evident as the source of wealth and plenty in the *Scotch union.* The will and pleasure of the *chancellor* in your *Oxford diploma,* or the scandalous profusion of the *prime minister* in the warrant which doubles your pay as *Hackney in Chief* to a *Scotch,* and consequently a *tory administration;* the greatest curse that can fall upon Great Britain. Again, the *articles, most redoubted doctor,* furnish a glorious contradiction to one of the basest of your positions in *Taxation no Tyranny,* namely, that there can be no such thing as *limited government.* Though I speak upon memory, (as I did in my former quotation) yet I am confident that this is your expression; its falsity and iniquity has fixed it in my mind. For such a one alone, you might well deserve to be burnt in effigy at *Salem,*[3] and in person *here.* Where there is no *limitation,* all must be *tyranny.* The rule of *right* is immutable and eternal. A government free from *kings,* and sons of *kings,* bids the fairest for preserving it. Such is a *Commonwealth,* (now in embryo in *America*) because it has *virtue* for its basis. If the justly celebrated *Montesquieu* (the noblest writer in the world except *Dr. Johnson*) were consulted, he would tell us that no government fit for man to live under, either can, or ought to be

---

3. "Casca" had in mind the Salem witchcraft hysteria of 1692, by then remembered with some embarrassment on both sides of the Atlantic, but in Massachusetts in particular.

unlimited; and that every such government (if it can deserve that name) must be complete *tyranny*.[4] The oppressed *Americans* have felt the worst effects of government *unlimited* not in its *constitution*, but in its late deviations from the line of *right* so justly drawn by our discerning ancestors. They have seen and felt how far a corrupt coalition of *three great estates*, wisely designed as checks upon each other, may form one *tyrannic mass of combination* against the liberties of their expiring country. With more than human fortitude they are wisely providing for their future peace in the midst of war. That a *limited monarchy* may degenerate into what may be truly called an unlimited *usurpation* (for there can be no such *government*) they have fatally experienced, and may therefore well abhor *kings* however restrained. The *Romans* (in no other respect braver than the *Americans*) had their *kings* at first. *The Americans*, in spite of threats, may now begin to date their æra as a *people*. They think so, and therefore, as suffering under sad experience, have laid the corner stone of government as far as possible from the *regal* plan. They sensibly admonish every colony to amend its constitution at the first outset, though they were not themselves permitted, under the protection of Great Britain, to enjoy even that which their ancestors had purchased with their blood. In the future government of *America*, *equality* will be the pole star of direction. No useful subjects are to be left *unrepresented*. There will be no *boroughs* visibly rotten, or invisibly consequential and important, but there is to be one representative for every 5000 polls. It is plain they have an eye to *commerce*; their situation for it is the noblest in the world. It is in no contemptible degree already opened, if *America* is faithful to herself, the utmost efforts of Great Britain cannot absolutely destroy it, though they may impede it for a time. She has planned her mode of *representation,* like a *commercial nation.* As such, she knows that the riches of the state must consist in the numbers of useful members; useful not to the aggregate body of *tyrants*, or to the single *tyrant* of the state, but to the *Commonweal* itself; not corrupt *voices*, but serviceable *hands*;

---

4. The author(s) could not resist coupling a sarcastic dig at Samuel Johnson with a compliment offered to the Baron de Montesquieu (for whom see n. XVI.6 supra).

not leaches, but *members* of society; not *drains* but *springs*. She has wisely and justly ordained, that one half of the members at every *Congress* shall be necessary to make a quorum, exclusive of *proxies*. If this was the rule in the house of Lords and Commons, *corruption* would neither be so easily effected, nor so cheaply maintained; great as the demands now are upon the people for the support of it, they must, in such case, have been still greater; the burthen more intolerable, the people more impatient, and this lingering, *persevering tyranny* sooner at an end. It is observable, that no *proxies* at all can be admitted, unless in case of *necessary absence*. An excellent precaution for the preservation of a virtuous government in its full vigour. A *proxy* can do no more than augment the number of votes on the one side or the other. *Content*, or *not content*, is all that such a shadow can advance, it can neither advise, reason, nor debate. It may be used as a passive agent to a crafty principal for the worst of purposes. It may, without a blush, in one single word espouse a decision which its iniquitous master could not dare to countenance in person. It may undo individuals, it may ruin kingdoms. The late case of *Thickness and Lee* in the House of Lords, supports me in this assertion. *Lord Mansfield* in that case voted by his *proxy* (his lord chancellor) against *Mr. Thickness*. He knew that *equity* and *Lord Camden* must and would declare clearly in his favour; but a private resentment was to be gratified by this man, who still bears upon his coach a motto* which the college of Heralds should sweep out. Junius, in a former *Crisis*, has given the world the story at large. Such a piece of judicial shamefaced iniquity can never be transacted in the *American Congress* by way of *proxy*; whilst the *shirking* principal is hearing a paultry cause of assault and battery, in a court almost adjoining to that, where almost the whole of a defrauded subject's property demanded his protection. In the next place, I must observe, that the *General Congress* are to appropriate all public monies for every separate and distinct service; no mass of public money will be suffered to fall into the hands of one man, or of any gang of men, to be disposed of in *secret services*; or in other words, for the sole emolument of themselves and their

---

*Soli æquus virtuti atq. ejus amicis.—A friend alone to virtue and her friends.

accomplices, in effecting the ruin of their country. For such monies, either the general, or executive *Congress*, are to draw on the general treasurer. Every single draft, by this means, becomes a public and notorious act, not transacted in *petto*. How differently do we proceed? With us, *Lord North* (the *proxy* of *Lord Bute*) draws upon *himself*. He has, not only the controll of all public monies, but the controll of all those among whom they are squandered or dispensed. *America* has thought it just to secure to the *six nations of Indians* all their landed property—we have, since the last war, deliberately and designedly invaded it; and within these five years have supported such invasions by a solemn decree at the council-board. This breach of national justice was a political stroke, in order to break the strength of those warlike people, and to render their association with the *Americans* (whom our government then viewed as enemies in embryo) of less importance. They were determined even then upon the speedy reduction of *America* to slavery, and therefore by these means among others, endeavoured to weaken and prevent all her natural resouces. *America* adheres, (and may heaven support in this just resolution!) to the terms of *reconciliation* proposed by her in her last petition, which has been trampled on in the despotic cabinet. She will have, and she ought to have, every act, made under the influence of *Bute* repealed. She demands, and justly, ample reparation and reimbursement. She requires the miserable remains of the finest part of the British army to be withdrawn: And then—(so far is she from a wish of *independence*) she declares herself ready and willing (though with victory in her hand) to return to her former connections and friendship (but not to *slavery*) under Great Britain. Hear this, *Lord Mansfield*, and recant your late flimsy speech in the House of Lords upon the vile restraining bill. It has exposed your principles, your politics, your party, and their execrable views, to public detestation. Abjure for ever the pitiful authority of *Montcalm's* letters. Disdain all selfish views, all insolent controul and influence in the close of life, and die at least, as a British nobleman ought to live, a friend to liberty and virtue. Learn from the present state of *America*, in the midst of her oppressions, that Providence is no friend to *tyrants*. In a land destined by your lordship and your associates to famine and desolation, behold granaries overflowing, marts erected, and ports opened to all the world, beside ourselves, for the exportation of redundant plenty. How impotent, how truly despicable, is all this parade of *royal vengeance,* when it cannot terrify even the husbandman, nor take off his attention from his field! When commerce is carried on even whilst the colours of the enemy are flying? All our West-India colonies in general will, nay they must of necessity resort to the great *American* mart, or perish. If they supply themselves from thence, their vessels will be seized and themselves deemed rebels; if they do not, they and their plantations must be ruined. They can be supplied from no other quarter, notwithstanding the ridiculous pretences of the ministry, and the more ridiculous provisions in the restraining bill. *Administration* to this moment are working in the dark. They know nothing of the colonies. But this I know, that the West-Indies must either submit to certain ruin, unless *America* will relieve them, or abide the vengeance of our *persevering tyrants* if they sue for her protection. These are miserable alternatives, and either way they will be lost to their mother country. In the mean time, will not this *American* resolution for the exportation of corn and other provisions, with which *America* at this moment abounds, open a most advantageous and extensive trade with the French, Spanish, and Dutch in particular, nay with our friends the Danes too, and with other powers? In this case can *America* want warlike supplies, or even warlike vessels? Are we in a condition at present to be regarded by either of these states, should we remonstrate, threaten, or declare war? Are our military and marine forces able at this juncture to cope with the most considerable states in Europe, and the combined force of all our American colonies at the same time? Will not France and Spain trade with *America* in defiance of, nay in hopes of making a breach with England at so favourable a period? Will the passive subjects of Great Britain submit patiently to be drained for the support of such a general war as may ensue in consequence of ministerial perseverance in the worst of causes, the destruction of civil liberty? Amidst these commotions, will Ireland, who had long been stripped of her undoubted rights, defrauded of her constitution, almost overwhelmed by taxes, pensions, plunder and oppression; will she forget her injuries, and exhaust her veins to serve the odious purposes of a rapacious and despotic government? At such a crisis will the influence of *Bute*, the craft of *Mansfield*, the lowering brow of an ungracious *tyrant*, appall an injured nation, or unnerve the arm of public justice? Will the general voice of discontent be checked by that false and slavish maxim "*a King can do no wrong?*" A maxim invented by *crown lawyers*, the worst of traitors to their country, and never seriously adopted since the late glorious *revolution*, but by the late *ministerial string* of *addressers*, the very dregs of the nation both in spirit and importance. These groveling wretches, under the false names of *merchants*, and *principal inhabitants*, (with those worshipful old women, the *Middlesex justices* at their head) have in their sagacious addresses, served up a splendid paraphrase upon that erroneous and detestable position, that "*a King* (though he were a *Nero*, or a *Driveler*, or a mixture of both) *can do no wrong.*" A position to which the *revolution* gives the lie; to which none would subscribe but slaves and sycophants, or such a majority of *ayes* and *noes, contents* and *not contents*, as have proscribed and massacred *America* by act of parliament: By such acts, which, if not repealed, *Great Britain* will be (as *Dr. Church* prophesies) *undone.*

C A S C A.

Printed and Published for the AUTHORS by T. W. SHAW, Fleet-Street, opposite Anderton's Coffee-House, where Letters to the Publisher will be thankfully received.

THE

CRISIS

NUMBER LX   *To be continued Weekly,*

DURING THE PRESENT BLOODY CIVIL WAR IN AMERICA.

SATURDAY, March 9, 1776   *Price* Two-pence Half-penny.

A   PROPHESY.

Good Georgy of Brunswick, Oh be not so bold;
For Britain thy Kingdom is bought, and is sold!
A *Stuart* to *Stuarts* most faithfull will be:
And the black cunning *Thane*'s too cunning for thee!
Soon driven thro' him to thy Hanover's Shore
Thy obstinate weakness there shalt thou deplore:
Like thy Ancestor James without hope of recall,
Betray'd by thy Friends, and deserted by ALL!

QUALIFICATIONS requisite for PRIME MINISTER in the present
Reign; the vilest that ever disgraced the Annals of this Kingdom.

TO be all Submission and Obedience to Lord Mansfield and
Earl Bute, by whose Omnipotence all the Affairs of this great
and extensive Empire, are and have long been governed with
the most absolute Sway.

527

To be particularly *adroit* in the Art of corrupting and bribing both Houses of Parliament, in order that every Point of Moment may be carried with a high Hand; to exercise the same laudable Talent in every Borough throughout the Kingdom; and whenever, through Inexperience and Want of Cunning, he finds himself at a Loss, to take the Advice and farther Directions of the above two great Masters in that noble Science.

To bestow Places, Pensions, Rewards, Titles, and Honours, Ecclesiastical, Civil and Military (unlimited) on Men without any Degree of Merit, except their having been avowed Enemies to the Family on the Throne.

To yield the Appointment of all the Judges, the Commission of the Great Seal, and even of the Lord High Chancellor, to Lord Mansfield's universal Power, *his own and his Family's distinguished Loyalty*, and his inviolate Observance of the fundamental Laws of this Realm; whereby, the whole Law Department being under his absolute Direction, we may soon be in a fair Way of enjoying our Lives, Liberties, and Properties, with the greatest Security.

To pay no Attention, except in Cases of Kindred, to filling up the Right Reverend Bench, as it must be the Duty of the Prime Minister to hold this Point in utter Contempt; that all Kinds of Vice, Immorality, and Infidelity, may flourish, the more easily to controul the Needy and Vicious of all Denominations.

N. B. Sir ROBERT WALPOLE filled these two Departments with the greatest *Dis*-Honour and *In*-Dignity to the Crown: as for Example.

Chancellors.	Chiefs and other Judges.	Church.
KING,	KING,	HOUGH,
TALBOT,	RAYMOND,	BOULTER,
HARDWICKE,	HARDWICKE,	GIBSON,
	LEE,	BENSON,
Rolls.	COMYNS,	HOADLEY,
JEKYLL,	PARKER,	POTTER,
VERNEY,	WILLS,	SHERLOCK,
FORTESCUE,	BURNET,	HARE,
STRANGE,	FOSTER,	HERRING.

To countenance, close under the Royal Palace and in Defiance of Law, excessive Gaming at Cards and Dice amongst the first Nobility and Gentry, to the utter Ruin of many great Families; thereby the better to secure their servile Dependance on the Court.

To establish yearly Lotteries, seldom practiced by former Ministers but in Time of War, or on some extraordinary Occasion; to suffer at least *Twenty Lottery-Offices* where *One* used to be sufficient; whereby a Variety of Tricks are practiced, in open Defiance of Law, to the manifest Injury and even Destruction of great Numbers of his Majesty's useful Subjects, such as laborious Mechanics, Servants, &c.

To suffer the *Stock-Jobbing Act* to continue Year after Year *unamended,*[1] notwithstanding the fatal Consequences from so shameful a Neglect appear every Day more and more shocking; such as numberless Suicides, Bankruptcies, with the greatest Scenes of Distress which naturally follow; public Credit mortally wounded, Confidence between Individuals destroyed, and our Trade and Manufactures stagnated.

Quære, Whether the late Earl of GUILFORD[2] did not follow this infamous Practice of *Stock-Jobbing* in 'Change-Alley almost every Day for many

1. Parliament had first passed the act that the author(s) had in mind in 1733, during the reign of George II, and it was subsequently renewed. It targeted "stock-jobbers"–in modern parlance, brokers who invested in highly speculative stocks, jeopardizing the public credit as well as private fortunes—but had so many loopholes that it did little to solve the problem, and may even have compounded it. Its inadequacies were a recurring grievance: see, for example, Thomas Mortimer's *Every Man His Own Broker*, 8th ed. (London: S. Hooper, 1775; orig. ed., 1761), which had been reissued just as *The Crisis* hit full stride. Its second chapter is titled "Of the mystery and iniquity of Stock-jobbing, in all its various branches."

2. This is one of the more interesting allusions in the entire run of *The Crisis*. It could be dismissed as wrong in the narrow sense because the first Earl of Guilford was still very much alive. His son would not succeed him for another fourteen years (see n. I.1 supra). But did the Earl's investments in trade run to the level of a "stock-jobber" (for which see the preceding footnote)? Matthew Kilburn, now with the History of Parliament Trust and who wrote the essay on the Earl for the *Oxford DNB*, 11:88–89, has not encountered any such activities. Nor did they sound familiar to Dr. Ruth Paley, also of the History of Parliament Trust. Perhaps this is just one instance of where *The Crisis* dipped to the level of a modern-day tabloid, making no clear distinction between innuendo and reliable information.

years before his Death, and in so low and pitiful a Way, as a dirty *Jew Broker* would have been ashamed of?

To plead the strictest Oeconomy, when the public Treasure is apparently squandering for the most infamous Purposes.

To shew less Regard to the Navy, our natural Bulwark, and the Nation's favourite Service, than to the Army, which, if not timely checked, may one Day or other be made use of for enslaving this *Free People, as they were formerly styled.*

To suffer the Flower of our *East-India* Trade to be uninterruptedly undetermined by Thousands of Smugglers; the Exchequer at the same Time being robbed of immense Sums, which would otherwise flow therein, from *Tea principally* and other Articles charged with the highest Duties.

To be an inanimate Spectator of such disgraceful and daring Abuses and Outrages: to wink at the Revenue-Officers and Military (employed for preventing them) receiving Bribes, in Imitation of their Betters, for facilitating Practices so injurious to fair Trade; to harangue upon the Insufficiency of our Finances, *in Trifles*, where Liberality and Justice claim the fairest Title; and whilst *Hundreds of Thousands of Pounds* are annually lost to the State by such criminal Neglects.

To take no Step whatsoever towards lessening or suppressing those numerous *Gangs* of *Banditti*, frequently consisting from 30 to 50, well mounted, well armed, and fully laden, who never before such *happy Times* dared *thus accoutred* to parade into the very Heart of the Capital.

To screen Men from Justice who have plundered the MOGUL'S harmless Subjects of Millions, and caused the shedding Rivers of their Blood to satiate their unbounded Avarice; whose immense and ill-acquired Wealth, so far from being punished, procure them Honours and Dignities, Seats in Parliament for themselves and Friends at any Expence, raise the Prices of Lands beyond their natural Value, and gain them the Respect and Protection of those who ought to be the foremost in stamping a Mark of Infamy, so justly due to their thus prostituting our national Honour.

To vindicate the Commitment of the most unprovoked and unjustifiable Barbarities upon a Colony of unoffending *Savages*, Subjects to the Sovereign, with the apparent Design of giving the fruitful Lands they possess to the rapacious Scotch:—As in a Case similar to that of *St. Vincent*'s.

To vindicate employing the Military in massacring six or seven, and wounding as many more, of his Majesty's innocent and unarmed Subjects, under the Pretence of quelling a tumultuous Mob; to screen the Perpetrators thereof from Justice, and even to glory in the Deed, by *Thanks* to the Assassins:—As in a Case similar to that in *St. George's Fields*.

To vindicate the Pardon of two notorious Murderers, convicted by the Laws of their Country; and after their Conviction, in order to give a colourable Sanction to so unexampled a Pardon, to unprecedently establish a Jury of *ten unsworn Surgeons* to reverse so solemn a Verdict:—As in a Case similar to that of *Balfe* and *McQuirk*, the *Brentford* Ruffians.

To vindicate the Pardon of two other notorious convicted Murderers (upon the Back of the former) at the infamous Sollicitation of several of the *Noble* Gallants to the Sister of such Convicts:—As in a Case similar to that of the two *Kennedys*.[3]

To countenance the Pardon of a convicted and most abandoned Sodomite:—As in a Case similar to that of *Robert Jones*.[4]

---

3. In February 1770 Patrick and Matthew Kennedy were convicted and sentenced to death (while two others were acquitted) in a trial at the Old Bailey for killing watchman John Bigby on the Westminster bridge three months before. They received a royal pardon, were ordered to be transported to America, then had their sentences commuted; critics claimed that they had only been spared because their sister, a London prostitute, had persuaded her high-placed clients to use their influence on her brothers' behalf.

4. Tried in the Old Bailey in July 1772 and sentenced to death for sodomizing a twelve-year-old boy, Jones was pardoned by the king and transported out of England the following October, the sentence stipulating that he never return. Since there was some question as to the boy's consent—which, legally speaking, he could not give—there were uncomfortable questions raised over the nature of homosexual relationships.

To trust for the Cure against the exorbitant Price of Provisions to mere Chance, by evading all Enquiries into the original Cause, from whence alone a Remedy to so dreadful a Calamity is to be found; to be deaf to the Lamentations of the starving Manufacturers, and to consider their Emigration into foreign Countries and our Colonies, as a Matter of no sort of Consequence to the Strength and Wealth of a commercial People.

To permit, out of downright Supineness, a District within the Bills of Mortality, consisting of 70 to 80,000 Souls, to continue for many successive Years with scarce a Magistrate or Constable to preserve the Peace:—As in the Case of *Spital-Fields*.

To persevere in the same Inattention with respect to the innumerable, illegal, and wicked Places of public Entertainment, although the most salutary Laws subsist for restraining them, as if it was the Interest of a Prime Minister, and the Glory of his Sovereign, to encourage the most extravagant Dissipation and Licentiousness; the Magistrates by such Example being *lulled asleep*, where GAIN is not the Object.

To give a more shining Lustre to his Accomplishments, let him, when the People are completely oppressed, screw out of their Vitals some *Hundred Thousands of Pounds* without Account, to supply the Deficiency of the *Civil List*, squandered in useless Places and Pensions; in bribing the Subject with the very Money levied upon them.

N O W or N E V E R!

B R I T O N S STRIKE H O M E !

No P O P E R Y,

No S L A V E R Y,   No FOREIGN T R O O P S,

No EXPORTING C A T T L E,   No S T A R V I N G,

No S C O T C H M I N I S T R Y,

No BRIBED P A R L I A M E N T,

No P L A C E M E N,   No P E N S I O N E R S,

But L I B E R T Y, LAW, and C O N S T I T U T I O N

B R I T O N S Revenge your Wrongs.

N. B. CASCA's spirited Letter against the Jesuitical *Wesley*, and the pensioned *Johnson* is received, and shall be made the Subject of our next Number.

Printed and Published for the AUTHORS by T. W. SHAW, Fleet-Street, opposite Anderton's Coffee-House, where Letters to the Publisher will be thankfully received.

T H E

C R I S I S

NUMBER LXI   *To be continued Weekly,*

DURING THE PRESENT BLOODY CIVIL WAR IN AMERICA.

SATURDAY, MARCH 12, 1776[1]   [Price Two-pence Half-penny.

————Hunc tota *armenta* sequuntur.

VIRG.[2]

As *Johnson noddles*, right or wrong's inferr'd;
He *stalks* the Leader of the *scribbling Herd*.

O F all the various ways by which *courtly and ministerial* Partisans have endeavoured, or pretended to serve their *King* and *Country*, there is but one way of serving them effectually; that is, neither by *bleeding*, by *voting*, nor by *writing* down the *Constitution*: but by *administering Restoratives*. Those who have endeavoured to write it down, are among the worst Traitors. Their Iniquity can admit of no excuse; because it is attended with all the Guilt of the most deliberate and serious Premeditation. They are not irritated and inflamed by the insulting approaches of an Enemy in the Field, or by a vigorous Opposition of *Patriots* in the Senate. Theirs is the cool Work of the pensive and sequestered Closet; the

1. This issue was misdated; it should have been March 16, 1776, as the printer noted in the closing of the next issue (on p. 549). For dating problems in general see I.1.

2. The herd (mindlessly) follows the leaders, from Virgil's *Aeneid*, Book 1.

infernal Product of a prostituted Pen, an itching Palm, and a rotten Heart. They are base enough to write for *Tyranny*, in Opposition to their Understandings, their Reading, their Reason, their inward Conviction, and their Conscience. When I say this, it is with an Eye only to the Head of this scribbling Fraternity, the great *Doctor Johnson*, and his pious Shadow Mr. *John Wesley*. I consider them but as *one*. As to the common Herd of *ministerial Hackneys*, they are but Echoes of their Master *Johnson*, without professing themselves so, as the Reverend Pastor Mr. *Wesley* does most zealously. *He* is the "Mimic of his Master's dance," the professed Admirer and Abridger of that elaborate Tract, *Taxation no Tyranny*, which has (together with Mr. Wesley's little *Two-penny* Manual) been already answered, more largely, but, I hope, neither more satisfactorily, nor more explicitly. I shall confine myself to the faithful *Abridgement* (by Mr. Wesley) only, which I took up casually the other Day. As it is manifestly intended for the use of the *Myriads of Moorfields* (an enthusiastic, hot-headed, clamorous Body, and therefore fit for despotic Purposes) though it excited my Attention for a Moment in a former Paper, yet I really think, as Mr. *Wesley* says, that I shall serve my King and Country, in good earnest, by animadverting upon it once more. So rank a Poison in so compact a form, calls for an Antidote in as small a Body as itself. Mr. Wesley has worked his Master's Tract into a small Drop of Comfort for his *Tribe*; my Observations upon his pigmy Composition will make but a little Pill, which I beg leave to present (like all my others) GRATIS to the Public.

To begin with Mr. *Wesley*'s Title of his Tract. He calls it, A CALM ADDRESS. It is the great Business and Master-stroke of all *Art* to conceal *Art*.—Under this specious Mark of a *Calm* Peace-maker, the reverend Epitomizer most insnaringly uses all his sacred Authority to bias his Flock in favour of *ministerial* and *despotic Measures*. I use Mr. *Wesley*'s new Edition, corrected and enlarged: in the Preface he professes to serve his *King* and *Country*:—but mark gentle Reader, that this Service can not be effected by endeavouring to instill *false Principles* into either; even such exploded Principles as Sir *Robert Filmer*'s Treatise upon Government abounds with.

Mr. Wesley asserts "that they are no *Slaves* who enjoy both civil and religious Liberty." I admit the Truth of this general Assertion; but it cannot be applied to *America*, who is now suffering in her Frontiers all the miseries of War for *constitutional Resistance* and in her back Settlements sees *Popery* established by Act of Parliament, that she may be driven by *Papists* in her rear, upon the Bayonets of *Tyrants*, *Parricides*, and *Assassins* in her Front. This *ministerial Divine* is then pleased to inform us, "who is a *Slave*,"—he points to the *Negræ*. But can it be any alleviation to the distressed *American* to behold another *Slave* of a darker Complexion than himself? Is this any Argument, or any Justification for introducing *Slavery* among *free Subjects?* Even the subjecting *Negræs* to Slavery, is against the Law of Reason, the Law of Nature, the Law of Nations, the Law of GOD, and the Laws of England.

In the next Paragraph, we are told what is the real difference between *Liberty* and *Slavery*. "It consists (says Mr. *Wesley*) in going where we will, and in the enjoying the *Fruits* of our Labour." Or in other Words, it consists in mere *Loco-motion*, and in the secure enjoyment of what we earn by the Sweat of our own Brows. We shall live to see Englishmen restrained from using this first Species of Liberty, should they *secede* (as probably they will) in large Bodies, to *America* within a very few Years; and a contrary Doctrine to this will be asserted *then*, perhaps even by Dr. *Johnson* and Mr. *Wesley* themselves; as to the other Species of Liberty, if *Money* is a Fruit of our Labour, we have already seen the most despotic Attempts made to wrest it from the *Americans without their Consent*. The English Government will not allow them the Right of *giving and granting* what they earn by their own Labour.

Mr. *Wesley* then arraigns the great *Montesquieu*, and *Judge Blackston*;[3] they prove too much it seems; be that as it may, since they are no Advocates for

---

3. Blackstone's *Commentaries*, as I mentioned above (see the Introduction and n. I.11), were as highly regarded in the colonies as they were in the mother country, even if, as John Phillip Reid contended, Blackstone's view represented a shift toward a "command" constitution and away from the constitution of "custom" favored by an earlier generation of English jurists like Coke. (See n. XXVI.2 supra.) For a counter to Reid's view see Jeffrey Goldsworthy, *The Sovereignty of Parliament* (Oxford: Clarendon Press, 1999); and a different approach altogether in Daniel J. Boorstin, *The Mysterious Science of the Law* (Cambridge: Harvard University Press, 1941).

Despotism, I shall not consider them as Opponents. Mr. *Wesley*'s Candour induces him to confess, that *he* only speaks according to the *Light* he has at present:—But why would a Man of his Calling and good Sense, as well as Reading, stoop to light his farthing Candle at *Doctor Johnson*'s Lamp, which was, even at that Instant, expiring in Stench? He abjures all lucrative Views; but could he seriously think that by inculcating *Anti-Revolution* Notions among his Congregation, he could really serve his *King*, who owes his Crown, and his Country who owes her present Constitution, to the happy *Revolution?*—Let us hear him further. He supposes in the outset of his *Address*, that all Emigrants owe the Origin of their Settlements to the *King's Charter*, "permitting them (as he says) to settle in some far Country." But the Truth is, that the first Settlers in *New England* had no *Charter* at first: They were *Puritans*, who, instead of emigrating under the Sanction of *Royalty*, flew from the Face of *Tyrannic Royalty* and *Oppression*. They made their first Settlement, (whereby they formed a Community distinct from their Mother Country) entirely at their own Expence; independent either of the Favours, Influence, or Authority of the Crown of England; yet to this *Authority* Mr. *Wesley* tells us they still continue subject. I admit it, as far as that *Authority* goes; but it must have been in consequence of a Charter obtained *subsequent* to their Settlement. But what was this *Authority?* no Authority that could *tax* them, for it was the *King's* alone. Mr. *Wesley*, conscious of this, artfully slides into the next Paragraph (p. 8.) from the Term *Authority*, to the Term *supreme Power*, as the Master *Johnson* does in his larger Lucubration; and then, as if the *King's* single Authority, and the *supreme Power* (i. e. the *King* in his Parliament) were one and the same Authority, he proceeds thus: "*Considering this* nothing can be more plain than that the *supreme Power* in England, has a right of laying *any Tax* upon them (the *Americans*) for any End beneficial to the whole Empire." Here is Reason and Argument! That because the *Americans* are subject to the *King's* controul under his Charter (that is, to an Observance of the Charter) *therefore*, they are subject to *unlimited Taxation* by the *supreme Power*, that is, by the King and Parliament. This is as much as to say, that because the *Executive Power* (the King) may do one thing; *therefore*, the *legislative and executive Power* (the King and Parliament) *joined together*, may do another. Upon this doughty Argument rest the whole Merits of

Dr. *Johnson's* laboured Tract, *Taxation no Tyranny*, which procured him a Doctor's Degree at Oxford, and a double Pension from the Minister. Mr. *Wesley's Calm Address* is but the Echo of it. Let us pursue the Sound again till we lose it. Mr. Wesley as if he had laid undeniable Premises, proceeds as Master of the Field. He attacks the *Americans* with this Argument, drawn, as it were, from an Absurdity. "If a Freeman, says he, cannot be *taxed* without his own Consent, neither can he be punished without it." The Argument will not hold. In a State of Nature every Individual is his own Avenger, his own Judge and Executioner. Upon entering into Society he tacitly yields up this personal Right to the supreme Power with whom he stipulates for Protection. That Protection, and the Dispensation of Rewards and Punishments, should flow from the supreme Hand, is the very Essence of Society. Were its Members still to remain Judges in their own Cause, it could exist no longer; all must be Anarchy and Confusion. Their natural Right therefore, which is no longer tenable by a Subject without the total Loss of the most substantial Benefits, is tacitly and necessarily yielded up to the supreme Power for the Good of the whole Community. But was it ever yet supposed, or can it with reason be asserted, that Individuals, when they form Societies, ever mean to yield up their present and future *Property*, the fluctuating eventual Acquisitions of their own Labours, to the sole will and pleasure of the supreme Power? Such a Supposition is absurd unless *all* are made for *one*; besides, the Demands of the Sovereign Power upon the Subject cannot, in justice, be unlimited, they must, in justice, be proportioned not only to the occasional Necessities of the State, but to the different Circumstances of the several Members; who must otherwise have exchanged their natural *free State* for a *State of Slavery*, if nothing remains to them which they can call their own. *Despotic* Government was never yet embraced; it has ever been usurped. This is one of its constant Badges, that a Subject should have no *peculium*, or Property of his own. Civilians tell us that *Slaves* can have none; but the having, or not having this, is one of the chief Distinctions made by all Writers on civil Law, between the *Freeman* and the *Slave*.

This *Peculium* is really and truely the very Thing which Mr. Wesley calls the *Fruit of a Man's Labours*; it can be no other. If then, a *Freeman* (to be a *Freeman*) must necessarily have some free Will and some Property (nay all his acquired Property) in his own disposal, why should he not be at Liberty to exercise that free Will in *giving* and *granting* for the use of the State; what must be his *own*, and only his, to give and grant? If he has neither this Degree of free Will, nor this Property left, then all must belong to this *supreme Power* (so often founded in our Ears by *Dr. Johnson*, and his Pupil *Wesley*) and all Mankind who have once entered into a State of civil Society must be neither more nor less than *Slaves*.

But Mr. *Wesley* (persevering like the *Doctor* and his ministerial *Paymaster*, in his mistakes and fallacies) insists "that the reception of any *Law* draws after it, by a Chain which cannot be broken the necessity of admitting *Taxation*." I think, I have just proved the very contrary to be true; I will therefore, only add one Position which is universally granted by all Writers on Civil and Municipal Law, and particularly by all English Lawyers, "That the Renunciation of a Subject's Right in one Case, or more, is not a Renunciation *in all*.

I now come to Mr. *Wesley*'s third Section, where he encounters one most true Position, with as much ferocity and assurance of Success, as *Quixot* did the Windmill. It is this: "That every *Freeman* is governed by Laws to which he has *consented*." This is most true, if by the Term *Consent*, is understood either an actual, or virtual, an express, or necessarily imply'd *Consent*. These must necessarily have obtained at first, in the Origin of every Government, between the *supreme Power* and the *People*. It must otherwise have been *Usurpation*, not *Government*; which always pre-supposes *a previous Compact*, either express, or imply'd, or both, between the Sovereign Power and the Subject. Every sensible and able Writer upon Government declares the same: Grotius, Puffendorff, Locke, Sidney, Milton, Nath. Bacon, Montesquieu, St. Armand, Archerley, and others.[4]

4. The authors no doubt meant George St. Amand, *An Historical Essay on the Legislative Power of England* (London, 1767; orig. ed., 1725) and Roger Acherley's *The Britannic Constitution*, 2nd ed. (London: T. Oborn, 1759; orig. ed., 1727). St. Amand was listed on the title page as "Of the Inner Temple"; see n. XXIV.6 supra for more on Acherley. Both treatises fall within the ancient constitution school of thought, contending that the king and people had always been joined by a reciprocal arrangement, a compact

In contradiction to these great Authorities, to History, Reason, common Sense, the general Opinion of Mankind, the essential difference between Freedom and Slavery, nay, in Contradiction to the Letter and Spirit of the British Laws and Constitution (under which the *Colonists* as well as we are born) in defiance of all these, *Doctor Johnson*, and his Scholar *Wesley*, pronounce this magisterial Sentence:—*"Absolutely false."*

[*To be concluded in our next.*]

Printed and Published for the AUTHORS by T. W. SHAW, Fleet-Street, opposite Anderton's Coffee-House, where Letters to the Publisher will be thankfully received.

to be honored by both parties. As Acherley put it, "tis the *Britannic Constitution* that gives this Kingdom a Lustre, above all other Nations." (p. vi) The Glorious Revolution, he emphasized, was a reaffirmation of rather than a departure from an arrangement between governor and governed that, unfortunately, had been violated by far too many monarchs, going back at least to King John 1.

THE

CRISIS

NUMBER LXII   *To be continued Weekly,*

DURING THE PRESENT BLOODY CIVIL WAR IN AMERICA.

SATURDAY, MARCH 23, 1776   [Price Two-pence Half-penny.

[Concluded from our last.]

MR. *Wesley* asks,—"How has any Man consented to those Laws which were made before he was born?" I answer, *virtually.* He has consented by his *Ancestors.* Why do Laws bind now, which were made three hundred Years ago? Because the *supreme Power* still survives; it is, by a rational Fiction, supposed never to die. By as rational a Fiction of Law the deceased *Ancestor* is supposed still to survive in his *Heirs*; otherwise, how could the *Heir* be bound by the solemn Acts and Covenants of his *Ancestor?* Every Man's *Heirs* are considered in Law as a Part (a surviving Part) of himself. For this very reason the brave *Americans* justly think themselves bound to deliver down to their Posterity such original Rights as they neither have, nor possibly could intend to surrender, by accepting a Charter from the *Crown.* Though *they* and *we* have consented *virtually,* or (as Mr. *Wesley* terms it) *passively,* to such Laws as bound our *Ancestors* (to the Laws at the *Revolution* for instance) yet by those very Laws, and by the Law of right Reason, (the Fountain of all other Laws) both *they* and *we* are bound to be *active,* and not *passive,* when the *inherent Right* of disposing of *our own,* of the *Fruits of our own Labours* (as Mr. *Wesley* says) is disputed with us; nay absolutely denied us. When I use the Word *us*, I mean to speak as an Advocate for *America*. The *Americans* do not complain of those Laws which bound their *Ancestors*, but they rightly insist upon being treated like free *Agents*, in such Laws as are at this instant intended to bind, and subject their *own peculiar Property*, acquired in a Community distinct from Great Britain. They will not sit like *passive Cyphers* with their Hands behind them, whilst their *Money* is taken out of their Pockets *without their own Consent*. This would argue the greatest pusillanimity, the basest inattention to Posterity, Freedom, and their Country.

This indubitable Right of disposing of *his own*, every Man does and must bring with him into a distinct Community, because every *Freeman* has it in himself previous to his Entrance into Society, and unless he gives it up it still remains in him. Mr. *Wesley* asserts, "that the Settlers in *America* had no Right to erect a *Legislature*, any more than those who have no Vote in England, have a Right to erect a *Parliament*." This he asserts contrary to the constant established usage in all the English Colonies (without exception) where legislative Assemblies of their own have not only been held from the first Settlements, but countenanced by the royal Instructions to the several Governors. This would hardly have been the Case, if the *Crown* had thought that the *Colonies* had no Right to form a *Legislature* of their own. So little does Mr. *Wesley* know of the Subject on which he writes; but he follows his Master *Johnson's* Steps, right or wrong. He is equally unfortunate in his application of the *American* Case to that of Persons who have no Vote in *England*. Is there no difference between the Case of a *distinct Community*, and that of Subjects still resident under the old Government, within the same Territory? In the first Instance, the Government is not as yet settled, nor can without such a *distinct Legislature*, be conveniently settled: In the other, it has been long established, and must not be overturned.

Mr. *Wesley* in his 7th Section, allows the *Americans* all they claim under royal Charters, "*Provided*, those Privileges are consistent with the *British Constitution*." Note, Reader, how very careful *Dr. Johnson* and *Mr. Wesley* are, to *exclude* the *Americans* from all *Benefits*, unless they are strictly agreeable to the *British Constitution*; yet, when these People are to bear *Burthens*, (*Taxes*) these may be laid without regard to the *Constitution*, that is to say, without the Consent of the People; and even their *Lives*, and *Liberties* and *Properties* in general, may be disposed of in the same Manner. This Mr. *Wesley* expressly asserts, page 10, and p. 20. This the reprobated Doctrine of Sir *Robert Filmer*, which has never dared to show it's Face since the great Mr. *Locke* opposed and confuted it, till *Doctor Johnson* wrote, and the Reverend Mr. *Wesley* held the Candle to him.

"The Legislature of a Colony (says *Mr. Wesley*) is like the *Vestry of a large Parish*, which may assess its own Inhabitants, but is still liable to *Taxes* laid by supreme Authority." I have shewn the difference in a former Paper; but to add another Word; The *Vestry* and *Parishioners* are all but a Part of one great Community, *taxed* on account of Property acquired by *themselves*, within one and the same Territory, under one and the same Legislature where they are actually represented, and entitled to no distinct Legislature of their own. The *Americans* form a *distinct* and distant Community, where they acquire a distinct Property, out of the Territory of Great Britain, entitled to a *distinct Legislature* of their own, and exercising distinct legislative Powers Time out of Mind, in all Cases relative to *internal* Burthens and civil Œconomy, and this too with the constant Assent of both King and Parliament.—'Till *Mr. Wesley* can prove that *America* lies in *Great Britain*, his Comparison will not hold.

Mr. *Wesley* has the Modesty in his 8th Section, to confess a gross Mistake in his former Edition. It would be more candid to recant his whole Supplement to Dr. *Johnson's* larger Work.

In his 10th Section, he seems to tremble at the Thought of a "*Commonwealth*, which is to be erected in England by a *few Men*." A wondrous Revolution this! like that of *Bayes* in the *Rehearsal*, to be effected, we know not by whom, or how, or why. But to treat this phantom of the Brain more seriously: A *Commonwealth* certainly followed the *Decollation* of that *unhappy Dupe*, that *persevering* Tyrant, Charles the First: but does Mr. *Wesley* see a stronger likeness between the reign of that weak Prince and his present Majesty, than there is between *America* and a *Parish Vestry?* Charles attempted to govern without a Parliament---George the Third never did; the Views of King and Parliament were *then* very different. The Parliament *then* were against the King and endeavoured to save the Constitution; Charles wished to destroy it. His present Majesty never fails of having a *Majority* of his Parliament with him, because the Views of King and Parliament are *now* the same. Is this the reason why *Mr. Wesley* trembles at the dreadful Thought of an approaching *Commonwealth*? *Oppression* is the Cause of every well founded *Revolution*; Monarchies may fall, and Commonwealths may rise from their Ashes. But Commonwealths ever are, and ever must be founded upon *Virtue*: They are the greatest Favourers both of civil and religious Liberty, and their ruling Principle, *Equality*, is better adapted, if not to bloodshed, yet to Peace and Commerce, than the despotic supremacy of a Tyrant *King* and a corrupt *Majority* of Parliament, formed into a determined Junto for the Destruction of civil Liberty.

I shall endeavour now to answer the several Interrogatories which *Mr. Wesley* puts to the *Americans* in his 11th Section.

"Can you hope for a more desirable *Form* of Government?"

Mr. Pope answered this Question long ago.

> "For *Forms* of Government let Fools contest;
> That which is best *administered* is best."

"What more *religious* Liberty can you desire than that which you enjoy already?"

Do you mean in *Canada*, Sir, where Popery is established by Act of Parliament?

"What civil Liberty can you desire which you are not already *possessed of*?"

We desire not to be *dispossessed*.

"Do you not sit, without *restraint*, every Man under his own *Vine*?"

We cannot say without *restraint*; for we are obliged to defend our *Vineyards*. The late blasts of *Tyranny* have so sower'd the *Grapes*, that 'the People's Teeth are set on Edge.' "

"Would the being independent of *England* make you more free?"

We only wish to be independent of *Tyranny.*

"Do you not enjoy the *Fruit* of your Labours?"

The *Fruit* of our Labours is our Wealth and Property: These you have already told us (page 10.) we have ceded to the King and Parliament; who have (you say) the Power of disposing, *without our Consent,* of both our *Lives, Liberties,* and *Properties.* The King and Parliament have intimated the same, though not quite in such direct Terms, but their Cannons speak the plainest Language in the Field.

"Would a *Republican* Government give you more Liberty?"

No Government can give us less than that which leaves us nothing that we can call our *own.*

"*Republics* (you say) shew no Mercy."

True, not to Sodomites and hired Slaughters of the People; but let *America* and *Wilkes* declare the Mercy which whole Territories, if not *passive,* and Individuals, if not *dumb,* have received from a Government which is no *Republic.*

The wholesome Advice which Mr. *Wesley* administers in his 12th and 13th Sections to *America,* must be well received from the same Mouth which tells them in his 4th Section, that their *Lives, Liberties,* and *Properties,* are at the disposal of the King and Parliament. A Doctrine to which the servile Bench of *Bishops* would hardly subscribe unanimously: Nay, I doubt, whether some of the *Crown Lawyers* would not hesitate, not, perhaps, from Conscience, but from Shame.

With the same strength of Features Mr. *Wesley* declares, that the Advocates for *America* have "exclaimed against Grievances, which either *never existed,* or are aggravated *above Measure.*" Did the *Fishery* (or *Famine*) Bill never exist? Does not the *Perseverance* of King & Parliament still exist? Have not Famine, Popery, Sword, and Fire, been carried into *America* by Act of Parliament? Are not these the worst of temporal Miseries? When these Grievances are let loose among Subjects, can the complaining

Sufferers be said to aggravate them *above Measure?* But, I congratulate myself upon my happy arrival at Mr. *Wesley*'s pious *Per-oration*, exhorting the oppressed *Americans* "to follow *after Peace.*" Smitten upon one Cheek, they are to turn the other:—As if the Sufferers were the Aggressors, he admonishes them with his parting Breath, "to fear GOD, and honour the *King.*" Mr. *Wesley* has given his Opinion freely (p. 14.) to the *Americans*; I take Leave to give my Opinion as freely to him. This it is: That Subject may be truely said to *fear God*, who defends with firmness and intrepidity, his *Life*, his *Liberty*, his *Property*, and the *Dignity of his Nature*, against every Effort of *Tyranny* and *Oppression*. When these Gifts are inhumanly invaded, Heaven itself is daringly insulted; for the due Employment of these distinguishing and peculiar Blessings Man is accountable to God; and therefore it would be the height of Impiety and Presumption, to submit them tamely to the disposal of any Power upon Earth. They are to be enjoyed and used to the Honour and Glory of our Maker; should we make a servile Offering of these choice Bounties at the feet of *Man*, we should offend and affront GOD, dishonour the *King*, enslave our Posterity, injure our Country, and debase our Nature.

C A S C A.

P. S. Mr. *Wesley* seems fond of *Secrets* (p. 17.) I will tell him one, known as yet, only at *St. James's.*—A considerable Part of our Provision-Transports, sent to the ROYAL TROOPS at *Boston*, are taken by the *Americans*, Guns and all; but the *ministerial Contractors* are to be paid, for all that, larger Prices than better Provisions sell for by retail in Newgate-Market. Another *Secret*;—*Press Warrants* are soon to issue for manning our second (or rather *third*) Fleet against *America*. Not a single Sailor enters willingly: They are of the same Opinion with our Soldiers, that *English* Throats ought to cut by *Foreigners*; especially by *Hanoverians*, whose *little Electorate* hangs like a *dependent Cob-web* upon the *British Crown*. As to the *ministerial Lies* circulated about the defeat of General *Montgomery* at *Quebec*, I give Mr. *Wesley* and his *Masters* Joy of them; but as that *Divine* deals in *probabilities* (p. 14.) no less flimsey than his *Logic*, I should be glad to know, what *probability* there is, that the *Canadians* should have *deserted* General *Montgomery*, as our News Writers say, on Account of the inclemency of the Weather. Would not a *Scotch Highlander*, who sleeps all Night upon a Mountain, and finds his Hair frozen down to it in the Morning, endure the inclemency of the Weather better than a *Macaroni* of the *Guards?* The Case is the same between the *Canadians* born in the back Settlements, and the Natives in the Frontiers and mid-land Parts of the Continent of North America. If our *Ministry* will *Lie*, they should remember PROBABILITY.

Errata. No. LXI. was by mistake dated 12th *March* instead of the 16th.

Printed and Published for the AUTHORS by T. W. SHAW, Fleet-Street, opposite Anderton's Coffee-House, where Letters to the Publisher will be thankfully received.

THE

CRISIS

NUMBER LXIII   *To be continued Weekly,*

DURING THE PRESENT BLOODY CIVIL WAR IN AMERICA.

SATURDAY, MARCH 30, 1776   [Price Two-pence Half-penny.

> Th' abuse of *Greatness* is, when it disjoins
> *Remorse* from *Power.*——

I SHALL confine my present thoughts chiefly to the *tyranny* of government, not in the least intimidated or convinced by the elaborate Doctor *Johnson's ipse dixit*, or by the Reverend Mr. *Wesley's* pontifical *Amen*. The Doctor may besmear the truth with sophistry, the master of arts may follow him with his priestly *trowel*, closing chinks, but truth will still prevail; neither pedant, enthusiast, jesuit or a *Mansfield*, can disguise her long. They may audaciously take upon them (like the *Devil* in Milton) "*to make the worse appear the better part;*[1] but their wicked

---

1. Book II of John Milton's *Paradise Lost*, which was widely available, as an individual title or in various collections of Milton's works, includes:

"But all was false and hollow, though his tongue
Dropt manna, and could make the worse appear
The better reason, to perplex and dash
Maturest counsels: for his thoughts were low."

labours must be lost, their fallacies must be detected, their infamous toils will be recorded, and their memories must be offensive to posterity.

Where is the man of reason or education (except the servile *Wesley*) who will expose himself to universal derision and contempt by denying this eternal truth: "That governments are instituted, not for the sake of *governors,* but of the *governed?*"—Yet Mr. *Wesley* in his calm address (p. 10.) is not ashamed to assert the contrary: he has the ignorance and the impudence to tell us, that our *all,* "our lives, our liberties, and our properties are, *without our consent,* at the absolute disposal of king and parliament.[2]—Neither *Mansfield* nor *Johnson,* have ventured so far: They have told us, however, that it behoves us now to contend with *America,* not to support our *right* (for that has been given up) but to maintain our *power.*

This is the grand principle of *tyranny,* this the vantage-ground (as *Lord Bacon* says) upon which every *despot* erects his bulwark against the liberties of the *people.* Upon this tremendous eminence flamed the bloody swords of *Cæsar, Phillip, Alexander,* and the mad *Swede Charles.*[3] Our *Charles* the first was struggling to ascend it, but fell in the attempt; that detested monarch, that real mass of perjury, ambition and *pious hypocrisy,* was not permitted by providence to satiate himself with *English blood*; with all the theory of *tyranny* at heart, he was but a pigmy in success to the *Roman,* the two *Macedonians,* and the *Swede.* These *despots* like the *fat* infatuated *Nimrod* of our day, were hunters of mankind, flattered by designing, selfish, sycophants into false ideas of *princely greatness* they aspired to be *Gods,* they thought,

---

Perhaps the author(s) worked from memory, conflating Milton with another source (where "part" takes the place of "reason"); or, more likely, the author(s) reworked the passage, as other passages had been in other issues. An earlier reference to *Paradise Lost* was more correct (see n. XXIII.1 supra).

2. John Wesley, *A Calm Address to Our American Colonies,* new ed. (London: Robert Hawes, 1775), p. 10.

3. Phillip II of Macedon is joined with his son Alexander the Great and Charles XII to Caesar as just another in a long line of tyrants who have blighted the western world. Note the allusion to Amurath later in the essay (and see n. LXIII.4 infra); all are foils to the proper British monarch who is committed to the rule of law and protection of the people.

(as Mr. *Wesley* instructs his *saints*) that every subject held his life, his liberty, and property, at their disposal, this was their *creed*, and they shewed their political *faith*, by their infernal *works*. Inflated with pride, and burning with an insatiable lust of *power*; they carried disolation, like a whirlwind, thro' the globe, like the tyrants of our nation, they provoked the resistance of the innocent, that they might indulge the kingly passion of revenge, they placed the glory of all sovereignty (as we do) not in *subordination* but in *slavery*, not in *submission,* but in *carnage*, they rejected (like us) all *supplication,* till they had depopulated the countries which they chose to ravage. From them we have learned to prefer the tribute of *slaves* to the benevolence of *freemen*, to follow the most unjust demands with inhuman *perseverance;* and without the colour or pretence of *right*, to invade with all our power, and to exterminate without remorse.

Thus do *Britons* (once magnanimous) follow the odious example of barbarous *ambition* and heathen *pride*, in an enlightened age, and a Christian country.

All civilized nations must think this the reign not of a *Brunswick* but of an *Amurath*.[4] We are now in the midst of a civil war with *America,* from whence it is agreed on all hands that no public *good* can possibly arise. Whether we conquer or are conquered, the decision must be equally fatal to the interest of Great Britain. We never shall, we cannot conquer (so truly brave is the *American* spirit) with out extermination; if that could be effected (which is impossible) what kind of dominion would the crown of England have to boast of upon that Continent? let every

4. This allusion is perhaps the best example in the entire series of the author(s)' literary sophistication—*and* the expectation that at least some devotees of *The Crisis* read on the same level. Shakespeare's *Henry IV*, Part I had already been drawn on (see XVI.3 supra); the allusion to Amurath here was most likely only an indirect reference to that Ottoman emperor, coming directly from *Henry IV*, Part II, Act V, scene 2, where the new king, Henry V, seeks to reassure those around him that "This is the English, not the Turkish court; not Amurath an Amurath succeeds, but Harry Harry." Shakespeare had Amurath (or Murad) stand in for an Asian despot unfavorably juxtaposed with an English king, bound by honor. In the line of Ottomans who went by that title, at least one had murdered his predecessor to take power.

reader answer this question for himself—Our *ministry* after one unsuccessful attempt upon the liberties of *America* by *famine, sword*, and *fire*, have found themselves *deceived*—They have confessed this in the House of Commons; nay more, they have been misled by Ignorance and misinformation, the consequence has been the loss of the very flower of the British army; there is now an handful of brave (but disgraced) forces left in *America*, the poor remains of thousands.

The Minister has, at last, been fairly beaten off his ground, he has with shame and reluctance, given up the *right of taxing America,* (at least *pro tempore)* and declares now, that *England* does not contend for *taxation*, but for *power*; these were *Lord North's* words lately in the House of Commons, all that his lordship could mean by this was (if put in plain *English*) that *administration* did not *now* mean *indirectly* to attack the *treasures*, but *directly* to attack the *throats* of the *Americans.* The ministerial hackneys (*Johnson* at their head) join in the united cry, that the contest with *America* now, is for power only. The midnight-murderer is satisfyed with a purse, the *ministerial cut-throats* expect a revenue, but from whence is this annual, this perpetual stream to issue? when a people are extinct, or reduced to a state of *slavery, cultivation* must cease of course, that being the basis of all national wealth, the rivers of wine and oil can no longer flow, when the fountain-head is dry; it cannot therefore, be the hope of annual plunder, it is the spur of vindictive pride that goads us on, it is unjust, irrational and impetuous desire of subduing, not only the persons and spirits, but of extinguishing the detested name and race of *Englishmen* in *America,* for what crime are they thus visited by every calamity of invasion and relentless war? for adhering to principles which brought the present family from a small *German Electorate* to the crown of *England*, to the sovereignty of a great nation, to more wealth, honour, and magnificence than the greatest *German prince* ever had a conception of, who had not travelled. In that little *Electorate, thirty thousand* men is the largest number, (including youth and age) which can be raised throughout all the territories, upon the most urgent necessity; yet so prodigal is the present elector of *English blood*, that near that number has been already sacrificed to the demon *revenge* upon the continent of *America;* *s*acrificed in subversion and defiance, not only of the principles, but of the *rights* of *Britons,* settled at the glorious revolution.

This most unwarrantable, attrocious and daring invasion, has been steadily enforced by *perseverance* and *persecution* on the one hand, and as bravely repelled by the truest spirit of insulted *liberty* on the other; has not a savage kind of *pride* impelled a rapacious *administration* to act ever against their own individual *interest?* I do not take the consideration of their *country* into the account, when I say this, but I consider (as they do) *self* alone. On a more extended view I should ask, whether *America* is not a child of commerce, and a horn of plenty to Great Britain? is she not the great support of all our *West India* colonies in general? can they exist without her? is she not the nurse and supplier of our navy? is she not able to produce such materials for its construction and support as we can no longer procure from those countrys which used to supply us? can our dock-yards be conveniently furnished with *timber,* from *Hanover?* or will the *mum, beer,* and *bacon* (the staple commodities of that *electorate*) preserve the vast numbers of our plantation-negroes in the *West-Indies* from famine, and their masters from inevitable ruin? will not these colonies be wise enough to throw themselves under the protection of *America,* who can feed them? If the consequence of this revolt should be extinction by more *British massacres,* an instant death will be preferable to a lingering one. I would tell our *despot* upon his throne, at the head of his venal parliament, that it would be cruelty to spare them, unless they should fall victims to his revengeful sword, *famine* will force them to prey upon each other. In such a case disolution would be mercy, and the utmost efforts of tyrannic power would be tenderness to the subject; but when the potent arm of *majesty* is extended (as in suffering *America*) to check industry, to blast cultivation, to ruin commerce, to destroy whole rising fertile colonies, to establish unjust demands (if possible) by the extinction of the human race: when the *British parliament,* once accustomed to protect, turn the violaters of *British rights,* and a paternal *senate* is transformed, at the back of a corrupting *minister,* into a hellish *pandemonium,* what tongues, what pens, what *swords,* but those of mercenary *aliens,* are fit to serve them? such *swords* have been at length procured; for assassinated *America* has not yet been "*locked into submission?*" as Lord North prophesyed, by a considerable army of the very best of our British troops; nor will she be *dragooned*; (for it is impossible she should ever be completely conquered) by the more tremendous appearance of *foreigners,* with larger hats, and harder faces. These German banditti let out like cattle, by their despotic masters for this slaughterous purpose, will serve to make the soil of *America* more fertile.

How happy is England in her *German* connections, and in her near alliance with the Landgrave of *Hesse-Castle?* what immence revenues is that *army-jobbing* prince likely to receive for hire of his *Germanic-wolves* to lay a country in disolation, where the *British lion* has roared in vain? to the honour of Great Britain these butcherly sons of death will, I hope, meet their deserved fate under a foreign commander in *chief. No English officer* wishes either to command, or to assist them; on the contrary, they are all making excuses, selling out at any loss, resigning, or absolutely refusing, and persisting in such refusal, at any hazard; in truth it is a service fit only for *savages* and *Germans,* who are let out by their *despotic owners,* in cool blood, for the perpetrating of *regal* and *imperial murder.*

Such are the venal instruments now to be used (for the edge of *Britons* is taken off) against *America.* We can neither raise forces of our own for this execrable purpose, nor spare those we have remaining. The truth is, they do not only murmur already at the service, but they have in *America* been more then once upon the brink of mutiny, and of laying down their arms, no notice has yet been taken of this in the *royal gazette*; but it is a fact. Our *American generals* who have so judiciously *slunk* out of the *American* business, would tell us so, if they dared.—but their service is necessary in England to instruct and inform a *trembling administration,* and to assert, deny, misrepresent, disguise, and colour over, (as they shall be directed) as often as enquiries disagreeable to the *minister* shall be set on foot in the House of Commons; for this purpose our admirals too have been suffered to return, I verily believe much to their satisfaction.

A further reason for keeping useful troops and officers at home is, that they will shortly be necessary to defend *Great Britain*, against the united forces of *France and Spain.*—A *Mansfield,* (lawyers have ever been the shallowest politicians) would smile at this suggestion; I know, our wise, unsuspecting *administration* are all *confidence*; but *England* will soon be all *confusion*—*France* and *Spain*, will strike. Had the same implacable, unrelenting spirit appeared against them in the last war, as rages now against our own vitals in *America*, we had bowed them to the dust, but with our natural and exhausted enemies we *negociate*, and against our *supplicating subjects* we *persevere. America* is to be crushed at all event, if possible; because, *"unless we get the better of her* (says Lord *Mansfield*) *she will get the better of us."*—And in so just a cause, it is but fit she should, if we still continue to *persevere.*

However, here is a plain confession from Lord *Mansfield* (the mouth of Lord *Bute)* that the attack now to be renewed against *America*, is for *power,* and for *power* only; this is the spirit of *tyranny* in perfection; what can be a truer definition of *despotism* then that it is an arbitrary exertion of *power,* without *right?* the right as I said before is given up, at least for the present; and the *minister* himself has declared, that the contest now is for *power* merely.

In the case of *America* every solemn profession she has made, disavowing her intent of *independence*, has (like her repeated supplications) been disregarded, on the other hand, *royal* and *ministerial* jealousies have prevailed, and still more formidable *armaments* are to be sent against a people, who have repeatedly offered to grant all we can ask, provided we will suffer them to give and grant *their own*, in the same manner the rest of his majesty's subjects do; they desire only to be permitted to enjoy the same rights as they did in the year 1763, when their persecution by the stamp act first commenced, upon being restored to the same state in which they stood at that period, they declare themselves ready to lay down their arms at the Kings feet, which they have been compelled to take up in their own defence: these they have used with the greatest magnanimity, temper

and humanity, in the justest cause; with the admiration and applause of all mankind, one detested *junto*, with their corrupt dependants, alone expected.[5]

This continued *perseverance* against *America* is irrational, savage and
unjust, because it is meant, confessedly not to determine the point of
right, (for that is waved for the present) but merely the point of *power*.
Such a principle might have obtained among the untutored, barbarous
Picts, but ill becomes the cultivated *Briton*; lions, tygers, bears, and
wolves, rely on *strength*; but civilized man in every contest should consult his *reason*, does *reason* prompt us first to wave our *right* and then
contend for *victory?* for a moment, suppose it did; yet we are still mistaken, our internal passion of *revenge* has blinded and misled us. The
contest upon the plan we now pursue it, will not determine even this
favourite point of *power*; we are attempting to subdue *America* not
by the proper strength of Great Britain, but by *hired foreign* forces;
will such *mercenaries* be for ever ready to assist us? can we be sure of
obtaining their aid upon every future rupture with *America?* or do we
flatter ourselves that these *German cut-throats*, will strike the decisive
blow at once? suppose they could; can this be called the *power* of
Great Britain? surely not, what then will be determined by this pusillanimous, disgraceful mode of conquest? not the magnanimity and
power of the English nation, but the cruelty and tyranny of an *English
king*; the baseness, servility, treachery, and *treason* of a corrupt *junto*
in a British parliament.

---

5. Imperial administrators could be forgiven if they thought a return to pre-1763 imperial policies would have placated protesting Americans. Even the Continental Congress
had given that impression, but its choice not to address grievances before that date was
a matter of political tactics, not a belief that they did not exist. See my "The First Continental Congress and the Problem of American Rights" *Pennsylvania Magazine of History and Biography* 122 (1998):353–83. On a basic level the empire had not changed fundamentally; there was no "mercantilistic" versus "imperialistic" dividing line at 1763,
as Oliver M. Dickerson would someday argue in *The Navigation Acts and the American
Revolution* (Philadelphia: University of Pennsylvania Press,1951). Dickerson was countered by Thomas C. Barrow in *Trade and Empire* (Cambridge: Harvard University
Press, 1967); and, much later, by Thomas M. Truxes, *Defying Empire* (New Haven: Yale
University Press, 2008).

By the *loan* of *German Butchers* the same despotic standard, which has been already dyed with the brave and guiltless blood of *America*, may and perhaps will, be reared in England; those who are weak enough to doubt it, must be strangers to the human heart, to the pride of *kings,* and but little versed in history. Under this standard of unlimited, presumptious and rapacious *majesty,* what devastations would not be made? what blood would not be spilt? what property would not be grasped? what liberties would not be trampled on? The *hand* would be the *king*'s, the *will* would be (as it now is) the *ministers*, Lord *Bute*, the actual minister, would then no longer lurk in holes and corners he would scorn to do his business any longer by his proxy *Mansfield*; he would break forth from his chamber, like the *sun* and rejoice "like a *giant* to run his course." a packed parliament would crouch to him, the mute and servile registers of his despotic *edicts*: in which *Wolsey's* triumphant *egotism (I; and my king)* would glare at us in audacious capitals. But the sovereign *will and pleasure* of this *Colossus*, who now bestrides the *English Empire*, will neither be able to re-unite AMERICA, nor prevent the *West-Indian Colonies* from adhering to their brethren on the continent, from whom alone they can expect support. The name of *Bute* cannot repel the united force of *France* and *Spain*, restore peace and commerce, raise a yearly revenue of *six millions* for the wanton carnage in AMERICA, quiet the approaching discontents in *Ireland*; allay the ferments of a civil war in *England*, or prevent another *revolution*.

C A S C A.

P. S. *Queries* addressed to *Lord North,* ostensible prime minister of Great Britain.

Your lordship having attempted to defend the late treaty with the Landgrave of *Hesse Castle* upon principles of *oeconomy* and *policy.* Query whether your lordship meant to contend for *truth*, or, according to your *American* politics, for *power* only? 2dly, whether it is *oeconomy* to increase the *national debt,* and grievous taxes, unless for national benefit? 3dly, If no benefit whatever possibly can (but the greatest *mischiefs* must) arise from the invasions, and slaughters in America, is it *policy* to persevere? As plain common sense must answer the two latter queries in the negative, your lordship will permit me to add two more.

Query, when we consider your lordship's argument, founded upon good *oeconomy* and good *policy*; which must we be most astonished at, the matchless *impudence,* or the wanton *inhumanity* of *administration?*

Query, how long will *England* patiently bear these *insults,* and still continue, servilely and basely, to contribute thus to the *massacre* of her fellow subjects in AMERICA, and to her own inevitable ruin?

Printed and Published for the AUTHORS by T. W. SHAW, Fleet-Street, opposite Anderton's Coffee-House, where Letters to the Publisher will be thankfully received.

THE

CRISIS

NUMBER LXIV   *To be continued Weekly,*

DURING THE PRESENT BLOODY CIVIL WAR IN AMERICA.

SATURDAY, April 6, 1776   [Price Two-pence Half-penny.

*GARDNER's GHOST,

A prophetic Ballad found in *Merlin's Cave, Richmond.*

L ET *little* villains conscience gor'd,
  Their fable vigils keep!
 GEORGE on his downy pillow snor'd:
  (How *R---l v----s* sleep!)

An hour ere day began to break,
  There *Gardner's spectre* stood:
The curtain shook,—it cried—"awake,
  Awake,—thou log of wood."

"Thy veins hath apathy congeal'd,
  Unthaw'd by pity's tear,
One spark a flinty heart may yield,
  Struck with the steel of FEAR!

*Colonel *Gardner* a gentleman of a most amiable character, and respectable family, in the Massachuset's Bay; slain by the tory army at Charles Town, 17th of June, 1775.

561

"Yes know,—that h—d so proud in crest,
 Sunk on the sygnet's plume,
Shall for the A-ᴇ and B—ᴋ dress'd,
 Shall meet a *Charles's* doom;

"Or, crouch'd in abject, care worn plight
 Beneath it's sorrows low,
Its bread by day—its rest by night,
 To Bourbon's mercy owe.

"Speak tyrant, which of Stuarts race
 Could match thy bloody work?
Go read when *Stafford was in place;
 A †Jeffries, and a ‡Kirk.

"Then failing history's *modern* page,
 Skill'd in her *ancient* lore,
Tell us if Nero in this age,
 ‖If Borgia could do more?

"Monster dismiss your ¶white rose clans,
 The impious task forbear!
Nor in their blood embrue those hands,
 Who plac'd a sceptre there!

"That liberty you now invade
 Gave you your ONLY right,
Thus in their sons our fires are paid,
 While you for Scotchmen fight.

---

*Earl of Stafford, temp. car. I.

†Judge Jeffries, the Mansfield of the last age,

‡General Kirk, that master piece of *inhumanity.*

‖Cæsar Borgia, if possible more cruel than the emperor Nero.

¶Query, are those of the *white* or the *red* rose rebels—ask the petitioning inhabitants of Mauchester, Lancaster, and Leicester.

"Satan for thee sunk deep in Hell
　　Shall forge his hottest tongs;
And fiends who gard his inmost cell,
　　Twine Scorpeons round their thongs.

"But hark!——I hear th' ill-omen'd cock,
　　The Gallic sun shall rise!
Lo *commerce founders on yon rock!
　　The British Lion dies."

GEORGE felt the dream, fetch'd many a shriek,
　　And tho' the ghost is gone,
Starts from his bed,—still hears it speak,
　　A cold,—damp sweat comes on.

With—that like Gloster in his tent,
　　He casts him on the ground,
And by these words seems to repent,
　　"Boston,— †bind up my wound

Just Heav'n give back the blood I've spilt,
　　My subjects lives restore;"
He wakes and to attone his guilt,
　　Bids *Gage* go butcher more.

REVOLVE your annals of mankind, and say, ye historians, which is the most horrible scene you have exhibited! the proscriptions of Rome, when three monsters twice marked the heads of their fellow citizens for destruction, condemned unheard.

When the most *virtuous* of *Rome's* defenders were MASSACRED, then the throne of the Cæsars was established, and the world was given up to the tyranny of the Emperors, whose ministers were informers, and whose soldiers executioners.

*The Prophesy,
†See Shakespear's Richard the 3d.

The fate of England is like thine? already has been heard the sound of proscription; she has already informers in her bosom, an informer* blackned the worthy Dr. Franklin—and her patricians were diverted with the barbarous mirth of the informer, instead of abhoring him; as patricians, under Nero and Domitian, smiled when good men were exposed to wild beasts in the Amphitheatre. The same *informer,* who is also a renegade, is prepared with further and bloodier prosecutions; he has described and *proscribed* those marked for sacrifice; he has already laid in caveats for excepting the chief patriots of *America* from pardon. He said there would be exceptions. So vengeance is determined, before the guilty are even known; that is Scotch jacobites have determined that the ghosts of so many of their countrymen who suffered in the rebellion, shall be appeased with the blood of immolated patriots—and the house of Hanover is to give up its friends to their revenge!

No rebellion has been proved on America, the greatest lawyers are divided in opinion whether the smallest degree has been committed—yet proscription is the word—and orders are already dispatched for seizing the victims. Americans are to be dragged across the Atlantic to be tried here—and not by juries—for here they have not, they cannot have *their peers.* The informer is ready to prosecute them—he has marked the criminals, tho' they are not yet accused —is this law? Is this England?— they are sent for—who are? let us know to whom this command for seizing is given—to a general—not to civil officers, is not this military law? citizens who have assembled to petition the king and parliament for justice and redress of grievances, are to be seized by a commander in chief and sent over hither—not to be tried—they cannot be tried here, they have not their peers here; these petitioners are already excepted from pardon by the informer—and since he has *solicited,* let him forever wear the infamous title of informer general.[1]

*Governor Hutchenson.

1. No Revolutionary American was ever tried for treason. Nonetheless, Parliament kept that prosecutorial option open, passing in 1777, and then renewing annually, a

Do we wonder at these shocking proceedings? when every jacobite is taken into favour, when every outlaw is pardoned and recalled, when *Shebbeare,* the defamer of the revolution and of the house of *Hanover,* is pensioned, when the brother and nephew of lord *Dunbar,* the Pretenders prime minister are in high trust, when the Pretender himself may be said to direct our councils, who can be surprized that war is declared against the Colonies? would not the Pretender naturally turn our swords against each other? can we think that so unnatural a civil war is not the effect of his and his creatures councils? *divide et impera;*[2] while we were united, could he hope to succeed? is it not a proof that his agents have influence, when we are on our knees to France, and proscribe our countrymen! fatal infatuation! blind besotted England! miserable merchants, ye petitioning scorned, rejected, merchants! fly, fly, with your wives and children—ruin will over take you—nobody listens to your prayers! you may be excepted from pardon, like your petitioning brethren in America, you are as culpable as they, for you have begged not to be undone.

Jefferies (*i.e.* Mansfield,') who will be courageous if *America* is *conquered,* will begin his campaign, with *the informer general* at his elbow, to try the rebels of *the West.* How merry and full of jokes will be his letters to his brother *Dunbar?* how he will compare the sufferers to those traytors Russel and Algernon Sidney! old Lovats ghost will be propitated by a hecatomb of whigs—and the two fields of Preston purified with English gore; with what humour will he relate the embassy of Dr. Murray, while signing warrants for execution! it will not be necessary in that Jovial hour of slaughter to employ a *Dun,* to take off Wilkes. Wilkes may be sworn, to have incited the Bostonians to rebellion; and a General Kirk will not be wanting to tuck him up.

Vain bloody men! you may for a while indulge your rage—but you are preparing your own downfall; the revolution sprung from the blood of

---

suspension of habeas corpus through the end of the war. That way captured Americans could be imprisoned without being brought to trial. See my "Imperial Impotence," pp. 696–701, and n. VIII.2 supra.

2. To divide and rule, or to some minds at the time, no doubt, to divide and conquer.

Russel and Sidney, as the liberty of Holland did from that of Count Egmont and Count Horne.[3] Jefferies the first after his sanguinary campaigne, was found pusillanimously disguised in an alehouse at Wapping; Mansfield the second Jefferies is not a greater hero, and though he has raised a civil war in a more covert manner than his family and countrymen have commonly done, he will not escape with impunity. The oppressed colonies, the ruined merchantry, the country groaning with new burthens, and swarming with poor will demand his head and those of his accomplices.

All England must blush with shame to think with what alacrity our ministers hurried into a shameful peace with France, and into an unnatural civil war with our own countrymen—and both with the same view, of paving the way to despotism, in a reign which will be remembered as long as time endures, for the inglorious peace and the unnatural war with which it has stained our annals.

T I B E R I U S.

To English S O L D I E R S.

YOU are Citizens, and when the rights of the people are invaded, every honest SOLDIER, will consider himself as injured. It is your duty to defend the liberties of Old England, and to protect the people by whom you are maintained; will you embrue your hands in the blood of your friends and brethren? to assist in depriving them of more then life; the inestimable blessing of freedom? consider the unjustifiable use which has

---

3. Given how little there was in the British press, beyond the reprinted writings of Sir William Temple, about the Dutch martyrs Count Egmont and Count Horn, who dared to stand against the Duke of Alba and were executed in 1568, it is quite possible that *The Crisis* actually went to a London reprint of an American source: John Dickinson's *A New Essay on the Constitutional Power of Great-Britain over the Colonies in America*, pp. 76–81, which John Almon took from the original 1774 text printed in Philadelphia by William and Thomas Bradford (as *An Essay...*). Dickinson, for his part, had drawn on Temple's writings about the Dutch wars for independence. For another example of Dickinson and transatlantic cross-fertilization in *The Crisis* see n. LXXX.3 infra.

already been made of the military power. Plead not your orders to commit murder in cool Blood. You are empowered by no law of man, to put unarmed defenceless persons to death on the spot, and remember the law of God declares, you are to fear him, and to do violence to no man.

An Alphabetical Catalogue of a few of OLD ENGLAND's present Grievances.

America enslaving	Oppressions numberless
BUTE still living	Popery established
Constitution violated	Quacks, political, medical, and
Duties excessive	religious
Englishmen neglected	Rogues in the cabinet
Foreign troops in British pay	Scotchmen preferred
Great Britain disgraced	Taxes enormous
Honour no where	Usurpation not opposed
Ireland out-pensioned	VENGEANCE ASLEEP
Jacobites court favourites	Wigs dispised
King George deceived	Christianity declining
Luxury encouraged	Yoke preparing
Mansfield Lord Chief	Zealous court parasites every
National debt increasing	where

Cum multis alis.[4]

Printed and Published for the AUTHORS by T. W. SHAW, Fleet-Street, opposite Anderton's Coffee-House, where Letters to the Publisher will be thankfully received.

4. That is to say, with many others (too numerous to name).

THE
CRISIS

NUMBER LXV   *To be continued Weekly,*

DURING THE PRESENT BLOODY CIVIL WAR IN AMERICA.

SATURDAY, APRIL 13, 1776   [Price Two-pence Half-penny.

Nullius addictus jurare in verba magistri.

HOR.[1]

Slave to no party *truth* alone I praise,
Nor swallow *falshood* tho' it comes from *Hayes.*

To LORD CHATHAM.*

My LORD,

I Have just read a letter given to the public in one of the daily papers, under the sanction of your lordship's name. As the style marks it for your lordship's and the sentiments coincide with those delivered by

---

*The letter which our correspondent alludes to has been contradicted, but not by Lord Chatham's authority as the public yet know: we have therefore thought proper to insert the following address to his lordship, from the high esteem we have for that nobleman, and in hopes he will satisfy the world, by publickly disavowing the nefarious production said to be HIS.

1. Horace's assertion that he was not bound by allegiance to any master; his only loyalty was to the truth. From his *Epistles*, Book 1, epistle 1.

Lord Temple in the house of peers, I cannot doubt of its authenticity.[2]
When I consider that your lordship (in and out of office) has always fig-
ured as a *patriot* in the senate, I cannot behold you without concern in
a sick bed transformed to a *tyrant* and a *parricide*. Your lordship's letter
is now before me, and I shall take leave to comment upon it with the
greatest freedom, forgive me, sir, but I cannot permit you to mislead
that nation in your retirement, which you once advanced to the highest
pitch of glory, in a short, but wise and spirited administration—your
lordship is pleased to declare that "your present sentiments *happily* coincide with those delivered by your brother *Temple*"—*happily* do you
say my lord?—very *unhappily* surely, both for *England* and *America*;
very *unhappily* for *yourself*—such a declaration from Lord *Chatham* argues great *instability*, if not *insanity* of mind. Are not you the identical

2. The extract from a purported letter written by Chatham on 9 March 1776 appeared
in the *Public Advertiser,* 22 March 1776, and was denounced as spurious in the *London
Evening Post* the very next day. The men behind *The Crisis* probably knew full well that
Chatham had written no such letter; still, its appearance gave them the opportunity to
chastise Temple as well as remind all true Whigs of where their allegiance should lie.
Chatham had gone into seclusion on his Hayes estate not long after failing to carry his
proposal to end the American crisis the year before, with North's proposal prevailing.
Whatever the nature of his malady, he did not return to Westminster until May 1777
and took virtually no part in public affairs during that long absence. In the "pretended
letter" Chatham laments his being confined to a sick bed at Hayes, but insists that his
views did "happily coincide" with what Earl Temple had stated in the House of Lords.
The Americans had gone too far, lamented Chatham, foolishly embracing republicanism and resisting Britain's efforts to restore the empire. Their only hope was to renounce
their republican folly and embrace the British constitution. Britain was fully within
its rights to use foreign troops to restore order. In his speech of March 5th Temple did
indeed state that Britain now had to "make peace, sword in hand," but he condemned
the ministry as sharply as he did the rebels. Temple had been drawn into a debate over
the Duke of Richmond's proposal that the king be requested to suspend hostilities and
that troops from Hesse, Hanau, and Brunswick not be sent across the Atlantic to help
suppress the rebellion. His speech was described as "so obscure" that it was difficult
to tell where he stood. He did not vote on Richmond's motion, which went down to
a sound defeat, 32 for, 100 against. See Simmons and Thomas, ed., *Proceedings and
Debates*, 6:427–53, for Temple; and Jeremy Black, *Pitt the Elder*, revised ed. (Phoenix
Mill: Sutton, 1999), pp. 209–61, for a succinct review of Pitt's position on the American
colonies in the larger British empire.

personage, who (when the propriety of the *stamp act* was agitated in the house of commons) *rejoiced* that *America* had *resisted?* were not these your lordship's words? does she do more at this present moment then persevere in that *resistance* which you once applauded? she certainly does not.

Give me leave to ask by what accident your lordship and your noble *brother* happened to think alike? did he submit so far as to deliver your sentiments, or did your lordship condescend to adopt his? the latter conjecture is highly improbable. Your lordship was never yet known to coincide with any man. In *politics* you have ever disclaimed all union where you was not allowed to *guide*. It is therefore most likely that your brother *Temple* pronounced your lordships sentiments; how greatly they are changed, with what reason, and through what *influence*, I shall proceed to observe, consider, and investigate.

Your lordship's letter informs us that "whilst *America* retained her *allegiance* you was the friend of *America*,"—with how ill a grace does this stricture upon *America* flow from the heart, or pen, of that man who first excited *America* to *resist?* yes, my lord, it was your oracular, applauding breath which first encouraged her to resent, consult, and *act*. She looked upon you as a tutelar-divinity. And are you to be drawn off by the sweet smelling favour of a little *ministerial sacrifice?* made almost to your lordship's *manics*, perhaps upon your *death bed?*— *America* has been so often and so fully cleared from every imputed breach of allegiance, not only in the public prints, but by the ablest and honestest members in both houses of parliament, that it would be impertinently tedious of me to take up her defence anew. In one word, who is so able to clear her from so false an imputation as your lordship? permit me therefore, to remind your lordship of your own defence of her upon this head in the House of Lords on the 20th of January, 1775, your lordships notions then were very different: your words were these: "The *constitution* and that alone limits both *sovereignty* and *allegiance?*—what has government done? they have sent an armed force consisting of above 17000 men to *dragoon* the Bostonians into what is called their *duty*.—is this the way to win men to their duty, and recover in them the principles of affection and British allegiance?"—your lordship closed thus: "when the inherent constitutional rights of *America* are invaded, I own myself an *American*; and feeling myself as such shall to the *verge of my life*, vindicate her rights"—now for the hole at which your lordship is endeavouring at present to creep out.—"But if *America* should at any time lose sight of this line (of *right*) I shall be an *Englishman*, and defend those *rights* against any power under heaven that would oppose them."—your lordship has at last thrown off your *American* mask, and not only resumed the *Englishman*, but commenced a *ministerial* man; and why? has *America* transgressed this *line of right*, (these limits of the *constitution*) by not submitting to be *dragooned* by 17000 men, by contending for her *inherent constitutional rights*, when they were invaded? by opposing the unjustifiable force of her *aggressors*, or by resisting *murderous* troops who dared to shed her *blood*? by whom was this *line of right* transgressed, my lord? you must own it was by *England*; a noble breast must disdain a *falsehood*. If your lordship will not now confess yourself an *American* once more, I must tell you that you are unworthy to be called an *Englishman*.—but your lordship is certainly under some stronger impulse than *ministerial*—you exclaim that "there is no treating with *rebels*, whilst *arms* were in the hands, honour, dignity, authority, interest, all forbid it." this is not the language of Lord *Chatham* in his senses, does your lordship forget the difference between constitutional *resistance* and unnatural *rebellion?* are you a *revolutionist* without a veneration for revolution principles? did not the renowned and immortal *rebels* of that glorious æra, take up arms against unconstitutional power and oppression? has *America* any greater sin to answer for? as to the honour and dignity of this, and every civilized nation, they consist in *justice* and *humanity*; it is authority must move (as your lordship has often said) within the limits of the constitution, and it is *interest* must be maintained by cherishing, protecting, and uniting, not by plundering, invading, and dismembering its dominions. A government thus principled would not have suffered (much less would it have aided) the executive power to break through *charters*, compacts, oaths and above all the sacred principles of the *revolution*, for the gratification of *regal pride* and *profusion*, for the sake of opening new sources of *ministerial corruption*, or indulging a pusillanimous spirit of impotent and ruinous *revenge*; ruinous my lord, it must be to this country, and heinously unjust, after every assurance of loyal attachment, every wise concession and earnest supplication had been made by injured *America*, and spurned from the senate and the *throne*, by the feet of unrelenting *tyrants*. Such they appear to all the world, and such your lordship will, at the last, appear, unless you dye as you have hitherto lived, a friend to *America* and *freedom,* and a determined foe to *despotic* men and measures.

But your lordship says, "the present state of things does not admit of *relaxation or concession.*"—who drove them to such a *crisis*, the *aggressors* or the *sufferers*, my lord? If justice and necessity require such *relaxation* and *concession* the pride of kings must stoop, or the nation be undone.—"All *conciliatory propositions* are futile"—There was a time when they ought to have been embraced, my lord, they were repeatedly tendered by the friends of *America* and *England;* by *America* herself, had rejected with disdain, under a pretence that they proceeded from the *Congress*, this alas! was a mere pretence to give a colour to unjustifiable despotic *perseverance.* How could a collective body of people join in an address without they met together? the terms *congress* and *meeting* are synonimous. A repulse grounded on a poor reason was rediculous and irrational; but *America* has lately, very lately, renewed her solicitations for peace in the humblest terms, in terms which must be the most satisfactory to any but determined and designing *tyrants*. Yet fresh *armaments* are mustered from *foreign countries* to continue an invasion commenced against every principle of Justice, humanity, sound policy, and the British constitution. The truth is, it would frustrate the despotic schemes of the present *administration* either to offer, or receive, any *conciliatory propositions*; confident in their hired *myrmidons* they rejoice to see the day when such *propositions* are become *futile* in the opinion of *Lord Chatham.*

"The colonies have levy'd open war against the present state." For the sake of truth, my lord, if that was ever an object of your veneration and respect, retract this rash, ill-grounded, false assertion. When your lordship made your last motion for a *conciliation* in the house of lords, was not a British army of *invasion* posted in the town of *Boston*? did they not shortly after make the *first* attack upon *America?* I am sorry to draw a blush from your lordship upon this occasion; no character however great can sanctify a *falsehood.*—"That expence is not to be regarded.—That *national honour* is above all estimate", I readily admit, but deny that the treasures of England are to be dissipated, like counters, in an unnatural, unjust, and impious war against *ourselves.* I deny that the honour of a nation ever has, or can appear, in such a contest; which was commenced upon narrow, false, impolitic, and selfish principles, (merely to seed rapine, prodigality, and corruption) and must terminate not only in the disgrace, but in the ruin of domestic peace, extended commerce, national reputation, and prosperity,

"*America*, says your lordship must be *brought back* to her *duty*," taking it for granted, (but not admitting) that the *Americans* have departed from their *duty*, (unless *self defence* is a departure) I should be glad to know why they have not been permitted to return *spontaneously* to what your lordship may now call their *duty*; but I call a free exercise of those rights which they have been stripped of?—why were their repeated *supplications* answered by famine, sword, and fire?—Again, "*America* must submit to the *constitutional* authority of Great Britain."—I concurr most heartily with your lordship, observing only that the *constitutional estates* of this kingdom have, in the case of *America*, proceeded most *unconstitutionally.*—But your lordship adds, that "the submission of *America* must be absolute, unlimited, and unconditional; then will be the time to temper *justice* with *humanity.*" This is the very language of the *minister* of *Bute, Mansfield,* and *George* himself, in his late answer to the last address of the city of London. Alas! my lords how does evil communications corrupt good manners! should *America* make so abject a submission, even in the dust, she will deserve not only to be deserted by your lordship and all her friends, but to be dispised and trampled into *slavery.*

That the time is not yet come for the exertion of *justice* and *humanity* towards her, is a disgrace not only to this free nation (as it is called) but to *humanity* itself.—Your lordship disclaims the defence of *all* the measures of *administration* most religiously—why so, my lord, if you have taken courage to defend the very *worst* of all? that your lordship may add a most remarkable phænomenon in the British annals in 1776, let me intreat you to make your *apostacy* complete. I will venture to foretell that neither your *conversion*, nor your brother *Temple's*, so near your dissolutions, can have the desired effect upon the *public*. Our wise *tampering* ministry is quite mistaken.

I pass over your lordships next expressions (applauding the hiring of *German* troops to cut the throats of *Englishmen,* and pitying the deluded colonists), and I pass them over with the greatest pity and contempt—they denote *insanity*—and to the next sentance, I believe your lordship dictated it to a *lucid interval*, because it is pregnant with a *paradox*. In such species of assertion your lordship has ever stood unrivalled and alone.—hear it, all ye listening world!—"I say the present armament will restore the Americans to *freedom*."—pardon me, my lord, but I can hardly suppress a laugh. It deserves no other answer—what your lordship says about *republicanism*, will but be answered by the event.—Your lordship in your close approves most of limited monarchy—I would ask your lordship whether ours is, at present a *limited* monarchy in reality and in truth, or whether it is only the shadow without the substance? be this as it may, I will aver that a *limited English* monarch at the head of a venal majority in parliament, is as absolute as the *Grand Seignior*.[3]

That I may not quit your lordship without some token of respect, permit me to assure you, that I should not have taken the liberty of a commentator with any correspondence between your lordship and your friends, which had not been manifestly designed for the public eye. Your late epistle has been a subject of general surprize, I wish I could say of general applause; various have been the conjectures formed. The *apostacy* of the great *Pulteny*, afterwards the little *Earl of Bath,* is frequently brought to mind; accomplished by a crafty *minister*, who knew the weakness of mankind, and a vain importunate woman.

Your lordship some time since upon a remarkable occasion declared, "you would live and dye with your noble brother,"—I now perceive, my lord, that your *suns* will set together. The *minister* has kept his eye upon them for some time, watching for their decline; the thane of *Bute* (under whose

---

3. That is to say, this or any Turkish sultan, who by definition was a tyrant (see n. LXIII.4 supra for another swipe at the Ottomans, borrowed from Shakespeare).

influence your lordship now begins to write, and your noble brother to harangue) knows that man is most accessible when he is upon the verge of *necessity*, or *death*. Both your lordships seem now to have lived (for your own glory) long enough; I know not who is lord *Chatham's amanuensis*, but lord *Temple* is his *mouth*; the speech and the letter have the honour of one common parent in your lordship. Thus have you two able lords given the triumphant thane a dutiful earnest of obedience for the future.

In the debate upon the *American* Stamp Act, I remember your lordship declared in the house of commons, that "you could give no ministry your *confidence*, because you could perceive a latent *influence*." you meant the influence of *Bute*. Alas! my lord, how little do the wisest of us know our-selves! what *American*, what *Englishman*, can *now* confide in either of your lordships? *now*, when this once-detested *influence* shines as strong upon the *noble Invalids* at *Hayes* and *Stowe*, as upon the rotten chapel of *St. Stephen?*

Your lordships have formerly spoken many applauded, *patriotic* truths in public; you have laid open the errors of a vile and wicked *administration* boldly; will your lordships condescend to hear your *own?* tottering (as ye both are) upon the verge of life, your lordships have at last consented to receive *extreme unction* from the gracious hand of *Bute*. His insured patronage to young Mr. *Grenville* (whose father produced the *Stamp Act*) the successor to the estate and title of *Earl Temple,* has melted down the *patriotism* of the stormy *brothers* into a *ministerial calm.*

Thus have I as a member of that collective body, the people of *England*, whom you have *deceived*, and as a firm friend to *America* (whom you have *deserted*), taken leave to send you, at once my poor ideas of your letter, you patriotism, and your principles. I am, my lord, with much less devotion then I ever wished to be, yours, &c.

C A S C A.

Printed and Published for the AUTHORS by T. W. SHAW, Fleet-Street, opposite Anderton's Coffee-House, where Letters to the Publisher will be thankfully received.

THE

CRISIS

NUMBER LXVI   *To be continued Weekly,*

DURING THE PRESENT BLOODY CIVIL WAR IN AMERICA.

SATURDAY, April 20, 1776   [Price Two-pence Half-penny.

They that resolve their Liberty to lose,
Heav'n is too just that Freedom to refuse,
But lets them have the Slav'ry which they choose.

TO THE KING.

SIR,

THIS Country is now reduced to a situation really alarming, through your weakness, obstinacy, revenge and cruelty. The treachery of *Lord Bute*, the villainy of *Mansfield*, and your ingratitude, are perhaps not to be paralleled in the history of this *island*. How can the people of England put any confidence in you, Sir, who pay no regard to their interest, or how can they be safe under a monarch, who almost every day falsifies his own word, violates the most solemn promises, and breaks the most sacred oaths? Your subjects for a time were willing to believe that your ministers kept from you the real state of public affairs, and that you were ignorant of the grievances they laboured under; they could not be persuaded that you was even acquainted with the violation of their dearest rights, much less concerned with an abandoned set of men in the destruction of that constitution, you was sworn to support and defend. The mask is at last thrown off, and you, sir, are no longer looked upon as the *father*, but as the *tyrant* of your people, ready to sacrifice their lives to your own savage revenge, and to the will of your minions. History too fatally informs us, that the *English* have been frequently driven to dangerous extremes by causes of less moment than those which have shaken the British Empire, during your reign. As you, sir, and your ministers have thought fit to copy the tyranny and despotism of the *Stuarts*; it ought to be now the chief object of your care, to avoid the dreadful catastrophe of one of them, and the ruin of your family. I am persuaded Sir, the English nation will soon proceed beyond remonstrating, unless the present measures of government are speedily altered, and some of your ministers delivered up a sacrifice, to appease the vengeance of a much injured and incensed people.

The crisis is not far distant when the fate of tyranny or the salvation of the constitution must be determined, fourteen years are not elapsed, since the last glorious war, under the conduct of lord Chatham, had humbled *France* and *Spain* to the dust. We had then in our hands sir, sufficient to have ruined them for ever as *naval powers*, sufficient to have reimbursed the expences of a war, great as they were, and to have added an imense revenue to the crown. We were in a condition at that time, to have kept for ever the invaluable conquest of our arms. What then, Sir, do you and those traitors deserve, who frustrated all the mighty toils and atchievements of the war, by the vile, crouching, rotten peace of Fontainbleau? A peace which, in so short a period, has inabled our vanquished foes openly to insult and disgrace us in the eyes of the world.

What *private* motives inspired these worst of *parricides* thus to abandon and betray their country, proof was at one time given, sufficient for conviction; sufficient, Sir, to have made your ministers tremble, and sufficient to have made them *suffer*, had they not found means to *bribe* those who were ready with undoubted evidence of their *guilt*.

The *public motive* for that dark and villainous transaction, was black envy; and an impatience to commence the present arbitrary Scotch system of government, formed by Lord Bute; under which the kingdom now groans, and which has reduced us from the highest pinnacle of glory and power to the brink of destruction; such has been the grateful return made by you, and your creatures to those brave *Englishmen*, who fought gloriously in defence of their country: and such has been your gratitude to the *whole people* of *England*, who raised you to *power*, that you have wantonly and wickedly destroyed their boasted liberties, reduced them to *beggery*, and are now attempting to bind them in chains; but, Sir, we have yet the means left within our constitution, to save ourselves and destroy all your despotic designs; against the common rights of mankind and the peace of society.

The most successful deluders of mankind have always acted in masquerade; and when the blackest villainies are meant, the most opposite spirit is pretended. Vice acts with security, and often with reputation, under the veil of virtue; as you have done, till this kingdom is now reduced to a state of misery and distress. Hence too, atheists have set up for the greatest piety; and to cover their own real want of it, have burnt those who really had it. The most *mirciless* tyrants have in the midst of oppression, set up for the patrons of liberty; and while their hands like yours were *deep in blood*, impudently adopted the title of clemency.

There are no such mighty talents requisite for government, as some, who pretend to them without *possessing* them, would make us believe: *Honest* affections, Sir, and common qualifications, are sufficient; and the administration has been always best executed, and the public liberty best preserved, near the origin and rise of states, when plain honesty and common-sense *alone* governed public affairs, and mens morals were not corrupted with riches and luxury, nor their understandings perverted by subtleties and distinctions.

You, Sir was never accused of being possessed of extraordinary abilities, but had you made an *honest use* of the little understanding you are blessed with, you would not have heard so many complaints from your people, and they had been happy under their native sovereign.

The people, Sir, have no biass to be knaves; the security of their persons and property is their highest aim. No ambition prompts them; they cannot come to be lords, to possess great titles and therefore desire none; they have no pimp or relation to raise: they have no occasion for dissimulation or intrigue, they can serve no end by faction; nor have they any interest but the general interest: would to God, Sir, that neither you, or your ministers had any other; but alas! the contrary is too fatally true; to gratify private passion, you would bring down public ruin, and to *save* your favourite, destroy the nation.

Consider well, Sir, your past conduct, and be advised in time, when the course of justice is entirely stopt, and the abused and enraged people can have no remedy, either real or imaginary, nor one victim to their fury, they will naturally and necessarily look higher, and who can foresee where their vengeance will end.

There seems to be in many respects, a fatal analogy between you and that unhappy prince *Charles* the *First* of the house of *Stuart*: you both came to the throne of the British empire, equally beloved, the very idols of the people, whose affections you never could have lost, had you not put your trust in private councils. *Charles* was undoubtedly a man of virtuous inclinations and just principles; and his reign would have been glorious and happy; but unfortunately for him, he found a set of depraved and abandoned ministers, who had been long used to lead their master which way they pleased. You found a set of honest men at the head of affairs, whom you thought proper to *dismiss*; and we have heard a great deal about your virtue and mildness, but we have not as yet experienced either one or the other. The ministers of *Charles*, set up an interest distinct from that of the people, and he fell in with and countenanced all their measures, which after a time brought a civil war on the nation; and he in the end lost his HEAD; if the House of Commons had been at that time, subservient to the designs of him and his ministers, the nation must have been enslaved. Your chosen ministers have likewise set up an interest distinct from that of the people; and you have not only countenanced them in their proceedings, but actually supported them by your authority in the most open and avowed manner, and what is still more fatal to this country, you have in conjunction with them packed a House of Commons, and through their survility, you have given full scope to your revenge, destroyed the property and lives of your subjects, and laid waste one part of the Empire. Whether these lawless and unconstitutional acts of government, may bring on a catastrophe as fatal to this country as those of *Charles the First*, time only can determine; this however we may safely take upon us to vouch, that without some alteration in your conduct and that of you ministers, we have all the misery to dread that can befall a nation. The laws are no longer the rule and measure of government; they cease to be a terror to public traitors; nor are they a protection for the innocent against oppression, cruelty, and injustice.

In a word, the situation of this country is much more deplorable now than at the last stupendous revolution. The danger of a total subversion of the government, and extinction of the laws and liberties of England is much greater now from the corrupt subserviency of the present House of Commons to your despotic designs and those of your ministers, than it was before the revolution, from the arbitrary and popish designs of King James. Indeed we have now hardly the shadow of our liberties left, and with them seems to be lost the heretofore invincible and free spirit of Englishmen. However, I still entertain a better opinion of my countrymen, than to believe they will degenerate so far from the virtue of their ancestors, as to resign up all their liberties at the shrine of despotism and passively submit to a state of slavery. I have yet a more generous opinion, of the bravest, and I hope the freest people in the world; I can conceive, they will soon see the necessity of leaving their wives, their children and dearest connections, to vindicate their own rights, against the wickedness, treachery and corruption of the three estates of the realm, who should be their *protectors*; but who are become their known and notorious enemies, who have been for some time endeavouring to destroy, the liberties and constitution of England. I am persuaded the day is not far distant, when we must all stand forth, and bravely attempt a restoration of our rights, or bravely die in the cause of freedom.

We are not only warranted but required to enter into association, and oaths for the preservation of our liberties and the constitution. The words of magna charta run thus. "That in case the King shall violate any part of it, and shall refuse to rectify what he had done amiss, it shall be lawful for the barons, and the *whole* people of England to distress him by all the ways they could think on; such as the seizing on his Castles, Lands, and possessions, provision being only made for the safety of the *persons* of the King and Queen and their children."[1]

I believe there is not in this Kingdom one man, when he seriously reflects (unless some ministerial hireling) who will deny that you have violated the GREAT CHARTER, and the laws of the land. There is often a necessity for speaking the truth, and this is a truth the generality of mankind believe, though they have not resolution enough to declare it openly. It appears to me the grosest absurdity, to suppose that the ministry would act daily in direct opposition to the laws of their country, and the chartered rights of the people; if they were not supported by you; no, it is certain you encourage them, we are sure they act with your consent, if not by your advice; otherwise they had been delivered up to the justice of their counrry, or at least dismissed from your presence and councils: it is therefore nonsense to throw the odium and gilt of public measures, entirely upon the ministry, when you only appear to be blameable, because it is in your power to prevent them. I hate flattery, and have always been of opinion, that fulsome adulation, and compliments paid to the King in petitions and addresses had a very bad tendency, and were unbecoming a FREE people; it is neither just nor decent to speak of the first magistrate, as the best of kings, as having many excellent qualities, and virtues, as being a tender father of his people; at the same time that he is putting his whole confidence in the worst of ministers, and treating every remonstrance from his people with sovereign contempt. What idea must you have of such encomiums given of *yourself*, from men who speak with the utmost dislike and bitter complaint; against the measures

---

1. This passage does not come from Magna Carta, either as first written in 1215 or as subsequently revised through 1297 under Edward I. Rather, it appears to have been taken, with small changes, from *The Present State of Great Britain and Ireland*, which appeared in eleven editions between 1707 and 1748. Guy Miege was the original author; Solomon Bolton edited the later printings. In this instance, I used the eleventh edition published in London by J. Brotherton, et al., quoting from p. 192 (Chapter 27 of Part I, "Of the Norman Line").

of your government; and in the same address worship you as a divinity. The people have generally been faulty in this particular: the stile of a free people, when approaching the throne should never speak any language inconsistent with this; *"Sir,* whilst you observe your coronation oath, we shall pride ourselves in our loyalty to you; if you violate that solemn engagement we consider ourselves as absolved from our allegience; and shall glory in resistance, if we find it necessary for the preservation of our liberties and the constitution.

Printed and Published for the AUTHORS by T. W. SHAW, Fleet-Street, opposite Anderton's Coffee-House, where Letters to the Publisher will be thankfully received.

THE

CRISIS

NUMBER LXVII   *To be continued Weekly,*

DURING THE PRESENT BLOODY CIVIL WAR IN AMERICA.

SATURDAY, April 27, 1776   [Price Two-pence Half-penny.

For the C R I S I S.

THE law is the great rule in every country, at least in every free country, by which private property is ascertained, and the public good, which is the great end of all laws, is secured; and the religious observance of this rule, is what alone makes the difference between *good* law and *none*. The terror and sanctity of the laws, are shewn by the execution of them; and to a *contempt* of the laws, or to a direct dispensing with them, have been owing, all the shocks and *revolutions*, that we have, for many ages sustained in *England*.

I speak here of those laws which have a direct and known tendency to secure to us what we have, and to preserve to us what we are: a free people, are kept so, by no other means, but an equal distribution of property; every man who has a share of *property*, having an equal share of *power*; and the first seeds of anarchy, which generally ends in tyranny, are produced from hence, that some are ungovernably rich, and many more miserably poor; that is, some are possessed of all the means of oppression, and others want all the means of self-defence.

What a progress we have lately made in *England*, towards such a blessed state of confusion and misery, by the credulity of the people; suffering all in the hands, and to the mercy of a set of base-born villains, mischievously trusted by the sovereign with a power to undo them, is too manifest, from the woeful condition we are in: the ruin is general, and every man has the miserable consolation to see his country undone, by a conspiracy of ministers, supported by the prince upon the throne.

These monsters stand single in the creation, they have served the people, as Satan served Job: and so far the Devil is injured, by any analogy we can make between him and them.

How far the people ought to carry their resentment, it may not perhaps be safe for me to pronounce; the measure of it must be determined by circumstances; still, keen resentment should be shewn, and some punishment, or punishments, inflicted; the dignity, the interest, and the liberty of this nation is at stake; mercy then, at such a time, would be cruelty indeed.

To this spirit of jealousy and revenge, the *Roman* common wealth was formerly beholden for the long preservation of its liberty; and since, the *Venetian* commonwealth owes its preservation to the same spirit; and liberty will not subsist long where this spirit is not exerted: for if any crimes against the public may be committed with impunity, men will be tempted to commit the greatest of all, I mean that of making themselves masters of the state; *Cæsar* thought he might do what he had seen *Marius* and *Sylly* do before him, and so enslave his country; whereas had they been hanged, he would perhaps never have attempted it.

I have mentioned these examples to prove, that nations should be quick in their resentments, and severe in their judgments: and no nation was ever more abused than this has been of late by the Sovereign, and a worthless tribe of *minions*; so no nation ever could, with more justice or greater security, take its full vengeance. Sometimes indeed the greatness and popularity of the offenders make strict justice unadviseable, because *unsafe*; but now it is not so; we may at present, load every gallows in England with detested ministers and their creatures, without the assistance of a sheriff's guard, or so much as a sigh from an old woman, tho' accustomed to shed tears at the untimely demise of a common felon. A string of those wretches well trussed up, besides the diverting sight, would be a cheap sacrifice to the manes of liberty and trade.

But, some will say, when did you see rogues covered with wealth brought to the axe or the gallows? I own the example is rare, more to the shame of this nation, which has had such rich temptations, and such frequent opportunities; we have public guilt in abundance, protected by party and by money. Faction on one side, and riches on the other; have, as it were, made a lane for the great criminals to escape. But all these escapes, which are indeed, our reproach, cannot give any ground to fear a present one.

This nation has formerly been bought and sold; but arts were used to blind the peoples eyes, and the effects of treachery were not immediately felt; and we know that the resentment of the vulgar never follows from their understanding, or their reflection, but from their feeling: a pick-pocket may tickle a plain fellows ear, till he has got his purse; but if he feels it going, he will knock the thief down.

We have felt our pockets picked, and we know who have done it: vengeance awaits them.

I am told, some of them have the face to pretend that they ought not to be put to death; but an honest legislature would effectually convince them, that this their partiality to themselves is groundless: all their hopes of safety must consist in their money; and without question, they will try to make the wages of their villainy protect their villainy: but I cannot see how any sums can save them; for as they have robbed and cheated all men, except their accomplices, so all men are concerned to see justice done to themselves; and if the ordinary channels of justice could be stopped by bags of money, or by partnership in original guilt, the inraged, and abused people, might be prompted by their upermost passion, and having their resentment heightened by disappointment, might it is to be feared; have recourse to extraordinary ways: ways that are often successful and justifiable.

Here are no parties in this case to disguise truth, and obstruct justice; the calamity is general, and so is the resentment: all are sufferers; all will be prosecutors. The cry of justice is loud and united; if it be balked, I can prophesy no good from so cruel an omission.

If this mighty, this destructive guilt, were to find impunity, nothing remains, but that every villain of a daring or voracious spirit may grow a great rogue, in order to be a great man: when a people can no longer expect redress of public and heavy evils, nor satisfaction for public and bitter injuries, hedious is the prospect they have before them. If they will tamely suffer a fall from plenty to beggery, they may soon expect another, and a worse, from that to slavery.

I have before my eyes a brave and honest people, lovers of trade and industery, free of their money and well deserving of the legislature, passionate for liberty, haters of chains; but deluded, drained of their money and abused beyond patience, beyond expression, by mean sharpers that swagger in the plunder of their country.

Where therefore there is so much capacity, and so many good dispositions to help us on one side; such loud and melancholly calls, for that help, on another side; and such open, such execrable, such public crimes from a third quarter; we might hope every thing from the *king and parliament;* but they alas! instead of our protectors, are become the infamous instruments of our destruction.

Few men have been desperate enough to attack openly, and barefaced, the liberties of a free people. Such avowed conspirators can rarely succeed: the attempt would destroy itself. Even when the enterprize is begun and visible, the end must be hid, or denied. It is the business and policy of traitors, so to disguise their treason with plausible names, and so to recommend it with popular and bewitching colours, that they themselves shall be adored, while their work is detested, and yet carried on by those that detest it.

Thus one nation has been surrendered to another, under the fair name of mutual alliance: The foretresses of a nation have been given up, or attempted to be given up, under the frugal notion of saving charges to a nation; and commonwealths have been trepanned into slavery, by troops raised or encreased to defend them from slavery.

It may therefore be of service to the World, to shew what measures have been taken by corrupt ministers, to ruin and enslave the people over whom they presided; and to shew by what steps and gradations of mischief nations have been undone, and consequently what methods may be hereafter taken to undo others.

Such traitors will probably endeavour first to get their prince into their possession, and like *Sejanus,* shut him up in a little island, or perhaps make him a prisoner in his court; whilst with full range, they devour his dominions, and plunder his subjects. When he is thus secluded from the access of his friends, and the knowledge of his affairs he must be content with such misrepresentations as they shall find expedient to give him. False cases will be stated, to justify wicked counsel; and wicked counsel will be given to procure unjust orders. He will be made to mistake his foes for his friends, and his friends for his foes; and to believe that his affairs are in the highest prosperity, when they are in the greatest distress, and that public matters go on in the greatest harmony, when they are in the utmost confusion.

They will be ever contriving and forming wicked and dangerous projects, to make the people poor, and themselves rich; well knowing that dominion follows property; that where there are wealth and power, there will be always crowds of servile dependants; and that on the contrary, poverty dejects the mind, and fashions it for slavery, and renders it unequal for any generous undertaking, and incapable of opposing any bold usurpation. They will squander away the public money in wanton presents to minions, and their creatures of pleasure, or of burden, or in pensions to mercenary and worthless men and women for evil ends and traiterous purposes.

They will prefer men of abandoned characters, and not suffer a man of knowledge to come near them or enjoy a place under them. They will disgrace men of virtue and rediculе virtue itself, and laugh at public spirit. They will put men into employments without any regard to their abilities or qualifications, only as they contribute to their designs, and shew a stupid alacrity to do what they are bid. They must be either fools or beggars; either void of capacity to discover their intrigues, or of credit and inclination to disappoint them.

They will by all practicable means of oppression provoke the people to disaffection; and then make that disaffection an argument for new oppression, for depriving them of liberties and privileges, to which they are entitled by their birth, and the laws of their country.

But if all these schemes for the ruin of the public, should fail them; and a few worthy patriots of a free country should prove obstinate, in defence of their country, and resolve to call its betrayers to a strict account; there is then but one thing left, for such traitors to do, that is to join with the enemy of their prince and country and so compleat their treason.

Printed and published for the AUTHORS by T. W. SHAW, Fleet-Street, opposite Anderton's Coffee-House, where Letters to the Publisher will be thankfully received. New Editions of all the Numbers of this spirited Paper, are now ready for Sale, and *complete sets* will be sent to any Part of *England, Carriage Free.*

THE

CRISIS

NUMBER LXVIII   *To be continued Weekly,*

DURING THE PRESENT BLOODY CIVIL WAR IN AMERICA.

SATURDAY, May 4, 1776   [Price Two-pence Half-penny.

TO THE KING.

SIR,

IT ought to be a reflection which you should often make, that in this
kingdom no man however exalted, is beyond the reach of punishment; you ought to reflect, that many things that begin *prosperously,*
often end *tragically.* You ought to consider, that the preservation of the
English constitution, hath, in all ages, appeared so dear, and valuable
to the people, that they would never suffer it to be destroyed either by
fraud, or the lawless power of their kings. In short Sir, did you but once
reflect on the many hard struggles, sharp encounters, and glorious resis-
tances made under tyrannical and powerful oppression; you could not
forbear to wonder at the fortitude, which hath hitherto inspired the souls
of Englishmen; you would then no longer join with an abandoned set of
ministers, in schemes destructive to the public welfare, and in attempts
to enslave the people: you may rest assured, Sir, that all your designs
will prove abortive, (notwithstanding the prostitution of both houses of
parliament) and instead of a *tame* submission to your plan of despotic

591

power, it is possible, you may feel the effects of their resentment, which now boils high; I would therefore have my countrymen take advantage of the humour they are in, and make a virtue of their present anger, and shew, that they who always scorned to be the property of tyrants, will not be the prey of slaves.

When the ancient Britons inhabited this island, they were renowned, for personal valour and an ardent love of liberty.—When they were inter-mingled with other nations, the same characteristics still marked them for a people—generous, humane, yet fearless of danger if contending for freedom, their *inherent birthright.* When, through length of time, and the natural course of things, monarchy was *permitted* by people, it was nevertheless so properly tempered, that the smallest encroachment upon their claims, the least violation of their privileges, was opposed with vigour; and the king who dared to countenance such proceedings, or plead his prerogative, as an excuse for his oppression, was instantly deemed an *enemy* to the state, a *traytor* to the commonwealth, and brand-ed with the epithet of *dastardly tyrant.*—When one of these miscreants, intoxicated with monarchical power, and not content to be looked upon only as the *first magistrate* in the kingdom presumed, of his own accord, to levy taxes and *encrease,* instead of *lessen,* public grievances—then, Sir, did our ancestors reduce this huge Leviathan: they made the lion crouch; and forced from his unweildly paw, *that ever-memorable charter,* which ought to be the loud boast of every *true born Englishman.* Sensible of the acquisition, and careful for their posterity, our great progenitors, taught by rueful experience, that truth seldom dwells in palaces, cared not to trust the *word* of future monarchs: but wisely exacted an *oath*, that they should hold their crown by the tenure of a strict adherence to MAGNA CHARTA, ONLY

Amongst your other *idle* amusements Sir, 'tis possible you may have read the history of a family, who by every tie of blood, succession, or heredi-tary right, deserved to wear the robe of royalty;—yet fascinated by the charms of arbitrary sway, they plunged the nation into civil discord; till oppressed beyond all bearing, the people, at length, *resumed* their awful power—and with one patriot blow, saved their sinking country from inevitable ruin. The heat of party however, soon subsiding, *British dignity,* roaming for safety in a foreign land, was a sight which touched the breasts of englishmen, with that compassion for which they are justly celebrated. The people therefore, exercised the christian virtue of forgiveness; buried their various wrongs, in silent oblivion; and with many an endearing mark of tenderness, invited over the descendant of a man, who however well qualified for the domestic purposes of *knitting* garters, *fabricating* buttons, *saluting* his lady, or dandling his children to sleep by the drone of a princely *lullaby* had yet none of the requisites, necessary in a king of England.

Charles the first, Sir, was chaste, timid, weak, pious, and shewed, if possible, as great an attachment to his wife as you do. His son, the second Charles, was abandoned, licentious and totally devoid of principle.

In short, Sir every branch of the Stuart race, displayed such a love for absolute rule; delighted so much in an extension of prerogative; that the abdication of that priest-ridden paltroon, James the second, only saved churchmen the trouble of making him a saint; or the nation, the formal ceremony, and expence, of *chopping* off his empty head in a solemn manner.

The mal-practices of this jesuitical family, ending at last in their total extermination, paved Sir, the way for the promotion, and astonishing elevation, of the house of Hanover, to the throne of those kingdoms.

The short reign of George the first, scarcely afforded us an opportunity of knowing, with precision, his real character. He was a perfect stranger to the manners, the genius, and the disposition of the English, But, when able to stammer our language, perceiving in the nation, a prodigious aversion at being governed by a foreigner; he discovered wisdom sufficient, to wish himself quietly reinstated in his *own* electorate. *Our late* monarch, wielded the sceptre, with the spirit of a soldier; acted, from himself; opposed with great vigour, two unnatural Scotch rebellions, that shook the fabric of our constitution; and died replete with honours and with age.

Now, Sir, indulge me, whilst I take a transiant view of your most *piteous* reign. Scarcely had *you* pronounced the lesson taught you by a

Scottish chieftain;—no sooner was the word BRITON sounded in our ears;—then we perceived, Sir, your mind strongly tainted with every highland notion, the despicable Caledonian could infuse. You stirred the very dregs of northan nobility, to find a favourite with whom to share the empire. *Lord Bute* from obscurity's obscurest corner, was summoned to bask himself at court; as a worm crawls forth from pu-trefaction, cherished by the sun's enlivening rays. Disgusted at the up-start insolence of such a mushroom, your ancient nobles blushed Sir, for a man, too *weak* to govern kingdoms; too *obstinate* to be advised; and too little *versed* in human nature to be capable of distinguishing real merit. What therefore, most mechanical Sir, was the powerful rea-son for this *undue* preferrence? what but some bewiching syren—an utter enemy to Britain's welfare, could have infatuated your untutored mind, or thus have rivetted your affections, upon a creature, in the shape of a man, possessed of every qualification bur intrinsic worth? if this all crafty Laird be endowed with any thing like abilities, they are, I will be answerable altogether *corporeal*; and therefore entirely unknown, to every person unless a certain lady long since dead; who much delighted in such *mysterious* charms. From this indissoluble, this jejune attachment, however, as from their real source and fountain, flow all the divided streams of infelicity, that will speedily deluge a land, *devoted*, by your headstrong weakness, to certain devastation. To make room for this insidious minion, the sacred ties of friendship were totally dissolved; former obligations were totally forgotten; rela-tions who presumed to remonstrate, were treated with cold indiffer-ence; and even gratitude, humanity's brightest ornament, was with the revolutions firmest friends, banished far distant from your habitation.

Think, Sir! brighten up your faculties! and, but for a moment, think of the dismal state, into which, by this precipitate unwary step, you threw Great Britain! deprived of all assistance, from men able to guide the complicated machine of Government,—distracted councils gave our en-emies fresh vigour—until most heartily despised abroad, a glorious and successful war, served by your *favourite's* mismanagement, only to render us more completely ridiculous.

You know, Sir, or it is now high time you was informed, that both the nations interest and honour were basely sacrificed to the sordid avarice of some ravenous harpies—who for the sake of gold, most chearfully, would exterminate the whole human race.

What followed the cession of hostilities, I scarcely need relate. Murmurs, discontents, accusations, and motions for impeachment were answered by *Scotch addresses, raggamuffin panegyrists, prostitute citizens, the votes of court-sycophants,* and by the resignation of a raw-bone prime *any-thing—* but minister.

Even, during such a peace, have the arts been assiduously cultivated? Hath science reared her dejected head? Has all due encouragement been given to men of illustrious merit? Lord Bute indeed *affected* to be thought a Mæcenas, a distinguished patron of literature.[1] As a proof of the extreme refinement of his taste, he made a *Scotch renegade parson,* his principal confident; delegated to the *quack, Hill,* who pretended to lengthen human life, by a leaf of sage, the care of Kew Gardens; pensioned that veteran self-important jacobite *Shebbeare* alias *Cinna;* and gave the man who whiped the cobwebs from his musty books, a seat in parliament— Whilst you, Sir, have been *ravished* with enchanting harmony; *exalted* beyond the limits of humanity, by the grace of Pianissimo; and *absorbed* in the various beauties of painting, building, or collecting *rareshows.*[2]

When his Lairdship was driven from the public theatre of life, he deputed certain engines to continue his pious work, of reducing us to an abject state of slavery. The friends of liberty pursued him Sir, with success. Worried him through all his haunts. He sheltered himself like another *Rogers,** under the foldings of a royal hoop petticoat: and when forced to fly

---

*Roger Mortimer lay with Isabella mother of young Edward the Third and by his influence over her almost ruined the nation.

---

1. Gaius Maecenas was remembered as a patron of the arts in Augustan Rome. He is commented upon by Suetonius in his *Twelve Caesars,* Tacitus in the *Annals,* and Horace wrote one of his *Odes* "To Maecenas" in gratitude for his support.

2. George Rousseau recently characterized Hill as "The Man Destroyed by Ambition in the Age of Celebrity" in *The Notorious Sir John Hill* (Bethlehem, Pa.: Lehigh University

for safety, to his cater cusin the *Pretender,* you Sir, was commanded, by a certain female, to commence his champion, and brave his cause, against such as should call in question his PARTS, his patriotism, or his honesty. Accordingly Sir you have been indefatigable in pursuing with rigour, the author of an harmless paper, meerly on account of his opposition to Lord Bute. Your time might, me-thinks have been employed to much better advantage. Your christian piety, Sir, should alone have taught you to forgive an injury: but your rank and station called for a nobleness of soul entirely exempt from, and far superior to resentment—an abject passion, calculated only for sordid base-borne minds. The firmness however of a man has before now totally defeated the merciless cruelty of an abstemious, chaste, virtuous sovereign.

Parliaments Sir, ought to be the guardians of our liberties. When we are legally represented, the House of Commons is the sacred magazine, wherein are deposited British priviliges and immunities;—curtailed of which, existence becomes a burthen, and a curse. A French writer, Sir, called Montesquieu, pronounces it impossible for this kingdom ever to be undone, unless by the corruption of its senators.

The present parliament, Sir—*Britons* I perceive your indignation rise! friends and fellow-countrymen, I entreat your pardon, for this hasty slip of my ungarded pen! the *motley* mixture at Westminster, I mean, is a self-created junto; the majority of whom, under the favour Sir, of your illus-

---

Press, 2012). Hill succeeded as a prolific man of letters and self-taught botanist; but he was also, as Rousseau put it, "a villain, a rascal, a cheat, a fraud, a fake, a plagiarist, a provocateur, a wag" (p. xiv)—and the list continues, as Hill importuned others to advance his own career. The "quack" allusion is to his practicing his own brand of herbal-based medicine, though he did have a medical degree from Edinburgh. As a political satirist John Shebbeare could wield a caustic pen; as a writer in support of the King he had been living off a pension granted over a decade before. "CINNA"—and was that indeed Shebbeare?—wrote in defense of the ministry, in essays that appeared in various London newspapers through 1775. See, for example, the *Middlesex Journal*, 7 February 1775 and the *Morning Post*, 15 February 1775, and occasional pieces in both papers through July; Shebbeare died in November. This was not the author(s)' first jab at Shebbeare—see n. XXVIII.1 infra; also see the *Oxford DNB* essay on Shebbeare by M. John Cardwell at 50:143–46.

trious auspices, are daily violating those rights purchased by the blood, the treasure, and the manly fortitude, of our gallant forefathers. Think you I venture beyond the limits of decency? for God's sake, Sir, by what name am I to call a meeting, which assumes to itself the right of judicature, determines upon incapacitation, and erects its own existence, upon the total ruin of our most hallowed laws? that it is degenerated from its original institution is a plain matter of fact, That a person was expelled because obnoxious—this is a truth that all Europe, who laugh at our puppet-show ministry, can amply testify:—the fatigues those wretches have undergone, to banish from their councils every person of worth and honour, are in reality, not to be compared with the steps they have pursued to people a chapel with a congregation quite of their own complexion. Sooner than suffer their schemes to prove *abortive,* murders were committed, and the parties, who gloried in the ministerial slaughter, pardoned by your clemency.

During your reign, to cut a throat with impunity, the hardy assassin needs but to have a *prostitute* sister, circumstances, which greatly alleviate his guilt, are instantly discovered by a sharp-sighted court-minion, who has a fellow-feeling in the case. Your acquiescing, Sir, in such complicated villainy, greatly lessens the high-flown opinion, we are taught to conceive about your pious virtues.

In short, great Sir, were your eyes but couched, clearly would you perceive, that your people are enslaved. You would see yourself grosly deceived, cajoled, bamboozled, and imposed upon. You would discover, that the nation is in a ferment; that factions, fomented by court-parisites, gather strength and that your very throne is so besprinkled with *innocent blood,* as to render it utterly impossible, for any thing but a general sacrifice of the whole banditti of a ministry, to wash out the stains.

If then you regard with an eye of paternal tenderness, your own offspring! if you wish well to this once happy island! call forth, Sir, for God's sake! call forth, your magnanmity! summon all your recollection! shake off the slumbers of *domestic* indulgence, nor longer let your own obstinacy, and the villainy of your minions destroy our chartered freedom!

Forgive me, Sir, thus presuming to advise: but hard is the condition of princes. Listen to the faithful voice of your unbiased people. They speak a language you are *bound* to *hear*. From them you need not fear deception.

Let sterling merit be a sufficient introduction to your presence. Build your now tottering Empire upon a solid basis. Reign in our hearts. Act with the dignity of a man:—nor borrow consequence from crowns. Be *mindful*, that you are born, Sir, for deeds far more exalted, than barely propigating the species, or excelling in mechanics. And as nature deals much in revolutions, wear always one truth near your heart. A single vote transferred three mighty kingdoms. Some short time hence, 'tis possible, *a resolute majority of millions* may, from the topmast pinnacle of greatness, hurl head-long an *incorrigable* Monarch; and send him to the book of sufferings to learn that all power is derived from, and lodged in the people only; and that Englishmen will never long tamely submit to *ministerial slavery,* nor *Kingly tyranny.*

Printed and Published for the Authors by T. W. SHAW, Fleet-Street, opposite Anderton's Coffee-House, where Letters to the Publisher will be thankfully received. New Editions of all the Numbers of this spirited Paper, are now ready for Sale, and *complete sets* will be sent to any Part of *England, Carriage Free.*

THE

CRISIS

NUMBER LXIX   *To be continued Weekly,*

DURING THE PRESENT BLOODY CIVIL WAR IN AMERICA.

SATURDAY, MAY 11, 1776   [Price Two-pence Half-penny.

A serious Warning to Great Britain, addressed

TO THE KING.

May it please your Majesty,

IF we examine the history of all nations that ever became famous for their power and greatness, and trace them to their dissolution, we shall find that a general corruption and depravity always prevailed and preceded their destruction. This great truth is particularly taught in the writings of the old testament, which Bishop Atterbury (in his Sermon intitled the wisdom of providence manifested in the revolutions of government, preached before the House of Commons the 29th of May 1701) says, is so full in what regards societies or civil bodies of men, "that there is no need of repeating lessons there so often inculcated, nor no room for improving upon them, which is the reason so little is said in relation to them in the gospel; And that the various and strange necessitudes the Jews underwent from their first erection into a people down to their final excision, is so punctually registered and transmitted to us, that we might in them as in the glass of providence distinctly see the several ways and methods of God's dealing with great states and kingdoms and be fully instructed in the rules of his raising or depressing, prospering or punishing them by the interposition of a divine power as visible almost as the virtues or vices that occasioned it."[1]

The Israelites a stiff necked and rebellious though chosen people, were not put in possession of the land of Canaan for their own righteousness or superior Virtue and merit above all other nations, but because of the great wickedness and impiety of the native inhabitants who had then compleated the measure of their iniquity, and were ripe for destruction; the Israelites in their turn, from the same causes experienced the same effects.

This being the usual method of the Almightys dealing with great states and kingdoms, whereby he sheweth himself to be a God that judgeth the earth; and when it is evident that a general corruption and depravity prevails, that laying house to house, and field to field till there is no place for the poor; pride, covetousness, dissipation of all kinds, oaths,* and adultery and all other vices that brought ruin and desolation even upon the jewish state, have deluged the land, and pervaded all ranks and degrees of people; ought not the nation in general, and the rulers in

---

*Custom House and Excise laws, and the corrupt practices at elections for members of parliament, have carried perjury with them throughout the kingdom; and children of the lower class of people, from the example of their parents, are taught to lisp out oaths and curses before they can speak plain.

---

1. From the sermon by Francis Atterbury, future Bishop of Rochester, in the House of Commons on 29 May 1701, marking the anniversary of the "Restoration" of Charles II. Ambitious Tory and high-church Anglican, Atterbury would end his days in exile, serving the Old Pretender (James III). He had begun publishing his sermons in his lifetime (including this one, soon after he delivered it) in a failed attempt to secure his position among the Tory leadership that tried to check the rising Whigs during the reign of Queen Anne. It is not clear which source the author(s) of *The Crisis* turned to, and, as often was the case, the quotations are reworked. I used Francis Atterbury, D.D., *Sermons and Discourses on Several Subjects and Occasion*s, 8th ed., 4 vols. (London: L. Davis et al., 1766), 1:254–55. See D. W. Hayton's essay in the *Oxford DNB*, 2:865–71.

particular seriously attend to such calamitous signs of the times and by a proper reformation endeavour to avert the wrath of heaven from being further poured out upon us.

So long ago as the year 1709 DEAN SWIFT published a pamphlet called, *a project for the advancement of religion and the reformation of manners*, In which he says, "It is in the power of the prince to make piety and virtue become the fashion of the age, if at the same time he would make them necessary qualifications for favour and preferment, by making it every mans interest and honour, to cultivate religion and virtue, by making vice a disgrace, and the certain ruin to preferment or pretensions." Having described the methods by which such a desirable event might be brought about, he adds, "And that some effectual attempt should be made towards such a reformation is perhaps more necessary than people commonly apprehend, because the ruin of a state is generally preceded by an universal degeneracy of manners and contempt of religion which is entirely our care at present;" and near the conclusion he writes thus, "The present queen is a princess of as many great virtues as ever filled a throne. How would it brighten her character to the present and future ages if she would exert her utmost authority, to instil some share of those virtues into her people, which they are too degenerate to learn only from her example? and be it spoken with all veneration possible, for so excellent a sovereign, her best endeavours in this most weighty affair, are a most important part of her duty, as well as of her interest and her honour."[2]

I believe if the dean was now living, he would say, that our iniquities were greatly increased, and that it was so much the more the duty of rulers, to set about a reformation at this time than it was then. And that men fearing God and hating covetousness ought to be the only counsellors to the king: and promoting religion and virtue the principal employment of the prince. From such men and such endeavours, we expect the favour of heaven, without which the greatest fleets and armies are

---

2. [Jonathan Swift], *Project for the Advancement of Religion and Reformation of Manners* (London: Benjamin Tooke, 1709), pp. 14–15, 16, 44–45, 58–59.

vain. For notwithstanding the omnipotence of parliament, neither their fleets nor their armies can advance one *foot* further than the *omnipotent* himself will give them leave. For instance, the proud Sinacherib *Isaiah* 37, v.24, "talks big, he had already put Jerusalem into consternation, and boasted of greater mischiefs he intended; But he that sits in heaven, laughs at him, and the great Jehovah derides the little talking insect, assures the prophet that beyond such a field he shall not step, and as he saith, he doth.—When Maxentius had filled Rome with murders, and the people feared not only greater injuries to their persons, but a total desolation, the almighty sets bounds to his brutish courage, and sends the great Constantine to remove him, and with him the yoke he had laid on the trembling people.—Selimus the Turk, in the year 1569, set out from Constantinople with Twenty-five thousand horse, and three thousand janizaries and joins an army of the Precopine Tartars, consisting of eighty thousand horse more, besides a navy at sea of a hundred and fifty gallies manned and provided with suitable amunition, to invade the kingdom of Astracan, he had already swallowed the empire in his hopes, distributed the various provinces to his Bashaws, and consulted how to govern the kingdom conquered already in imagination, its true the inhabitants of Astracan were in great confusion, but the mighty God, who fits up one and pulls down another, comes in, dashes all the swelling hopes of the haughty Sultan, and beyond expectation all that mighty army pines and dwindles away on their march, some of them come as far as Azeph, and of that vast multitude only two thousand returned to Constantinople."

The Spanish Armada in the famous year 1588, is another instance of the controuling power of the almighty, mentioned with the foregoing, in an old sermon on the 30th of January now in my possession. And doubtless our rulers are arrived at that degree of infidelity the jews were, who said, the Lord hath forsaken the earth, the Lord seeth us not.* They must acknowledge an over ruling providence, that hath hitherto frustrated their designs against America. Because they were full of blood and distruction, not contrived in his fear, and therefore unsupported by his favour.

---

*Ezekiel 9 v. 9.

Above eight years ago I wrote to your majesty, and in that letter I thought it my duty to say in the words of the prophet. That I believe great was the anger and the wrath of the lord against this people* which now begins to appear to our very great confusion, and except we turn to him that smiteth us we shall smart under still severer judgments. Though the signs of the times, and the great iniquity of the band might alone justly warrant such belief, I have more particular reasons for it, derived from a most wonderful surprizing appearance I saw in the air, an account of which I sent to the late Archbishop of Canterbury, the 17th of September, 1767, (the day the Duke of York died,) as follows.

"The Almighty is unchangeable, and unless we amend our ways and doings, we can have no reason to expect but he will as certainly punish us for our vices, as he did the nations of old. Nay, we may justly now say, he has begun to lay his hand upon us, for we have felt some severe tokens of an angry providence; Nothing of late has prospered in our hands, but even the very nature of things has been inverted!" of which I gave several instances, and then thus proceeded to relate what I had seen.—"On the 4th of September between five and six o'clock in the evening, walking in the City Road, near Islington, I saw, what I believe your grace will acknowledge to be a very uncommon appearance in the air, looking up I was particularly struck with a large blue cloud, like a mountain, the sides and top of which were covered with a most resplendent border resembling silver lace, but far exceeding it in brightness and many little lighter blue coloured clouds, with the same kind of border, detached from the great one, formed the most beautiful sight that was ever seen by mortal eyes. I stood still near a quarter of an hour, if not more, to survey this splendid appearance, in which time I saw, as plain as I now see this paper I am writing upon, on the top of the great blue cloud, the likeness of the hind part of a large white horse, and the form of a man with a plume upon his head riding upon it. Soon after the figure of a lion made its appearance on the north side, which I attentively surveyed for some time, and said to myself a lion in the air, what can this mean! and turning my

*Jeremiah 36 v. 7.

eyes to the south, in a white cloud at a distance from the blue one, I beheld the figure of a man with all the marks of death in his face, stretched out on his back, his arms laying extended close by his side, a woman standing at his feet, leaning towards him, with her arms stretched out as if inclined to help him. This appearance remained I believe five minutes in full proportion, and then gradually sunk away; the shining border I had before seen, disappeared and nothing but common clouds remained. The great author and governor of the universe does nothing in vain, nor for no purpose; and in times like these, when we see the nature of things inverted on earth, and uncommon appearances in the air, ought they not to awaken our attention, and incline us to consider our ways and be wise."

Two copies of the above, I sent to your majesty, one the 1st of November, 1767, the other the 11th of January, 1770, and it was published in the Whisperer the 9th of June 1770, and in the Ledger the 10th of August 1774. The colour of the lion was red as blood, which I at that time thought unnatural, but it then struck me no otherways than as a mark that the dying person was of the royal family, which was the case, for according to the Gazette it was the day after the severity of the Duke of York's illness began, that this extraordinary sight appeared, in which it was remarkable, that there were three signs, the last of which, was at that very time fulfilling, and the second is now accomplished; for, whether those sanguinary degrees, which have filled America with blood, took their rise from a man or men from the North, or Lord North himself, I appeal to your majesty if the wit of men or angels, could devise a more comprehensive striking emblem of the present times than a blood red lion issuing from the North.

Only one sign now remains to be fulfilled, which appears to me to have a very fatal meaning both to king and people, particularly to the royal family, the accomplishment of which, as it is our duty, it will be our greatest interest and happiness, by a speedy reformation to prevent.

As the preservation of the house of Hanover upon the throne and saving Great Britain from the horrors of internal war, are not unworthy of the particular interposition of providence, I would flatter myself the aforementioned supernatural appearance was sent from above, to give the nation warning of the impending danger, that by a suitable conduct it might be averted.

Whether your majesty and the people will take warning or not, I have done what I apprehend to be my duty, and leave the event to the sovereign disposer of all things, who bringeth low and lifteth up, whose works are all truth and his ways judgment and those that walk in pride he is able to abase—Daniel 4.v.34.

I am, may it please your majesty,

Your majesty's most faithful subject,

William Stewardson.

Cottons Wharf, Southwark,
May 11, 1776.

Printed and Published for the AUTHORS by T. W. SHAW, Fleet-Street, opposite Anderton's Coffee-House, where Letters to the Publisher will be thankfully received. New Editions of all the Numbers of this spirited Paper, are now ready for Sale, and *complete sets* will be sent to any Part of *England, Carriage Free.*

THE

CRISIS

NUMBER LXX   *To be continued Weekly,*

DURING THE PRESENT BLOODY CIVIL WAR IN AMERICA.

SATURDAY, MAY 18, 1776   [Price Two-pence Half-penny.

For the C R I S I S.

BY liberty, I understand the power which every man has over his own actions, and his right to enjoy the fruits of his labour, art, and industry, as far as by it he hurts not the society, or any members of it, by taking from any member, or by hindering him from enjoying what he himself enjoys. The fruits of a man's honest industry are the just rewards of it, ascertained to him by natural and eternal equity, as is his title to use them in the manner which he thinks fit: and thus with the above limitations, every man is sole lord and arbiter of his own private actions and property.—A character of which no man living can divest him but by usurpation, or his own consent.

The entering into political society, is so far from a departure from his natural right, that to preserve it was the sole reason why men did so; and mutual protection and assistance is the only reasonable purpose of all reasonable societies. To make such protection practicable, magistracy was formed, with power to defend the innocent from violence, and to punish those that offered it; nor can there by any other pretence for magistracy in the world. In order to this good end, the magistrate is entrusted with conducting and applying the united force of the community; and with exacting such a share of every man's property, as is necessary to preserve the whole, and to defend every man and his property from foreign and domestic injuries. These are boundaries of the power of the magistrate, who deserts his function when ever he breaks them. By the laws of society, he is more limited and restrained than any man amongst them; since, while they are absolutely free in all their actions, which purely concern themselves; all his actions, as a public person, being for the sake of society, must refer to it, and answer the ends of it.

It is a mistaken notion in government, that the interest of the majority is only to be consulted, since in society every man has a right to every man's assistance in the enjoyment and defence of his private property; otherwise the greater number may sell the lesser, and divide their estates amongst themselves; and so, instead of a society, where all peaceable men are protected, become a conspiracy of the many against the minority. With as much equity may one man wantonly dispose of all, and violence may be sanctified by mere power.

And it is as foolish to say, that government is concerned to meddle with the private thoughts and actions of men, while they injure neither the society, nor any of its members. Every man is, in nature and reason, the judge and disposer of his own domestic affairs; and, according to the rules of religion and equity, every man must carry his own conscience. So that neither has the magistrate, or any body else any manner of power to model people's speculations, no more than their dreams. Government being intended to protect men from the injuries of one another, and not to direct them in their own affairs, in which no one is interested but themselves: it is plain that their thoughts and domestic concerns are exempted intirely from its jurisdiction: in truth, men's thoughts are not subjected to their own jurisdiction.

Idiots and lunatics indeed, who cannot take care of themselves, must be taken care of by others, but while men have their five senses, I cannot see what the magistrate has to do with his actions by which the society cannot be affected; and where he meddles with such, he meddles impertinently or tyrannically. Must the magistrate tie up every man's legs, because some men fall into ditches? or must he put out their eyes, because with them they see lying vanities? or, would it become the wisdom and care of governors to establish a travelling society, to prevent people by a proper confinement, from throwing themselves into wells or over precipices: or to endow a fraternity of physicians and surgeons all over the nation, to take care of their subjects health, without being consulted; and to vomit, bleed, purge and scarify them at pleasure, whether they would or no, just as these established judges of health shall think fit? If this were the case what a stir and hubbub should we soon see kept about the established potions and lancets? Every man, woman, or child, though ever so healthy, must be a patient, or woe be to them! the best diet and medicines would soon grow pernicious from any other hand; and their pills alone, however rediculous, insufficient, or distasteful, would be attended with a blessing.

Let people alone, they will take care of themselves, and do it the best; and if they do not, a sufficient punishment will follow their neglect, without the magistrate's interposition and penalties. It is plain, that such busy care and officious intrusion into the personal affairs, or private actions, thoughts and imaginations of men, has in it more craft than kindness; and is only a device to mislead the people, and pick their pockets, under the false pretence of the public and their private good. To quarrel with any man for his opinions, humours, or the fashion of his cloaths, is an offence taken without being given. What is it to a magistrate how I wash my hands, or cut my corns; what fashion or colour I wear, or what notions I entertain, or what gestures I use, or what words I pronounce, when they please me, and do him and my neighbour no hurt? as well may he determine the colour of my hair, and controul my shape and features.

True and impartial liberty is therefore the right of every man to pursue the natural, reasonable, and religious dictates of his own mind; to think what he will, and act as he thinks, provided he acts not to the prejudice of another; to spend his own money himself, and lay out the produce of his labour his own way; and to labour for his own pleasure and profit, and not for others who are idle, and would live and riot by pillaging and oppressing him, and those that are like him.

So that evil government is only a partial restraint put by the laws of agreement and society upon natural and absolute liberty, which might otherwise grow licentious: and tyranny is an unlimited restraint put upon natural liberty, by the will of one or a few. Magistracy, amongst a free people, is the exercise of power for the sake of the people; and tyrants abuse the people, for the sake of power. Free government is protecting the people and their liberties by stated rules: tyranny is a brutish struggle for unlimited liberty to one or a few, who would rob all others of their liberty, and act by no rule but lawless lust.

So much for an idea of civil liberty. I will now add a word or two, to shew how much is it the delight and passion of mankind; and then shew its advantages.

The love of liberty is an appetite so strongly implanted in the nature of all living creatures, that even the appetite of self-preservation which is allowed to be the strongest, seems to be contained in it; since by the means of liberty they enjoy the means of preserving themselves, and of satisfying their desires in a manner which they themselves choose and like best. Many animals can never be tamed, but feel the bitterness of restraint in the midst of the kindest usage; and rarher than bear it, grieve and starve themselves to death; and some beat out their brains against their prisons.

This passion for liberty in men, and their possession of it, is of that efficacy and importance, that it seems the parent of all the virtues: and therefore in free countries there seems to be another species of mankind, than is to be found under tyrants. Small armies of *Greeks* and *Romans* dispised the greatest hosts of slaves; and a million of slaves have been some times beaten and conquered by a few thousand freemen, Insomuch that the difference seems greater between them than between men and sheep; it was therefore well said by *Luculius*, when being about to engage the great king *Tigranes*'s army, he was told by some of his officers, how prodigious great the same was, consisting of between three and four hundred thousand men: *no matter*, said the brave *Roman*, drawing up his little army of fourteen thousand, but fourteen thousand *Romans*:

no matter, the lion never enquires into the number of the sheep. And these royal troops proved no better; for the Roman's had little else to do but to kill and pursue; which yet they could scarce for laughing; for more were they diverted than annimated by the rediculous dread and sudden flight of those imperial slaves and royal cowards.

Education alters nature, and becomes stronger. Slavery, while it continues, being a perpetual awe upon the spirits, depresses them, and sinks natural courage; and want and fear, the concomitants of bondage, always produces dispondency and baseness; nor will men in bonds ever fight bravely, but to be free. Indeed, what else should they fight for; since every victory that they gain for a tyrant, makes them poorer and fewer; and, increasing his pride, increases his cruelty, with their own misery and chains?

Indeed liberty is the divine source of human happiness. To possess in security, the effects of our industry, is a most powerful and reasonable incitement to be industrious: and to be able to provide for our children, and to leave them all that we have, is the best motive to beget them. But where property is precarious, labour will languish. The privileges of thinking, saying, and doing, what we please, and of growing as rich as we can, without any other restriction, than that by all this we hurt not the public, nor one another, are the glorious privileges of liberty; and its effects, to live in freedom, plenty, and safety.

These are previleges that increase mankind. and the happiness of mankind. And therefore countries are generally peopled in proportion as they are free, and are certainly happy in that proportion: and upon the same tract of land that would maintain a hundred thousand freemen in plenty, five thousand slaves would starve. In *Italy*, fertile *Italy*, men die sometimes of hunger amongst the sheaves, and in a plentiful harvest; for what they sow and reap is none of their own; and their cruel and greedy governors, who live by the labour of their wretched vassals, do not suffer them to eat the bread of their own earning, nor to sustain their lives with their own hands.

Liberty naturally draws new people to it, as well as increases the old stock; and men as naturally run when they dare from slavery and wretchedness, when ever they can help themselves. Hence great cities loosing their liberty become deserts and little towns, by liberty grow great cities; as will be fully proved before I have gone through this argument. I will not deny, but there are some great cities of slaves: but such are only imperial cities, and the seats of great princes, who draw the wealth of a continent to their capital, the center of treasure and luxury. *Babylon, Antioch, Seleucia*, and *Alexandria*, were great cities peopled by tyrants; but peopled partly by grants and indulgencies, their power great and boundless as it was, could not alone people their cities; but they were forced to soften authority by kindness; and having brought the inhabitants together by force, and by driving them captive like cattle, could not keep them together, without bestowing on them many privileges, to encourage the first inhabitants to stay and invite more to come.

This was a confession in those tyrants, that their power was mischievous and unjust; since they could not erect one great city, and make it flourish, without renouncing in a great measure their power over it; which by granting it these privileges, in effect they did. These privileges were fixed laws, by which the trade and industry of the citizens were encouraged, and their lives and properties ascertained and protected, and no longer subjected to the laws of mere will and pleasure: and therefore while these free cities, enjoying their own liberties and laws, flourish under them; the provinces were miserably harassed, pillaged, dis-peopled, and improverished, and the inhabitants exhausted, starved, butchered and carried away captive.

This shews that all civil happiness and prosperity is inseparable from liberty; and that tyranny cannot make men, or societies of men, happy, without departing from its nature, and giving them privileges inconsistent with tyranny. And here is an unanswerable argument, amongst a thousand others, against, absolute power in a single man. Nor is there one way in the world to give happiness to communities, but by sheltering them under certain and express laws, irrevocable at any man's pleasure.

There is not, nor can be any security for a people to trust to the mere will of one, who while his will is the law, cannot protect them if he would. The number of sycophants and wicked counsellors, that he will always and necessarily have about him, will defeat all his good intentions, by representing things falsely and persons maliciously; by suggesting danger where it is not, and urging necessity where there is none; by filling their own coffers, under colour of filling his, and by raising money for themselves, pretending the public exigencies of the state, by sacrificing particular men to their own revenge, under pretence of public security; and by engaging him and his people in dangerous wars, for their own profit or fame; by throwing public affairs into perpetual confusion, to prevent an enquiry into their own behaviour, and by making him jealous of his people, and his people of him, on purpose to manage and mislead both sides.

But if the disposition of such a prince be evil, what must be the condition of his people, and what door of hope can remain for common protection! The best princes have often evil councellers, the bad shall have no other: and in such a case what bounds can be set to their fury, and to the havock they will make? The instruments and advisers of tyranny and depradation always thrive best and are nearest their ends, when depradation and ryranny run highest: when most is plundered from the people, their share is greatest; we may therefore suppose every evil will befall such a people, without supposing extravagantly. No happiness, no security, but certain misery, and a vile and precarious life, are the blessed terms of such a government—A government which necessarily includes all evils, and from the same necessity neither must nor can redress any, which is a true and faithful picture of the present government in England under George the obstinate.

Printed and Published for the AUTHORS by T. W. SHAW, Fleet-Street. opposite Anderton's Coffee-House, where Letters to the Publisher will be thankfully received. New Editions of all the Numbers of this spirited Paper, are now ready for Sale, and *complete sets* will be sent to any Part of *England, Carriage Free.*

THE

CRISIS

NUMBER LXXI   *To be continued Weekly,*

DURING THE PRESENT BLOODY CIVIL WAR IN AMERICA.

SATURDAY, May 25, 1776   [Price Two-pence Half-penny.

For the C R I S I S.

S I R,

By your leave I mean to shew how much it is the interest of the king and his ministers to use the people well; by making these observations the subject of your next paper, you will particularly oblige

Your's A. B.

IT is altogether impossible for one man or a small number of men, to support themselves in power upon their own proper strength, without taking in the assistance of a great many others, and they can never have that assistance, unless they take in their interest too; for men will laugh at bare arguments brought to prove, that they must labour, be robbed of that labour, and want; that others may live in idleness, riot, and plunder. Those governments therefore which are founded upon oppression, always find it necessary to engage interests enough in their tyranny to overcome all opposition from those who are tyrannized over,

615

by giving *separate* and *unequal* privileges to the instruments and accomplices of their oppression and cruelty.

But, when a government is founded upon liberty and equal laws, it is rediculous for those in the administration to have any hopes of preserving themselves long there, but by just actions, or the appearance of just actions; and by letting the people find, or fancy they find, their own happiness in their submission. It is certain that the people have so just a dread of public disturbances, that they will bear a great deal before they will involve themselves in tumults and wars;[1] and mankind are so prone to emulation and ambition, and to pursue their separate interests, that it is easy to form them into parties, and play those parties in their turns upon one another; but all parties will at last compare notes, and find out that they are only made use of as cudgels in the hands of wicked men, to assault each other by turns, till they are both undone. It is downright madness, to hope long to govern ALL against the interest of ALL.

People will for some time be dallied with, and amused with false reasonings, misrepresentations, and promises, wild expectations, vain terrors and imaginary fears; but all these hopes and apprehensions will vanish by degrees, will produce a quite contrary effect, and no wise man will think it prudent to provoke a whole people. What could king James do against his whole people? His ministers betrayed him, his family deserted him, his soldiers revolted from him, and it was foolish to expect any thing else; for how could he hope, that those who could have no motive to stand by him, besides their own personal interest, and every motive to oppose him arising from conscience and honour, would not leave him when that interest changed, and when they could serve themselves better by serving their country.

I laugh at the stupid notions of those who think that more is due from them to their patrons, who are trusted to dispose of employments for the public benefit, than to their country, for whose sake, and by whose

---

1. Locke is being echoed here on the reluctance of people to rise in rebellion—see Laslett, *Second Treatise*, "Of the Dissolution of Government," section 225 at p. 415 (and n. IX.5 supra), which would later be written into the Declaration of Independence.

direction, those employments were first instituted, out of whose pocket the profits of them arise, and from whose confidence or credulity their pretended benefactors derive all their power to give them. Those who receive them, accept the gift upon the terms of the constitution, that is to execute them faithfully for the public good, and not to take the people's money to destroy the people.

What did the whole power of Spain do against a few revolted provinces, when all the people were enraged by oppression? how many armies were lost, how many millions foolishly squandered, to recover by force what a few just concessions would have done at once? Her generals no sooner took one town, but two revolted; and they sometimes lost ten without striking a stroke, for one that they gained by the sword: What by the mutinies of her own soldiers, and other common events, which usually happen in such cases, they twice lost altogether, and were forced to begin their game anew; and so destroyed a mighty empire, to oppress a little part of it, whose affections might have been regained by doing them but common justice.

It is senseless to hope to overcome some sorts of convulsive distempers, by holding the patient's hands, and tying him with ropes, which will only encrease the malady; whereas the softest remedies ought to be used: Violent methods may stop the distemper for a little time, but the cause of the grief remains behind, and will break out again more furiously. What did king James get by all his bloody executions in the West, by his manacling us with chains, and keeping up a military force, to lock them on, but to frighten his friends, still more to provoke his enemies, and at last to unite them all against himself? And yet, I believe, I may venture to assert, that if, instead of throwing the broad seal into the Thames, and deserting his people, he had suffered his parliament to sit, and given up some of the instruments of his tyranny, and had permitted them to have taken a few proper precautions to have hindred it for the future, he need not have been a fugitive through the world.

It is certain, that if king Charles had made at first, and with a good grace, but half of those concessions which were extorted from him afterwards, that bloody war, so fatal to himself and family, had been prevented, and the ambition or malice of his personal enemies had been suppressed, or turned to their own confusion, and he himself might have reigned a happy prince, with as much power as he had a right to by the constitution: Whereas, if my Lord *Clarendon* is to be believed; the whole kingdom (very few excepted) took part against the court at first, and continued to do so 'till some leading men in the House of Commons discovered intentions to overturn the monarchy itself.

It is foolish therefore to be frightened with apprehensions which may be removed at pleasure: the way to cure people of their fears, is, not to frighten them further, but to remove the causes of their fears. If the kingdom be disaffected, (as its enemies of all sorts would make us believe) let enquiry be made into the motives of that disaffection. It cannot be *personally* to his Majesty, who is a *most excellent* Prince; and his greatest opponents neither do nor can object to him those vices, which too often accompany and are allied to crowns: nor is there the least pretence to accuse him of any *Designs* of enlarging his *Prerogative* beyond its due bounds. It is certain, that when he came to the crown, he had a large share in the affections of his people, *and he himself has done nothing to make it less.*

It cannot be to his title, which is the best upon earth, even the positive consent of a great and free nation.

Whence therefore should such disaffection arise, if there be any such as I hope there is not? and it plainly appears that there is not or that it is not general, by the dutiful *reception* which his majesty meets with in *all places.* And the same loyal disposition would appear more and more every day, if those who have the honour to be admitted to his more immediate confidence would represent honestly to him what he ought to know.

It is childish to say, that a few flies and insects can rise a great dust; or, that a small number of disappointed and unpreferred men can shake a great kingdom, with a wise prince at the head of it, supported with such power and dependances. A great fire cannot be raised without feuel, and the materials which make it must have been combustible, before. And if this be our case we ought to ask how came they so? and who made them inflamable? Who laid the Gunpowder? as well as who fired or intended to fire it? When we have done this, we ought to remove the causes of the distemper, allay the heat of the fever by gentle lenatives, throw no more fiery spirits to inflame the constitution, but do all that we can to soften and cool it.

Every Country in the world will have many malcontents; some through want and necessity; others through ambition and restlesness of temper; many from disappointments and personal resentment; more from the fear of just punishment for crimes: but all these together can never be dangerous to any state, which knows how to seperate the peoples resentment from theirs. Make the former easy, and the others are disarmed at once. When the causes of general discontent are removed, particular discontents will signify nothing.

The first care which wise governors will always take is, to prevent their subjects from wanting, and to secure to them the possession of their property, upon which every thing else depends. They will raise no taxes but what the people shall see a necessity for raising; and no longer than that necessity continues: and such taxes ought to be levied cautiously, and laid out frugally. No project ought to be formed to enrich *a few,* and to ruin thousands: for when men of fortune come to lose their fortunes, they will try by all means to get new ones; and when they cannot do it fairly, they will do it as they are able; and if they cannot do it at all, will throw all things into confusion, to make others as miserable as themselves. If people are poor, they will be desperate and catch at every occasion, and join with every faction, to make public disturbances, and to make their own condition better, when they find it cannot be worse.

Wise statesmen will see all this at a distance; will use the best precautions, and most prudent measures, to procure general plenty, encrease trade and manufactures, and keep the people usefully employed at home, instead of starving, and prating sedition in the streets. They will not be perpetually provoking them with constant injuries, giving them eternal occasions and reasons for dissatisfaction, and then quarrel with them for shewing it, and be still encreasing their discontents, by preposterously endeavouring to put a stop to them by new shackles, armed bands, bribery and corruption, and by laying on them fresh burdens and impositions to maintain such oppressions; and so when they have raised resentment to the highest pitch vainly hope to stop the tide. This is what the king of Spain did formerly in the Dutch provinces, and king James the Second in England, but what, I hope, will never be seen here again.

But it will be said, that people will be sometimes dissatisfied without any just provocations given to them by their governors; the necessities of all states will sometimes subject themselves to greater taxes and other seeming oppressions, than they can well bear.

When this happens to be the case, there ought to be double diligence used to prevent the ill consequences from such disaffection: no more money ought to be raised than is strictly necessary, for the peoples protection; and they are to be shewn that necessity, and are to see from time to time, the accounts of what they give, that it is disbursed frugally and honestly, and not engrossed by private men, lavished upon minions, or squandered away in usless pensions to undeservers, and that the product of the whole peoples labour and substance is not suffered to be devoured by a few of the worst of men.

What can be more invidious, than for a nation staggering under the weight and oppression of its debts, eaten up with usury, and exhausted to have the additional mortification to see private and worthless men riot in their calamities, and grow rich whilst they grow poor; to see the town every day glittering with new and pompous equipages, whilst they are mortgaging and selling their estates, without having spent them; to see blazing meteors suddenly exhalted out of their jakes, and their mud, as in Egypt, warmed in monsters.

Printed and Published for the AUTHORS by T. W. SHAW, Fleet-Street, opposite Anderton's Coffee-House, where Letters to the Publisher will be thankfully received. New Editions of all the Numbers of this spirited Paper, are now ready for Sale, and *complete sets* will be sent to any Part of *England, Carriage Free.*

THE

CRISIS

NUMBER LXXII   *To be continued Weekly,*

DURING THE PRESENT BLOODY CIVIL WAR IN AMERICA.

SATURDAY, JUNE 1, 1776   [Price Two-pence Half-penny.

For the C R I S I S.

To the worst and most infamous minister that ever disgraced
this Country, LORD NORTH,

WHAT is government, but a trust committed by all or the most, to one, or a few, who are to attend upon the affairs of all, that every one may with the more security, attend upon his own? a great and honourable trust; but too seldom honourably executed; those who possess it having it often more at heart to encrease their power, than to make it useful; and to be terrible rather than beneficient. It is therefore a trust which ought to bounded with many and strong restraints, because power renders men wanton, insolent to others and fond of themselves. Every violation therefore of this trust, where such violation is considerable, ought to meet with proportionable punishment; and the smallest violation of it ought to meet with some, because indulgence to the least faults in magistrates may be cruelty to the whole people.

Honesty, diligence, and plain sense, are the only talents necessary for the executing of this trust; and the public good is its only end: as to refinements and finesses, they are only the false appearances of wisdom and parts, and oftener tricks to hide guilt and emptiness; and they are generally mean and dishonest: they are the arts of jobbers in politics, who, playing their own game under the public cover, subsist upon poor shifts and expedients; starved politicians, who live from hand to mouth, from day to day, and following the little views of ambition, avarice, revenge, and the like personal passions, are ashamed to avow them, yet want souls great enough to forsake them; small wicked statesmen, who make a private market of the public, and deceive it in order to sell it.

These are the poor parts which great and good governors scorn to play, and cannot play; their designs like their stations, being purely public, are open and undisguised. They do not consider their people as their prey, nor lie in ambush for their subjects; nor dread, and treat and surprise them like enemies, as all ill magistrates do; who are not governors but jaylors and spunges, who chain them and squeese them, and yet take it very ill if they do but murmur; which is yet much less than a people so abused ought to do. There have been times and countries, when public ministers and public enemies have been the same individual men. What a melancholy reflection is this, that the most terrible and mischievous foes to a nation should be its magistrates! and yet in every enslaved country, which is almost every country, this is their woful case.

Honesty and plainness, go always together, and the makers and multipliers of mysteries, in the political way, are shrewdly to be suspected of dark designs. *Cincinnatus* was taken from the plough to save and defend the *Roman* state; an office which he executed honestly and successfully, without the grimace and gains of a stateman. Nor did he afterwards continue obstinately at the head of affairs, to form a party, raise a fortune, and settle himself in power: as he came into it with universal consent, he resigned it with universal applause.

It seems that government was not in those days a trade, at least a gainful trade.—Honest *Cincinnatus* was but a farmer: and happy had it been for the *Romans*, if when they were enslaved, they could have taken the administration out of the hands of the emperors, and their refined politicians, and committed it to such farmers, or any farmers. It is certain many of their imperial governors acted more rediculously than a board of ploughmen would have done, and more barbarously than a club of butchers could have done.

But some have said *it is not the business of private men to meddle with government*. A bold, false and dishonest saying; and whoever says it either knows not what he says, or cares not, or slavishly speaks the sense of others. It is a cant now in England, and which never prevailed but when liberty and the constitution were attacked, and never can prevail but upon the like occasion.

It is a vexation to be obliged to answer nonsense, and confute absurdities: but since it is and has been the great design of this paper to maintain and explain the glorious principles of liberty, and to expose the arts of those who would darken or destroy them; I shall here particularly shew the wickedness and stupidity of the above saying; which is fit to come from no mouth but that of a tyrant or a slave, and can never be heard by any man of an honest and free soul, without horror and indignation: it is in short, a saying, which ought to render the man who utters it for ever incapable of place or credit in a free country, as it shews the malignity of his heart, and the baseness of his nature, and as it is the pronouncing of a doom upon our constitution.—A crime or rather a complication of crimes, for which a lasting infamy ought to be but part of the punishment

But to the falshood of the thing, public truths ought never to be kept secrets; and they who do it, are guilty of a solecism, and a contradiction: every man ought to know what it concerns all to know. Now nothing upon earth is of a more universal nature than government; and every private man upon earth has a concern in it, because in it is concerned, and nearly and immediately concerned, his virtue, his property and the security of his person: and where all these are best preserved and advanced, the government is best administered; and where they are not, the government is impotent, wicked or unfortunate; and where the government is so, the people will be so, there being always and every where a certain sympathy and analogy between the nature of the government and the nature of the people. This holds true in every instance. Public men are the patterns of private; and the virtues and vices of the governors become quickley the vrtues and vices of the governed.

Nor is it example alone that does it. Ill governments, subsisting by vice and rapine, are jealous of private virtue, and enemies to private property. They must be wicked and mischievous to be what they are; nor are they secure while any thing good or valuable is secure. Hence it is, that to drain, worry, and debauch their subjects, are the steady maxims of their politics, their favourite arts of reigning. In this wretched situation, the people to be safe, must be poor and lewd: there will be but little industry where property is precarious; small honesty where virtue is dangerous.

Profuseness or frugality, and the like virtues or vices, which affect the public, will be practiced in the city, if they be practiced in the court, and in the country if they be in the city. Even NERO that royal monster in man's shape, was adored by the common herd of Rome, as much as he was flattered by the great; and both the little and the great admired, or pretended to admire his manners, and many to immitate them. TACITUS tells us, that those sort of people long lamented him, and rejoiced in the choice of a successor that resembled him, even the profligate OTHO.

Good government does on the contrary, produce great virtue, much happiness, and many people. Greece and Italy, while they continued free, were each of them for the number of inhabitants, like one continued city; for virtue, knowledge, and great men, they were the standards of the world; and that age and country which could come nearest to them, has ever since been reckned the happiest. Their government, their free government, was the root of all these advantages, and of all this felicity and renown; and in these great and fortunate states the people were the principals in the government; laws were made by their judgment and authority, and by their voice and commands were magistrates created and condemned. The city of Rome could conquer the world; nor could the great Persian monarch, the greatest then upon earth, stand before the face of one Greek city.

But what are *Greece* and *Italy* now? *Rome* has in it a herd of pampered Monks, and a few starving lay inhabitants; the Campania of Rome, the finest spot of earth in Europe, is a desert. And for the modern Greeks, they are a few abject contemptible slaves, kept under ignorance, chains and vileness by the Turkish monarch, who keeps a great part of the globe intensely miserable, that he may seem great without being so.

Such is the difference between one government and another, and of such important concernment is the nature and administration of government to a people. And to say that private men have nothing to do with government, is to say that private men have nothing to do with their own happiness and misery.

What is the public, but a collective body of private men, as every private man is a member of the public? and as the whole ought to be concerned for the preservation of every private individual, it is the duty of every individual to be concerned for the whole, in which himself is included.

One man or a few men have often pretended the public and meant themselves, and consulted their own personal interest, in instances essential to its well-being; but the whole people, by consulting their own interest, consult the public, and act for the public by acting for themselves: this is particularly the spirit of our constitution, in which the whole nation is represented; and our records afford instances, where the house of commons have declined entering upon a question of importance, till they had gone into the country, and consulted their principals, the people: so far were they from thinking that private men had no right to meddle with government. In truth our whole worldly happiness and misery (abating for accidents and diseases) are owing to the order and mismanagement of government; and he who says that private men have no concern with government, does wisely and modestly tell us, that men have no concern in what concerns them most; it is saying that people ought not to concern themselves whether they be naked or clothed, fed or starved, deceiv'd or instructed, and whether they be protected or destroyed: what nonsense and servitude in a free and wise nation!

By the bill of rights, and the act of settlement, at the revolution, a right is asserted to the people of applying to the king and to the parliament, by petition and address. for a redress of public grievances and mismanagements, when such there are, of which they are left to judge: and the difference between free and enslaved countries lies principally here, that in the former, their magistrates must consult the voice and interest of the people; but in the latter, the private will, interest, and pleasure of the governors, are the sole end and motives of their administration. Under this plan you and your infamous colleagues in office, have regularly proceeded during the whole course of the present diabolical reign.

Such is the difference between England and Turkey; which difference they who say that private men have no right to concern themselves with government, would absolutely destroy; they would convert magistrates into bashaws, and introduce *popery* into politics. The late revolution stands upon the very opposite maxim; and that any man dares to contradict it since the revolution would be amazing, did we not know that there are, in England, wretches who would betray their God and their country for *hire?*

On Tuesday *next will be published*, by T. W. SHAW, *Price* One Shilling.

The late ADDRESSES for Blood and Devastation,
and the ADDRESSERS

E X P O S E D;

Together with the

I D O L A T R O U S   W O R S H I P of Kings and Tyrants,

AND

The Americans justified by several precedents from Scripture,
in their Resistance to the Depredations and Lawless Violence
of an English King, and his bribed servile Parliament.

WHICH MAY SERVE AS AN ANSWER TO

TAXATON no TYRANNY, *Wesley's* CALM ADDRESS,
and all the ministerial Pamphlets that have been, or may be Wrote.

FIAT JUSTITIA RUAT COELUM.[1]

By W I L L I A M   M O O R E,

Author of the NORTH BRITONS Extraordinary, and the WHISPERERS. &c

---

1. Which has passed into legal Latin as "let justice be done, though the heavens fall." The original source—and whether it is truly classical—is a matter of some debate. It had been in use in England well over a century by the time of its appearance here.

Printed and Published for the AUTHORS by T. W. SHAW, Fleet-Street, opposite Anderton's Coffee-House, where Letters to the Publisher will be thankfully received. New Editions of all the Numbers of this spirited Paper, are now ready for Sale, and *complete sets* will be sent to any Part of *England, Carriage Free.*

THE

CRISIS

NUMBER LXXIII   *To be continued Weekly,*

DURING THE PRESENT BLOODY CIVIL WAR IN AMERICA.

SATURDAY, JUNE 8, 1776   [Price Two-pence Half-penny.

To the Inhabitants of this once flourishing Nation.

Friends and Fellow Subjects.

NAKEDNESS, poverty, and every species of Misery which human nature can experience, must soon be the wretched fate of millions of industrious subjects in this country, if speedy means cannot be devised of driving from the presence of the *Grand Seignor* a set of the greatest miscreants that ever disgraced the annals of any country. The two principal traitors are of northern extraction; the one at the head of a great law department: the other of the accursed Stuart line—both titled scoundrels. May those traitors be the first victims of a long abused nation's vengeance: In this prayer all honest men most fervently unite.

The wicked ministers of the *Grand Seignor* must be removed from his presence and councils for ever, or peace and plenty will never more visit your humble mansions: poverty will not only be yours but posteritys miserable lot, if you shrink from the call of your injured country.

The enemies of public liberty, and the dispoilers of your property, are placemen, pensioners, dependants on the court, and a numerous train of scotch jacobite agents, and a bloody minded ministry, who to encrease our distress at home, have bought up many thousand head of catle in the country, and are still contracting for more to export, not only for the maintenance of our own soldiers, but a large army of foreigners, who are hired to cut the throats of our own brethren in America, which will raise the price of meat and other necessaries (already very dear) too high for us to purchase. If they prosecute this war which they intend, our taxes will be increased, and our manufactures, Trade and commerce ruined. Besides if they conquer America, we shall and well deserve to be enslaved at home. We are therefore too deeply concerned, to remain silent and inactive. A winter is approaching, in which many of us will remain unemployed, and ourselves, wives and children starving, without money in the midst of riches, and without food in a land of plenty. Then seeing the dreadful calamities which threaten us; though the ministry have deprived us of our right and liberties yet if we have any spirit of Englishmen left, we shall never patiently submit to be starved to death.

Let us therefore endeavour to save ourselves and families from famine and ruin, which must come upon us if the ministers effect their wicked intentions against trade, commerce, and America; call to mind all your former exertions, against the oppressions of wicked and unjust task-masters. Dare to be FREE and you will be so. God will sanctify the designs of good men in all stations, he has no respect to persons, but loves and will assist all his creatures, high and low, poor as well as rich, and though the ministers are sending our food out of the land, let us shew we are determined not to be starved, or see our wives and children perish miserably before our eyes.

> No B R I B E R Y and C O R R U P T I O N,
> No imprisonment of Englishmen without trial, conviction or
>   sentence.
> No Ex Officio informations.
> No tampering with juries.
> No attorneys to be at once party, accuser, judge and jury.

In this country, where obedience only to the laws, which each individual has a share in assenting to, forms the idea of subordination, how can we account for the conduct of him, who appointed to put those laws in execution, in *actions redicules them*, and in words disavows subjection to them; who pleased with the bauble of prerogative, thinks himself born to command, not to obey; who frowns upon his friends and cherishes his enemies; who laughs reason to scorn, and piques himself on making folly fashionable: and wasting his time in amusements, disgraceful even to human weakness.

If our sovereign, were the unhappy being here depictured, what anguish of mind would not sensibility force him to suffer; yet, in this portrait we see every lineament, every feature of his life and conduct and can trace in him, no marks of sorrow, no signs of remorse, no eagerness for reformation. He still treads the same *dull, unmeaning,* round of pleasure, and armed with the sword of obstinacy, exercises it only in repelling the entry of prudence into the vacuity of his understanding. Folly, in an amiable dress, attracted affection to his father, clad in all the horrors of willful ignorance and unsociableness, to him it has insured universal hatred.

Declamation alone, I am an enemy to; let us then proceed to particulars; and if my labour, labour I can justly call it, when bestowed on so undeserving an object, is crowned with the smallest success, I shall not think my time mispent.

His father was a man remarkable for what is termed good nature. Harmless as the dove, he traveled through life, and made his escape to the other world, without laying a foundation for scandal to defame his character, or praise to extol it. With a taste neither rude nor refined, his amusement gave employment to the mechanic, and his generosity, pleasure and contentment to all around him, his heart felt for the widow and fatherless, and his liberality, though not applied with all the propriety imaginable, was seldom heaped on the most unworthy of the creation. Mean oeconomy never disgraced his board and though his pecuniary wants were frequent, yet the public supplied them without grudging them, knowing that they only took their money out of their pocket, and put it in anothers, and that what they gave would in a trifling space of time return among them. With patience and complacency he listened to the requests or complaints of the meanest of his fellow subjects; with affibility he answered them; and if he did not serve or relieve every petitioner, he gave all kind words and pleasant looks. He was a faithful husband, as far as the warmth of his constitution would admit; a loving and tender father, and a good friend.

In which act of life hath he imitated what in his father was praiseworthy? I believe we may wait for Syrus's reigning in the month of March before this question can be answered. From his very childhood he betrayed a tincture of pride unqualified by decency; for in the most exalted walk of life, pride, without that qualification, is burthensome to the breast that harbours it, and disagreeable to all who feel its effects. Without a genius equal to the weight, he pored over folios, and by the most studious application, acquired a knowledge as quickly shook off as it was slowly gained.

The good Bishop, who was entrusted with the care of his education often regretted the hardship of his employment. He knew the small share of credit that would accrue to him from the indocility of his pupil. He saw passions destructive of quiet rising into muturity, and mourned the fatal consequences that would unavoidably ensue from them. Anger and revenge, his good sense told him, were incompatiable with royalty, would deform the most amiable disposition, and render abortive all his lessons of humility and benevolence. Yet his ardent affection for him and his family, determined him to withstand, if possible, the swelling torent, and choak up, if not totally eradicate by his precepts, the weeds that opposed the cultivation of his mind.

An unforeseen event blasted all his hopes, and removed from his person a faithful servant and learned instructor. His mother for reasons to herself best known, did him an injury which he now seems not to feel a sense of, yet may rue when irreparable.

An upright Scot, sprung from a very honest and opulent family, made him unread the lessons of his predecessor, and with savage avidity, wormed out of his youthful breast every sentiment which he had with Herculean force laboured to implant, and which might have prevented his natural disposition making him miserable.

It is inherent in man to imbibe with facility what is pleasing to them in preference to that which they have no taste for. Under Lord Bute's tuition his understanding became of a sudden illuminated and the doctrines he instructed him in took immediate root, and have ever since flourished in the generous soil.

To this Scotchman and his mother's cherishing care, conjoined with his own inclinations, he owes his present happy situation. Permitted when a boy, to tyrannize over his domestics, he carried the same spirit with him to that seat which blind fortune elevated his family to. Inspired by his tutor with an affection for arbitrary and despotic power, he became its first victim by suffering Lord Bute to hold his mind in subjection intolerable to thought. Conceiving a high opinion of *jus divinum* of rulers, he unfortunately fell in the snare, and now walks with as much self importance, as much content in the trammels of slavery, as if he had been born in a *scotch coal mine*. Passive obedience and non-resistance were pleasing ideas to a weak mind, and to believe that he could not be free except he ruled over slaves, can be ascribed only to his narrowness of sentiment.

When the news of his grandfathers death was brought him, he received it with an indecent joy, and seemed to think that the moment which gave him the means of becoming rediculous in the eyes of all Europe, was the happiest in his life.

His first act of power presents us a specimen of the spirit of contradiction that reigned within him, or of his not knowing how to think. He instantly banished from his presence every man who was esteemed for his integrity of life, love to his subjects, and affection to his family. In their room took those whose vices had made them conspicuous, who without the least spark of honour, cared not by what means they procured riches and promotion, and are better adapted for farmers general to the Grand Monarch, than to guide the councils of, and discharge the trust reposed in them by a king of a free people. Those men he still continues particularly to countenance, and in every scene of iniquity that they have been concerned in, has, by his not expressing a disapprobation of it, been by him tacitly applauded, the magistrates and citizens of the first city in the world, he, as a mark of contempt to his predecessors for treating them with the necessary compliments becoming politeness, turns his back on while he clasps in his arms the very man they complain of; and hugs himself in the thought of having shewed so great a spirit.

As every action of his life discovers his unfitness to govern, and as the misconduct, and villany of his ministers, or those people he calls his friends, threatens him with a catastrophe, dreadful even in thought: it would be better he would resign the reigns which trembles in his hands; or advise with those he takes to be his enemies; but who are his real friends, about the method to preserve and guide them.

On Tuesday last was Published by T. W. SHAW. Price 1s.

The late ADDRESSES for Blood and Devastation, and the ADDRSS-ERS Exposed; together with the IDOLATROUS WORSHIP of KINGS and TYRANTS.

By W I L L I A M   M O O R E,
Author of the North Britons Extraordinary, Whisperers, &c. &c.

Printed and Published for the AUTHORS by T. W. SHAW, Fleet-Street, opposite Anderton's Coffee-House, where Letters to the Publisher will be thankfully received. New Editions of all the Numbers of this spirited Paper, are now ready for Sale, and *complete sets* will be sent to any Part of *England, Carriage Free.*

THE

CRISIS

NUMBER LXXIV   *To be continued Weekly,*

DURING THE PRESENT BLOODY CIVIL WAR IN AMERICA.

SATURDAY, JUNE 15, 1776   [Price Two-pence Half-penny.

S I R,

By inserting speedily if you can, this letter in the Crisis, you will oblige
many of your constant readers.

To the right honourable JOHN Earl of Sandwich,
first lord of the Admiralty, &c.—alias Twitcher.

"I will my lord, speak of you, as you are.
Nothing extenuate or set down ought in malice."

My Lord,

I Have not the honor of being personally known by your lordship, tho'
as an individual, I have been in your presence at several of your naval visitations: I should almost despair of thus publickly addressing
you, (for it is allowed by all, that your lordship has never blushed at any
misconduct you have been guilty of; since the crimson hue o'er spread
your countenance, when the Essay on Woman was read in the house
of Peers, which gave such a shock to your delicate sense of things, and

greatly offended your lordships ears, whose chastity, and whose morals are so well known to the world, (that no comment is required to make them conspicuous) but as I hope there may be a moment, (and now is that crisis) when you may see your error; thro' the chanel of this paper I will urge some truths, which I sincerely desire both you, and the public will consider.

Your religious principles my lord, I shall slightly touch upon; not that I consider deism, and irreligion necessary in a statesman, if I did your lordship should be the only person I would recommend, not only to any other important trust under this virtuous administration; but likewise to retain your present employ, as absolutely necessary to support your extravagance, by putting annually some thousands into your pocket, to sport with at Newmarket, at Arthur's, or Almacks, or where ever your lordships sharping companions may assemble, to ease you of your specie; or that you might with the greater facility pension off some cloystered nymphs at Charlotte Haye's, and by that means ease the venerable matron of many corroding troubles.

You will, I hope, my lord, accept this traite of your religious conduct, as the dedication of my letter (not that I expect a place or pension) but as a prelude to my considering your lordships conduct in another point of view.

First then, as to your acting when consulted on American affairs, (that now alarms the nation in general, and shakes the monarch's throne;) in respect to this case, it is well known that the will of lord Mansfield governs you as it does the lord Chancellor in every thing, and both your understandings are under as much subjection to him, as the iron is to the attractive impulse of the magnet.

And now my lord, I will secondly consider you as preciding at the head of the admiralty board.

It has been puffed oft to the world by your venal writers; the great assiduity, care, and trouble that attends you, in your annual visitations to the several dock-yards, this will appear as a proof of your diligence and under the head œconomy, to those not acquainted with naval affairs; but upon due consideration of the whole, it will be found the reverse; your frequent visits will be justly deemed unnecessary, your knowledge gained thereby but superficial, and all those boasted acts of œconomy futile, and void of any just foundation; for let me ask those writers this question, where is the great hardship in a pleasant season of the year, for your lordship to take a voyage to the different ports? it is but very seldom you are in a storm; but suppose it true, that Neptune is sometimes displeased with your expedition, and causes the channel to be rough and disagreeable for some hours; you may soon recover the fatigue, forgeting all the toil by relaxing over the fumes of a bottle, and then sink into a sweet sleep folded in the arms of some enchanting Dulcinea; for we know your lordship always furnishes your seraglio on the water as compleatly with sea nymphs; as that on shore with silvan Deities. Where then can be your lordships great hardship on this watry element? as these hired garreteers would make us believe.

The œconomy practised by your lordship in this affair, can never with justice be vindicated, if considered impartially; for it will appear the travelling charges of yourself, and those that consequently attend you on these annual visitations, amounts to more money than you can by any means save by this your personal attendance; the business would be carried on with the same care and attention, if your visits were as seldom as the bishops of the diocese; who once in three years comes to confirm his lambs and that is full as often as either of you are wanted.

I have thus considered your lordships fatigues, and also the œconomy practised in these visitations; I will now consider the knowledge acquired thereby. Let us view the wonderful discoveries of this sagacious inquisition, and the mighty effects it has produced.

In the beginning of the year, the shiprights of the royal yards were informed, that your lordship had appointed their work to be performed by contract, under a number of articles. This greatly alarmed them in respect to future evils; but the bait being gilded over with its being calculated for their good, they resolved to make trial in obedience to your instructions. But now by practice having discovered many inconveniences not provided for; the distant yards of Portsmouth and Plymouth, (where some of these evils were more immediately felt) on your lordships last visitation, petitioned you to redress them, which being refused they absented from their work.

I will give a specimen of some of their complaints, and leave it to the consideration of the impartial part of mankind.

They petitioned for an advance price on some articles, which are so disproportioned, that by hard labour a man can hardly get his usual pay. Secondly in working timber that proves defective, which in some large pieces requires hours, nay I might say days to accomplish, (and when nearly or quite finished, proving bad, it is thrown away) they desired to be paid some adequate allowance for such loss of time.

Thirdly, in rainy weather when they could not work, to be permitted to go home, and not be detained within those walls when they could do nothing; for it is well known by proper judges, their work not being always portable, it cannot be removed under cover without a manifest hindrance.

These were the heads complained of to your lordship, and which you was desired to alter, if not, then set aside task work, and let things proceed in their former channel. But you having imbibed the principles of arbitrary power, (like the king your master) will force an implicit obedience to things unjust.

This shews that you have gained but a superficial knowledge of the true internal welfare of that body of men, to whose art, and to support whom as useful to the community, it becomes you my lord to cherish; for without them, there will be no occasion for one to fill that post which now your lordship enjoys.

These are the happy effects of your late visitation; where peace resided, is now anarchy and uproar, and the crys of injured thousands imprecating of vengeance on you! reflect my lord but a few moments on the present Crisis; it is not too late to remove the evil; take away the first cause of complaint, *viz. the task work*, and the consequence will most assuredly be this; these useful men will unanimously strive to entice each other, in the diligent discharge of their duty.[1]

M   A   R   C   U   S.[2]

Extract of a letter from a gentleman at Grantham,
to his friend at Lincoln.

Dear Sir,

As I write to you I can write freely, that is, I can write my heart, though you must excuse my blotting this paper with the blood of it.

I am sorry to find you were so much indisposed with your old complaint, as not to attend your family to the races; but perhaps at this time of life you may be beginning to think of running a better, if so, I pray God, sir, to give me also his grace to think of setting out after you; for to tell you the plain truth of the matter, I am really weary and ashamed of having run such a one as I have; but to leave moralising and proceed to politics.

---

1. The shipwrights at the Portsmouth royal dockyards were first to strike; workers at other royal dockyards followed, demanding that the "task work"—piece rate pay—not displace daily wages, and complaining about various other issues, as reported in *The Crisis*. The walkout that began in June had ended by August, with a compromise being agreed to between the contesting parties. An incensed Sandwich, who saw himself as the man the King depended on to rebuild the navy, beginning with the yards, insisted that the ringleaders not be allowed back, and they were not. For details see James M. Haas, "The Introduction of Task Work into the Royal Dockyards, 1775" *Journal of British Studies* 8 (1969):44–68; Peter Linebaugh, *The London Hanged* (Cambridge: Cambridge University Press, 1982), pp. 371–401; and Rodger, *Insatiable Earl*, pp. 149–54.

2. This is the only instance where "Marcus" is used as a nom de plume; likewise, it is the only issue where Sandwich is the direct target, though it is hardly the first issue where Sandwich is lumped in with others for criticism. See no. VIII of *The Crisis*, 11 March 1775, supra, as the first instance of over a dozen caustic allusions before the one made here. The Roman emperor Marcus Aurelius, noted for his sage advice in his still popular *Meditations*, available in various English translations published in London, could be the intended reference point; it could just as easily have been Marcus Junius Brutus as well (as n. VII.9 supra).

However ill or indisposed you may have been, I doubt not but some late alarming occurrences have before now reached your ears, I mean in particular the late accounts from America, where the *state Blood hounds* have been infernally employed in hunting after, running down, and then cutting the throats of some of the best and most valuable subjects of the British Empire.

This grand *Neronian* hunting match began to take good effect in the villages of *Lexington* and *Concord* on the 18th and 19th of April 1775 and on the 17th of June, when under the directions and by the express orders of his majesty's *executioner general* for the time being *Thomas Gage*, among other *murders* then and there committed by the PACK called out for that purpose, the Village of *Charles Town*, near *Boston*, was as that monster of barbarity most *soldierly* expresses it, at CRITICAL moment set on fire, and burnt to ashes, and where doubtless the cries, shrieks, and agonies of the poor roasted inhabitants, men, women, and children must have been (till the fire and smoke had suffocated their power of utterance) beyond all expression.

This single exploit was enough to have immortalised the royal memory of a *Nero*—but infernal as it was; it has not been the last.

O! *George*, may there never be wanting a hand to revenge, any more than a pen to record the infamy of that execrable æra, when from the order and authority of a *Brunswick*, thousands of the most loyal, affectionate, and best deserving of their posterity, who raised thy ancestrors from the dunghill of a paltry electorate were (to please the resentment of an abandoned and papistical junto, and for no other crime than that of defending their liberties, to which mankind had a right before tyrants existed), devoted to be the carnage of their countrymen.

Printed and Published for the AUTHORS by T. W. SHAW, Fleet-Street, opposite Anderton's Coffee-House, where Letters to the Publisher will be thankfully received. New Editions of all the Numbers of this spirited Paper, are now ready for Sale, and *complete sets* will be sent to any Part of *England, Carriage Free*.

THE

CRISIS

NUMBER LXXV   *To be continued Weekly,*

DURING THE PRESENT BLOODY CIVIL WAR IN AMERICA.

SATURDAY, JUNE 22, 1776   [Price Two-pence Half-penny.

For the C R I S I S.

A S there must be in all well regulated states, a variety of offices, in a due subordination one to another, for the management and carrying on the business of the public! so the nature and power of these offices vary, in different nations, according to the different constitutions of their respective governments. For this reason in absolute monarchies, we generally find a person invested by the prince with the sole management and direction of all his affairs, under the title of Prime Minister, who is, by virtue of his office, as he commonly proves himself to be by his actions, an *arbitrary viceroy* or *deputy tyrant*. But the power of such a minister seems to be inconsistent with the nature of a free state, whether a common wealth or a limited monarchy, (unless it be upon extraordinary occasions, as the Roman Dictators were created of old) because the absolute, uncontroulable will of one man has been generally found to end in the destruction of liberty in general; and though it may be said that a limited monarch cannot delegate more power than he is invested with himself, and therefore cannot make any of his ministers absolute; yet every such prince has too much power to be reposed in the hands of any of his servants; for experience shews us, that a worse use is commonly made of the regal authority, when in the possession of a private subject, then under the direction of the prince himself; and there seems to be an obvious reason for this; since a king, who is possessed, during life, of all the power, prerogative, and jurisdiction, which are agreeable to the fundamental laws of the country over which he reigns, and has the same rights intailed on his posterity, cannot, without being a man of very ill principles, have any farther views, because his true interest, upon a little recollection, will instruct him to confine his thoughts within those sacred barriers: whereas a minister, who is in great power to-day, and perhaps afraid of loosing it to-morrow (especially if he be a man of a small, paternal inheritance) will be tempted to amass exorbitant wealth by indirect methods, and aggrandize his own family at the expence of the public. Nay, even supposing the case of a bad prince, who through the instigations of ambition, or a cruel tyrannical disposition, should be inclined to oppress his subjects, I believe the bulk of the people would be much more easy under any hardships, which could be laid upon them by their sovereign, than such as they should suffer from one of their equals.

This is sufficient to shew, that the office of Prime Minister is, in its nature, of dangerous consequence to a free people: but there is another consideration, which though it be not of the same importance, ought to make every rational Briton join his voice and his interest against such an over-grown power in any of his fellow subjects; for

When the prince reserves the prerogative in his own hands, or divides it amongst a certain number of his subjects, to be administered in an equal manner (as it has been most usual in this kingdom) the royal smiles, favours, and honours, as well as the office of the kingdom, both great and small, are commonly distributed in the same *equal* and impartial manner. Whereas when the whole power of the crown has been lodged in a single hand, we may observe that grants, titles and preferments, have been generally monopolized, and the whole bounty of a court, thought little enough to satiate the craving hungry appetites of one family.

Nay, we have seen this spirit of rapine and rapaciousness carried to such a height under some administrations, that, not content with all the crown has had in its power to bestow, they have attempted to engross the favours and suffrages of the people; nor do I want instances to shew, that opposing only a Welch cousin of a great man has been called opposing the ministry, and looked on as a mark of malignancy and disaffection.

As inconsiderable and self-interested as this observation may seem, yet it certainly ought to have some weight in a free nation; for as a bishop of SARUM very justly observed, in answer to one of his opponents in a controversy, that although no man has a natural right to a place at court; yet every man has a right to get one if he can. And if the old beaten topick, of all the whig-writers can justify that a kingdom was not made for one man, meaning the Prince, it could not surely be designed only to gratify the pride, avarice and ambition of a private subject.

But as such power in any minister is contrary to the interest of the People; so it is also of dangerous consequence to the Prince himself, especially in a limited government.

An absolute monarch indeed, who is under no restraint but his own will, may raise a favourite to what height of power he pleases without being under any great apprehensions from his treachery or ambition, because he can pull him down when he begins to grow insolent, with the same high hand that lifted him up.

But a limited monarch, who, in order to reign happily, is obliged to preserve an harmony and good understanding with his people, (who are, by the constitution join'd with him in the legislative power) ought to be very cautious how far he aggrandizes any of his servants, or trusts the power out of his own hands; because a minister who has the disposition of preferments and honours, may thereby strengthen himself so much by cabals, alliances, obligations, and immense wealth that it may become dangerous for the prince to displace him, even though he should be, personally, as ill beloved by himself, as he is by the generality of his subjects.

I have now before me a little book intitled, "Rules of Government, or a true balance between Sovereignty and Liberty; said to be written by a person of honour, immediately after the civil war, in Charles the First's time;" which contains many useful directions upon this subject, some of them I beg leave to transcribe.

He tells us, in one place (speaking of counsellors) that over greatness in one, or over strict combination in a few, may be both dangerous to a PRINCE. In another place he says, that it is a great fault in a Prince "to look upon no man himself, but through a glass, or as the image of a man is reflected unto him from a favourite, or some great officer; for this is to strengthen their root, and weaken his own; for here, though the guilt is his, the obligation is another's. This makes him have many attendants, but few servants; for servants placed about him by great men, are rather their spies than his servants: such unconcernedness as this, who are about him, makes him appear like a town blocked up; he can freely receive no provisions he stands in need of; and his own servants are disheartened by perceiving great men's friends or servants every day preferred or gratify'd before them. This course chills all public spiritedness; for men, introduced by favourites, think they shall last no longer than their patrons, who are often changed or in the wain; and so they come unto a court like harvest men, who serve only in a short time to reap that, which others, plowed and harrowed; or they work only in fair weather, and when the corn is carrying into the barn."

The same author gives this wholesome advice to Ministers of state in the following paragraph, which I beg leave to recommend to the serious consideration of all great men in the several courts of Europe.

"A wise councellor says he will not engross too many affairs into his own hands, nor encroach upon other men's offices, nor be apt to undervalue them in it to raise his own credit, by the loss of other men's; for he that does good offices to others, is in the best way to make hearty friends to himself: and he must be patient to hear other men's advices; nay with some respectfulness, bear their follies: And he must be unconcerned when his own counsels are not complyed with, or are laid aside."[1]

---

1. *Rules of Government: Or, a true Balance between Sovereignty and Liberty* had been printed in 1710 in London by Bernard Lintott. According to the title page it was written "By a Person of Honour, immediately after the late Civil War. And now Published, to

I shall leave these wholesom directions to those whom they may concern, and conclude with observing in general, that the office of a Prime Minister seems to be calculated for an absolute government; though, in my opinion, even such a government would fare much better, if the prince would vouchsafe to manage his affairs himself. But the power of such an officer is intirely repugnant to the safety of a free state, which is so fully demonstrated by history and experience, that I need not insist upon it any further. In governments purely popular, I cannot at present recollect any instance of such a minister, unless it be of the famous *de Witt* in Holland, whose terrible fate should deter others from attempting such a power.[2]

In England, we have been often pestered with these over-grown, rapacious wretches in former times; but for several years past we were free from them, till that upstart Scotchman, Lord Bute, made his appearance in the miserable reign of George the Third!

A Recept to make a LORD, occasioned by a late Promotion.

TAKE a man who by natures a true son of earth,
By rapine enrich'd, though a beggar by birth;
In genius the lowest, ill bred, and obscene,
Of mortals most wicked, most nasty in mien,

---

prevent Another." In any event, it cautions that monarchy comes from God and, even if God allows people the freedom to depose their rulers, that does not mean they act as his agents. The wise monarch therefore chooses wise men to serve him, thereby not giving the people a reason to rebel and destroy the only governmental form that God truly sanctioned. Sir Philip Warwick is often listed as the actual author. David L. Smith's essay on Warwick in the *Oxford DNB*, 57:522–25 does not include *Rules* among Warwick's writings.

2. Hero and martyr of the Dutch Republic, Jan de Witt, struggled to keep the Netherlands united and to end the Anglo-Dutch trade wars, but without falling too far under the domination of the House of Orange. He was lynched by supporters of the Stadtholder (the future William III) in 1672. Readers of *The Crisis* most likely knew de Witt from the English translation of his *Political Maxims of the State of Holland* (London: J. Nourse, 1743), which drew from Aristotle (for general principles) and the Roman republic (for what happened when those principles were violated).

By none ever trusted, yet ever employ'd,
In blunders most fertile, in merit quite void;
A scold in the senate, abroad a buffoon,
The scorn and the jest of all courts but his own.
A slave to that wealth, which ne'er made him a friend,
And proud of that cunning, which ne'er gain'd an end.
A dupe in each treaty, a swiss in each vote,
In manners and form a compleat hottontot.

Such a one could you find, of all men I'd commend him,
But be sure let the curse of each Briton attend him:
Thus fitly prepar'd add grace to the throne,
The folly of monarchs, and skreen of a crown,
Take a prince for his purpose without ears or eyes,
And a long parchment patent, stuff'd brimful of lyes,
These mingled together, a fiat shall pass,
And that thing strut a peer, who before was an ass.

Printed and Published for the AUTHORS by T. W. SHAW, Fleet-Street, opposite Anderton's Coffee-House, where Letters to the Publisher will be thankfully received. New Editions of all the Numbers of this spirited Paper, are now ready for Sale, and *complete sets* will be sent to any Part of *England, Carriage Free.*

THE

CRISIS

NUMBER LXXVI   *To be continued Weekly,*

DURING THE PRESENT BLOODY CIVIL WAR IN AMERICA.

SATURDAY, JUNE 29, 1776   [Price Two-pence Half-penny.

For the C R I S I S.

POPULAR affection, when justly obtained, (that is by truly promoting the interest of the people) is the highest honour which a mortal can enjoy, and one of the surest marks of public felicity; for when a man possesses the general love of any community, it is natural to infer that the community esteem him their general benefactor; and certainly no respect, honours, or reward, which the people can bestow, are too great to testify their gratitude to him, who approves himself worthy of that character.

Popularity therefore, in this sense, on this foundation, and under these restrictions, is due to every true patriot (a character indeed somewhat scarce!) and is a good presumptive proof of the happiness of that nation, under which it is obtained. But this desirable blessing is so often acquired by false means, bestowed on worthless objects, and applied to bad ends, that an honest man cannot be too cautious on whom he confers it, nor how he is influenced by it, when conferred on others.

The vulgar multitude judge honestly of public affairs, as far as they come within their knowledge; and, having no hopes of sharing in the administration themselves, desire only to live quietly and easily, in the free enjoyment of what they daily earn, incumbered with as few taxes and drawbacks, as the real necessities of the public will admit of. For this reason they always respect, and, in a manner, venerate those, who seem to consult their interest, and endeavour to preserve them in the secure possession of their rights and privileges. But they are so liable to be imposed on by false shews, and artful pretences, that we are not always to look upon their favour as the badge of real patriotism, and a truly public spirit; for on the contrary, we shall find that it is too often acquired by sinister methods, in order to carry on some crafty and pernicious design.

The wisest and best constituted governments of old, especially the famous republicks of Greece and Rome, were sensible of this, that it was made criminal for any of their members to affect uncommon popularity, and conciliate too much the minds of their fellow subjects: accordingly we find, in the histories, several instances of the most eminent patriots, who were banished, and otherwise treated as enemies to their country, only for rendering themselves too much beloved by general largesses and donations, or other extraordinary acts of public beneficence; for which severities, those nations have been often reproached, by succeeding ages, with injustice, barbarity, and ingratitude; but if we examine their conduct, in this particular, with candour and impartiality, I believe we shall find that they acted a very prudent and commendable part; they seemed to judge very rightly of human nature; they knew the temptations of power, and how popularity is apt to turn the wisest heads, and corrupt the purest hearts; for which reason they thought it impolitic to let the most deserving of their fellow subjects possess a power, which he might turn against them, or trust their liberties to the private virtue and integrity of any man whatsoever.

Indeed the histories of all nations, as well of theirs, abound with so many instances, in which the favor of the People has been most traiterously abused and perverted to wicked purposes, that to a serious and thoughtful mind, their conduct stands in need of no justification; for whenever we read of any great, professed patriot, who falls under signal disgrace or punishment, on account of his popular interest and esteem, though acquired by the justest methods, we ought not to interpret it as proceeding from any ill will to virtue or public good, but as the effect of political precaution, and of the jealousy of a wise people for their antient rights and liberties.

But there is another sort of popularity, which is infinitely more dangerous than what I have been speaking of, and has been more studied, in these latter ages, by ambitious and designing men; I mean popularity among the chief persons of a nation; which becomes still more dangerous and vile, when it is cultivated by venal and corrupt methods. This is indeed the most comprehensive method of becoming popular, as it saves abundance of trouble in cajoling the affections of the vulgar, and stooping to a thousand, little pleasing arts, to which some modern great spirits do not care to submit.

A man, who sets up for a diffusive and universal love of the people, must put himself under several uneasy restraints in his behaviour, and guide every action of his life with the utmost caution, tenderness, and circumspection. He must be courteous, affable and generous; must submit to the wayward tempers of a fickle multitude, and adapt himself to every character; he must be all things to all men, and honour them in all their various appetites, different views, and fantastical opinions, he must humble himself to the pride of the lofty, consult the interest of the avaritious, and conform to the intemperance of rhe libertine; he must drink or pray, whore or cant, be a saint or a sinner, just as his company shall please to prescribe, or set him an example.

Whereas a man, who is master of the other compendious method, and has it in his power to put it in practice, will find no occasion to study the inclinations of the people, nor even so much as pretend to a zeal for their interest; he knows a much shorter way to compass his designs, by bringing over a whole Borough, a City or a County at once into his interest, and obtaining by these means, the general assent of the nation to his own ambitious designs, he becomes in this sense, very popular, at the same time that he is universally odious, and retains the vox populi on his side, in spite of their teeth.

Nor is it at all difficult to accomplish such a design, in a vicious and depraved age, when profuseness, extravagance, and a general spirit of libertinism, grew predominent in any nation, especially among persons of a superior rank, who are intrusted with the rights and liberties of the people; for when once luxury has fixed a deep root in their minds, it will soon get the better of their noble faculties; it will effeminate, soften and melt down all those stubborn virtues, which are the natural effects of temperance and frugality; the consequence of which is, that a man thus debauched and effeminated will in order to support himself, in the same vicious manner, fall into any measures, which are dictated to him with a prospect of advantage, and sacrifice the most valuable rights of his country for a fashionable town-house, a splendid equipage, and an elegant table.

But as it is very easy for any man in power to acquire this sort of popular affection; so it is hardly possible to withstand its influence, or disappoint its designs.

There are some hopes that a man, who arrives at popularity, by courte-ousness, affability and munificent Spirit may really be in earnest, and exert these amiable virtues from a good natural disposition, and without any private view; for if it is possible at least, even in this age, that a disin-terested zeal for the public good, may be the prevailing passion in some breasts; and that there may still exist a few, particular men, in whom the innate love of their Country remains uncorrupted with any sordid and mercenary considerations.

There may be others, who, though they have not the same noble and sincere affection for the public, yet are fond of popularity, for the sake of popularity, and find their ambition sufficiently gratified by the shouts and acclamations of a numerous multitude. Nay, even supposing that a man endeavours to insinuate himself into the popular favour, with a bad design; yet if he does not attempt it by corrupting the leaders and guardians of the people, the danger to the public is not very great; for it is impossible for the craftiest brain to impose very long on the majority of a nation; He may for some time reign in esteem, and trepan the affec-tions of his countrymen by plausible pretences, artful declarations and a seeming concern for their service, but when his latent designs appear, (as at length they must) the people will withdraw their affection; his general popularity will be turned into a general odium, and he will feel the resentments and indignation of those, whose favour he has abused. Perhaps two more remarkable instances cannot be produced than of those treacherous apostate traitors OLIVER and TOWNSEND.[1]

But the case is quite otherwise with those who make themselves popular by venal and corrupt methods. Money the root of all evil, is also the strongest cement in the world; it binds together persons of the most opposite complexions, and is a more lasting tie than honour, friendship, relation, consanguinity, or unity of affections.

When any person therefore takes an annual or other salary for giving his opinion, that black is white, it is in vain for us to endeavour to convince him of the contrary; persuasion to such a man is of no effect, and reasoning is thrown away upon him; the strongest arguments leave no impression on his mind, and the clearest truth has no charms in his eyes. He is inlisted in the service of his patron, and must always fight on that side, let the cause be what it will, from which he receives his pay. It is rediculous to talk of Right to a man, who is pre-engaged, and hired to judge wrong; or to argue about justice, conscience and equity with one, who has tasted the sweets of acting upon different principles; witness the callous souls of the present piratical ministry, they have been deaf to reason and the most sacred truths, their hearts have been steeled against every feeling of humanity, through interested views in all their proceedings against America.

Ambitious and ill-designing men, in former ages, were not ignorant of this. They knew how precarious, as well as troublesome, that sort of

1. The author(s) probably had in mind the late Charles Townshend, for the policies that he pushed through Parliament in 1767 forever associated with his name, and the more recently deceased Lieutenant Governor Andrew Oliver of Massachusetts. Accusations had poured out of the Bay Colony for the previous several years, repeated in the London press, that Oliver had undercut the liberties of the people by conniving with Governor Thomas Hutchinson to unconstitutionally extend the royal prerogative and strengthen imperial authority there.

popularity is, which subsists only upon the foundation of worthy actions; and how permanent that, which is established upon self-interest, bribery, and subornation.

Tacitus informs us, that Augustus paved his way to dominion by these methods; having laid aside the title of Triumvir, and taking upon himself only the character of Consul, under a specious pretence that he had nothing at heart but the good of the people (whose favour he at first cultivated by several generous actions), he grew insolent by degrees, and at lenth engrossed the whole power of the empire into his own hands.[2]

Printed and Published for the Authors by T.W. SHAW, Flect-Street, opposite Anderton's Coffee-House, where Letters to the Publisher will be thankfully received. New Editions of all the Numbers of this spirited Paper, are now ready for Sale, and *complete sets* will be sent to any Part of *England, Carriage Free.*

---

2. From Tacitus's *Annals*, Book 1, possibly from Thomas Gordon's *The Works of Tacitus*, 3rd ed., 5 vols. (London: T. and T. Longman, et al., 1753), 1:3–15, to which I turned, or perhaps the fourth edition of 1770.

THE

CRISIS

NUMBER LXXVII   *To be continued Weekly,*

DURING THE PRESENT BLOODY CIVIL WAR IN AMERICA.

SATURDAY, JULY 6, 1776   [Price Two-pence Half-penny.

For the C R I S I S.

A S the present government of England, under his piratical Majesty GEORGE the THIRD, his Blood-Thirsty Parliament and Ministers, is by much the worst in Europe, or perhaps the World, it may not be amiss to shew what all Governments ought to be.

All government, under whatsoever form they are administered, ought to be administered for the good of the society; when they are otherwise administered, they cease to be government, and become usurpation. This being the end of all government, even the most despotic have this limitation to their authority: in this respect, the only difference between the most absolute princes and limited magistrates, is, that in free governments there are checks and restraints appointed and expressed in the constitution itself; in despotic governments, the people submit themselves to the prudence and discretion of the Prince alone; but there is still this tacit condition annexed to his power, that he must act by the unwritten laws of discretion and prudence, and employ it for the sole interest of the people, who give it to him, or suffer him to enjoy it, which they ever do for their own sakes.

Even in the most free governments, single men are often trusted with discretionary power: but they must answer for that discretion to those that trust them. Generals of armies and admirals of fleets have often unlimited commissions? and yet are they not answerable for the prudent execution to those commissions? the council of ten, in Venice, have absolute power over the liberty and life of every man in the state; but if they should make use of that power to slaughter, abolish, or enslave the senate; would it not be lawful for those who gave them that authority, for other ends, to put those ten unlimited traitors to death, any way they could? the crown of England has been for the most part entrusted, with the sole disposal of the money given for the civil list, often with the application of great sums raised for other public uses, yet, if the lord treasurer had applied this money to the dishonour of the king, and ruin of the people, though by the private direction of the crown itself, will any man say that he ought not to have been compensated for his crime, by the loss of his head and his estate.

I have said thus much, to shew that no government can be absolute in the sense, or rather nonsense, of our modern dogmatizers, and indeed in the sense too commonly practiced. No barbarous conquest; no extorted consent of miserable people, submitting to the chain, to escape the sword; no repeated and hereditary acts of cruelty, though called succession; no continuation of violence, though named prescription; can alter, much less abrogate, these fundamental principles of government itself, or make the means of preservation the means of destruction, and render the condition of mankind infinitely more miserable than that of the beast of the field, by the sole privilege of that reason which distinguishes them from the brute creation.

For it can give no title but to revenge, and to the use of force again; nor could it ever enter into the heart of any man, to give to another power over him, for any other end but to be exercised for his own advantage: and if there are any men mad or foolish enough to pretend to do otherwise, they ought to be treated as idiots or lunaticks, and the reason of their conduct must be derived from their folly and frenzy.

All men are born free; liberty is a gift which they receive from God himself; nor can they aleniate the same by consent, though it is possible they may forfeit it by crimes. No man has power over his own life; or to dispose of his own religion; and cannot consequently transfer the power of either of them to any body else: much less can he give away the lives and liberties, religion or acquired property of his posterity, who will be born as free as he himself was born, and can never be bound by his wicked and rediculous bargain.

The right of the magistrate arises only from the right of private men to defend themselves to repel injuries, and to punish those who commit them, that right being conveyed by the society to their public representative, he can execute the same no further than the benefit and security of that society requires he should. When he exceeds his commission, his acts are extrajudicial, as are those of any private officer, usurping an unlawful authority, that is, they are void; and every man is answerable for the wrong which he does. A power to do good can never become a warrant for doing evil.

But here arises a grand question, which has perplexed and puzzled the greatest part of mankind: yet, I think, the answer to it easy and obvious. The question is, who shall be judge whether the magistrate acts justly, and pursues his truth? to this it is justly said, that if those who complain of him are to judge him, then there is a settled authority above the chief magistrate, which authority must be itself the chief magistrate; which is contrary to the supposition; and the same question and difficulty will recur again upon this new magistracy. All this I own to be absurd; and I aver it at least to be as absurd to affirm, that the person accused is to be the decisive judge of his own actions, when it is certain that he will always determine in his own favour; and thus the whole race of mankind, will be left helpless under the heaviest injustice, oppression and misery, that can afflict human nature.

But if neither magistrates, nor they who complain of magistrates, and are aggrieved by them, have a right to determine decisively, the one for the other; and if there be no common established power, to which both are subject; then every man interested in the success of the contest, must act according to the light and dictates of his own conscience, and inform it as well as he can.

If the senate and people of Rome had differed irreconcilably, there could have been no common judge in the world between them; and consequently no remedy but the last; for that government consisting in the union of the nobles and the people, when they differed no man could determine between them; and therefore every man must have been at liberty to provide for his own security, and the general good in the best manner he was able. In that case the common judge ceasing, every one was his own; the government becoming incapable of acting, suffered a political demise: the constitution was dissolved, and there being no government, the people were in the state of nature again.

The same must be true, where two absolute princes, governing a country, come to quarrel, as sometimes two Cæsars in partnership did, especially towards the latter end of the Roman Empire; or where a sovereign council govern a country, and their votes come equally to be divided. In such a circumstance, every man must take that side which he thinks must be for the public good, or chuse any proper measures for his own security; for, if I owe my allegiance to two princes agreeing or to the majority of a council; when between these princes there is no longer any union, nor in that council any majority, no submission can be due to that which is not; and the laws of nature and self-preservation must take place, where there are no other.

Now I would fain know, why private men may not as well use their judgment in an instance that concerns them more; I mean that of a tyrannical government, of which they hourly feel the sad effects, and sorrowful proofs; whereas they are not by far the equal means of coming to a certainty about the natural incapacity of their governors. The persons of great princes are known but to few of their subjects and their parts to much fewer, and several princes have by management of their wives or ministers, or murderers reigned a good while after they were dead.

In Poland, according to the constitution of that country, it is necessary, we are told, that in their diets, the consent of every man present must be had to make a resolve effectual: and therefore, to prevent the cutting of people's throats, they have no remedy to cut the throats of one another; that is, they must pull out their sabres, and force the refractory members (who are always the minority) to submit. And amongst us in England, where a jury cannot agree, there can be no verdict; and so they must fast till they do, or till one of them is dead, and then the jury is dissolved.

This, from the nature of things themselves, must be that constant case in all disputes between dominion and property. Where the interest of the governors and that of the governed clash, there can be no stated judge between them: to appeal to a sovereign power, is to give up the sovereignty; for either side to submit, is to give up the question, and therefore, if they themselves do not amicably determine the dispute between themselves, Heaven alone must. In such case recourse must be had to the first cause of government itself.

Suppose, for example, the grand monarch as he is called, had bought a neighbouring kingdom, and all the lands in it, from the courtiers, and the majority of the peoples deputies; and the church lands into the bargain, with the consent of their convocation, or synod, or by what other name that assembly was called; would the people and clergy have thought themselves obliged to have made good this bargain, if they could have helped it? I dare say that neither would? but on the contrary, that the people would have had the countenance of these reverend patriots to have told their representatives in round terms, that they were chosen to act for the interest of those that sent them, and not for their own; that their power was given them to protect and defend their country, and not to sell and enslave it.

This supposition, as wild as it seems, yet is not absolutely and universally impossible. King John actually sold the kingdom of England to his holiness: and there are people in all nations ready to sell their country at home; and such can never have any principles to with-hold them from selling it abroad.

Obedience to authority is so well secured, that it is wild to imagine that any number of men, formidable enough to disturb a settled state, can unite together and hope to overturn it, till the public grievances are so enormous, the oppression so great, and the disaffection so universal, that there can be no question remaining, whether their calamities be real or imaginary, and whether the magistrate has protected or endeavoured to destroy his people.

Upon this principle of people's judging for themselves, and resisting lawless force, stands our late happy revolution, and with it the *just and rightful* title *of our most excellent* Grand Seignor *King George*, to the scepter of these realms; a scepter which his predecessors swayed to their own honour, and the honour, protection, and prosperity of the people.

Printed and Published for the AUTHORS by T. W. SHAW, Fleet-Street, opposite Anderton's Coffee-House, where Letters to the Publisher will be thankfully received. New Editions of all the Numbers of this spirited Paper, are now ready for Sale, and *complete sets* will be sent to any Part of *England, Carriage Free.*

THE

CRISIS

NUMBER LXXVIII   *To be continued Weekly,*

DURING THE PRESENT BLOODY CIVIL WAR IN AMERICA.

SATURDAY, July 13, 1776   [Price Two-pence Half-penny.

————*Neque amissos Colores*
Lana resert medicata suco;
Nec vera Virtus, sum semel occidit,
Curat reponi deterioribus.
                                Hor.[1]

Nor *Place,* nor *Title,* nor *Corruption's* lore,
Nor *George's* smile, lost *Honor* can restore.
No change of *Name* can wipe out *Mindon's* stain;
The blasted *Sackville's* blotch still marks *Germaine.*

1. Horace's musing on cowardice and virtue, from Book 3 of the *Odes*: when wool absorbs the dyer's stain, its native color can never be restored.

For the C R I S I S.

To Lord G E O R G E G E R M A I N E,[2]

My Lord,

THE profound respect I bear to the memory of your illustrious father, the late *Lionel* duke of *Dorset*, whose useful life was shortened by the blast he received from MINDEN, prompts me though late, to congratulate your lordship, (before I proceed further) as well upon your change of *name* as station; I am rejoiced to find that you remain no longer a disgraceful *memento* to *the Dorset* family, under the once unblemished name of *Sackville*, I might have snatched an earlier opportunity, but I thought it beneath a man to wound an object on the ground; your late abject state (unfeathered and unnoticed) debased you beneath the censure of the most obscure pen, but your lordship is now rising rapidly into meridian luster. Our discerning *monarch* has deigned to furbish up your long tarnished *honour*, by raising you to a height where your *merits* must become fatally conspicuous; so wise a prince well knew that an excess of wisdom and *valour* rarely meets, in your lordship they are most happily united.

In spite of all the convincing testimony of a great General, and many brave officers unsullied in point of honour, in spite of the detestation and resentment of your late good and gallant sovereign; your lordship has sprung up upon wings of merit, from the lowest pit of infamy, to the very pinnacle of all earthly happiness; from the contempt of the meanest subject, into the bosom of the most pious, wise, and courageous *monarch* in the universe. Your lordship (whilst a *Sackville*) had unfortunately sunk beneath the *chastisement* of a *Ferdinand*, that prince consigned you and your saucy *challenge*, with the utmost scorn, to the *cane* of his *domestic*, but you are now become *Germaine*, a minister, a councellor, a favourite, and one of the *saviours* of this unhappy kingdom, *deaf, bashful,* and slow

---

2. Since November 1775 the secretary of state for American affairs, Germain having succeeded Dartmouth. For more on Germain see n. L.5 supra.

of apprehension, as you was at *Minden*; you are now become quick, confident and intelligent, no order, hint, nor *whisper* can escape you. With open ears, steady execution, and clear conception, you are now become alert in obedience, and dextrous even in guessing at the pleasure of your *masters*. *Bute's* beck, *Mansfield's* eye, and *George's* lowering frown, are now intelligible and explicit.

In the latitude of *St. James's*, your lordship can understand even *signs* and *gestures*. In the latitude of *Minden*, repeated *orders*, in the clearest terms were wholly *unintelligible*; for the future service of your country, you nobly consulted the safety of your person in the *field*, that you might one day figure in the *cabinet*, dead to every sense of honour and of shame in *Germany*, your lordship now lives to plan the ruin of *America*, in an *office* of the greatest importance to this kingdom.

Your lordship's great experience in the art of war, may well give a sanction to all your schemes as a politician. What hand so fit to draw a plan of military operations against injured and oppressed subjects as that which forced the lines of a *foreign enemy* with such vigour and intrepidity? What *head* so proper to defeat the patriotic spirits of a *Washington* or a *Putnam*, as that which was puzzled by a plain *order* from Prince *Ferdinand*, no less than three times delivered in the most distinct terms? At whose name will the glorious leaders of true *revolutional resistance* in *America*, so soon turn pale, as at his (the great *Germaine's*) whose lips quivered with fear, on receiving a command to charge on a dastardly enemy, just on the brink of flight? But how can your lordship advise and plan an *English massacre* in the *cabinet*, who dared not assist the completion of an *English victory* in the *field?* How can you support and contrive *ministerial tyranny*, without a blush? you, my lord, who could not join a *British conquest*, without a *panic?* for shame my lord, give up the persecution of *America*. Methinks, your hands should tremble more in planning schemes of national slaughter in *America* than it did when you attempted to draw your reluctant sword upon the plains of *Minden*, was your lordships heart chilled with fear in the cause of *honour*, and does it beat high now in the cause of *assassination?* was you *once* afraid to partake of *glory*, and do you now dare to imbrue your hands in *murder?* were you timid in a just war, that you might reserve yourself for *despotic butchery?* will you, who *industriously* declined the gallant orders of your General, stain, once more, the honour of your family by enforcing the bloody instructions of a *tyrant*, or a set of *tyrants?*

Permit me to remind your lordship with what compassion your own deplorable case was treated by your late humane *sovereign*, your lordship had the effrontry and folly to add the character of *bravo* to that of *coward*, you rashly demanded a *court martial* more than once, you repeated, you insisted, persisted, and at last prevailed—Your noble father felt for the disgrace his timerous son had brought upon the name of *Sackvile*, he knew your guilt, was convinced that your dastardly behaviour deserved *death*, and trembled lest the *court marshal* should observe a Roman strictness in their sentence; over whelmed with grief, he implored the lenity of his late *majesty*, who, with his wonted goodness of heart, dropped a sympathetic tear; but justly determined that *death* should, at all events, be the portion of a *coward*, if your lordship was pronounced so.—I will not say that the *court marshal* were partial, my lord, but I will say that they were very, very kind; I will say that they felt more for a noble family than for you, they pronounced you *bashful* at Minden.

This verdict, my lord, has left such a stain upon you as none but *yourself* would survive.—you was *broke*, dishonoured, and dispised.—you tried but in vain to make yourself popular, by a kind of half-faced temporary *opposition*; but the patriotic party disdained such an associate, and even the *ministry* kept a loof, till necessity obliged them to put their trust in numbers, and to enlist men into their service of the worst principles. Your father, my lord, was a *whig*, and served a prince whose principles were truly *revolutional*, who detested *hypocrisy* and *tyranny*, and deserved to have been *immortal* on the throne of *England*. In such a reign, your lordships useful talents must ever have rested unemployed; your late *sovereign* had seen actual service as a *soldier*, he was truly brave, his soul disdained a *coward*; had your lordship by any mistake, gained a seat at the council board, in *his* reign he would have done you the honour to have struck your hateful name out with his own hand, that good prince would not have sat with smiling patience, in his closet, whilst your lordship had laid *military traps* before him for the destruction of his wronged, irritated and repulsed *subjects* in *America*.

You should have shewn yourself a *Soldier* in a better cause, my lord, but you are still actuated by the same principles which possessed your soul at *Minden*—FEAR—There you feared *death,* and here you fear *obscurity;* your lordship has *vanity,* but you cannot be said to have *ambition;* the first you share in common with the lowest clerk in your office; the latter cannot be gratified in such an *office* and such a reign, under such an *administration,* and by such talents as your lordship is possessed of. The wretch, who can temporize in *politics,* will want honour in the *cabinet,* integrity in *office,* virtue in the *senate,* and fortitude in the *field,* yet no other men than such can *safely* be employed at present. Among these your lordship stands conspicuously branded with the opinion of all mankind.

You are now raised to an happy eminence, from whence you look down with indifference and contempt upon all wordly censure; the gracious eye of *majesty* has healed your wounded honour, and brought you once more into favour with yourself, your mental faculties begin to brighten up, and now your lordship, who was once at a loss to comprehend the clearest instructions, as a *soldier,* can pen the bloodiest, as an *agent* of *tyranny, ambition, rapacity* and *revenge*; at a happy distance from all danger, your lordship, in your official capacity, conveys, commands, you dare not *execute.* Upon *paper* your hand is steady, in the *field* it shakes. Were the brave *Colonel Sloper* now to see your lordship brandishing your servile goose quill at *Whitehall,* he must admire your alacrity, your adroitness, your martial air, your steady perseverance, and the placid composure of your visage, he would view you with astonishment, planning schemes of carnage upon paper, without a *change of features,* even you, my lord, whose *pale cheeks* and *quivering lips* denoted what you was, (and what you still are) at *Minden.* That *Colonel Sloper,* my lord, saw a noble contrast to your lordship in the gallant *Granby;* the bare mention of his name, turns your lordship pale again, it is with envy, or detestation, of so much virtue? most probably the latter.[3]

Whilst that brave nobleman survived, your patron *Bute* would not venture to raise your lordship from the ground, where the justice of your late *sovereign* at his lamented death had left you. The *Thane* was given to understand that the noble *marquis* would have looked upon such an elevation of your lordship, whilst he was at the head of our *army,* as an insult, as an indignity, which he could not brook, he looked upon your lordship as a *deserter,* as a disgrace to every administration, every government, to this nation, and to the very name of a *soldier,* he industriously avoided the very air your lordship breathed in. Beloved, adored as he was by the whole army, even your godlike *Thane* did not dare to give him reason for *offence;* thus your lordships intrinsic merit laid smothered for a while; you had otherwise, mourned long ago among the number of those *faithful servants of the crown* whom the *king* delights to honour, and whom the nation most detests.

Your lordship is, at last, advanced; tho' late, yet alas! too early for your country. Had you either perished, or preserved your honour upon the plains of *Minden,* your memory would have been dear, or your life useful, to *Great Britain,* but, my lord, the better half of you is now dead, and that which survives, is dedicated to the worst of services, the designs of a corrupt and abandoned *ministry*; a profligate, revengeful, stupid, and ambitious *tyrant,* and the ruin of your country. I shudder my lord when I add that your lordship, with the heart of a *deer,* and the effrontery of a *dog,* (these expressions are *Homerical*[4]) is now laying military *plans* for the destruction of the most valuable part of the empire of Great Britain

---

3. Colonel Robert Sloper and the Marquis of Granby had both been at Minden with Germain (see n. L.5 supra) and both appeared for the prosecution in Germain's subsequent court martial. Sloper testified that Germain had waited too long to execute Prince Ferdinand's order to attack with the cavalry; Granby added that, once under way, Germain advanced too slowly.

4. Pope, *Iliad of Homer,* 1:31 (Book I, lines 295–300) describes Achilles' anger at Agamemnon (Atrides) for bringing the wrath of the gods down on the Greek camp:

in *America;* yet who so proper to project a *massacre* of *brave subjects,* as the palid wretch who did not dare to spur his horse, or use his sword at MINDEN?

Before I take my leave of your lordship, as the present fabricator of all our military achievements in *America,* suffer me to congratulate you upon your *masters* late success in raising recruits, against *conscience,* against *revolutional resistance,* against every *principle* which advanced his family to the throne of these kingdoms; your lordship may now with the greatest confidence, feed the hopes of your *despotic baby,* with the assurance of future victories in *America;* you may boldly sketch out decisive battles upon *paper;* for your lordship now can produce *men,* just half a degree better than *Lord Barrington's paper-men,* to fight thereon.

I have lately seen, with the greatest pity, some scores of these military *shadows,* the formidable *bull calves,* conducted with drum and fife, in a state of intoxication, from a certain country town, immediately to the water side, to be from thence wafted, in privacy to tenders which lay ready to receive them, on board these, and in their passage over, they are taught the use of *arms,* that is to know the *muzzle* from the *but-end* of the musquet. The poor boys (for mere *boys* they are) destined thus as *food for powder,* most of whom have hardly reached their *teens,* are, indeed, figures too slender to be marched up to *London,* too laughable to be seen by day light; they are therefore conveyed away, as fast as they are *kidnapped* before the first crowing of the cock.

This, my lord, is a pregnant instance of the great alacrity with which English *men* take up arms against their *injured fellow subjects,* when mere children are eagerly transported to intimidate *America* by dint of numbers; they are mere pegs to hang red coats upon, they are, my lord,

---

"Nor yet the rage his boiling breast forsook,
Which thus redoubling on Atrides broke.
O monster! Mix'd of insolence and fear,
Thou dog in forehead, but in heart a deer!
When wert thou known in ambush'd fights to dare,
Or nobly face the horrid front of war?"

likely to be just as much real service in the battle as your lordship was at MINDEN.

I am sensible that your lordships promotion (like the waters of *Lethe*)[5] has washed away all remembrance of your former self, when *Sackville,* you will therefore call me libeller; if you can find a single man of *real honour* who will pedge himself (as *proxy* for your lordship) that I shall be prosecuted as *libeler* in the court of *common pleas*; I will immediately discover who I am, so much do I long to hear the doctrine of *libels* discussed by the very candid *chief justice* of that court; who in the late case of *Sayer* against *Lord Rochford*, has out shone all his predecessors upon the doctrine of *treasons*: the upright *court judges* of *James the second*, were fools to him. With the *statute* of *treasons* staring him in the face, he has *dared*, even in these enlightened days, and in this *mild and pious* reign, (even in the life time of a *Camden*) to give an opinion, in the very teeth of that statute, and of the statute of *king William*. Had *Hales, Holt,* or that friend to the *revolution* and the *truth*, the late learned and venerable *Foster,*[6] heard him they must have fainted.

This is the man, my lord, who will pour *jesuitical balm*, into the wounds of all your *tory* party, who shall be stabbed by *wiggish* libellers. To this consolation, the only one (besides *court sun shine*, and your pay) which a man in your lordships circumstances can receive in this life, I now leave you, with all the honest contempt of an *Englishman*; who wishes you had fallen bravely, in the service of a *good* king, and *better* cause, upon the plains of *Minden*.

C A S C A.

---

5. The Lethe was a river that ran through the underworld of Greek mythology. Those who came in contact with its waters forgot everything about their lives on the Earth beyond Hades. Lethe as river, or Lethe as the goddess of forgetfulness, was scattered throughout the classical canon—from Horace's *Odes* to Virgil's *Aeneid* to Ovid's *Metamorphoses* to various tragedies by Seneca.

6. Sir Mathew Hale (1609–1676) was remembered for his jurisprudential skill as a judge on the court of common pleas. Sir John Holt (1642–1710) and Sir Michael Foster (1689–1763) had earned a similar high regard for their years on the court of king's bench.

Printed and Published for the AUTHORS by T. W. SHAW, Fleet-Street, opposite Anderton's Coffee-House, where Letters to the Publisher will be thankfully received. New Editions of all the Numbers of this spirited Paper, are now ready for Sale, and *complete sets* will be sent to any Part of *England*, *Carriage Free*.

THE

CRISIS

NUMBER LXXIX   *To be continued Weekly,*

DURING THE PRESENT BLOODY CIVIL WAR IN AMERICA.

SATURDAY, JULY 20, 1776   [Price Two-pence Half-penny.

Reflections on the present conspiracy of the King and Parliament
of Britain against the *Americans*.

TAXES imposed without the consent of the people, or their representatives, who are so circumstanced, that they cannot tax their
constituents, without taxing themselves, breaks down every
barrier of liberty. Remove this constitutional check, and the people are
no longer a controul upon the House of Commons, nor they upon the
minister. Empire follows the balance of property and confers sovereign
power to the possessor, though he may not have more wisdom, honour,
humanity, or justice, than that malignant influence which secretly prevails in the closet, debauches the senate and seems to be traitorously
gnawing out the vital principles of the constitution. He who holds the
national purse, holds life, liberty, and every thing valuable to society, at
his absolute disposal. Every act of the present administration verifies the
position. Hence it is we behold, with secret indignation, an addressing,
obsequious parliament, and a petitioning, discontented, insulted people,
calling loud for impeachments; a pensionary commons, voting supplies
with an unconfined liberality, and the nation demanding account. The

wise and virtuous pining in obscurity, or secretly retiring from court, while honours. pensions, and the most lucrative employments, the rewards of great and eminent service, are conferred upon splendid villains, for the meanest prostitutions. The first servant of the state, insulting the religion of his country, with impunity, within those consecrated walls, where one would have imagined, common decency, in the absence of religion, and virtue, would forever held her in legal reverence.

The most august judicature of the nation, deaf to all reason and argument, obstinately persisting in a system of violence, with the evidence of repeated experience, has demonstrated to be fatal to commerce; subversive of natural justice; the clearest principles of law; derogratory to its own honour, incongrous with the usage of all deliberate and judicial assemblies; and finally, pregnant with the most unnatural scenes of bloodshed, murder and devastation. If such are the melancholly effects of an inordinate attachment to gain, in a luxurious dissipated age, can we wonder that the first step, always taken by artful ministers, is to command, without controul, the property of the subject, when the people are to be deprived of their freedom, and independency? The unhappy Charles knew the weight of the argument; but happily for this nation, his virtuous parliament felt its full force; and therefore in a contest for a few shillings, this island was made to run down with the best and richest blood of the nation.

Whoever, dispassionately considers, the nature of the controversy, between administration and the colonies, will find it very nearly resembles that which was maintained between the Stuart race, and the people of Great Britain. The same arguments may, with equal propriety, be urged in favour of the colonists, which were made use of by the patriots of those times. There is, I confess, some difference in the mode, by which Tyranny is now supported, from what it was at that period. In that virtuous age, Parliament was the controuling power for the people, the redresser of grievances, and guardian of the the public welfare. But in the unnatural times of degeneracy, parliament is become the violent instrument, under the baneful influence of a flattering minion, by which the very throne is undermined, and a brave and loyal people persecuted with the most relentless cruelty.

Fully sensible that there would be no end of impositions and oppressions, if once they should submit to the reasonable claims of Britain,
after solemn deliberation, they are reduced to the fatal necessity of an
appeal to heaven, and the justice of their cause. In imitation of their
illustrious progenitors, they are determined to undergo every species of
misery! Nay, all the horrors of the last century, rather than abandon their
own native rights, or servilely bend their necks to the yoke of domestic
tyranny! It is equal to them, whether they are enslaved by a few, or the
many; by the prerogative of the crown, the false towering dignity of Parliament, or the head-long savage resentment, and blind-fold ambition, of
an unfeeling administration.

By what tenure do the colonists hold their liberties; when, after encoun-
tering, almost insuperable hardships, toils, and difficulties, the fruits of
their industry is to be torn from them by the lords and commons of Britain, who have no property in America, to serve as a controul upon their
actions? Men who have solemnly professed they will be restricted by
no limitations, and who by their remote distance, must be incompetent
judges of their abilities, or the ways and means taxes can be imposed,
least burthensome to them: men, who are under an undue bias, from
motives of popularity and interest in their respective districts, to throw
an unequal proportion of the national burthens, upon the shoulders of
the colonists, to ease themselves, and the estates of the gentry of this
kingdom.

Why does the law require legal qualifications for members to sit in the
British house of Commons? was it not wisely judged a measure absolutely
necessary, for every member to have three hundred pounds per year for a
Borough, and five for a county, as a security for the people against unlimited taxation? Have the colonists this security? Does an American estate give
this qualification? Why do the Commons so pertinaciously insist upon the
exclusive privileges of framing money bills, and granting annual supplies
to support the prince, the army, and navy establishments? let the people
of Great Britain give up this controul upon their representatives, and they
immediately become absolute: let the commons relinquish this right and
they cease to have an existence. The will of the Prince becomes the law of

land, and the army paid with the peoples money, becomes the executioner of the arbitrary mandates of the minister.

But say, the advocates for the British supremacy, are there not millions in Great Britain, who have no imediate share in sending representatives to parliament? do not the towns of Birmingham, Sheffield, and Manchester, stock-holders, and copyholders, come under this description? But is not this reasoning from a defect in the constitution of Great Britain? how happens it those towns are not represented? Had they existed when writs was first issued, to call members to Parliament, would they have been neglected? Do not stockholders and copyholders, vote frequently as freeholders, citizens and freemen? They are not parallel cases, for the following obvious unanswerable, reasons.

I. The Commons of Britain are chosen from a class of men, to whom the rights of those towns, are as dear as those other towns, which have a share in the election of members.

II. There is, from the nature of things, an inevitable and inseparable reciprocation of interest, between all the people of Great Britain, whither electors, non-electors, or representatives.

III. The laws know no difference between the electors, nonelectors, or the elected: they are all equally obnoxious to the same inconveniences, contributors to the same taxes: therefore stockholders, copy-holders and the inhabitants of those towns, having no taxes levied upon them, but what equally bind the Lords and Commons of Great Britain, are in no worse condition than those electors, who have actually and personally a right of representation.

If some advocate for the British Supremacy, laying aside the falacious subterfuges of sophistry and deceit, will point out to my conviction, how the colonies, circumstanced as they are, stand in the same predicament with those towns, I will give up the controversy, and confess, the complainants have no right to accuse Britain of tyranny and injustice. The claim of virtual representation is manifestly defective. It does not provide for the safety of the colonists. It discovers an overweening attachment to our own interest; and being partial, tends to work that disunion we all dread, as ruinous to the whole empire. The litigants on both sides seem to be insensible, that the constitutional principles they appeal to, were established before the colonies were discovered; whereas the truth is, the empire, long after the constitution was formed, acquired a new adventitious state; and the question therefore is, not what the constitution was, or is; but what, present circumstances considered, it ought to be? Britain having made a vast accession to her dominions, by discovery, by conquest, and by cession, the disputants, instead of idly spending their time in collecting arguments, all changeable with a *non sequitur,* should have pointed to measures, conducive to the common weal of both countries, because to that the constitution (be it what it will) ought to bend, and sooner or later, will bend, unless it is the design of heaven to forsake the British councils, and infatuate and destroy us as a nation.

Can the lives, or the religion of the colonists be secure, when a military force is quartered upon them, without the controul of law to bleed them into obedience? Call such a constitution what you will, it is the sword that governs. Are they not equally entitled to welfare and happiness, security in their persons and properties, freedom in their governments, with the people of Great Britain? Can we attempt to dispossess them of these things, upon any pretence whatever? The very idea is insupportable to every true Britain, and cannot be viewed, even in contemplation, without horror and detestation! Was not an attempt to take away the property of the subject; without his consent, a just foundation for that resistance which brought the first Charles and his ministers to the block, and drove James the second an exile into France, where he at last died in disgrace, a terrible monument of the vengeance of God upon arbitrary princes?

The regulations which have been made in the different departments of our legislative and executive government, respecting the colonies, dispassionately considered, favour more of the inquisition than the common law of England, of the constitution of a free state.

To deprive the subject of the inestimable trial by jury—change the constitution of government—violate charters—abolish the sacred privilege of habeas corpus—proscribe a large and capital city—starve the innocent, and under the colour of justice, sport with their calamities—impose taxes without consent, and compel obedience by new, unconstitutional tribunals—"excite commotions and then scourge for being excited" by a standing army raised without their consent, and paid with their money—exempt murderers from the hands of justice—drag their venerable patriots the principle pillars of their liberties, whom they now behold with an eye of gratitude and affection to be tried at an unequal bar, three thousand miles distance, where, without witnesses and friends, they have not the least chance of acquittal, or even the miserable consolation of beholding, in the gloomy hour of death, that they fell victims upon the alter of liberty bewailed and lamented by their countrymen.

Printed and Published for the AUTHORS by T. W. SHAW, Fleet-Street, opposite Anderton's Coffee-House, where Letters to the Publisher will be thankfully received. New Editions of all the Numbers of this spirited Paper, are now ready for Sale, and *complete sets* will be sent to any Part of *England, Carriage Free.*

THE

CRISIS

NUMBER LXXX   *To be continued Weekly,*

DURING THE PRESENT BLOODY CIVIL WAR IN AMERICA.

SATURDAY, JULY 27, 1776   [Price Two-pence Half-penny.

Continued from our last.

P ROSECUTE those who expose the licentiousness of power, and imprison the subject for delivering truths—declare the means of obtaining redress of grievances, high treason—seize private property by military force—insult the sovereign, by establishing a religion professedly intolerant, perfidious, and Bloody—pervert the course of justice, and finally carry dessolation, ruin and wonton cruelty, through the peaceful vales of industry! Does such an uncontrouled barbarous phrenzy of oppressing, accord with the benign, liberal genious of the British nation, and the maxims under which we have prospered for ages? Were the laws of nature the ends of government, the principles of religion, the constitution, or the finer feelings of humanity, consulted? Does it not excite astonishment, that brutal power and the influence of the treasury, could have thus debauched the principles, and affections of a British Legislature? Have not such violent outrages excited most alarming apprehensions in the breast of every sober minded man, both in England and America? and must eventually justify a firm, intrepid resistance in both countries? Have we not reason to apprehend, that the expiring

675

virtue of Britain, the pride, profligacy, avarice, luxury, and effeminacy, into which she has sunk, will shortly call down the righteous vengeance of heaven, unless there is a speedy change in the system of these affairs?

In the course of human events, those who fall on such outrageous measures, and daringly dispise the remonstrances of the people, will most assuredly fall victims to their own arbitrary contrivances. What ever may be the language of court sycophants, we, notwithstanding, find, that though they had stoned the kings treasurer to death, and taken up arms against their lawful king, yet God himself would not support even his own theocracy, in the oppression of the people.*

Fathers provoke not your children to anger, is a divine precept, founded on an intimate knowledge of the feelings and conduct of men. "When once they begin to be in earnest against those who would enslave them, their power is irresistible".[1]

The great author of nature, has so linked causes, and their correspondent effects, that we find even those princes were *sic volo, sic jubeo, stet proratione voluntas,*[2] is the express written in the law of the land, do nevertheless frequently fall a sacrifice to their own slaves, when pushed to the last extremeties. How many Turkish monarchs have been strangled by their own mutes? How few of the Roman emperors died natural deaths, though they had their Court Jannissaries and prætorian bands to protect them? The wheels of government do not depend alone upon the secret

---

*Chron. Book II. Chap. XI.

---

1. The author(s) quoted from James Otis's *The Rights of the British Colonies Asserted and proved* (Boston: Edes and Gill, 1764), p. 22, which had been reprinted in London by John Almon in just a matter of months. Otis noted his debt to John Locke's comments on the dissolution of government, the people deciding to "rouze themselves" when they could stand the abuses of government no longer. Locke's *Two Treatises of Government* had come out in a new London edition in 1764 as well; see p. 396 (section 225) for the relevant passage.

2. "This I want, this I command; my will stands in place of reason," from Juvenal's *Satires,* Book 6 (see n. VII.7 supra).

machinations of a court cabinet, or the policy of princes. Nature has its laws, and when her rights are trampled upon, she will find executioners. The observation is founded on historical facts, and contains an admirable lesson for the direction of our conduct in the present critical juncture. I do not mean to threaten or inform: the first would be rashness, the last presumption. But I conceive it is the duty of every member of the community, to warn those who are going down a precipice of their danger. We are passing the rubicon; add however it may be received this side the Water, by an infatuated Administration, it is a solemn truth; the people we are contending with, are three millions in number, and hold in their hands the richest veins of our commerce, the source of our power and opulence. What then are we to think of the present contest? it is a disease which affects life, and, as it spreads fast, the remedy must be speedily administered. Every temporary violent quack medicine has been tried, they have exasperated the disease, and if not immediately discontinued, will shortly put the malady beyond all manner of prescription. The affection of three millions of people, situated as they are at the distance of three thousand miles, with so many distinguishing peculiarities, in soil and climate, are not to be dispised or insulted: Commerce is not a matter of compulsion: no dominion is good but what is lasting: to make it permanent it must be founded on love and interest, otherwise we shall fix such a deep rooted rancor, in the minds of the Colonists, which we shall never be able to eradicate, and must eventually reap the bitter fruits of. This general proposition, true in *all* conditions, becomes more evident, when applied to a country, doubling by its own growth in five and twenty years, besides the accession of foreigners, and must, in fifty, equal the present inhabitants of Great Britain, and Ireland.

While we are thus valiantly, over-leaping the bounds of law, and the constitution, it might be prudent to reflect that they have a numerous well disciplined militia, who are as yet hardy, brave determined, and undebauched, by the effeminacy of the present age, and we an imense national debt of a hundred and forty millions to discharge. Thus circumstanced, is alieniating the affections of a brave spirited people, drying up the distant springs of our commerce and revenue, become the primary object of our policy? Will such a system of measures furnish raw materials for our manufactures, naval stores for our ships, multiply seamen, increase the value of our lands, inrich our merchants, pay our debts, feed our poor, furnish employment for our labouring people, decrease the interest of the national debt, or enable us to meet our natural enemies in another war? Can the history of mankind furnish an example of a nation exhausted by its own efforts, and trembling under its own weight, destroying its own markets, ruining its own resources, massacring its customers, who supply her with those things, essentially necessary to her, taking in return, the fruits of her industry, at her own price, balancing the difference with their gold and silver?

It is an incontrovertable truth, that a branch of commerce, once lost, is irretrievably lost; no human institutions will be able to direct it into its antient channels. The present fruitless endeavours of Parliament, to restore the Spanish trade to Jamaica, from whence it was injudiciously drove, by the interference of government, is a strange flagrant proof of the position, and one would imagine, affords a useful lesson to those, who would profit by experience. The interest of the merchants, if left to the natural bias of their own inclinations, is the interest of the community at large; as the individual becomes rich, so must the state to which they belong; the legislature here can do little more than give encouragement, and protection to the commerce, when ever much more is attempted, she commits *felo de se,* and repentance follows close at her heels.

The Colonies are, in general, inhabited by men of small fortunes, four-fifths of whom, are employed in agriculture, and, if left in the peaceable possession of their indubitable rights, would never think of entering into manufactures; if they be permitted a reasonable trade, it would be neither their inclination, nor their interest, to contend with old and popular countries, which must be able to excell them in cheapness, and workmanship; but, if the present obnoxious scheme is pursued, it will drive them into habits of oeconomy, and the necessity of promoting manufactures among themselves, and convince us, that nothing is too difficult for men to effect, whose hearts are filled with a generous love to their country.

It was palpable blundering, to restrain the trade of the Colonies to the foreign plantation in the West Indies, and prohibit the paper currency.

These were the resources, from whence they were enabled to make their remittances, to the British merchants at home, and at the same time, increased the vent of our manufactures abroad, thereby converting them into British Colonies, without the expence of protection. Britain ought to be contented with her sovereignty in commerce. The Colonists demand, only an exemption from parliamentary taxations, as a *right,* recognizing the supremacy of Britain, every other instance. Her prosperity and strength depends upon commanding a market for her manufactures, and their supplying her with such articles, in preference to other nations, as are essential to her manufactures, and her strength at sea: hence their importance to her. This will produce all the advantages she ought to wish, or they can grant, consistent with the duty they owe us, and themselves; any further restrictions is risquing all, by being in too great haste to gain; distressing them , without enriching ourselves.

Our foreign trade is confessedly lost, or very much decayed; other nations have interfered with us, and the boasted omnipotence of Parliament, cannot extend to them; they have each a commercial police of their own, and we have already felt the inconvenience of their commercial regulations; so as to induce us to lay large bounties upon such articles, as they used to furnish us with, to encourage the importation of them from our Colonies, which has made us almost independant on the world, in point of Trade but if the present contest should continue, the balance of trade with foreign countries, will be so much against us, for raw materials to supply our manufactures, as will shortly render us, from being one of the most opulent, the most indigent nation in Europe, and threaten our very existence as a state, in short the benefit of the Northern Colonies, have been hitherto immense; "before their settlement. says Devenant,[3] our

3. These lines are not from any of the works of political economist Charles Davenant, who had died in 1714. Even so the thinking expressed there was in line with what Davenant, who warned that foolish policies might drive Americans to seek independence, had written. The lines were most likely taken from the London edition of John Dickinson's (anonymous) *Letters from a Farmer in Pennsylvania, to the Inhabitants of the British Colonies,* printed by John Almon. They appear in a footnote to the fifth "letter," on p. 40, after Dickinson had indeed quoted from Davenant, but Dickinson attributed

manufacturers were few, and those but indifferent; and the number of English merchants and the whole shipping of the nation, much inferior to what belongs to the Northern Colonies alone"; they are essential to the strength, and form the very basis of the British power.

All these advantages, must, if wise system is pursued, and we return to the antient policy of the kingdom, be encreased in the same proportion as they encrease. If our successes are wisely improved, the last glorious war, will prove profitable to the nation, the vast encrease of the national debt notwithstanding. By the conquest of Canada, we have acquired, the dominion of all North America; and henceforth, by expeditions from that Continent, in conjunction with a British fleet, we may be in a condition to seize, all the West India islands at pleasure, humble France and Spain, and secure the tranquility of Europe.

The West India produce, imported into France, in 1754, was near ten million sterling; she holds these sources of wealth, at the mercy of Britain! What an immence operation in favour of the revenue! an object much more worthy for a great ministers attention, than wantonly laying waste the rights and properties of the subject, governing by corruption, and influence, and throwing the whole empire into confusion, by vigourously inforcing unconstitutional claims.

Printed and Published for the AUTHORS by T. W. SHAW, Fleet-Street, opposite Anderton's Coffee-House, where Letters to the Publisher will be thankfully received. New Editions of all the Numbers of this spirited Paper, are now ready for Sale, and *complete sets* will be sent to any Part of *England, Carriage Free.*

---

the lines to Malachy Postlethwayt, who died in 1767. That the author(s) of *The Crisis* conflated the works of two Englishmen, and did that while drawing from a pamphlet written by a colonist, serves as a nice example of the transatlantic nature of imperial protest, and that certain ideas about how the empire should—and should not—be run carried through the generations as well back and forth across the ocean. For another possible borrowing from Dickinson see n. LXIV.3 supra.

THE

CRISIS

NUMBER LXXXI   *To be continued every Saturday,*

DURING THE PRESENT BLOODY CIVIL WAR IN AMERICA.

SATURDAY, August 3, 1776   [Price Two-pence Half-penny.

Continued from our last.

THE salvation of the people and the king's lands, was the tyrants plea for unlimited power over the property of the subject in the last century. *To ease the estates of the gentry of this kingdom,** is the present claim of the British Parliament; to bind the Colonies in all cases whatsoever. No power can be safe but what is limited. Reason, justice, and the latent principles of society, all declare, that there are bounds, which, by God and nature are fixed, beyond which Parliament cannot pass, without violating the first and clearest principles of law, and all those barriers set up as marks, whereby kings, ministers, and parliaments, are equally obliged to conduct themselves. The venerable sages of the law have solemnly adjusted, that acts of parliament, against natural equity, are void: *jura natura, sunt immutabilia.*[1] The business of parlia-

---

*See the protest of the House of Lords against the repeal of the *Stamp Act.*

1. "The laws of nature are unchangeable," which had long before passed in legal Latin.

ment is to declare the rights of the people not to give them. This without derogating from its dignity, is beyond its prerogative. If right, belongs only to him, who views with an equal eye both prince and people; who neither slumbers nor sleeps: whose rain falls equally upon the just and the unjust. Though the business of parliament is to declare, what is for the welfare and happiness of the people, yet it is by no means inferred that the declaration makes any law so: consequently, if the legislature shall have enacted any laws which shall appear palpably, and by "evident consequence," to have a direct tendancy to destroy the inherent primary, and essential rights of freemen, they must in their own nature, be illegal, necessarily void, and not binding upon the subject. It is equally evident, that they who attempt to make or enforce such laws, supersede reason, and that great charter given by God to all men at their creation, and which no power under heaven, can take away, without waging war upon the subject, and incurring the censure of tyranny and violence.

It has been apprehended, by some, that such extensive colonies, like an over-grown child, will exhaust the parent-state. The Cases of the antient Phoenecians, and modern Spaniards, have been mentioned, on this occasion, and even urged as an argument, to justify administration, in the violation of their rights. But all who read history are not able to apply it, and make the proper distinctions.

If Great Britain is to be ruined, as these speculatists imagine, by the flight of her inhabitants to America, it is high time to set the new house in order, for our comfortable accommodation, and welcome reception: if any unforeseen catastrophe, should render these favourite islands, no longer tenable in this quarter, we may retreat to America, and the present is a most advantageous season, for laying a solid foundation, for the speedy re-establishment, of a dominion which no power on earth will be able to annoy.

Though the wars of Asia, drove the feeble and defenseless Phoenecians to Carthage, and the mines of Mexico and Peru, depopulated Spain, yet Great Britain, by a wise conduct, may improve her Colonies, even for the encrease of her population, as well as the agrandizement of her power; every body knows that the number of her inhabitants, is vastly encreased, since the discovery of the New World: and can any man be ignorant that this is owing, to the augmentation thereby given to her commerce? The encrease of people depends upon the encouragement given to marriages; trade and commerce give that encouragement, manufactures exported, draw subsistance from foreign countries for numbers, who are thereby enabled to marry and raise families. But if by violence and oppression, Great Britain impedes or loses her American trade, and no new employment is found for our manufacturers, occupied in that trade, she will soon be deprived of so many inhabitants.

As the inhabitants of Great Britain, emigrate to America, in a treble proportion, will be the increase of the inhabitants from the parent stock: there is no bound to the prolific nature of men, but what is made, by their interfering with each others subsistance: if all the nations in Europe were obliterated in one instant, Polipus like, they would in a small period of time, be replenished by the natural generation of Great Britain alone: The same causes, will produce the same effects; the spanish emigrations drained the old state, chiefly because they sent her money instead of merchandize; Spain was converted into a castle of indolence and pride; she acquired silver and gold from her colonies, not real wealth. Money begets luxury and indolence; the consequences are evident, commerce drops her head; manufacturers are at a stand; uncrouded ports: fields mourn; the hand of cultivation is with-held; a warm climate, bad religious police enervated the body, dryed up the fountain of health, and the springs of nature stood still.

If Great Britain is attentive to her own, and the trade of her colonies, she may dismiss all fear of her own depopulation, or their increase; nay, it will be her interest, to encourage their increase.

The Colonies are universally agitated by suspicion, fear, and disgust, let Britain abandon her unreasonable jealousy, it is become a national disease, and will if it continues, be the ruin of us all: if she means to oppress her colonies, their common danger, will, in spite of all opposition, unite them together; the present offensive laws are a proof of it. A people are never weak, while the principles remain, which made them strong; prosperity may make them wanton; but the history of mankind, will scarce furnish an instance of Provinces, setting up an independancy for themselves, unless the yoke of oppression galls; if there is a recourse to a dominion, founded only on fear, it can last no longer, than till the controuling power is distressed by a general war; the revival of the contest for liberty, at such a crisis must produce tragical consequences, defying all calculation.

The nation will rejoice at our madness and folly, and leave us nothing, but the miserable consolation of unavailing complaints, and wishes for the recovery of lost opportunity. But if we abandon our partiality, and generously consult the common weal, by devising a constitution friendly to every branch of the general whole, linking Great Britain and her Colonies, by indisoluble ties, what ground can there be for jealousy*? when once secured in their lives, religion, liberty, and property, their affections will revive, and ten thousand cords may be contrived to tye us together, by the bonds of love and interest, and give peace, health and vigour to the whole.

One cannot take the state, nature, climate, and prodigious extent of the American continent, into contemplation, without high prospects in favor of the state to which it belongs; it is sufficient to be the granary, of all the rest of the British dominions: fed by the American plough, Britain may attend more the cultivation of sheep, by that staple, and the collection of raw materials from them, and by them, she may convert the whole island, into a great town of manufacturers, undersell every nation in Europe, and maintain and exalt her supremacy, until heaven blots out all the empires in the world.

All is at present sunshine, and we are now at the meridian of our political career; but night with all his gloomy horrors may come, and from a quarter little expected; futurity must determine on which side the scale of fortune will turn; the race is not always to the swift nor the battle to the strong, did the history of the two last wars prove the Americans less

---

*See a sketch of the constitution of the Colonies, recommended to Parliament, in a Pamphlet, entitled, America vindicated.

brave, than the inhabitants of this island? does the estimate, the religion, the government, the education of the people, furnish sufficient grounds, in favour of that idea? I know there have been men, high in military employ, who have ventured to propogate that opinion, not withstanding the evidence of facts; and, to the honour of the present administration, with too much success.

How well the Americans were disciplined at the commencement of the last war, the unprejudiced pen of a faithful historian may best relate: and is it to be supposed they have degenerated in point of military skill, by the large proportion they bore in the actual service of the late war? It should be remembered, the Colonies raised twenty thousand Provincials, who were disbanded, after three years service, and at the end of that period new regiments raised in their room. These men are most of them now residing in America, and are equally concerned with the rest, in defending their just rights: such a body of disciplined troops, at the head of their numerous militia, may bring *the haughty Minister at their feet*, a deaf ear to their complaints, has already begot, a sullen abhorrence to their masters; oppression has made the wisest, mad, and the weakest strong; America may prevail and triumph over those who would enslave them. history is full of events, which at the time they happened seemed more improbable. The states of Holland and Switzerland are cases in point: they have been often recited; they ought to instruct and alarm us: it is not with America alone, we have to contend; will the nations of Europe, remain patient spectators, and not engage their interposition? Would such a conduct be consistent with past experience, and the invariable policy of princes? Enraged, even to madness, at the loss of conquered provinces, it would be the very perverseness of folly notwithstanding the most prolific assurances, to suppose, that France and Spain will stand neuter in the general confusion of our affairs; the cause of America is theirs; it is for this we fought, for this we conquered? Shall our blood be spilt, and our treasures expended in defence of maxims, cruel beyond barbarism, which leads to our own disgrace, and the success of our enemies? shall we destroy the very end of our acquisitions, and victories?

Should America prove successful in the present contest, she may demand as the terms of reconciliation, monuments of public Justice, for the bloody sacrifice of her sons: the smiles of a gracious sovereign, may not always afford a safe retreat to the instruments of oppression; they may be turned into frowns! I have been deceived, I have been abused may be the language from the throne; a dispirited minority may become the major voice! and in that day of trial the whole nation at length, be convinced, that supreme right, must, in its own nature, finally get the better of wrong! that men are only bound by benefits! that no dominion is secure, but what is founded on affection, or on the practice of the eternal, unalterable laws of moderation and justice.

To be concluded in our next.

Printed and Published for the AUTHORS by T. W. SHAW, Fleet-Street, opposite Anderton's Coffee-House, where Letters to the Publisher will be thankfully received. New Editions of all the Numbers of this spirited Paper, are now ready for Sale, and *complete sets* will be sent to any Part of *England, Carriage Free.*

THE

CRISIS

NUMBER LXXXII   *To be continued every Saturday,*

DURING THE PRESENT BLOODY CIVIL WAR IN AMERICA.

SATURDAY, August 10, 1776   [Price Two-pence Half-penny.

Concluded from our last.

IT is an attempt full of danger, for a state to depart from those anti-ent, fundamental maxims, by which she has grown into wealth, and prosperity: maxims, an attention to which, at this great crisis, must determine Great Britain's future fortune and importance. The conduct of Rome towards her Colonies, and the oppressions of her pro-consuls, was one great cause of the downfall of that once glorious republic. This fact ought to furnish us with matter of very useful reflection, and serious circumspection: an erroneous policy, always preceeds a declining power: a haughty spirit before a fall, and pride before destruction. *Quem Deus vult perdere, prius dementat.*[1]

Armies stationed over Provinces, as guards, to keep them in subjection, are learning from their superiors a dreadful lesson to princes: the prince who holds out measures of violence and injustice to his subjects, has

---

1. "Whom God wishes to destroy he first makes mad," a proverb, the precise origins of which have been long disputed.

reason to apprehend the same treatment in his turn: James found the observation verified, by woeful experience, when he pathetically exclaimed, Good God! my people and my children, have forsaken me! Extraordinary powers granted to Caesar furnished him with an opportunity, by largesses, to win the distant legions; whereby an astonishing senate beheld the servant of the state, the tyrant of his country. By what means Cromwell wrested the supreme power out of the hands of government, and finally laid the law, the peerage, the sovereign, and constitution, in the dust, needs no comment. History is full of examples where the army have profited by the court-precept, and even exceeded their worse; making advantageous terms for themselves; they have joined the cause of the oppressed, or seized the prey for their general, at the expence of the prince, by whom they were employed. The same causes will produce the same effects; and America has many distinguishing peculiarities, in favour of such a project, too delicate for public disquisition.

The thunder of the British navy can reach no further than the sea coasts of America: the truly brave are always just and generous; they are inseparable companions from true manly courage. Will good sense, honour, justice and the finer feelings of humanity, operate with less force, in the breast of a british officer, than it does upon the rest of mankind? The iniquity of the experiment must disarm him, from the unnatural carnage of his fellow-citizens! Shall the sword which was never drawn, but in the common cause of liberty and our country, be stained with the blood of the companions of our dangers, and victories? shall he tarnish the lustre of well-earned laurels, by enforcing acts, which take away the property of his fellow-subjects, in direct opposition to the essential rights of human nature, and the vital principles of the constitution? shall the honourable character of soldier, be thus degraded, into the disgraceful name of an unfeeling ruffian? under such banners, the bravest troops, may convince those at the helm, that fidelity and attachment cannot be expected, in support of measures, so execrable in their nature, and horrid in their execution! the still voice of conscience, that faithful monitor within, will doubtless speak more irresistibly to them, than the voice of the prophet Shemaiah did the houshold-troops of Rehoboam, upon a similar occasion —*Ye shall not go up nor fight against your brethren: return every man to his house: for this thing is done of me.*[2]

Having thus submitted a few thoughts on this alarming crisis, in behalf of the Colonists, who are justly moved with a spirit of general discontent, permit me further, to intreat your seasonable interposition, and spirited remonstrances, by insisting that a constitution be immediately formed for the Colonies, consistent with the genius and spirit of the English government, and friendly to the future peace, welfare, and prosperity of both countries. Every moment, your supine inactivity in this great national concern, becomes more and more dangerous. you have hitherto, with patience acquiesced under an unpardonable procrastination, and criminal indifference to your own interests, and the sufferings of your brethren: you cannot, any longer, plead ignorance: your justice and honour, have been solemnly appealed to, by three million of people, and you must be sensible, from the incontrovertable evidence of facts, that large strides have been made, by your rulers, to deprive your fellow-subjects of that security in their persons and properties, inseperable from freedom, and which is due from the legislature, without partiality to every individual of the empire. If you are not dead to all sense of shame, and totally calous to those fine feelings and honourable sentiments, which have hitherto distinguished you as a nation: such unprecedented deviations from all the rules of justice, humanity, and the sound policy of your ancestors, accompanied with an open defiance and matchless violation of the principles of law and the constitution, will rouse you into action, and demand your serious attention. These outrageous measures, you must be convinced, are not the effect of accident, oversight, or in advertency, but one uniform, deep laid system of enslaving. In direct contradiction to the repeated pressure of severe experience, they have been persisted in with an obstinacy, which threatens nothing less than the total ruin of your commerce, revolt of the Colonies, and general bankruptcy of the

2. A passage from 1 Kings 12:24 (KJV), where the prophet Shemaiah forbids the king, Rehoboam (son of Solomon), from leading warriors of Judah and Benjamin against the other ten tribes of Israel.

mother kingdom. Their repeated humble remonstrances and petitions to our astonishment, have not only been treated with contempt and indifference, but their misfortunes imbittered with scorn and insult to the peculiar disgrace of these times, and dishonour of the british nation. Remember you are contending, not only for yourselves, but a people with whom hitherto you have been connected by the ties of reciprocal interest and long intercourse, improved by the maturing hand of time and mutual benefits, in real friendship.

Lord Camden's *Speech in the House of Lords, in 1765, on the declaratory Bill of the sovereinty of Great Britain over her Colonies,*[3]

My Lords,

WHEN I spoke last on this subject, I thought I had delivered my sentiments so fully, and supported them with such reasons, and such authorities, that I apprehended I should be under no necessity of troubling your lordships again. But I am now compelled to rise up and to beg your further indulgence. I find that I have been very injuriously treated; have been considered as the broacher of new-fangled doctrines, contrary to the laws of this kingdom, and subversive of the rights of parliament. My lords, this is a heavy charge, but more so when made against one stationed as I am in both capacities, as peer and judge, the defender of the law and the constitution. When I spoke last, I was indeed replied to, but not answered. In the intermediate time, many things have been said. As I was not present, I must now beg leave to answer such now as have come to my knowledge. As the affair is of the utmost importance, and in its consequences may involve the fate of kingdoms, I took the strictest view of my arguments; I re-examined all my authorities; fully determined if I found myself mistaken, publickly to own my mistake, and

---

3. For Camden's speech in the House of Lords on 3 February 1766, with the Earl of Mansfield's retort, see Simmons and Thomas, eds., *Proceedings and Debates*, 2:124–33, passim; and his speech of March 7th (again with a counter by Mansfield) in ibid., 2:318–23.

give up my opinion: but my researches have more and more convinced me, that the British parliament have no right to tax the Americans. I shall not therefore consider the declaratory bill now laying on your table; for to what purpose, but loss of time, to consider the particulars of a bill, *the very existence of which is illegal, absolutely illegal, contrary to the fundamental laws of nature, contrary to the fundamental laws of this constitution?* a constitution grounded on the eternal and immutable laws of nature; a constitution whose foundation and center is liberty, which sends liberty to every subject that is or may happen to be or may happen to be within any part of its ample circumference. Nor my lords, is the doctrine new, 'tis as old as the constitution. It grew up with it, indeed it is its support; taxation and representation are inseperably united; God hath joined them, no British parliament can separate them: to endeavour to do it, is to stab our very vitals. Nor is this the first time the doctrine has been mentioned; seventy years ago, my lords, a pamphlet was published, recommending the leveying a parliamentary tax on one of the colonies; this pamphlet was answered by two others, then much read; these totally deny the power of taxing the colonies: and why? because the colonies had no representatives in parliament to give their consent; no answer public or private was given to these pamphlets, no censure passed upon them: men were not startled at the doctrine, as either new or illegal, or derogatory to the rights of parliament.

I do not mention these pamphlets by way of authority, but to vindicate myself from the imputations of having first broached this doctrine.

My position is this—repeat it—I will maintain it to my last hour, taxation and representation are inseperable;—this position is founded on the laws of nature; it is more, it is itself an eternal law of nature; for whatever is a man's own, is absolutely his own: no man hath a right to take it from him without his consent, either expressed by himself or representative; whoever attempts to do it, attempts an injury, whoever does it, commits a robbery; he throws down and destroys the distinction between liberty and slavery.

Taxation and representation are coeval with and essential to this constitution. I wish the maxim of Machiavel was followed, that of examining a constitution, at certain periods, according to its first principles; this would correct abuses and supply defects.

I wish the times would bear it, and that mens minds were cool enough to enter upon such a task, and that the representative authority of this kingdom was more equally settled. I am sure some histories, of late published, have done great mischief; to endeavour to fix the Æra when the house of commons began in this kingdom, is a most pernicious and destructive attempt; to fix it in an Edward's or Henry's reign, is owing to the idle dreams of some whimsical ill-judging antiquarians: but my lords, this is a point too important to be left to such wrong-headed people.

When did the house of commons first begin? when my lords? it began with the constitution: it grew up with the constitution; there is not a blade of grass growing in the most obscure corner of this kingdom, which is not, which was not ever represented since the constitution began; there is not a blade of grass, which when taxed, was not taxed by the consent of the proprietor.

Printed and Published for the AUTHORS by T. W. SHAW, Fleet-Street, opposite Anderton's Coffee-House, where Letters to the Publisher will be thankfully received. New Editions of all the Numbers of this spirited Paper, are now ready for Sale, and *complete sets* will be sent to any Part of *England, Carriage Free.*

THE

CRISIS

NUMBER LXXXIII   *To be continued every Saturday,*

DURING THE PRESENT BLOODY CIVIL WAR IN AMERICA.

SATURDAY, AUGUST 17, 1776   [Price Two-pence Half-penny.

I Cannot help thinking it an astonishing event in the history of human affairs, (said the emperor Justinian) that a whole people, consisting of free born men, and equal all by nature, should with one joint assent resign their rights into the hands of a single person, a weak individual, a feeble mortal like themselves, subject to the same infirmities, open to imposition, liable to self-delusion, and prone to errors, which in a moment may prove destructive to millions! And do you imagine, says, Belisarius, that in a senate, or an assembly of the people there is more safety, greater wisdom, or a steadier administration of justice?[1]

---

1. The emperor Justinian, who presided over the eastern Roman (Byzantine) empire based in Constantinople (527–565 CE), was often depicted very favorably as the lawgiver whose code had even inspired elements of what became English common law. When paired with his general, Belisarius, however, he comes off in a less flattering light. According to various tales passed down over the centuries, Justinian turned his back on this, his most successful general, allowing him to die impoverished and forgotten. In 1767 there had been an English translation, with several printings, of the French novel *Belisarius* by Jean-Francois Marmontel that perpetuated the theme. Benjamin Franklin had already tapped into it in 1766 when lobbying for repeal of the stamp act. He had a

693

Was it under a monarchy that Camillus, Themistocles, and Aristides, were proscribed?[2] to multiply the members of government is to multiply its vices; for every individual mingles his own: the most simple form of government is the most eligible; and whether states were founded upon conquest or original compact; whether mankind agreed to transfer their natural rights to the civil magistrate, or' where by force subdued into political society; in either case it was reasonable, that the most renowned for wisdom or for valour, should attract popular regard, and gain the general suffrage in his favour. I am not therefore, surprised that the magistrate, or the hero, should be selected for the government of the whole; but that a single person could be found willing to accept so painful a pre-eminence, is matter of astonishment. This part of the argument says Tiberius, is not sufficiently clear to my apprehension.[3] To form a distinct idea, replied Belisarius; it will help you much, if you will figure to your fancy the first formation of a state, and place yourself alternately in the different characters of the people and the sovereign.

Where is the risk the people may be supposed to say, what hazzard do we run in giving supremacy to a king? with the good of the people we blend his happiness; we make them but one thing? the force of the community becomes the strength of the crown; *upon the general weal his glory is grafted*; and the regal character is at once derived from the people, and supported by them. The general love of his subjects will be his true

card printed that showed a dismembered man, his arms and legs labeled with American colonies, carrying an inscription *"Date Obolum Belisario"* (Give a Penny to Belisario). Franklin's use of this fallen classical hero to chasten the modern British minister is discussed in Labaree, et al., eds., *Papers of Franklin*, 13:66–72.

2. Plutarch celebrated Camillus as a great Roman statesman of the 4th century BCE in his *Lives*; Herodotus did likewise in his *History* for Themistocles and Aristides, Athenians who fought to keep Greece free from Persia in the 5th century BCE. There had been no new London edition in English of Herodotus since 1737; the Langhorne brothers' popular translation of Plutarch had appeared just two years before.

3. See footnote 1 of these notes for the source of this paraphrased dialogue between Belisarius and a young Tiberius, who would later become emperor of the Byzantine empire, written by Marmontel for his novel.

self-love, and his best interest will be found in justice, moderation, and beneficence.

This must have been the political creed of mankind.—But they did not take into their account, said Justinian, the passions and the complication of motives that encompass a prince. Very true replied Belisarius; they only thought of an inseperable union of interests between the sovereign and his people: that there ever could be a separation of those interests, and that the two parts of the body-politic, could live in a state of mutual hostility, did not enter into their idea. Usurpation appeared to them a kind of suicide, that could only proceed from a fatal deprivation of reason; and should the prince be seized with so extravagant a phrenzy. they relied upon the wisdom of the legislature, to controul the passions of a man grown an enemy to himself. They foresaw, indeed, that many might find their interest in mischief and evil deeds: but they persuaded themselves that such a confederacy in vice would be a small minority, against which a great superiority of good and honest men, with the prince at their head, would always preponderate. And indeed, till *fatal experience* opened the eyes of them, who could foresee that kings would sink to such a degree of infatuation, as to devorce themselves from their people, and combine with the avowed enemies of all the rights of man? a conduct like this is such an outrage to nature and to reason, that it was necessary it should actually happen, before the possibility of it could be believed.—It was not in the simplicity of antient manners to expect so shocking a revolution.

To consider on the other hand the feelings of sovereigns in that early period of mankind, he on whom the supreme authority devolved, must be deemed the party that had most reason, to be alarmed: for if the father of a family, who has the charge of five or six children to educate and to establish in the world, feels an incessant anxiety that plants thorns upon his pillow, what must be the case with the chief family which is counted by millions?

He must have reasoned with himself in this manner: "The compact which I make with my people, binds me to live for their good only: the repose of my life must be devoted to their happiness, I engage myself by a solemn oath to regard the good of the community in every legislative act, and submit my own will to the spirit of the law. In proportion to the power committed to me, my natural liberty is abridged, the more my subjects confide in me, the stronger are the obligations I am under:—for the frailties of my nature, my errors, and my passions, I render myself accountable: I give my people a kind of jurisdiction over me; and in short by consenting to resign, I abdicate myself."—The private man is as it were annihilated, to make room for royalty to engross the soul. Can there be a more generous sacrifice? an engagement of so solemn a nature: and yet these were the sentiments of Antoninus and Marcus Aurelius. "I have nothing properly my own" said one of them, "My very palace is not mine," was the declaration of the other,—The few of their stamp thought the same.[4]

In the appendage of sovereignty, vulgar error marks only some external circumstances of parade, which serve to awaken envy, such as palaces, the splendor of a court, the homage that is paid, together with the pomp and magnificence which policy attached to the regal state, in order to give it sanction and authority. And yet, amidst all this brilliancy, the sovereign is no more than mere man, overwhelmed with splendid cares, distracted with anxieties, a self-consuming votarist for the public good and a victim to his duty if he be zealous to perform it, an object of scorn if he neglect it, and of detestation should he betray it. Under perpetual restraint, and fluctuating for ever between good and evil, he finds himself environed with enemies to his quiet, with painful vigils, devouring cares, a tedious apathy that makes him weary of himself, and ends in a distaste of every thing: Behold there the portrait of a king! it is true invention has exhausted itself to make his enjoyments counter-balance

---

4. Roman emperor from 161–80 CE, Marcus Aurelius was best remembered as a Stoic philosopher whose *Meditations* had long been translated, the most recent English edition being printed in Glasgow in 1764. Marcus Aurelius had served as a consul under the emperor Antoninus Pius (who ruled from 138–61 CE) and was named his heir. Most of what the author(s) of *The Crisis* knew of both men would have come from the *History* of Cassius Dio, which had also been translated into English. Both men turned up as well in modern commentaries on classical ways, such as in the essays of Joseph Addison and, long before him, Francis Bacon, which were still being reprinted.

his cares; but his cares are numberless, and his pleasures are confined within the scanty circle of his wants. The highest luxury is not ingenious enough to give him one new organ of sensation; and while pleasures solicit him on every side, nature, quite harrassed down forbids enjoyment, and the palled appetite refuses all.

Thus every thing about him is superfluity; his extensive palace is but a void immense, of which he occupies a little corner; under crimson curtains and gilded ceilings he seeks in vain that sweet repose which dwells in the peasant's cottage; and at his table the pleasure of the monarch ends, when appetite craves no more.

I perceive said Tiberius, that every thing cannot be enjoyed, where every thing abounds;—but is the pleasure of chusing nothing in the account?

"Alas! young man! (explained Belisarius) my worthy young man! you are not acquainted with that incurable disease, satiety. It is the most fatal languor of the mind. Are you acquainted with the cause of it? the power of enjoying with facility makes us listless, and disgusted at every thing. Either our desires have not time to revive, or they revive to loath the affluence that invites too soon. Art has wearied itself in studying delicacies to provoke and quicken the languid appetite; but the powers of perception are decayed, the inlets of pleasure are obstructed, the incentives to action are extinguished in the soul, and delight itself has lost both its allurements, and its gratifications. Woe to the man who can command every thing with a wish! for as, on the one hand, the predominant idea of a total privation saps all the vigor of the mind, by fixing a train of corroding reflections; so, on the other, a constant habit of enjoyment gives insipidity to what were otherwise exquisite, and thus life loses its relish.

You will grant me, however, interposed Tiberius, that there are refined and sensible delights, in their nature proper for the gratification of a monarch, which are always sure to give rational enjoyment, without the danger of disgusting by repetition—As for instance? says Belisarius—The love of glory, for instance replied the young man—But what sort of glory?—Why, of all the various classes of glory, renown in arms must hold the foremost place—Very well that is your position and do you think the pleasure that springs from conquest has a sincere and lasting charm in it? Alas! when millions are stretched in mangled heaps upon the field of battle, can the mind in that situation taste of joy? I can make allowance for those who have met danger in all its shapes; they may be permitted to congratulate themselves that they have escaped with their lives; but in the case of a king, born with a sensibility of heart, the day that spills a deluge of human blood, and bids the tears of natural affection flow in rivers round the land; that cannot be a day of true enjoyment. I have more than once traversed a field of battle: I would have been glad to have seen a Nero in my place; the tears of humanity must have burst from him. I know there are princes who take the pleasure of a campaign, as they do that of hunting; and who send forth their people to the fray, as they let slip their dogs: but the rage of conquest is like the unrelenting temper of avarice, which torments itself and is at last insatiable. A province has been invaded; it has been subdued; it lies contageous to another not yet attempted; desire begins to kindle; invasion happens after invasion; ambition irretates itself to new projects, till at length comes a reverse of fortune, which exceeds, in the mortification it brings, all the pride and joy of former victories.

But to give things every flattering appearance, let us suppose a train of uninterrupted success; yet, even in that case the conqueror pushes forward; like another Alexander, to the limits of the world; and then, like him, re-measure back his course, fatigued with triumphs, a burthen to himself and to all mankind; at a loss what to do with the immense tracts which he has depopulated, and melancholy with the reflection that an acre of his conquests would suffice to maintain him, and a little pit-hole to hide his remains from the world. In my youth I saw the sepulphre of Cyrus; a stone bore this inscription.

"I am Cyrus; he who subdued the Persian empire. Friend, whoever thou art, or wherever thy native country, envy me not this scanty space that covers my clay-cold ashes."—Alas! said I, (turning aside from the mournful epitaph,) is it worth while to be a conqueror!

Tiberius interrupted him with astonishment; Can these be the sentiments of Belisarius?—Yes, young man, thus thinks Belisarius, he is able to decide upon this subject. Of all the plagues which the pride of man has engendered, the rage of conquest is the most destructive.

Printed and Published for the AUTHORS by T. W. SHAW, Fleet-Street, opposite Anderton's Coffee-House, where Letters to the Publisher will be thankfully received. New Editions of all the Numbers of this spirited Paper, are now ready for Sale, and *complete sets* will be sent to any Part of *England, Carriage Free.*

THE

CRISIS

NUMBER LXXXIV   *To be continued every Saturday,*

DURING THE PRESENT BLOODY CIVIL WAR IN AMERICA.

SATURDAY, August 24, 1776   [Price Two-pence Half-penny.

The following is the Declaration of INDEPENDENCE of the BRAVE, FREE, and VIRTUOUS *Americans,* against the most dastardly, slavish, and vicious TYRANT, that ever disgraced a Nation, whose savage cruelties are covered under a mask of Religion. Horrid Impiety! Execrable Hypocrisy!

A Declaration by the Representatives of
the united States of America, in General Congress
assembled. July 4, 1776

When in the course of human events it becomes necessary for one people to dissolve the political bonds, which have connected them with another, and to assume among the powers of the earth the seperate and equal station to which the laws of nature, and nature's God entitles them, a decent respect to the opinions of mankind requires that they should declare the causes which impel them to the separation.

We hold these truths to be self evident; that all men are created equal; that they are endowed by their creator with certain unalienable rights, that among these are life, liberty, and the pursuit of happiness. That to secure these rights, governments are instituted among men, deriving their just powers from the consent of the governed; and whenever any form of government becomes destructive of these ends, it is the right of the people to alter or to abolish it, and to institute new government; laying its foundation on such principles, and organizing its powers in such form, as to them shall seem most likely to effect their safety and happiness. Prudence indeed will direct that governments long established should not be changed for light and transient causes, and accordingly all experience hath shewn, that mankind are more disposed to suffer, while evils are sufferable than to right themselves by abolishing the forms to which they are accustomed. But when a long train of abuses and usurpations, pursuing invariably the same object, evinces a design to reduce them under absolute despotism, it is their right, it is their duty, to throw off such government, and to provide new guards for their future security.

Such has been the patient sufferance of these colonies, and such is now the necessity that constrains them to alter their former systems of government. The history of the present King of Great Britain, is a history of repeated injuries and usurpations; all having in direct object the establishment of an absolute tyranny over these states. To prove this let facts be submitted to a candid world.

He has refused to assent to laws the most wholesome and necessary for the public good.

He has forbidden his governors to pass laws of immediate and pressing importance, unless suspended in their operations till his assent should be obtained; and when so suspended he has utterly neglected to attend them.

He has refused to pass other laws for the accommodation of large districts of people, unless those people will relinquish the rights of representation in the legislature; a right inestimable to them and formidable to tyrants only.

He has called together legislative bodies at places unusual, uncomfortable, and distant from the depository of their records, for the sole purpose of fatiguing them into compliance with his measures.

He has dissolved representative houses repeatedly, for opposing with manly firmness, his invasions on the rights of the people.

He has refused for a long time, after such dissolutions, to cause others to be erected; whereby the legislative powers, incapable of annihilation, have returned to the people at large for their exercise; the state remaining in the mean time exposed to all the dangers of invasion from without, and convulsions within.

He has endeavoured to prevent the population of these states; for that purpose, obstructing the laws for naturalization of foreigners, refusing to pass others to encourage their migrations hither, and raising the conditions of new appropriations of land.

He has obstructed the administration of justice, by refusing his assent to laws for establishing judiciary powers.

He has made judges dependent on his will alone, for the tenure of their offices, and the amount and payment of their salaries.

He has erected a multitude of new offices, and sent hither swarms of officers to harrass our people, and eat out their subsistence.

He has kept among us in times of peace, standing armies without the consent of our legislatures.

He has affected to render the military independent of and superior to, the civil power;

He has combined with others to subject us to a jurisdiction foreign to our constitution, and unacknowledged by our laws; giving his assent to their pretended acts of legislation.

For quartering large bodies of armed troops among us.

For protecting them, by a mock trial, from punishment for any murders which they should commit on the inhabitants of these states.

For cutting off our trade with all parts of the world.

For imposing taxes on us without our consent.

For depriving us in many cases, of the benefit of trial by jury.

For transporting us beyond seas to be tried for pretended offences.

For abolishing the free system of English laws in a neighbouring province; establishing therein an arbitrary government, and enlarging its boundaries, so as to render it at once an example and fit instrument for introducing the same absolute rule in these colonies.

For taking away our charters, abolishing our most valuable laws, and altering fundamentally the forms of our governments.

For suspending our own legislatures, and declaring themselves invested with power to legislate for us in all cases whatsoever.

He has abdicated government here, by declaring us out of his protection, and waging war against us.

He has plundered our sea, ravaged our coasts, burnt our towns, and destroyed the lives of our people.

He is, at this time, transporting large armies of foreign mercenaries, to compleat the works of death, desolation, and tyranny already begun with circumstances of cruelty and perfidy, scarcely paralleled in the most barbarous ages, and totally unworthy the head of a civilized nation.

He has constrained our fellow citizens, taken captive on the high seas, to bear arms against their country, to become the executioners of their friends and brethren, or to fall themselves by their hands.

He has excited domestic insurrections amongst us, and has endeavoured to bring on the inhabitants of our frontiers, the merciless Indian savages, whose known rule of warfare is an undistinguished destruction, of all ages, sexes, and conditions.

In every stage of these oppressions we have petitioned for redress, in the most humble terms, our repeated petitions have been answered only by repeated injuries.—A prince, whose character is thus marked by every act which may define a tyrant, is unfit to be the ruler of a free people.

Nor have we been wanting in attention to our British brethren. We have warned them from time to time, of attempts, by their legislature, to extend an unwarrantable jurisdiction over us. We have reminded them of the circumstances of our emigration and settlement here. We have appealed to their native justice and magnanimity, and we have conjured them by the ties of our common kindred, to disavow these usurpations which would inevitably interrupt our connections and correspondence. They too have been deaf to the voice of justice and consanguinity. We must therefore acquiesce in the necessity which denounces our separation, and hold them, as we hold the rest of mankind, enemies in war, in peace friends.

We, therefore, the representatives of the united States of America, in General Congress assembled, appealing to the supreme judge of the World, for the rectitude of our intentions, do, in the name and by the authority of the good people of these colonies, solemnly publish and declare, that the united Colonies are, and of right ought to be, FREE and INDEPENDENT STATES, and that they are absolved from all allegiance to the British Crown, and that all political connection between them and the State of Great Britain, is, and ought to be totally dissolved; and that, as free and independent states, they have full power to levy war, conclude peace, contract alliances, establish commerce, and to do all other acts and things, which independent states may have a right to do. And for the support of this declaration, with a firm reliance on the protection of divine providence, we mutually pledge to each other our lives, our fortunes, and our sacred honour.

Signed by order, and in behalf of the Congress,

JOHN HANCOCK, President.

Attest. CHARLES THOMSON, Secretary.[1]

---

1. For the making of the text see John Hazelton, *The Declaration of Independence* (New York: Dodd, Mead and Company, 1906); for the component parts see Edward Dumbauld, *The Declaration of Independence and What It Means Today* (Norman: University of Oklahoma Press, 1950); for the text itself see Julian Boyd, *The Declaration of Independence* (Washington, D.C.: Library of Congress, 1999); and for context see Pauline Maier, *American Scripture* (New York: Alfred A. Knopf, 1997).

Extract of a L E T T E R

I Have looked over the memorials to you, and as I conceive, to all lovers of liberty, I approve of their contents, purport, and design; and shall be ready to contribute towards their promotion and completion. I am persuaded that calamities are hanging over our heads, and that the blackest attempts on our liberties are in agitation.

Every intelligent man who regards posterity, must be under dread-apprehensions; but as I am a feeble old man, without heirs, and just going out of the world, and being too in a delicate and ticklish state of health, cannot act in this most noble cause with a vigour proportioned to my zeal, and good wishes: and hence likewise you will reflect that I have no consideration at all, but philanthrophy, to incite the stuper of old age, and warm the ice of superannuation. If I could look on a race of children and grand children just on the brink of slavery, it would rouse my pity and compassion, as well as fire my indignation; but, thanks be to Heaven, I shall have none such to be made slaves of to any weak and ungrateful prince.

I should be glad to see you, and any other hearty friends to the cause of Liberty, at my House, in order to consult of the best means of carrying the intention of the patriots who have addressed you, into execution. I should glory in being instrumental in promoting so good a cause, which I am sure Heaven must look down upon with pleasure and approbation. Believe me to be very much a friend to the cause, to the friends of the Bill of Rights, as well as,

Dear Sir,

Your most humble servant,

Printed and Published for the AUTHORS by T. W. SHAW, Fleet-Street, opposite Anderton's Coffee-House, where Letters to the Publisher will be thankfully received. New Editions of all the Numbers of this spirited Paper, are now ready for Sale, and *complete sets* will be sent to any Part of *England, Carriage Free.*

THE

CRISIS

NUMBER LXXXV   *To be continued every Saturday,*

DURING THE PRESENT BLOODY CIVIL WAR IN AMERICA.

SATURDAY, August 30, 1776   [Price Two-pence Half-penny.

From the LONDON GAZETTE of August 24.

Whitehall, August 24.

CAPTAIN HOPE arrived on Wednesday evening last from South Carolina, with dispatches from Commodore Sir Peter Parker and Lieutenant General Clinton.

Extract of a letter from Sir Peter Parker to Mr. Stephens,
Secretary of the Admiralty, dated within Charles-Town Bar, July 9.[1]

IT having been judged adviseable to make an attempt upon Charles Town, in South Carolina, the fleet sailed from Cape Fear on the 1st of June, and on the 4th anchored off Charles Town Bar. The 5th sounded the Bar, and laid down buoys preparatory to the intended entrance of the harbour. The 7th all the frigates and most of the transports

---

1. The excerpt ran on the first page of the issue and carried over to the second. The note dated Whitehall, August 24, that follows immediately after above, in the newspaper

got over the Bar into Five-fathom Hole. The 9th Gen. Clinton landed on
Long Island with about 400 or 500 men. The 10th the Bristol got over
the Bar with some difficulty. The 15th gave the captains of the squadron my arrangement for the attack of the batteries on Sulivan's Island,
and the next day acquainted Gen. Clinton that the ships were ready.
The General fixed on the 23d for our joint attack, but the wind proving
unfavourable, prevented its taking effect. The 25th the Experiment arrived, and the next day came over the Bar, when a new arrangement was
made for the attack. The 28th, at half an hour after nine in the morning,
informed General Clinton, by signal, that I should go on the attack. At
half an hour after ten I made the signal to weigh; and about a quarter
after eleven the Bristol, Experiment, Active, and Solebay, brought up
against the fort. The Thunder Bomb, covered by the Friendship armed
vessel, brought the sailant angle of the East bastion to bear N. W. by N.
and Colonel James (who has ever since our arrival been very anxious to
give the best assistance) threw several shells a little before and during the
engagement in a very good direction. The Sphynx, Actæon, and Syren,
were to have been to the westward, to prevent fire-ships or other vessels
from annoying the ships engaged, to enfilade the works, and, if the rebels
should be driven from them, to cut off their retreat if possible. This last
service was not performed, owing to the ignorance of the pilot, who ran
the three frigates aground. The Sphynx and Syren got off in a few hours,
but the Acrœon remained fast till the next morning, when the Captain
and officers thought proper to scuttle and set her on fire. I ordered a
court-martial on the Captain, officers, and company, and they have been
honourably acquitted. Captain Hope made his armed ship as useful as

---

came after a list of the warships (and their commanders) involved in the action. Within
a few days a half dozen other London papers had reprinted what first appeared in the
Gazette (the *Daily Advertiser*, *Lloyd's Evening Post*, *Morning Chronicle*, *Morning Post*,
and *Daily Advertiser* on the 26th, and the *London Chronicle* on the 27th). The London
press in fact ran more about the war when it erupted than about events leading up to
it, with excerpts from official reports as well as private correspondence being routinely
printed in one paper and then reprinted in others. See n. I.1 supra for a comment on
misdating; this issue should be dated August 31st, not the 30th.

he could on this occasion, and he merits every thing that can be said in his favour. During the time of our being abreast of the fort, which was near ten hours, a brisk fire was kept up by the ships, with intervals, and we had the satisfaction, after being engaged two hours, to oblige the rebels to slacken their fire very much. We drove large parties several times out of the fort, which were replaced by others from the main. About half an hour after three, a considerable reinforcement from Mount Pleasant hung a man on a tree at the back of the fort, and we imagine that the same party ran away about an hour after, for the fort was then totally silenced, and evacuated for near an hour and a half; but the rebels finding that our army could not take possession, about six o'clock a considerable body of people re-entered the fort, and renewed the firing from two or three guns, the rest being, I suppose, dismounted. About nine o'clock, it being very dark, great part of our ammunition expended, our people fatigued, the tide of ebb almost done, no prospect from the eastward, and no possibility of our being of any farther service, I ordered the ships to withdraw to their former moorings. Their Lordships will see plainly by this account, that if the troops could have co-operated in this attack, his Majesty would have been in possession of Sulivan's island. But I must beg leave here to be fully understood, lest it should be imagined that I mean to throw the most distant reflection on our army: I should not discharge my conscience, were I not to acknowledge, that such was my opinion of his Majesty's troops, from the General down to the private soldier, that after I had been engaged some hours, and perceived that the troops had not got a footing on the north end of Sulivan's Island, I was perfectly satisfied that the landing was impracticable, and that the attempt would have been the destruction of many brave men, without the least probability of success; and this, I am certain, will appear to be the case, when Gen. Clinton represents his situation. The Bristol had 40 men killed, and 71 wounded; the Experiment 23 killed, and 56 wounded, and both of them suffered much in their hulls, masts, and rigging: the Active had Lieutenant Pike killed, and 6 men wounded; and the Solebay 8 men wounded. Not one man who was quartered at the beginning of the action on the Bristol's quarter-deck escaped being killed or wounded. Capt. Morris lost his right arm, and received other wounds, and is since dead; the master is wounded in his right arm, but will recover the use of it: I received several contusions at different times, but as none of them are on any part where the least danger can be apprehended, they are not worth mentioning. Lieutenants Caulfield, Molloy, and Nugent, were the Lieutenants of the Bristol in the action; they behaved so remarkably well that it is impossible to say to whom the preference is due; and so indeed I may say of all the petty officers, ship's company, and volunteers. At the head of the latter I must place Lord William Campbell, who was so condescending as to accept of the direction of some guns on the lower gun deck. His Lordship received a contusion on his left side, but I have the happiness to inform their Lordships that it has not proved of much consequence. Captain Scott, of the Experiment, lost his left arm, and is otherwise so much wounded. that I fear he will not recover. I cannot conclude this letter without remarking, that when it was known that we had many men too weak to come to quarters, almost all the seamen belonging to the transports offered their service with a truly British spirit, and a just sense of the cause we are engaged in. I accepted of upwards of 50 to supply the place of the sick. The masters of many of the transports attended with their boats, but particular thanks are due to Mr. Chambers, the master of the Mercury.

All the regiments will be embarked in a few days. The first brigade, consisting of four regiments, will sail in a day or two, under convoy, for New York; and the Bristol and Experiment will, I hope, soon follow with the remainder.

Whitehall, Aug. 24. It appears by Lieutenant Gen. Clinton's letter to Lord George Germain, dated July 8, 1776, from the camp on Long Island, Province of South Carolina, that Sir Peter Parker and the General having received intelligence that the fortress erected by the rebels on Sulivan's Island (the key to Charles Town Harbour) was in an imperfect and unfortified state, resolved to attempt the reduction thereof by a coup de main; and that, in order that the army might co-operate with the fleet, the General landed his troops on Long Island, which had been represented to him as communicating with Sulivan's Island, by a ford passable at low water; but that he, to his very great mortification, found the channel, which was reported to have been 18 inches deep at low water, to be seven feet deep; which circumstance rendered it impossible for the army to give that assistance to the fleet in the attack upon the fortress that the General intended, and which he, and the troops under his command, ardently wished to do.

R E M A R K S.

THE Gazette of Saturday contains more of the truth than is to be found in any government relation of any American battle fought since the commencement of the war. There is an honest bluntness in naval officers which renders them averse to say the thing which is not. A very good sailor is a very bad courtier. He scorns the art of misrepresentation, and without the cardinal virtue of lying to perfection, it is impossible to figure as a man of conesquence in a drawing-room. Had the whole of Sir Peter Parker's letter been published, remarks would have been superfluous, and any supplement would have been unnecessary. As the hand of official interpolation is evident in several parts of the composition, a few observations may be forgiven.

The public will recollect, what threats were denounced against the southern colonies. There is not any necessity to remind the people of the wonders which were to have been achieved in South Carolina. Mark but the event of the very first attack. A fleet commanded by an experienced commodore. Troops commanded by two very able generals, all fail in the capture of a single fort, which stands only at the entrance of the river leading to Charles Town. It is of no avail to talk of the ignorance of a pilot, or of the misinformation received by the Commodore, relative to the fathomage of the ford reaching from Long Island.

The gentlemen to whom Sir Peter Parker writes, may see things so plainly as to descry what infinite wisdom may have determined shall never happen. Mortals of a coarser mould, are only clearsighted enough to see what has actually happened.

From the facts narrated in the Gazette, there is not any general inference to be drawn of utility to the public. The war is to be carried on with vigor. Ministry are now as certain of conquest, as they were at the commencement of the dispute.

As all the government accounts confirm the cowardice of the Americans, we have every reason to believe the fact. There can be no doubt, but that the Provincials always RUNAWAY. The cursed misfortune is, that whenever it is judged adviseable to attack them, they do incredible mischief by—their FLIGHT.

*** The Publisher sincerely hopes the Public and his Friends will excuse the Delay that has unavoidably happened this Week, and which was not in his Power to prevent, as the Printer was taken suddenly ill.

Printed and Published for the AUTHORS by T. W. SHAW, Fleet-Street, opposite Anderton's Coffee-House, where Letters to the Publisher will be thankfully received. New Editions of all the Numbers of this spirited Paper, are now ready for Sale, and *complete sets* will be sent to any Part of *England, Carriage Free.*

THE

CRISIS

NUMBER LXXXVI   *To be continued every Saturday,*

DURING THE PRESENT BLOODY CIVIL WAR IN AMERICA.

SATURDAY, SEPTEMBER 8, 1776   [Price Two-pence Half-penny.

The PRINCIPLES of a REAL WHIG.[1]

MANY books and papers have been published since the late revolution, tending to justify the proceedings of the people of England at that happy juncture: by setting in a true light our just rights and liberties, together with the solid foundations of our constitution: which, in truth, is not ours only, but that of almost all Europe besides; so wisely restored and established (if not introduced) by the Goths and Franks, whose descendants we are.

---

1. Molesworth had been dead a half century. His *Principles of a Real Whig* were first published in 1711 as a a preface to his translation of Francis Hotman's *Franco-Gallia*. The *Principles* appeared under separate cover, printed in London by J. Williams in 1775, before being printed that same year in a reissue of *Franco-Gallia*. The London Association underwrote publication and dedicated Molesworth's essay "*To every true, free Englishman, in the British Empire,* who is willing and ready to maintain a *steady opposition* to the introduction of POPERY and SLAVERY into these realms." Molesworth is most accessible in Justin Champion's *An Account of Denmark* (Indianapolis: Liberty Fund, 2011), which includes the "Principles" and *Francogallia*; and also Robbins, *Eighteenth-Century Commonwealthman*, pp. 88–133, and passim. In yet another dating error, it should be Saturday, September 7th, not the 8th (a Sunday). See supra n I.1.

These books have as constantly had some things, called *answers,* written to them by persons of different sentiments; who certainly either never seriously considered, that they were thereby endeavouring to destroy their own happiness, and overthrow her Majesty's title to the crown; or, if they knew what they did, presumed upon the *lenity* of that government they decried; which, were there no better reason, ought to have recommended it to their approbation, since it could patiently bear with such as were doing all they could to undermine it.

Not to mention the railing, virulency, or personal false reflections in many of those answers, (which are always the signs of a weak cause, or a feeble champion) some of them assert the divine right of an hereditary monarch, and the impiety of resistance upon any terms whatever, notwithstanding any authorities to the contrary.

Others (and those more judicious) denied positively, that sufficient authorities could be produced to prove, that a free people have a just power to defend themselves, by opposing their prince, who endeavours to oppress and enslave them: and alledged, that whatever was said or done tending that way, proceeded from a spirit of rebellion, and antimonarchial principles.

To confute, or convince this last sort of arguers (the first not being worthy to have notice taken of them) I set about translating the *Franco-Gallia* of that most learned and judicious civilian, Francis Hotoman; a grave, sincere, and unexceptionable author, even in the opinion of his adversaries. This author gives an account of the ancient free state of above three parts in four of Europe; and has appeared to me so convincing and instructive in those important points he handles, that I could not be idle whilst it remained unknown, in a manner, to Englishmen: who, of all people living, have the greatest reason and need to be thoroughly instructed in what it contains; as having, on the one hand, the most to lose, and on the other, the sense of their right to that, which hitherto they seem, at least in a great measure, to have preserved.

It will be obvious to every reader, that I have taken no great pains to write elegantly. What I endeavour at, is as plain a stile as possible, which on this occasion I take to be the best: for since the instruction of mankind ought to be the principal drift of all writers, especially of history, whoever writes to the capacity of most readers, in my opinion, most fully answers the end.

I am not ignorant, how tiresome and difficult a piece of work it is to translate, nor how little valued in the world. My experience has convinced me, that it is more troublesome and teazing than to write and invent at once. The idiom of the language out of which one translates, runs so in the head, that it is next to impossible not to fall frequently into it. And the more barren and incorrect the stile of the original is, the more shall that of the translation be so too.

I take this author to be one of those few that has escaped the envy of the snarling critics, and *pensioned* scribler; and I make use of this occasion to declare, that the chief motive which induces me to publish this treatise to the world, is a sincere desire of instructing the only possessors of true liberty, what right and title they have to that liberty; of how much value it is; what misery follows the loss of it; how easily, if care be taken in time, it may be preserved: And if this either opens the eyes, or confirms the honourable resolutions of any of my worthy countrymen, I have gained a glorious end; and accomplished that in my study, which I should have promoted any other way had I been called to it.

I hope to die with the comfort of believing, that Old England will continue to be a free country, and *know* itself to be such; that my friends, relations and children, with their posterity, will inherit their share of this inestimable blessing, and that I have contributed my mite towards it.

The names of *Whig* and *Tory* will, I am afraid, last as long among us, as those of *Guelf* and *Ghibbeline* did in Italy. I am sorry for it: but to some they become necessary for distinction sake; not so much for the principles formerly adapted to each name, as for particular and worse reasons. For there has been such chopping and changing both of names and principles, that we scarce know one from another.

I think it therefore necessary, in order to appear in my own colours, to make a public profession of my political faith; not doubting but that it may agree in several particulars with that of many worthy persons, who are as undeservedly aspersed as I am.

My notion of *Whig,* I mean of a real *Whig,* for the nominal are worse than any sort of men, is, that he is one who is exactly for keeping up to the strictness of the true old Gothic constitution, under the three estates of king, or queen, lords and commons; the legislature being seated in all three together, the executive entrusted with the first, but accountable to the whole body of the people, in case of mal-administration.

A true *Whig* is of opinion, that the executive power has as just a title to the allegiance and obedience of the subject, according to the rules of known laws enacted by the legislative, as the subject has to protection, liberty and property. And so on the contrary.

A true *Whig* is not afraid of the name of a *commonwealthsman,* because so many foolish people, who know not what it means, run it down. The anarchy and confusion which these nations fell into near sixty years ago, and which was falsly called a *commonwealth,* frightening them out of the true construction of the word. But Queen Elizabeth, and many other of our best princes, were not scrupulous of calling our government a *commonwealth,* even in their solemn speeches to parliament.

And indeed if it be not one, I cannot tell by what name properly to call it: for where in the very frame of the constitution, the good of the whole is taken care of by the whole, as it is in our case, the having a king or queen at the head of it, alters not the case; and the softening of it by calling it a *limited monarchy,* seems a kind of contradiction in terms, invented to please some weak and doubting persons.

And because some of our princes in this last age, did their utmost endeavour to destroy this union and harmony of the three estates, and to be arbitrary or independent, they ought to be looked upon as the aggressors upon our constitution.

This drove the other two estates, for the sake of public preservation, into the fatal necessity of providing for themselves; and when once the wheel was set a running, it was not in the power of man to stop it just where it ought to have stopped. This is so ordinary in all violent motions, whether mechanic or political, that no one can wonder at it.

But no wise men approved of the ill effects of those violent motions either way, could they have helped them. Yet it must be owned they have (as often as used, through an extraordinary piece of good fortune) brought us back to our old constitution again, which else had been lost; for there are numberless instances in history, of a downfall from a state of liberty to a tyranny, but very few of a recovery of liberty from tyranny, if this last have had any length of time to fix itself and take root.

Let all such, who either through interest or ignorance are adorers of absolute monarchs, say what they please; an English *Whig* can never be so unjust to his country, and to right reason, as not to be of opinion, that in all civil commotions, which side soever is the wrongful aggressor, is accountable for all the evil consequences. And through the course of his reading, though my Lord Clarendon's be thrown into the heap, he finds it very difficult to observe, that ever the people of England took up arms against their prince, but when constrained to it by a necessary care of their liberties and the constitution.[2]

It is certainly as much a treason and rebellion against this constitution, and the known laws, in a prince to endeavour to break through them, as it is in the people to rise against him, whilst he keeps within their bounds, and does his duty. Our constitution is a government of laws, not

2. Edward Hyde, first Earl of Clarendon, was a major player in English politics, beginning in the reign of Charles I and extending through that of Charles II. Chancellor of the exchequer under the first Charles, lord chancellor under the second, Clarendon, the Middle Temple-trained barrister, attempted to apply the rule of law as the standard for all legitimate political conduct, which may help explain how he had an appeal that transcended cavalier-roundhead divisions, both during his life and after. He eventually fell from grace at Charles II's court and went into exile on the Continent, where he died. For his defense of the Isle of Jersey during the last days of Charles I's reign, Charles II had made him a proprietor in both the Jersey and Carolina grants in North America. Clarendon lived on for the American Revolutionary generation through his reprinted writings, most notably *A Complete Collection of Tracts* (London: C. Davis, 1747) and in his autobiography, *The Life of Lord Clarendon* (Oxford: Clarendon Press, 1759). See Paul Seaward's essay on Clarendon in the *Oxford DNB*, 29:120–38.

of persons. Allegiance and protection are obligations that cannot subsist separately; when one falls, the other falls of course.

The true etymology of the word *loyalty,* which has been so strangely wrested in the late reigns, is an entire obedience to the prince in all his commands according to law; that is to the laws themselves, to which we owe both an active and passive obedience.

By the old and true maxim, that *the King can do no wrong,* no one is so foolish as to conclude, that he has not strength to murder, to offer violence to women, or power enough to disposses a man wrongfully of his estate, or that whatever he does, how wickedly soever, is just; but the meaning is, he has no lawful power to do such things; and our constitution considers no power as irresistible, but what is lawful.

[*To be continued.*]

Printed and Published for the Authors by T. W. SHAW, Fleet-Street, opposite Anderton's Coffee-House, where Letters to the Publisher will be thankfully received. New Editions of all the Numbers of this spirited Paper, are now ready for Sale, and *complete sets* will be sent to any Part of *England, Carriage Free.*

THE

CRISIS

NUMBER LXXXVII   *To be continued every Saturday,*

DURING THE PRESENT BLOODY CIVIL WAR IN AMERICA.

SATURDAY, SEPTEMBER 14, 1776   [Price Two-pence Half-penny.

The P R I N C I P L E S of a R E A L W H I G.[1]

[*Continued from our last.*]

WHIGGISM is not circumscribed or confined to any one or two of the religions now professed in the world, but diffuses itself among all. We have known Jews, Turks, nay, some Papists, (which I own to be a great rarity) very great lovers of the constitution and liberty. And could there be any rational grounds to expect that a majority of them could be so, I should be against using severities or distinctions upon account of religion. For a Papist is not dangerous, nor ought to be ill used by any one, because he prays to saints, believes purgatory, or the real presence in the Eucharist, and pays divine worship to an image or picture, which are the common topics of our writers of controversy against the Papists, but because Popery sets up a foreign jurisdiction paramount to our laws. So that a real Papist can neither be a

1. For Molesworth's *Real Whig* see supra LXXXVI.1.

true governor of a Protestant country, nor a true subject; and besides, is the must priest-ridden creature in the world.

I profess myself to have always been a member of the Church of England, and am for supporting it in all its honours, privileges, and revenues: but as a Christian and a Whig, I must have charity for those that differ from me in religious opinions, whether Pagans, Turks, Jews, Quakers, Socinians, Presbyterians, or others. I look upon bigotry to have always been the very bane of human society, and the offspring of interest and ignorance, which has occasioned most of the great mischiefs that have afflicted mankind.

We ought no more to expect to be all of one opinion, as to the worship of the Deity, than to be all of one colour or stature. To stretch or narrow any man's conscience to the standard of our own, is no less a piece of cruelty, than that of Procrastes the tyrant of Attica, who used to fit his guests to the length of his own iron bedstead, either by cutting them shorter, or racking them longer.

What just reason can I have to be angry with, to endeavour to curb the natural liberty, or to retrench the civil advantages of an honest man (who follows the golden rule of doing to others as he would have others do to him, and is willing and able to serve the public) only because he thinks his way to Heaven surer or shorter than mine? No one can tell which of us is mistaken till the day of judgment, or whether any of us be so, for there may be different ways to the same end, is not certain, and I am not for circumscribing the mercy of the Almighty: This I am sure of, one shall meet with the same positive opinions in some of the priests of all those sects; the same want of charity, engrossing Heaven by way of monopoly to their own corporation, and managing it by a joint stock, exclusive of all others; the same pretences to miracles, martyrs, inspirations, merits, mortifications, revelations, austerity, antiquity, &c.

I think it to the honour of the reformed part of the Christian profession, and the church of England in particular, that it pretends to fewer of these unusual and extraordinary things, than any other religion we know of in the world; being convinced, that these are not the distinguishing marks as the truth of any religion; and it would not be amiss, if we further enlarged our charity, when we can do it with safety, or advantage to the state.

Let us but consider how unjust and impolitic it is to condemn all people, but such as think of the Divinity just as we do. May not the tables of persecution be turned upon us? A Mahometan, in Turkey, is in the right; and I, if I carry my own religion thither, am in the wrong: They will have it so. If the Mahometan comes with me to Christendom, I am in the right, and he in the wrong; and hate each other heartily for differing in speculations, which ought to have no influence on moral honesty.

But, as on the one hand, a true Whig thinks that all opinions purely spiritual and notional ought to be indulged; so on the other, he is for severely punishing all immoralities, breach of laws, violence and injustice. A minister's tythes are as much his right, as any layman's estate can be his; and no pretence of religion or conscience can warrant the subtracting of them, whilst the law is in being which makes them payable: For a Whig is far from opinion that they are due by any other title.

It would make a man's ears tingle to hear the divine right insisted upon for any human institutions; and to find the Almighty brought in as a principal, when there is not the least occasion for it, to support those absurd institutions.

To affirm that monarchy, episcopacy, synods, tythes, the hereditary succession to the crown, &c. are jure divino;[2] is to cram them down a man's throat, and tell him in plain terms, that he must submit to any of them under all inconveniencies, whether the laws of his country are for it or against it

Every Whig's own submission to government to be an ordinance of God. "Submit yourselves to every ordinance of man, for the Lord's sake," says

---

2. The author(s) may have two references in mind here—the simple translation from Latin as "divine law" and, perhaps, for the better read, an allusion to Daniel Defoe's *Jure Divino* (1706), which mocked the idea of divine right monarchy. Defoe dedicated it to "Lady Reason," the "First Monarch of the World."

the Apostle.[3] Where, by the way, he calls them ordinances of man; and gives you the true notion how far any thing can be said to be jure divino; which is far short of what your high-flown assertors of the jus divinum would carry it, and proves as strongly for a republican government as a monarchial; though in truth it affects neither, where the very ends of government are destroyed.

A real Whig looks upon frequent parliaments as such a fundamental part of the constitution, that even no parliament can part with this right. High Whiggism is for annual parliaments, and low Whiggism for triennial, with annual meetings. I leave it to every man's judgment, which of these would be the truest representative; would soonest ease the house of the numerous swarm of placemen and pensioners, the very fountain from whence all our national evils flow; or which of the two is most agreeable to ancient custom.

But I think it seems inconsistent with the reason of the thing, and preposterous, for the first parliament after a prince's accession to the crown, to give the public revenue arising by taxes, for a time longer than that parliaments duration. I cannot see why the members of the first parliament should engross to themselves all the power of giving, as well as all the merit and rewards due to such a gift: and why succeeding parliaments should not, in their turn, have it in their power to oblige the prince, or to strengthen him, if they saw occasion; and to withdraw such support, if they were convinced he made an ill use of such a revenue. I am sure we have had instances of this kind; and a wise body of senators ought always to provide against the worst that can happen.

An old Whig is for chusing such sort of representatives to serve in parliament as have estates in the kingdom; and those not fleeting ones, which may be sent beyond sea by bills of exchange by every packet-boat, but fixed and permanent. To which end every merchant, banker, or other monied man, who is ambitious of serving his country as a senator, should

---

3. As excerpted from 1 Peter 2:13 (KJV).

have also a competent, visible land estate, as a pledge to his electors that he intends to abide by them, and has the same interest with theirs in the public taxes, gains and losses.

I have heard and weighed the arguments of those who, in opposition to this, urged the unfitness of such, whose lands were engaged in debts and mortgages, to serve in parliament, in comparison with the monied man who had no land: but these arguments never convinced me.

A Whig is against the raising or keeping up a standing army in time of peace: but with this distinction, that if at any time an army (though even in time of peace) should be necessary to the support of the state, a Whig is not for being too hasty to destroy that which is to be the defender of his liberty.

I desire to be well understood. Suppose then, that persons, whose known principle and practice it has been, during the attempts for arbitrary government, to plead for and promote such an army in time of peace, as would be subservient to the will of a tyrant, and contribute towards the enslaving the nation. should, under a legal government, cry down a standing army in time of peace, during the time of a national ferment; I should shrewdly suspect, that the principles of such persons were not changed, but that either they do not like the hands that the army is in, or the cause that it espouses; and look upon it as an obstruction to another sort of army, which they should like even in time of peace.

The arming and training of all the freeholders of England, as is our undoubted ancient constitution, and consequently our right, so it is the opinion of most Whigs, that it ought to be put in practice. This would put us out of all fear of foreign invasions, or disappoint any such when attempted. This would soon take away the necessity of maintaining standing armies of mercenaries in time of peace. This would render us a hundred times more formidable to our neighbours than we are; and secure effectually our liberties against any king that should have a mind to invade them at home; which, perhaps was the reason some of our late kings were so averse to it.

As the case now stands, ten thousand disciplined soldiers, once landed, might march without considerable opposition from one end of England to the other. Were our militia well regulated, we need not fear an hundred thousand enemies, were it possibie to land so many among us. At every river and pass, the enemy would meet with men resolutely determined to conquer or die in support of their country, liberty and laws.

[*To be concluded in our next.*]

Printed and Published for the AUTHORS by T. W. SHAW, Fleet-Street, opposite Anderton's Coffee-House, where Letters to the Publisher will be thankfully received. New Editions of all the Numbers of this spirited Paper, are now ready for Sale, and *complete sets* will be sent to any Part of *England, Carriage Free.*

THE

CRISIS

NUMBER LXXXVIII   *To be continued every Saturday,*

DURING THE PRESENT BLOODY CIVIL WAR IN AMERICA.

SATURDAY, SEPTEMBER 21, 1776   [Price Two-pence Half-penny.

The PRINCIPLES of a REAL WHIG.[1]

[*Continued from our last.*]

THE farther such an army advanced into the country, the stronger and more resolved it would find us; as Hanibal did the Romans, when he encamped under the walls of Rome, even after such a defeat as that at Cannae. And why? because they were all trained soldiers, they were all freemen that fought for the preservation of their liberty; and scorned to trust to the valour and assistance of mercenaries and slaves, though ever so able-bodied: They thought weapons became not the hands of those who had nothing to lose, and upon that account were unfit defenders of their masters properties; so that they never tried the experiment but in the utmost extremity and danger.

That this is not only practicable but easy, the modern example of the Swissers and Swedes is an undeniable indication. Englishmen have as

---

1. See supra LXXXVII.1.

much courage, as great strength of body, and capacity of mind, as any people in the universe: and if our late monarchs had the enervating their free subjects in view, that they might give a reputation to mercenaries, who depended only on the prince for pay, I know no reason why their example should be followed in the days of liberty, when there is no such prospect. The preservation of the game is but a very slender pretence for omitting it. I hope no wise man will put a hare or a partridge in balance with the safety and liberties of Englishmen; though after all, it is well known to sportsmen, that dogs, snares, nets, and such silent methods as are daily put in practice, destroy the game ten times more than shooting with guns.

The militia, upon the footing it now stands, will be of little use to us: it is generally composed of servants, and those not always of the same, consequently not well trained; rather such as wink with both eyes at their firing their musquets, and scarce know how to keep them clean, or charge them aright.

It consists of people whose reputation, especially the officers, has been industriously diminished, and their persons, as well as their employment, rendered contemptible, on purpose to enhance the value of those that serve for pay; insomuch that few gentlemen of quality will now stoop so low as to accept of the command of a company or a regiment in the militia.

A right Whig thinks no prince fit to govern, whose principle it must be to ruin the constitution, as soon as he can acquire unjust power to do so. He judges it nonsense for one to be the head of a charch, or defender of a faith, who thinks himself bound in duty to overthrow it.

He cannot satisfy himself with any of the foolish distinctions trumped up of late years, to reconcile base interest with a show of religion; but deals upon the square, and plainly owns to the world, that he is not influenced by any particular spleen: but that the exercise of an arbitrary illegal power in the nation, so as to undermine the constitution, would incapacitate either a King James, King William, or any other, from being his king, whenever the public has a power to hinder it.

Lastly, the supporting of parliamentary credit, promoting of all public buildings and highways, the making all rivers navigable that are capable of it, employing the poor, suppressing idlers, restraining monopolies upon trade, maintaining the liberty of the press, the just paying and encouraging of all in the public service, especially that best and most useful of all people, the seamen, are all articles of my Whiggish belief, and I hope none of them are heterodox. And if all these together amount to a republican or commonwealthsman, I shall never be ashamed of the name, though given with a design of fixing a reproach upon me, and such as think as I do.

₊ *As we think it our Duty to insert whatever may tend to serve the Cause of Liberty, we trust our Renders will not be displeased with the Perusal of the following circular Letter and Resolutions from the London-Association.*

CIRCULAR LETTER

FROM THE

LONDON ASSOCIATION.

LONDON,²

THE present awful and calamitous situation of Great Britain and its colonies, cannot but alarm and grieve every true friend to Liberty and his Country, who considers the ruinous consequences, inevitable to the

---

2. The London Association circular letter and resolutions of 25 August 1775 had been included in the reprint of Molesworth's *Real Whig*, pp. 22–26 (see supra LXXXVII.1). "The London Association seems to have been an autonomously organized society which raised the spectre, without threatening the reality, of insurrection," observed John Sainsbury in his *Disaffected Patriots*, p. 113. "In national impact, as well as in ideology and membership, it typified in microcosmic form the metropolitan pro-American movement as a whole."

most essential interests of this nation, its commerce and freedom, in the alienation, perhaps the total loss of America.

While the present arbitrary ministers have, in so many instances, openly violated, and endeavoured to subvert our excellent constitution, recognized and established at the late glorious revolution, and the consequent accession of the illustrious house of Brunswick to the throne of these realms—many sincere friends to Liberty, conformable to ancient usage, have associated, in support and maintenance of the principles confirmed at those two great and important periods, and to defeat the designs of men, who seem determined to destroy all their excellent effects.

This Association, formed for the honor of the King, the preservation of religion, the revival of trade, the glory and happiness of the whole empire, we trust will meet with your approbation; and that you will use your best endeavours to promote this great and necessary work, by recommending and instituting associations on the same excellent principles in your county and neighbourhood.

And as nothing can more contribute to our good designs, than mutual fidelity, unanimity, and resolution, together with a reciprocal communication between us, we have, for this purpose, appointed a COMMITTEE of CORRESPONDENCE; who will pay due attention to such intelligence of your progress, in this business, as you shall think proper to transmit.

RESOLUTIONS
OF THE
LONDON ASSOCIATION.

GLOBE TAVERN, *Fleet Street, Aug. 25.*

RESOLVED, That this Association, duly sensible of the many blessings we enjoy from the Revolution and Accession, to which, under

God, we owe the free constitution of our country, will use our best and most unwearied endeavours to extend and transmit to posterity their excellent principles and consequences; and that we will embrace every opportunity to evince our zeal, affection, and fidelity, to his present Majesty KING GEORGE THE THIRD, and his ROYAL FAMILY, for whose honor and safety whilst we manifest the highest regard, we hold the truest concern for the freedom, peace, and welfare of the whole British empire, convinced that under a prince of the House of Brunswick we only CAN be free, and at the same time resolutely determined, that under a prince of the House of Brunswick we WILL BE FREE.

RESOLVED, that the present high price of the necessaries of life, the decay of trade, and consequent distresses of the industrious poor, those most useful members of the state, demand our best consideration, that PEACE may no longer be the parent of poverty and misery, instead of the source of riches and happiness.

RESOLVED, That as it is declared by the BILL OF RIGHTS, (Art. V.) that it is the RIGHT of the SUBJECT to petition, we will use our best endeavours to bring to the justice of their country, those men who have prevented the cries of the nation from being heard by his Majesty, and consequently their miseries and complaints from being redressed.

RESOLVED, That if any descendants of those illustrious noblemen, who by their undaunted and zealous endeavours, brought about and established the GLORIOUS REVOLUTION, and effected the ACCESSION, shall determine to join this Association, for the great purposes of CONSTITUTIONAL FREEDOM and NATIONAL HAPPINESS, we will pay due regard to their RANK and BIRTH, though we shall always keep their zeal for the PUBLIC CAUSE, and their uniform support of the principles and proceedings of their gallant and patriotic ancestors FOREMOST in our view, our gratitude, and respect.

Printed and Published for the AUTHORS by T. W. SHAW, Fleet-Street, opposite Anderton's Coffee-House, where Letters to the Publisher will be thankfully received. New Editions of all the Numbers of this spirited Paper, are now ready for Sale, and *complete sets* will be sent to any Part of *England, Carriage, Free.*

THE

CRISIS

NUMBER LXXXIX   *To be continued every Saturday,*

DURING THE PRESENT BLOODY CIVIL WAR IN AMERICA.

SATURDAY, SEPTEMBER 28, 1776   *Price* Two-pence Half-penny.[1]

From the Virginia Gazette, and other American papers, dated August 3d, 1776, we have the following intelligence, brought by the ship Christian, which arrived at Greenock on Friday, September 20th, 1776.

New York, July 15,

YESTERDAY Lord Howe sent up a flag with the Captain and Lieutenant of the Eagle man of war; the Adjutant General met them, after some little ceremony, but as the letter was directed for George Washington, Esq. he could not receive it; the officers insisted much on his receiving it, saying it was of a civil nature, his Lordship being invested with unlimited powers, and was sorry he had not arrived

---

1. What follows was lifted, virtually verbatim, from either the *Gazetteer and New Daily Advertiser* or the *Morning Chronicle*, 25 September 1776–an indication, like reprinting the long extracts from Molesworth, that the author(s) of *The Crisis* were becoming intellectually disengaged. For the Howes and their dealings with Congress see O'Shaughnessy, *Men Who Lost America*, pp. 83–122; and Ira D. Gruber, *The Howe Brothers and the American Revolution* (Chapel Hill: University of North Carolina Press, 1972).

a few days sooner. This morning we have accounts that the ships, &c. which passed the town, are 50 miles up, opposite to Tary Town, where the river is four miles wide, and they may be safe.

On Tuesday another flag from the fleet appeared, and was met as before, when a letter was again offered, but for the same reason as the former rejected.

PHILADELPHIA.
I n   C O N G R E S S, July 19, 1776.

RESOLVED, That General WASHINGTON, in refusing to receive a letter said to be sent from Lord Howe, addressed to GEORGE WASH-INGTON, Esq. acted with a dignity becoming his station; and therefore this Congress do highly approve the same, and do direct that no letter or message be received, on any occasion whatever, from the enemy, by the Commander in Chief, or other the Commanders of the American army, but such as shall be directed to them in the characters they respectively sustain. By order of the Congress,

J O H N   H A N C O C K, President.

CONGRESS, JULY 19, 1776.

RESOLVED, That a copy of the circular letters, and the declarations they enclosed from Lord Howe to Mr. W. Franklin, Mr. Penn, Mr. Eden, Lord Dunmore, Mr. Martin, and Sir James Wright, late Governors, sent to Amboy by a flag, and forwarded to Congress by General Washington, be published in the several Gazettes, that the good people of these united states may be informed of what nature are the commissioners, and what the terms, with the expectation of which the insidious court of Great Britain has endeavored to amuse and disarm them; and that the few who still remain suspended by a hope founded either in the justice or moderation of their late King, may now, at length, be convinced, that the valour alone of their country is to save its liberties.

Extracts from the Journals,

C H A R L E S   T H O M S O N, Secretary.

EAGLE, off the Coast of the Province of Massachusetts Bay, *June* 20, 1776.

"S I R,

"BEING appointed Commander in Chief of the ships and vessels of his Majesty's fleet employed in North America, and having the honour to be by his Majesty constituted one of his COMMISSIONERS for restoring peace to his colonies, and for granting pardon to such of his subjects therein as shall be duly solicitous to benefit by that effect of his gracious indulgence; I embrace this opportunity to inform you of my arrival on the American coast, where my first object will be an early meeting with General Howe, whom his Majesty has been pleased to join with me in the said Commission.

"In the mean time I have judged it expedient to issue the inclosed declaration, in order that all persons may have immediate information of his Majesty's most gracious intentions. And I desire you will be pleased forthwith to cause the said declaration to be promulgated, in such manner, and at such places within the province of New Jersey, as will render the same of the most public notoriety.

"Assured of being favoured with your assistance in every measure for the speedy and effectual restoration of public tranquility, I am to request you will communicate, from time to time, such information as you may think will facilitate the attainment of that important object, in the province over which you preside.

"I have the honour to be,

With great respect and consideration,

Sir, your most obedient humble servant,

H O W E."

By RICHARD VISCOUNT HOWE, of the Kingdom of Ireland, one of the King's Commissioners for restoring Peace to his Majesty's Colonies and Plantations in North America, etc.

D E C L A R A T I O N.

WHEREAS, by an Act passed in the last session of Parliament, to prohibit all trade and intercourse with the colonies of New Hampshire, Massachusett's Bay, Rhode Island, Connecticut, New York, New Jersey, Pennsylvania, the three lower countries on Delaware, Maryland, Virginia, North Carolina, South Carolina, and Georgia, and for other purposes therein mentioned, it is enacted, "That it shall and may be lawful, to and for any person, or persons, appointed and authorized by his Majesty, to grant a pardon, or pardons, to any number or description of persons by proclamation in his Majesty's name, to declare any colony or province, colonies or provinces, or any county, town, port, district, or place, in any colony or province, to be at the peace of his Majesty; and that, from and after the issuing such proclamation, in any of the aforesaid colonies or provinces, or if his Majesty shall be graciously pleased to signify the same by his Royal proclamation, the said act, with respect to such colony or province, colonies or provinces, county, town, port, district or place, shall cease, determine, and be utterly null and void."

And whereas the King, desirous to deliver all his subjects from the calamities of war, and other *oppressions which they now undergo,* and to restore the said colonies to his protection and peace, as soon as the constitutional authority of government therein may be replaced, hath been graciously pleased, by letters patent, under the great seal, dated the sixth day of May, in the sixteenth year of his Majesty's reign, to nominate and appoint me, Richard Viscount Howe, of the kingdom of Ireland, and William Howe, Esquire, General of his forces in North America, and each of us, jointly and severally, to be his Majesty's commissioner and commissioners, for granting his *free and general pardon* to all those who, in the tumult and disaster of the times, may have deviated from their just allegiance, and who are willing, by a speedy return to their duty, to reap the benefits of the Royal favour; and also for declaring, in his Majesty's name, any colony, province, county, town, port, district, or place, to be at the peace of his Majesty. I DO, THEREFORE, hereby declare, that due consideration shall be had to the meritorious services of all persons who shall aid and assist in restoring the public tranquility in the said colonies, or any part or parts thereof; that pardons shall be granted, dutiful representations received, and every suitable encouragement given, for promoting such measures as shall be conducive to the establishment of legal government and peace, in pursuance of his Majesty's most gracious purposes aforesaid.

Given on board his Majesty's ship, the Eagle, off the coast of the province of Massachusett's Bay, the twentyeth Day of June, 1776.

H O W E.

By Order of the Congress,

JOHN HANCOCK, President.

Extract from the Minutes.

CHARLES THOMPSON, Secretary.

From the Virginia Gazette, *Williamsburgh, July* 5.

The following are the Appointments under the new
Plan of Government:

PATRICK HENRY, junior, Esq. Governor.—John Page, Dudley Digges, John Taylor, John Blair, Benjamin Harrison of Berkley, Bartholomew Dandridge, Charles Carter of Shirley, and Benjamin Harrison of Brandon, Counsellors of State.—Thomas Whiting, John Hutchins, Champion Travis, Thomas Newton, jun. and George Webb, Esqrs. Commissioners of Admiralty.—James Husband, Joseph Prentis, and John Tyler, Esqrs. Judges of Admiralty.—Edmund Randolph, Esq. Attorney Ceneral.—Thomas Everard and James Cooke, Esqrs. Commissioners for settling Accounts.

GOD Save the Commonwealth!

In C O N G R E S S, June 26, 1776.

RESOLVED, That a Bounty of TEN DOLLARS be given to every non-commissioned officer and soldier, who will enlist to serve for the term of three years.

Extract from the Minutes.

CHARLES THOMPSON, Secretary.

New York, July 11. On Wednesday last, the Declaration of Independence was read at the head of each brigade of the Continental army, posted at and near New York, and every where received with loud huzzas, and the utmost demonstrations of joy.

"The same evening the equestrian statue of George III. raised in the year 1770, was, by the sons of freedom, laid prostrate in the dirt. The lead wherewith this monument was made, is to be run into bullets, to assimulate with the brain of our infatuated adversaries, who, to gain a pepper-corn, have lost an empire."

The passengers arrived in the Christian say, that the grand attack by his Majesty's troops, amounting to 26,000 men, was intended to be made upon New York about the 13th of August.

Printed and Published for the Authors by T. W. SHAW, Fleet-Street, opposite Anderton's Coffee-House, where Letters to the Publisher will be thankfully received. New Editions of all the Numbers of this spirited Paper, are now ready for Sale, and *complete sets* will be sent to any Part of *England, Carriage Free.*

THE

CRISIS

NUMBER XC   *To be continued every Saturday,*

DURING THE PRESENT BLOODY CIVIL WAR IN AMERICA.

SATURDAY, OCTOBER 6, 1776   [Price Two-pence Half-penny.

An EXTRACT from the Freeholder's Political Catechism, *written by the late* Earl of Bath, *containing a short but judicious Summary of the Duty, as well as Rights, of every English Freeholder*[1]

Q. WHO are you?

A. I am T—M— a freeholder of Great Britain.

Q. What privilege enjoyest thou by being a freeholder of Great Britain?

A. By being a freeholder of Great Britain, I am greater in my civil capacity than the greatest subject of an arbitrary prince; because I am governed

---

1. *The Freeholders's Political Catechism*, first published in 1733, is usually attributed to Bolingbroke (see Dickinson's *Bolingbroke*, pp. 239–40). It was reprinted in 1757 (no place or printer given) and again in 1769, not only in London but in New London, Connecticut, by Timothy Green, who admonished that it was "very necessary to be studied by every Freeman in *America.*" The date for this issue should be October 5th, not the 6th; see n. I.1 supra for errors in dating.

by laws, to which I gave my consent; and my life, liberty, and goods cannot be taken from me, but according to those laws.— I am a freeman.—

Q. Who gave thee this liberty?

A. No man gave it me. Liberty is the natural right of every human creature. He is born to the exercise of it, as soon as he has attained to that of his reason; but that my liberty is preserved to me, when lost to a great part of mankind, is owing (under God) to the wisdom and valour of my ancestors, freeholders of this realm.

Q. Wherein does this liberty which thou enjoyest consist?

A. In laws made by the consent of the people, and the due execution of those laws. I am free from the law, by the law.

Q. Wilt thou stand fast in this liberty, whereunto thou art born and entitled by the laws of thy country?

A. Yes, I will; and I thank the great Author of my Being, that I am born a member of a community governed by laws, and not by arbitrary power.

Q. What dost thou think incumbent upon thee, to secure this blessing to thyself and posterity?

A. As I am a freeholder, I think it incumbent upon me to believe aright concerning the fundamental articles of the government, to which I am subject; to write, speak, and act on all occasions conformably to this orthodox faith; to oppose, with all the powers of my body and mind, such as are enemies of our good constitution, together with all their secret and open abettors, and to be obedient to the king, the supreme magistrate of the society.

Q. Is it not a maxim in the law, that the king can do no wrong?

A. It Is; for since kings do not act immediately by themselves, but immediately by their officers, and inferior magistrates; the wisdom of the law provides sufficiently against any undue exercise of their power, by charging all illegal acts, and all kinds of mal-administration upon their ministers; by the great regard which is paid to the king by this maxim, laying him under an indisputable obligation, not to skreen his ministers from public justice, or public enquiry.

Q. What dost thou mean by the royal prerogative?

A. A discretionary power in the king to act for the good of the people, where the laws are silent, never contrary to law, and always subject to the limitations of law.

Q. Is not the king above the laws?

A. By no means; for the intention of government being the security of lives, liberties, and properties of the members of the community, they never can be supposed, by the law of nature, to give an arbitrary power over their persons and estates. King, is a title which, translated into several languages, signifies a magistrate with as many different degrees of power as there are kingdoms in the world; and he can have no power but what is given him by law; yea, even the supreme, or legislative power is bound, by the rules of equity, to govern by laws enacted, and published in due form, for what is not legal is arbitrary.

Q. How comes it that those, who endeavour to destroy the authority and independence of any of the branches of the legislature, subvert the constitution?

A. By the fundamental laws of the constitution, the free consent and mutual concurrence of the three members is necessary to the making of a law: therefore if the consent of any of the three is wilfully omitted or obtained by terror or corruption, the legislature is violated; and in stead of three, there may be really and effectually but one branch of the legislature.

Q. Canst thou illustrate this by an example.

A. The royal authority, and that of the house of peers, were both destroyed by the house of commons, and by a small part of that, in the late civil war; so that the very form of government was annihilated.

Q. Can you give me an instance where the form of government may be kept, and yet the constitution destroyed?

A, Yes. The forms of the free government of Rome were preserved under the arbitrary government of the emperors. There was a senate, consuls, and tribunes of the people: as one might say king, lords and commons: and yet the government under the emperors was always despotic, and often tyranical; and indeed the worst of all governments is tyranny sanctified by the appearance of law.

Q. By what means fell that great people into this state of ruin and slavery?

A. I have read the Roman history, and by what I can judge, it was by faction, corruption, and standing armies.

Q. All those things might happen to Romans; but did ever any parliament of this nation give up the liberty of the people?

A. Yes. A packed parliament, in Richard the Second's time, established by a law the king's arbitrary power, and with leave to name a commission with parliamentary authority. Parliaments in Henry the Eighth's time were slaves to his passions, and one gave the king a legislative authority. And there are many instances of parliaments making dangerous steps towards the destruction of the liberty of the people.

Q. Who were the English monarchs who were most indulgent to the liberties of the people?

A. The great king Alfred, who declared that the English nation was as free as the thoughts of man; the glorious monarchs, Edward the First, Edward the Third, and Henry the Fifth, who would not let his people swear to him till he had an opportunity of swearing to them at his coronation. And the immortal Queen Elizabeth, who declared it by law high treason, during her life, and a premunire afterwards, to deny the power of parliament in limiting and binding the descent, or inheritance of the crown, or the claim to it.

Q. When were those slavish imaginations of hereditary, indefeaible right and prerogative, superior to law, first introduced?

A. In the time of James the First; who, by endeavouring to establish them, laid the foundation of all the miseries which have since happened to this family; and it is the greatest security to the present branch of it, that such doctrines which sow the seeds of jealousy between the king and his people, are by the present establishment quite exploded.

Q. What dost thou learn from those histories?

A. That a king of this realm, in the full possession of the affections of his people, is greater than any arbitrary prince; and that the nation can never be effectually undone but by a wicked parliament; and lastly to be thankful to God, that under our present most gracious king, our constitution is preserved entire, though at the same time there are many circumstances which call loudly for vigilance.

Q. What are those?

A. Such as have been the forerunners and causes of the loss of liberty in other countries; decay of virtue and public spirit, luxury and extravagance in expence, venality and corruption in private and public affairs.

Q. How comes there to be a decay of public spirit, when there is more than usual a desire to serve the public?

A. If a desire to live upon the public be a public spirit, there is enough of it at this time, when extravagance makes people crave more, and the administration of a public revenue (perhaps treble what it was before the revolution) enables the crown to give more than formerly.

Q. What dost thou fear from this?

A. That such as serve the crown for reward, may in time sacrifice the interest of their country to their wants; that greediness of public money may produce a slavish complaisance, as long as the crown can pay; and mutiny when it cannot; and in general, that motives of self-interest will prove an improper and weak foundation for our duty to our king and country.

Q. What wouldst thou do for thy country?

A. I would die to procure its Prosperity; and I would rather my posterity were cut off, than that they should be slaves: I discharge the duties of my station, and exhort my neighbours to do the same.

[To be concluded in our next.]

Printed and Published for the Authors by T. W. SHAW, Fleet-Street, opposite Anderton's Coffee-House where Letters to the Publisher will be thankfully received. New Editions of all the Numbers of this spirited Paper, are now ready for Sale, and *complete sets* will be sent to any Part of England, *Carriage Free.*

THE

CRISIS

NUMBER XCI   *To be continued every Saturday,*

SATURDAY, OCTOBER 12, 1776   [Price Two-pence Half-penny.

An EXTRACT from the Freeholder's Political Catechism, *written by the late* Earl of Bath *containing a short but judicious Summary of the Duty as well as Rights, of every English Freeholder.*[1]

[Concluded from our last.]

Q. WHAT are the Duties of your station?

A. To endeavour, as far as I am able, to preserve the public tranquility; and, as I am a freeholder, to give my vote for the candidate whom I judge most worthy to serve and benefit his country; for if for any partial motive I should give my vote to one unworthy, I should think myself justly chargeable with his guilt.

Q. Thou hast perhaps but one vote of five hundred, and the member perhaps one of five hundred more; then your share of the guilt is but small?

A. As he, who assists at a murder, is guilty of murder, so he who acts the lowest part in the enslaving his country, is guilty of a much greater crime than murder.

---

1. See supra n. XC.1.

Q. Is enslaving one's country a greater crime than murder?

A. Yes; inasmuch as the murder of human nature is a greater crime than the murder of a human creature: or as he who debaseth and rendereth miserable the race of mankind, is more wicked than he who cutteth off an individual.

Q. Why is enslaving mankind murdering human nature?

A. Because mankind in the state of slavery and freedom is a different sort of creature; for proof of this I have read what the Greeks were of old, and what they are now, in a state of slavery.

Q. What is become of the heroes, philosophers, orators, and free citizens of Greece?

A. They are now slaves to the Great Turk.

Q. What is become of the Scipio's and Cato's of Rome?

A. They sing now on the English stage.

Q. Does not the tranquility occasioned by absolute monarchy, make the country thrive?

A. Peace and plenty are not the genuine fruits of absolute monarchy; for absolute monarchies are more subject to convulsions than free governments, and slavery turneth the fruitful plains into a desart: whereas liberty, like the dew from Heaven, fructifieth the barren mountains. This I have learned from travelers who have visited countries in both conditions: therefore, as I said before, as I observed before, I should reckon myself guilty of the greatest crime human nature is capable of, if I were any ways accessory to the enslaving my country. Though I have but one vote, many units make a number; and if every elector should reason after the same manner, that he has but one, what must become of the whole? A law of great consequence, and the election of the member who voteth for that law, may be both carried by one vote. Great and important services for the liberties of their country have been done by ordinary men. I have read that the institution of the Tribunes of Rome, was owing to a word spoke in reason by a common man.

Q. Is it not lawful then to take a bribe from a person otherwise worthy to serve his country?

A. No more than for a judge to take a bribe for a just sentence; is it any more lawfnl to corrupt, than to commit evil that good may come of it? Corruption converts a good action into wickedness. Bribery of all sorts is contrary to the law of God; it is a heinous sin, often punished with the severest judgments; it involves in it the sin of perjury, as the law stands now, and is, besides, the greatest folly and madness.

Q. How is it contrary to the law of God?

A. The law of God saith expressly, "Thou shalt not wrest judgment:[2] Thou shalt not take a gift." If it is a sin in a judge, it is much more in a law-giver, or an elector, because the mischiefs occasioned by the first, reach only to individuals; that of the last may affect the whole nation, and even generations to come. The Psalmist describing the wicked, saith, "His right hand is full of bribes." The prophet describing the righteous, tells us, "He shaketh his hands at a bribe?" The leprosy adhered to Gehazi, (the servant of Elisha) and his house for ever, for taking a bribe from Naaman, a rich minister of a great prince. Therefore he that taketh a bribe, may justly expect what is threatened in holy writ, "He shall nor prosper in his way, neither shall his substance continue: his silver and gold shall not be able to deliver him in the day of the wrath of the Lord."[2]

Q. What thinkest thou of those who are bribed by gluttony and drunkenness?

A. That they are viler than Esau, who sold his birth-right for a mess of pottage.

Q. Why is taking a bribe folly or madness?

2. These Biblical excerpts were taken from, respectively, Deuteronomy 16:19 ("not wrest judgment" and "not take a gift"); Psalms 26:10 ("right hand full of bribes"); Isaiah 33:15 ("shaketh his hand"); Deuteronomy 28:29 ("shall not prosper") Job 15:29 ("substance continue") and Zephaniah 1:18 ("silver and gold"). As quoted from the KJV.

A. Because I must refund ten-fold in taxes of what I take in elections; and the member who bought me, has a fair pretence to sell me; nor can I, in such case, have any just cause of complaint

Q. Is not the justice of a king sufficient security for the liberty of a people?

A. The people ought to have more security, for all that is valuable in the world, than the will of a mortal and fallible man. A king of Britain may make as many peers, and such as he pleaseth; therefore the last and best security for the liberties of the people is a house of commons, genuine and independent.

Q. What meanest thou by a genuine house of commons?

A. One that is the lawful issue of the people, and no bastard.

Q. How is a bastard house of commons produced?

A. When the people, by terror, corruption, or other indirect means, chuse such as they otherwise would not chuse; when such as are fairly chosen are not returned, when such as are returned are turned out by partial votes, and others, not fairly chosen, set in their places.

Q. Can a king have a more faithful council than a house of commons, which speaketh the sense of the people?

A. None; for they will not only give him impartial council, but will powerfully and cheerfully assist him to execute what they advise.

Q. Who is most likely to accept of a bribe?

A. He who offers one.

Q. Who is likely to be frugal of the people's money?

A. He who puts none of it in his own pocket.

Q. Who are those who are careful of the trade of the nation?

A. Such as are willing to keep it from all vexatious interruptions by inspections, entering into houses, seizures, suits, and the oppression of tax-gatherers, as much as possible; such as are willing to take off the burthensome duties which encrease the expence of the workman, and consequently the price of the manufacture.

Q. But as you have a freehold, would you not be willing to be excused from paying the land-tax, by laying excises upon other parts of our consumption?

A. No doubt;—every landed man would be glad to be free from paying it; but it is utterly impossible to raise by excise what shall be equivalent to land-tax, without the ruin of trade; for the excises which are settled already, generally speaking, raise double the duty upon the people, of what they bring in to the government.

T H E   E N D.

An ADDRESS from the AUTHORS to the PUBLIC.

WE have carried on the CRISIS near Two Years from the most disinterested principles for the HONOUR and INTEREST of our Country; with a View to expose the horrid Deformity of Tyranny, Rapine, and lawless Power, and to shew the Blessings and Advantages of LIBERTY. We have braved every Danger with a Spirit and Resolution which, we flatter ourselves, few Men would have done:—We have attacked Vice, Corruption and Folly in whomsoever they were found. We now lay down this PAPER, with grateful Thanks to the Public, and as LIBERTY and VIRTUE have taken their Flight to AMERICA, the only Asylum for Freemen, we are determined to follow, and not longer struggle in vain to animate our dastardly, degenerate Countrymen with the noble Spirit of their Forefathers, against the Ingratitude of a Tyrant, whose bare-faced System of Despotism and Blood, must soon end in the Ruin of England, and the Slavery of the present BASTARD Race of Englishmen.

Printed and Published for the AUTHORS by T. W. SHAW, Fleet-Street, opposite Anderton's Coffee-House, where Letters to the Publisher will be thankfully received. New Editions of all the Numbers of this spirited Paper, are now ready for Sale, and *complete sets* will be sent to any Part of England, *Carriage Free.*

Index

A Note on the Type

This book is set in Adobe Garamond, an adaptation by Robert Slimbach of the typeface cut around 1540 by the French punchcutter, typographer, and printer Claude Garamond. The original Garamond face, with its small lowercase height and restrained contrast between thick and thin strokes, is a classic old-style face and has long been one of the most influential and widely used typefaces. Slimbach based the italic on type designed by the French engraver, type founder, and printer Robert Granjon.

Printed on paper that is acid-free and meets the requirements of the American National Standard for Permanence of Paper for Printed Library Materials, z39.48-1992. ⊗

Book design by Otto Barz, as guided by the original page design of *The Crisis*
Typography by Publishing Synthesis, Ltd., New York
Index by Kate Mertes
Printed and bound by Edwards Brothers/Malloy, Ann Arbor